ANNUAL REVIEW OF SOCIOLOGY

ANNUAL REVIEW OF SOCIOLOGY

VOLUME 12, 1986

RALPH H. TURNER, *Editor*

University of California, Los Angeles

JAMES F. SHORT, JR., *Associate Editor*

Washington State University

ANNUAL REVIEWS INC.   4139 EL CAMINO WAY   P.O. BOX 10139   PALO ALTO, CALIFORNIA 94303-0897

⟨R⟩ ANNUAL REVIEWS INC.
Palo Alto, California, USA

International Standard Serial Number: 0360–0572
International Standard Book Number: 0–8243–2212–6
Library of Congress Catalog Card Number: 75-648500

Annual Reviews Inc. and the Editors of its publications assume no responsibility for the statements expressed by the contributors to this *Review*.

Typesetting by Kachina Typesetting Inc., Tempe, Arizona; John Olson, President
Typesetting coordinator, Janis Hoffman

PRINTED AND BOUND IN THE UNITED STATES OF AMERICA

PREFACE

With the opening chapter of this volume we initiate a new feature. The Editorial Committee asked George Homans to look back on his distinguished career and to write whatever personal reflections on sociology and his own intellectual development he chose. As a continuing series, such personal intellectual documents by our most distinguished sociologists should be of great current interest. We hope they may also become an important resource for historians of the discipline.

In 12 years of planning and editing these review volumes, we have learned that fields within sociology grow by shifting directions. When we ask authors of reviews from five years earlier whether developments merit a new review of the same topic, very few answer in the affirmative. But most former authors identify one or two closely related problem areas in which there has been a flurry of exciting activity. These areas of fresh activity are usually offshoots from earlier lines of development or the products of the intersection of two earlier strands of sociological work. Most of our current reviews address these areas of recent activity.

In spite of sociology's erratic pattern of development, a 12-year perspective reveals more continuity than discontinuity. The themes of most of the reviews in this volume were adumbrated in earlier volumes. For example, themes such as life course, gender roles, bureaucracy and its alternatives, race relations in the United States, social impact and evaluation research, contemporary social movements, social conditions of mental health, sampling problems, and political participation and the state appear in both this volume and Volume One.

As many of our readers will recall, in 1969 the Sociology Panel of the joint Behavioral and Social Science Survey of the National Academy of Sciences and the Social Science Research Council formally recommended publication of an annual review of sociology as a step toward strengthening sociological knowledge. The Council of the American Sociological Association agreed, and ASA entered into a collaborative enterprise with Annual Reviews, Inc. to publish the *Annual Review of Sociology*. The Review has now become the indispensable record of trends and developments in the discipline.

As originally conceived, the purpose of the *Annual Review of Sociology* was to provide authoritative surveys of recent important sociological theory and research in specialized fields (or of recent literature from other disciplines that

(continued)   v

is important for the development of a specialty in sociology). The reader with a general background would be brought up-to-date on the nature and status of rival points of view and the variety of empirical work in the field. In addition, reviews were to be interpretative and critical.

In order to ensure a proper diversity of topics in each volume, the Editorial Committee uses the 12 broad categories that appear in the cumulative title index as an organizing framework and checklist. These categories serve as a heuristic device rather than a rigid structure. Within this loose framework, the specific topics for review change each year. The rate of accumulation of sociological knowledge and the pattern by which the discipline advances could not justify reviewing the same topics in successive years. Many problems and seminal ideas in sociology stimulate a flurry of relatively transient interest and may justifiably be reviewed only once. Others produce a slow accumulation of knowledge and—more importantly—a slow change in perspective that would merit recurrent review, but only perhaps at five- to ten-year intervals. Our editorial policy is to reassess specific topics about five years after publication of the initial review so as to decide which ones ought to be reviewed again.

The Editorial Committee is never satisfied that the articles appearing in a volume are perfectly representative of the most vital recent developments in sociology. We therefore invite specific proposals from all members of the discipline. What areas of activity have we overlooked? What specialized developments may not otherwise come to the Committee's attention on a timely basis? It is especially helpful to the Committee when a recommendation is accompanied by a paragraph describing the proposed topic, some key bibliographic examples, and the names of persons qualified to prepare the review. In a few instances, sociologists who have proposed topics and volunteered themselves as expert reviewers have been commissioned to prepare chapters.

THE EDITORS AND THE EDITORIAL COMMITTEE

Annual Review of Sociology
Volume 12, 1986

CONTENTS

viii   CONTENTS   *(Continued)*

RELATED ARTICLES FROM OTHER ANNUAL REVIEWS

From the *Annual Review of Anthropology,* Volume 15 (1986)

Language Socialization, Bambi B. Schieffelin and Elinor Ochs
The Anthropology of Emotions, Catherine Lutz and Geoffrey M. White
Systems and Process 1974–1985, Joan Vincent

From the *Annual Review of Psychology,* Volume 37 (1986)

Program Evaluation: The Worldly Science, Thomas D. Cook, and William R. Shadish, Jr.
Expectancies and Interpersonal Processes, Dale T. Miller and William Turnbull
Culture and Behavior: Psychology in Global Perspective, Marshall H. Segall
Emotion: Today's Problems, Paul R. Pintrich, David R. Cross, Robert B. Kozma, and Wilbert J. McKeachie

From the *Annual Review of Public Health,* Volume 7 (1986)

Medical Care at the End of Life: The Interaction of Economics and Ethics, A. A. Scitovsky and A. M. Capron
Occupational Ergonomics—Methods To Evaluate Physical Stress on the Job, W. Monroe Keyserling and Don B. Chaffin
Mediating Solutions to Environmental Risks, Sam Gusman and Philip J. Harter

---

ERRATUM

Professor Charles Hirschman calls attention to an error in his article, "America's Melting Pot Reconsidered," in Volume 9 of the *Annual Review of Sociology* (1983). On page 398, he incorrectly attributed a quotation to Herbert Hoover.

For the convenience of readers, a detachable order form/envelope is bound into the back of this volume.

Photograph by Christopher S. Johnson.

George C. Homans

Ann. Rev. Sociol. 1986. 12:xiii–xxx

FIFTY YEARS OF SOCIOLOGY

George C. Homans

Department of Sociology, Harvard University, Cambridge, Massachusetts 02138

Abstract

What follows is a personal appraisal of the development of sociology over the past 50 years. The 1930s were a time of high hopes, empirically (field studies, new statistical techniques) and theoretically (for instance, functionalism and operationalism). The great achievement of sociology has been its development of statistical techniques, but these have had the effect of inhibiting field studies. In theory, sociology has remained divided into a number of different schools, a condition maintained by the failure of most sociologists to consider what a theory *is*. The condition can be overcome only by sociologists' accepting the "covering law" view of theory, the covering laws referring to the behavior of individual persons as members of a single species, and the laws themselves being the laws of behavioral psychology. Recent favorable developments in sociology include network analysis, historical sociology, and sociobiology.

INTRODUCTION

In what follows I reflect, from my own point of view and from my experience with, and practice of, the discipline of sociology for 50 years, on what successes and failures the subject has met over this era, what new issues it faces, and what these have to teach us about the directions sociology should take in the future.

THE HOPES OF THE 1930S

I published my first book in sociology in 1934 (Homans & Curtis 1934), and I cannot be expected to publish many, if any, more. Age, together with many unpleasant things, brings a kind of freedom. In the societies of the East, we are told, an old man gives up his worldly responsibilities and goes off on pilgrimage, with nothing but a begging bowl in his hand. He feels free to act like an old

0360-0572/86/0815-0000$02.00

rogue, exempt from the conventions and allowed to say anything he pleases, however outrageous, at the price, naturally, of being disregarded. I propose to take advantage myself of this privilege. I propose, indeed, to take advantage of it to the point of hurting some persons' feelings.

For American society at large, 1934 was a dreary year, because we were still in the grip of the depression. But in the social sciences it was a year of exhilaration. Many new statistical techniques were being invented, under the leadership of such men as Samuel Stouffer and Paul Lazarsfeld. At the other end of the technical spectrum, field work (the direct observation of small groups and the interviewing of their members) was being introduced into sociology from anthropology and was soon to show brilliant results in such studies as Arensberg & Kimball's *Family and Community in Ireland* (1941) and W. F. Whyte's *Street Corner Society* (1943). We were excited by the community studies of the Lynds (1928) and of W. L. Warner (1941–1963). Elton Mayo was beginning to introduce us to experimental and field studies of modern industry through the Western Electric researches (see Roethlisberger & Dickson 1939). I should even mention Moreno's invention of what was called sociometry in a book strangely entitled *Who Shall Survive?* (1934). I could mention others.

More important than the techniques were the ideas. The Russian Revolution had made Marxism almost unchallenged among some intellectual groups, especially Jews of poor parents who had yet managed to get a good education in New York City. This was also the time when Freud's ideas began to achieve general acceptance among intellectuals. These new ideas may have been the most prominent examples, though certainly not the most important in the long run. Keynsian economics and logical positivism also flourished, stimulated in the long run by the work of Whitehead and Russell, the popular philosophers of the age. Bridgman's operationalism (1936), Skinner's behaviorism (1938), at once broader and more rigorous than J. B. Watson's, and various forms of functionalism, derived again from anthropology, all attracted adherents. Closer to my own intellectual base, Talcott Parsons had begun his teaching at Harvard and was developing an extraordinary group of students which included Kingsley Davis and Robert Merton. Parsons introduced them to what are now considered the European classics of sociological thought: Durkheim, Weber, and Pareto (though I believe that Durkheim, at least, was already well known at Chicago). Why Tocqueville was not admitted to the canon, I have never discovered. Above all, Parsons and Merton made the idea of sociological theory respectable and even a means of gaining status, though they had no clear idea what a theory was.

More important still, what did we young social scientists believe we were going to be able to do? With our new techniques and ideas we were going to be able to solve, at least intellectually, most of the ills besetting the world. Certainly our first students, returning from World War II, were convinced of it and made our field among the most popular on our various campuses. Unfortunately we vastly and irresponsibly oversold ourselves, and disillusion rightly set in. (I myself was more skeptical, but my teacher Elton Mayo certainly was sure we could stop the rot, if not produce positive improvement.) We also thought that we were going to create an integrated and cumulative social science, cumulative because one piece of research would, with the help of a better theory, build on another.

STATISTICAL METHODS AND EMPIRICAL RESEARCH

Looking back over 50 years, how much have we done to realize the dreams of our youth? I have the impression of some advances, much wasted effort, some hopes disappointed, certainly much intellectual disarray, and even some losses. In one area at least we have made great progress. Our advances in statistical and mathematical techniques have been huge and consolidated. Multivariate- and path-analysis, coupled with high-speed computers, have made possible investigations that would have been impossible or impossibly costly even a few years ago. I am thinking especially of studies, notably the famous report by James Coleman (1966), on the effect of the character of schools on the intellectual attainments of their students. It was not Coleman's fault that the use of his findings by the Supreme Court and the federal hierarchy has, together with other factors, made conditions worse rather than better, at least in my own city of Boston.

I also have the impression that the new techniques are often used mechanically to produce some, indeed any, findings from data that just happen to be available. I am thinking here of one study of the wage differentials between supervisors and workers in a sample of factories. The data were readily available, but after the author had applied his statistical techniques to them, I still had the impression that he had never been inside a factory nor ever looked carefully at what a supervisor and his workers actually *did*.

Yet the general tendency has still been favorable. In the years immediately after World War II, if some group such as a government committee asked a sociologist what was known about a particular social problem, the best answer available was apt to be: "We know little about it, but give us enough money and we'll find out." Today in a number of fields a body of fairly solid knowledge is at once on hand. In this sense our subject has indeed become more cumulative. It has not become more cumulative in developing a powerful general theory, or at least in accepting such a theory.

The rise of the new statistics has actually encouraged us to abandon a technique—call it that—which was one of our glories in the period just before and after World War II. So powerful were the new statistics and so quickly could they generate findings that they made field studies of small groups seem almost a waste of time. Where are now such studies as that of the Bank Wiring Room in the Western Electric researches (Roethlisberger & Dickson 1939), of Whyte's *Street Corner Society* (1943), of Peter Blau's *The Dynamics of Bureaucracy* (1955)? I can think of some, but in no such quantity or quality.

The decline of these studies has had three unfortunate results. First, science begins, as L. J. Henderson used to say, with the scientist's acquiring an intuitive familiarity with the facts (see Barber 1970:67). In our field, this can only be acquired by the scientist's watching and talking to people at first hand, and field studies alone provide the opportunity. Science, of course, does not end there, but it certainly begins there.

Second, I believe that the fundamental principles of social behavior (an adequate microsociology, if you will) can best be worked out after direct observation and interviewing—and I do not mean with formal questionnaires— of a few people interacting with one another. At least since the time of Edgeworth (1881), economics has had an adequate microeconomics, on which it could fall back when its macrotheories yielded contradictory intellectual or practical results—as they do now, when Keynsianism has lost its dominance and macroeconomics is in disarray. We have no such microsociology. I tried to produce one, based on behaviorism, but I cannot say that it has been generally accepted (Homans 1961, 1974). Others have done microsociological work but have failed to produce a microsociology.

Third, we are unable to understand some (at least) of the results of survey research without the help of small-group research. Some years ago, Stanley Seashore (1954) made a survey of the workers in a large factory in the Middle West. Among other things he found that behavior interpretable as "restriction of output" was particularly likely to occur in departments that held high status. The survey itself provided no evidence by which one could explain this finding. I bet that, if the survey had been accompanied by detailed field studies of at least two departments (say, one of high status and one of low), the elements of an explanation would have been forthcoming. Why can we not combine our methods more often? Expense?

These considerations lead me to another technique, one which social psychology with its psychological tradition introduced into sociology: experimental methods. We used to argue about the degree to which these experiments corresponded to something we were pleased to call "real life." The underlying issue now seems to me a little different. It is whether in the course of establishing strong experimental controls the investigator may not destroy the very phenomena he is interested in. I have an example in mind, one unfortunately carried out by persons I otherwise admire and, what is more, published in a *festschrift* in my honor (Burgess & Nielsen 1977). The research was directed at what I call distributive justice, the relation between the rewards the members of a group receive in relation to what they contribute. I believe that some of the findings of the research were confused, but that is not the point I want to raise here. The subjects in the experiment used consoles through which they could deliver various sums of fictitious money to the parties with which they were in exchange, and to this extent each had some control over the others' behavior. With this exception, to ensure the purity of the findings, "every effort was made to prevent the subjects from meeting or identifying one another. During the course of the experimental sessions, no verbal communication between the subjects was possible." But it is only through social interaction, and repeated social interaction, that members of real groups discover what the others are gaining from or contributing to the exchange between them, and only thus do they manage to reach some degree of consensus as to the values of their rewards and contributions or the other resources by which they reckon distributive justice. Moreover, the rewards and contributions are not single but multiple. Here I think the experimenters, in a justifiable endeavor to establish strong experimental controls, managed to destroy the conditions under which problems of distributive justice manifest themselves in real life. So much for our obvious strengths and some of their ambiguities.

SOME DISAPPOINTING IDEAS

Let me turn now to the fate of some of the ideas of the 1930s; I will begin with Marxism. There are probably more American sociologists now who claim they are Marxists than there ever have been. But they are not the same young intellectuals who embraced Marx in one form or another in the New York universities before World War II. Glazer, Kristol, Bell, and the like are Marxists no longer. How then account for the recrudescence of Marxism? After all, it is now some 137 years since the publication of the Communist Manifesto. Through there are still great virtues in the ideas of historical materialism—after all, technology and the social organization the technology may favor are very good places from which to start the study of any society—none of Marx's specific predictions has been borne out, though they have had plenty of time. And Marxism has divided into a number of hairsplitting sects, which address themselves to what their rivals say rather than to how humans behave (the latter is, after all, what Marx himself tried to do).

The Bible has, in the Sermon on the Mount, a good adage: "By their fruits ye shall know them!" If ideas have consequences (and we are always being told they have), we should look at the consequences of trying to put into practice some Marxist ideas—if indeed they are Marxist and not Leninist. The results have been economic inefficiency and political repression, without even much progress towards a classless society. Under these conditions one might expect honest scientists to desert Marxism, and many of them have. But the recruits have more than replaced the deserters. Why? I think the reasons are what Pareto

(1917) would have called nonlogical (See Homans & Curtis 1934). Using Marxist language shows that you are on the side of the underdog or (which may not be quite the same thing) that you hate the bourgeoisie, though most Marxists are members of the bourgeoisie. Taking such impeccably moral positions gives many people a great deal of satisfaction. Indeed, for some there is no greater pleasure than embracing a good, simple, self-righteous moral position. Some few Marxists may believe that capitalism will collapse even in the Western democracies and that, by declaring themselves Marxists now, they will entitle themselves to positions of power in the ensuing Communist regime. Their hopes are almost wholly unfounded. As they ought to know by now, the revolution has a way of devouring its own.

At any rate, I think sociology would be much better off by abandoning Marxism and its controversies and, above all, by abandoning its language, for its substance being hollow, its language is about all Marxism has left. Abandoning Marxism would not mean that its adepts would have to change their concrete research interests. All they would have to abandon is a jargon that is increasingly hypocritical and out of touch with reality.

In a different way, the same is true of Freud, another of the thinkers who looked in the 1930s as if they would become intellectual liberators. Today what is left of Freud besides the concept of the unconscious, which even the behaviorists are eager to accept (and which does not always work in the ways Freud said it would), and some of his earlier clinical reports? The latter part of his work, if not merely the embodiment of old metaphors, is only speculation. Again, "By their fruits ye shall know them!" The application of Freud's ideas to psychotherapy has never been shown to have significant positive results. Statistically, that is, the Freudian cures have never been shown to be more numerous than those that would have occurred if the patients had just been left to the mercies of *vis medicatrix naturae* (see Brown & Herrnstein 1975, pp. 594–99.) Moreover, many psychic ills that once fell into the hands of Freudian and other psychotherapists whose techniques were limited to talking with the patient have now been shown to yield to treatment by drugs. And like Marxism, Freudianism has been riven by quibbling schools and by idiocies such as those of Jacques Lacan (see Turkle 1978). Happily, unlike Marxism, social scientists seem to me to use the ideas and language of Freudianism less and less often. It keeps its place as a convenient popular psychology for use at cocktail parties.

As for the other intellectual developments of the 1930s—functionalism in its old sense, as taken over by sociologists from anthropologists, is dead, at least in its collectivistic form, though Jeffrey Alexander (1982:55–63) promises to revive it. The individualistic form of functionalism can easily be identified with behavioral psychology (Homans 1984:343–45). Bridgman's operationalism certainly added rigor to our formulations of hypotheses, but the philosophers of science have shown that the doctrine cannot be generally applied. That is, all theories of any complexity must contain terms that cannot be defined operationally but only implicitly in the form of propositions. Thus, Newton's force law (f = ma) is not a proposition in which all the terms can be operationally defined (see Braithwaite 1953:50–87). Instead the proposition is an implicit definition of the concept *force* (f).

Strangely, the one intellectual enthusiasm of the 1930s that has shown it can maintain itself and develop scientifically is the one that has always been least popular. I mean behaviorism, a stripped-down form of which is called utilitarianism or rational-choice theory. I shall have much more to say about it later.

THE PROBLEM OF THEORY

If the chief strength of current sociology lies in its empirical studies controlled by new and powerful statistical and mathematical methods, its chief weakness lies in theory, which was once expected to redeem it from "mere fact-finding." Sociology is divided into a number of theoretical schools, each claiming to be different from the others: the Marxisms, symbolic interactionism derived from G. H. Mead (1934), exchange theory, dramaturgical theory (Goffman), ethnomethodology (Garfinkel), conflict theory (R. Collins), and others. Each has interesting empirical findings to its credit, but to my mind it is impossible to discover what the alleged theoretical differences are.

Among sociologists there is hardly anyone who does not sometimes set up to be a theorist. A theorist has high prestige. What really surprises me about the theorists is that, so far as I can tell, almost none of them, with the notable exception of myself, ever states what he or she believes a theory *is*. (See Homans 1967; another possible exception is Kaplan 1964.) True, there may be more than one definition of the word *theory*, but the theorists never specify which one is theirs. Perhaps they take the characteristics of a theory to be a matter of common knowledge. Or they may mean by *theory* simply *generalization*. If so, they are mistaken, for the issue is a tricky one, and the philosophers of science have been preoccupied with its trickiness. At any rate, the failure of sociologists even to discuss the nature of theory has meant that we cannot tell what it is they are trying to do. Or rather, we can see what in fact they do. They spend little time on developing a theory of actual human behavior and much time and enormous erudition in discussing the words of theorists like themselves. They produce words about words.

I myself as a confessed theorist have at least not neglected to consider what a theory *is*. Basing my description on the work of some, but not all, of the philosophers of science and a study of some, but not all, examples of what are accepted as good theories in the natural sciences, I have adopted and tried to use what is conventionally called the "covering law" view of theory.

I have said what follows many times, and I shall repeat it as long as I live or as long as I feel that repetition is necessary, whichever lasts longer. A theory of a phenomenon is also an explanation of the phenomenon. It consists of at least three propositions, as in a syllogism. A proposition is a statement of a relationship, often only approximately true, between properties of nature (variables). At least one of the propositions is more general than the others, in the sense that we cannot derive it logically from the conjuncture of the others, just as we cannot derive "All men are mortal" from the combination of "Socrates is a man" and "Socrates is mortal." Other propositions state the given conditions (parameters) to which the general propositions are to be applied. When the empirical proposition, the phenomenon, can be shown to follow deductively from the other propositions in the set (the deductive system), then the phenomenon is said to be explained. The deductive system is the theory of the phenomenon.

The "covering law" view takes its name from the general propositions. These can often in time be shown to follow from propositions still more general. Note that if the given conditions (parameters) change, different, though sometimes related, propositions will follow from the deductive system. And the nature of the given conditions can often themselves be explained. Indeed, what we usually call a theory is not a deductive system explaining a single phenomenon but a set of general propositions, a variety of given conditions, and a number of different empirical propositions which can be shown to follow from the general ones under different combinations of the given conditions.

The chief difference between real theories lies, it seems to me, in differences between their general propositions. Not only do sociological theorists never discuss what they mean by theory, a fortiori they never state what they consider their general propositions to be. In philosophical language, their logic is *enthymematic*. And since they do not state what they take their general propositions to be, we cannot tell whether or not, or in what ways, their theories are similar. They may well differ in their empirical content because they deal with different given conditions. That is not what counts. What does count is the nature of the general propositions.

I believe that, if theorists of sociology did make their general propositions explicit, they would find that they were all using some variety of the same set. The tragedy of sociology is that, since they do not do this (and perhaps are afraid of trying), the actual unity of our science and hence its possibilities for cumulative theoretical growth go unrecognized, and our intellectual chaos persists.

The theoretical unity of our science is well worth working toward. A good theory organizes a science, simplifies it by showing how its empirical propositions are related to one another, and often allows its adepts to predict new propositions that are worth testing.

UTILITARIANISM AND BEHAVIORISM

If it were made explicit, I think the set of general propositions in question would turn out, at the simplest level, to be something that is called rational-choice theory or utilitarianism. I do not like the word *rational* in rational-choice because *rational* is a normative term: it often refers to what someone believes to be a better way for a person to behave in order to achieve a particular result, rather than to how the person in question actually behaved. The latter is what sociologists, in the first instance, should be interested in. *Utilitarianism* does not bother me in the same way. No matter. The simplest way of putting the main proposition of rational-choice or utilitarian theory is this: In choosing between at least two alternative courses of action, a person is apt to choose the one for which the perceived value of the result multiplied by the perceived possibility that the action will achieve the result is the greater (Homans 1974:43–47).

Note that the two chief variables in the proposition are the value (degree of reward) of the result and the probability of attaining that result. The perceptions are the actor's own perceptions, which may be mistaken. They depend on his past experience of the degree of reward and success that have attended his actions and on the other circumstances (stimuli) accompanying his past actions in their bearing on value and success in the present case. They may depend on his observation of others performing similar actions and their success in obtaining valued results. (For model learning, see especially Bandura 1969.)

Rational-choice theory or utilitarianism is a first approximation to, or a simplification of, behavioral psychology. The two hold in common the main proposition cited above. Utilitarianism is a stripped-down version of behaviorism in a number of different ways. It often tends to take the perceived rewards and success of various actions as given—a statistically reasonable assumption for numerous actors pursuing widely shared values, when their success in obtaining them is virtually certain. But the more general science of behaviorism insists that individuals often learn different values, differ in their success in obtaining them, and acquire different perceptions. That is, utilitarianism has little to say about the effect of past history on present behavior. It also has little to say about emotional behavior and pays little attention to the niceties of behaviorism, such as the effect on behavior of different schedules of reward (Ferster & Skinner 1957). For instance, actions performed under intermittent schedules of reward (reinforcement) are particularly resistant to extinction (their elimination when reinforcement ceases). Utilitarianism will serve well enough as the general proposition in theories of many kinds of human behavior, but not for all. For the wider reach the full panoply of behavioral psychology is needed.

Behavioral psychology, together with cognitive psychology (which some take to be a separate science), is a set of propositions about human nature, or so much of it as we know now. It states the characteristics of behavior that human beings share as members of a single species. It obviously does not imply that all human beings behave exactly alike. The variables in the propositions remain; their coefficients, so to speak, differ. Individuals differ genetically in their behavior. They differ in what they have learned and therefore in their current behavior. Indeed, if we know enough about their pasts, including their genetic differences (which we rarely do), we can use the general propositions to explain why they differ in what they have learned. By the same token, human cultures differ because their past histories have differed, though we are often at a loss to explain why, because many differences were already present before the historical record begins. But the general propositions still hold, and human nature in this sense is indeed the same the world over—a view that would have been treated as a heresy in the heyday, again in the 1930s, of the "culture and personality" school of anthropology.

The general propositions of behaviorism are the general propositions not only of sociology but of all the social sciences. That does not mean that every social science uses them to explain the same phenomena, for the different disciplines apply them to different given conditions. The conditions of the classical market are not those of an enduring small group. What should serve as a warning to sociologists is that the other social sciences are increasingly using behaviorism, usually in its utilitarian form, to explain phenomena that used to lie within the field of sociology. Consider, just to take a few instances, the work of Olson (1965), Schelling (1984), and Barry (1970). Sociology is in danger of losing potentially important parts of its field to other disciplines because most sociologists (though, I am glad to say, not all) refuse to use this powerful theoretical tool.

I say that they *refuse* to use it because I observe that behaviorism and utilitarianism are sometimes mentioned by sociologists and then rejected, usually without familiarizing themselves with what they have rejected. The rejection also seems to vary by nationalities. Although most often rejected by British and American sociologists, behaviorism and utilitarianism are making their way even among them. For a few examples see Burgess & Bushell (1969), Hamblin (1971), Scott (1971), Kunkel (1975), and Hechter (1983). These theories seem to be most often accepted in West Germany, though the emphasis there is less often on behaviorism than on utilitarianism and methodological individualism. For a few examples, see Malewski (1967), Schwanenberg (1970), Opp (1972, 1985), Vanberg (1975), and Raub (1984). Since most American sociologists do not read German—another example of the weakness of language instruction in American schools—they do not know what they are missing. What are the reasons for this "great refusal"?

REASONS FOR THE REJECTION OF BEHAVIORISM

Six reasons have been put forward for the rejection of behaviorism as a theory.

1. By the very name of their subject, sociologists have to do with social behavior. But the propositions of behavioral psychology are individualistic. That is, the propositions apply to the behavior of individuals, not of groups. In the language of philosophy, such propositions should be formally stated, for instance, as "For all individuals, if a particular kind of action taken by an individual is rewarded, then . . . ." But this has nothing to do with individualism as a moral philosophy, which is repugnant to many persons. Behaviorism does not imply that the largest part of human behavior has ever been anything but social—that is, consisting of interactions between individuals. What it does imply is that no new proposition is needed to explain a person's behavior when his action is rewarded by another person from when it is rewarded by the nonhuman environment, as by his catching a fish. Of course the effects of social behavior may be much more complicated, because the given conditions to which the general propositions apply are more complicated too. Sociologists should heed statements like a recent one by Pierre Boudon (1984:39): "A fundamental principle of the sociologies of action is that social change ought to be analyzed as the resultant of an ensemble of individual actions" (my translation). The ensemble may be very complicated, requiring complicated mathematics for its analysis, and the resultant, one that no single individual intended.

   Behavioral psychology as a set of individualistic propositions implies that there can be no general laws of history as such, which so many historians have so long sought for in vain. The only general laws of history are the laws of human nature. There are many true historical, as there are sociological, propositions of less than full generality, because some social conditions may favor the appearance of similar "ensembles of individual actions;" but these conditions are never universal. Boudon's whole book *La Place du désordre* (1984) is devoted to this argument, though as an implication of individualism, not behaviorism.

2. Behaviorism, it has been said, robs human beings of purposes, which are one of their most precious perquisites (Coleman 1975:79). Behaviorism does no such thing. All it insists on is that purposes do not come to human beings out of the blue. Purpose does not imply teleology. Drives may be given genetically, but an individual must learn the particular actions that will satisfy these drives. He learns them from past experience, and he applies them under contingencies (stimuli) whose relevance he has also learned in the past. And the same is true of actions that receive secondary rather than primary rewards. A purpose is an action, or an approxima-

tion of that action, that has been rewarded in the past—that has been conditioned.

3. As a study of the effects of reward and punishment, behaviorism is hedonism in its crudest form, and good people—sociologists are of course good people—are never hedonists. Early behaviorist writings did often sound pretty crude. But modern behaviorism recognizes that altruism can be acquired through classical (respondent) conditioning which depends on genetically determined rewards. As H. J. Eysenck remarked, "Conscience is a conditioned reflex" (quoted in Wilson & Herrnstein 1985:48).

4. Behaviorism is a psychological doctrine. Indeed, once treated as a pariah, it has now become a part of mainstream psychology. What is worse, its propositions can be used to reduce sociology to psychology. What this means is that sociological propositions—to speak crudely, propositions of the sort usually put forward by sociologists—can be shown to follow under specified given conditions from psychological propositions. Many sociologists feel that this robs their subject of its status as an independent science; and its status is none too high as it is. But chemistry, for instance, does not seem to have lost its identity from being shown to be reducible to physics. And if sociology loses its sense of identity through psychological reductionism, so should all the social sciences. But they will not, because though they use the same psychological general propositions, they usually apply them to different given conditions. Perhaps the real source of the difficulty many sociologists (not the social psychologists) find with behaviorism derives from their limited knowledge of psychology. They prefer to read Habermas and forgo the greater advantage of really learning about social behavior in humans and animals.

5. A rather different kind of criticism is one that accuses some of the propositions of behaviorism of being tautological. For one example, consider the proposition: The more valuable a reward, the more likely a person is to take action that is followed by the reward. This is tautological, it is said, because there is no independent measure of value other than the frequency of action taken to get it. In this sense the proposition is indeed tautological. But we must always examine how statements like this are actually used in theories. The formula is a useful catchall. A large number of different kinds of result are known empirically to be reinforcing. Instead of enumerating them, which cannot be done, for new ones are being discovered all the time and learned, we substitute into our formula particular values that are relevant. After all, the statement that a person deprived of food is, until satiated, apt to take frequent action that is followed by food is true but *not* tautological. Braithwaite (1953:50–87) has shown that the kind of tautological statement which is an implicit definition of theoretical terms

must occur in many, if not all, scientific explanations. Incidentally, this is one of the most important arguments against strict operationalism.

6. I am not saying that the sociological theorists do not often have good ideas. They do. I am saying that their theories are inadequate because they leave their major premises unstated. Indeed, they seem to be unaware of what their major premises are. Let me take an example. One of the charges that some of the sociologists bring against their behaviorist colleagues is that they neglect the effects of social structures on the behavior of individuals. By social structures I shall mean—and I think the critics mean—more or less enduring practices followed by a number of persons, whether or not these practices are made explicit in norms or defended by sanctions. Structures include what we usually call institutions. To this controversy, Anthony Giddens introduces the idea of *structuration,* which he describes as follows: "The concept of structuration involves that of the *duality of structure,* which relates to the *fundamentally recursive character of social life, and expresses the mutual dependence of structure and agency.* By the duality of structure I mean that the structural properties of social systems are both the medium and the outcome of the practices that constitute those systems" (1979:69; Giddens' emphases).

If I understand it right, I think this is a good idea. I would translate it into what I think is clearer, less abstract, though more lengthy language: Individuals by their actions (agency), in concert or even at cross-purposes, intentionally or unintentionally, are always in the process of creating and maintaining social structures, at least for a time, for no structure endures forever. Indeed, the structures *are* the actions. But while structures are thus being created and maintained by the acts of individuals, these same structures are providing new contingencies (rewards, stimuli, possibilities of success or failure) for the maintenance, again by the actions of people, of old structures or the creation of new ones. This is the "fundamentally recursive character of social life." If I have translated *structuration* adequately, this is a sound view and one I have long held myself.

But the acute reader of Giddens will note that he provides no explanation how and why the actions of people create or maintain structures, nor how and why structures in turn maintain or change the actions of people by affecting the contingencies of their behavior. To do so, Giddens would have had to bring in behaviorism, under that name or another, and he does not even begin to do so. To that extent, his theory is a good description but an inadequate explanation.

The reasons for rejecting or ignoring behaviorism are often emotionally, but never intellectually, compelling.

RECENT DEVELOPMENTS

I have spoken of the failures and disappointments, except in the mathematical and technical fields, of the hopes entertained by sociologists in the 1930s. Especially disappointing have been the results of so-called theoretical work. They have not even produced conclusions on what a theory *is*. But at the end I want to mitigate the gloom and mention three recent developments I think are especially hopeful.

Social Networks

The first is the study of social networks, an application of mathematics to the analysis of small (and potentially to large) social structures. A social network is a pattern of positive or negative choices, on some criterion such as liking or disliking, made by individuals for or against other individuals in a small group or much larger assemblage of persons. The study of social networks grew out of such psychological researches as "balance theory" (Heider 1946) and the description of concrete networks in Homans (1950). The mathematical problem is that of devising equations from which the underlying and nonobvious characteristics of concrete networks can be generated. More generally, it is that of "generating quantified statements about the pattern of social relations in a community" (Barnes 1979:412). Network research has recently attracted an extremely able group of sociologists and mathematicians, such as Harrison White, James A. Davis, and their associates, Scott Boorman, Ronald Breiger, Mark Granovetter, Paul DiMaggio and many others. I am not enough of a mathematician myself to evaluate the work, but I can see that it can add an important dimension to our understanding of social structures. A good survey of recent research on social networks will be found in Holland & Lienhardt (1979).

But about one thing I believe I am clear: Social network theory cannot be a general sociological theory, for the existence of networks themselves still has to be explained. Social networks arise out of the choices individuals make for interacting with other individuals, from the development of cliques, and the development of hierarchies within cliques and among them. Social network research, with the exception of a part of "balance theory," cannot deal with these matters. They will have to be explained by a more general theory of social behavior, derived from an individualistic behavioral psychology. Indeed "balance theory" can itself be derived from such a psychology (see Homans 1974:59–65). But network analysis should help a behavioral psychology be much more clear about what social phenomena it has to explain.

Sociology and History

The second encouraging development is the increasing interest of sociologists in history. This too was, I believe, originally stimulated by work in the 1930s, especially by Marc Bloch (1931) and the *Annales* school in France, concentrating on the fields of economic and social history. But in those days American sociologists seemed to know no history except of the most contemporary American sort. Yet economic and social history obviously shares certain interests with sociology. No sharp line can be drawn between them, and history adds a dynamic dimension to sociology.

This condition has now changed, and American sociology in recent years has produced a number of interesting social and economic historians such as Barrington Moore, Jr. (1966), Charles Tilly (1975), Emmanuel Wallerstein (1974), Theda Skocpol (1979), and Arthur Stinchcombe (1978). The early members of the *Annales* school had usually limited themselves to close studies of particular countries or even districts. Perhaps under the influence of later *Annaliens* such as Fernand Braudel (1973), some of the Americans have taken on historical problems of much greater scope. Perhaps the most notable example is Wallerstein's attempt to delineate the development of a world economic system.

The problem faced by historians of this kind is that, with important exceptions such as Moore and Tilly, they must depend on secondary sources and on their own judgment of what sources are reliable. They lack the training in the use of primary sources which is one of the strengths of the professional historians. Their ambitions are so vast that they have not the time for this kind of training. The result is that professional historians often find gaps and weaknesses in particular steps in their arguments. My own suggestion is that sociologists should acquire training in the use of primary sources in at least some area of their interests. That experience would teach them to hold the other secondary sources in some abeyance of belief. With this reservation, I think many of the conceptions of the new sociological historians are undoubtedly important. This kind of work is promising; it enlarges our discipline and should be encouraged.

Charles Tilly is somewhat different from the others. The scope of the problems he tackles is a little smaller. He works systematically with certain kinds of primary sources and exploits them with modern statistical techniques. He can do this work only with the help of a team of well-integrated and well-trained colleagues. Indeed, I doubt if sound history on a grand scale can be carried out by individuals, in the manner of Spengler and Toynbee. But again the work is promising and should be encouraged.

Sociobiology

The third new, or revived, area of interest is that of genetic influences on behavior. Again, this interest goes back to the 1930s and to the controversy in psychology between the advocates of nature (genetics) or nurture (learning) as the main kind of influence on behavior. At that time the overwhelming weight of opinion and research came down on the side of nurture. Indeed, the question appeared to be settled, and nature was almost forgotten.

But later, stimulated by such pioneers in the study of the social behavior of animals as Lorenz and Tinbergen, the question was reopened, particularly in two books by Edward O. Wilson—*Sociobiology* (1975) and *On Human Nature* (1978). In one sense it had never been closed. Not just scholars but ordinary persons of sense had always known that animals, including humans, inherited their physical characteristics from their ancestors. And such persons of sense often shrewdly surmised that they had inherited some of their psychological characteristics too, and by physical genetics at that, not just because their parents had brought them up in the ways the parents themselves had learned.

The sociobiologists turned that shrewd surmise into a real scientific possibility. The new statistics then made it possible for social scientists to estimate *how much* of a given psychological trait (which of course would manifest itself in social behavior) could be attributed to genetic inheritance and *how much* to learning. The issue is highly controversial for three reasons. First, it raises the possibility of racial differences in such traits as intelligence—and I want to make it clear that for my part I am only concerned with individual differences. Second, the statistical techniques can be applied only under special and rather rare conditions, such as the existence of identical twins reared by different foster-parents. And third, genetic inheritance, which resists quick change, would inhibit the efforts of those high-minded persons who think human nature is a blank slate on which benign social arrangements can write through learning whatever behavior they wish. Will the Old Adam, for instance, abort the birth of the "new Communist man"?

Many sociologists are such high-minded persons, and others as usual are afraid that sociobiology will destroy the identity of sociology as a distinct science.

The most interesting question turns out not to be that of the place of genetics versus that of learning in human behavior, but rather of how the two interact. Thus, a person born genetically to be large and strong will learn to behave under contingencies different from those faced by one born to be small and puny, and therefore, the phenotypical behavior of the two is apt to be different for a combination of both kinds of reasons. Or again, some kinds of behavior that are certainly of genetic origin can be changed by learning much less easily than can some others.

But I shall say no more about sociobiology since both the research and the debate are young and still developing. The time is not ripe for firm conclusions. Yet the issues sociobiology raises for the understanding of human social behavior are momentous, and sociologists cannot afford to dismiss them, at least so long as they are more interested in the pursuit of truth than in the identity of their subject. Indeed if they ignore genetics as they have so long tried to ignore behavioral psychology, they will find their field contracting, not expanding.

Let me give an example of the possible shape of things to come. Sociologists have had for years a practical monopoly of the field of criminology; by and large they have adopted some form of the view that crime rates are determined by purely social conditions, and to some degree they are correct. But the best recent book on criminology, *Crime and Human Nature,* by James O. Wilson and Richard Herrnstein (1985), brings to the study of the subject both behaviorism and genetics. Yet neither of the authors are sociologists—one is a political scientist and the other a psychologist.

In the last 50 years, the great success of sociology has lain in its development of statistical and mathematical methods, which have added greatly to the soundness of our empirical knowledge in many fields. This success has been accomplished to some extent at the expense of field research. The weakness of sociology has continued to lie in theory. Not only have most sociologists failed to accept an adequate conception of what a theory *is,* but they have allowed themselves to fragment into a number of allegedly incompatible theoretical schools. These could be united by an individualistic behavioral psychology. Most sociologists have not been willing to write in this way, and their reluctance has allowed social scientists of other disciplines to make advances in areas that should be (and have been in the past) of great interest to sociology. The increasing interest of sociologists in historical problems is a favorable development, but their ambivalence towards sociobiology perpetuates their old and mistaken fears about the independent status of their discipline. Our field ought to be expanding, not contracting, and it should be open, as any great science must be, to all kinds of ideas and research that may have something to add to knowledge not only of our own field but of the behavior of all humankind.

Literature Cited

Alexander, J. 1982. *Theoretical Logic in Sociology,* Vol. 1. Berkeley: Univ. Calif. Press

Arensberg, C. M., Kimball, S. T. 1941. *Family and Community in Ireland.* Cambridge, Mass: Harvard Univ. Press

Bandura, A. 1969. *Principles of Behavior Modification.* New York: Holt, Rinehart & Winston

Barber, B. 1970. *L. J. Henderson on the Social System.* Chicago: Univ. Chicago Press

Barnes, J. A. 1979. Network analysis: Orienting notion, rigorous technique, or substantive field of study. See Holland & Lienhardt 1979, pp. 403–21.

Barry, B. 1970. *Sociologists, Economists, and Democracy.* London: Collier-Macmillan

Blau, P. M. 1955. *The Dynamics of Bureaucracy.* Chicago: Univ. Chicago Press

Bloch, M. 1931. *Les Caractères originaux de l'histoire rurale française.* Oslo: Inst. Sammenlignende Kulturforskning

Boudon, R. 1984. *La Place du désordre.* Paris: Presses Univ. France

Braithwaite, R. B. 1953. *Scientific Explanation.* Cambridge: Cambridge Univ. Press

Braudel, F. 1973. *The Mediterranean and the Mediterranean World in The Age of Philip II.* Vols. 1, 2. New York: Harper & Row. (Originally published as *La Méditerranée et le Monde Méditerranéen a l'Époque de Philippe II.* Paris: Armand Colin, 1949)

Bridgman, P. W. 1936. *The Nature of Physical Theory.* Princeton: Princeton Univ. Press

Brown, R., Herrnstein, R. J. 1975. *Psychology.* Boston: Little, Brown

Burgess, R. L., Bushell, D. Jr., eds. 1969.

Behavioral Sociology. New York: Columbia Univ. Press

Burgess, R. L., Nielsen, J. M. 1977. Distributive justice and the balance of power. In *Behavioral Theory in Sociology: Essays in Honor of George C. Homans*, ed. R. L. Hamblin, J. H. Kunkel, pp. 139–69. New Brunswick, NJ: Transaction

Coleman, J. S. 1975. Social structure and a theory of action. In *Approaches to the Study of Social Strucure*, ed. P. M. Blau, pp. 76–93. New York: Free Press

Coleman, J. S. et al 1966. *Equality of Educational Opportunity*, Vols. 1, 2. Washington, DC: Office Educ.

Edgeworth, F. Y. 1881. *Mathematical Psychics.* London: Kegan Paul

Ferster, C. B., Skinner, B. F. 1957. *Schedules of Reinforcement.* New York: Appleton-Century-Crofts

Giddens, A. 1979. *Central Problems in Social Theory.* Berkeley: Univ. Calif. Press

Hamblin, R. L. et al 1971. *The Humanization Processes.* New York: Wiley Intersci.

Hechter, M. ed. 1983. *The Microfoundations of Macrosociology.* Philadelphia: Temple Univ. Press

Heider, F. 1946. Attitudes and cognitive organization. *J. Psychol.* 21:107–12

Holland, P. W., Lienhardt, S., eds. 1979. *Perspectives on Social Network Research.* New York: Academic

Homans, G. C. 1950. *The Human Group.* New York: Harcourt Brace

Homans, G. C. 1961 (Rev. ed. 1974). *Social Behavior: Its Elementary Forms.* New York: Harcourt Brace Jovanovich

Homans, G. C. 1967. *The Nature of Social Science.* New York: Harcourt, Brace & World

Homans, G. C. 1984. *Coming to My Senses: The Autobiography of a Sociologist.* New Brunswick, NJ: Transaction

Homans, G. C., Curtis, C. P. Jr. 1934. *An Introduction to Pareto.* New York: Knopf

Kaplan, A. 1964. *The Conduct of Inquiry.* San Francisco: Chandler

Kunkel, J. H. 1975. *Behavior, Social Problems, and Change.* Englewood Cliffs, NJ: Prentice-Hall

Lynd, R. S., Lynd, H. M. 1929. *Middletown.* New York: Harcourt, Brace

Malewski, A. 1967. *Verhalten und Interaction.* Tübingen: Mohr. (Originally published 1964. *O zastosowaniach teorie zachowania.* Warsaw: Państowowe Wydawnictwo Naukowe)

Mead, G. H. 1934. *Mind, Self, & Society.* Chicago: Univ. Chicago Press

Moore, B. Jr. 1966. *Social Origins of Democracy and Dictatorship.* Boston: Beacon

Moreno, J. L. 1934. *Who Shall Survive?* Washington, DC: Nervous and Mental Disease Publ.

Olson, M. Jr. 1965. *The Logic of Collective Action.* Cambridge, Mass: Harvard Univ. Press

Opp, K-D. 1972. *Verhaltens-theoretische Soziologie.* Hamburg: Rohwolt

Opp, K-D. 1985. Sociology and Economic Man. *Zeitschrift für die gesamte Staatswissenschaft.* 141:213–43

Pareto, V. 1917. *Traité de sociologie générale,* Vols. 1, 2. Paris: Payot

Raub, W. 1984. *Rationale Akteure, institutionelle Regelungen und Interdependenzen.* Frankfurt am Main: Peter Lang

Roethlisberger, F. J., Dickson, W. J. 1939. *Management and the Worker.* Cambridge, Mass: Harvard Univ. Press.

Schelling, T. S. 1984. *Choice and Consequence.* Cambridge, Mass: Harvard Univ. Press

Schwanenberg, E. 1970. *Soziales Handel—Die Theorie und ihr Probleme.* Bern: Hans Huber

Scott, J. F. 1971. *The Internalization of Norms.* Englewood Cliffs, NJ: Prentice-Hall

Seashore, S. E. 1954. *Group Cohesiveness in the Industrial Work Group.* Ann Arbor, Mich: Univ. Mich. Inst. Soc. Res.

Skinner, B. F. 1938. *The Behavior of Organisms.* New York: Appleton-Century

Skocpol, T. 1979. *States and Social Revolutions.* Cambridge: Cambridge Univ. Press

Stinchcombe, A. L. 1978. *Theoretical Methods in Social History.* New York: Academic

Tilly, C., Tilly L., Tilly, R. 1975. *The Rebellious Century.* Cambridge, Mass: Harvard Univ. Press

Turkle, S. 1978. *Psychoanalytic Politics.* New York: Basic

Vanberg, V. 1975. *Die zwei Soziologien.* Tübingen: Mohr

Wallerstein, E. 1974. *The Modern World-System,* Vol. 1. New York: Academic Press

Warner, W. L. et al 1941–1963. *Yankee City Series,* Vols. 1–6. New Haven: Yale Univ. Press

Whyte, W. F. 1943. *Street Corner Society.* Chicago: Chicago Univ. Press

Wilson, E. O. 1975. *Sociobiology.* Cambridge, Mass: Harvard Univ. Press

Wilson, E. O. 1978. *On Human Nature.* Cambridge, Mass: Harvard Univ. Press

Wilson, J. Q., Herrnstein, R. J. 1985. *Crime and Human Nature.* New York: Simon & Schuster

Ann. Rev. Sociol. 1986. 12:1–21

ASSOCIATIONS AND INTEREST GROUPS

David Knoke

Department of Sociology, University of Minnesota, Minneapolis, Minnesota 55455

Abstract

A review of the past decade's research on American associations reveals significant growth in empirical findings across three levels of analysis: the individual member, the organization, and the political system. The social correlates of joining and participation, particularly gender and race differences, and the effect of incentives on individual decisions continued to attract the interest of many researchers. At the organization level, the structure of incentives and the impact of collective decision-making processes received less attention than the social ecology of association growth and differentiation. The advocacy explosion of recent years that brought many new groups and lobbying methods to Washington stimulated much research on associations in the pressure group system. The field of association research as a whole, however, still suffers from a lack of theoretical consensus on the central issues and of means for studying them.

INTRODUCTION

Elements for a comprehensive theory of associations lie scattered across diverse disciplines, including sociology, political science, business, organizational analysis, social work, labor economics, recreation and leisure, and law. This review describes many of the major writings on American associations and interest groups of the past decade. A comprehensive bibliography, which would easily run to 400 books and articles, is not attempted. (For the large literature on associations before 1976, the reader may consult several excellent bibliographic essays, including Smith 1975, Smith & Macauley 1980, and Salisbury 1975). Neither can I do justice to the vast literature on social

1

0360-0572/86/0815-0001$02.00

movements, which includes analysis of the interplay of formal movement organizations with more diffuse kinds of collective behaviors (e.g. McAdam 1982, Lo 1982). Space limitations necessitate a narrower examination of the part played by established American associations in group differences with respect to political participation and power.

To anticipate my overall assessment, research on associations expanded steadily during the decade. However, its surface diversity and richness mask the field's underlying anarchy. Put bluntly, association research remains a largely unintegrated set of disparate findings, in dire need of a compelling theory to force greater coherence upon the enterprise. Without a common agreement about central concepts, problems, explanations, and analytic tools, students of associations and interest groups seem destined to leave their subject in scientific immaturity. Now to the particulars of that indictment.

A DEFINITION AND A FRAMEWORK

A minimal definition of an association is "a formally organized named group, most of whose members—whether persons or organizations—are not financially recompensed for their participation." (Whether significant differences in structure arise from membership based on natural persons vs organizations has not been a focus of investigation.) These criteria serve to distinguish associations on the one hand from primary groups, such as families, and on the other hand from bureaucratic organizations, such as private-sector firms and government bureaus (see Knoke & Prensky 1984, for a systematic comparison among these types of social organization). Within this broad compass, associations span the range of functionally specialized societal subsystems: labor unions, churches and sects, social movement organizations, political parties, professional societies, business and trade associations, fraternal and sororal organizations, recreational clubs, civic service associations, philanthropies, social welfare councils, communes, cooperatives, and neighborhood organizations. Most associations embrace principles of egalitarian and voluntary participation, perform essential integrative tasks for a society, and account collectively for significant amounts of economic and political activity in advanced industrial nations. Whenever associations attempt to influence governmental decisions, they are acting as interest groups.

In recent years, I have advocated a political economy framework as the most useful structure for organizing the literature on associations, and I will employ it again here. Since an exposition appears elsewhere (Knoke 1985), I will not recapitulate it in detail. The political economy approach emphasizes the processes of acquisition and allocation of organizational resources to collective objectives. These processes occur at three analytic levels, each asking a basic question about how different social actors decide to apply their resources to achieve their goals. These levels of analysis, elaborated below, are: the individual, the organization, and the polity.

MEMBERS IN RELATION TO THEIR ASSOCIATIONS

The unit of analysis at the individual level is a person who is a potential member of an association. Such persons face, first, a decision about whether or not to join an association and second, once they are members, a decision about an appropriate level of participation. The latter decision basically concerns what amount of personally controlled resources should be relinquished to the association. That is, what degree of "loss of power" (Coleman 1973) can be tolerated in return for other benefits? Research on individuals' association behavior may be roughly dichotomized into analyses examining the joining process and those inquiring into participatory consequences, both internal and external to the organization.

Causes of Participation

SOCIAL CORRELATES   Despite America's image as a nation of joiners—inaugurated in 1835 by Tocqueville's (1961:141) famous observation that "Americans of all ages, all conditions, and all dispositions, constantly form associations"—participation is neither exceptionally widespread nor deep. At any time, perhaps a third of US adults belong to no formal voluntary organization, and only a third hold membership in more than one association, not counting churches (Verba & Nie 1972:41–42, Olsen 1982:128). The amount of active participation is even lower, since many of these memberships are nominal.

Research attention to the social correlates of joining and participating continued steadily during the past decade. Many researchers, using cross-sectional surveys, largely confined themselves to empirical analyses of relationships between association involvement and such "background" variables as age, education, income, marital status, community size, gender, race, and the like (e.g. Cutler 1976, Knoke & Thomson 1977, Hanks & Eckland 1978, Klobus-Edwards et al 1978, Sutton 1980, Hanks 1981, Gordon & Long 1981). Reanalysis of a longitudinal Nebraska survey using multivariate techniques demonstrated that differences in membership rates across social categories "are most likely due to differences in the rate of joining associations, rather than in leaving them" (McPherson & Lockwood 1980:80). The effects uncovered in these various studies were sometimes contradictory and their magnitudes tended to range between the modest and the trivial. One article, on the basis of small R-squares, concluded pessimistically that "no definitive statement can be made regarding the seemingly ineffectual nature of the correlates in predicting social involvement" (Edwards & White 1980:71). Such uncertainty will likely persist until research is conducted on a representative national sample, in which theoretically guided data are collected about individuals' joining and participating decisions. For example, no one seems to have pursued Palisi & Jacobson's (1977) intriguing suggestion that association participation is systematically structured by a set of "dominant statuses," such as class, race, gender, and age. While such empirical covariations are frequently observed, researchers have yet to explain in more than ad hoc ways just how such status dimensions come to be related to greater or lesser levels of involvement.

GENDER AND RACE   Two areas in which considerable progress was made in the past decade were the study of gender and race differences in association involvement. Data spanning 20 years suggest some blurring of the gender gap in overall participation rates. Comparative surveys from five nations in the early 1960s showed that men belong to organizations at a higher rate then women, even when greater male trade union involvement is taken into account (Gustafson et al 1979, see Sutton 1980). However, women's increasing employment in the labor force seems to equalize their role in instrumental (business-related and union) organizations, a finding also supported by American national data from the late 1970s (Klobus-Edwards et al 1984). Such apparent equalization of aggregate gender participation rates belies substantial persistent differences in the types of association and their consequences, as shown in perceptive analyses by McPherson & Smith-Lovin (1982, 1984). Direct evidence on the sex composition of associations in 10 Nebraskan communities revealed a high degree of gender segregation, with half of the organizations exclusively female and another fifth wholly male. Female memberships generate an average of 30 network contacts, while men's memberships offer them 38 connections, and the latter tend to be more sexually heterogeneous (McPherson & Smith-Lovin 1984). Viewed as opportunity structures for "weak tie" channels to the larger community's economy and polity, these gender affiliation patterns thus give men a decided advantage.

A lively debate about race differences in participation flourished during the past decade. Verba & Nie (1972:205–8) provided a benchmark, with their finding that the deficit in political participation of blacks relative to whites is reduced by multiple active affiliations with associations. However, the higher proportion of organizational activists in the white population yields greater gains in overall political participation to whites. The racial gap was not as severe as that between lower and upper socioeconomic status (SES) groups. Subsequent researchers generally found that blacks' participation rates fell below whites' but disagreed on whether the gap could be traced to black SES disadvantages.

Recent controversy swirled around whether black participation can be explained as a strong ethnic community process. This hypothesis argues that many blacks, to change social conditions, exert efforts beyond what can be predicted by their SES. The excess derives from the high participatory motivation of those blacks with strong ethnic-racial consciousness, engendered by the civil rights and black power movements since the 1960s. Evidence for this ethnic community process was initially mixed, with some studies supporting (London 1975, McPherson 1977) and others rejecting it (Cohen & Kapsis 1978, Klobus-Edwards et al 1978, Thomson & Knoke 1980). However, Guterbock & London (1983) in a definitive study used the 1967 Verba-Nie national survey to perform exhaustive tests of four competing models of racial participation. They compared observed and expected rates of black and white formal membership in voluntary associations and political participation under varying political trust and efficacy orientations. They rejected the compensatory, isolation, and cultural-inhibition models but found strong evidence for the ethnic community process, involving low trust (or high system blaming) and high efficacy. Distrustful blacks participated politically at much higher rates than expected on the basis of their SES and demographic characteristics. Blacks as a whole participated politically and socially at levels comparable to whites of equivalent class levels and trust-efficacy orientations. The Guterbock & London analyses demonstrated the usefulness of a conflict model for explaining racial differences in individual sociopolitical participation.

Much less attention has been devoted to understanding the larger participatory differentials among groups with different socioeconomic status. Building upon these well-known empirical generalizations, McPherson (1981) specified a simple stochastic process model of the turnover in voluntary affiliations. It satisfactorily accounted for observed SES differences within six nations, due to the tendency of high-status persons to join at greater rates and to remain longer in organizations. Negative consequences for lower-status persons are apparent, for example, in restricted access to network contacts and political resources.

THE IMPACT OF SELECTIVE INCENTIVES   The most prominent exemplar of rational choice explanations of participation in associations is Mancur Olson's classic *The Logic of Collective Action* (1965). Olson challenged the conventional assumption that individuals will join an organization in order to produce a public good, the benefits of which they may enjoy whether they join or not. In the political economy literature, the concept of a public good has a precise meaning: A good or service from whose consumption no group member can be excluded regardless of the level of an individual's contribution towards the provision of that good. Olson's central insight was that even when all potential group members with an interest in a public good might benefit if the good were produced, many persons would fail to make adequate contributions towards its production if the group relies solely on the value of the collective good to induce the contributions. In other words, the temptation to take a "free ride" threatens the demise of nascent organizations.

While philanthropy, coercion, or irrationality may compel a few people to join some groups, these motivations are inadequate to account for the prevalence of associations (Olson 1965:159–65). Olson argued the necessity for groups to induce members to make resource commitments for collective ends by persuasive means other than the utility inherent in the public goods themselves. Selective incentives, benefits unavailable to persons outside an organization, are offered to potential members, contingent upon their contribution to collective action (Olson 1965:51). Associations offer newsletter and journal subscriptions, group travel and insurance plans, seminars and workshops, and the solidary attractions of social activities such as parties and picnics to attract potential free riders. Thus, an organization's efforts for the public good are reduced to a "by-product" of members' rational pursuit of private goods (Olson 1965:132–35).

In the past two decades, considerable effort was poured into refining Olson's theoretical insights (Brubaker 1975, Smith 1976, Fireman & Gamson 1979, Oliver 1980). Other theorists argued that Olson's analysis is more widely applicable to organizations that offer mainly public policy goals as inducements to join, such as Common Cause (Salisbury 1975, Berry 1977, Moe 1980) or trade associations (Staber & Aldrich 1983). However, these modifications still maintain the central thrust of Olson's economic rationality approach: Individual decision-making is a cost-benefit calculus weighing the values of selective private-good incentives against the public goods produced by an association.

Empirical tests of hypotheses drawn from Olson's collective action theory are inconclusive. Moe's (1980:201–18) analysis of survey data from members of five economic associations suggested that members join and remain primarily because of the material services, but also because of the public policy objectives sought by the associations. However, Tillock & Morrison (1979), using survey data from Zero Population Growth, showed that many members willingly contributed to the organization in the absence of selective incentives. In a reply, Olson argued that selective incentives were indispensable, given the fact that many people with interests in population control did not join ZPG. On the other hand, using member data from several environmental interest groups, Mitchell argued that "private goods supplement the public goods and bads incentives that have a powerful motivating force of their own" (Mitchell 1979:121). Further, Godwin & Mitchell's (1982) formal models, applied to the same environmental data, found evidence that both free riding and norms of fairness in allocating rewards are present in decisions to join public interest groups, to participate in their internal affairs, and to contact public officials (but see the exchange between Hardin and the two authors in the same issue). Finally, Oliver (1984) showed that joining a neighborhood organization was positively affected by a belief that others would be active on community issues. But, leadership and activity level among members was inversely related to optimism about the prospects for collective action. She concluded that members rejected their neighbors' free riding: If others are unlikely to produce a collective good, one must either provide it herself or do without.

Perhaps the most damaging empirical critique of the Olson model was Marwell & Ames' field experiments on the free-rider problem (1979, 1980). They asked high school students to allocate $5 in tokens between a private good with a fixed interest rate and a public good having higher rates of return depending upon the amounts contributed by the other group members. Contrary to Olson's free-rider hypothesis that either suboptimal or no investments in the public good would be made, about 66% of the subjects invested half their tokens, while only 13% invested nothing in the public good. Although the optimum investment point was not reached, the strong free-rider hypothesis was clearly refuted. Postexperimental debriefing of subjects suggested that normative expectations of fairness accounted for much of the subjects' behavior.

> [N]ormative factors such as fairness seem to have strongly influenced economic decisions. It appears that subjects see the claims of groups for public goods as intrinsically normative in nature and their participation in the provision of goods as at least one major goal to be weighed in their matrix of motives (Marwell & Ames 1979:1359).

Intriguing as the Marwell & Ames findings are, their external validity remains to be demonstrated in relation to the behavior of adults in real collective-goods associations. While rational-choice explanations of participatory behavior remain popular, the accumulating evidence is pointing researchers toward more multifaceted accounts of individual motivations.

The Consequences of Participation

Associations enjoy a privileged position in various theories of mass society (Halebsky 1976). They are crucial mechanisms for social integration, bastions of democracy, and bulwarks against centripetal impulses towards communal fragmentation. Some initial efforts have examined the dynamics of association life and shown how variation in member participation is linked both to organizational commitment within the association and to the mobilization of external political efforts.

THE COMMITMENT PROCESS   Some evidence has been uncovered that associations' internal structures have important intrapersonal consequences for their participants. Using an exchange approach, Cafferata (1979) found that leaders of a national medical specialty association were more satisfied with and more positively valued the organization than did the regular members. Given their greater involvement, leaders benefited more from the organization's actions, and hence they expressed greater commitment to the collectivity. Hougland & Wood (1980) applied Tannenbaum's "control graph" measures to 58 Indianapolis Protestant churches and found that members' commitment (satisfaction, identification, and involvement) rose as a function of the total amount of control rather than the distribution of control across roles. Finally, Knoke & Wood (1981) examined psychological and behavioral commitment in 32 local chapters of social influence associations (i.e. groups with public policy influence as a major goal). They found that membership support was greatly enhanced by an associational control system that promoted organizational democracy. The more widespread a person's participation in collective decision-making and the greater her integration into the communication structure, the higher the member's commitment to the association (positive affect, loyalty, and efforts to realize group goals), and the lower the detachment (personal remoteness and feelings of inability to influence collective actions and policies). These relationships held both at the aggregate level and at the individual level, as shown by a contextual effects analysis where organization-level participation patterns exerted effects on individual commitment that were independent of individual participation (Knoke 1981). Because these commitment studies were limited to subtypes of associations, the degree to which the participation-commitment relationship is common to all types of associations under all conditions remains to be determined.

THE POLITICAL MOBILIZATION PROCESS   One thriving topic attracting much empirical and theoretical effort in recent years is the role of association involvement in stimulating individuals' external political activities. Associations act as mobilizing mechanisms in democratic societies, transforming nonpolitical organizational involvements into political participation through several related processes:

> (1) Association membership broadens one's sphere of interests and concerns, so that public affairs and political issues become more salient to the individual. (2) It brings one into contact with many diverse people, and the resulting social relationships draw the individual into a wide range of new activities, including politics. (3) It gives one training and experience in social interaction and leadership skills that are valuable in the political sphere. (4) It provides one with multiple channels through which he or she can act to exert influence on politicians and the political system. (Olsen 1982:32)

Political mobilization by associations is most effective when the organization becomes the object of an individual's commitment, that is, an intense psychological bonding occurs in which the member "is willing to let the group serve as a source of identification and direction for his own beliefs and behaviors" (Wilson & Orum 1976:194, also Knoke & Wood 1981:8–14). Such reference group processes are shaped by symbolic, interpersonal, and ideological devices.

Several empirical efforts tried to specify further the components of the mobilization model. Rogers & Bultena (1975, Rogers et al 1975) concluded that organizational involvement of people in three Iowa counties explained more of the variation in their political participation than did their social status and political attitudes, although the relationship was stronger for "instrumental" than for "expressive" associations. The researchers concluded that the overall mobilization effect of voluntary group involvement serves to widen class differences in political participation. Schulman's (1978) Buffalo survey found little support for hypotheses that formal democratic structures or direct organizational involvement enhances external political participation, although he suggested that some instrumental task learning may take place.

Olsen's (1982) analyses of surveys in Indianapolis and Gavle, Sweden, supported the proposition that the political mobilization process takes place across all types of organizations, from labor unions and business associations to fraternal, recreational, and church-related groups. Political discussions, voting turnout, partisan activities, and contacting of government officials all covaried positively with the number of associations to which individuals belonged, net of age, education, income, and occupation. However, contrary to Verba & Nie's (1972) conclusion, mobilization did not seem to depend upon an individual's activity level within an association, at least in the US data: "sheer number of memberships by itself may lead to political participation, even with age and socioeconomic status held constant" (Olsen 1982:138). Knoke's (1982) analyses of political influence efforts by members of 32 Indianapolis social influence associations disclosed that mobilization may depend both upon members' degree of associational involvement (measured by frequency of communication) and upon the organization's attempts to rouse its membership to contact government officials. That is, when no contact opportunities were available, member communication frequency did not affect contacting; but when the association attempted to mobilize its members, those persons in heavy communication with others were much more likely to contact officials. This interaction effect did not generalize to the conventional external behaviors studied by Olsen, such as voting turnout or campaigning, implying that the mobilization process may be quite specific with regard to the targets and objectives of political participation.

ASSOCIATIONS AS ORGANIZATIONS

At the organizational level, the unit of analysis is the association as an organizational entity, consisting of a complex set of interrelated social role positions. The fundamental decision here is how the organization collectively decides to which purposes it will apply the pooled associational resources over which it has gained collective control. Questions of internal democracy in the allocation of resources to these various goals have predominated, at least among observers of Western liberal societies. This section begins with an overview of research on the question of incentive systems, turns to internal decision-making processes, and concludes by looking at recent theorizing on the social ecology of the association.

Incentive Systems

From an association's vantage point, the organizational provision of incentives is the major economic exchange mechanism through which a collectivity secures the resources necessary for its maintenance and growth. Almost all analyses of incentive systems begin with some form of exchange theory, usually of the rational-choice type expounded by economists such as Olson. But they frequently incorporate affective incentives (friendships, social gatherings) and normative appeals (global values, altruistic goals) as part of their schemas. Each element of Clark & Wilson's classic trilogy of incentives—material, purposive, and solidary—was asserted to occur in pure form, since "few organizations can easily combine the three values (or three incentive systems)" (1961:240). Other theorists have proffered more elaborate systems, such as Knoke & Wright-Isak's (1982) 8-fold typology and Zald & Jacobs' (1978) 16-fold categories, generated by crossing 3 and 4 basic dimensions, respectively. Such elaborations of fundamental property spaces are useful theoretical exercises, but they stimulated little systematic empirical research on the actual frequency of incentive systems among associations.

A basic proposition of incentive system theory is that substantial covariation occurs between an organization's incentive offerings and its membership's needs, dispositions, and resources. A mismatch between supply and demand may disrupt the association's internal economy and render it unable to achieve its collective goals. Evidence for a basic congruence between incentive provisions and member "tastes" for benefits, at least among well-functioning associations, can be found in surveys of economic associations (Moe 1980:208–9), social influence associations (Knoke & Wood 1981:50–69), a professional medical society (Cafferata 1979), and the American Agricultural Movement (Cigler & Hansen 1983). In some instances, an organization's need to assure a regular, dependable flow of resources may lead to creation of an incentive system that attracts substantial numbers of members with scant interests in the primary goals (often its public policy objectives). For example, the American Farm Bureau Federation's urban contingents are attracted mainly by cheap insurance and tires and not by agricultural concerns (Wilson 1981:19–26). As an association develops a complex incentive system to satisfy the needs of a diverse membership, it must channel an increasing proportion of its internal economy into member service activities, to the relative eclipse of public legitimation and public-policy-influence objectives (Knoke 1985). Greater incentive system complexity, made possible by the resource growth produced from an expanding membership base, should necessitate internal structural differentiation. New positions are created to perform advertising, public relations, information collation and dissemination, newsletter and magazine editing, and social affairs. Association leaders find themselves increasingly engaged in daily incentive management decisions, which may absorb the bulk of their energies.

The equilibrium between maintenance and externally focused activities has received little attention (but see Browne 1977 for his impressions of four municipal interest associations). While mixed-incentive systems probably have greater longevity and survival value for an association (Knoke & Wright-Isak 1982:45), their corresponding increase in membership heterogeneity may become an unwelcome source of friction over the goals and directions the group should take (e.g. Cigler & Hansen 1983). These theoretical arguments lack a firm basis in extensive observations of numerous associations. Analyses are now underway on a sample of 459 national associations (Knoke & Adams 1986) that will soon expand knowledge about the relative efficacy of various inducements and their organizational consequences.

Collective Decision-Making Processes

An association's internal polity is its decision-making procedures for allocating its collective resources, acquired through its incentive system, among diverse goals. Collective choices among various goals—including member services, public legitimation, and public policy influence—are reflected in many specific binding decisions: proportions of the annual budget allocated to various categories; new programs undertaken and old ones dropped or expanded; leaders elected or hired to manage the daily business. Thus, any inquiry into an association's political economy must include its formal and operating procedures for deciding major issues. These procedures include both the constitutional authority structure (the division of rights and responsibilities among various role positions) and the actual division of power and influence among these actors. A crucial question is how decision procedures encourage or suppress mass membership participation in and support for collective actions. To date, associational decision-making remains one of its least understood areas.

An oligarchic polity centralizes decision-making in one faction, typically a minority that controls the formal authority positions and exercises decisive influence over every important policy in the face of any opponents. Oligarchic leadership is often unresponsive to the interests and preferences of significant proportions of the membership. This polity form is notorious in trade unions (Warner & Edelstein 1978, Hemingway 1978, Hartman 1979, Anderson 1979, Dickerson 1982), but also appears among public interest groups (Berry 1977:187), fraternal organizations (Schmidt 1973), and even some churches, although altruistic rather than self-serving objectives may be promoted by the oligarchs (Hougland & Wood 1979, Wood 1981). The hypothesized detrimental effects of oligarchic regimes, in addition to their blatant affronts to democratic norms, include membership alienation and apathy, and the eruption of internal struggles and faction splits, culminating in a debilitating impact upon associational performance [e.g. Brill's (1978) in-depth portrait of the Teamster's union]. Most theorists assume that oligarchic control of organizations is enhanced by the membership's social and attitudinal homogeneity, and by the centralizing and rationalizing imperatives of bureaucratic growth, both of which promote values and substantive practices contrary to democratic principles and rules. Applying embryological principles of development, Cafferata (1982) argued that bureaucracy's alleged oligarchic propensities may be controlled and regulated by formal democracy. Her assertions remain to be tested.

Many organizational theorists imply that a democratic-participatory polity, in contrast to an oligarchy, is more conducive to garnering optimal levels of resources and membership support for the collectivity. A core proposition—almost a truism despite relatively limited empirical support—is that widespread membership involvement in collective decision-making promotes greater personal commitment and attachment to the association, which in turn increases an association's ability to acquire personal resources for collective use. Knoke & Wood (1981) and Knoke (1981) found evidence for this dynamic in a sample of local social influence association chapters. Gamson's (1975) analysis of historical social movement organizations, however, suggested a more complex process in which centralized power, bureaucracy, and factionalism interact to affect the success of efforts at influence in the larger polity. Centralization constrains the crippling effects of factions, but a bureaucratic structure can help decentralized polities succeed in the face of factional splits (Gamson 1975:88–109).

Because association researchers have largely neglected internal processes, very little is known about either collective decision-making or its consequences at the individual, organizational, and system levels. Association size, goal diversity, member apathy, and an absence of effective mechanisms to reinforce participation may conspire to restrict the effective scope of decision participation. Few associations go to the length of the League of Women Voters in relying upon numerous small, local, face-to-face units that successively aggregate members' preferences for collective decisions (McFarland 1976). More typically, influence is biased in ways that depart significantly from textbook ideals of participatory democracy. The extent to which such departures from normative standards of membership control create problems in associational functioning, under varying conditions, remains to be determined.

The Social Ecology of Associations

During the past decade, organizational theorists devoted increasing attention to the ways that macroenvironmental forces shape organizational behaviors. Borrowing from natural selection models of biology, social ecologists investigated changing distributions in populations of organizations, emphasizing how environmental constraints and contingencies select certain attributes for reproduction or attrition (e.g. Hannan & Freeman 1977, Hatch & Mocroft 1977, Pfeffer & Salancik 1978). The major exponent of this approach to studying voluntary associations is J. Miller McPherson, whose theories offer a bridge from the individual to the interorganizational levels of analyses. A methodological paper (McPherson 1982) established the validity of hypernetwork sampling techniques for measuring systemic characteristics from the reports of respondents sampled in a community survey. Data from the 1977 Nebraska social indicators survey (McPherson 1983a) revealed that association size increases with community size, with affiliation into umbrella organizations, and with location in the economic sector. In turn, large size confers greater stability of membership and more central location within interorganizational networks. In his most formal treatment, McPherson (1983b) explicitly adapted such biological ecology concepts as competition for environmental resources, niches, and carrying capacity. The Nebraska data were used again to estimate rates of membership creation and dissolution, overlapping affiliations, and niche breadths based on multivariate distributions of age, occupation, gender, and education for members of 12 types of associations. McPherson's social ecology model opens up a powerful new approach to conceptualizing interorganizational relationships at the community level. Recent data incorporating time, geography, subjective orientations, and a broader range of nonvoluntary organizations promise to yield rich new insights into organizational demography and macrosocial structures.

In a continuing project on the creation and transformation of national trade associations, Staber & Aldrich also apply population-ecology principles. A preliminary study of 71 organizations in 19 manufacturing industries (Staber & Aldrich 1983) discovered that most trade associations today are largely noncompetitive specialists, although they may have devolved by spinoffs and mergers from more generalist associations in an earlier era. A strong emphasis on the historical dynamics of this volatile association form underpins Aldrich & Staber's on-going expanded study of trade associations since World War II. They hypothesize that much of the impetus for the rapid creation of new associations was a response to a perception that the federal government was overregulating business, for example, with environmental protection and occupational safety and health measures. The State's impact upon business conditions provoked the formation of associations to influence public policies. At this point we enter the third level of analysis, the polity.

ASSOCIATIONS IN THE POLITY

At the polity level of analysis, the central question is: How does a system of interacting cooperative and competitive organizations—including associations, firms, and bureaus—reach binding collective decisions about public policies? The polity may be a small community or a large nation state, but in either case the dynamics of interest group influence activity constitute the classic "pressure group system" studied for so long by political scientists. In such systems, an interest group is any "organized body of individuals who share some goals and who try to influence public policy" (Berry 1984:4). The interest group concept embraces not only membership associations but other types of institutions, such as corporations, nonprofit organizations, and even government agencies, whenever they act to affect governmental decisions (Salisbury 1984). Data from my recent survey of national association leaders found that almost half agreed that "influencing public policy decisions of the government [is] a moderate or major goal." Labor unions were four times as likely to act as interest groups (85%) as were social and recreational organizations (22%), while trade associations (58%) and professional societies (53%) fell in between.

Space limitations prevent any extended discussion of the comparative literature on interest group systems, especially those involving European nations (e.g. Panitch 1977, Berger 1981, Lehmbruch & Schmitter 1982). Central debates include the socioeconomic determinants of group interest formation, the impact of national historical development, the intraorganizational dynamics of interest articulation, the role of the State in creating new interests, and the growing "ungovernability" of contemporary systems of interest representation. In restricting my attention just to recent American interest group research, I obviously truncate the set of explanatory concepts available through a comparative approach. Unfortunately, the large comparative literature and the limited space necessitate foregoing that review until a later volume.

Two Theoretical Perspectives

Two alternative theoretical approaches have been proposed to account for the presence of organizational activity in liberal democratic polities. The conventional wisdom, growing out of mass society (Halebsky 1976) and pluralist (Dahl 1982) writings, depicts interest associations as demand aggregators, mediating relations of the State and its citizenry:

> Each intermediate organization brings together a number of people with similar concerns and goals, provides means through which these members can acquire information about relevant public issues, enables them to pool their resources to generate greater collective influence than could be exercised by a single individual, and provides an established channel through which they can exert this influence "upward" on political decisions and policies. (Olsen 1982:33)

Associations provide government officials, in turn, with channels to communicate information and provide political benefits to selected constituencies. American interest group proliferation is encouraged by a federal constitutional structure that fragments power among hundreds of separate policy domains.

Each domain comprises a subgovernment ("cozy triangle"), consisting of Congressional subcommittees, government bureaus, and interest group clientele, that resists the intrusion of a strong central authority (McFarland 1983). This conventional wisdom lay behind Truman's (1951) assertion that interest groups would form almost spontaneously within any group of persons experiencing a common disturbance that might be redressed through collective action. This proposition has been effectively refuted, not only theoretically (Olson 1965, Lowi 1979), but empirically by such findings as the difficulty oppressed groups encounter in entering the American pressure group system (Gamson 1975), the vital importance of well-heeled patrons (including foundations and the government itself) to keep interest groups in operation (Taub et al 1977, Walker 1983), and the evident system biases towards corporate policy interests (Schlozman 1984, Gais et al 1984).

An alternative perspective on the interest group system depicts it as a conflict arena in which various groups engage in political struggles to impress their policy preferences on the authorities at the expense of other groups whose interests are either less powerful or simply never organized in the first place (Hayes 1978). In this view, organizations do not only articulate member interests. They create demands, instill them in their members, and participate in governmental policy-making on equal terms with political parties and public bureaucracies. Subgovernments rapidly became unable to contain the contentious regulatory and redistributive issues—environmental protection, civil rights, consumer and occupational safety—that spilled over into the full Congress and the White House for collective resolution (Gais et al 1984). This widened scope of political conflict nudges the polity toward a more national structure, dominated increasingly by institutions (Salisbury, 1984). The system may eventually evolve into a mass society in which interest group executives become remote from, and unresponsive to, their mass memberships (Hayes 1983). At the extreme, a corporatist polity could emerge in the US, similar to those in European liberal democracies (Lehmbruch & Schmitter 1982), where peak associations are directly incorporated into governmental deliberations in return for guaranteed control of their fractious mass bases. However, most scholars argue that American exceptionalism will delay that future indefinitely (Wilson 1982).

An Advocacy Explosion

Over the past two decades, an advocacy explosion in the nation's capital triggered renewed academic attention to the phenomenon. Several surveys used interest groups' founding dates to estimate rapid rates of growth in lobbying organizations in Washington since the 1960s (Walker 1983, Schlozman & Tierney 1983, Berry 1984:18–26). Citizen lobbies (so-called public interest groups, or PIGS) were especially likely to be born in this era (Berry 1977:34), although the rate of increase is distorted to some unknown degree by mortality prior to the survey. Of the nearly 7000 organizations that maintain a continuing presence in Washington, either by keeping an office or hiring counsels to represent them, nearly half are corporations (Schlozman 1984). Probably more than 2000 associations are headquartered today in the DC area.

Speculations about the causes of this expanded activity abound. Congressional reorganization provided additional points of political access and leverage (Schlozman & Tierney 1985). Post-Watergate election reforms created those ubiquitous political action committees (PACS) with coffers overflowing with political money (Malbin 1980, Conway 1983). Successive waves of regulatory and deregulatory policies stimulated citizen, labor, business, and professional counter mobilizations (Gais et al 1984). An unravelling two-party system left a vacuum into which interest groups flowed (Berry 1984). And ideological polarization in the populace promoted liberal and conservative insurgencies through single-interest social movements (Hershey & West 1983). To date, no one has attempted the ambitious, systematic, quantitative model-building that will be necessary to winnow the anecdotal chaff from the substantive wheat. Such an undertaking must necessarily track the changing structure of the pressure group system over several decades, possibly at multiple levels of aggregation ranging from the organizational, to the policy domain, to the entire polity. Although much of the information for this project is available in secondary sources or through reconstruction from informant interviews, the costs of assembling and analyzing the vast volume of data can be prohibitive, to judge from research on just one decade of policymaking in the energy and health domains (Laumann et al 1985, Laumann & Knoke 1986).

Modes of Interaction

Several recent empirical efforts concentrated upon modes of interaction between interest groups and government targets. The expanded numbers of participants accompanied an enlarged repertoire of political influence tactics and strategies. Especially noteworthy were greater use of electronic mass media, computerized direct mail (Godwin & Mitchell 1984), constituency-legislator linkages, and more reliance upon conventional lobbying practices such as Congressional hearing testimony and personal contacts (Schlozman & Tierney 1983). PIGS are especially likely to use grass-roots mobilizations, appealing to the public through the mass media, launching letter-writing campaigns, and mobilizing local lobbying efforts (McFarland 1984, Gais et al 1984). Corporations are more prone to work through law firms, consulting or public relations firms, and other institutional representation (Salisbury 1984, Laumann et al 1985, but see Loomis 1983 on the Chamber of Commerce's grass-roots politicking). The relative availability of members or money as resources undoubtedly explains much of the variation in choice of interaction modes. Less attention has been paid to coalitional strategies among interest groups as a means to pooling their scarce resources for collective action. Studies of collective decision-making at both local and national levels often find extensive collaborative efforts, suggesting that networks of interorganizational exchange may be a significant factor shaping the dynamics and outcomes of influence activities (Heclo 1978, Chubb 1983, McFarland 1984, Berry 1984:202–5, Galaskiewicz 1979, Knoke 1983, Knoke & Laumann 1983).

Whether viewed primarily as demand aggregators or combat organizations, interest groups have clearly entrenched themselves as significant players in the political game. However, assessing their impact on public policy decisions remains clouded. Association activity is considerably easier to measure than the effectiveness of such activity in securing desired policy decisions. Because the American polity is so intricately convoluted, tracing input demands through to policy outcomes is a herculean task for which both theory and data are wanting. Given the concern aroused about these matters, however, especially over whether the proliferation of narrow interest groups is stalemating liberal democracy (Thurow 1980, Olson 1982), we can anticipate a vigorous assault on the question in the years ahead.

ASSESSMENT AND PROSPECTS

This brief review of the past decade's major research on American associations and interest groups reveals a diverse specialty that has continued to uncover interesting findings about these forms of social organization. The volume of factual knowledge at all levels of analysis has grown significantly. But association research as a field failed to achieve a sustained take-off into scientific maturity. Lacking consensus about the central issues and appropriate ways to study them, it remains a fragmented and unfocused enterprise at the margins of its parent disciplines. Sorely missing is an overarching paradigm that could crystallize attention and confer cachet upon the specialty. A fundamental theoretical goal must be to create coherence among the myriad empirical findings, particularly those bridging multiple levels of analysis from the individual, to the organizational, to the societal.

Lest this indictment appear overly harsh, I will close on an upbeat note by suggesting several especially promising research lines.

* How are new associations created and what are their developmental dynamics? How important are organizational entrepreneurs and environmental selection processes in the births, deaths, and mergers of various associations?
* What are the relative efficacies of different incentive systems for eliciting membership participation in collectivities, and how do these inducements change across the life cycle of associations?

18   KNOKE

* What are the connections between microlevel internal processes and the macrolevel activities of associations in the larger society and polity? Particularly, how does associational governance constrain the allocation of resources to organizational goals?
* Are the relationships uncovered among American associations and interest groups similar to or different from those in other liberal democracies and less-developed countries?

Answers to these questions require creation of new data, especially those having longitudinal and multilevel dimensions. Equally important is the sharpening and refinement of cogent theoretical explanations of association behaviors. For only through the continual interplay of data and theory can we expect major advances in the years ahead.

ACKNOWLEDGMENT

The writing of this paper was facilitated by a grant from the National Science Foundation (SES82-16927).

Literature Cited

Anderson, J. C. 1979. Local union democracy: In search of criteria. *Rel. Ind.* 34:431–51

Berger, S. D., ed. 1981. *Organizing Interests in Western Europe.* Cambridge: Cambridge Univ. Press

Berry, J. M. 1977. *Lobbying for the People: The Political Behavior of Public Interest Groups.* Princeton: Princeton Univ. Press

Berry, J. M. 1984. *The Interest Group Society.* Boston: Little, Brown

Brill, S. 1978. *The Teamsters.* New York: Simon & Schuster

Browne, W. P. 1977. Organizational maintenance: The internal operation of interest groups. *Public Admin. Rev.* 37:48–57

Brubaker, E. R. 1975. Free ride, free revelation, or golden rule? *J. Law Econ.* 18:147–61

Cafferata, G. L. 1979. Member and leader satisfaction with a professional association: An exchange perspective. *Admin. Sci. Q.* 24:472–83

Cafferata, G. L. 1982. The building of democratic organizations: An embryological metaphor. *Admin. Sci. Q.* 27:280–303

Chubb, J. 1983. *Interest Groups and the Bureaucracy: The Politics of Energy.* Stanford: Stanford Univ. Press

Cigler, A. J., Hansen, J. M. 1983. Group formation through protest: The American Agricultural Movement. See Cigler & Loomis 1983:84–109

Cigler, A. J., Loomis, B. A., eds. 1983. *Interest Group Politics.* Washington, DC: CQ

Clark, P. B., Wilson, J. Q. 1961. Incentive systems: A theory of organizations. *Admin. Sci. Q.* 6:129–66

Cohen, S. M., Kapsis, R. E. 1978. Participation of blacks, Puerto Ricans, and whites in voluntary associations: A test of some current theories. *Soc. Forc.* 56:1053–71

Coleman, J. S. 1973. Loss of power. *Am. Sociol. Rev.* 38:1–17

Conway, M. M. 1983. PACS, the new politics, and Congressional campaigns. See Cigler & Loomis 1983:126–44

Cutler, S. T. 1976. Age differences in voluntary association membership. *Soc. Forc.* 55:43–58

Dahl, R. 1982. *Dilemmas of a Pluralist Democracy.* New York: Oxford Univ. Press

Dickerson, M. 1982. *Democracy in Trade Unions: Studies in Membership Participation and Control.* St. Lucia, Australia: Univ. Queensboro Press

Edwards, J. N., White, R. P. 1980. Predictors of social participation: Apparent or real? *J. Voluntary Action Res.* 9:60–73

Fireman, B., Gamson, W. A. 1979. Utilitarian logic in the resource mobilization perspective. In *The Dynamics of Social Movements: Resource Mobilization, Social Control and Tactics,* ed. M. N. Zald, J. D. McCarthy, pp. 8–44. Cambridge, Mass: Winthrop

Gais, T. L., Peterson, M. A., Walker, J. L. 1984. Interest groups, iron triangles, and representative institutions in American national government. *Br. J. Polit. Sci.* 14:161–86

Galaskiewicz, J. 1979. The structure of community interorganizational networks. *Soc. Forc.* 57:1346–64

Gamson, W. A. 1975. *Strategy of Social Protest.* Homeword, Ill: Dorsey

Godwin, R. K., Mitchell, R. C. 1982. Rational models, collective goods and nonelectoral political behavior. *West. Polit. Q.* 35:161–81

Godwin, R. K., Mitchell, R. C. 1984. The implications of direct mail for political organizations. *Soc. Sci. Q.* 65:829–39

Gordon, M. E., Long, L. N. 1981. Demographic and attitudinal correlates of union joining. *Ind. Relat.* 20:306–11

Gustafson, K., Booth, A., Johnson, D. 1979. The effect of labor force participation on gender differences in voluntary association affiliation: a cross-national study. *J. Voluntary Action Res.* 8:51–56

Guterbock, T. M., London, B. 1983. Race, political orientation, and participation. *Am. Sociol. Rev.* 48:439–53

Halebsky, Sandor 1976. *Mass Society and Political Conflict.* Cambridge: Cambridge Univ. Press

Hanks, M. 1981. Youth, voluntary associations, and political socialization. *Soc. Forc.* 60:211–23

Hanks, M., Eckland, B. K. 1978. Adult voluntary associations and adolescent socialization. *Sociol. Q.* 19:481–90

Hannan, M., Freeman, J. 1977. The population ecology of organizations. *Am. J. Sociol.* 82:929–64

Hartman, H. 1979. Work councils and the iron law of oligarchy. *Br. J. Ind. Relat.* 17:70–82

Hatch, S., Mocroft, I. 1977. Factors affecting the location of voluntary organization branches. *Policy Polit.* 6:172–83

Hayes, M. T. 1978. The semi-sovereign pressure groups: A critique of current theory and an alternative typology. *J. Polit.* 40:134–61

Hayes, M. T. 1983. Interest groups: Pluralism or mass society? See Cigler & Loomis 1983:110–25

Heclo, Hugh 1978. Issue networks and the executive establishment. In *The New American Political System,* ed. A. King. Washington: Am. Enterprise Inst.

Hemingway, J. 1978. *Conflict and Democracy: Studies in Trade Union Government.* Oxford: Oxford Univ. Press

Hershey, M. R., West, D. M. 1983. Single-issue politics: Prolife groups and the 1980 senate campaign. See Cigler & Loomis 1983:31–59

Hougland, J. G. Jr., Wood, J. R. 1979. Determinants of organizational control in local churches. *J. Sci. Study Relig.* 18:132–45

Hougland, J. G. Jr., Wood, J. R. 1980. Control in organizations and the commitment of members. *Soc. Forc.* 59:85–105

Klobus-Edwards, P., Edwards, J. N., Klemmack, D. L. 1978. Differences in social participation: Blacks and whites. *Soc. Forc.* 56:1035–52

Klobus-Edwards, P., Edwards, J. N., Watts,

A. D. 1984. Women, work, and social participation. *J. Voluntary Action Res.* 13:7–22

Knoke, D. 1981. Commitment and detachment in voluntary associations. *Am. Sociol. Rev.* 46:141–58

Knoke, D. 1982. Political mobilization by voluntary associations. *J. Polit. Militar. Sociol.* 10:171–82

Knoke, D. 1983. Organization sponsorship and influence reputation of social influence associations. *Soc. Forc.* 61:1065–87

Knoke, D. 1985. The political economies of associations. In *Research in Political Sociology,* ed. R. G. Braungart, M. Braungart, 1:211–42. Greenwich, Conn: JAI

Knoke, D., Adams, R. E. 1986. The incentive systems of associations. In *Research in the Sociology of Organizations* ed. S. B. Bacharach, N. DiTomaso. Vol. 5. Greenwich, Conn: JAI. In press

Knoke, D., Laumann, E. O. 1983. *Issue publics in national policy domains.* Presented at Ann. Meet. Am. Sociol. Assoc., Toronto

Knoke, D., Prensky, D. 1984. What relevance do organization theories have for voluntary associations? *Soc. Sci. Q.* 65:3–20

Knoke, D., Thomson, R. 1977. Voluntary association membership trends and the family life cycle. *Soc. Forc.* 56:48–65

Knoke, D., Wood, J. R. 1981. *Organized for Action: Commitment in Voluntary Associations.* New Brunswick: Rutgers Univ. Press

Knoke, D., Wright-Isak, C. 1982. Individual motives and organizational incentive systems. In *Research in the Sociology of Organizations,* ed. S. B. Bacharach, 1:209–54. Greenwich, Conn: JAI

Laumann, E. O., Heinz, J. P., Nelson, R., Salisbury, R. H. 1985. Washington lawyers—and others: The structure of Washington representation. *Stanford Law Rev.* 37:465–502

Laumann, E. O., Knoke, D. 1986. *National Policy Domains: An Organizational Perspective on Energy and Health.* Madison, Wis: Univ. Wis. Press. In press

Laumann, E. O., Knoke, D., Kim, Y. 1985. An organizational approach to State policymaking: A comparative study of energy and health domains. *Am. Sociol. Rev.* 50:1–19

Lehmbruch, G., Schmitter, P. C., eds. 1982. *Patterns in Corporatist Policy-Making.* Beverly Hills: Sage

London, B. 1975. Racial differences in social and political participation: It's not simply a matter of black and white. *Soc. Sci. Q.* 56:274–86

Loomis, B. A. 1983. A new era: Groups and the grass roots. See Cigler & Loomis 1983:169–90

Lo, C. Y. H. 1982. Countermovements and

conservative movements in the contemporary U.S. *Ann. Rev. Sociol.* 8:107–34

Lowi, T. J. 1979. *The End of Liberalism.* New York: Norton. 2nd ed.

McAdam, D. 1982. *Political Process and the Development of Black Insurgency 1930–1970.* Chicago: Univ. Chicago Press

McFarland, A. S. 1976. *Public Interest Lobbies: Decision Making on Energy.* Washington: Am. Enterprise Inst.

McFarland, A. S. 1983. Public interest lobbies versus minority faction. See Cigler & Loomis 1983:324–53

McFarland, A. S. 1984. *Common Cause.* Chatham, NJ: Chatham

McPherson, J. M. 1977. Correlates of social participation: A comparison of the ethnic and compensatory theories. *Sociol. Q.* 18:197–208

McPherson, J. M. 1981. A dynamic model of voluntary affiliation. *Soc. Forc.* 59:705–28

McPherson, J. M. 1982. Hypernetwork sampling: Duality and differentiation among voluntary organizations. *Soc. Networks* 3:225–50

McPherson, J. M. 1983a. An ecology of affiliation. *Am. Sociol. Rev.* 48:519–32

McPherson, J. M. 1983b. The size of voluntary organizations. *Soc. Forc.* 61:1044–64

McPherson, J. M., Lockwood, W. 1980. The dynamics of voluntary affiliation: A multivariate analysis. *J. Voluntary Action Res.* 9:74–84

McPherson, J. M., Smith-Lovin, D. L. 1982. Women and weak ties: Differences by sex in the size of voluntary associations. *Am. J. Sociol.* 87:883–904

McPherson, J. M., Smith-Lovin, D. L. 1984. *Sex segregation in voluntary associations.* Presented at Ann. Meet. Am. Sociol. Assoc., San Antonio

Malbin, M. J., ed., 1980. *Parties, Interest Groups, and Campaign Finance Laws.* Washington: Am. Enterprise Inst.

Marwell, G., Ames, R. E. 1979. Experiments on the provision of public goods. I. Resources, interest, group size, and the free rider problem. *Am. J. Sociol.* 84:1335–60

Marwell, G., Ames, R. E. 1980. Experiments on the provision of public goods. II. Provision points, stakes, experiences, and the free-rider problem. *Am. J. Sociol.* 85:926–37

Mitchell, R. C. 1979. National environmental lobbies and the apparent illogic of collective action. In *Collective Decision-Making,* ed. C. Russell, pp. 187–221. Baltimore: Johns Hopkins Univ. Press

Moe, Terry M. 1980. *The Organization of Interests: Incentives and the Internal Dynamics of Political Interest Groups.* Chicago: Univ. of Chicago Press

Oliver, P. 1980. Rewards and punishments as selective incentives for collective action: Theoretical investigations. *Am. J. Sociol.* 85:1356–75

Oliver, P. 1984. Active and token contributors to local collective action. *Am. Sociol. Rev.* 49:601–10

Olsen, M. E. 1982. *Participatory Pluralism: Political Participation and Influence in the United States and Sweden.* Chicago: Nelson-Hall

Olson, M. Jr. 1965. *The Logic of Collective Action.* Cambridge, Mass: Harvard Univ. Press

Olson, M. Jr. 1982. *The Rise and Decline of Nations.* New Haven: Yale Univ. Press

Palisi, B. J., Jacobson, P. E. 1977. Dominant statuses and involvement in types of instrumental and expressive voluntary organizations. *J. Voluntary Action Res.* 6:80–88

Panitch, L. 1977. The development of corporatism in liberal democracies. *Comp. Polit. Stud.* 10:61–90

Pfeffer, J., Salancik, G. R. 1978. *The External Control of Organizations.* New York: Harper & Row

Rogers, D. L., Bultena, G. L. 1975. Voluntary associations and political equality: an extension of mobilization theory. *J. Voluntary Action Res.* 4:172–83

Rogers, D. L., Bultena, G. L., Barb, K. H. 1975. Voluntary association membership and political participation: An exploration of the mobilization hypothesis. *Sociol. Q.* 16:305–18

Salisbury, R. H. 1975. Interest groups. In *Handbook of Political Science,* ed. F. I. Greenstein, N. W. Polsby, 4:171–228. Reading, Mass: Addison-Wesley

Salisbury, R. H. 1984. Interest representation: The dominance of institutions. *Am. Polit. Sci. Rev.* 78:64–76

Schlozman, K. L. 1984. What accent the heavenly chorus? Political equality in the American pressure system. *J. Politics.* 46:1006–32

Schlozman, K. L., Tierney, J. T. 1983. More of the same: Washington pressure group activity in a decade of change. *J. Polit.* 34:351–77

Schlozman, K. L., Tierney, J. T. 1985. *Organized Interests and American Democracy.* New York: Harper & Row

Schmidt, A. J. 1973. *Oligarchy in Fraternal Organizations.* Detroit: Gale Res.

Schulman, D. C. 1978. Voluntary organization involvement and political participation. *J. Voluntary Action Res.* 7:86–105

Smith, D. H. 1975. Voluntary action and voluntary groups. *Ann. Rev. Sociol.* 1:247–70

Smith, D. H., Macauley, J., eds. 1980. *Participation in Social and Political Activities.* San Francisco: Jossey-Bass

Smith, J. 1976. Communities, associations, and the supply of collective goods. *Am. J. Sociol.* 82:291–308

Staber, U., Aldrich, H. 1983. Trade association stability and public policy. In *Organization Theory and Public Policy,* ed. R. H. Hall, R. E. Quinn, pp. 179–94. Beverly Hills: Sage

Sutton, J. R. 1980. Some determinants of women's trade union membership. *Pacific Sociol. Rev.* 23:377–91

Taub, R. P., Surgeon, G. P., Lindholm, S., Otti, P. B., Bridges, A. 1977. Urban voluntary associations, locality based and externally induced. *Am. J. Sociol.* 83:425–42

Thomson, R., Knoke, D. 1980. Voluntary associations and voting turnout of American ethnoreligious groups. *Ethnicity* 7:56–69

Thurow, L. C. 1980. *The Zero-Sum Society.* New York: Basic Books

Tillock, H., Morrison, D. E. 1979. Group size and contribution to collective action: A test of Mancur Olson's theory on Zero Population Growth, Inc. In *Research in Social Movements, Conflict, and Change,* ed. L. Kriesberg, 2:131–58. Greenwich, Conn: JAI

Tocqueville, A. 1961. *Democracy in America.* Garden City, NJ: Doubleday

Truman, D. B. 1951. *The Governmental Process.* New York: Knopf

Verba, S., Nie, N. H. 1972. *Participation in America.* New York: Harper & Row

Walker, J. L. 1983. The origins and maintenance of interest groups in America. *Am. Polit. Sci. Rev.* 77:390–406

Warner, M., Edelstein, J. D. 1978. The meaning and dimensions of democracy in work-related organizations. *J. Ind. Relat.* 20:113–37

Wilson, G. K. 1981. *Interest Groups in the United States.* Oxford: Clarendon

Wilson, G. K. 1982. Why is there no corporatism in the United States? See Lehmbruch & Schmitter 1982:219–36

Wilson, K., Orum, T. 1976. Mobilizing people for collective political action. *J. Polit. Militar. Sociol.* 4:187–202

Wood, J. R. 1981. *Legitimate Leadership in Voluntary Organizations.* New Brunswick: Rutgers Univ. Press

Zald, M. N., Jacobs, D. 1978. Compliance/incentive classifications of organizations: Underlying dimensions. *Admin. Soc.* 9:403–24

Ann. Rev. Sociol. 1986. 12:23–45

SOCIAL PATTERNS OF DISTRESS

John Mirowsky and Catherine E. Ross

Department of Sociology and College of Medicine, University of Illinois, Urbana, Illinois 61801

Abstract

This paper reviews survey research explaining the social patterns of distress. There are four basic patterns: (*a*) The higher one's social status the lower one's distress; (*b*) women are more distressed than men; (*c*) married persons are less distressed than unmarried persons, and; (*d*) the greater the number of undesirable events in one's life the greater one's distress. The major forms of distress are malaise (such as lethargy, headaches, and trembling hands), anxiety (such as feeling afraid, worried, or irritable), and depression (such as feeling sad, worthless, or hopeless). Sociological theory suggests that alienation, authoritarianism, and inequity produce distress. The research indicates that distress is reduced by control, commitment, support, meaning, normality, flexibility, trust, and equity. The presence or absence of these accounts for the social patterns of distress.

INTRODUCTION

One of the goals of sociology is to understand the connections between social and personal problems. We can look at the personal problems of someone who left an inner city high school at the first opportunity, without a degree and without basic skills; who spent years unemployed and underemployed; who finally got a factory job and managed to hold onto it long enough to make a down payment on a house and to start a family; who was among the first laid off when the product the factory produced could not compete with ones made where labor costs are lower; and whose unemployment compensation has run out. The despair this person feels is deeply personal, but the problems are deeply social. More than that, it is the despair that identifies the social fact as a

23

0360-0572/86/0815-0023$02.00

social problem—and as a research problem. One of the core areas of sociology is the study of social stratification—of inequalities in wealth, power, and prestige. Would we be as interested in these inequalities if the poor and powerless were as happy and fulfilled as the wealthy and powerful? It is the inequality in misery that makes the other inequality so meaningful.

The sociologist's interest in the subjective quality of life is often unstated and indirect. Pearlin & Lieberman (1979) note that the traditional division of academic turfs may mask the connection between personal and social problems: Those who study personal problems often rely on speculation in drawing connections to the social milieu, and those who study the structure of society and its institutions often guess about consequences for the subjective quality of life. Guessing has its hazards. The inference that a particular social condition is distressing may erroneously assume that one's own values, preferences, and emotional responses are shared by persons in the situation. An inference of this sort would be unacceptable in sociology. The cautious researcher often concentrates on the social condition while leaving its emotional consequences unmentioned. This creates a reassuring sense of objectivity. We can speak of status mobility and leave unmentioned the bitterness of failure or the pride of success. This avoids the problem of attributing one's own feelings to others. An alternative is to measure, explicitly and objectively, feelings such as fear, anxiety, frustration, anger, guilt, despair, depression, demoralization, joy, fulfillment, and hope, and to map the relationship of these feelings to social conditions and positions. It is this alternative research that we review.

Before discussing research on the social patterns of distress, it is useful to say what we mean by distress and what is typically measured. The term refers broadly to a number of uncomfortable subjective states (and to the absence of positive subjective states). There are three main forms of distress: (a) malaise, such as lethargy, weakness, headaches, cold sweats, acid stomach, trembling hands, fainting spells, and heart palpitations; (b) anxiety, such as feeling afraid, worried, irritable, fidgety, or tense; and (c) depression, such as feeling sad, blue, lonely, worthless, hopeless, unhappy, or joyless.

The indexes used in early research focused on malaise and anxiety (Gurin et al 1960, Langner 1962), whereas indexes used in recent research tend to focus on depression (Radloff 1977). Several discoveries prompted the shift. First, questions about malaise were used partly to mask the intent of measuring emotional states, but people are far more willing to report their feelings in community surveys than anyone expected. Second, malaise may indicate physical health problems as well as emotional ones, thus potentially confounding results (e.g. Johnson & Meile 1981, Wheaton 1982). Studies of the emotional impact of chronic and acute disease, hospitalization, injury, and disability use purely psychological indicators to avoid bias (Aneshensel et al 1984, Thoits 1981). On the whole, "physiogenic bias" exists but is not great and does not account for the major social patterns of distress (Johnson & Meile 1981). Measures of malaise, anxiety, and depression are interrelated and interchangable for most purposes (Dohrenwend et al 1980). Sometimes different types of distress have different patterns that provide insight into the nature of a particular social condition (e.g. Mirowsky & Ross 1984, Wheaton 1983), but more often the patterns match and tell the same story about who is distressed and why.

Four basic social patterns of distress were found in early community surveys and in many surveys conducted since then: (a) The higher one's socioeconomic status the lower one's level of distress; (b) women are more distressed than men; (c) married persons are less distressed than unmarried persons; and (d) the greater the number of undesirable events in one's life the greater one's level of distress. At first these findings stood as new discoveries, then as core facts in the growing body of research. After it became clear that these are robust and replicable findings, the focus of research switched from *demonstrating* the facts to *explaining* them. Just as astronomy was once driven by the desire to explain the recorded motions of the sun, moon, planets, and stars, research on distress is currently driven by the desire to explain its recorded association with status, sex, marriage, and events. All of the studies of distress discussed in this paper attempt to explain one or more of the four associations. Although there is great diversity in the specific models proposed as explanations, most share a single abstract form: (a) Status, sex, marriage, and events mark the objective conditions of social life; (b) conditions shape people's beliefs about the nature of society, human relations, themselves, and their relationship to others and to society; (c) the level of distress depends on the nature of these beliefs. Three themes in the individual's understanding of self and society stand out as explanations of the known social patterns of distress: alienation, authoritarianism, and inequity. These are the link between the external reality of objective social conditions and the internal reality of subjective distress.

ALIENATION

Most explanations of the social patterns of distress refer to alienation in one or more of its forms. On the most general level, alienation is any form of social detachment or separation. Although alienation may be defined in terms of objective social conditions, studies of distress more commonly follow Seeman's (1959) classic definition of alienation in terms of expectations and beliefs. He described five major types of alienation: powerlessness, self-estrangement, isolation, meaninglessness, and normlessness. Seeman hoped that subsequent research would uncover their consequences and the social conditions that produce them. As the material that follows shows, distress is one of the major consequences of alienation. In reviewing the relevant literature we will describe each type of alienation, its social causes, and its emotional consequences. Although Seeman's definitions of the five types of alienation provide a core set of concepts, 25 years of research has broadened the topics considered (Seeman 1983). We will discuss five issues that incorporate Seeman's original ideas, their variations, and related concepts: control, commitment, support, meaning, and normality.

Control

Of all the beliefs about self and society that might affect an individual's distress, belief in control over one's own life may be the most important. Seeman ranked the sense of powerlessness as the primary type of alienation, defining it as, "the expectancy or probability, held by the individual, that his own behavior cannot determine the occurrence of the outcomes, or reinforcements, he seeks" (Seeman 1959:784). He was careful to point out that powerlessness, as a social-psychological variable, is distinct from the objective conditions that may produce it and from the frustration an individual may feel as a consequence of it. Thus, Seeman clearly stated the central position that powerlessness fills in a three-part model of conditions, understandings, and feelings, while he called for an end to the practice (common at the time) of measuring alienation as a jumble of causes and effects. The importance of powerlessness is recognized in other social and behavioral sciences, where it appears in a number of forms with various labels. In psychology the concept of powerlessness appears in two major forms, depending on whether the psychologist has a behavioral or cognitive orientation. The behaviorists speak of "learned helplessness," which results from exposure to inescapable, uncontrollable negative stimuli and is characterized by a low rate of voluntary response and low ability to learn successful behaviors (Seligman 1975). Even the purist has difficulty refraining from attributing unpleasant feelings to the whimpering, apathetic animal that has been exposed to uncontrollable punishment, and it is clearly the researchers' intent to produce an analogue of human depression. ("Learned helplessness" refers to the behavior, though, and not the imputed emotion.) The cognitive psychologists speak of an "external versus internal locus of control" (Rotter 1966). Belief in an external locus of control is a learned, generalized expectation that outcomes of situations are determined by forces external to one's self such as powerful others, luck, fate, or chance. The individual believes that he or she is powerless and at the mercy of the environment. Belief in an internal locus of control (the opposite) is a learned, generalized expectation that outcomes are contingent on one's own choices and actions. The individual believes that he or she can master, control, or effectively alter the environment. In anthropology the concept appears as the "man-nature orientation" (Kluckhohn & Strodtbeck 1961), or "fatalism" (Madsen 1973). In sociology, beliefs about control appear under a number of different names in addition to "powerlessness," notably such terms as the sense of personal efficacy (Kohn 1972), self-directedness (Kohn & Schooler 1982), mastery (Pearlin et al 1981), and fatalism versus instrumentalism (Wheaton 1980). These concepts are not precisely the same but, as with the various types of distress, they are roughly interchangeable in a wide range of instances.

An individual learns through social interaction and personal experience that his or her choices and efforts are usually likely or unlikely to affect the outcome of a situation (Wheaton 1980, 1983; Mirowsky & Ross 1983a, 1984). Socio-logical theory points to several conditions likely to produce a belief in external control: Powerlessness, defined as an objective condition rather than a belief, is the inability to achieve one's ends or, alternatively, the inability to achieve one's ends in opposition to others. Structural inconsistency is a situation in which society defines certain goals, purposes, and interests as legitimate and desirable and also defines the allowable procedures for moving toward the objectives but does not provide adequate resources and opportunities for achieving the objectives through legitimate means. Alienated labor is a condi-tion under which the worker does not decide what to produce, does not design and schedule the production process, and does not own the product. De-pendency is a situation in which one partner in an exchange has fewer alterna-tive sources of sustenance and gratification than the other. In looking for the correlates of a sense of powerlessness and belief in external control the re-searcher looks for variables associated with conditions of powerlessness, structural inconsistency, alienated labor, and dependency.

Surveys find several major sociodemographic correlates of a sense of powerlessness. General socioeconomic status, as measured by family income, the occupational prestige of the respondent or breadwinner, and ratings of the social class of the neighborhood, home, and respondent are negatively related to a sense of powerlessness and positively related to a sense of mastery and control (Mirowsky & Ross 1983a, Wheaton 1980). Education also increases the sense of mastery and control, net of the impact of general status (Mirowsky & Ross 1983a). Jobs are important for a number of reasons. Low status jobs produce a sense of powerlessness because the job, and the opportunities and income it provides, are seen as barriers to achievement (Wheaton 1980), and because the work is uncomplex (primarily with things rather than data or people) and does not require or allow responsibility and self-direction (Kohn & Schooler 1982). Job disruptions such as being laid off, downgraded, or fired decrease the worker's sense of mastery, partly by lowering income and increas-ing difficulties in acquiring necessities such as food, clothing, housing, and medical care (Pearlin et al 1981). In addition to the effects of status and occupation, gender plays a role; women have a greater sense of powerlessness than men (Ross, Mirowsky & Cockerham 1983; Mirowsky & Ross 1983a, 1984). Although the reason women feel more powerless has not been established, it may be due to dependency, restricted opportunities, or low substantive complexity of housework and women's jobs. Finally, after taking into account lower education, income, and status, Mexican heritage is associated with belief in external control (Ross et al 1983; Mirowsky & Ross 1983a, 1984). Although the effect could be due to a purely cultural orientation toward fatalistic beliefs, it could also be due to an emphasis on subordination to the family or to restricted opportunity in the Anglo-dominated economic system.

The sense of powerlessness can have two effects on distress: It can be demoralizing in itself, and it can hamper effective coping with difficult events or situations. People who believe they have little influence over the things that happen to them (that what is going to happen will happen, that we might as well decide what to do by flipping a coin, and that success is mostly a matter of getting good breaks) tend to be more distressed, whereas those who believe that when they make plans they can make them work, that people's misfortunes result from the mistakes they make, that there is really no such thing as luck, and that what happens to them is their own doing tend to be less distressed (Wheaton 1980). Similarly, an increasing belief that "There is really no way I can solve some of the problems I have," or that "I have little control over the things that happen to me" increases distress over time whereas an increasing belief that "I can do just about anything I really set my mind to," or that "What happens to me in the future mostly depends on me" decreases distress over time (Pearlin et al 1981).

In addition to its direct, demoralizing impact, the sense of not being in control of one's own life can diminish the will and motivation to cope actively with problems. Wheaton (1983) argues that fatalism decreases coping effort. Belief in the efficacy of environmental rather than personal forces makes active attempts to solve problems seem useless. The result is less motivation and less persistence in coping and, thus, less success in solving problems and adapting. Taking Wheaton's arguments a step further, the fatalist has a reactive, passive orientation whereas the instrumentalist has a proactive one. Instrumental persons are likely to search the environment for potentially distressing events and conditions, to take preventive steps, and to accumulate resources or develop skills and habits that will reduce the impact of unavoidable problems. When undesired events and situations occur, the instrumental person is better prepared and less threatened. In contrast, the reactive, passive person ignores potential problems until they actually happen. The result is that problems are more likely to happen and the person is less prepared when they do. Furthermore, passive coping—such as trying to ignore the problem until it goes away—fails to limit the consequences of problems. Thus, the instrumentalist is constantly getting ahead of problems whereas the fatalist is constantly falling behind. The theoretical result is a magnification of differences, with the fatalists suffering more and more problems, which reinforce the sense of powerlessness and lack of control, thus producing greater passivity in the face of difficulties.

The impact of instrumental coping is revealed in two ways—as a set of dynamic reciprocal effects, and as modified or contingent effects. The first is exemplified by the work of Kohn & Schooler (1982). Their research shows that self-direction plays a central role in a dynamic, three-way relationship with problem-solving flexibility and distress. Jobs that are routine, closely supervised, and uncomplex reduce self-direction, and this leads to greater inflexibility and distress. These effects are then boosted by self-amplifying feedback: Inflexibility and distress reduce subsequent self-direction, which creates more inflexibility and distress, and so on. (However, the impact of self-direction on distress is much larger than the rebound effect of distress on self-direction.) The circle of effects magnifies the impact of job characteristics, and of sociodemographic variables, on distress.

The impact of instrumental coping is revealed, secondly, when an individual's belief in internal control interacts with stressful events or situations. In interaction models, "two or more conditions must be present; together they set off a process that neither alone could produce, and literally, the resultant whole is greater than the sum of its parts" (Wheaton 1983:221). Kessler & Cleary (1980) find that undesirable events and physical health problems are more distressing to low-status persons than to middle- or high-status persons. Furthermore, the differences in distress between social strata are attributable to differences in emotional response more than to differences in the level of undesirable events and health problems (although differences in the level of problems do exist and do account for some of the differences in distress). Further analysis shows that the protective effect of higher status is actually due to the presence of upwardly mobile persons in the high-status groups. Kessler & Cleary speculate that, "the experience of success associated with upward mobility creates the sort of assertive coping skills needed to avoid the psychological damage that can result from undesirable life events. . . . success in overcoming adversity can help create in an individual the sort of personal characteristics—feelings of self-esteem, confidence, perseverance—that are the stuff of competent problem management" (Kessler & Cleary 1980:472). In support of this idea, Kessler & Cleary argue that the use of tranquilizing drugs is a form of passive coping. They find no association between exposure to undesirable events and the use of tranquilizers among the upwardly mobile; whereas among people in the same social class who are not upwardly mobile, exposure to undesirable events increases the probability of using tranquilizers.

In a study of women in southwestern Ontario who recently gave birth, Turner & Noh (1983) replicated the finding that undesirable events are more distressing to lower-class persons than to middle- or upper-class persons. Turner & Noh went a step further and measured perceptions of control. Women who express a sense of powerlessness and fatalism are distressed by low socioeconomic status; this distress is not shared by women who express a sense of efficacy and instrumentalism and are members of a network in which they feel valued and esteemed. However, lower-status women are more likely than middle- and upper-status women to lack a sense of control, which in part accounts for the greater impact of events on lower-status women and thus for the higher level of distress among them.

Wheaton (1983) developed the theory of instrumental coping further; he extended the model to include chronic stressors, in addition to acute events, and distinguished among three psychological outcomes. Wheaton defines chronic stress as the perception of barriers to the achievement of one's goals or stagnation in the improvement of one's condition; the perception of inequity (inadequate rewards in comparison to one's effort or qualifications); excessive or inadequate demand in the environment compared to the capacity of the individual; frustration of role expectations; and the absence of necessary objective resources. Wheaton looks at three psychological consequences of acute and chronic stressors: (a) depression, such as feeling unhappy, useless, lethargic, or in low spirits; (b) anxiety, such as heart palpitations, cold sweats, trembling hands, restlessness, irritability and worrying; (c) schizophreniform hallucinations and delusions, such as hearing voices, seeing things, thinking your mind is dominated by forces beyond your control, or believing you are being plotted against. He finds that instrumentalism reduces or eliminates the impact of acute and chronic stressors on depression and schizophrenia but does not modify the impact of stressors on anxiety. Stated another way, a fatalistic orientation is a necessary condition for a depressed or schizophrenic response to stressful events and situations, but it is not necessary for an anxious response. Wheaton speculates that anxiety in response to stressors does not depend on a passive coping style because much of anxiety is psychophysiologic arousal, which may be a natural response to stressors and is not necessarily dysfunctional (even though uncomfortable).

Looking broadly at the ideas and findings, we see that people in higher socioeconomic positions tend to have a sense of personal control and people in lower socioeconomic positions tend rather to have a sense of personal powerlessness. The sense of powerlessness is depressing and demoralizing in itself, but worse than that, it undermines the will to seek and take effective action. People in lower socioeconomic positions have a triple burden: They have more problems to deal with; their personal histories are likely to have left them with a deep sense of powerlessness; and that sense of powerlessness discourages them from marshaling whatever energy and resources they do have in order to solve their problems. The result for many is a multiplication of despair.

Commitment

It is difficult to find an English word that is an unambiguous label for the second concept of alienation. We have chosen to refer to the absence of this form of alienation as commitment, but words such as freedom, self-expression, involvement, identification, and pride each tap a part of the concept. Although commitment can occur in many areas of life, the issue is probably best known from Marx's discussion of "alienated labor." Marx argued that in working for someone else the wage laborer belongs to another person and not to himself. The work is a means of satisfying other needs rather than a satisfaction in itself; work is external, rather than part of the worker's nature, and imposed rather than voluntary. Workers deny themselves in work rather than fulfill themselves (Kohn 1976). The set of ideas and orientations thought to result from alienated labor are called "self-estrangement" (Seeman 1959). Alienated labor is the *condition* in which the worker does not decide what to produce, does not design the production process, and does not own the product. Self-estrangement is the *sense* of being separate from that part of one's thoughts, actions, and experiences given over to the control of others; of work being foreign to oneself rather than an expression of oneself (Mirowsky & Ross 1983a). Work is seen as drudgery. It has no intrinsic value. There is no pride in it. Any rewards lie outside the activity itself. At best one is compensated, and at worst one is forced by circumstances to submit.

Although the idea of self-estrangement is quite clear, measures of it are often ambiguous or mixed with indicators of other concepts. Some researchers ask people if they are satisfied or dissatisfied with their work and interpret the response as an indication of self-estrangement. However, many workers may think of satisfaction as a question of adequate compensation and good relations with coworkers and the boss. A worker could claim to be completely satisfied and yet find the idea of intrinsic gratification from work utterly incomprehensible and a contradiction in terms. To many, work is, by definition, that which you would not do if no one was paying you to do it. To the alienated worker, pay is the only reason for working. To the committed worker, on the other hand, pay makes it *possible* to work and, beyond that, signifies recognition of the quality and value of one's work. Thus, measures of self-estrangement often include statements about intrinsic gratification and the meaning of pay: "I can put up with a lot on my job as long as the pay is good" (Pearlin & Schooler 1978:21); "I find it difficult to imagine enthusiasm for my work" (Kobasa et al 1981:372). Our discussion of self-estrangement suggests several other items it might be useful to include in indexes: "I feel lucky because I get paid to do work I like to do anyway," "My job is like a hobby to me," "My job gives me a chance to do things I enjoy doing," or, alternatively, "Work is a grind," "If it wasn't for the pay, I'd never do the things I do at work."

The existing research on occupational self-estrangement shows it is more common among workers who are older, have lower incomes, are less educated, and come from lower-status backgrounds (Schooler 1972, Pearlin & Schooler 1978). It is also correlated with a sense of external control and powerlessness, and with a focus on the goals of security and freedom from want (Kobasa et al 1981). Studies of distress have looked at its association with conditions of alienated labor but have not yet addressed the issue of whether self-estrangement is the mental link between the objective working conditions and the emotional response. Kohn (1976) argues cogently that closeness of supervision, routinization, and the substantive complexity of work are the crucial characteristics of jobs, more than ownership, position in the hierarchy, status, income, or coworker relationships. Kohn & Schooler (1982) show that work requiring initiative, thought, and independent judgment instills habits of self-direction and an open-minded, flexible approach to solving problems that reduce distress. Overall, there are surprisingly few studies of the impact that alienated labor and self-estrangement have on distress. The ones that do exist suggest that the impact of alienated labor is much as theory predicts.

Commitment is an issue in the wider social arena as well as in the workplace. Many people are deeply involved in churches, political parties, civic or charitable organizations, clubs, and hobbies. Because participation in these activities is voluntary and without pay, it is self-expressive rather than self-estranged. Mutran & Reitzes (1984) studied the social patterns and consequences of participation in voluntary organizations and cultural activities among persons 65 years old and over. They find that the amount of time spent in clubs, volunteer groups, political activities, or hobbies and the frequency of attendance at movies, museums, concerts, and sports increase with education and income and decrease with age and poor health. These community activities are, in turn, associated with greater feelings of being excited or interested in something, a greater sense of pride and pleasure in having accomplished something, and a "feeling of being on top of the world with things going your way." Community activities are also associated among the elderly with feeling less upset, lonely, bored, and depressed when data are controlled for family social support. Using panel data on adult heads of households in rural Illinois, Wheaton (1980) finds that memberships in voluntary organizations increased with socioeconomic status and the number of major changes in one's life in preceeding years. Memberships are decreased by fatalism and by the sense that one's income, present job, and job opportunities are barriers to achievement. The number of memberships in voluntary organizations is negatively correlated with psychological and psychophysiological distress. However, when data are controlled for fatalism, there is no significant association between the number of memberships and the level of distress. This appears to contradict the results of Mutran & Reitzes. The different results could be due to the fact that Wheaton measured the number of memberships rather than the frequency and amount of participation, or to the fact that Mutran and Reitzes did not adjust for fatalism in their analysis. As it stands now, participation in voluntary organizations and social activities may itself reduce distress, or it may simply indicate an instrumental orientation that reduces distress.

Support

In all forms of alienation the individual feels detached from society in some way. Social isolation is detachment from personal relationships—a sense of not having anyone who is someone to you and not being someone to anyone. The opposite of isolation is commonly called social support, which is the sense of being cared for and loved, esteemed and valued as a person, and part of a network of communication and obligation (Kaplan et al 1983). Although Seeman (1959:789) originally excluded "the warmth, security, or intensity of an individual's social contacts" from his definition of isolation, it is precisely this meaning that has greatest currency today and that is most important in research on the social patterns of distress (Seeman 1983).

Studies of the relationship between distress and support fall into two categories: Those looking at objective social conditions indicative of more or less isolation, and those looking at the individual's sense of having fulfilling personal relationships. Those of the first type are actually studies of social integration rather than of social support (e.g. Myers et al 1975). Presumably the structural density of a person's network, the number of relationships, and the frequency of contact, increase the probability of fulfilling personal relationships, but they don't guarantee it. For example, marital status is generally considered an important indicator of social integration. As we noted in the introduction, studies consistently find that married persons are less distressed than people who are divorced, separated, widowed, or have never been married. It is an unresolved issue whether married persons have a greater sense of social support that accounts for their lower distress. Unmarried persons can have supportive relationships with their parents, children, other relatives, and friends. On the other side, marriage is no guarantee of a supportive relationship, and many married persons report a lack of reciprocity, affection, and communication that is strongly associated with distress (Pearlin 1975, Gove et al 1983).

Results concerning the impact of social integration on distress are mixed. Williams et al (1981) found that increases in psychological well-being over time are associated with an index of social integration that includes contact with neighbors, friends, and relatives, as well as participation in religious and social groups. However, it is not clear whether integration into personal networks or participation in community groups is the active factor, or both. Hughes & Gove (1981) have looked at the impact of living alone on distress. Counter to theoretical expectation, Hughes & Gove find that within categories of marital status (never married, separated or divorced, widowed) there is *no* difference in distress between those who live alone and those who live with relatives or friends. The difference in distress is between married persons and everyone else rather than between those who live alone and everyone else. Hughes & Gove speculate that social integration may involve a psychological trade-off: ". . . just as persons may gain substantial satisfaction and personal gratification from family relations, they may also suffer frustration, aggravation, hostility, and repressed anger from being constrained to conform to the obligations necessary to meet socially legitimated demands of others in the household" (Hughes & Gove 1981:71).

This speculation is given credence by the results of other studies. Eaton & Kessler (1981) find that depression is lower in two-person households than in households with only one person or with three or more persons (adjusting for marital status, age, sex, education, income, employment, race, and urban versus rural residence). This suggests that the trade-off between social support and social demands is typically optimized in two-person households. Mirowsky & Ross (1984) and Krause & Markides (1985) note that Mexican culture emphasizes the mutual obligations of family and friends, and that responsibility to the group places constraints on the individual, who must take into account the expectations, desires, and well-being of family and friends. These constraints produce a sense of being not in control of one's own destiny, which increases depression; yet, the group is also responsible to the individual, which decreases anxiety (Mirowsky & Ross, 1984). Similarly, Mutran & Reitzes (1984) find that among widowed persons 65 years old and over, receiving financial help, personal services, and practical advice from relatives is associated with lower distress, but *giving* similar forms of help to relatives is associated with *greater* distress. Finally, Kessler & McLeod (1984) find that women have more friendship and family ties than men and are more distressed by the undesirable events that happen in the peripheries of their networks. It appears that integration into personal networks may have costs as well as benefits.

Discussions of social integration often assume that imbeddedness in a social network indicates the availability of social support. However, Pearlin et al (1981) argue that support in times of trouble is not automatic simply because one has family, friends, and associates. "Support comes when people's engagement with one another extends to a level of involvement and concern, not when they merely touch at the surface of each other's lives. . . . The qualities that seem to be especially critical involve the exchange of intimate communications and the presence of solidarity and trust" (Pearlin et al 1981:340). Social support in this sense is emotional intimacy, which Pearlin et al measure by asking if the respondent feels his or her spouse is someone, "I can really talk with about things that are important to me," and by asking if the respondent has a friend or relative (other than the spouse) he or she can tell just about anything to and count on for understanding and advice. In a study over time of the impact on men of job disruptions such as being laid off, fired, or on sick leave, Pearlin et al find that emotional support indirectly reduces the impact of the disruption on depression. Job disruption typically decreases the sense of self-esteem and mastery, which in turn increases depression. However, emotional support reduces the impact of job disruption on self-esteem by as much as 30%, and it reduces the impact of job disruption on the sense of mastery by as much as 50%.

In a study of job stress among employed men, LaRocco et al (1980) find that overwork, conflicting demands, uncertainty, insecurity, lack of opportunity to use one's skills, abilities, and training, and little ability to influence the decisions that affect you all increase depression, irritation, anxiety, and malaise. However, social support from one's supervisor, coworkers, wife, family, or friends tends to reduce the psychological impact of job pressures. Similarly, Turner & Noh (1983) find that women who lack either a sense of support or a sense of mastery are distressed by low socioeconomic status, but women who feel loved, wanted, valued, and esteemed, who feel that others in their network can be counted on, and who have a sense of mastery are not more distressed by low status.

Although some studies, such as the ones described above, find support acts as a buffer that reduces the impact of potentially stressful events and situations, many others do not find an interaction between stressors and support. In a review of 22 studies that tested the possible interaction of stressors and social support, Wheaton (1983) reports that 7 find some evidence of interaction, but the other 15 do not. In 4 of the 7 that find interactions, the evidence pertains to job-related stressors, and in 2 of the other 3 studies the central indicator of support is marital status. In a review of 23 studies, Kessler & McLeod (1985) found that the largest studies with the most reliable and valid measures of social support tend to find a significant buffering effect, presumably because the power of the significance test is better. Thoits (1982) argues that the importance of social support does not rest solely on whether it reduces the effect of stressors on well-being. Love, understanding, appreciation, and mutual commitment may reduce distress in and of themselves, aside from any value they may have as protection against stressful events and situations.

Meaning

An unintelligible world can be disturbing for a number of reasons. Clearly, a world that cannot be understood also cannot be controlled. However, the importance of meaninglessness may go beyond its implications for the sense of control. People may require a sense of purpose in their lives—of knowing where they want to go as well as believing they know how to get there. Furthermore, people may require a sense of the inherent significance and value of their existence. This is what Thoits (1983) speaks of as "existential security." It is the self-assurance of believing that you know what is, that you know what is right, and that your life is a valid expression.

Although the concept of meaninglessness has a prominent place in some explanations of the social patterns of distress, this prominence is based on theory rather than on empirical evidence. None of the studies we reviewed developed or used an index of meaninglessness, and only a few used indexes that might be interpreted as measures of meaninglessness: Kobasa et al's (1981) "alienation from self," and Thoits' (1983) "identity accumulation." Several things are necessary to transform the concept of meaninglessness from a plausible explanation of distress to a valid one: A definition of meaninglessness that makes clear both its essence and its distinction from other concepts such as self-esteem, depression, powerlessness, etc; a reliable index of beliefs that have face validity as indicators of meaninglessness and are not indicators of self-esteem, depression, etc—which may require purging indicators of meaning-lessness from indexes measuring other concepts; tested models showing that variations in the sense of meaninglessness account for social patterns of distress, net of other forms of alienation. Theory and circumstantial evidence strongly suggest that this would be a productive effort.

Normality

Detachment from the normal order of social life constitutes the fifth and final type of alienation that links social conditions to distress. Expectations can be disappointed or violated if actions do not follow usual, discernible, or socially desirable patterns. The failure of others, society, or one's own life to conform to expectations can be distressing. Research on normality and distress has developed around three topics, each of which is discussed below: Normlessness, role stress, and the life cycle.

Normlessness is the belief that socially unapproved behaviors are required to achieve one's goals (Seeman 1959). If the community fails to convince the individual of the legitimacy of its standards for behavior, the individual may choose the most efficient means towards ends, whether legitimate or not: Efficiency displaces social desirability as a guide. A related problem that can be discussed under the same heading for our purposes occurs when community values such as prestige and respect are displaced by elementary pleasures. The essence of normlessness, as broadly defined, is the rejection of the community as a source of standards. Good advice and exemplary behavior are seen as invalid guides. In rejecting standards that arise from the expressed needs, preferences, and rights of others, the individual falls back on intrinsic satisfactions and pragmatic efficiency as guides that do not require faith in others.

Next to powerlessness, normlessness is the form of alienation with the most developed measures and indexes. Some focus on insensitivity to anything but crude enforcement, as indicated by the belief that if something works it doesn't matter if it's right or wrong, and that it is all right to do anything you want as long as you stay out of trouble (Kohn 1976). Other measures focus on antisocial attitudes and behaviors, such as believing that people are honest only out of fear of getting caught if they are dishonest and that people should take everything they can get (Mirowsky & Ross 1983b).

Theory suggests that normlessness is most common under conditions of structural inconsistency, where access to effective legitimate means is limited. In a study of the effects of occupation, Kohn (1976) finds that normlessness is greatest among nonowners in low hierarchical positions. The association is explained by low education and by the routine, closely supervised, uncomplex work. However, with these factors adjusted, ownership and high position actually *in*crease normlessness. This may be a sign that pressure or the desire to win creates some temptation to cheat. The consequences of normlessness are mistrust and anxiety. In the extreme, a person who is despised by the community and wanted by the law is one person against the world. Other people exist to be manipulated, cheated, robbed, or used. Others can provide gratification but not comfort. The normless person must disguise his or her actions and purposes, or otherwise protect against preemption and retaliation. As a result, normlessness is correlated with signs of mistrust and paranoia, such as believing you are being plotted against and feeling it is safer to trust no one, and with symptoms of distress such as brooding and worrying (Mirowsky & Ross 1983b).

The second link between normality and distress is disjunction in the system of roles. Each role involves a set of expectations concerning the behavior of the person in the role and of people in other articulating roles (e.g. husband and wife, mother and child, employee and employer). The expectations are standards or norms in two senses. First, they are understandings and assumptions about the usual behavior of people in particular social categories or situations. As such, they are like maps or guide books that represent the behavioral topography and provide handy information for the social traveler. The planning and coordination of action is greatly enhanced by knowing what to expect of others and knowing what others expect of you. Second, the expectations are required and enforced. If sociology had propositions akin to the laws of thermodynamics in physics, one would surely be that the usual is required and the unusual is forbidden. By demanding the usual of each other and ourselves we simplify decisions and plans, minimize the amount of negotiation necessary to coordinate our lives, and create a workable order. Because the violation of expectations disturbs this order, it carries an onus that threatens both self-evaluations and one's relationships with others.

Role stress arises when expectations are not met. Aside from the situation in which the individual chooses not to meet expectations, which we discussed above as normlessness, there are three types of role stress. Role conflict exists when two legitimate expectations produce incompatible or mutually exclusive demands; role ambiguity exists when it is not clear what is expected; role overload exists when expectations imply demands that overwhelm the resources and capabilities of the individual. Most studies of role stress focus on jobs and the workplace. For example, La Rocco et al (1980) find that an excessive amount of work and conflicting demands on the job are distressing. However, the impact of role conflict and overload on distress can be reduced by emotional and instrumental support from the worker's family, friends, coworkers, and supervisor. In other words, open-minded understanding and a willingness to adjust to the worker's plight can reduce the distress produced by conflicting or excessive demands. This makes sense. If our expectations put somebody on the spot, readjustment of our expectations can ease the tension.

Although studies of the workplace tend to support the role-stress hypothesis, studies of employment among married women appear to contradict it. Since the turn of the century there has been a trend toward greater rates of employment among married women. However, the trend toward approval of such employment tended to lag over much of the period, and the trend toward readjustment of household and family roles was even further behind—only getting under way in the last decade (Ross, Mirowsky & Huber 1983; Ross, Mirowsky & Ulbrich 1983). One would expect overwhelming role-stress among employed wives and their families, including conflict between the demands of the job and those of home and family; ambiguity and uncertainty concerning the proper obligations and rights of an employed wife and mother; and overload among women struggling to do all the things a good mother and wife should do while simultaneously holding a job. Thus, one would expect sharply elevated distress among employed wives and their husbands. However, the research results either did not confirm this prediction or contradicted it. Studies comparing wives who were employed to those who were exclusively housewives either found no difference (e.g. Radloff 1975) or found that the employed wives were actually less distressed than the housewives (e.g. Kessler & McRae 1982). Studies comparing the husbands of employed wives to the husbands of women who were exclusively housewives sometimes found greater distress (e.g. Kessler & McRae 1982), sometimes found less (e.g. Booth 1976), and sometimes found no difference (e.g. Roberts & O'Keefe 1981).

Further research showed that the apparent inconsistencies are due to the fact that marital and family roles are in transition. Some couples are living according to the traditional norms, some according to new egalitarian norms, and many are in between. Husband and wife are both less distressed if the wife's employment status matches their role preferences and are both more distressed if her employment status contradicts their preferences. The pattern of differences in distress suggests that, in the transition from traditional to egalitarian roles, the central problem for husbands is one of self-esteem—of getting over any embarrassment, guilt, or apprehension associated with their wives' employment. For the wives the central problem is getting their husbands to share the housework (Ross, Mirowsky & Huber 1983).

The third and last link between normality and distress is the normal sequence of roles, statuses, and transitions over the life cycle. Transitions that happen out of their usual sequence create practical and moral dilemmas and may also threaten the sense of the meaningful, predictable, and secure social reality. Even a highly undesirable event, such as the death of a parent, can have very different effects depending on whether it happens in childhood or late adulthood (Brown & Harris 1978). Many of the effects of expectation on distress can be thought of as contextual effects. Expectations are mental representations of general social conditions. If we ask ourselves what qualities of social conditions will change expectations and thus modify the impact of events, one answer is the prevalence of the events or sequence of events among others in the same social category. The higher the prevelance the less unusual it is and, thus, the greater the cultural, social, and personal preparation for it. For example, Lennon (1982) looked at the impact of menopause on distress. Although it is commonly believed that menopause is a "natural" period of distress for women, Lennon argues that the appropriate timing of life course change is socially defined and that individuals are aware of these age expectations and evaluate their own experience against the normative standard. Life-course changes are not ordinarily traumatic if they occur on time because they have been anticipated and rehearsed. Major distress is caused by events that upset the *expected* sequence and rhythm of life.

Menopause marks the beginning of "midlife"—the period between parenthood and old age. The median age at menopause is 49.7 years, and three quarters of natural menopauses happen between ages 45 and 54. Using data from the Health and Nutrition Examination Survey, Lennon finds that women of ages 25–43 currently going through menopause have 72% more symptoms of depression than premenopausal women of the same age, and women 54–74 currently going through menopause have 78% more depression than postmenopausal women of the same age, but among women ages 44–53 there is no difference in depression between those who are premenopausal, currently menopausal, and postmenopausal (controlling for race, marital status, education, income, and number of children). Thus, the impact of menopause on distress depends entirely on whether it happens inside or outside the usual age range.

In the coming decade we may see many more studies of the effects of contextual expectations. To the extent possible, they should try to demonstrate two things: First, that the amount of distress associated with the event or situation in question is lowest in the sociodemographic groups where it is most common, or alternatively that the most common pattern or sequence in a group is the least distressing one; second, that the prevalence of the event or situation in a person's sociodemographic group increases his or her preparation or even preference for it, or increases the availability of institutional and personal support; and that these are the proximate factors that modify the impact of events and situations on distress and thus explain the effect of prevalence.

Summary

Sociological theory about the forms, causes, and consequences of alienation has inspired much of the recent research on social patterns of distress. Perceptions of control, commitment, support, meaning, and normality can reduce distress either by meeting basic psychological needs or by reducing the impact of potentially threatening or disturbing events and situations. Although social variations in alienation are a major source of social variations in distress, two other factors also play a part: Authoritarianism and inequity.

AUTHORITARIANISM

Authoritarianism is a complex world view with a number of thematically related elements. Chief among these is a sense that tradition and authority are compelling guides to behavior, and a belief that ethical conduct and compliance with the dictates of tradition and authority are identical. Theoretically, authoritarianism has many consequences. Two are particularly important in explaining social patterns of distress: (a) inflexibility in dealing with practical and interpersonal problems, and (b) suspiciousness and mistrust.

Inflexibility

Cognitive flexibility is an open-ended, open-minded approach to solving problems characterized by the ability to elaborate and weigh arguments and evidence both for and against a proposition, by the ability to imagine a complex set of actions necessary to solve a practical problem, and by the ability to imagine and compare multiple solutions to a single problem. Inflexibility is characterized by a tendency to favor particular modes of coping in all stressful situations, by a dearth of strategies for solving problems, by reliance on conformity and obedience as coping strategies, by rigid application of rules and standards, by an inability to imagine contradictory views and complex solutions, and by dedication to tradition as a means of adaptation (Kohn & Schooler 1982, Wheaton 1983).

According to the theory, inflexibility is learned as an habitual style of thought and action in social situations that limit the individual's horizons and demand conformity and obedience. Insular personal networks and a lack of exposure to the views of other cultures, historical periods and sectors of society can create a sense that the familiar, traditional order has a universal and unique validity that transcends time, place, and situation; and low-status jobs often require un-reflecting compliance with rules and plans the individual did not have a part in making. Studies find that education increases intellectual flexibility, and that the characteristic demands of one's occupation also have an effect. Jobs that are routine, closely supervised, simple, and involve things rather than people or data tend to reduce the individual's flexibility in solving cognitive and social problems. Furthermore, educational and occupational experiences shape the values and beliefs that parents pass on to their children (Kohn 1972, Kohn & Schooler 1982, Schooler 1972). The result is that inflexibility is associated with low current status and with a low status of origin.

Wheaton (1983) compares the theoretical effect of inflexibility on distress to that of fatalism. As discussed earlier, the belief that outcomes are determined by external forces beyond one's control implies a lack of coping *effort*. If luck, fate, chance, and powerful others are the controlling forces in your life, then there is no point in trying. By comparison, inflexibility reduces coping *ability*. The individual who lacks the mental skill to imagine all aspects of a problem or multiple solutions to a problem, who cannot understand other points of view, and who thus finds it difficult to negotiate and compromise, will have trouble solving personal, interpersonal, and social problems. Both theory and labora-tory studies of animals suggest an intimate link between fatalism and inflexibil-ity with the two reinforcing each other. Learned helplessness is created by exposing animals to inescapable electric shock. It is characterized by subse-quent failure to attempt escape when an avenue of escape is available *and* by a diminished ability to learn escape behaviors even when forcibly and repeatedly demonstrated (Seligman 1975). It is as if the animal learns inattention to the connections between signs, actions, and outcomes. Similarly, fatalism may produce inflexibility by reducing the individual's efforts to understand events and situations. Not only will this tend to produce a rigid, habitual response to problems, but it will also limit the development of intellectual problem-solving skills. This inflexibility in turn reduces the ability to cope, and the consequent failures increase the sense of not being in control.

Kohn & Schooler (1982) find evidence of this pattern in their study of the cognitive and emotional impact of job characteristics. They find that flexibility reinforces self-directedness, boosts the impact of job characteristics on self-directedness, and leads to jobs with characteristics that produce self-directedness. Wheaton (1983) found that flexibility reduces the amount of depression associated with acute and chronic stressors and that flexibility eliminates the association between stressors and schizophrenic symptoms. Overall, it appears that flexibility improves the individual's ability to cope, reinforces coping effort, and eventually leads the individual into situations that demand and produce greater flexibility and instrumentalism—all of which reduce distress.

Mistrust

The second characteristic of authoritarianism associated with distress is mistrust, which is an absence of faith in other people based on a belief that they are out for their own good and will exploit or victimize you in pursuit of their goals. Theory points to three related causes of mistrust: awareness that one's internal impulses are frustrated and controlled by external authority, which means others also have selfish motives that must be restrained; belief that there is an inherent scarcity of wealth, power, and prestige, so that one person's gain is always another person's loss; and belief that victimization and exploitation are common and have dire consequences for the victim.

Theory thus implies that mistrust is most common where control is external, resources and opportunities are scarce, and crime and exploitation are common. Research shows that mistrust is greatest among persons with low education; who have low family income, live in low-status neighborhoods, and have low-prestige jobs; and who believe in external control. Furthermore, there is an interaction between low socioeconomic status and belief in external control, so that the combination of the two greatly increases mistrust. Among those with a strong sense of mastery and instrumentalism low status is not associated with mistrust. This suggests that people who feel in control of their own lives and take an active approach to problems feel they can deal with situations where the threat of exploitation is great (Mirowsky & Ross 1983a).

Trust allows pairs of individuals to establish cooperative relationships whenever doing so is mutually beneficial (Rotter 1980). In contrast, the mistrusting individual may not seek social support when in need, may reject offers of such support, and may be uncomfortable with any support that is given. Suspicious individuals can help create and maintain the very conditions that seem to justify their beliefs: Their preemptive actions may elicit hostile responses; without allies they are easy targets; when victimized or exploited they cannot share their economic or emotional burden with others; and by not providing aid and assistance to others they weaken the community's power to forestall victimization and exploitation and to limit its consequences (Mirowsky & Ross 1983a). Recent studies find that mistrust tends to develop into paranoid beliefs that enemies are conspiring against you and that mistrust is highly related to distress (Mirowsky & Ross 1983a,b).

INEQUITY

A third classic theme has engendered less research than alienation and authoritarianism, but in theory should be at least as relevant to emotional well-being. It is the theme of unfairness, injustice, and inequity. The sense of right and wrong, feelings of guilt or grievance, and the relation of exploiter and victim are concerns as old as the earliest stories and writings. Emotions are deeply related to the sense of fairness. Unfairness produces guilt and anger. It may also produce anxiety and depression.

The current work on equity and distress is entirely concerned with marital relations. Pearlin (1975) finds that married people feel distressed if the other partner expects more than he or she is willing to give back, acts like the only important person in the family, and demands more compliance than he or she is willing to give. How does the selfish partner feel? Equity theory is distinct from other theories in its prediction that exploiters of unfair relationship are distressed too. Schafer & Keith (1980) confirm this prediction. They find that married persons are more depressed if their partner's effort at cooking, housekeeping, earning income, companionship, and childcare seems too small *or too great* compared to their own effort. Mirowsky (1985) also confirms the prediction. He finds depression is lowest if the married person's influence in major family decisions is neither too small nor too large.

Equity is clearly an important factor in depression relating to the quality and nature of marital relationships. Does equity also mediate the impact of larger, more impersonal social relationships? It is possible that large-scale, impersonal relationships free individuals from the emotional consequences of exploiting others. It is also possible that such freedom is rarely complete. Future research on equity and distress should explore the larger social relationships, paying special attention to comparison with equity in personal relationships.

CONCLUSION

In the past 15 years, research on social patterns of distress has moved beyond the simple reiteration of basic facts toward *explanations* of those facts. The explanations suggest that distress is reduced by control, commitment, support, meaning, normality, flexibility, trust, and equity. In some ways this may seem like progress backwards. The four basic facts—that low status, undesirable events, being female, and being unmarried are distressing—have generated far more than four explanations. In future research we must order, prune, and synthesize our explanations, developing a lean, coherent theory of the social patterns of distress.

Literature Cited

Aneshensel, C. S., Frerichs, R. R., Huba, G. J. 1984. Depression and physical illness: A multiwave, nonrecursive causal model. *J. Health Soc. Behav.* 25:350–71

Booth, A. 1976. Wife's employment and husband's stress: A replication and refutation. *J. Marriage Fam.* 39:645–50

Brown, G. W., Harris, T. 1978. *Social Origins of Depression.* New York: Free Press

Dohrenwend, B. P., Shrout, P. E., Egri, G., Mendelsoln, F. S. 1980. Nonspecific psychological distress and other dimensions of psychopathology. *Arch. Gen. Psychiatry* 37:1229–36

Eaton, W. W., Kessler, L. G. 1981. Rates of symptoms of depression in a national sample. *Am. J. Epidemiol.* 114:528–38

Gove, W. R., Hughes, M., Style, C. B. 1983. Does marriage have positive effects on the psychological well-being of the individual? *J. Health Soc. Behav.* 24:122–31

Gurin, G., Veroff, J., Feld, S. 1960. *Amer-*

icans View Their Mental Health. New York: Basic

Hughes, M., Gove, W. R. 1981. Living alone, social integration, and mental health. *Am. J. Sociol.* 87:48–74

Johnson, D. R., Meile, R. L. 1981. Does dimensionality bias in Langner's 22-item index affect the validity of social status comparisons? *J. Health Soc. Behav.* 22:415–33

Kaplan, H. B., Robbins, C., Martin, S. S. 1983. Antecedents of psychological distress in young adults: Self-rejection, deprivation of social support and life events. *J. Health Soc. Behav.* 24:230–44

Kessler, R. C., Cleary, P. D. 1980. Social class and psychological distress. *Am. Sociol. Rev.* 45:463–78

Kessler, R. C., McRae, J. A. 1982. The effect of wive's employment on the mental health of married men and women. *Am. Sociol. Rev.* 47:216–27

Kessler, R. C., McLeod, J. D. 1984. Sex differences in vulnerability to undesirable life events. *Am. Soc. Rev.* 49:620–31

Kessler, R. C., McLeod, J. D. 1985. Social support and mental health in community samples. In *Social Support and Health,* ed. S. Cohen, S. L. Syme. New York: Academic

Kluckholn, F. R., Strodtbeck, F. L. 1961. *Variations in Value Orientations.* Westport, Conn: Greenwood

Kobassa, S. C., Maddi, S. R., Courington, S. 1981. Personality and constitution as mediators in the stress-illness relationship. *J. Health Soc. Behav.* 22:368–78

Kohn, M. L. 1976. Occupational structure and alienation. *Am. J. Sociol.* 82:111–30

Kohn, M. L., Schooler, C. 1982. Job conditions and personality: a longitudinal assessment of their reciprocal effects. *Am. J. Sociol.* 87:1257–86

Krause, N., Markides, K. S. 1985. Employment and psychological well-being in Mexican American women. *J. Health Soc. Behav.* 26:15–26

Langner, T. S. 1962. A twenty-two item screening score of psychiatric symptoms indicating impairment. *J. Health Human Behav.* 3:269–76

LaRocco, J. M., House, J. S., French, J. R. P. 1980. Social support, occupational stress, and health. *J. Health Soc. Behav.* 21:202–18

Lennon, M. C. 1982. The psychological consequences of menopause: The importance of timing of a life stage event. *J. Health Soc. Behav.* 23:353–66

Madsen, W. 1973. *The Mexican-Americans of South Texas.* New York: Holt, Rinehart, Winston. 2nd ed.

Mirowsky, J., Ross, C. E. 1983a. Paranoia and the structure of powerlessness. *Am. Sociol. Rev.* 48:228–39

Mirowsky, J., Ross, C. E. 1983b. The multidimensionality of psychopathology in a community sample. *Am. J. Community Psychol.* 11:573–91

Mirowsky, J., Ross, C. E. 1984. Mexican culture and its emotional contradictions. *J. Health Soc. Behav.* 25:2–13

Mirowsky, J. 1985. Depression and marital power: An equity model. *Am. J. Soc.* 91: In press

Mutran, E., Reitzes, D. G. 1984. Intergenerational support activities and well-being among the elderly: A convergence of exchange and symbolic-interaction perspectives. *Am. Soc. Rev.* 49:117–30

Myers, J. K., Lindenthal, J. J., Pepper, M. P. 1975. Life events, social integration and psychiatric symptomatology. *J. Health Soc. Behav.* 16:421–27

Pearlin, L. I. 1975. Status inequality and stress in marriage. *Am. Sociol. Rev.* 40:344–57

Pearlin, L. I., Lieberman, M. A. 1979. Social sources of emotional distress. In *Research in Community and Mental Health,* ed. R. G. Simmons. Greenwich: JAI

Pearlin, L. I., Schooler, C. 1978. The structure of coping. *J. Health Soc. Behav.* 19:2–21

Pearlin, L. I., Menaghan, E. G., Lieberman, M. A., Mullan, J. T. 1981. The stress process. *J. Health Soc. Behav.* 22:337–56

Radloff, L. 1975. Sex differences and depression: the effects of occupational and marital status. *Sex Roles* 1:249–65

Radloff, L. 1977. The CES-D scale: A self-report depression scale for research in the general population. *Appl. Psychol. Measurement* 1:385–401

Roberts, R. E., O'Keefe, S. J. 1981. Sex differences in depression reexamined. *J. Health Soc. Behav.* 22:394–400

Ross, C. E., Mirowsky, J., Cockerham, W. C. 1983. Social class, Mexican culture, and fatalism: Their effects on psychological distress. *Am. J. Community Psychol.* 11:383–99

Ross, C. E., Mirowsky, J., Ulbrich, P. 1983. Distress and the traditional female role: A comparison of Mexicans and Anglos. *Am. J. Sociol.* 89:670–82

Ross, C. E., Mirowsky, J., Huber, J. 1983. Dividing work, sharing work, and in-between: Marriage patterns and depression. *Am. Sociol. Rev.* 48:809–23

Rotter, J. B. 1966. Generalized expectancies for internal vs. external control of reinforcement. *Psychol. Monogr.* 80:1–28

Rotter, J. B. 1980. Interpersonal trust, trustworthiness, and gullibility. *Am. Psychol.* 35:1–7

Schafer, R. B., Keith, P. M. 1980. Equity and depression among married couples. *Soc. Psych. Q.* 43:430–5

Schooler, C. 1972. Social antecedents of adult

psychological functioning. *Am. J. Sociol.* 78:299–323

Seeman, M. 1959. On the meaning of alienation. *Am. Sociol. Rev.* 24:783–91

Seeman, M. 1983. Alienation motifs in contemporary theorizing: the hidden continuity of classic themes. *Soc. Psychol. Q.* 46:171–84

Seligman, M. E. P. 1975. *Helplessness.* San Francisco: Freeman

Thoits, P. A. 1981. Undesirable life events and psychological distress: A problem of operational confounding. *Am. Sociol. Rev.* 46:97–109

Thoits, P. A. 1982. Conceptual, methodological, and theoretical problems in studying social support as a buffer against life stress. *J. Health Soc. Behav.* 23:145–59

Thoits, P. A. 1983. Multiple identities and psychological well-being: A reformulation and test of the social isolation hypothesis. *Am. Sociol. Rev.* 48:174–87

Turner, R. J., Noh, S. 1983. Class and psychological vulnerability among women: The significance of social support and personal control. *J. Health Soc. Behav.* 24:2–15

Walster, E., Walster, G. W., Berscheid, E. 1978. *Equity: Theory and Research.* Boston, Mass: Allyn & Bacon

Wheaton, B. 1980. The sociogenesis of psychological disorder: An attributional theory. *J. Health Soc. Behav.* 21:100–24

Wheaton, B. 1982. Uses and abuses of the Langner Index: A reexamination of findings on psychological and psychophysiological distress. In *Psychosocial Epidemiology: Symptoms, Illness Behavior, and Help-Seeking,* ed. D. Mechanic. New York: Watson

Wheaton, B. 1983. Stress, personal coping resources, and psychiatric symptoms: An investigation of interactive models. *J. Health Soc. Behav.* 24:208–29

Williams, A. W., Ware, J. E., Donald, C. A. 1981. A model of mental health, life events, and social supports applicable to general populations. *J. Health Soc. Behav.* 22:324–36

Ann. Rev. Sociol. 1986. 12:47–66

POPULAR CULTURE

Chandra Mukerji and Michael Schudson

Sociology and Communication Departments, University of California at San Diego, La Jolla, California 92093

Abstract

Popular culture studies have until recently been treated as more or less unworthy of serious scholarly attention. But developments in anthropology, history, communication, American studies, and literary criticism have given the study of popular culture new analytic tools and legitimacy. This article reviews some of the more noteworthy contributions to this body of scholarship. Interpretive anthropology by Clifford Geertz, Victor Turner, and others, historical work influenced by the *Annales* school, studies of mass media, and the work of structuralists and post-structuralists from many disciplines are all discussed. This work, as well as sociological analyses of leisure, art, and mass culture are shown to have provided rich and vital insights into the social power and forms of popular culture.

INTRODUCTION

Much more than with most objects of study, a leading question with popular culture has traditionally been whether it deserves serious consideration at all. But an extraordinary new interest in popular culture has emerged in the past two decades in the humanities and the social sciences. Part of it stems from the growing conviction among Marxist scholars that popular culture plays a crucial role in mobilizing political action. And part of it has emerged from the development of new interpretive techniques for making sense of the content of popular forms.

The resulting field of popular culture does not have distinct borders. Indeed, recent works by DiMaggio (1982) and Levine (1984) excavate the social origins of the distinction between "high" or "elite" culture and popular culture and offer deep skepticism about the honorific quality of the distinction. The study of popular culture also crosses disciplines, and it would be impossible to discuss a

47

sociology of popular culture without attention to work in history, anthropology, and folklore. Within sociology, the sociology of art, music, religion, language, education, mass media, and everyday life contribute to an analysis of popular culture.[1]

Popular culture as it is discussed here includes both "folk" or "popular" beliefs, practices, and objects rooted in local traditions as well as "mass" beliefs, practices, and objects generated from political and commercial centers. Conventionally, objects taken to be part of popular culture are *readable* objects, written or visual materials for which there are available traditions of interpretation and criticism. In recent years, the range of what is considered "readable" has expanded; now spatial arrangements (Sennett 1976, Dyos & Wolff 1973, Lynch 1960), household objects (Csikszentmihalyi & Rochberg-Halton 1981), advertisements (Schudson 1984, Goffman 1979, Ewen 1976, Boorstin 1963), television (Newcomb 1982, Ellis 1982, Fiske & Hartley 1978, Tuchman et al 1978, Williams 1975), food and drink (M. Douglas 1982, Messer 1984), dress (Barthes 1983, Mukerji 1983, Lurie 1981, Bell 1976), and youth cultural styles (Grossberg 1983, Frith 1981, Hebdige 1979, Hall & Jefferson 1978) are all parts of readable cultural systems. The special task of "interpretation," for many years left to departments of literature and art, has become a more general subject to which symbolic anthropology, sociolinguistics, and psychoanalysis have contributed, creating a new convergence of the social sciences and humanities (Hirsch 1981).

What remains most impressive in the recent sociological study of popular culture are the theoretical developments that have begun to integrate the study of culture into a general understanding of social life. These changes might seem to have emerged exclusively from the revival of Marxist thought and new theories of interpretation born in the 1960s, but they owe so much to contemporaneous developments in anthropology and history that we begin with a look at recent scholarship in these fields.

Developments in Anthropology

Anthropology's catholic approach to the study of human societies has helped make popular culture a legitimate object of study, especially when anthropologists have studied popular culture in industrial as well as tribal societies. There have been at least two significant lines of influence from anthropolo-

---

[1]Some pertinent areas have been treated in recent *Annual Review* volumes: the sociology of leisure (Wilson 1980), the sociology of sport (Luschen 1980), the sociology of secular ritual and ceremony (Gusfield & Michalowicz 1984), the sociology of tourism (Cohen 1984), and the sociology of culture (Peterson 1979). Relevant work in social and cultural history is reviewed in the tenth anniversary number of the *Journal of Social History* (1976) and the tenth anniversary issue of *Reviews in American History* (Kutler & Katz 1982). The sociology of popular culture has also been surveyed in a special issue of the *Journal of Popular Culture* (Fine 1977).

gy. We can label these the *structuralist* branch, inspired by the conceptual tools of linguistics and the work of Claude Levi-Strauss, and the *interpretivist* branch, a variety of approaches centered on the importance of the symbolic and the communal in modern society. The interpretivist branch involves something of a rediscovery of the Durkheim of *Elementary Forms* and a consequent focus of research on ceremony, celebration, spectacle, and ritual in both traditional (religious) and modern (mass media, professional sports, etc) forms. (For a recent review of anthropological approaches to culture, see Ortner 1984.)

The structuralist approach begins with the premise that the human mind (universally) orders the flux of experience into categories of binary oppositions: on/off, male/female, sacred/profane, up/down, in/out, pure/impure. People make sense of the world through these binary oppositions and make use of the sense data of the world—plants, animals, colors, human bodies—to arrive at cognitive order. Things that are thought to bridge across categories are "anomalous" and take on special powers of danger, magic, or meaningfulness. Religious systems, such as totemism and myths in primitive societies, are cultural constructions that elaborate and master a society's cognitive categories (Levi-Strauss 1966; 1963). The cultural constructions of industrial societies should equally be subject to a structuralist analysis; Will Wright (1975) directly applied a Levi-Straussian framework to a study of cowboy films; Williamson (1978) did the same for advertisements, and E. A. Lawrence (1982) for the rodeo. However, the influence of structuralism on popular culture studies has been more general than any specific applications; structuralism in its various guises has helped produce a heightened theoretical sophistication, a point we take up in the last section of this essay.

One inspiration for interpretivist anthropology has been Clifford Geertz, who elaborates a notion of the cultural system that strictly distinguishes it from the social system. Geertz takes the capacity for and reliance on the symbolic as the defining feature of the human species. Symbols exercise a cybernetic control over human behavior, expressing the social system and personality systems of a culture without being *merely* expressive. Geertz accords significance to symbols (and relationships within the symbol system) *without* bowing to one or another formalist method of analysis that would divorce the symbolic from its relationship to the social (Geertz 1980).

For the study of popular culture, the single most influential work by Geertz has been his famous essay, "Deep Play: Notes on the Balinese Cockfight" (1973). This essay gave the green light to scholars who wanted to believe that the neglected parts of a culture, the popular parts of a culture, contained profundities usually located only in elements of "high culture." The cockfight essay does three things. First, it shows the ways in which the Balinese cockfight represents and heightens important social solidarities and social divisions in Balinese society. Second, and more incidentally, it shows how the cockfight represents and heightens important psychological tendencies in Balinese personality, especially that surrounding the relationship between the Balinese man and his "cock." Most importantly, Geertz demonstrates that the cockfight is not a mere reflection of underlying tendencies but is a point of focus for society and forms a powerful influence directed back onto society. The cockfight, Geertz argues, provides a "sentimental education" for the Balinese. It does not express what Balinese society is but what—in a kind of collective thought-experiment—Balinese society *might be* if certain emotional tendencies were taken to their logical extreme.

The anthropologists who might be called neo-Durkheimians, especially Victor Turner and his students, have concentrated attention on ceremony, celebration, and spectacle, those features of social life that step self-consciously out of social life to negate and counterpoise daily existence with moments of high contrast or "anti-structure" (Turner 1967, 1969).

Turner himself focuses on "social dramas." These are "sustained public actions" in which social conflicts are *dramatized*, be it in a court of law, an assembly of elders, or some other ritual mode of redress. These dramas do not simply restate or mirror underlying social structure and social divisions. They are performances that belong to what Turner calls society's "subjunctive" mood. Ritual, carnival, festival, theater, and other cultural performances express "supposition, desire, hypothesis, possibility" rather than fact (Turner 1984). For anthropologists in both the Geertzian and Turnerian lines, popular cultural forms can be read as a culture thinking out loud about itself (MacAloon 1984a; Babcock 1984).

One of the contributions of anthropologists (and folklorists) has been to draw attention to the concept of "performance" as a key form of cultural behavior (Hymes 1975). Performance is a kind of activity that is formally staged or an aspect of everyday life in which a person is oriented to and intends to have some effect on an audience. Studies of Afro-American culture emphasize that a great deal of everyday verbal interaction is performance-oriented (Abrahams 1970, 1976). Erving Goffman's interest in "focused interaction" or a "sociology of occasions" has contributed to the study of performance, too (1967). Studies of oral poetry show that the structure and form of poems like the *Iliad* and the *Odyssey* derive from their roots in an oral, memorized, improvised, and performed mode of composition (Finnegan 1977, Lord 1960). From the work of sociolinguists, anthropologists, and folklorists of performance, there has been strong emphasis on reintegrating the study of texts into their social (and often "performed") contexts (Bauman & Sherzer 1974, Moore & Meyerhoff 1977).

Another anthropologist who has influenced studies of popular culture is Mary Douglas. Coming out of a tradition of British social anthropology but influenced also by French structuralism, she broadened her studies of African cultures to consider issues of ritual and taboo, and native understandings of purity and defilement, in contemporary British and American societies (Douglas 1966). She extended this work, in one direction, to a study of the meaning of food in different cultures. She shows how to "decipher" the social meaning of a meal, taking food as a system of cultural communication. In another direction, she has examined consumer goods as a medium through which culture is constituted. For her, as for many other anthropologists, and in sharp contradistinction to economists, human beings are meaning-making animals more than they are profit-maximizing animals, and "the essential function of consumption is its capacity to make sense." Commodities, in her view, are not good for eating, clothing, and shelter so much as they are, as Levi-Strauss had said of totems, "good for thinking; treat them as a nonverbal medium for the human creative faculty" (Douglas & Isherwood 1979). In theoretical terms, the argument that culture precedes and becomes the necessary context for practical activity has been most powerfully made by Marshall Sahlins (1976).

Historical Studies: Early Modern Europe

Popular culture studies in sociology until recently concerned themselves with contemporary culture and the roots of that culture in the late nineteenth century. This perspective made reasonably good sense. Modern culture was thought the main province of sociology; mass culture was viewed as the pattern of popular culture most powerful in this era; and the growth of mass culture was associated with nineteenth-century industrialization. Even interest in so-called folk cultures did not really push studies of culture earlier than the nineteenth century; that is when the idea of folk culture we live with today was formulated.

This pattern was changed by members of the *Annales* school of French historians. The *Annales* group was not intent on changing our visions of popular culture; they were initiating an experiment in historiography. They wanted to see what would happen to the history of the West if it were viewed not through the documents of the literate elite but through the objects and habits of the people. Marc Bloch (1953) argued that this approach was particularly necessary in the medieval period, for which written records are scarce and so a poor basis for writing history. Others found this method of writing history equally useful in the early modern period when the literate elite was still small, and written documents presented information primarily about the social worlds of elites.

Fernand Braudel was among the historians who began to approach the history of the early modern era with this new perspective; he produced a new image of popular culture in the period. He started from the theoretical premise that history is made and experienced differently at the various levels of the social structure (Braudel 1977). At least three discrete streams of history coexist and change at different paces. Starting from this insight, Braudel wrote his monumental book, *The Mediterranean and the Mediterranean World in the*

Age of Phillip II (1966). Where Bloch formulated for historians a kind of anthropological concept of culture as *mentalité,* a way of thinking, Braudel developed a more materialist history that attempted to locate patterns of culture in the geography, economy, and material culture of common people. These men worked at different ends of the continuum linking ideational and material culture, but they shared the commitment to using their new approaches to culture to write history of "the people," which could reveal modes of thought quite antithetical to their own (Clark 1983; see also Darnton 1984, Ginzburg 1980, Foucault 1973).

LeRoy Ladurie helped to tie popular culture in the early modern period to larger political life in his *Carnival in Romans* (1980). He described a moment in which a carnival celebration turned into a peasant revolt, explaining how the disrespect for elites made legitimate in carnival turned into a serious political event. Natalie Davis in *Society and Culture in Early Modern France* (1965) counters potential arguments that the culture of the people in this early era was too simple or thin to deserve much attention *as culture.* She describes how popular culture was enriched by the Reformation and the invention of printing and how these larger cultural patterns grew powerful through their translation into the world of popular culture.

All these historians provide new insights into popular culture in the early modern period, but they do not discuss its character and importance directly. In contrast, Peter Burke in *Popular Culture in Early Modern Europe* (1978) does precisely this. He describes a flowering in the popular culture of the early modern period and suggests that the increased urbanization and wealth of the period allowed traditional forms of popular culture (such as celebrations for Saints' Days or street performances in cities) to reach new levels of aesthetic development and cultural elaboration. He also indicates how two forces—(a) efforts to reform popular culture during the Reformation and Counterreformation and (b) the social transformation of European society brought about by expansion of trade to the East and the Americans—brought an end to many of these patterns of culture.

If the beginning of the early modern period was characterized by expansion and elaboration of traditional popular culture, the end of this period was more aptly characterized by the development of a new form of popular culture: commercial or mass culture. McKendrick et al in *The Commercialization of Society in 18th-Century England* (1982) contend that mass marketing techniques such as advertising and the use of displays for promoting goods were used successfully during the eighteenth century. They show how new values associated with commercial development were affecting a variety of realms of public and private life from politics to the raising of children. They not only provide evidence of the ubiquity of this new culture even in the lower ranks of

English society in this period, they also argue its importance to the industrial growth there.

The sociology of Norbert Elias also addresses the culture of this period. Although he is concerned with court culture and other elements of elite civility in the period, he also looks at early efforts to spread elite civility to the middle class. His classic discussion of table manners is a study of the mass dissemination of patterns of taste in a period when social mobility was great enough and the elaboration of manners complicated enough that people had difficulty knowing how to act. A form of mass culture, printed books of manners, filled the gap (Elias 1978).

The sociological argument implicit in this work is elaborated in Chandra Mukerji's *From Graven Images: Patterns of Modern Materialism* (1983). She argues that the mass culture that most sociologists locate in the nineteenth century and describe as an offshoot of industrialization actually predated industrialization and helped to create it. She details the commercial development of pictorial prints during the sixteenth century to show how early mass production techniques put in the service of commercial enterprise were able to create a new group of consumers among the less affluent.

In its attention to the materiality of cultural forms, Mukerji's work and that of the more materialist historians of early modern Europe are kin to a number of studies about communication technologies as simultaneously material and cultural forces. Studies in the history of literacy (Goody 1977), print (Eisenstein 1979), the newspaper press (Schudson 1977, Williams 1961, Schiller 1981), the telegraph (Czitrom 1982) and the impact of mass media on rural society (Weber 1976) have made a sharp division of the material from the cultural world difficult to sustain.

Historical Research: The Nineteenth Century

Historical studies of the nineteenth century have also undergone profound change, focusing increasingly on the experiences of laborers, slaves, women, children, and other disadvantaged groups. There has also been increased interest in patterns of public ritual, from parades (Davis 1986) and court proceedings (Isaac 1982) to the language of popular political rhetoric (Sewell 1980). Historians have come to view the "rituals of journeymen's brotherhoods, the recruitment patterns of stonemasons, the organization of production in hatters' workshops, the piece-rate schedules that determined artisans' wages, all as meaningful statements, as a set of interrelated texts that demand close reading and careful exegesis" (Sewell 1980).

Two of the most significant developments in social history for the study of popular culture have been the new history of the working class and the new women's history. It is hard to think of a work with more profound impact on a field than E. P. Thompson's *Making of the English Working Class* (1963), which has deeply influenced the study of the working class and Marxist historiography in general. Thompson found that the emergence of a working class "consciousness" in nineteenth century England came from traditional artisans, not new industrial laborers. There is now "almost universal agreement" that the nineteenth century labor movement was "born in the craft workshop, not in the dark satanic mill" (Sewell 1980; see also Gutman 1976, Wilentz 1984). Thompson shows that forging a new working class consciousness and working class organizations relied on the artisans' sense of inheriting the rights of Englishmen, in other words, on a *backward-looking* sense of entitlements as a basis for claims on the political system. This suggests that political struggle does not grow naturally out of particular economic conditions, but that economic conditions themselves are understood by the people who live them through available cultural frames. There is some danger, however, that the increasing focus of historians on cultural experience may obscure the importance of the political altogether (Genovese & Fox-Genovese 1976). It could be entirely wrong-headed to take the elaboration of a rich working class culture as evidence of effective political consciousness or incipient political rebellion (Murdock 1982, Stedman Jones 1983). Similar issues arise in the study of slave culture (Levine 1977). Debate continues in history as well as in sociology as to whether working class culture is a source of working class resistance or "false consciousness" (Aronowitz 1973).

In the history of women, among a great many important recent works, Ann Douglas's work is of special interest to the study of popular culture. In *Feminization of American Culture* (1977) she argues that modern mass culture was first given its peculiar sentimentality and superficial allusions to morality in nineteenth-century popular literature written for (and often by) women. Douglas is interested in this corpus because she sees it as one that women had the power to influence, and she is disappointed with the result. Rather than attempting as writers and readers of literature to inaugurate serious discussions of power in society and the relative powerlessness of women, women created and found refuge in a world of simple sentimentality.

The role of women as consumers in the nineteenth century and the power of consumerism in that period has been explored by Rosalind Williams in *Dream Worlds* (1982). Like Douglas, Williams tries to locate the origins of modern mass culture in nineteenth-century consumption patterns. But Williams turns her attention more to class than to gender. She looks at the articulation of an aesthetic for mass culture in the nineteenth century that drew on the aristocratic traditions of taste from an earlier era but was used to market consumer goods to middle-class consumers. She is sensitive (like Pierre Bourdieu) to the use of taste for the maintenance of power and to the ways "corruptions" of taste may mark shifts in power. On another level, she is a careful reader of the department store as a social icon and teacher of middle-class tastes (cf Barth 1980 and Miller 1981). (On early responses to mass culture, see Thompson 1977 and Lears 1981.) Baltzell's studies of the American aristocracy are valuable in documenting the development of an upper class's social patterns and cultural tastes as a response to and intentional effort at creating a preserve apart from mass culture (1964; DiMaggio 1982).

A challenging study of political utopianism and its material expression in the nineteenth century is Dolores Hayden's *The Grand Domestic Revolution* (1981). She describes a little-known American radical feminist movement that focused on domestic architecture as a source of liberation for women. Hayden's work brings to bear on studies of popular culture the voluminous literature on the spread of feminist theories and movements in the nineteenth century as well as the literature on housing, interior design, and social engineering that was so important to the culture of cities and suburbs in this period (Wright 1980, Barth 1980).

Related to work in history, the field of American studies has also begun to change, especially, to rethink *how* to study literature. The study of literature has become more sociological. Jane Tompkins has addressed the subject of literary reputation and the "canon" itself (1985). More attention has been paid to the act of reading, not just the act of writing, and to a study of what audiences *get* from texts, not just what texts *give* to certain privileged readers (the critics and scholars). Rarely does this "reader-response theory" go so far as to examine empirically what audiences really think about books. Yet exceptions to this are noteworthy for sociology. Janice Radway (1984) examines the industry of romance novel publishing and interviews a group of women romance readers in great detail. Since she is able to look at the readers' interpretation of the novels in the context of their lives, she is able to study not only what interpretation the readers place on the books but how these readers *use* the books socially.

American studies has provided new life for popular culture studies, while the work begun at Bowling Green State University and developed through the Popular Culture Association and the *Journal of Popular Culture* has at least begun to accommodate the new developments in anthropology and history (Browne 1982). The Bowling Green movement saw critics of mass culture in the 1950s and 1960s throwing out the baby (of deeply-felt proletarian and folk cultures) with the bath water (of empty media messages). Their impulse, like that of many early anthropologists, was to document a threatened culture and to show its beauty and depth (Nye 1972). But these collectors have often been dismissed by other scholars who *assume* the importance of popular culture and want to find the means to read it more deeply.

Work in history, American studies, and folklore has legitimated a vast range of new topics for study: sports, games, and play (Guttmann 1978, Rader 1983); film (Sklar 1976); material culture (Schlereth 1982, Deetz 1977, Quimby

1978); and technology as culture, including works on the automobile in American life (Flink 1975, Rae 1971, Belasco 1979). Studies of technology are reviewed in a bibliographic essay by Carroll Persell (1983), in one of a series of annual bibliographic reviews in *American Quarterly*. With respect to the nineteenth century and since, one definition of the subject matter for the history of popular culture has been the rise of "semipublic city spaces" and the activities associated with them. These spaces are privately owned but afford relatively free public access—department stores (Barth 1980), theaters (Barth 1980), symphony halls (DiMaggio 1982), railroad terminals (Schivelbusch 1977), ball parks (Barth 1980, Lever 1983), dime museums (Harris 1978), saloons (Duis 1983), amusement parks (Kasson 1978), circuses (Harris 1973), and so forth.

The Sociology of Mass Culture

The most celebrated discussion of popular culture in sociology is the debate over "mass culture." The concept of "mass society" or "mass culture" has origins that go very far back (Brantlinger 1983) but that received modern statement especially after World War II with essays both by conservative intellectuals (T. S. Eliot 1968) and by Marxist thinkers of the Frankfurt School (Jay 1973). It was also very quickly criticized by mainstream sociologists who believed it mistakenly pictured a world with no social institutions mediating between the mass of individual citizens and the centralized structures of power (Rosenberg & White 1957).

The idea of "mass society," associated especially with emigre German intellectuals like Hannah Arendt, Erich Fromm, Karl Mannheim, and others, emerged as a way to understand Nazi Germany and the rise of "totalitarian" societies. Hannah Arendt (1958), for instance, saw people in "mass society" as unusually susceptible to authoritarian regimes because of their isolation from major social and political institutions. The individual in mass society has been seen as alienated, isolated, lonely, and privatized. Politically, this makes the modern person susceptible to the siren song of an authoritarian leader. Culturally, it is said to be produced by the suffusion of the population in the manipulatory machinery of the "culture industry" (Horkheimer & Adorno 1972, Benjamin 1968).

In the 1950s and 1960s, the debate over mass society and mass culture became a heated battle between those who felt revulsion, political or aesthetic or both, at advanced capitalist society and those who argued that the revulsion was itself a class-based reflex that ignored the empirical reality of contemporary society and culture. The debate was comprehensively reviewed, from the side that rejected the Frankfurt School position, by Herbert Gans in 1974. Gans argued that the critical theorists' views were empirically false, that American citizens' understandings of the world were shaped by their own local culture and own social experience more than by mass-mediated images, that "high culture" was not threatened by popular culture, and that high culture differed in degree, not in kind, from popular culture. It is better, he argued, to recognize a plurality of "taste cultures" than a hierarchy of "high" and "low" cultures.

The debate over mass culture has taken several important turns in the past decade. New critiques of mass culture have been formulated. Daniel Bell has developed a conservative version of the critique (1976), and a new left-wing critique has rejected both the extreme (and aristocratic) positions of the Frankfurt School and the liberal pluralism of Herbert Gans and others. The new left version has sought inspiration not in Horkheimer & Adorno but in Antonio Gramsci and the concept of "hegemony" (Lears 1985).

Second, the critique of mass culture has led to studies of audiences and the ways people modify or resist the products of the culture industry. This work has been especially strong in Britain (Curran et al 1977, Cohen 1972). Willis (1977) studied twelve nonacademic "lads" in an ethnographic study in and around their school and documented their opposition to authority, their "counter-school culture," and its links to the "shopfloor culture" they were headed for. This line of research has also grown out of Marxism but in a way that runs counter to the emphasis of "hegemony" theorists (Murdock 1982).

Third, sociologists have shown that there is an unequal distribution of cultural items across classes. The most theoretically ambitious effort to date has been that of Pierre Bourdieu (1984), who tried to show how the unequal distribution of cultural items across social classes represents and reproduces social and political inequality. Similar, though theoretically less ambitious, work in the US looks at what Peterson (1983) calls "patterns of cultural choice."[2]

Fourth, the concept of "culture industry," something of a metaphysical entity in the original Horkheimer & Adorno essay, has been appropriated to justify the empirical study of culture-producing organizations. The resulting "production-of-culture" work has in many cases been a self-conscious reaction *against* mass culture studies (DiMaggio 1977). DiMaggio argues that left-wing critics of mass culture implicitly assume a "monopoly" situation—that the public will absorb whatever the culture offers—while right-wing critics of mass culture implicitly assume a "perfect competition" situation where the public will get whatever it desires. In contrast, the central features of mass culture, in DiMaggio's view, are the "attributes of industries, not of societies." Some mass culture industries *are* in monopoly—like the television industry (before cable), or elementary- and secondary-school textbook publishers that produce the same materials for everyone in the population. But other mass culture industries—trade books, records, movies, magazines—create objects for specialized au-

[2]Surveys of time use and "cultural indicators" examine the distribution of culture. See Robinson 1983, Peterson 1983, Katz & Gurevitch 1976, Szalai 1972.

diences, and their situation more closely resembles one of free competition. What DiMaggio goes on to argue, following insights from Peterson & Berger's work on the popular music industry (1975), is that "the extent of diversity and innovation available to the public—and, conversely, the degree of massification of culture—has more to do with the market structures and organizational environment of specific industries than with strongly felt demands of either the masses or their masters for certain kinds of homogeneous cultural materials" (DiMaggio 1977:448).

Where the focus in conventional sociology of art has been on the unique meaning of a work of art or the unique genius of an artist, the focus in the production-of-culture perspective is on the set of constraints that limit the originality of and determine the form of the produced work. Production-of-culture studies are not, of course, all of a piece. Some works are oriented to economic sociology and emphasize the relationship of the culture-producing organization to the marketplace (Hirsch 1972, Mukerji 1978). Some emerge from a symbolic interactionist tradition and an ethnographic method of study and emphasize much more the development and consolidation of resources, work routines, and ideological perspectives among the workers in the culture industries (Tuchman 1978, Rosenblum 1978a,b; McCall 1977). Others are set within a framework of the sociology of occupations and professions (Faulkner 1983, Kealy 1979; Cantor 1971). Howard Becker's *Artworlds* (1982) is the most developed version of this perspective.[3]

Production-of-culture studies have examined a variety of spheres of cultural production, including "elite" as well as popular culture. Among the best developed areas of study have been the works on popular and country music (Frith 1981, Denisoff 1975, Peterson & Berger 1975, Peterson & DiMaggio 1975), works on television and newspaper news (Turow 1984, Schudson 1983, Golding 1981, Gitlin 1980, Fishman 1980, Gans 1979, Epstein 1973, Tuchman 1972); pieces on television entertainment (Gitlin 1983, Intintoli 1984, Cantor & Pingree 1983); and works on publishing (Powell 1985, Coser et al 1982, Tuchman 1982, Griswold 1981).

Theoretical Perspectives

The most radical changes in studies of popular culture since the 1960s have resulted from an increasing concern with theory—both with theoretical reasons for studying popular culture and with theories about the proper conceptual frames and analytical categories for making such studies. These changes have been radical in two senses. On the one hand, they have infused a particularly

---

[3]Perhaps the best ethnographic works on popular culture remain community studies in which popular culture is not a special focus. See Blythe 1969, Lynd & Lynd 1929, Gans 1962, Hannerz 1969, and Liebow 1967.

atheoretical subfield with such an abundance of concepts and conceptual controversies that they have made the student of popular culture today quite unlike earlier practitioners in the field. In another sense, the changes have been radical because the theoretical schools that have entered into the analysis of popular culture have been (or at least claimed to be) voices of the political left.

Marxism's relationship to popular culture began to change with the "discovery" of Althusser and Gramsci (Althusser 1971, Gramsci 1971). These two theorists redirected attention to the role of mass culture in the functioning of the state, and they made its analysis seem more necessary than ever. Althusser borrowed from Saussurian linguistics and Lacan's theory of dreams to argue that ideology is the purely imaginary; ideologies may be used historically to maintain the power of the ruling class, but ideology as a form of consciousness is not tied to historical moments. It is instead a world of fantasy in which individual, social, and personal identities are made up (Althusser 1971). Thus, Althusser provided a reason and a means for studying the sources of ideology in popular culture, to understand the fictional aspect of all consciousness, i.e. false consciousness. And he helped to bridge Marxist structuralism with the work of theorists concerned with the structure of mind, such as Lacan and Levi-Strauss (Eagleton 1983, Bruss 1981, Kurtzweil 1980, Hall 1977, De-George & DeGeorge 1972).

Gramsci, on the other hand, was much more concerned with the political functioning of ideology. He developed the idea of hegemony as the means by which the ruling class gains the assent of those it rules. Hegemony is achieved in large part through the use of ideology, by defining a reality in which the ruling class seems to have some natural or inevitable right to be in charge (Gramsci 1971, Gottdiener 1985, Sassoon 1982; see also Berger 1980, Gitlin 1980, Hall 1977, Berger 1972).

The other structuralist tradition that has entered into studies of popular culture, structuralism/semiology, is in many ways the antithesis of Marxist structuralism, because it has taken the cultural object out of social context instead of finding its meaning in its social location and function. Both traditions of structuralism share, however, a commitment to finding the meaning of objects not in their surface characteristics but in their deeper structural significance. Marxist structural analyses look at the ideological structures of popular culture while the semiological/structural tradition looks at the structure of signs.

The latter structuralism had its roots in Saussurian linguistics and Levi-Strauss's anthropology. Students of culture wanted to do with the objects of Western culture something similar to what Levi-Strauss had done with myths, and they extended the idea of culture as a communication system to do so (Eagleton 1983, Kurtzweil 1980, DeGeorge & DeGeorge 1972). Roland Barthes was perhaps the best-known of the semioticians to move in this direction.

Barthes started by trying to dissect the sign systems in Western culture to uncover layers of ideology in capitalist societies. His political interests and debt to Levi-Strauss were both apparent in the title of his early book, *Mythologies* (1957).

The type of structural analysis that Barthes helped to create and that came to be known simply as structuralism (or, in some cases, semiotics) posits that language is a system of signs whose meaning does not inhere in the sign but in the *difference* between one sign and another. The relation between the signifier (the word on the page) and the signified (the object in the world the word refers to) is arbitrary; a dog could as easily be called "chien" as "dog." "Dog" has meaning as a sign not in its relationship to the real-world dog but in its difference from other possible signs—for instance, in its difference from "log" or "doff" or "dig." The role of the analyst is to find those systems of relationships among signs that give them their meanings. Because it is arbitrary *differences* among signs that give them meaning, great emphasis is placed on the oppositions and reversals of the signs themselves (Eagleton 1983).

While structuralists exclude from their repertoires social analyses that take the reader outside of the text, structuralist analysis (as a school of thought) treats meaning as fundamentally social in the sense that language is social; it is collective and constructed. Structuralism also treats meaning as fundamentally anonymous (an expression of language rather than of an author). By this theory, the subject is a romantic myth, a construction of language rather than the source of all communication (Eagleton 1983, Kurtzweil 1980, Harari 1979). These ideas, usually developed for and applied to the study of literature, were also surprisingly easy to transfer to the study of popular culture, where culture production is often collective and anonymous. Semioticians indicated how one could treat objects other than words using this perspective.

Christian Metz was particularly successful in developing a semiotics to apply to film (1974). In the wake of auteur theory in film [Arnheim 1957, Sarris (1962) 1985, Wollen 1972], which had pushed the idea of subjectivity in filmmaking to a level of the absurd, Metz's insistence that film theorists should be reading film content for sign systems was invigorating. And in contrast to a growing number of scholars who were writing on the institutions which produced, distributed, and exhibited films (Balio 1976, Guback 1969, and more recently Wasko 1982), it also seemed high time that someone wrote about films themselves. Metz not only broke with tradition, but also made it seem perfectly natural. His notion that one could look at the sign-making strategies of individual filmmakers made his semiology seem a logical extension of auteur theory. And his idea that one can see the effects of film institutions in the content of films themselves (the cinematic in the filmic) made semiotics also seem totally compatible with institutional analyses of film. Thus, he made a very quiet revolution in film theory (Mast & Cohen 1985).

But as Metz was drawing film theorists away from the "author" of films, Derrida was beginning to challenge the fundamental assumption of structuralism that cultural objects and readings of them can be made without a subject. Like the structuralists, post-structuralists from Derrida to Foucault continued to deny the romantic visions of the author, a concept underlying the structuralist project, but they paid increasing attention to language as something wielded by individuals in interaction with the language system presented to that individual (Eagleton 1983, Harari 1979). Communication through culture was seen as dialogic (Bakhtin 1981).

The growing concern with subjectivity paralleled an increased attention to the psychological aspects of culture. Drawing from Lacanian psychoanalysis, many scholars, including Metz (1982), broadened the world of linguistic analysis and cultural interpretation into the world of dreams and sexuality. The latter was particularly interesting to feminists who were trying to see how sex and gender were inscribed into the communications patterns in their culture. A reviving interest in Freud thus ironically stimulated new directions in feminist criticism (Mulvey 1985, Glendhill 1985, Erens 1979).

As with the type of "thick description" championed by Geertz, the detailed readings stimulated by these efforts in cultural criticism have led to an increase in the level of detail used in analyses of popular culture. And like Geertz again, analysts from the structuralist and post-structuralist camp(s) have drawn increasing attention to the objects of culture themselves. But the structuralists and post-structuralists have maintained an interest in theory and fashions of theoretical development that makes them almost the opposite of Geertz. For Geertz is urging scholars to write about an empirical world, while the structuralists and post-structuralists deny the possibility of a world apart from the apparatus that analyzes and describes it. This radical vision makes these theories difficult to reconcile with more social and empirical theories of meaning (Geertz 1983, Eagleton 1983, Kurtzweil 1980).

In spite of conflicting theoretical assumptions among many schools of popular culture studies, numerous scholars, such as Hall (1977), Gottdiener (1985), Murdock (1983), and Hebdige (1979), have created hybrid analyses. These and other (frequently but not exclusively British) students of popular culture have treated much of the theory emanating from France as a means for educating the critical eye rather than as vessels carrying the truth. Thus, they have felt quite comfortable integrating the two directions of structural analysis and including ideas from post-structuralism as revisions of structuralism. They have taken these tendencies in theories of interpretations and converted them into techniques for *cultural* interpretation by using them to describe and explain empirical phenomena, particularly life-styles in subcultures. Their work has helped to make the theoretical richness of the past two decades more available to traditional students of popular culture.

Critical analyses of popular culture, structuralism and post-structuralism, Marxism and linguistic analysis, have created new definitions of the human mind and its social location. The objects that lie between the two, since they are extensions of the human mind and are also produced materially (and socially), seem much more interesting and consequential because of these developments. Students of popular culture are among the scholars who have benefited from the results.

Literature Cited

Abrahams, R. D. 1976. *Talking Black*. Rowley, Mass: Newbury. 102 pp.

Abrahams, R. D. 1970. *Deep Down in the Jungle*. . . . Chicago: Aldine. 278 pp.

Althusser, L. 1971. Ideology and ideological state apparatuses. In *Lenin and Philosophy and Other Essays*, pp. 127–86. New York: Monthly Rev.

Arendt, H. 1958. *The Human Condition*. New York: Anchor. 385 pp.

Arnheim, R. 1957. *Film as Art*. Berkeley: Univ. Calif. Press. 230 pp.

Aronowitz, S. 1973. *False Promises*. New York: McGraw-Hill. 465 pp.

Babcock, B. A., 1984. Arrange me in disorder: Fragments and reflections on ritual clowning. See MacAloon 1984:102–28

Bakhtin, M. M. 1981. *The Dialogic Imagination*. (ed. M. Holquist) Austin, Tex: Univ. Tex. Press. 444 pp.

Balio, T. 1976. *The American Film Industry*. Madison, Wis: Univ. Wis. Press. 499 pp.

Baltzell, E. D. 1964. *The Protestant Establishment: Aristocracy and Caste in America*. New York: Vintage. 429 pp.

Barth, G. 1980. *City People: The Rise of Modern City Culture in Nineteenth-Century America*. New York: Oxford Univ. Press. 289 pp.

Barthes, R. 1964. *Elements of Semiology*. New York: Hill & Wang. 111 pp.

Barthes, R. (1957) 1972. *Mythologies*. New York: Hill & Wang. 160 pp.

Barthes, R. 1983. *The Fashion System*. New York: Hill & Wang. 303 pp.

Bauman, R., Sherzer, J., eds. 1974. *Explorations in the Ethnography of Speaking*. Cambridge: Camb. Univ. Press. 501 pp.

Becker, H. 1982. *Artworlds*. Berkeley: Univ. Calif. Press. 392 pp.

Belasco, W. J. 1979. *Americans on the Road: From Autocamp to Motel, 1910–1945*. Cambridge: MIT Press. 212 pp.

Bell, D. 1976. *The Cultural Contradictions of Capitalism*. New York: Basic. 301 pp.

Bell, Q. 1976. *On Human Finery*. New York: Schocken. 134 pp.

Benjamin, W. 1968. The work of art in the age of mechanical reproduction. In *Illuminations*, ed. H. Arendt, pp. 219–53. New York: Schocken. 280 pp.

Berger, J. 1972. *Ways of Seeing*. Harmondsworth: Penguin. 165 pp.

Berger, J. 1980. *About Looking*. New York: Pantheon. 198 pp.

Bloch, M. 1953. *The Historian's Craft*. New York: Vintage. 197 pp.

Blythe, R. 1969. *Akenfield*. New York: Dell. 318 pp.

Boorstin, D. 1963. *The Image*. New York: Atheneum. 315 pp.

Bourdieu, P. 1984. *Distinction: A Social Critique of the Judgement of Taste*. Cambridge: Harvard Univ. Press. 613 pp.

Brantlinger, P. 1983. *Bread and Circuses: Theories of Mass Culture as Social Decay*. Ithaca: Cornell Univ. Press. 307 pp.

Braudel, F. (1949) 1966. *The Mediterranean and the Mediterranean World in the Age of Phillip II*. New York: Harper & Row. 1375 pp.

Braudel, F. 1974. *Capitalism and Material Life, 1400–1800*. New York: Harper & Row. 462 pp.

Braudel, F. 1977. *Afterthoughts on Material Civilization*. . . . Baltimore: Johns Hopkins Univ. Press. 144 pp.

Browne, R. 1982. *Objects of Special Devotion*. Bowling Green, Ohio: Popular. 364 pp.

Bruss, N. H. 1981. Lacan and literature. *Mass. Rev.* 22:62–92

Burke, P. 1978. *Popular Culture in Early Modern Europe*. London: Temple Smith. 351 pp.

Cantor, M. 1971. *The Hollywood Producer*. New York: Basic. 256 pp.

Cantor, M. G., Pingree, S. 1983. *The Soap Opera*. Beverly Hills: Sage. 167 pp.

Clark, S. 1983. French historians and early modern popular culture. *Past & Present* 100:62–99

Cohen, E. 1984. The sociology of tourism:

Approaches, issues and findings. *Ann. Rev. Sociol.* 10:373–92

Cohen, S. 1972. *Folk Devils and Moral Panics: The Creation of the Mods and Rockers.* London: MacGibbon & Kee. 224 pp.

Coser, L. A., Kadushin, C., Powell, W. W. 1982. *Books: The Culture and Commerce of Publishing.* New York: Basic. 411 pp.

Curran, J., Gurevitch, M., Woollacott, J. 1977. *Mass Communication and Society.* Beverly Hills: Sage. 478 pp.

Csikszentmihalyi, M., Rochberg-Halton, E. 1981. *The Meaning of Things: Domestic Symbols and the Self.* New York: Cambridge Univ. Press. 304 pp.

Czitrom, D. 1982. *Media and the American Mind: From Morse to McLuhan.* Chapel Hill: Univ. NC Press. 254 pp.

Darnton, R. 1984. *The Great Cat Massacre and Other Episodes in French Cultural History.* New York: Basic. 298 pp.

Davis, N. 1965. *Society and Culture in Early Modern France.* Stanford: Stanford Univ. Press. 346 pp.

Davis, S. 1986. *Parades and Power: Street Theater in 19th Century Philadelphia.* Philadelphia: Temple Univ. Press.

Deetz, J. 1977. *In Small Things Forgotten: The Archaeology of Early American Life.* Garden City, NY: Anchor Press. 184 pp.

DeGeorge, R., DeGeorge, F. 1972. *The Structuralists from Marx to Levi-Strauss.* Garden City, NY: Doubleday Anchor. 323 pp.

Denisoff, R. S. 1975. *Solid Gold: The Popular Record Industry.* New Brunswick, NJ: Transaction. 504 pp.

Derrida, J. 1978. *Writing and Difference.* Chicago: Univ. Chicago Press. 342 pp.

DiMaggio, P. 1977. Market structure, the creative process, and popular culture: Toward an organizational reinterpretation of mass-culture theory. *J. Popular Cult.* 111:436–452

DiMaggio, P. 1982. Cultural entrepreneurship in nineteenth-century Boston: The creation of an organizational base for high culture in America. *Media, Cult. Soc.* 4:33–50

Douglas, A. 1977. *The Feminization of American Culture.* New York: Avon. 481 pp.

Douglas, M. 1982. *In The Active Voice.* London: Routledge & Kegan Paul. 306 pp.

Douglas, M. (1966) 1970. *Purity and Danger.* Harmondsworth: Penguin. 220 pp.

Douglas, M., Isherwood, B. 1979. *The World of Goods.* New York: Basic. 228 pp.

Duis, P. R. 1983. *The Saloon: Public Drinking in Chicago and Boston, 1880–1920.* Urbana: Univ. Ill. 380 pp.

Dyos, H. J., Wolff, M., eds. 1973. *The Victorian City: Images and Realities.* London: Routledge, Kegan Paul. 957 pp.

Eagleton, T. 1976. *Marxism and Literary Criticism.* London: Methuen, 87 pp.

Eagleton, T. 1983. *Literary Theory: An Introduction.* Minneapolis: Univ. Minn. Press. 231 pp.

Eisenstein, E. 1979. *The Printing Press as an Agent of Change.* Cambridge: Cambridge Univ. Press. 794 pp.

Elias, N. 1978. *The History of Manners.* New York: Pantheon. 310 pp.

Eliot, T. S. (1940, 1949) 1968. Notes towards the definition of culture. In *Christianity and Culture,* pp. 79–170. New York: Harcourt Brace Jovanovich

Ellis, J. 1982. *Visible Fictions.* London: Routledge & Kegan Paul. 295 pp.

Epstein, E. J. 1973. *News From Nowhere: Television and the News.* New York: Random House. 321 pp.

Erens, P. 1979. *Sexual Stratagems: The World of Women in Film.* New York: Horizon. 336 pp.

Ewen, S. 1976. *Captains of Consciousness: Advertising and the Social Roots of Consumer Culture.* New York: McGraw-Hill. 261 pp.

Faulkner, R. 1983. *Music on Demand.* New Brunswick, NJ: Transaction. 281 pp.

Fine, G. A., ed. 1977. Sociology and popular culture. *J. Popular Cult.* 11:379–526

Finnegan, R. 1977. *Oral Poetry.* Cambridge: Cambridge Univ. Press. 299 pp.

Fishman, M. 1980. *Manufacturing the News.* Austin: Univ. Tex. Press. 189 pp.

Fiske, J., Hartley, J. 1978. *Reading Television.* London: Methuen, 223 pp.

Flink, J. J. 1975. *The Car Culture.* Cambridge: MIT Press. 247 pp.

Foucault, M. 1973. *The Order of Things.* New York: Vintage. 387 pp.

Foucault, M. 1975. What is an Author? *Partisan Rev.* 4:603–14

Foucault, M. 1979. *Discipline and Punish.* New York: Vintage. 325 pp.

Frith, S. 1981. *Sound Effects: Youth, Leisure, and the Politics of Rock and Roll.* New York: Pantheon. 294 pp.

Gans, H., 1962. *The Urban Villagers.* New York: Free. 367 pp.

Gans, H. J. 1974. *Popular Culture and High Culture.* New York: Basic. 179 pp.

Gans, H. J. 1979. *Deciding What's News.* New York: Pantheon. 393 pp.

Geertz, C. 1973. *The Interpretation of Cultures.* New York: Basic. 470 pp.

Geertz, C. 1980. *Negara: The Theatre State in Nineteenth-Century Bali.* Princeton: Princeton Univ. Press. 295 pp.

Genovese, E., Fox-Genovese, E. 1976. The political crisis of social history: A Marxian perspective. *J. Soc. Hist.* 10:205–20

Gillett, C. 1970. *The Sound of the City*. New York: Outerbridge & Dienstfrey. 375 pp.

Ginzberg, C. 1980. *The Cheese and the Worms*. New York: Penguin. 172 pp.

Gitlin, T. 1978. Media sociology: the dominant paradigm. *Theory Soc.* 6:205–53

Gitlin, T. 1980. *The Whole World Is Watching: Mass Media in the Making and Unmaking of the New Left*. Berkeley: Univ. Calif. Press. 327 pp.

Gitlin, T. 1981. *Inside Prime Time*. New York: Pantheon. 369. pp.

Glendhill, C. 1985. Recent developments in feminist criticism. See Mast & Cohen 1985:817–45

Goffman, E. 1967. *Interaction Ritual*. Garden City, NY: Doubleday Anchor. 270 pp.

Goffman, E. 1979. *Gender Advertisements*. New York: Harper & Row, 84 pp.

Golding, P. 1981. The missing dimensions—news media and the management of social change. See Katz & Szecsko 1981:63–82

Goldman, R., Wilson, J. 1983. Appearance and essence: The commodity form revealed in perfume advertisements. *Curr. Persp. Soc. Theory* 4:119–42

Goody, J. 1977. *The Domestication of the Savage Mind*. Cambridge: Cambridge Univ. Press. 179 pp.

Gottdiener, M. 1985. Hegemony and mass culture: A semiotic approach. *Am. J. Sociol.* 90:979–1001

Gramsci, A. 1971. *Selections from the Prison Notebooks*. New York: Int. 483 pp.

Griswold, W. 1981. American character and the American novel. *Am. J. Sociol.* 86:740–65

Grossberg, L. 1983. The politics of youth culture: Some observations on rock and roll in American culture. *Soc. Text* 8:104–126

Guback, T. 1969. *The International Film Industry: Western Europe and America since 1945*. Bloomington: Ind. Univ. Press. 244 pp.

Gusfield, J. R., Michalowicz, J. 1984. Secular symbolism: Studies of ritual, ceremony, and the symbolic order in modern life. *Ann. Rev. Sociol.* 10:417–35

Gutman, H. 1976. *Work, Culture, and Society in Industrializing America*. New York: Vintage. 343 pp.

Guttmann, A. 1978. *From Ritual to Record: The Nature of Modern Sports*. New York: Columbia Univ. Press. 198 pp.

Hall, S. 1977. Culture, the media and the "Ideological Effect." In *Mass Communication and Society*, eds. J. Curran, pp. 315–48. Beverly Hills: Sage

Hall, S. 1981. Cultural studies: two paradigms. In *Culture, Ideology and Social Process: A Reader*, eds. T. Bennett, G. Martin, C. Mercer, J. Woollacott, pp. 19–37. Open Univ. Press

Hall, S., Jefferson, T., 1978. *Resistance Through Ritual*. London: Hutchinson. 287 pp.

Hannerz, U. 1969. *Soulside*. New York: Columbia Univ. Press. 236 pp.

Hardy, S. 1982. *How Boston Played: Sport, Recreation, and Community, 1865–1915*. Boston: Northeastern Univ. Press. 272 pp.

Harari, J. 1979. *Textual Strategies: Perspectives in Post-Structuralist Criticism*. Ithaca, NY: Cornell Univ. Press. 463 pp.

Harris, N. 1973. *Humbug: The Art of P. T. Barnum*. Boston: Little, Brown. 337 pp.

Harris, N. 1978. Museums, merchandising, and popular taste: The struggle for influence. See Quimby 1978:140–74

Hayden, D. 1981. *The Grand Domestic Revolution*. Cambridge: MIT Press. 367 pp.

Hebdige, D., 1979. *Subculture: The Meaning of Style*. New York: Methuen. 195 pp.

Hirsch, P. M. 1972. Processing fads and fashions: An organization-set analysis of cultural industry systems. *Am. J. Sociol.* 77:639–59

Hirsch, P. M. 1981. Institutional functions of elite and mass media. See Katz & Szecko 1981:187–200

Horkheimer, M., Adorno, T. W. [1944] 1972. *Dialectic of Enlightenment*. New York: Seabury. 258 pp.

Hymes, D. 1975. Breakthrough into performance. In *Folklore: Performance and Communication*. ed. D. Ben-Amos, K. S. Goldstein, pp. 11–74. The Hague: Mouton

Intintoli, M. J. 1984. *Taking Soaps Seriously: The World of Guiding Light*. New York: Praeger. 260 pp.

Isaac, R. 1982. *The Transformation of Virginia: 1740–1790*. Chapel Hill: Univ. NC Press. 451 pp.

Jay, M. 1973. *The Dialectical Imagination: A History of the Frankfurt School and the Institute of Social Research, 1923–1950*. Boston: Little, Brown. 382 pp.

Kasson, J. F. 1978. *Amusing the Million: Coney Island at the Turn of the Century*. New York: Hill & Wang, 119 pp.

Katz, E., Szecko, T., eds. 1981. *Mass Media and Social Change*. Beverly Hills: Sage. 271 pp.

Katz, E., Gurevitch, M., 1976. *The Secularization of Leisure: Culture and Communication in Israel*. Cambridge: Harvard. 288 pp.

Kealy, E. 1979. From craft to art: The case of sound mixers and popular music. *Sociol. Work Occup.* 6:3–29

Keil, C. 1966. *Urban Blues*. Chicago: Univ. Chicago Press

Kurzweil, E. 1980. *The Age of Structuralism*. New York: Columbia Univ. Press. 246 pp.

Kutler, S. I., Katz, S. N., eds. 1982. *The Promise of American History: Progress and

Prospects. Special issue of *Rev. Am. Hist.* 10(4):1–423
Ladurie, L. R. 1980. *Carnival in Romans.* New York: Braziller. 426 pp.
Lawrence, E. A. 1982. *Rodeo: An Anthropologist Looks at the Wild and the Tame.* Knoxville: U. Tenn. Press. 288 pp.
Lears, T. J. J. 1981. *No Place of Grace: Antimodernism and the Transformation of American Culture, 1880–1920.* New York: Pantheon. 375 pp.
Lears, T. J. J. 1985. The concept of cultural hegemony: problems and possibilities. *Am. Hist. Rev.* 85:567–93
Lever, J. 1983. *Soccer Madness.* Chicago: U. Chicago Press. 200 pp.
Levine, L. W. 1977. *Black Culture and Black Consciousness.* New York: Oxford. 522 pp.
Levine, L. W. 1984. William Shakespeare and the American people: A study in cultural transformation. *Am. Hist. Rev.* 89:34–66
Levi-Strauss, C. 1963. *Structural Anthropology.* New York: Basic. 410 pp.
Levi-Strauss, C. (1962) 1966. *The Savage Mind.* Chicago: Univ. Chicago Press. 290 pp.
Liebow, E. 1967. *Tally's Corner.* Boston: Little Brown. 260 pp.
Lord, A. B. 1960. *The Singer of Tales.* Cambridge: Harvard. 307 pp.
Lowenthal, L. 1961. *Literature, Popular Culture, and Society.* Englewood Cliffs, NJ: Prentice-Hall. 169 pp.
Lurie, A. 1981. *The Language of Clothes.* New York: Random House. 273 pp.
Luschen, G., 1980. Sociology of sport: Development, present state, and prospects, *Ann. Rev. Sociol.* 6:315–47
Lynch, K. 1960. *The Image of the City.* Cambridge: MIT Press. 194 pp.
Lynd, R. S., Lynd, H. M. 1929. *Middletown.* New York: Harcourt, Brace & World. 550 pp.
MacAloon, J. J., ed. 1984a. *Rite, Drama, Festival, Spectacle: Rehearsals Toward a Theory of Cultural Performance.* Philadelphia: Inst. Stud. Hum. Iss. 280 pp.
MacAloon, J. J. 1984b. Olympic games and the theory of spectacle in modern societies. See MacAloon 1984a:241–80
Mast, G., Cohen, M. 1985. *Film Theory and Criticism.* New York: Oxford. 852 pp. 3rd ed.
McCall, M. 1977. Art without a market: Creating artistic value in a provincial art market. *Symb. Interact.* 1:32–43
McKendrick, N., Brewer, J., Plumb, J. H. 1982. *The Birth of a Consumer Society.* Bloomington: Ind. Univ. Press. 334 pp.
Messer, E. 1984. Anthropological perspectives on diet. *Ann. Rev. Anthropol.* 13:205–49
Metz, C. 1974. *Language and Cinema.* The Hague: Mouton. 294 pp.

Metz, C. 1982. *The Imaginary Signifier.* Bloomington: Ind. Univ. Press. 327 pp.
Miller, M. 1981. *The Bon Marche.* Princeton: Princeton Univ. Press. 272 pp.
Modleski, T. 1982. *Loving With a Vengeance: Mass-Produced Fantasies for Women.* New York: Methuen. 125 pp.
Moore, S. F., Meyerhoff, B. 1977. *Secular Ritual.* Amsterdam: Van Gorcum. 293 pp.
Mukerji, C. 1978. Artwork: Collection and contemporary culture. *Am. J. Sociol.* 84:348–65
Mukerji, C. 1983. *From Graven Images: Patterns of Modern Materialism.* New York: Columbia Univ. Press. 329 pp.
Mulvey, L. 1985. Film and visual pleasure. See Mast & Cohen 1985:803–16
Murdock, G. 1982. Mass communication and social violence. In Marsh, P., Campbell, A., eds. *Aggression and Violence,* pp. 69–90. Oxford: Blackwell.
Murdock, G. 1983. *Televising "Terrorism": Political Violence in Popular Culture.* London: Commedia. 181 pp.
Newcomb, H., ed. 1982. *Television: The Critical View.* New York: Oxford Univ. Press. 549 pp. 3rd ed.
Nye, R. B. 1972. *New Dimensions in Popular Culture.* Bowling Green, Ohio: Popular. 246 pp.
Ortner, S. 1984. Theory in anthropology since the sixties. *Comp. Stud. Soc. Hist.* 26:126–66
Park, R. 1955. Natural history of a newspaper. In *Society,* pp. 89–104. Glencoe: Free
Persell, C. W. 1983. The history of technology and the study of material culture. *Am. Q.* 35:304–15
Peterson, R. A., Berger, D. G. 1975. Cycles in symbol production: The case of popular music. *Am. Sociol. Rev.* 40:158–73
Peterson, R. A., ed. 1976. *The Production of Culture.* Beverly Hills: Sage. 144 pp.
Peterson, R. A. 1979. Revitalizing the culture concept. *Ann. Rev. Sociol.* 5:137–66
Peterson, R. A., ed. 1983. Patterns of Cultural Choice. *Amer. Behav. Sci.* 26:419–552
Peterson, R. A., DiMaggio, P. 1975. From region to class, the changing locus of country music: A test of the massification hypothesis. *Social Forces* 53:497–506
Powell, W. W. 1985. *Getting Into Print: The Decision-Making Process in Scholarly Publishing.* Chicago: Univ. Chicago Press. 260 pp.
Quimby, I. M. G., ed. 1978. *Material Culture and the Study of American Life.* New York: Norton. 250 pp.
Rader, B. 1983. *American Sports: From the Age of Folk Games to the Age of Spectators.* Englewood Cliffs: Prentice-Hall. 376 pp.
Radway, J. A. 1984. *Reading the Romance:*

66   MUKERJI & SCHUDSON

Women, Patriarchy, and Popular Literature. Chapel Hill: Univ. NC Press. 274 pp.
Rae, J. B. 1971. *The Road and the Car in American Life*. Cambridge: MIT Press. 390 pp.
Robinson, J. P. 1983. Cultural indicators from the leisure attitude survey. *Am. Behav. Sci.* 26:543–52
Rosenberg, B., White, D. M., eds. 1957. *Mass Culture*. Glencoe: Free. 561 pp.
Rosenblum, B. 1978a. Style as social process. *Am. Sociol. Rev.* 43:422–38
Rosenblum, B. 1978b. *Photographers at Work*. New York: Holmes & Meiers. 140 pp.
Sahlins, M. 1976. *Culture and Practical Reason*. Chicago: Univ. of Chicago Press. 252 pp.
Sarris, A. 1985 (1962). Notes on the auteur theory in 1962. In Mast & Cohen 1985:500–15
Sassoon, A. S. 1982. *Approaches to Gramsci*. London: Writers & Readers. 254 pp.
Schiller, D. 1981. *Objectivity and the News*. Philadelphia: Univ. Pa. Press. 222 pp.
Schivelbusch, W. 1977. *The Railway Journey: Trains and Travel in the 19th Century*. New York: Urizen. 213 pp.
Schlereth, T. J. 1982. *Material Culture Studies in America*. Nashville: Am. Assoc. State Local Hist. 419 pp.
Schudson, M. 1978. *Discovering the News: A Social History of American Newspapers*. New York: Basic. 228 pp.
Schudson, M. 1984. *Advertising, the Uneasy Persuasion*. New York: Basic. 288 pp.
Schudson, M. 1983. Why news is the way it is. *Raritan* 2:109–25
Sennett, R. 1976. *The Fall of Public Man*. New York: Knopf. 373 pp.
Sewell, W. H. Jr. 1980. *Work and Revolution in France: The Language of Labor from the Old Regime to 1848*. Cambridge: Cambridge Univ. Press. 340 pp.
Sklar, R. 1976. *Movie-Made America*. New York: Vintage. 340 pp.
Sombart, W. (1913) 1967. *Luxury and Capitalism*. Ann Arbor: Univ. Mich. Press. 200 pp.
Stedman Jones, G. 1983. *Languages of Class: Studies in English Working Class History*. Cambridge: Cambridge Univ. Press. 256 pp.
Szalai, A., ed. 1972. *The Use of Time*. The Hague: Mouton. 868 pp.
Thompson, E. P. 1977. *William Morris: from Romantic to Revolutionary*. New York: Pantheon. 829 pp.
Thompson, E. P. 1963. *The Making of the English Working Class*. New York: Vintage. 848 pp.
Tompkins, J. 1985. Masterpiece Theater: The politics of Hawthorne's literary reputation. *Am. Q.* 36:617–42
Tompkins, J., ed. 1980. *Reader-Response Criticism: From Formalism to Poststructuralism*. Baltimore: Johns Hopkins Univ. Press. 275 pp.
Tuchman, G. 1972. Objectivity as strategic ritual: An examination of newsmen's notions of objectivity. *Am. J. Sociol.* 77:660–679
Tuchman, G., Daniels, A. K., Benet, J., eds. 1978. *Hearth and Home: Images of Women in the Mass Media*. New York: Oxford Univ. Press. 333 pp.
Tuchman, G. 1978. *Making News: A Study in the Construction of Reality*. New York: Free. 244 pp.
Tuchman, G. 1982. Culture as resource: actions defining the Victorian novel. *Media, Cult. Soc.* 4:3–18
Turner, V. W. 1967 *The Forest of Symbols*. Cornell: Cornell Univ. Press. 405 pp.
Turner, V. W. 1969. *The Ritual Process: Structure and Anti-Structure*. Chicago: Aldine. 213 pp.
Turner, V. W. 1984. Liminality and the performative genres. See MacAloon 1984a:19–41
Turow, J. 1984. *Media Industries: The Production of News and Entertainment*. New York: Longman. 213 pp.
Wasko, J. 1982. *Movies and Money: Financing the American Film Industry*. Norwood, NJ: ABLEX. 247 pp.
Weber, E. 1976. *Peasants Into Frenchmen: The Modernization of Rural France, 1870–1914*. Stanford: Stanford Univ. Press. 615 pp.
Wilentz, S. 1984. *Chants Democratic: New York City and the Rise of the American Working Class, 1788–1850*. New York: Oxford Univ. Press. 446 pp.
Williams, R. 1961. *The Long Revolution*. New York: Columbia Univ. Press. 370 pp.
Williams, R. 1975. *Television: Technology and Cultural Form*. New York: Schocken. 160 pp.
Williams, R. H. 1982. *Dream Worlds*. Berkeley: Univ. of Calif. Press. 451 pp.
Williamson, J. 1978. *Decoding Advertisements*. London: Boyars. 180 pp.
Willis, P. 1977. *Learning to Labor: How Working Class Kids Get Working Class Jobs*. New York: Columbia Univ. Press. 226 pp.
Wilson, J. 1980. Sociology of leisure. *Ann. Rev. Sociol.* 6:21–40
Wollen, P. 1972. *Signs and Meaning in the Cinema*. Bloomington: Ind. Univ. Press. 175 pp.
Wright, G. 1980. *Moralism and the Modern Home*. Chicago: Univ. of Chicago Press. 382 pp.
Wright, W. 1975. *Sixguns and Society: A Structural Study of the Western*. Berkeley: Univ. Calif. Press. 217 pp.

Ann. Rev. Sociol. 1986. 12:67–92

RECENT DEVELOPMENTS IN ROLE THEORY

B. J. Biddle

Center for Research in Social Behavior, University of Missouri-Columbia, Columbia, Missouri 65211

Abstract

Role theory concerns one of the most important features of social life, characteristic behavior patterns or *roles*. It explains roles by presuming that persons are members of *social positions* and hold *expectations* for their own behaviors and those of other persons. Its vocabulary and concerns are popular among social scientists and practitioners, and role concepts have generated a lot of research. At least five perspectives may be discriminated in recent work within the field: functional, symbolic interactionist, structural, organizational, and cognitive role theory. Much of role research reflects practical concerns and derived concepts, and research on four such concepts is reviewed: consensus, conformity, role conflict, and role taking. Recent developments suggest both centrifugal and integrative forces within the role field. The former reflect differing perspectival commitments of scholars, confusions and disagreements over use of role concepts, and the fact that role theory is used to analyze various forms of social system. The latter reflect the shared, basic concerns of the field and efforts by role theorists to seek a broad version of the field that will accommodate a wide range of interests.

INTRODUCTION

Role theory poses an intriguing dilemma. On the one hand, the concept of *role* is one of the most popular ideas in the social sciences. At least 10% of all articles currently published in sociological journals use the term role in a technical sense, chapters on role theory appear in authoritative reviews of social psychology, essay volumes on role theory appear regularly, endless applications of role ideas may be found in basic texts for sociology and social

67

0360-0572/86/0815-0067$02.00

psychology, and role theory provides a perspective for discussing or studying many social issues. On the other hand, confusion and malintegration persist in role theory. Authors continue to differ over definitions for the role concept, over assumptions they make about roles, and over explanations for role phenomena. And formal derivations for role propositions have been hard to find.

This dilemma has prompted some authors to write damning reviews of role theory. Nevertheless, substantial reasons exist for the popularity of the role concept. Role theory exhibits an agreed-upon set of core ideas, and empirical research that uses these ideas flowers. The philosophical stance of role theory is attractive and useful in efforts to ameliorate human problems. Role theory offers opportunities to integrate key interests of researchers in sociology, psychology, and anthropology. Recent contributions also suggest that explanation in role theory is now becoming more formal. Consequently, the focus of this essay is more upon synthesis than criticism of the field. I review ideas basic to role theory, examine treatment of these ideas in several perspectives of social thought, and review empirical research for key issues in role theory. The essay ends with a discussion of issues and propositional theory for the field.

BASIC IDEAS AND ORIENTATION

Role theory concerns one of the most important characteristics of social behavior—the fact that human beings behave in ways that are different and predictable depending on their respective social identities and the situation. As the term *role* suggests, the theory began life as a theatrical metaphor. If performances in the theater were differentiated and predictable because actors were constrained to perform "parts" for which "scripts" were written, then it seemed reasonable to believe that social behaviors in other contexts were also associated with parts and scripts understood by social actors. Thus, role theory may be said to concern itself with a triad of concepts: patterned and characteristic social behaviors, parts or identities that are assumed by social participants, and scripts or expectations for behavior that are understood by all and adhered to by performers.

Confusion entered role theory because its basic theatrical metaphor was applied only loosely and because its earliest proponents (Georg Simmel, George Herbert Mead, Ralph Linton, and Jacob Moreno) differed in the ways they used role terms. Unfortunately, these differences persist in current literature. Thus, whereas some authors use the term *role* to refer to characteristic behaviors (Biddle 1979, Burt 1982), others use it to designate social parts to be played (Winship & Mandel 1983), and still others offer definitions that focus on scripts for social conduct (Bates & Harvey 1975, Zurcher 1983). Although these differences appear substantial, the problem is more terminological than substantive. Agreement persists among role theorists that the basic concerns of the orientation are with characteristic behaviors, parts to be played, and scripts for behavior. For convenience, in this essay I shall designate these basic concepts of role theory by the familiar terms of *role, social position,* and *expectation,* respectively.

Somewhat more serious are disagreements by role theorists over the modality of expectations presumably responsible for roles. Whereas many role theorists assume that expectations are *norms* (i.e. prescriptive in nature), others assume them to be *beliefs* (referring to subjective probability), and still others view them as *preferences* (or "attitudes"). Each mode of expectation generates roles for somewhat different reasons, so different versions of role theory result, depending on the mode of expectation assumed. (Later I will argue that all three modes should be retained.)

Even more serious is the retention, in role theory, of concepts whose definitions involve improbable, undetectable, or contradictory conditions. To illustrate this latter problem, one influential source defines a role as "a particular set of norms that is organized about a function" (Bates & Harvey 1975: 106). Another describes role as a "comprehensive pattern for behavior and attitude" (Turner 1979: 124). And still another conceives role as "behavior referring to normative expectations associated with a position in a social system" (Allen & van de Vliert 1984a: 3). These definitions overlap, but each adds one or more conditions not given in the others. This leaves the reader in confusion over how to conceptualize or study events that do not meet these conditions. (Are patterned behaviors then not roles when they are *not* associated with a function, *not* tied to attitudes, or *not* associated with norms or social positions?) Role theory would be better off if its major proponents could be persuaded to agree upon, or better yet, to eschew, such limiting conditions.

Although role theorists differ in the assumptions they build into basic concepts, they are largely similar in philosophic orientation and in the methods used for their research. Most versions of role theory presume that expectations are the major generators of roles, that expectations are learned through experience, and that persons are aware of the expectations they hold. This means that role theory presumes a thoughtful, socially aware human actor. As a result, role theorists tend to be sympathetic to other orientations that presume human awareness—for example, cognitive and field theories in social psychology or exchange theory and phenomenological approaches in sociology. And because of this sympathy, role theorists also tend to adopt the methods of research prevalent in these orientations, particularly methods for observing roles and those that require research subjects to report their own or others' expectations.

Given its basic focus, one might assume that empirical research by role theorists would focus on the origins, dynamics, and effects of roles, social positions, and expectations. Surprisingly, this has not been the case. Instead, much of role research has concerned practical questions and derived concepts such as role conflict, role taking, role playing, or consensus. The practical concerns of role research have been both a blessing and a curse. On the positive side, they have brought attention to role theory and funds for needed research efforts. On the negative, they have tended to expand and confuse the application of role ideas. This has led to widespread adoption of the role vocabulary as well as the generation of new concepts that might not have appeared had research been more focused. But formal development of the theory has suffered, and role theorists often have worked at cross-purposes. In addition, the fact that role concepts have been employed by scholars representing several different theoretical perspectives has meant that, in the views of some authors, "role theory" is merely an expression of those perspectives. This has led some reviewers to praise or damn role theory because they approve or disapprove of the perspective with which they associate it—failing to recognize that role concepts are employed for various purposes by other social scientists. These problems are serious ones, and role theory will prosper in the future to the extent that it adopts its own distinctive theoretical orientation, one that stands apart from the theoretical perspectives with which it has been historically associated.

PERSPECTIVES AND THEIR CONTRIBUTIONS

As suggested above, interest in role theory has appeared in some of the central arenas of sociology and social psychology. Five such perspectives are discriminated here.

Functional Role Theory

The functional approach to role theory began with the work of Linton (1936) but was not formalized until the publications of Parsons (1951; Parsons & Shils 1951). In general, functional role theory has focused on the characteristic behaviors of persons who occupy social positions within a stable social system. "Roles" are conceived as the shared, normative expectations that prescribe and explain these behaviors. Actors in the social system have presumably been taught these norms and may be counted upon to conform to norms for their own conduct and to sanction others for conformity to norms applying to the latter. Thus, functional role theory became a vocabulary for describing the differentiated "parts" of stable social systems as well as a vehicle for explaining why those systems are stable and how they induce conformity in participants.

A recent work that represents the thought of functional role theory is the text by Bates & Harvey (1975). This work views social structures as collections of designated social positions, the shared norms of which govern differentiated behaviors. Some of the norms applying to a given position govern general conduct, but others govern only relationships between a focal position and a specific, counter position, and among the latter, "roles" are those that apply to the accomplishment of specific functions. Building on these concepts, the authors offer insightful analyses of various forms of social systems, ranging from groups to complex organizations and human communities. In addition, they discuss problems of the individual as a participant in particular social systems and examine the phenomena of stratification and social change. Thus, Bates & Harvey cover many of the traditional concerns of role theory and also reach out toward a synthesis of role theory with other orientations in sociology.

Functional theory was once very popular; indeed, it was the dominant perspective in role theory until perhaps the mid-1970s, and some writers of introductory texts as well as some sociologists interested in applying role concepts (e.g. Nye 1976) still embrace a functionalist stance. The assumptions of functionalism have been criticized, however, and this perspective has lost its former, dominant position in American sociology. Among other things, it has been pointed out that many roles are not associated with identified social positions, that roles may or may not be associated with functions, that social systems are far from stable, that norms may or may not be shared within the system and may or may not lead to conformity or sanctioning, and that roles may reflect other cognitive processes as well as normative expectations. Contemporary role theory seems debilitated by its lingering association with functionalism.

Symbolic Interactionist Role Theory

Interest in the role concept among symbolic interactionists began with Mead (1934) and gives stress to the roles of individual actors, the evolution of roles through social interaction, and various cognitive concepts through which social actors understand and interpret their own and others' conduct. Although many symbolic interactionists discuss the concept of norm and assume that shared norms are associated with social positions, norms are said to provide merely a set of broad imperatives within which the details of roles can be worked out. Actual roles, then, are thought to reflect norms, attitudes, contextual demands, negotiation, and the evolving definition of the situation as understood by the actors. As a result of these emphases, symbolic interactionists have made strong contributions to our understanding of roles in informal interaction, and their writings are replete with insights concerning relationships among roles, role taking, emotions, stress, and the self concept.

Recent works within the symbolic interactionist tradition have included major reviews of the role field (Heiss 1981, Stryker & Statham 1985), a volume of reprinted works (Heiss 1976), and others concerned with applications of theory (Ickes & Knowles 1982, Zurcher 1983). Contributors have also continued to explore implications of role ideas. Gordon (1976) discusses the development of evaluated role identities, and Gordon & Gordon (1982) examine how the changing of roles also alters one's goals and self-conceptions. McCall

(1982) applies role concepts to the topic of discretionary justice; Stryker & Macke (1978) explore similarities between status inconsistency and role conflict; and Stryker & Serpe (1982) discuss commitment, identity salience, and role behavior. Turner continues his extensive contributions by examining rule learning (1974), the role and the person (1978), a strategy for developing role propositions (1979), issues over which role theorists disagree (1985), and the effect of others' responses on interpretation of role behavior (Turner & Shosid 1976).

Other writers, influenced by symbolic interactionism, have continued to explore implications of role theory's basic theatrical metaphor. Dramaturgical role theory can be traced to an early paper by Simmel (1920), but classic works expressing the perspective did not appear until midcentury. As a rule, this perspective has focused upon the details of role enactment and on the effects of that enactment on the actor and observers. This has led to discussions of self-presentation, impression and identity management, involvement, deviancy, and the impact of social labeling. Recent works representing these efforts may be found in Gove (1975), Lyman & Scott (1975), Scheibe (1979), Sarbin (1982), and Hare (1985).

Symbolic interactionism has also attracted its share of criticism. Not all symbolic interactionists use the role concept, but those who do tend to exhibit many of the problems associated with the perspective. Among these are tendencies to use fuzzy and inapplicable definitions, to recite cant, and to ignore the findings of relevant empirical research. Symbolic interactionists often fail to discuss or to study the contextual limits for application of their insightful ideas. Little formal attention is given to actors' expectations for other persons or to structural constraints upon expectations and roles. In addition, it is not always clear from the writings of symbolic interactionists whether expectations are assumed to generate, to follow from, or to evolve conjointly with roles—and if the latter, what we are to understand about the relationship between expectations and conduct. These problems have reflected both the unique history of symbolic interactionism and its epistemological approach, which favors ethnography over survey and experimental evidence. Such problems have weakened contributions from the perspective and have prompted additional attacks on role theory because of its presumed identification with symbolic interactionism.

Structural Role Theory

Linton's early statement of role concepts also influenced anthropologists and others interested in social structure (see Levy 1952, Nadel 1957), and this has prompted the development of mathematically expressed, axiomatic theory concerning structured role relationships (Burt 1976, 1982; Mandel 1983; White et al 1976; Winship & Mandel 1983). Within this effort, little attention is given to norms or other expectations for conduct. Instead, attention is focused on "social structures," conceived as stable organizations of sets of persons (called "social positions" or "statuses") who share the same, patterned behaviors ("roles") that are directed towards other sets of persons in the structure. Such concepts lead to formal discussions of various concerns including social networks, kinships, role sets, exchange relationships, comparison of forms of social systems, and the analysis of economic behaviors. Thus, as with functionalists, structuralists are attempting to take on some of the central concerns of sociology and anthropology. Their treatment of these subjects is far different, however. The assumptions they make are simpler, their focus is more on the social environment and less on the individual, and their arguments are more likely to be couched in mathematical symbols.

Structural role theory has not yet achieved a large following. Work representing this effort has the advantage of clarity and of explicit logic. On the other hand, most social scientists seem unwilling to read arguments that are expressed in mathematical symbols, and the assumptions made by structuralists are limiting. How does such an approach deal with the nonconforming person, for example, with social systems whose structures are not well-formed, with social change? Moreover, role theory is popular, in part, because it portrays persons as thinkers, thus purporting to explain both behaviors and phenomenal experience, while much of structural role theory ignores the latter. It is certainly possible to build a role theory that merely describes social structure, but one wonders whether the gain is worth the effort.

Organizational Role Theory

However insightful the work of functionalists, structuralists, and symbolic interactionists, most empirical research in the role field has not come from these perspectives. Instead, it has reflected other perspectives that have generated their own traditions of effort. One of these has appeared among researchers interested in the roles of formal organizations. Their efforts have built a version of role theory focused on social systems that are preplanned, task-oriented, and hierarchical. Roles in such organizations are assumed to be associated with identified social positions and to be generated by normative expectations, but norms may vary among individuals and may reflect both the official demands of the organizations and the pressures of informal groups. Given multiple sources for norms, individuals are often subjected to role conflicts in which they must contend with antithetical norms for their behavior. Such role conflicts produce strain and must be resolved if the individual is to be happy and the organization is to prosper.

Organizational role theory may be said to have begun with the seminal books of Gross et al (1958) and Kahn et al (1964). Recent work includes review articles on role conflict research (Van Sell et al 1981, Fisher & Gitelson 1983), others on role conflict resolution (van de Vliert 1979, 1981), volumes of original essays (van de Vliert et al 1983, Visser et al 1983), and an edited work seeking to extend the theory to the phenomena of role transition (Allen & van de Vliert 1984b). The latter work, in particular, presents theory and application papers focused on problems generated when the actor must cope with changes in social position or expectations for the actor's position. Such experiences typically cause strain, and the core of the theory concerns variables that affect the actor's choice of strategies for coping with the situation.

Organizational role theory has had considerable impact in business schools and among industrial psychologists and sociologists. It is also subject to criticism. Among other problems, its assumptions appear to be limiting and to preclude the study of roles that evolve or roles that are generated by nonnormative expectations. As well, the perspective implies that organizations are rational, stable entities, that all conflicts within them are merely role conflicts, and that the participant will inevitably be happy and productive once role conflict is resolved. These latter conclusions are questionable. Nevertheless, substantial empirical research has appeared based on this perspective, and much of what we know about role conflict and its resolution today has come from that effort.

Cognitive Role Theory

The remaining bulk of empirical role research has largely been associated with cognitive social psychology. As a rule, this work has focused on relationships between role expectations and behavior. Attention has been given to social conditions that give rise to expectations, to techniques for measuring expectations, and to the impact of expectations on social conduct. Many cognitive role theorists have also concerned themselves with the ways in which a person perceives the expectations of others and with the effects of those perceptions on behavior.

Several subfields of effort can be recognized within cognitive role theory. A first began with Moreno's (1934) early discussion of *role playing*. As Moreno had it, role playing appears when the person attempts to imitate the roles of others. Role playing is said to appear naturally in the behavior of children and can be practiced as an aid in both education and therapy. The latter assertion has led to scores of studies on the effectiveness of therapeutic role playing; many of these confirm the value of the technique (McNamara & Blumer 1982). Role playing has been found an effective way to produce changes in expectations (Janis & Mann 1977). It has also been touted as a way of operationalizing dependent variables in social psychological experiments, but the latter application is questionable (Yardley 1982, Greenwood 1983).

A second subfield was stimulated by Sherif's (1936) early work on group norms but was given additional impetus by the subsequent work of others on group norms and the roles of leaders and followers. Research on group norms and the roles of leader and follower continues to this day (see Moreland & Levine 1982, Rutte & Wilke 1984, Hollander 1985).

A third subfield has focused on theories of anticipatory role expectations originally suggested by Rotter (1954) and Kelly (1955). Emphasis within this tradition has *not* been upon normative expectations. Instead, expectations have been conceived as beliefs about likely conduct, and researchers have examined both subjects' beliefs about their own behavior and those beliefs that they attribute to other persons. Research stimulated by these insights has focused on counseling and the interpretation of mental illness, although recent work seeks to extend the orientation to an understanding of family interaction (see Brewer et al 1981, Carver & Scheier 1981, Duckro et al 1979, Mancuso & Adams-Webber 1982, Tschudi & Rommetveit 1982).

Finally, a fourth subfield has appeared as research on *role taking,* stimulated by contributions of Mead (1934) and Piaget (1926). Although other interpretations of role taking have also appeared, one group of investigators has assumed that this term refers to the degree to which persons attribute sophisticated thoughts to others. Standardized methods have been developed for measuring sophistication of role taking, and sophistication is generally found to be greater among persons who are older, wiser, and more mature (see Enright & Lapsley 1980, Underwood & Moore 1982, Eisenberg & Lennon 1983).

Other cognitive social scientists have also contributed to role theory, although they may not have used the role concept in their writings. To illustrate, Fishbein & Ajzen (1975) have conducted research examining the comparative impact of "attitudes" and of attributed norms on conduct. Schwartz (1977) has investigated subjects' responses to moral norms. Good and his colleagues (Brophy & Good 1974, Good 1981, Cooper & Good 1983) have studied the impact of teacher expectations about pupils on teacher classroom behavior and pupil achievement. And this list might be extended indefinitely.

Integrative works representing cognitive role theory appeared in the past, but given the breadth of this perspective, it is not surprising to learn that few such works have recently surfaced. An exception to this generalization appears in Biddle's (1979) text, a work that offers separate chapters on the concepts of role, social position, expectation, derived concepts, and applications of role theory to the social system and individual adjustment. In addition, Biddle explores the assumptions of role theory and provides reviews of applicable empirical evidence.

Unlike most role theorists, Biddle assumes that role expectations can appear simultaneously in at least three modes of thought: norms, preferences, and beliefs. These modes of expectation are learned through somewhat different experiences. However, each may (or may not) be shared with others in a given context, each can affect behavior, and all may be involved in generating a role.

Such an approach suggests a sophisticated model for the person's thoughts about roles and allows integration of role theory with various traditions of research on "attitudes," the self-concept, and related topics. In addition, Biddle, Bank, and their colleagues have published research on the origins and comparative effects of norms, preferences, and beliefs (Bank et al 1977, 1985; Biddle et al 1980a,b, 1985).

Cognitive role theory is also subject to criticism, of course. As a rule, the insights of this perspective tend to rely too heavily on contemporary American culture, its research fails to explore the contextual limitations of effects, and it tends to ignore the dynamic and evolving character of human interaction. As well, cognitive role theorists, by focusing on the individual, often slight role phenomena associated with social positions or with temporal and structural phenomena. For the present, however, cognitive role theory appears to have a broader empirical base than other perspectives in the field.

KEY CONCEPTS AND RESEARCH

One of the strengths of role theory is that its concepts are easily studied. This has led to considerable research effort which, in turn, has produced information concerning basic issues in role theory. It is appropriate that I review some of this information here. For convenience, the review will focus on four key concepts that have stimulated research traditions.

Consensus

The term *consensus* is used by role theorists to denote agreement among the expectations that are held by various persons. The significance of this concept was first argued by functionalists who asserted that social roles appear because persons in the social system share norms for the conduct of social-position members. Thus, such persons know what they should do, and all persons in the system can be counted on to support those norms with sanctions. And for this reason, social systems are presumably better integrated, and interaction within them proceeds more smoothly, when normative consensus obtains. As well, functionalists often built assumptions about normative consensus into their definitions of concepts for role theory. To illustrate, a social norm has been defined as "a standard shared by members of a social group" (Kolb 1964:472), and definitions such as these are often accepted today by role theorists who have little sympathy for the rest of functional theory.

Enthusiasm for consensus has not been universal, however. Role-conflict researchers have often pointed out that assumptions about consensus are sometimes untenable, and critical theorists have questioned the usefulness of focusing on consensus as the sole mechanism for producing social order. (Social order might be produced, for example, through negotiation, social exchange, chicanery, or applications of force, and normative consensus may well result from hegemonic domination by powerful interest groups.) These arguments pose two questions about consensus that can be addressed through empirical research. *First,* to what extent do persons actually agree on norms, and what factors affect their agreement? *Second,* is it true that the integration of social systems is facilitated by normative consensus, and what factors affect this relationship?

As it turns out, research does not provide satisfactory answers to these questions. Early research produced a number of studies of normative consensus in small groups (see McGrath & Altman 1966), but this research tradition has largely lapsed today. Early research also generated good discussions of the norm concept and methods for measuring consensus (Jackson 1960, 1966; Leik 1966; Gibbs 1965), but these had little apparent impact on research. Indeed, recent research on normative consensus appears to be rediscovering measurement issues and to be largely concerned with posing criteria by which one might detect when sufficient consensus is present to conclude the "existence" of a social norm (see Labovitz & Hagedorn 1973, Hamilton & Rytina 1980, Jacobsen & van der Voordt 1980, Markoff 1982, Rossi & Berk 1985). Research on small groups suggests that normative consensus is greater within longer-lasting groups and when group cohesiveness obtains (Hollander 1985). Consensus also appears likely when persons are asked about their norms for easily identified social positions in the society-at-large (Deux 1984, Rossi & Berk 1985). But factors that would affect normative consensus seem not to have been studied for most social system forms, and it is difficult to find studies that address the presumed relationship between normative consensus and social-system integration.

Arguments concerning the advantages of consensus need not be confined to the normative mode of expectations. It is often asserted that social systems will also be better integrated when their members share beliefs about social conduct. (After all, such beliefs should lead to collective action that anticipates the effects of conduct thought likely.) This, too, is an attractive idea, but little research seems to have been conducted concerning it.

In contrast, considerable research has appeared concerning the effects of preferential consensus (or "attitude similarity"). Few of these studies have controlled for the possible presence of effects generated by norms or beliefs, and some studies have used scales for the measurement of preferences that are contaminated by normative or belief-oriented items (for discussion of this issue and an example, see Bank et al 1977). But within these limits, much of the available research supports the premise that preferential consensus promotes social integration. To illustrate, this consensus mode has been found associated with interpersonal attraction (Fishbein & Ajzen 1972), friendship formation (Hill & Palmquist 1978), and marital adjustment (White & Hatcher 1984).

However, there appear to be limits to the generality of the effect. It is less likely to appear if persons differ significantly in status (White 1979) or if the behavior at issue is disliked (Novak & Lerner 1968, Taylor & Mettee 1971). For these reasons, among others, preferential consensus is only weakly related to success in counseling (Ross 1977). Why should these effects occur? It is argued that when persons share preferences they are likely to respond similarly to a common stimulus, thus to coordinate their activities easily. But coordination is less likely when these persons differ in status or are responding to a stimulus they dislike.

The arguments for preferential-consensus effects appear to be weaker than those for normative consensus, and role theorists who have focused their theories on the latter are unlikely to be impressed with evidence concerning the former. But traditions of research on preferential consensus have been strong among cognitive psychologists, whereas sociologists have more often merely argued about or assumed the presence of normative consensus. This is a serious deficiency. Role theorists must provide more evidence concerning normative consensus or they will presently find that their arguments concerning it are ignored. And once they take up the empirical challenge, it seems likely that they will discover limits to the normative-consensus model. Some social systems involve deception, others are "staged," still others involve conflicts of interest, and many appear to be integrated through the mass media or the imposition of power. Normative consensus appears unlikely in such systems, and its appearance would not necessarily be integrative.

In the face of such thoughts, why do some role theorists continue to make assumptions about consensus? In part, this behavior seems to be generated by conceptual confusion. Thus, for some theorists a social norm or role "is" an entity that involves a state of normative consensus, and such persons find it difficult to think about role phenomena that might violate this assumption. In part, also, role theorists are merely reflecting an assumption that is commonly made in the society at large. Social psychologists have known for years that persons are likely to perceive consensus when none exists, and this phenomenon has recently attracted a good deal of empirical research (see, for example, Crano 1983, Sherman et al 1984, or van der Pligt 1984). But to make unwarranted assumptions about consensus seems a poor basis for constructing theory.

Conformity

Conformity connotes compliance to some pattern for behavior. Sometimes that pattern is conceived as the modeling of behavior by others, and a good deal of research has been published on conformity as social imitation. But why do persons imitate the behaviors of others? Most role theorists answer this question by invoking the concept of expectation. They argue that others' actions either reflect or lead the person to form expectations and that it is the latter that induce conformity. Thus, for role theorists, studies of conformity generally investigate the relationship between expectations and behaviors.

The idea that expectations generate behavior is endemic to most versions of role theory, and propositions about conformity may be found in functionalist, symbolic interactionist, organizational, and cognitive role literature. Much of this writing assumes that conformity is a good thing, that social integration and personal satisfaction are greater when persons conform to their own and others' expectations. But enthusiasm for conformity is also mixed. Symbolic interactionists often question the degree to which roles are actually generated through conformity, and ideological commitments of the past two decades have tended to favor nonconformity, creativity, and the questioning of traditional expectations. As well, role theorists have differed concerning their explanations for the relationship between the expectation and behavior. Such challenges suggest various questions for empirical research. How likely is it that people will conform to expectations, and what factors govern this? Why should persons conform to expectations? What are the effects of conformity, and when will those effects appear?

Most research on conformity has been conducted within modally specific traditions of effort. Some of it has reflected the idea that behaviors conform to norms. The argument for normative conformity goes something like this: Others often hold norms concerning the behaviors of persons. People are led to verbalize norms or to bring pressure to bear on others for conformity to them. As a result, those persons become aware of others' norms, and they conform thereafter either for instrumental reasons or because they internalize the norms. Instrumental conformity appears because persons perceive that others are powerful and are likely to sanction them for noncompliance. Internalized conformity, in contrast, results because persons accept others' norms as their own and conform because they believe it "right" to do so.

Evidence is available that tends to support normative conformity theory. To illustrate, scores of studies have confirmed the likelihood of conformity to norms in small groups (Stein 1982) and compliance to norms that persons attribute to others (Fishbein & Ajzen 1975; van de Vliert 1979). Much of this conformity appears to be instrumental; thus, persons are more likely to conform when others can view their behaviors, have power, and are thought likely to exercise sanctions over the person. Moreover, instrumental conformity is efficacious, and persons who conform are also likely to accrue status or "idiosyncrasy credits" for their actions (Santee & VanDerPol 1976, Thelen et al 1981, Hollander 1985). But not all normative conformity is instrumental, and Schwartz (1977) offers research confirming that persons will also conform to moral norms.

Although research support for normative conformity appears to be impressive, it fails to deal with several crucial issues. For one, research provides little evidence that others will actually sanction the person for nonconformity nor even that assumptions about sanctions are necessary for instrumental conformity. For another, little seems to be known yet concerning the determinants or effects of internalized conformity. But above all, the evidence does not tell us when persons will fail to conform to norms. Clearly, some persons violate norms. Some do this unknowingly, some do it secretly, some continue to do it until discovered, some continue to do it in spite of sanctions or apparent guilt, but programmatic research on nonconformity to norms seems hard to find.

Other theorists argue that conformity is associated with beliefs, and two traditions of research have appeared that support their arguments. One concerns *self-fulfilling prophecies,* a concept first suggested by Merton (1948) who noted that some beliefs cause others to behave, inadvertently, in ways that encourage conformity to those beliefs by the person. This idea has spawned substantial research (see Jones 1977, Snyder 1984), and the evidence supports the proposition that others' beliefs can generate conformity. But again, this form of conformity seems to be a contingent matter. To illustrate, Rosenthal & Jacobson (1968) suggested that schoolteachers inadvertently encourage pupils to conform to teacher-held beliefs for success and failure. Subsequent studies have confirmed the effect but have also found that it appears only for certain teachers and is likely to disappear once those teachers are alerted to its presence (Brophy & Good 1974).

Another belief-oriented tradition concerns influence strategies that are presumed to induce changes in self-concept in persons who are exposed to them. A number of such strategies have been suggested, among them *altercasting, labeling the person,* the *foot-in-the-door-technique,* and others. Most of these have been found effective in producing conformity, but again the effects are contingent, and it is not always clear from the research that the conforming response was, in fact, induced by shifts in beliefs (see Gove 1975, Shrauger & Schoeneman 1979, DeJong 1979). Nevertheless, conformity is sometimes easier to achieve through manipulation of beliefs than through normative means. This fact was illustrated in a study by Miller et al (1975) who report achieving more conformity, among school children, with altercasting than with strategies based on normative advocacy. Miller et al argue that this effect was obtained because persons resent and resist the sanctions they associate with normative conformity but have few defenses against attributions of favorable identities.

Yet another group of theorists have argued that conformity may occur because of preferential (or "attitudinal") processes. The latter theories do not usually concern themselves with others' preferences, nor is much attention given to the possibility that persons may attribute preferences to others. However, it is argued that when a person is exposed to others' actions, the person forms, or shifts, preferences for behavior, and it is the latter that induces conformity. In support of this argument, many studies have reported investigations of "attitude change" and the impact of "attitudes" on behavior (Seibold 1975; Ajzen & Fishbein 1977; Eagly & Himmelfarb 1978; Cialdini et al 1981). Regarding the former, shifts in preferences have been found to follow exposure to behavior modeling, advocacy, and the contingent use of sanctions and threats. Regarding the latter, whereas earlier reviewers questioned whether preferences affect behavior (Deutscher 1966, Wicker 1969), recent reviewers have found abundant evidence that preferences can affect conduct (Calder & Ross 1973; Schuman & Johnson 1976; Fishbein & Ajzen 1975). However, preferential conformity is by no means a certainty; indeed, it is more likely to occur when preferences are socially supported in some way. By no means will persons always do what they prefer to do.

Which, then, is a stronger generator of conformity: norms, beliefs, or preferences? Moreover, what happens when the person holds norms, beliefs, or preferences that are at odds? Unfortunately, studies concerning such questions have only begun to appear (see Fishbein & Ajzen 1975; Schwartz 1977; Triandis 1977; Bank et al 1985; Biddle et al 1985). So far the available evidence indicates that all three modes of expectation can have independent effects and that those effects vary from situation to situation. Other research, however, suggests that Americans today are generally less driven by norms and more affected by preferences than they were in earlier generations (see Turner 1976, Zurcher 1977). If confirmed, this may reflect the decline in importance of community, church, and family in our lives and the ascendancy of mass-media influences. One hopes that the next decade will produce more research on the comparative origins and effects of expectation modes.

In sum then, the evidence suggests that persons often conform to expectations that are held by others, are attributed to others, or are held by the person for his or her conduct. Conformity is by no means a certainty, and its appearance reflects somewhat different processes depending on the modality of the expectation involved. In fact, recent studies suggest that if conformity occurs it probably results from the resolving of several, modally distinct expectations, which may or may not favor the conforming response. Simple assumptions about conformity are no more useful in role theory than simple assumptions about consensus.

Is conformity a good thing? Our answer will depend on the context and criterion of goodness. Thelen et al (1981) note that persons gain status through conformity only when that response is not perceived as "calculating." Duckro et al (1979) report that, despite widespread assumptions concerning its necessity, therapist conformity to client-held expectations is *not* required for success in counseling. Conformity seems a useful response where coordination of behaviors or safety are at stake (Ley 1982, Epstein & Cluss 1982, Schoen 1983), but in other contexts it may prove useless or counterproductive. Social systems must evolve in order to survive in a changing world, and evolution requires the programming of nonconformity.

Role Conflict

What happens when others do *not* hold consensual expectations for a person's behavior? One possibility is that those others are formed into sets of persons whose expectations are distinct and incompatible. In such cases, it is argued, the person will be subjected to conflicting pressures, will suffer stress, will have to "resolve" the problem by adopting some form of coping behavior, and that the person and system will both be disrupted. These ideas have given rise to the concept of *role conflict,* which is normally defined as the concurrent appearance of two or more incompatible expectations for the behavior of a person. The ideas associated with role conflict are attractive and appear to capture some of the subjective problems associated with participation in the complex social system. But role conflict theory has also attracted criticism, and critics have sometimes viewed research on role conflict as an activity that diverts our attention from concern for the real conflicts that appear in social systems or from the possibility that persons might cope by changing those systems.

Be that as it may, a lot of research on role conflict has appeared over the past three decades. Most if not all studies have focused on normative role conflict, and discussions of these findings have largely reflected the theory of instrumental conformity. And whereas early studies tended to focus on actual disparities in the expectations that were held by others, recent research has more often examined conflicts among expectations that are attributed by the person to others.

What have we learned from role conflict research? A host of studies have found role conflicts in the formal organization and have suggested that role conflict is associated with stress in that context (for reviews see Stryker & Macke 1978, van de Vliert 1979, Van Sell et al 1981, Fisher & Gitelson 1983). Moreover, role conflicts have also been associated with various indices of personal malintegration in the work place, such as poor job performance, lower commitment to the organization, and higher rates of accidents and resignations. Many writers have also argued that women in Western societies are subjected to conflicts between expectations associated with traditional roles, such as homemaking, and those for occupational or professional careers. These arguments have also been supported by studies demonstrating the prevalence of role conflicts and associations between role conflicts and stress for women (Stryker & Macke 1978; Lopata 1980; Skinner 1980).

Findings such as these appear to suggest that role conflict is a frequent experience and is inevitably stressful, but one should be cautious about accepting these conclusions. Investigators have not thought to study role conflicts in many settings, so the real range and effects of such phenomena are as yet unexplored. And role-conflict research has also been subject to conceptual and methodological confusion. As it happens, role conflict is only one of several structural conditions that are thought to cause problems in social systems. Others have included *role ambiguity* (a condition in which expectations are incomplete or insufficient to guide behavior), *role malintegration* (when roles do not fit well together), *role discontinuity* (when the person must perform a sequence of malintegrated roles), and *role overload* (when the person is faced with too many expectations). As well, the person may have difficulty in performing a role because of lack of skill or incongruence between expectations and his or her personal characteristics. Each of these conditions may produce stress for the individual. Unfortunately, most have been confused with role conflict by one or more authors, and instruments presumably designed to measure role conflict have sometimes involved operations that are more appropriate for the study of these other phenomena. Bank & Janes (submitted) argue that these confusions have caused investigators to overestimate the relationship between role conflict and stress. Sieber (1974) argued that persons will sometimes prefer to take on multiple roles, despite the fact that this nearly always exposes them to increased role conflict. And, in support of this proposition, Sales et al (1980) and Bank & Janes both report weak, positive relationships between role conflict and satisfaction for women who are simultaneously mothers and university students.

Certainly some role conflicts are stressful, however, and when this happens how does one cope with the matter? Gross et al (1958) posed a theory of role-conflict resolution which suggested that persons would choose among the incompatible norms and that their choice could be predicted if one understood the degree to which the person considered others powerful and their norms legitimate. This theory has since been studied by many researchers, and a summary of their work appears in van de Vliert (1979, 1981) who concludes that three steps may be taken to resolve stressful role conflict: If possible, choice among norms (in which case, anticipated sanctions and judgments of legitimacy come into play); if that is not possible, a compromise among norms; if all else fails, withdrawal from the situation. Most of the research reviewed by van de Vliert was focused on role conflicts in the organization, and the range of coping strategies considered appears limited. Fortunately, other theories consider a broader range of coping strategies. To illustrate, Hall (1972) discusses three types of response: negotiating with others to change their expectations; restructuring one's views so that the problem is less worrisome; and adjusting one's behavior. Hall and others (see Harrison & Minor 1984) have applied this typology to the coping behaviors of women who experience role conflict.

To date, role conflict research has not focused on several questions that appear central to our understanding. It does not tell us how frequently the person is likely to encounter role conflict, nor with what structural factors role conflict is likely to be associated. It has given but little attention to role conflicts that involve incompatible beliefs, preferences, or internalized norms. As a rule, it has not explored relationships between role conflicts and true conflicts-of-interest among persons. And it provides little evidence bearing on the presumed relationship between role conflict and social malintegration. Some years ago Goode (1960) suggested that role strain was endemic in complex social systems and provided a positive force that promoted system evolution. It would appear that Goode's conjectures have yet to be tested.

Role Taking

The theory of *role taking,* first articulated by Mead (1934), suggests that adequate development of the self and participation in social interaction both require that the person "take the role of the other." This theory focuses attention on the importance of attributed expectations, but scholars have often differed over the exact meaning of Mead's concepts. In the case of role taking, differing interpretations have produced two distinct traditions of effort. Some scholars have thought that successful role taking meant *accuracy* of attributed expectations, that persons are more effective role takers when the expectations they attribute to others match those that others actually hold. Other scholars have thought that successful role taking involved *sophistication* of social thought, that the person is a better role taker if he or she presumes that others also hold expectations that map the thoughts and actions of other persons. These two interpretations have spawned independent traditions of research that are conducted in apparent ignorance of one another. Both traditions have assumed that role-taking ability was a blessing and that successful role taking would facilitate personal development and social integration. Has any evidence appeared that would justify such assumptions?

Many early studies of role-taking accuracy constituted a search for the presumed trait of "empathy," conceived as a general ability to judge persons' expectations accurately. If some persons do have such a trait, they would surely make better group leaders, counselors, therapists, or confessors. This belief stimulated a good deal of early research, but by the mid-1950s, critical papers began to appear that questioned the methods of the research (Cronbach 1955, Gage & Cronbach 1955). These papers noted that artifacts might appear in scores from empathy scales and suggested that such scores might represent not one but several judgment components. These criticisms were devastating, and research on the presumptive trait of empathy has largely disappeared today.

Not all such research reflected a search for the trait of empathy, however. Other studies appeared from researchers representing several traditions in role theory (see Chowdhry & Newcomb 1952; Stryker 1956; Wheeler 1961; Biddle et al 1966; Preiss & Ehrlich 1966; Howells & Brosnan 1972; Thomas et al 1972; Kandel 1974). These latter studies involved research with all three modes of expectation and reported considerable variation in subjects' role-taking ability. Moreover, this variation was found to be associated with contextual conditions. Persons who interact regularly or have similar backgrounds were found to take one anothers' roles more accurately than those who do not. Persons of low status were also found to be more accurate role takers (possibly because they have greater need to predict others' conduct), although greater role-taking accuracy was also found among those chosen for group leadership. Role-taking accuracy was found to be low when the subject and others had reason to restrict communication concerning crucial topics. These findings imply that accurate role taking is neither universal nor requisite for successful interaction in all cases. Unfortunately, this research tradition, too, seems to have declined during the past decade.

Research on the sophistication of role taking has been conducted by cognitive and developmental psychologists and is now a substantial enterprise (for reviews see Enright & Lapsley 1980; Underwood & Moore 1982; Eisenberg & Lennon 1983). These studies also report considerable variation among subjects in role-taking ability, but studies have associated that variation with personality variables in the main. Role-taking sophistication is greater among older and more mature subjects, and role taking correlates positively with altruism. Some persons have thought that role-taking sophistication would be greater among women than among men, but the evidence does not bear this out. Women and young girls *are* found to respond more emotively to the plights of others, however.

In sum, research on role taking appears to be more fragmented than research for the other three concepts I have reviewed. Research on role-taking accuracy is suggestive, but early studies within the tradition were often flawed, and research on the problem seems to have declined recently. Research on role-taking sophistication is more active but is focused largely on personality variables. Both traditions suggest that role-taking ability varies among persons, but neither has yet generated much information about the presumed positive effects of role taking for the person and social system.

Role-taking ideas have had considerable impact within developmental psychology. They have had less impact on discussions of social integration, however, and many contemporary theories about the latter are based on assumptions about negotiation, exchange, power, or the economy and presume little about role taking. This does not mean that assertions about the advantages of role taking are right, nor are they necessarily wrong. It will take more focused research to establish the effects of role taking within the social realm.

ISSUES AND PROPOSITIONAL THEORY

Many commentators have remarked on the absence of an explicit, explanatory, propositional theory for the role field. Why has such a theory been slow to develop?

A couple of reasons are suggested by problems associated with the history of the role field. Propositions are hard to generate when a field is plagued by conceptual and definitional confusions, and by employment of its terms by persons who promote radically different perspectives. Clearly, the development of role theory will accelerate as the field adopts a set of agreed-upon definitions for basic concepts and sloughs off associations with perspectives from which it clearly differs.

Other reasons for the weak development of propositions may be found in the reviews of empirical research just completed. For one thing, much of role theory seems to be driven by simple assumptions about such phenomena as consensus, conformity, role conflict, and role taking, and yet the evidence suggests that these simple assumptions are not always valid. In addition, the reviews suggest a lack of integration between the efforts of theorists and researchers in the role field. An interest in applying role concepts to solving human problems seems to have generated much of the research. In so doing, researchers have produced practical information, particularly information about the impact of role phenomena on the individual. But basic research issues for role theory have remained underresearched, particularly those concerning the effects of role phenomena in the social system. Propositional development would benefit were research to be linked more closely to key questions in role theory.

These reasons for the weakness of theory are serious but correctable; were they the only ones troubling the role field an integrated propositional theory might have already appeared. Unfortunately, role theory has also been hampered because its proponents disagree over major issues that concern the stance and scope of the field. One issue concerns whether role theory is to focus attention on the person as an individual or the person as representative of a social position. Symbolic interactionists and cognitive theorists prefer the former approach, functionalists and structuralists the latter. The former approach leads one to think of roles as the evolving, coping strategies that are adopted by the person, the latter conceives roles as patterns of behavior that are typical of persons whose structural positions are similar. Neither stance is necessarily "correct," but propositions about individuals may not be those that one would make about representatives of a social position.

Other issues concern the assumptions that one makes about expectations. A few role theorists avoid the expectation concept altogether. Others assume that roles are an amorphous amalgam of thought and action and take no position on the possible relationships between these two realms. Most role theorists assume that expectations are formed in response to experience and that roles are largely generated by expectations, but even these latter differ over the mode of expectation they discuss and the explanations they advance for social integration. Each of these stances will also generate a propositional system that differs from the others.

And still other issues are implied by constraints created by definitions of role concepts used by theorists. For some authors, roles are tied to functions, for others they are inevitably directed towards another actor in the system; for yet others, roles are those behaviors that validate one's position or that project a self image. Constraints such as these also lead to somewhat different versions of propositional role theory.

The fact that role theorists differ over issues of stance and scope reflects not only the histories of perspectival thought but also the fact that various groups of role theorists are wrestling with different forms of social systems. Thoughtful contributors have stated role propositions for the family, the jury trial, the kinship, the classroom, the counseling session, the doctor-patient relationship, the formal organization, the community, the political forum, the ethnic, racial, and sexual identity, the society and nation-state. But assumptions that seem reasonable in one of these arenas seem foolish in others. This suggests that, in part, the role field will evolve in the near future as a set of propositional theories for specific social systems—theories that may have little in common with one another.

But this is not the total picture. Centripetal forces are also at work within role theory, not the least of which are a common vocabulary and a set of shared, basic concerns. But if role theory is to accommodate the differing stances that have appeared within the field—if it is to develop propositions that apply to many contexts—role theory must separate its basic concepts from context-specific assumptions and be prepared to incorporate a wide range of insights that have appeared in the differing, limited, current versions of itself. This suggests the gradual evolution of an integrated version of role theory in which some propositions concern the roles of individual actors *and* some concern roles that are common to persons in the same social position, a role theory in which roles may be generated by norms, beliefs, *and* preferences, a theory that can examine role sectors, role functions, *and* self-validation. Not all of these insights need be applied to a given context, of course. But the integrated version of role theory must be prepared to accommodate such insights and is likely to explain a lot more about human conduct than current, limited versions of theory.

What, then, should one conclude about role theory in the mid-1980s? In several senses role theory is alive, well, and prospering. Interest in role ideas remains high among theorists, and authors continue to apply those ideas in new and innovative ways. Research that uses role ideas is vigorous, and insights from role theory are widely applied in discussions of social problems and their alleviation. But confusion and malintegration persist in role theory. The latter partly reflects problems associated with the development of the field, unwise perspectival commitments, and lack of integration between the efforts of theorists and researchers. Some of role theory's problems also reflect the fact that proponents are trying to deal with differing forms of social systems and in so doing make assumptions that are inappropriate in other realms. Role theory will prosper as proponents recognize these problems and expand their efforts to accommodate one anothers' insights within an integrated version of the field.

Literature Cited

Ajzen, I., Fishbein, M. 1977. Attitude-behavior relations: A theoretical analysis and review of empirical research. *Psychol. Bull.* 84:888–918

Allen, V. L., van de Vliert, E. 1984a. A role theoretical perspective on transitional processes. See Allen & van de Vliert 1984b, pp. 3–18

Allen, V. L., van de Vliert, E., eds. 1984b. *Role Transitions: Explorations and Explanations.* New York: Plenum

Bank, B. J., Biddle, B. J., Anderson, D. S., Hauge, R., Keats, D. M., et al. 1985. Comparative research on the social determinants of adolescent drinking. *Soc. Psychol. Q.* 48:164–77

Bank, B. J., Biddle, B. J., Keats, D. M., Keats, J. A. 1977. Normative, preferential, and belief modes in adolescent prejudice. *Sociol. Q.* 18:574–88

Bank, B. J., Janes, D. P. 1985. The consequences of role conflict: Ideology or evidence? Submitted.

Bates, F. L., Harvey, C. C. 1975. *The Structure of Social Systems.* New York: Wiley

Biddle, B. J. 1979. *Role Theory: Expectations, Identities, and Behaviors.* New York: Academic

Biddle, B. J., Bank, B. J., Anderson, D. S., Hauge, R., Keats, D. M., et al. 1985. Social influence, self-referent identity labels, and behavior. *Sociol. Q.* 26:159–84

Biddle, B. J., Bank, B. J., Marlin, M. M. 1980a. Parental and peer influence on adolescents. *Soc. Forc.* 58:1057–79

Biddle, B. J., Bank, B. J., Marlin, M. M. 1980b. Social determinants of adolescent drinking: What they think, what they do, and what I think and do. *J. Stud. Alcohol* 41:215–41

Biddle, B. J., Rosencranz, H. A., Tomich, E., Twyman, J. P. 1966. Shared inaccuracies in the role of the teacher. In *Role Theory: Concepts and Research,* ed. B. J. Biddle, E. J. Thomas, pp. 302–10. New York: Wiley

Brewer, M. B., Dull, V., Lui, L. 1981. Perceptions of the elderly: Stereotypes as prototypes. *J. Pers. Soc. Psychol.* 41:656–70

Brophy, J. E., Good, T. L. 1974. *Teacher-Student Relationships: Causes and Consequences.* New York: Holt

Burt, R. S. 1976. Positions in networks. *Soc. Forc.* 51:93–122

Burt, R. S. 1982. *Toward a Structural Theory of Action: Network Models of Social Structure, Perception, and Action.* New York: Academic

Calder, B. J., Ross, M. 1973. *Attitudes and Behavior.* Morristown, NJ: General Learning

Carver, C. S., Scheier, M. F. 1981. *Attention and Self-Regulation.* New York: Springer-Verlag

Chowdhry, K., Newcomb, T. M. 1952. The relative abilities of leaders and nonleaders to estimate opinions of their own groups. *J. Abnorm. Soc. Psychol.* 47:51–57

Cialdini, R. B., Petty, R. E., Cacioppo, J. T. 1981. Attitude and attitude change. *Ann. Rev. Psychol.* 32:357–404

Cooper, H. M., Good, T. L. 1983. *Pygmalion Grows Up: Studies in the Expectation Communication Process.* New York: Longman

Crano, W. D. 1983. Assumed consensus of attitudes: The effect of vested interest. *Pers. Soc. Psychol. Bull.* 9:597–608

Cronbach, L. J. 1955. Processes affecting scores on "understanding of others" and "assumed similarity." *Psychol. Bull.* 52: 177–93

DeJong, W. 1979. An examination of self-perception mediation of the Foot-In-The-Door effect. *J. Pers. Soc. Psychol.* 37:2221–39

Deutscher, I. 1966. Words and deeds: Social

science and social policy. *Soc. Probl.* 13:235–54

Deux, K. 1984. From individual differences to social categories: Analysis of a decade's research on gender. *Am. Psychol.* 39:105–16

Duckro, P., Beal, D., George, C. 1979. Research on the effects of disconfirmed client role expectations in psychotherapy: A critical review. *Psychol. Bull.* 86:260–75

Eagly, A. H., Himmelfarb, S. 1978. Attitudes and opinions. *Ann. Rev. Psychol.* 29:517–54

Eisenberg, N., Lennon, R. 1983. Sex differences in empathy and related capacities. *Psychol. Bull.* 94:100–31

Enright, R. D., Lapsley, D. K. 1980. Social role-taking: A review of constructs, measures, and measurement properties. *Rev. Educ. Res.* 50:647–74

Epstein. L. H., Cluss, P. A. 1982. A behavioral medicine perspective on adherence to long-term medical regimens. *J. Consult. Clin. Psychol.* 50:950–71

Fishbein, M., Ajzen, I. 1972. Attitudes and opinions. *Ann. Rev. Psychol.* 23:487–544

Fishbein, M., Ajzen, I. 1975. *Belief, Attitude, Intention and Behavior: An Introduction to Theory and Research.* Reading, Mass: Addison-Wesley

Fisher, C. D., Gitelson, R. 1983. A meta-analysis of the correlates of role conflict and ambiguity. *J. Appl. Psychol.* 68:320–33

Gage, N. L., Cronbach, L. J. 1955. Conceptual and methodological problems in interpersonal perception. *Psychol. Rev.* 62:411–22

Gibbs, J. P. 1965. Norms: The problem of definition and classification. *Am. J. Sociol.* 70:586–94

Good, T. L. 1981. Teacher expectations and student perceptions, a decade of research. *Educ. Leadership* 38:415–23

Goode, W. J. 1960. A theory of role strain. *Am. Sociol. Rev.* 25:483–96

Gordon, C. 1976. Development of evaluated role identities. *Ann. Rev. Sociol.* 2:405–33

Gordon, C., Gordon, P. 1982. Changing roles, goals, and self-conceptions: Process and results in a program for women's employment. See Ickes & Knowles 1982:243–83

Gove, W. R. 1975. *The Labelling of Deviance: Evaluating a Perspective.* New York: Wiley

Greenwood, J. D. 1983. Role playing as an experimental strategy in social psychology. *Eur. J. Soc. Psychol.* 13:235–54

Gross, N., Mason, W. S., McEachern, A. W. 1958. *Explorations in Role Analysis: Studies in the School Superintendency Role.* New York: Wiley

Hall, D. T. 1972. A model of coping with conflict: The role of college educated women. *Admin. Sci. Q.* 4:471–86

Hamilton, V. L., Rytina, S. 1980. Social consensus on norms of justice: Should the punishment fit the crime? *Am. J. Sociol.* 85:1117–44

Hare, A. P. 1985. *Social Interaction as Drama: Applications from Conflict Resolution.* Beverly Hills, Calif: Sage

Harrison, A. O., Minor, J. H. 1984. Interrole conflict, coping strategies, and satisfaction among black working wives. In *Work and Family: Changing Roles of Men and Women,* ed. P. Voydanoff, pp. 251–60. Palo Alto, Calif: Mayfield

Heiss, J., ed. 1976. *Family Roles and Interaction: An Anthology.* Chicago: Rand McNally. 2nd ed.

Heiss, J. 1981. Social roles. In *Social Psychology: Sociological Perspectives,* ed. M. Rosenberg, R. H. Turner, pp. 95–129. New York: Basic

Hill, J. P., Palmquist, W. J. 1978. Social cognition and social relations in early adolescence. *Int. J. Behav. Dev.* 1:1–36

Hollander, E. P. 1985. Leadership and power. In *Handbook of Social Psychology,* ed. C. Lindzey, E. Aronson, 2:485–537. New York: Random. 3rd ed.

Howells, J. M., Brosnan, P. 1972. The ability to predict workers' preferences: A research exercise. *Hum. Relat.* 25:265–81

Ickes, W., Knowles, E. S., eds. 1982. *Personality, Roles, and Social Behavior.* New York: Springer-Verlag

Jackson, J. M. 1960. Structural characteristics of norms. In *The Dynamics of Instructional Groups: Sociopsychological Aspects of Teaching and Learning,* ed. N. B. Henry. Yearbook of the National Society for the Study of Education 59(II):136–63

Jackson, J. M. 1966. A conceptual and measurement model for norms and roles. *Pacific Sociol. Rev.* 9:35–47

Jacobsen, C., van der Voordt, T. J. M. 1980. Interpreting modal frequencies to measure social norms. *Sociol. Meth. Res.* 8:470–86

Janis, I. L., Mann, L. 1977. *Decision Making: A Psychological Analysis of Conflict, Choice and Commitment.* New York: Free

Jones, R. A. 1977. *Self-fulfilling Prophesies: Social, Psychological, and Physiological Effects of Expectancies.* Hillsdale, NJ: Lawrence Erlbaum

Kahn, R. L., Wolfe, D. M., Quinn, R. P., Snoek, J., Rosenthal, R. A. 1964. *Organizational Stress: Studies in Role Conflict and Ambiguity.* New York: Wiley

Kandel, D. 1974. Interpersonal influences on adolescent illegal drug use. In *Drug Use: Epidemiological and Sociological Approaches,* ed. E. Josephson, E. E. Carroll, pp. 207–40. New York: Wiley

Kelly, G. A. 1955. *The Psychology of Personal Constructs.* New York: Norton

Kolb, W. L. 1964. Norm. In *A Dictionary of the Social Sciences*, ed. J. Gould, W. L. Kolb, p. 472–73. New York: Free

Labovitz, S., Hagedorn, R. 1973. Measuring social norms. *Pacific Sociol. Rev.* 16:283–303

Leik, R. K. 1966. A measure of ordinal consensus. *Pacific Sociol. Rev.* 9:85–90

Levy, M. J. 1952. *The Structure of Society*. Princeton, NJ: Princeton Univ.

Ley, P. 1982. Satisfaction, compliance and communication. *Br. J. Clin. Psychol.* 21:241–54

Linton, R. 1936. *The Study of Man*. New York: Appleton-Century

Lopata, H. Z., ed. 1980. *Research in the Interweave of Social Roles: Women and Men—A Research Annual*, Vol. 1. Greenwich, Conn: JAI

Lyman, S. M., Scott, M. B. 1975. *The Drama of Social Reality*. New York: Oxford Univ. Press

McCall, G. J. 1982. Discretionary justice: Influences of social role, personality, and social situations. See Ickes & Knowles 1982:285–303

McGrath, J. E., Altman, I. 1966. *Small Group Research: A Synthesis and Critique of the Field*. New York: Holt

McNamara, J. R., Blumer, C. A. 1982. Role playing to assess social competence: Ecological validity considerations. *Behav. Mod.* 6:519–49

Mancuso, J. C., Adams-Webber, J. R., eds. 1982. *The Construing Person*. New York: Praeger

Mancuso, J. C., Adams-Webber, J. R. 1982. Anticipation as a constructive process: The fundamental postulate. See Mancuso & Adams-Webber, pp. 8–32.

Mandel, M. J. 1983. Local roles and social networks. *Am. Sociol. Rev.* 48:376–86

Markoff, J. 1982. Suggestions for the measurement of consensus. *Am. Sociol. Rev.* 47:290–98

Mead, G. H. 1934. *Mind, Self and Society*. Chicago: Univ. Chicago Press

Merton, R. K. 1948. The self-fulfilling prophecy. *Antioch Rev.* 8:193–210

Miller, R., Brickman, P., Bolen, D. 1975. Attribution versus persuasion as means for modifying behavior. *J. Pers. Soc. Psychol.* 31:430–41

Moreland, R. L., Levine, J. M. 1982. Socialization in small groups: Temporal changes in individual-group relations. In *Advances in Experimental Social Psychology*, ed. L. Berkowitz, 15:137–92. New York: Academic

Moreno, J. L. 1934. *Who Shall Survive?* Washington, DC: Nervous and Mental Dis. Publ.

Nadel, S. F. 1957. *The Theory of Social Structure*. Glencoe, Ill: Free

Novak, D. W., Lerner, M. J. 1968. Rejection as a consequence of perceived similarity. *J. Pers. Soc. Psychol.* 9:147–52

Nye, F. I., ed. 1976. *Role Structure and Analysis of the Family*. Beverly Hills, Calif: Sage

Parsons, T. 1951. *The Social System*. Glencoe, Ill: Free

Parsons, T., Shils, E. A. 1951. *Toward a General Theory of Action*. Cambridge, Mass: Harvard Univ. Press

Piaget, J. 1926. *The Language and Thought of the Child*. New York: Harcourt, Brace, World

Preiss, J. J., Ehrlich, H. J. 1966. *An Examination of Role Theory: The Case of the State Police*. Lincoln, Neb: Univ. Neb. Press

Rosenthal, R., Jacobson, L. 1968. *Pygmalion in the Classroom: Teacher Expectation and Pupils' Intellectual Development*. New York: Holt

Ross, M. B. 1977. Discussion of similarity of client and therapist. *Psychol. Rep.* 40:699–704

Rossi, P. H., Berk, R. A. 1985. Varieties of normative consensus. *Am. Sociol. Rev.* 50:333–47

Rotter, J. B. 1954. *Social Learning and Clinical Psychology*. Englewood, Cliffs, NJ: Prentice-Hall

Rutte, C. G., Wilke, H. A. M. 1984. Transition to the leader's role in small groups. See Allen & van de Vliert 1984b:197–209

Sales, E., Shore, B. K., Bolitho, F. 1980. When mothers return to school: A study of women completing an MSW program. *J. Educ. Soc. Work* 16:57–65

Santee, R. T., VanDerPol, T. L. 1976. Actor's status and conformity to norms: A study of students' evaluations of instructors. *Sociol. Q.* 17:378–88

Sarbin, T. R. 1982. A preface to a psychological theory of metaphor. In *The Social Context of Conduct: Psychological Writings of T. R. Sarbin*, ed. V. L. Allen, K. E. Scheibe, pp. 233–49. New York: Praeger

Scheibe, K. E. 1979. *Mirrors, Masks, Lies, and Secrets: The Limits of Human Predictability*. New York: Praeger

Schoen, S. F. 1983. The status of compliance technology: Implications for programming. *J. Spec. Educ.* 17:483–96

Schuman, H., Johnson, M. P. 1976. Attitudes and behavior. *Ann. Rev. Sociol.* 2:161–207

Schwartz, S. 1977. Normative influences on altruism. In *Advances in Experimental Social Psychology*, ed. L. Berkowitz, 10:221–79. New York: Academic

Seibold, D. R. 1975. Communication research

and the attitude-verbal report overt behavior relationship: A critique and theoretic reformulation. *Hum. Commun. Res.* 2:3–32

Sherif, M. 1936. *The Psychology of Social Norms.* New York: Harper

Sherman, S. J., Chassin, L., Presson, C. C., Agostinelli, G. 1984. The role of the evaluation and similarity principles in the false consensus effect. *J. Pers. Soc. Psychol.* 47:1244–62

Shrauger, J. S., Schoeneman, T. J. 1979. Symbolic interactionist view of the self-concept: Through the looking glass darkly. *Psychol. Bull.* 86:549–73

Sieber, S. D. 1974. Toward a theory of role accumulation. *Am. Sociol. Rev.* 39:567–78

Simmel, G. 1920. Zur Philosophie des Schauspielers. *Logos* 1:339–62

Skinner, D. A. 1980. Dual-career family stress and coping: A literature review. *Family Relat.* 29:473–81

Snyder, M. 1984. When belief creates reality. In *Advances in Experimental Social Psychology,* ed. L. Berkowitz, 18:248–305. New York: Academic

Stein, R. T. 1982. High-status group members as exemplars: A summary of field research on the relationship of status to congruence conformity. *Small Group Behav.* 13:3–21

Stryker, S. 1956. Relationships of married offspring and parent: A test of Mead's theory. *Am. J. Sociol.* 52:308–19

Stryker, S., Macke, A. S. 1978. Status inconsistency and role conflict. *Ann. Rev. Sociol.* 4:57–90

Stryker, S., Serpe, R. T. 1982. Commitment, identity salience, and role behavior: Theory and research example. See Ickes & Knowles 1982:199–218

Stryker, S., Statham, A. 1985. Symbolic interaction and role theory. In *Handbook of Social Psychology,* ed. C. Lindzey, E. Aronson, 1:311–78. New York: Random. 3rd ed.

Taylor, S. E., Mettee, D. R. 1971. When similarity breeds contempt. *J. Pers. Soc. Psychol.* 20:75–81

Thelen, M. H., Frautschi, N. M., Roberts, M. C., Kirkland, K. D., Dollinger, S. J. 1981. Being imitated, conformity, and social influence: An integrative review. *J. Res. Pers.* 15:403–26

Thomas, D. L., Franks, D. D., Calonico, J. M. 1972. Role-taking and power in social psychology. *Am. Sociol. Rev.* 37:605–14

Triandis, H. C. 1977. *Interpersonal Behavior.* Monterey, Calif: Brooks/Cole

Tschudi, F., Rommetveit, R. 1982. Sociality, intersubjectivity, and social processes. See Mancuso & Adams-Webber, pp. 235–61

Turner, R. H. 1974. Rule learning as role learn-ing: What an interactive theory of roles adds to the theory of social norms. *Int. J. Crit. Sociol.* 1:52–73

Turner, R. H. 1976. The real self: From institution to impulse. *Am. J. Sociol.* 81:986–1016

Turner, R. H. 1978. The role and the person. *Am. J. Sociol.* 84:1–23

Turner, R. H. 1979. Strategy for developing an integrated role theory. *Humboldt J. Soc. Rel.* 7:123–39

Turner, R. H. 1985. Unanswered questions in the convergence between structuralist and interactionist role theories. In *Micro-Sociological Theory: Perspectives on Sociological Theory,* ed. J. H. Helle, S. N. Eisenstadt, 2:22–36. Beverly Hills, Calif: Sage.

Turner, R. H., Shosid, N. 1976. Ambiguity and interchangeability in role attribution: The effect of alter's response. *Am. Sociol. Rev.* 41:993–1006

Underwood, B., Moore, B. 1982. Perspective-taking and altruism. *Psychol. Bull.* 91:143–73

van der Pligt, J. 1984. Attributions, false consensus, and valence: Two field studies. *J. Pers. Soc. Psychol.* 46:57–68

van de Vliert, E. 1979. Gedrag in rolkonfliktsituaties: 20 jaar onderzoek rond een theorie. *Ned. Tijdschrift Psychol.* 34:125–45

van de Vliert, E. 1981. A three-step theory of role conflict resolution. *J. Soc. Psychol.* 113:77–83

van de Vliert, E., Visser, A. Ph., Zwaga, P. G. J., Winnubst, J. A. M., ter Heine, E. J. H., eds. 1983. *Rolspanningen.* Amsterdam: Boom Meppel

Van Sell, M., Brief, A. P., Schuler, R. S. 1981. Role conflict and role ambiguity: Integration of the literature and directions for future research. *Hum. Relat.* 34:43–71

Visser, A. Ph., van de Vliert, E., ter Heine, E. J. H., Winnubst, J. A. M., eds. 1983. *Rollen: Persoonlijke en Sociale Invloeden op her Gedrag.* Amsterdam: Boom Meppel

Wheeler, S. 1961. Role conflict in correctional communities. In *The Prison: Studies in Institutional Organization and Change,* ed. D. R. Cressy, pp. 229–59. New York: Holt

White, C. J. M. 1979. Factors affecting balance, agreement and positivity biases in POQ and POX triads. *Eur. J. Soc. Psychol.* 9:129–48

White, H. C., Boorman, S. A., Breiger, R. L. 1976. Social structure from multiple networks: I. Blockmodels of roles and positions. *Am. J. Sociol.* 81:730–80

White, S. G., Hatcher, C. 1984. Couple complementarity and similarity: A review of the literature. *Am. J. Fam. Therapy* 12:15–25

Wicker, A. W. 1969. Attitudes versus actions: The relationship of verbal and overt behavioral responses to attitude objects. *J. Soc. Issues* 25:41–78

Winship, C., Mandel, M. 1983. Roles and positions: A critique and extension of the blockmodeling approach. In *Sociological Methodology 1983–1984*, ed. S. Leinhardt, pp. 314–44. San Francisco: Jossey-Bass

Yardley, K. M. 1982. On engaging actors in as-if experiments. *J. Theory Soc. Behav.* 12:291–304

Zurcher, L. A. 1977. *The Mutable Self: A Self-Concept for Social Change*. Beverly Hills, Calif: Sage

Zurcher, L. A. 1983. *Social Roles: Conformity, Conflict, and Creativity*. Beverly Hills, Calif: Sage

Ann. Rev. Sociol. 1986. 12:93–108
Copyright © 1986 by Annual Reviews Inc.

A SOCIOLOGY OF JUSTICE

Harold E. Pepinsky

Department of Criminal Justice, Indiana University, Bloomington, Indiana 47405

Abstract

Although literature on causes and prevention of crime now transcends disciplinary lines, it can still be categorized by the questions addressed. One line of research expands upon questions posed and answers given in the nineteenth century. Another line of research is predicated on a series of criticisms of the nineteenth-century approach, criticisms that appeared in the 1920s and 1930s. This latter line goes well beyond Marxism, offering fundamentally different ways to define and study justice that go beyond conventional political, philosophical, and social scientific debate. The major literature of this sociology of justice is identified and emergent directions indicated.

SCOPE OF THIS REVIEW

This is a review of current trends in the literature on causes and prevention of crime. Traditionally, this body of literature has been called *criminology,* and in the United States it originated as a branch of sociology. More recently, criminology has been extended to include literature by people trained in a wide range of disciplines and in interdisciplinary programs known by such names as "administration of justice," "criminal justice," "criminology," "social ecology," and in the last several years, "justice studies." For a while, there were attempts to distinguish genres of this literature, for example, by asserting that criminologists studied causes of crime while criminal justice researchers studied responses to crime. Issues and persons kept transcending and confounding these distinctions, however, and the attempts to draw them have now largely ceased. Disciplinary boundaries have mostly dropped out of the study of what causes and what cures crime.

While disciplinary distinctions have faded, a new kind of distinction has arisen: one between those who ask and answer questions as did criminologists of the nineteenth century, and those who are posing new kinds of issues. The

93

0360-0572/86/0815-0093$02.00

former try both to explain and address distinctions between citizens who are law abiding and those who are criminals, and to evaluate responses to offenders. The latter researchers try to look beyond such distinctions, asking why some people find it less necessary than others to distinguish criminals from others or to inflict pain of any kind on offenders (Christie 1981). In this review, the former approach is called by the traditional name for the study of crime, *criminology*. The latter is called *the sociology of justice—justice* to connote transcending distinctions between criminals and law-abiding citizens (Myren 1980), and *sociology* to connote that the study is an empirical science of social relations.

The review begins by tracing trends over the past couple of decades in criminology. Here leading studies are cited that exemplify the kind of work being done. The purpose is not to tell readers where to find all the most-cited recent studies of this genre but to indicate the general direction that the work has taken.

The major part of the review is devoted to describing and surveying the emerging sociology of justice. As a basic departure from nineteenth-century criminology, the sociology of justice may offer ways to obtain genuine relief from crime and punishment. At least it suggests some options that have only begun to be tried, as we shall see.

RECENT CRIMINOLOGY

Rothman's (1971) history of nineteenth-century ideas about crime and punishment is the first of a number of recent works to help make criminologists aware of our own intellectual tradition. Among these works are Foucault (1977), Newman (1978), Haney (1982), Kramer (1982), Rafter (1985), Rothman (1980) again, and now in mental health, Dwyer (1986). What Rothman alone makes clear, and the other works substantiate, is that today's theories of what distinguishes criminals from law-abiding citizens and of what ought to be done to criminals had virtually all been stated and empirically supported by 1900 (Pepinsky 1980a). Today's data sets may be larger, today's statistics more complex by far, but the results come and go pretty much as they did a hundred years ago.

Until recently, ideas of what goes wrong with offenders and how society should respond had moved in cycles. As criminology moved into the twentieth century, there was an extended period of belief that offenders were socially disadvantaged and that community treatment alternatives to prison could help them (Rothman 1980). After World War I, this view gave way to determination to punish and incapacitate "habitual offenders." On the surface, the shift looks remarkably like the one from the penchant for rehabilitation and community treatment in the 1960s toward that for retribution and incapacitation of "career criminals" which began in the mid-1970s (Kramer 1982).

Surface appearances are deceptive. For now at least the cycles have ended. Instead of one set of theories and responses to criminality being supplanted, now previously incompatible theories and responses are accumulating and coexisting. Christie (1981) has traced this post–World War II development of criminology. He purports to speak only of Scandinavian developments, but in reality the sources he cites and the developments he describes are first and foremost American.

As Christie describes it, the most prominent criminology of the 1950s, which followed the lead of the Gluecks (1950), concentrated on understanding why poor youth turned to crime, so that their illness might be diagnosed and they might be rehabilitated. Rehabilitation took hold in the 1960s. While police-recorded crime began a steep climb, Americans took the lead in establishing diversionary, rehabilitative treatment programs—earlier outside penal institutions than inside; in consequence, our incarceration rates dropped.

Struggle for Justice (American Friends Service Committee 1971) heralded a new stage of mainstream criminology. Coerced treatment, enforced rehabilitation, was bound to fail, the AFSC suggested. Opponents of the infliction of pain, such as Christie, were attracted to this message, for in part, it represented a recognition that what we do to offenders is (let's not kid ourselves) painful. Richard Nixon's federal funding to fight crime prompted the recipients of funds to reduce crime reporting, so that police-recorded rates dropped for a couple of years in the early 1970s. But to Christie's chagrin, rationalizations for punishment continued to mount. The police did not want the American public to forget that recorded crime far exceeded its level in 1960, and the American public was prepared to accept that message at face value (Seidman & Couzens 1974; Selke & Pepinsky 1982). Instead of deciding that the failure of punishment was reason to reject the infliction of pain itself, the leading government-funded criminologists sought to find another justification for inflicting pain on offenders. First, claims [as by Erlich (1975) and Wilson (1975)] that more punishment generally deterred crime took hold. But since research on deterrence was a time-honored criminological pursuit with an accompanying tradition of skepticism, these claims as well soon came under attack, and punishment came to be defended as a moral end in itself (Van den Haag 1975, Von Hirsch 1976). Commentators like Van den Haag and Von Hirsch held that criminal justice was corrupt, but not inherently so. Rather, we needed to be more rational, more systematic and "scientific," ensuring that the degree of punishment corresponded to the seriousness of the crime.

This time, though, making the punishment fit the crime did not preclude making the punishment fit the offender, nor did it preclude pursuit of diagnosis and treatment within prisons. The computer made it possible to process data about offenses and offenders so as to compound these factors. As Christie (1981:50–52) points out, the Von Hirsch (1976) report lays down just this kind of ambiguous justification for infliction of pain. After rejecting rehabilitation and deterrence claims, the report in effect tells readers that punishment has to be accepted simply because crime is wrong. It goes on to build in allowance for the dangerousness of offenders as individuals. In a dissent, part of the report stresses that it remains to be seen whether making the punishment fit the crime will serve as a general deterrent. Every justification for punishment remains viable according to the report; the additive statistical models so easy for the criminologists to program into data analysis allow the independent justifications to be tested simultaneously, with repeated variations, on a limited part of large data sets. Officials who want to expand the use of punishment can justify themselves because with enough analyses, some "proof" can be found to affirm that systematically punishing offenders this way or that accomplishes some crime control objective.

Adding independent justification together allowed broad expansion both of criminology and of punishment. American incarceration rates began to rise rapidly in the mid-1970s, just as the Von Hirsch report appeared. It has continued its rapid rise to this day. Legislative reform, as in New York in the later 1970s, encouraged putting more offenders away longer. Academic and official cooperation and unity of purpose now enjoyed a renaissance.

Finally by 1980 (Christie 1981: 65–69), treatment of crime-related parent/child problems was welcomed back into the criminological fold. Expert diagnosticians and therapists were encouraged to open up a growing array of preventive, precriminal justice treatments. Those treated now included potential and actual victims and perpetrators not merely of crimes like child abuse and vehicular homicide but generally of alcoholism, drug dependence, learning disabilities, suicidal tendencies, and the like. Some of these approaches to treatment are, whether providential or diabolical, remarkably inventive. Recently, for instance, my local newspaper carried a boldly illustrated major feature on the newly recognized problem of "sexual addiction," complete with a diagnostic test and information on how to contact an Alcoholics Anonymous–like group for help (*Bloomington/Bedford Sunday Herald-Times,* February 3, 1985: Sec. E, p. 1). One case study centered on a "brilliant" and highly successful, but reportedly tormented, lawyer. Those for whom we cannot prescribe punishment as offenders can instead be systematically gathered into treatment networks. By now, every justification for punishment—retribution, deterrence, incapacitation, and rehabilitation—has assumed a prominent, legitimate place in the criminological and political mainstream. Never has punishment received such broad acceptance in criminal justice; never in American history has it been so pervasive. Today, for example, one in four black men in his twenties is in an American jail or prison.[1] In the whole population, well over twice as many people are on probation and parole (US Dep. of Justice 1984b) as are in jail and prison combined. The system has grown far beyond the capacity of its managers (Pontell 1984). Never have so many criminologists been paid to do so much. As one index, the American Society of Criminology drew over 1000 people as participants in its 1984 annual meeting. But while the bulk of prominent criminological research is more comprehensive than ever, it continues to be a synthesis of old knowledge—new data perhaps, but old findings. That is why Christie calls it at once "neo-classicist" and "neo-positivist."

This revival of nineteenth-century criminology has nothing to do with the political right or left. Indeed, Marxist criminology had been incorporated into the American criminological mainstream even before World War II and, in pure form, is a part of today's complement of notions of how and why poor young men are our worst crooks (Pepinsky 1980a). Those at both ends of the political spectrum accept suppression by the state as the primary means of crime control; their argument is over who ought to be in charge of the state.

The sociology of justice that has emerged in this century transcends distinctions of political left and right. While the ideas in this new field may be branded as radically left by some and radically right by others, the field actually lies off the conventional spectrum; it departs equally from the criminology of the right and of the left.

Nor is the distinction between traditional criminology and the emergent sociology of justice one of good versus evil social scientists. Such sociologists of justice as Christie criticize criminologists not for having bad motives but for failing in their analyses to transcend governmental distinctions between who is law-abiding and who is criminal or in need of treatment. Like criminology, the sociology of justice has expanded in recent years. Its roots, however, lie in scholarship done between the two World Wars.

POINTS OF DEPARTURE FROM NINETEENTH-CENTURY CRIMINOLOGY

Cultural Anthropology

Brogden (1982) has recently observed the remarkable breadth of consensus among social classes in the nineteenth- and twentieth-century that the underclass—the chronically unemployed of the industrial city—deserve to be

---

[1]This estimate is the product of three government figures: (a) that 1.5% of all black men were in prison as of 1982 (US Dep. of Justice 1984c:23); (b) that the rate of imprisonment for men in their twenties is 12 times the average rate for men of all other ages (US Dep. Justice 1983: 1); and (c) that more than half again as many men are in jail as in prison (US Dep. Justice 1984a).

policed. His is an analysis of the growth of police authority in England but applies to many other peoples, including Americans. The consensus unites people from the working class through the elites regarding the legitimate exercise of government power. Even the Communist Manifesto denounced the underclass as "scum." This consensus preceded the Enlightenment in Western societies; Chambliss (1964) and Melossi & Pavarini (1981) have described how it operated centuries earlier with respect to vagrants. Stereotypes about crime and criminality, as manifested for instance in the concept of the "normal primitive" (Swigert & Farrell 1977), are deeply ingrained in many cultures, including our own. It has been recognized in criminological literature for nearly half a century that when the stereotypes are applied to people who happen on some occasion to have misbehaved, a self-fulfilling prophecy can be created so that they become confirmed members of a delinquent or criminal class (Tannenbaum 1938; see also Lemert 1967).

One way of escaping this kind of cultural bind is to study cultures where the concepts or stereotypes we use are not applied. Cultural anthropologists have paved the way for this quest for new knowledge (see Nader & Parnell 1983). The first to draw the concept of crime into question was Malinowski (1951, originally 1926). He was unable to let go of the concept itself but broadened it to include an "outburst of passion" that might or might not entail violation of a taboo. Radcliffe-Brown (1933) called acts "crimes" when they generated moral outrage throughout a community and noted that responses could be restitutive rather than punitive. Llewellyn & Hoebel (1941) brought to our attention a Native American tradition among the Cheyenne of resolving disputes by empowering "offenders" to rejoin normal community life rather than by incapacitating or hurting them. Offenders, then, could be seen as normal people who occasionally slipped, rather than as a dangerous class that needed to be policed. The line between criminals and law-abiding citizens might not necessarily be drawn as Americans particularly and Westerners generally had become wont to do. Hurtful behavior might instead be viewed as a temporary, reparable rupture in the fabric of social relations.

White-Collar Crime

Sutherland (1940) coined the term "white-collar crime" in his 1939 Presidential Address to the American Sociological Society. He completed a more exhaustive study of the topic before his untimely death in 1950 (Sutherland 1949, 1983). Even within legally proscribed categories, Sutherland found crime to be especially prevalent (and especially harmful to society) among persons of wealth and position, persons who were virtually immune from ordinary law enforcement, prosecution, and punishment for their crimes.

Sutherland began with the observation that the apparent extent of undetected, unreported, and unpunished crime among the well-to-do called the full range of traditional explanations of criminality into serious question. Correlates of poverty had been used to explain crime, but suppose in fact that the poor on average committed fewer and less serious crimes than the rich?

It is a challenge to detach oneself from one's political ethos to examine this supposition. It has become clear that whether we consider an act a crime depends crucially on our preconceptions about who looks like an offender or a victim (see generally Wilkins 1984, or specifically Joseph 1979). If we give respondents cues that we are asking about "crime" in victim and self-report surveys, crime may appear to be associated with poverty. This is so because we depend primarily on government for news about crime, and government tells us that the crooks it finds, in the places where it looks, are poor (Pepinsky 1980b:120–42, 197–244). But if, for instance, we start from the premise that doctors as portrayed in hospital and medical insurance records are no less suspect than poor people as portrayed in police reports, we can apply FBI operational definitions to show that physicians alone are involved in more murders and thefts than all street criminals put together (Reiman 1984; Pepinsky & Jesilow 1985). Is the common finding, the common "knowledge," that poverty breeds more and worse crime than wealth and power a sign that the poor are more crooked or that the transgressions of the rich are more likely to be overlooked or more readily rationalized (Cressey 1953)? Proof one way or the other may be impossible. Meanwhile, Sutherland's theoretical breakthrough was to recognize that as long as we remain free of political bias, we must remain agnostic about who is more crooked than whom (Pepinsky 1976:25–43).

History of Punishment

In the fertile period of criminological inquiry prior to World War II, Rusche & Kirchheimer (1939) made another fundamental breakthrough. They noted that trends and means of punishing offenders could be analyzed independently of the causes of crime or the identity of offenders. While the anthropologists had begun to indicate the rich variety of ways people might manage human conflict, Rusche & Kirchheimer suggested that the ways offenders were punished (a subclass of the ways we manage conflict) varied not in response to sins but rather as a function of our various means of establishing and maintaining different forms of political and economic organization. As industrial laborers became necessary, workhouses became a dominant form of punishment for offenders. When industrial development lagged behind expansion of the available work force, "work" in prison became nonproductive punishment, aimed at what Foucault (1977) has since called discipline. Thus, independently of the study of the causes and cures of criminality, one might study trends and shifts in the history of punishment.

A SOCIOLOGY OF JUSTICE

A New Order of Problem

Building on these departures from nineteenth-century criminology is like trying to solve a Zen *koan* or riddle: We know the fear and pain that crime causes, and we know many ways to inflict pain (to punish criminals) in response. Yet for all we can see or do, the classes of criminals we punish may be those that harm us less than certain classes of persons we respect and emulate. Thus, for all we know, the pain we reserve for those we brand criminal may be as unjust and hurtful as the pain wrought by criminals. If we cast aside the arbitrary class bias in legislation, the punishment we inflict may be no less "criminal" than the crime we suffer. Might we explain and lessen the pain of crime more by committing the crime of punishment less ourselves? Or, can we explain and address the injustice criminals do their victims without doing injustice to isolated classes of offenders?

Over the past two or three decades, a growing number of criminologists have confronted this riddle and begun to spell out a solution: Crime may be defined to entail the kinds of physical loss and pain the law recognizes (see Sellin & Wolfgang, 1964), or it may not. Regardless of what the law says, the emerging genre of literature says *people are offended and threatened by being unable to share information with significant others*. This theory holds that you can be hurt by others without being offended. You will be offended if you sense that people you believe yourself dependent upon are unaccountable or will not listen to you, even if you suffer no tangible loss or injury at their hands. Offenses may include, but not be limited to, acts known as crime and the counter-offenses called punishment. Violence generally is traceable to blockages in information flow. According to this theory, peace depends on information flowing freely among people, a state of affairs particularly well described by Buddhists as "compassion" (Ikeda 1982; see also Quinney 1982). In the remainder of this review, I describe and illustrate foundations of this emerging theoretical framework for analyzing problems of justice.

The major threat that social isolation poses to many of today's urban elderly is a case in point [a plight well described by Merry (1981) in the United States and by Balvig (1979) in Scandinavia]. Many older people in cities today fear that people around them will not notice if they get hurt or are dying. The threats caused by isolation can be pervasive: Older people fear that if they get sick or fall while alone in their apartment, no one may find them for days or weeks; that if they run short of money, no one may offer food or warm clothing; that if a stranger on the streets wants their money, there may be no one willing to defend them. People who are thus threatened and offended by their circumstances may attribute their apprehension to delinquent kids in the neighborhood, if only because other people take their complaints seriously only when they speak in terms of street crime and criminals. These victims of social isolation may even convince themselves that neighborhood youths embody the global threat they face. As Merry (1981) has discovered, however, (*a*) such victims' fear of crime is far out of proportion to the risk of unlawful behavior they face, and (*b*) the youths they identify as threats are usually not the ones who steal from and assault neighborhood residents. The victimization is real, but describing the victimization conventionally in terms of street crimes and criminals is highly misleading. A person who is socially secure can experience a burglary or theft as a fleeting annoyance; a person who is isolated may experience terror at the mere prospect of such an event. Measuring the threat in terms of goods stolen or blows inflicted by criminals ignores the heart of the problem and leaves the victim's pain largely unaddressed.

Christie's (1981) thesis is people's failure to share information—which he calls failure of "knowledge"—is the first of several basic conditions that permit people to inflict pain on one another, either as crime or as punishment. To be willing to rape, steal from, or imprison people, you have to detach yourself from them (see also Milgram 1965), neither accounting to them for your actions nor observing their responses to your actions. As long as people exchange information freely with one another, Christie believes they will be virtually incapable of the intent, let alone the act, of inflicting pain on one another. Opening channels of communication thus becomes a primary means to reduce violence of all kinds, including conventional street crime and punishment of offenders.

Leslie Wilkins has been working for over 20 years to understand and articulate the significance of patterns of information flow. He became world-renowned in the 1950s for developing an instrument to predict whether boys would violate the law once released from juvenile institutions (Mannheim & Wilkins 1955). In the early 1960s, he abandoned efforts to predict and explain criminal behavior entirely; he began to examine and design systems people could use to process information about crime and punishment (beginning with Wilkins 1964). He disclaimed the ability to discern either real crime or right decisions about what to do to offenders. He held that levels of crime depended on varying propensities of people to be offended. What mattered was not prejudging what ought to be deemed crime or what ought to be done to offenders, but rather opening to the participation of all concerned the systems by which such decisions were made. Thus, in the design of parole guidelines, his major concern was to inform inmates about parole board policies and to keep such policies open to review and change as inmates presented new kinds of cases (see Gottfredson et al 1978). In his latest book, his emphasis is on analyzing how to "democratize" the systems by which citizens learn of and inform criminal justice policy (Wilkins 1984). Wilkins makes explicit a causal connection between crime and punishment on the one hand and exchange of information on the other.

Some other general works in the field fall into a similar line of argument, finding that crime and punishment increase as information gets locked into certain channels, proposing that we resolve problems of crime and punishment by freeing the flow of information among the parties concerned. Tifft & Sullivan (1980) speak of the free flow of information in economic terms, as "mutual aid," in much the same way that Kennedy (1970) speaks of moving "beyond incrimination." Quinney (1970) won wide attention for describing crime and punishment as arising from restricted definitions of situations or "social realities" that perpetuate and extend fear and violence. Most recently, in the speech he gave accepting the American Society of Criminology's 1984 Edwin H. Sutherland Award, Quinney suggested that if we let ourselves know our immediate surroundings more closely and directly, we might succeed in freeing ourselves from crime, which he calls "one of the predominant myths of our contemporary culture" (Quinney 1985:9). Those who have begun to articulate the sociology of justice find that crime and punishment are not particular acts, but forms of the human failure to attend to one another throughout courses of action. Christie and Wilkins, in particular, suggest that criminologists should focus on mechanisms for accountability for those who pass judgment on others, and for granting complainants standing to be heard—giving and hearing information. In so doing, they join others who would extend criminology beyond its current study of why people break laws and what criminal justice officials can do about it. Such scholars recommend asking broader questions: How does violence arise; what are the mechanisms of social control people use publicly and privately; are those mechanisms just or unjust (see e.g. Streib 1977; Myren 1980; Cavender 1984; Williams 1984)?

The emerging sociology of justice has begun to suggest new ways to reduce the threat of crime and punishment. As addressed in the following section, some of the research concerns how to organize people to help keep problems of crime and punishment from arising in the first place—on general prevention— while other research concerns how to resolve problems that are called crime without resort to punishment—specific prevention.

Research on the General Prevention of Crime and Punishment

Galtung (1969) begins to distinguish general prevention as traditionally approached in criminology from general prevention in the emerging sociology of justice. Violence, he observes, can be opposed in two ways: Negatively, by using further violence, or positively, by reorganizing violent social structures peacefully, without repressing personal villains. Fellow Norwegian criminologist Christie (1981) turns from his critique of criminology to a description of two Scandinavian communities, Vidaraasen in Norway (see also Christie 1982a) and Kristiania in Denmark, where crime and punishment are virtually inconceivable. He infers five structural conditions that appear to enable members of these communities to coexist, in his terms, without inflicting pain on one another: Members know one another personally; power is not monopolized by any group; those who pass judgment on others are likewise vulnerable to their subjects; members are manifestly interdependent [much as Tifft & Sullivan (1980) call for "mutual aid"]; and members believe each human body contains a "sacred soul" (this is much like the position taken by Quinney 1980). Elsewhere, Christie argues that such communities must be small and "tight" (Christie 1982b). In these ways, he summarizes elements of a social structure that enable information to flow relatively freely among a community's members.

Most research on general prevention of this kind has been done by noncriminologists. Assuming the trend continues of broadening programs from "criminology" to "justice studies," these researchers should become more visible in the field. Among them are anthropologists studying groups, such as the Hutterites, which behave peaceably while living in much the structural form Christie outlined (for instance, dividing communities before they grow much past 100 members and choosing leaders by lot so as to resist the arrogance of power; see Bennett 1967). This kind of research, specifically as it concerns law and social control, has sometimes been done by nonanthropologists explicitly. We may hope to see more work like Schwartz's (1954) classic comparative study of Israeli kibbutzim in years to come.

But what about general crime prevention in the industrialized city? Urban planner Jacobs (1961) has described architectural ways of enhancing flows of information among those who circulate through "healthy" neighborhoods. Her prescription for maintaining variety in and around city blocks dovetails nicely with implications of studies of urban burglary patterns, or—once again—findings by cultural anthropologists (Pepinsky 1980b:109–10).

There is a rapidly expanding literature on organizing workplaces so as to enhance accountability and the standing that allows workers to be heard. Oakeshott (1978) has evaluated well the viability and justice of various forms of distributing ownership rights. Mondragon, a thriving community of 150 worker-owned enterprises in Basque Spain exemplifies the careful planning of shared ownership and managerial rights and duties [see Gutierrez-Johnson (1984) for a recent update of trends there]. Worker satisfaction is high in Mondragon, absenteeism and labor strife low—the one strike in more than a quarter century occurred at the only enterprise larger than several hundred worker-owners (Henk & Logan 1982).

The relation between patterns of ownership and crime has repeatedly been established. Contrast, for instance, the pattern of owner complicity in employee theft in *Talley's Corner* (Liebow 1967) to the dramatic drop in inventory loss in a pair of supermarkets in South Philadelphia when workers bought out A & P (Lindenfeld 1984). Jesilow (1982), who found that risk of auto repair fraud drops when the owner is on the work premises, concluded that Adam Smith (1937, originally 1776) was correct: When forces like laws of incorporation help aggrandize and depersonalize ownership, customers get cheated. This is the theoretical foundation Pepinsky & Jesilow (1985:143–56) used to build their proposals for crime prevention.

In sum, the theoretical and empirical groundwork for research, in the sociology of justice, on general prevention has been laid, but the work has just begun.

Research on Specific Prevention of the "Crime and Punishment" Syndrome

Research on how to respond peacefully once cases of crime or punishment have occurred flows more directly from past work in criminology. Findings suggest that the starting point is to let conflicting parties speak for themselves—to include their perspective on the conflicts in the criminological information network. Criminologists have long done such studies but recently have begun expanding them to include persons not previously interviewed, such as prison guards (Lombardo 1981) and families of death-row inmates (Smykla 1984).

Criminology researchers have gone on to suggest how we might extend the hearing we give offenders and victims. Korn (1971) proposes that we give poor defendants in our courts the same standard of justice that persons in business commonly accord elite members of their own group. Christie (1977) speaks of letting conflicts belong to the parties involved. Brady (1981a,b, 1982) and Longmire (1981) argue on some points but agree generally on the necessity for a "popular justice" much like that which Christie describes. Specific proposals are beginning to emerge from studies of how police can be made more closely accountable, both for their policies and their practices, to residents of the communities they patrol (Jones & Winkler 1982; Pepinsky 1984).

A few experiments have been made at reforming conflict management squarely within our own criminal justice system. The accountability that Wilkins built into parole guidelines has already been mentioned. Until the governor fired him, Tom Murton (the prototype for the film character "Brubaker") managed to end violence in and around Arkansas prisons by giving inmates genuine self-government both on matters of policy and in disciplinary proceedings (Murton & Hyams 1970). Witty (1980) is at the forefront of the anthropological study of mediation mechanisms in other societies; she has used her knowledge to help design and evaluate one of the more innovative "Neighborhood Justice Centers," in Boston. Created out of the experience of the Mennonite community in Northern Indiana, victim and offender reconciliation programs (VORPs) have sought to give victims a safe outlet for fear and anger, offenders an opportunity to be seen and heard in their own defense, and the two together a chance to work out a way to transcend retribution and settle their differences (Immarigeon 1984). Similar programs are being started in Britain (Marshall 1985). It is a challenge for these programs to escape cooptation into doing the courts' business of punishing offenders; some apparently succeed. As Immarigeon (1984) notes, the idea of reconciliation is radically opposed to that of punishment—even to milder variants like restitution. Reconciliation seeks to *increase* the involvement of the offender in the victim's life and hence also to increase the offender's power to heal the conflict. Punishment and its variants, by contrast, are ways of taking power away from offenders and of isolating them from victims. Underlying this entire genre of experimentation is the idea of making those who would handle disputes accountable to offenders and victims and of increasing the standing of offenders and victims to be heard on how to manage and prevent conflict.

Within the emerging sociology of justice, the study of prevention rests on the finding that crime and punishment increase where accountability and standing to be heard are curtailed among community members—where some members monopolize the flow of the information that affects others. The research is in its infancy but offers new hope for preventing the cycle of crime and punishment, either by forestalling its beginning, or by preventing escalation once the cycle has begun.

CONCLUSION

Within the sociology of justice, punishing offenders is considered a part of the crime problem, not a solution. Sociologists of justice explore the possibility that crime and punishment arise together out of violent social structures— violent, in the sense that the flow of information among groups of people is confined and restricted. Building on work begun a half century ago, today's sociologists of justice are beginning to find ways that communities can organize both to forestall crime and to help victims without punishing offenders when crime does occur. We live in a time and place where fear of crime and punishment of offenders escalate in a vicious spiral, from which traditional criminology offers no means of escape. The sociology of justice suggests an alternative.

ACKNOWLEDGMENTS

Special thanks go to Jim Short, Bob Bohm, Jill Bystydzienski, David Friedrichs, Bob Lilly, Dick Myren, Graeme Newman, Harold B. Pepinsky, Pauline N. Pepinsky, Henry Pontell, John Smykla, and Larry Tifft, who have helped me to rethink and rewrite what appears here, although they may continue to take issue with what I say.

Literature Cited

American Friends Service Committee. 1971. *Struggle for Justice*. New York: Hill & Wang

Balvig, F. 1979. Om aeldre kvinders angst for kriminalitet (On older women's anxiety about criminality). Rapport fra Kontaktseminaren, Sundvolden, 1979. Oslo: Scand. Council Criminol.

Bennett, J. W. 1967. *Hutterite Brethren: The Agricultural Economy and Social Organization of a Communal People*. Stanford, Calif: Stanford Univ. Press

Bloomington/Bedford Sunday Herald-Times. 1985. Sexual addiction. February 3, 1985: Sec. E, p. 1. Bloomington, Ind.

Brady, J. P. 1981a. The revolution comes of age: Law, order, and political development in Cuba. In *Crime, Justice, and Underdevelopment*, ed. Colin Sumner, pp. 248–315. London: Heinemann

Brady, J. P. 1981b. Towards a popular justice in the United States: The dialectics of community action. *Contemp. Crises* 5:155–92

Brady, J. P. 1982. *Justice and Politics in People's China: Legal Order or Continuing Revolution?* New York: Academic

Brogden, M. 1982. *The Police: Autonomy and Consent*. London/New York: Academic

Cavender, G. 1984. A critique of sentencing reform. *Justice Q.* 1:1–16

Chambliss, W. J. 1964. A sociological analysis of the law of vagrancy. *Soc. Probl.* 12:66–77

Christie, N. 1977. Conflicts as property. *Br. J. Criminol.* 17:1–19

Christie, N. 1981. *Limits to Pain*. New York: Oxford Univ. Press

Christie, N. 1982a. Det er vi som taper (It is we who lose). *Forskningsnytt* 27(1/2):46–47

Christie, N. 1982b. *Hvor Tett et Samfunn?* (How tight a society?) Oslo: Univ. Press

Cressey, D. T. 1953. *Other People's Money: The Social Psychology of Embezzlement*. New York: Free Press

Dwyer, E. 1986. *Homes for the Mad: Life Inside Two Nineteenth-Century Lunatic Asylums*. New Brunswick, NJ: Rutgers Univ. Press. In press

Ehrlich, I. 1975. The deterrent effect of capital punishment: A question of life and death. *Am. Econ. Rev.* 65 (June):397–417

Foucault, M. 1977. *Discipline and Punish: The Birth of the Prison*. Transl. A. Sheridan. New York: Pantheon

Galtung, J. 1969. Violence, peace, and peace research. *J. Peace Res.* 6:167–91

Glueck, S., Glueck, E. T. 1950. *Unraveling Juvenile Delinquency*. Cambridge, Mass: Harvard Univ. Press

Gottfredson, D. M., Wilkins, L. T., Hoffman,

P. B. 1978. *Guidelines for Parole and Sentencing*. Lexington, Mass: Lexington

Gutierrez-Johnson, A. 1984. The Mondragon model of cooperative enterprise: Conditions concerning its success and transferability. *Changing Work* 1:35–41

Haney, C. 1982. Criminal justice and the nineteenth-century paradigm: The triumph of psychological individualism in the 'Formative era.' *Law Hum. Behav.* 6(3/4):191–235

Henk, T., Logan, C. 1982). *Mondragon: An Economic Analysis*. London/Boston: Allen & Unwin

Ikeda, D. 1982. *Life: An Enigma, a Precious Jewel*. Transl. C. S. Terry. New York: Harper & Row

Immarigeon, R. 1984. Victom-offender reconciliation programs and the criminal justice system: Confusion and challenge. *VORP Network News* 3(4):7–9

Jacobs, J. 1961. *The Death and Life of Great American Cities*. New York: Random

Jesilow, P. 1982. Adam Smith and white-collar crime. *Criminology* 20:319–28

Joseph, J. M. 1979. *The effects of cost to the victim and legitimate freedom on character evaluation, blame and decision to punish*. PhD thesis. Albany: State Univ. NY.

Jones, J., Winkler, W. T. 1982. Beyond the beat: Policing in the riotous city. *J. Law Soc.* 9:103–14

Kennedy, M. D. 1970. Beyond incrimination: Some neglected facets of the theory of punishment. *Catalyst* 5:1–17

Korn, R. 1971. Of crime, criminal justice and corrections. *Univ. San Francisco Law Rev.* 6:27–75

Kramer, R. C. 1982. From 'habitual offenders' to career criminals: The historical development of criminal categories. *Law Hum. Behav.* 6(3/4):273–93

Lemert, E. M. 1967. *Human Deviance Social Problems, and Social Control*. Englewood Cliffs, NJ: Prentice-Hall

Liebow, E. 1967. *Tally's Corner*. Boston: Little, Brown

Lindenfeld, F. 1984. O & O markets: The labor and cooperative movements get together. *Changing Work* 1:42–46

Llewellyn, K. N., Hoebel, E. 1941. *The Cheyenne Way: Conflict and Case Law in Primitive Jurisprudence*. Norman: Univ. Okla. Press

Lombardo, L. X. 1981. *Guards Imprisoned: Correctional Officers*. New York: Elsevier

Longmire, D. 1981. A popular justice system: A radical alternative to the traditional criminal justice system. *Contemp. Crises* 5:15–30

Malinowski, F. 1951. *Crime and Custom in*

Savage Society (Originally published in 1926). New York: Humanities

Mannheim, H., Wilkins, L. T. 1955. *Prediction Methods in Relation to Borstal Training.* London: Her Majesty's Stat. Off.

Marshall, T. F. 1985. British initiatives in mediation and dispute resolution. *Home Off. Res. Plan. Unit Res. Bull.* 19:5–8

Melossi, D., Pavarini, M. 1981. *The Prison and the Factory: Origins of the Penitentiary System.* Transl. C. Gousin. Totowa, NJ: Barnes & Noble

Merry, S. E. 1981. *Urban Danger.* Philadelphia: Temple Univ. Press

Milgram, S. 1965. Some conditions of obedience and disobedience to authority. *Hum. Rel.* 18:57–75

Murton, T. O., Hyams, J. 1970. *Accomplices to the Crime.* New York: Grove

Myren, R. A. 1980. Justiciology: An idea whose time has come. *Just. Rep.* 1(April 19):1–7

Nader, L., Parnell, P. 1983. Comparative criminal law and enforcement: Preliterate societies. In *Encyclopedia of Criminal Justice,* ed. S. Kadish, pp. 200–7. New York: Macmillan

Newman, G. R. 1978. *The Punishment Response.* Philadelphia: Lippincott

Oakeshott, R. 1978. *The Case for Workers' Co-ops.* London/Boston: Routledge & Kegan Paul

Pepinsky, H. E. 1976. *Crime and Conflict: A Study of Law and Society.* New York: Academic

Pepinsky, H. E. 1980a. A radical alternative to 'Radical' criminology. In *Radical Criminology: The Coming Crises.* ed. J. A. Inciardi. Beverly Hills, Calif: Sage

Pepinsky, H. E. 1980b. *Crime Control Strategies.* New York: Oxford Univ. Press

Pepinsky, H. E. 1984. Better living through police discretion. *Law Contemp. Probl.* 47:249–67

Pepinsky, H. E., Jesilow, P. 1985. *Myths That Cause Crime.* Cabin John, Md: Seven Locks. Rev. ed.

Pontell, H. N. 1984. *A Capacity to Punish: The Ecology of Crime and Punishment.* Bloomington: Ind. Univ. Press

Quinney, R. 1970. *The Social Reality of Crime.* Boston: Little, Brown

Quinney, R. 1980. *Providence: Reconstruction of Social and Moral Order.* New York: Longman

Quinney, R. 1982. *Social Existence: Metaphysics, Marxism, and the Social Sciences.* Beverly Hills, Calif.: Sage

Quinney, R. 1985. Myth and the art of criminology. *Legal Stud. Forum.* In press

Radcliffe-Brown, A. R. 1933. Primitive law. In *Encyclopedia of Social Sciences,* ed. E. R.

A. Seligman, pp. 202–6. New York: Macmillan

Rafter, N. H. 1985. *Partial Justice: Women in State Prisons, 1800–1935.* Boston: Northeastern Univ. Press

Reiman, J. 1984. *The Rich Get Richer and the Poor Get Prison.* New York: Wiley. 2nd ed.

Rothman, D. J. 1971. *Discovery of the Asylum: Social Order and Disorder in the New Republic.* Boston: Little, Brown

Rothman, D. J. 1980. *Conscience and Convenience: The Asylum and Its Alternatives in Progressive America.* Boston: Little, Brow

Rusche, F., Kirchheimer, O. 1939. *Punishment and Social Structure.* New York: Columbia Univ. Press

Schwartz, R. D. 1954. Social factors in the development of legal control: A case study of two Israeli settlements. *Yale Law J.* 63 (Feb.):471–91

Seidman, D., Couzens, M. 1974. Getting the crime rate down: Political pressure and crime reporting. *Law Soc. Rev.* 8:457–93

Selke, W. L., Pepinsky, H. E. 1982. Police reporting in Indianapolis, 1948–78. *Law Hum. Behav.* 6(3/4):327–42

Sellin, T., Wolfgang, M. E. 1964. *Can Delinquency Be Measured?* New York: Wiley

Smith, A. 1937. *An Inquiry into the Nature and Causes of the Wealth of Nations.* (Originally published 1776.) New York: Modern Library

Smykla, J. 1984. *The people on death row only die once but the family dies a hundred times.* Paper presented at Ann. Meet. Acad. Crim. Just. Sci., Chicago, March 27, 1984

Streib, V. L. 1977. Expanding a traditional criminal justice curriculum into an innovative social control curriculum. *J. Crim. Just.* 5:165–69

Sutherland, E. H. 1940. White-collar criminality. *Am. Sociol Rev.* 5:1–12

Sutherland, E. H. 1949. *White-Collar Crime.* New York: Dryden Press

Sutherland, E. H. 1983. *White-Collar Crime: The Unexpurgated Edition.* (Ed. G. Geis.) Westport, Conn. Greenwood

Swigert, V. L., Farrell, K. A. 1977. Normal homicides and the law. *Am. Sociol. Rev.* 42 (Feb.):16–32

Tannenbaum, F. 1938. *Crime and the Community.* Boston: Ginn

Tifft, L., Sullivan, D. 1980. *The Struggle to be Human: Crime, Criminology, and Anarchism.* Over the Water, Sanday, Orkney, UK: Cienfuegos

United States Department of Justice, Bureau of Justice Statistics. 1983. Prisoners in 1982. *Bur. Just. Stat. Bull.* (April)

United States Department of Justice. 1984a. The 1983 jail census. *Bur. Just. Stat. Bull.* (November)

United States Department of Justice. 1984b. Probation and parole 1983. *Bur. Just. Stat. Bull.* (September)

United States Department of Justice, Bureau of Justice Statistics. 1984c. Prisoners 1982 in State and Federal Institutions. *Prisoner Stat. Bull.* (August)

Van den Haag, E. 1975. *Punishing Criminals: Concerning a Very Old and Painful Question.* New York: Basic

Von Hirsch, 1975. *Doing Justice: The Choice of Punishment.* New York: Hill & Wang

Wilkins, L. T. 1984. *Consumerist Criminology.* London: Heinemann

Wilkins, L. T. 1964. *Social Deviance: Social Action, Policy, and Research.* Englewood Cliffs, NJ: Prentice-Hall

Williams, F. P. III. 1984. The demise of the criminological imagination: A critique of recent criminology. *Just. Q.* 1:91–106

Wilson, J. Q. 1975. *Thinking About Crime.* New York: Basic

Witty, C. J. 1980. *Mediation and Society: Conflict Management In Lebanon.* New York: Academic

Ann. Rev. Sociol. 1986. 12:109–30

THE TRANSITION TO ADULTHOOD

Dennis P. Hogan and Nan Marie Astone

Department of Sociology, University of Chicago, Chicago, Illinois 60637

INTRODUCTION

An enormous amount of research on the transition to adulthood in America is founded on early landmark studies that include *Elmtown's Youth* by August B. Hollingshead (1961), *The Adolescent Society* by James Coleman (1961), and the report of the Presidential Panel on Youth (1974). Research culminating in what has become known as the Wisconsin model of status attainment focused attention on the transition to adulthood; the study found that social psychological and institutional factors operating in adolescence mediated the effects of socioeconomic origins on educational attainment, occupational attainment, and earnings (Sewell & Hauser 1975). More recently, concern with high levels of premarital adolescent pregnancy among blacks and rising levels among whites prompted a great many studies on the antecedents and consequences of a premature transition to parenthood (Chilman 1980). Similarly, high levels of youth unemployment stimulated investigation of the process by which young people make the transition to full-time worker (Stephenson 1979). Scholarly interest in changes in the family life course has led to research on historical changes in the transition to adulthood (Modell et al 1976, Winsborough 1978, Hogan 1981). Researchers' work on labor markets and socioeconomic attainments led to study of the nature of careers (Spenner et al 1982, Elder 1985a). At the same time, new and better techniques for the collection and analysis of event history data have been developed (Hannan & Tuma 1979).

The transition from adolescent to adult has long been of interest to students of human development. During the period of adolescence, young people grow to their full adult size, undergo the hormonal and physical changes associated with puberty, and attain reproductive maturity. Piaget has defined the cognitive task of adolescence as the achievement of formal operational reasoning (see Mussen 1970, Keating 1980). Personality development during adolescence has been

109

0360-0572/86/0815-0109$02.00

characterized by Erikson (1950) as the acquisition of the individual identity necessary for intimacy in adulthood. The social transitions characterizing the passage to adulthood include the completion of school, labor-force entry, marriage, and parenthood (Panel on Youth 1974).

Sociological research on these social demographic transitions has provided us with an enormous amount of information about the transition to adulthood, much of it intended to address particular policy issues rather than advance our general understanding. As a result many studies have focused on one kind of transition at a time, largely neglecting population-level cultural and in-stitutional influences on, and the social historical context of, the process. Potential between-group differences in the transition process too often have been ignored. Intentionality in transition behavior continues to be neglected, in part because longitudinal data on preferences and behaviors is lacking. To overcome these problems, we advocate the use of a population perspective in studies of the transition to adulthood.

Research on human development has specified a series of ordered stages through which an individual passes in his or her life and which are associated from one stage to the next with age (that is, age-grading). Though some persons may fail to progress from one stage to the next, each stage represents a launching point for the next, and thus individuals cannot skip a developmental stage or reverse a developmental transition (Clausen 1985). Featherman (1985) has observed that such a conceptualization of development is overly restrictive, since the analyst must specify a priori both origin and destination states and the reversibility of transitions is ignored.

Featherman suggests that development minimally involves any state-to-state transition in which the transition rate increases or decreases with duration of time in the origin state. To determine whether the rate of transition from one state to another increases or decreases accordingly, or whether or not the rate is duration dependent, it is necessary to study the transition at the population level.

Consideration from the population level of the transition to adulthood clari-fies the role institutional factors play in shaping people's lives. Because we believe that institutional arrangements are of crucial importance in choices people make, throughout this paper we will use *pathway* when we refer to the life course of an individual. We believe that *pathway* (a course laid out for people, strongly encouraging them to take a particular route to get from one place to another) is a more accurate way to describe the particular series of transitions an individual makes than *trajectory* (which implies a greater amount of individual initiative than actually occurs).

A final advantage of a population-level perspective is that it simplifies the consideration of subgroup differences in the transition to adulthood. In America the experience of becoming an adult is different for individuals in different race and class groups as well as different for those of the two sexes. The meaning and mechanisms of these differences are easier to discern when the focus is on individuals viewed in their social and institutional contexts, and on the multi-dimensional character of the life course.

Although we acknowledge the importance of the biological and psychological dimensions of the transition to adulthood, page limitations prevent us from reviewing that literature in detail. Useful reviews of these aspects of the transition to adulthood are available in Adelson (1980). In what follows we selectively review research on the demographic transitions that make up the transition to adulthood. We emphasize the research's shortcomings in the hope of provoking sociologists to move on to more interesting research questions in future studies.

BECOMING AN ADULT IN AMERICA

Multidimensionality of the Transition to Adulthood

In small societies with a simple division of labor, a single age system may be used to determine a multiplicity of familial, work, religious, and political roles (Neugarten & Datan 1973). Foner & Kertzer (1978) described 21 African age-set societies in which named age groups are recognized and there are formal rites of passage marking the transition of age-group members to the next named age-grade. In such societies, individuals become adults at a particular age, upon accomplishment of some specified task, or on a particular date with others born within some specified period of time, and this passage to adulthood is formally signified. In more complex societies certain ceremonies (for example, Jewish bar mitzvoth, Christian confirmations, and debutante balls) symbolize that a young person is growing up. However, the society makes no formal, explicit association between the physical, psychological, and social transitions that take place as individuals move from adolescence to adulthood. There is, rather, an implicit association by members of society of these roles with each other and with a person's age.

Age-Grading of Transitions

Transitions are age-graded if exposure to the risk of a transition begins at birth, or some other specified age, and the rate of transition depends on the length of time in the exposed state. The extent of age-grading varies across individuals depending on their biological heritage and the cultural and social environment in which they are growing up (Featherman & Lerner 1985). This means that the pace of biological, psychological, and social development may differ between individuals, and there need be no uniformity in the ordering in which developmental stages on the different dimensions occur. Thus, the lives of young people are made up of various pathways to adulthood, producing differences in the aging process for each individual (Featherman 1985, Featherman & Lerner 1985, Riley 1985).

Transition To Adulthood As a Process

In light of this complexity, the transition to adulthood is better described as a process than as an event. Childhood, youth, and adulthood are defined by the role-complex characteristic of each (Fry & Keith 1982, Riley 1985). Although most young persons eventually achieve all of the roles that define adulthood, some persons (for example, those who remain childless) do not, but they are socially recognized as adults nonetheless (Modell et al 1976). More generally, the occurrence, timing, and sequence of social roles in different spheres of public and private life define the unique life-course pathways of Americans (Elder 1978, Hagestad & Neugarten 1985, Neugarten & Datan 1973). The distribution of persons across developmental states and the movement of people from one state to another are relevant. Differences in transition rates are the focus of much empirical research in this area (Hannan & Tuma 1979, Hogan 1984, Sørensen 1980, Teachman 1982), although Featherman (1985) has suggested that differences in duration dependence of rates also are of critical importance to understanding different processes of development (for example, see Featherman & Sørensen 1983).

Duration Dependence

In the case of positive duration dependence, the rate of moving from one state to the next increases as an individual spends more time in an origin state, acquiring the skills or resources needed to move on to the next developmental state. The most common examples of positive duration dependence involve psychological or social transitions that are based on the biological changes associated with adolescence. For example, young black women who are virgins are increasingly likely to initiate sexual activity during each succeeding month as they grow older (Hogan & Kitagawa 1985; also see Presser 1978). Rapid initiation of sexual activity may result from the persuasive skills of a dating partner (who at successive ages is increasingly likely to be a nonvirgin), the reduced parental supervision and more permissive living situations associated with later adolescence, and an increased desire on the part of the teenager to become sexually active like her peers (Antonovoski et al 1980, Bolton 1980, Chilman 1979, Coleman 1980, Collins 1974, Miller & Simon 1980).

Negative duration dependence indicates that a particular transition becomes less likely as more time is spent in the origin state. For example, the reversibility of a transition may become less likely as individuals become more practiced in the skills or roles entailed in the destination state, as with departure from the parental home and establishment of an independent residence. Intermediate transition states (such as student dormitories or military barracks) may provide an institutional framework for this learning process (Goldscheider & DeVanzo 1986). There has been considerable interest in part-time employment while in school as a mechanism for socializing students for full-time employment (Shore 1972), although the types of jobs commonly held by teens seem to minimize such effects (Greenberger & Steinberg 1981, Steinberg 1982, Stephenson 1979).

The analyst must be cautious in attempting to measure duration dependence of rates. Some transitions may not display positive or negative duration dependence at all ages. This situation occurs when the transition is biologically based, with some individuals never exposed to risk. For example, the rate of first pregnancy among black women displays positive duration dependence through age 20, but at older ages this will change to negative duration dependence as the population at risk increasingly consists only of those persons who are unable to bear a child or wish to remain childless (Hogan & Kitagawa 1985). Other transition events may temporarily modify the duration dependence of a transition. For example in nineteenth century Italy, rates of migration from the community of birth displayed negative duration dependence but became positive for women of marriageable age, since many husbands came from other communities, and patterns of postnuptial residence were patrilocal (Hogan & Kertzer 1985). Thus, the duration dependence of rates will only be correctly measured if the analyst has controlled for relevant sources of population heterogeneity.

Linkages Between Transitions

The researcher must thus be aware that the transition to adulthood occurs in a variety of dimensions and that the individual demographic transitions and developmental stages occur in different orders and times for different individuals. In addition the researcher needs to recognize that the various transitions and stages influence each other. Although this area is critically important, it is plagued by methodological problems.

Several researchers have used simultaneous equation models to represent the reciprocal effects of two or more transition events (such as schooling and marriage) in the lives of individuals (Marini 1978a, 1984c; Moore & Hofferth 1980; Voss 1975). The statistical estimation of unique effects in such models requires the careful selection of instrumental variables (Clarridge 1985). This may be particularly difficult in cases of closely linked transitions with common determinants. While the magnitude of the effects remains a subject of contention, this research indicates that an additional year of schooling delays marriage more among women than among men, and that early marriage hinders additional schooling for both sexes.

Alexander & Reilly (1981) have attacked the use of simultaneous equation methods. They note that such methods use inference about how variables are related to each other in the lives of individuals, and these inferences are drawn from comparisons across individuals in the currently stable situation. They argue that this procedure makes little sense in the case of variables that occur only once in an individual's life and which are invariant thereafter (and cannot be mutually adjusting). They propose analyzing the educational attainment process by examining segments of single and married life separately. However, such a procedure does not suggest the nature of the overall relationship between the two variables insofar as it seems to distort the delaying effect of additional schooling on marriage (Clarridge 1985). A related problem arises in that the temporal sequencing of two events need not indicate their causal relationship at the individual level since one transition may be triggered by the anticipated occurrence of the other (Marini 1984c).

In sum, adulthood in America, as well as childhood and adolescence, is a complex of social roles and psychological stages associated with age. The transition to adulthood is a developmental process. In order to further our understanding of this process, it will be helpful to adopt a perspective and to use a methodology that allow the formulation and testing of hypotheses about this process in its full complexity.

AGE STRATIFICATION

Age stratification refers to the association of social roles or role constellations with the people who move through these roles as they grow older (Riley & Waring 1976). While all societies have some form of age stratification, they differ in the degree to which age groups are expected to fill certain roles and avoid others, the explicitness of those expectations, and the nature of the sanctions (if any) against those who fail to conform to these expectations (Foner 1982, Fry & Keith 1982, Riley 1985). These expectations are culturally embedded so that the very conception of what constitutes developmental aging varies between populations (Featherman 1985).

Institutional and Organizational Bases of Age Stratification

In societies characterized by mechanical solidarity, normative expectations about the appropriate ages for life transitions are enforced by direct social pressures for conformity. In more modern societies, in which a complex division of labor creates patterns of organic solidarity, there are far fewer direct pressures for social conformity. In this situation, the age-graded organization of social institutions produces age-regularities in individual lives.

Schools in the United States provide an instructive example for the transition to adulthood. They are highly structured; most districts have either an elementary and high school system or primary, middle, and high school system. Appropriate ages at entry and exit have become much more uniform over the years (Kaestle & Vinovskis 1978). Age is a major basis for the assignment to school grades, creating the conditions necessary for the formation of adolescent groups that exert peer influences on individual behaviors (Coleman 1961). Schools simultaneously have become more bureaucratized organizations that are isolated from the community, complicating the job search and placement of young people when schooling is completed.

Examples of age-graded institutions that affect age patterns of the transition to adulthood are not restricted to schools. Non–career military service is strongly age-graded; living arrangements and duty assignments for soldiers reflect an organizational assumption that soldiers are unmarried. Colleges are organized on similar age bases but have developed specific institutional arrangements to deal with students who are married (married student housing) or employed full-time (evening programs). Apprentice programs for craft positions usually select people within certain narrowly defined age limits, while the age-similarity of college graduates promotes patterns of age uniformity among persons entering white collar occupations. Thus, the organizational structures of schools, military service, and labor markets differ across societies, producing unique institutional bases of age-grading, and societal variability in age-stratification systems.

Unfortunately, analysts studying the timing of early life transitions rarely consider the effects of such institutional patterns in the society they are studying. For example, research on age-graded patterns of school enrollment and of age at school completion (Featherman et al 1984, Hogan 1981, Winsborough 1978) has not taken into account the increased likelihood that an individual will terminate schooling at the end of a level rather than between grades within levels, nor has it considered the age-graded pattern of school grade enrollment. Research on the age at school completion could be improved by formulating a model of the rate of school completion that includes a time-varying independent variable which indicates whether a given level of schooling was completed during the age interval in question. Similarly, the availability of entry-level jobs in each year should be considered in studies of the timing of labor force entry and of decisions about timing of military service.

Changes in Age Stratification

Age-stratification systems may be relatively static in the absence of other social change. But even age-set societies experience conflict and change with respect to the age system (Foner & Kertzer 1979). Age-stratification systems may change in response to the increasingly complex division of labor and the extended school attendance associated with modernization, and these changes are reinforced by laws mandating compulsory minimal school attendance and minimum ages for labor-force entry (Coleman 1961, Cosner & Larson 1980, Modell et al 1976, Panel on Youth 1974). Socially important historical events such as depressions or wars, in combination with age conflict and cohort succession, also have changed the age-stratification system (Elder 1980).

As a result of such influences the number of age strata in the United States has increased since colonial times, and boundaries between age groups have become more distinct (Foner 1982). Age at school completion and at labor force entry has risen, and the establishment of an independent residence and family formation have occurred at earlier ages and more universally than before (Modell et al 1976, Winsborough 1978). These changes are associated with an increased compactness of the transitions marking the achievement of adult status and with a greater overlap between the public and private life transitions.

Wartime military service caused interruptions in schooling and occupational careers, and delays in marriage and parenthood (Elder & Meguro 1985, Hogan 1981, Winsborough 1979). The interruption of other life-course transitions by military service sometimes may provide the opportunity to escape an early life history of disadvantage and begin a different life pathway (Elder 1986). Intercohort changes in mortality have reduced the likelihood that a young person will be orphaned before reaching adulthood (Uhlenberg 1978). Reductions in child mortality increase the expected returns to parental and societal investment in children (Cain 1984, Haines 1984). The declining age at first menses, higher rates of premarital sexual activities, and improved contraceptive technologies have substantially altered the transition to parenthood (Chilman 1979, Miller & Simon 1980, Presser 1978, Zelnik et al 1981). Thus, historical changes in the biological life course and the pace of psychological development also change age-stratification systems.

INTERCOHORT CHANGE   Because the age-stratification system of any society is continually changing, individuals born at different times are subject to different societal expectations about the aging process (Riley 1979, 1985). This is a key source of historical influences on the process of human development (Hareven 1978, Riley 1973). Cohort succession permits societies to respond relatively rapidly to changing social environments (Ryder 1965). Moreover, the variable sizes of birth cohorts may disrupt existing institutional arrangements in the age-stratification system and create further pressures for change (Riley et al 1972, Waring 1975).

Transition Norms

Neugarten and her associates (1965, 1973, 1976) have elaborated this sociocultural perspective on aging, arguing that people's lives are ordered by societal norms regarding age-appropriate behaviors, roles, and statuses. Each society imposes its own schedule for the appropriate developmental process; persons internalize normative timetables by which they can describe themselves as early, on-time, or late with regard to familial and occupational events.

These timetables are embedded in each culture, structuring the ways in which individuals conceive of development and plan and interpret their own life course. Normative timetables vary by gender, reflecting pervasive cultural differences in the age stratification of men and women.

Some researchers contend that there are culturally determined age norms that specify appropriate ages for life transitions and age ranges outside of which transitions are inappropriate. These contentions have been supported by sample surveys in which middle-aged, middle-class Americans indicated their attitudes about age-appropriate behavior (Neugarten et al 1965). New surveys are beginning to be done to update these findings (Passuth et al 1984). It is imperative that additional studies be done on samples that are nationally representative and which include a wide range of age groups, including adolescents. Such relatively crude sample-survey evidence should be supplemented by intensive ethnographic studies of youth behavior in local communities (Liebow 1967; Suttles 1968, 1976).

The identification of cultural norms of behavior in communities has been a focus of ethnographic studies in anthropology. This research has produced a wealth of evidence describing cultural differences in what are considered appropriate age-related behaviors (Brown 1981, 1982; Kertzer & Keith 1984). Among industrial societies, these include differences in appropriate ages to marry, and whether or not economic self-sufficiency is necessary at marriage (Hogan & Mochizuki 1985, Morgan et al 1984, Plath & Ikeda 1976).

It is unclear whether to expect normative timetables to be more or less salient during the transition to adulthood. On the one hand, since this is a time of so many transitions and also since late adolescence marks the culmination of the most intense period of socialization a person will ever experience, we may expect normative timetables to be highly salient. On the other hand, the research to date (done on samples of adults) on normative timetables indicates that older individuals have stronger age norms and that older people more frequently see themselves as being aligned with the normative standards of others (Neugarten et al 1965, Passuth et al 1984, Plath & Ikeda 1976).

Normative standards are likely to become a focus of conflict between parents and children during periods of rapid change in the age-stratification system (Bengtson & Cutler 1976). Initially, young people may continue to express traditional norms while accepting behaviors that depart from the ideal (Walters & Walters 1980). However, such conflict ultimately is resolved as changes in behavior become accepted normative standards. For example, Modell (1980) has shown that post–World War II shifts in opinions about appropriate ages at marriage were led by young people, but that other members of the society began to shift their opinions to conform with new standards of behavior.

Since World War II, the United States has witnessed major changes in marriage, divorce, and remarriage behaviors (Cherlin 1981, Thornton & Freedman 1983). These changes in marital behaviors have outmoded models of the family life course based on an idealized family in which all births occur within marriage and the parental family remains intact until the youngest child leaves home (Hogan 1984; Spanier et al 1979; Spanier & Glick 1980). Even among middle-class white Americans, the degree of consensus about the ages preferred for making key life transitions has declined over the past two decades, while judgments about age-inappropriate behavior have persisted (Passuth et al 1984). It seems likely that unmarried motherhood has become a much more acceptable path to adulthood among young blacks, as increased numbers grow up in homes where the mother is the head of the household (Furstenberg et al 1983, Wilson & Neckerman 1985).

Marini (1984a) has posed a strong challenge to the normative model for understanding age-graded behaviors in the United States, citing the lack of nationally representative survey evidence on age norms and their mode of acquisition, the apparent lack of sanctions by which such norms are enforced, the differences in transition behaviors between population subgroups, and the tendency of age norms to change over time so as to reflect behaviors. Certainly there is a substantial need for supporting evidence for Neugarten's sociocultural perspective. However, we think acceptance of Marini's suggestion that the normative model should be dropped would not help to advance our understanding of the transition to adulthood. Her point may apply to the study of the 1957 cohort of Illinois high school students she has analyzed so intensively, in which her interest centers on differentials in the timing of early life transitions. But the point loses any force when our attention shifts to comparative (historical and cross-cultural) analyses in which expected forms of behaviors, and the institutional arrangements to deal with them, provide radically different contexts for life-course development, particularly youth-to-adult transitions.

Age Stratification as a Population Phenomenon

As our discussion above indicated, Featherman (1985) has suggested that it is useful to conceptualize the impact of the age-stratification system as it is revealed by the magnitude of duration dependence for transitions, a characteristic that can only be measured for a population. Differences in developmental processes resulting from age-stratification systems for populations subgroups (such as men and women) can be measured in a similar fashion. Hogan (1978) has used procedures for the analysis of contingency tables to argue that American men tend to delay marriage until after they have completed school, an argument that accounts for the differing age patterns of the two transitions. Alternatively, this linkage has been analyzed by identifying age-specific rates of the marriage transition for students and nonstudents (Winsborough 1979). However, the measurement of linkages between transition events is much more complex than the analysis of a single transition, and the researcher must be aware of a variety of potential methodological pitfalls (Winship 1986). Other researchers have analyzed the linkages between transitions as stochastic phenomena that should be measured at the population level.

Regardless of the statistical methodology used, one should not expect to observe the effects of age-stratification norms at the individual level. These culturally embedded expectations should instead be regarded as providing a context for transitions. Individual departures from such normative behaviors then become a legitimate subject of inquiry, and the consequences of lack of fit between transitions that actually occur and those expected by social institutions become a subject for investigation (Elder 1974).

Significant numbers of individuals marry prior to finishing their schooling, even though such behaviors do not conform to apparent population patterns of normative linkages between transitions. Differences in the ordering of transitions between individuals reflect their socioeconomic origins, educational attainments, and the social histories of birth cohorts (Hogan 1978, 1981; also see Marini 1984b). Men who marry prior to completing their schooling subsequently experience higher rates of marital instability and lower educational returns to education, perhaps as a result of lack of fit between individual behaviors and the structure of schools and labor markets (Hogan 1980). We believe that it is important that researchers attend to the culturally determined age-graded character of institutions in analyses of life transitions because such bureaucratic structures are the basis of social solidarity in modern societies.

In advocating a population level approach to the study of age stratification and the transition to adulthood, we are not advocating analyses that use only aggregate level data. Rather, we are calling for the inclusion of contextual and institutional effects in both theory and analyses of the individual life course. In addition, we call for research to include a variety of subgroups of the population, since comparison of these groups affords insight into the institutional mechanisms that maintain the age-stratification system.

HETEROGENEITY IN TRANSITIONS

Even within societies there may be different cultural expectations about what constitutes the stages of youth-to-adult development for major subgroups. In the United States major differences in the transition to adulthood exist between males and females, racial and ethnic groups, and social classes, as well as for groups experiencing the transition to adulthood at different times. Some of these differences are due to factors of selection; for example, insufficient funds can prevent high school graduates from attending college, or racial discrimination can make it difficult for young blacks to find full-time employment after finishing school. Other subgroup differences are due to socialization. For example, public life (i.e. work and education) has traditionally been more important for males than females, and differences in the patterns of transition from full-time student, and to full-time worker, may be due to such sex role socialization.

Much research to date has concentrated on the documentation of subgroup differentials in the transition to adulthood. In order to expand our understanding now, it is important to look at population-level factors that create and maintain heterogeneity. Historical events and change, culture, and socioeconomic resources—all affect the transition to adulthood directly; they also create circumstances in which the salience of transitions differs for different groups, and levels of intentionality about transitions vary.

Cohort Differentials

The social historical conditions that characterize birth cohorts critically affect the context of the transition to adulthood because the age-stratification system changes over time (Elder 1980). Research on this subject has proceeded by matching the aggregate transition characteristics of birth cohorts to the social and economic conditions they faced, in order to understand these effects (Easterlin 1980, Evans 1983, Hogan 1981). Unfortunately, researchers with data for multiple birth cohorts who have studied individual behaviors typically have grouped populations arbitrarily into five-year or ten-year birth cohorts that do not coincide with variations in cohort histories. Then they have engaged in ad hoc speculations about cohort effects. Research on the transition to adulthood would be improved significantly if analysts would estimate contextual models of the effects of these cohort-level variables on the behaviors of individuals.

Too often research on the transition to adulthood has analyzed a single birth cohort, without considering how the unique histories of this cohort may differentiate its transition history. As Elder (1980) pointed out, Coleman (1961) ignored the unusually high proportion of adolescents whose fathers were absent when they were children (due to military service) in formulating his theory of the adolescent society. Marini (1978a,b; 1984a,c) has been careful to compare her follow-up sample of these Illinois adolescents to other studies of high school students sampled in the late 1950s, but in interpreting her results she has largely ignored the unique historical situation of this cohort. Surely sex differences in the transition to adulthood may have changed for subsequent birth cohorts in which women were more exposed to nontraditional sex role ideologies, had mothers who were more likely to work, and who could be sexually active prior to or within marriage with a much lower probability of a career interruption due to an unplanned birth (Lipman-Blumen & Tickamyer 1974, Miller & Garrison 1982).

Such an ahistorical approach to the transition to adulthood has been characteristic of much of the research in this area (Card & Wise 1978, Hofferth

& Moore 1979, Haggstrom & Associates 1981, Moore & Waite 1977, 1981, Sewell & Hauser 1975). Of course, the study of a single birth cohort is one useful method of controlling for contextual effects associated with birth cohort, but such research may lead us to misunderstand the transition to adulthood if care is not taken to locate fully the cohort studied in its unique historical context. Analysts need to go beyond their statistical equations to speculate on how the cultural and social historical context of the life course of the cohort under study may have structured its transition to adulthood.

A useful illustration is the work of Elder (1975, 1981; Elder & Rockwell 1979) on the effects of the Great Depression on young people. He finds that these effects depended on the age of the subjects at the time the economic crisis occurred, the extent of income loss experienced by their family, and the social class position of their family. The impact of World War II on the transition to adulthood differed by a person's age at the War and by whether military service interrupted a single man's schooling or the career of a married man (Elder 1986). The salience of male wartime military service probably was greater for the transitions of women who were married and had childcare responsibilities when their husbands entered military service than for single women who were forced to postpone marriage until after the war.

Race and Social Standing

A further complicating factor is that period conditions need not uniformly affect members of birth cohorts (Elder 1980). In the United States race and socioeconomic standing are important characteristics differentiating members of birth cohorts because of their role in determining access to valued social resources that are institutionally controlled. This is a critical consideration in studies of the transition to adulthood since this is the time in which young people convert their ascribed attributes and social origins into attainments in public life.

Educational and career opportunities differ between communities and have substantial impacts on achievements in public life (Alexander et al 1975, Blau & Duncan 1967; Sewell & Hauser 1975). It is not sufficient to measure such characteristics for the population at the SMSA level and to include them as control variables in a statistical model. The effects of such contextual variables may differ critically by the extent of access to these opportunities. For example, geographic proximity to a quality school or university would have had little effect on the educational attainments of blacks prior to the desegregation of schools. A low unemployment rate in a community may not indicate favorable employment prospects for an uneducated Latino entering the labor market, if available positions are for educated and skilled workers. Research on the transition to adulthood will be improved if analysts more carefully specify these contextual variables. Statistical models should then be estimated to determine whether the process of the transition to adulthood differs according to these contextual conditions or whether they directly affect the rate of youth-to-adult transitions.

Socioeconomic Resources

Socioeconomic resources in families of origin also affect the transition to adulthood, as may be seen by comparing individuals with similar cultural origins and social histories. Marini (1978a,b; 1984a,b,c) has convincingly demonstrated the effects of parental education, occupation, number of siblings, family income, and other characteristics of family background on the timing of school completion, labor force entry, marriage, and parenthood, and on their sequencing (also see Duncan et al 1972, Hogan 1981). Educational attainment is a key intervening variable in this process, because of the effects of prolonged schooling on the timing of other life transitions.

In effect, young people may delay the completion of the transition to adulthood in order to facilitate their educational and lifetime career attainments. As the delays in school completion become prolonged (for example, with graduate or professional schools), it becomes increasingly likely that postponed transitions (such as labor force entry, marriage, and parenthood) will occur, even though such patterns may not conform to cultural expectations (Hogan 1981). These linkages between the transition marking adulthood and the socio-economic life cycle thus become a critically important subject for investigators interested in explaining life histories in a sociological framework.

Gender

Virtually all age-stratification systems differ by gender; the social allocation of roles by age is always accompanied by the consideration of sex (Fry & Keith 1981). Murty (1978) has suggested that in industrial societies the move to the adult female role, with its prescription of passivity and its emphasis on family, is far less of a sharp transition with youth than the move to the adult male role. The adult role complex combines roles that fall broadly in the two spheres of work and family or public and private life. Traditional gender role ideology accords primacy to the public life among males and the private life among females. Sex differences abound within the role complexes of American adults (Bayer 1969, Gilligan 1979, Hout & Morgan 1975). Marini (1978a,b) argues, for example, that although educational attainment affects both occupational standing and marriage market position for both sexes, the mechanism by which it affects social standing is different for the two sexes since the routes to status attainment for the two sexes are different.

The organization of social institutions is of major importance in the study of gender differences in occupational careers and the relationship of careers to family life. Occupations in the United States are highly segregated by sex (Baron & Bielby 1984, Bielby & Baron 1984). Wolf & Rosenfeld (1978) found that occupations held primarily by women permit late entry and exit and reentry in the labor force to a greater degree than do male occupations of similar occupational status. Women who plan their labor force participation around family goals may choose low-paying occupations that permit them to enter the labor force after childbearing or to interrupt their labor force participation for childbearing (Miller & Garrison 1982, Tittle 1981, Moen 1985). Because such jobs rarely are embedded in career chains that lead to more skilled and better paying jobs, the wages of women continue to lag long after their childbearing responsibilities are completed (Sewell et al 1980). Furthermore, employers may come to expect women employees to have erratic work histories, and this may lead to the creation of patterns of institutionalized discrimination that penalize all women, even those who give first priority to their career achievements (Reskin 1984).

Differentials in Salience of Transitions

Other research has suggested that there are subgroup differences in the salience of particular private or public life transitions for young persons. The achievement of sexual maturity among whites may be signified primarily by sexual intercourse, and among blacks by motherhood (Gabriel & McAnarney 1983, Johnson 1974, Stack 1974). Young women who have been socialized to fill a passive maternal role (Falk et al associates 1981, Protinsky et al 1982, Stewart 1981) or who lack access to marriage partners and career roles (Spanier & Glick 1980, Wilson & Aponte 1985) may emphasize single motherhood as a path to adulthood. Limitations on black access to entry-level labor market positions and the lesser likelihood that the initial job will provide entree to the primary labor market have been associated with these racial differences in patterns of family formation (Wilson & Neckerman 1985). Research generally has found significant gender and ethnic differentials in the degree of emphasis placed on education as a route to adult success (Hout & Morgan 1975, Tenhouten et al 1971).

Transition Intentions

Considerable evidence suggests that the aspirations and plans of young people have a significant impact on their transition to adulthood. Intentions very likely play a major role in creating and maintaining some of the between-group differences in the transition to adulthood. Educational aspirations have major effects on the post–high school educational achievements of young persons (Sewell & Hauser 1975). Educational aspirations and marriage plans are consistently related, with a later age at marriage associated with higher educational aspirations (Bayer 1969). Adolescent expectations about the timing of school completion, labor force entry, independent residence, marriage, and parenthood depend on family socioeconomic resources, parental expectations, and educational aspirations (Hogan 1985). These anticipations appear to influence subsequent behaviors. While most demographers have regarded teenage parenthood as a stochastic result of high levels of unprotected sexual intercourse (Alan Guttmacher Institute 1981, Chilman 1980), other social scientists have argued that the high rate of premarital parenthood among black adolescents may reflect a conscious choice of that pathway to adulthood in the absence of viable alternatives (Hogan & Kitagawa 1985, Stack 1975, Wilson & Neckerman 1985). Other black teenagers expect to remain childless so that they can capitalize on relatively favorable social origins in their occupational careers (Astone 1984).

Research on the transition to adulthood would be much more informative if analysts were able to consider adolescent intentions (Marini 1984a). Such data could be used at the population level to determine culturally embedded notions about the timing of life transitions (Elder 1974). At the individual level, the sources of transition expectations could be investigated in order to elaborate the process by which family background influences the transition to adulthood. The causal connections between two or more transition events could be more certainly established, without resort to complex statistical models that provide uncertain results. Such analyses ultimately would provide a better understanding of the degree of personal control individuals exert on their development (Brandtstadter 1984).

Analysts have been handicapped by the absence of longitudinal data on transition expectations and behaviors (see, for example, the papers in Elder 1985). This shortcoming promises to be remedied by data from the *High School and Beyond* survey conducted by NORC. This study provides a nationally representative sample of American high school sophomores and seniors in Spring 1980. Study respondents were reinterviewed in 1982 and 1984, and additional survey waves are being planned. Data on expected ages at school completion, first job, independent residence, first marriage, and parenthood have been collected in the 1980 and 1982 waves of the survey, along with complete event histories on these behaviors at each interview. We anticipate that the *High School and Beyond* data will prove to be an important research resource for future studies of the transition to adulthood.

CONSEQUENCES OF THE TRANSITION TO ADULTHOOD

The transition to adulthood is of general interest to social scientists because of its importance for understanding the adult life pathway. The adult roles initially assumed provide entry ports for subsequent familial and occupational careers. The manner in which these adult roles are entered (in terms of intentionality, timing, sequencing in relation to other roles) influences the subsequent life course.

The best data on these connections is for the timing of marriage and parenthood. A teenage pregnancy sometimes prompts a marriage to legitimate the child, but marriages involving teenagers end more frequently than others in separation and divorce (Furstenberg 1976, Moore & Caldwell 1976, Moore & Hofferth 1978a,b). Among whites, marital instability is higher for women marrying before age 19, regardless of age at first childbirth. Among blacks, an early age at parenthood is associated with greater marital instability (Moore & Waite 1981). Young women who become pregnant first at an early age have higher rates of subsequent fertility and thus shorter intervals between births (Bumpass et al 1978). During the late 1960s and early 1970s, early parenthood decreased educational attainment among all women, although the effects were somewhat greater among whites (Moore & Waite 1977). Controlling for social origins, researchers found that couples in the Detroit area during the 1960s who were pregnant premaritally had economic attainments inferior to those of couples who were not (Coombs et al 1970). Welfare dependency is increased and family income is reduced as a result of teenage motherhood (Card & Wise 1978, Hofferth & Moore 1979, Trussell 1976, Trussell & Menken 1978). Also, parenthood before 18 decreases the perceived personal efficacy of young women (McLaughlin & Micklin 1983).

Other research has examined the effects of discontinuties in schooling on career achievements (Duncan et al 1972, Ornstein 1976), the effects of disorder in public life transitions on the timing of parenthood (Rindfuss et al 1985), and the effects of the ordering of school completion, first job, and marriage on marital stability, and occupational and earnings attainments (Hogan 1980). This research all demonstrates the importance of the temporal patterning of early life transitions on the subsequent life history, although the relative importance attached to the timing and the sequencing aspects of temporal patterns varies, depending on the transitions studied and the outcomes of interest. Thus, the transition to adulthood influences the adult life course because it represents a critical juncture in personal life histories and connects social origins with subsequent adult attainments and life satisfaction.

CONCLUSION

Inquiries into the transition to adulthood remain critically important for understanding human development, the age-stratification system, and individual life histories. The frequency of multiple transitions during adolescence and the relatively good life-history data available make the transition to adulthood an especially promising area of inquiry for methodologists interested in the linkages between transition events. For these reasons, studies of the transition to adulthood will remain of interest to many social scientists.

If research on the transition to adulthood is to fulfill its potential, a population perspective must be taken, to correct the shortcomings of previous research. It is important to include in future research consideration of the transition to adulthood in its full complexity, including both its multidimensionality and the larger societal context in which the transition takes place. Attention must be paid to the culturally determined institutional bases of life transitions and the ways in which these bases vary between and within birth cohorts. Between-group differentials in the transition process, and the roles that salience and intentionality play in creating and maintaining these differentials, deserve investigation. A population level perspective on the transition to adulthood will provide a framework that includes all this and, in combination with thoughtful and careful use of new data sources and techniques for the analysis of event histories, should lead to further understanding of this important period of the life course.

ACKNOWLEDGMENTS

We thank Glen Elder, David Featherman, Sandra Hofferth, David Kertzer, Margaret Mooney Marini, Matilda White Riley, and Alice Rossi for their helpful comments on earlier drafts of this paper.

Literature Cited

Adelson, J. 1980. *Handbook of Adolescent Psychology*. New York: Wiley

Alan Guttmacher Institute. 1981. *Teenage Pregnancy: The Problem That Hasn't Gone Away*. New York: Guttmacher Inst.

Alexander, K. L., Eckland, B. K., Griffin, L. J. 1975. The Wisconsin model of socioeconomic achievement: A replication. *Am. J. Sociol.* 81:324–42

Alexander, K. L., Reilly, T. W. 1981. Estimating the effects of marriage timing on educational attainment: Some procedural issues and substantive clarifications. *Am. J. Sociol.* 87:143–56

Antonovski, H. F., Shoham, I., Kavenaki, S., Lancet, M., Modan, B. 1980. Gender differences in patterns of adolescent sexual behavior. *J. Youth Adolesc.* 9:127–41

Astone, N. M. 1984. *Sex role attitudes and fertility expectations in white and black adolescent girls*. Presented at Ann. Meet. Midwest. Sociol. Soc., St. Louis, Mo.

Baltes, P. B., Brim, O. G. Jr. eds. 1984. *Life Span Development and Behavior*. Vol. 6. New York: Academic

Baron, J. N., Bielby, W. T. 1984. Organizational barriers to gender equality: Sex segregation of jobs and opportunities. See Rossi 1984, pp. 233–51

Bayer, A. 1969. Marriage plans and educational aspirations. *Am. J. Sociol.* 75:239–44

Bengtson, V. L., Cutler, N. E. 1976. Generations and intergenerational relations: Perspectives on age groups and social change. See Binstock & Shanas 1976, pp. 130–59

Bielby, W. T., Baron, J. N. 1984. A woman's place is with other women: Sex segregation in organizations. In *Sex Segregation in the Workplace: Trends, Explanations, Remedies*, ed. B. Reskin. Washington, DC: Natl. Acad.

Binstock, R. H., Shanas, E., eds. 1976. *Handbook of Aging and the Social Sciences*. New York: Van Nostrand. 2nd ed. 1985. Van Nostrand Reinhold. 3rd ed. In press

Blau, P. M., Duncan, O. D. 1967. *The American Occupational Structure*. New York: Wiley

Bolton, F. G. Jr. 1980. *The Pregnant Adolescent: Problems of Premature Parenthood*. Beverly Hills: Sage

Brandtstadter, J. 1984. Personal and social control over development: Some implications of an action perspective in life-span developmental psychology. See Baltes & Brim 1984, pp. 2–32

Brown, J. K. 1981. Cross-cultural perspectives on the female life cycle. In *Handbook of Cross-Cultural Human Development*, ed. R. H. Munroe, R. L. Munroe, B. B. Whiting. New York: Garland

Brown, J. K. 1982. Cross-cultural perspectives on middle-aged women. *Curr. Anthropol.* 23:143–56

Bumpass, L. L., Rindfuss, R. R., Janosik, R. B. 1978. Age and marital status at first birth and the pace of subsequent fertility. *Demography* 15:75–86

Cain, M. 1984. Fertility as an adjustment to risk. See Rossi 1980, pp. 145–159

Card, J. J., Wise, L. L. 1978. Teenage mothers and teenage fathers: The impact of early childbearing on the parents' personal and professional lives. *Fam. Planning Perspec.* 10:199–205

Cherlin, A. J. 1981. *Marriage, Divorce, Remarriage.* Cambridge: Harvard Univ. Press

Chilman, C. S. 1979. *Adolescent Sexuality in a Changing Society: Social and Psychological Perspectives.* Bethesda: Dep. Health, Educ., Welfare, Publ. Health Serv.

Chilman, C. S. 1980. Social and psychological research concerning adolescent childbearing: 1970–1980. *J. Marriage Fam.* 42:793–805

Clarridge, B. 1985. *School completion and age at first marriage.* University of Wisconsin-Madison. Unpublished

Clausen, J. A. 1985. *Sociology of the Life Course.* New York: Prentice-Hall. In press

Coleman, J. C. 1980. Friendship and peer group in adolescence. See Adelson 1980, pp. 408–31

Coleman, J. S. 1961. *The Adolescent Society.* New York: Free Press

Collins, J. K. 1974. Adolescent dating intimacy: Norms and peer expectations. *J. Youth Adolesc.* 3:317–28

Coombs, L. C., Freedman, R., Freedman, J., Pratt, W. F. 1970. Premarital pregnancy and status before and after marriage. *Am. J. Sociol.* 75:800–20

Cosner, T. L., Larson, G. L. 1980. Social fabric theory and the youth culture. *Adolescence* 15:99–104

Duncan, O. D., Featherman, D. L., Duncan, B. 1972. *Socioeconomic Background and Achievement.* New York: Seminar

Easterlin, R. 1980. *Birth and Fortune: The Impact of Numbers on Personal Welfare.* New York: Basic

Elder, G. H. Jr. 1974. *Children of the Great Depression: Social Change in Life Experience.* Chicago: Univ. Chicago Press

Elder, G. H. Jr. 1975. Age differentiation and the life course. *Ann. Rev. Sociol.* 1:165–90

Elder, G. H. Jr. 1978. Approaches to social change and the family. *Am. J. Sociol.* (Suppl.) 84(S):1–S38

Elder, G. H. Jr. 1980. Adolescence in historical perspective. See Adelson 1980, pp. 3–46

Elder, G. H. Jr. 1981. History and the life course. In *Biography and Society,* ed. D. Bertaux. Beverly Hills: Sage

Elder, G. H. Jr. 1985a. *Life Course Dynamics: Trajectories and Transitions, 1968–1980.* Ithaca: Cornell Univ. Press

Elder, G. H. Jr. 1985b. Perspectives on the life course. See Elder 1985a, pp. 23–49

Elder, G. H. Jr. 1986. Military times and turning points in men's lives. *Develop. Psychol.* In press

Elder, G. H. Jr., Meguro, Y. 1985. *Wartime in men's lives: A comparative study of American and Japanese cohorts.* Presented at Ann. Meet. Am. Sociol. Assoc., Washington, DC

Elder, G. H. Jr., Rockwell, R. W. 1979. Economic depression and postwar opportunity in men's lives: A study of life patterns and health. In *Research in Community and Mental Health,* ed. R. G. Simmons. Greenwich: JAI

Erikson, E. H. 1950. *Childhood and Society.* New York: Norton

Evans, M. D. R. 1983. *Modernization, economic conditions and family formation: Evidence from recent white and nonwhite cohorts.* Ph.D. thesis. Univ. Chicago. 401 pp.

Falk, R., Gispert, M., Baucom, D. H. 1981. Personality factors related to black teenage pregnancy and abortion. *Psychol. Women Q.* 5(Suppl.):733–46

Featherman, D. L. 1985. Biography, society and history. In *Human Development and the Life Course: Multidisciplinary Perspectives,* ed. A. B. Sorensen, F. Weinart, L. Sherrod. Hillsdale, NJ: Erlbaum. In press

Featherman, D. L., Carter, T. M. 1976. Discontinuities in schooling and the socioeconomic life cycle. In *Schooling and Achievement in American Society,* ed. W. H. Sewell, R. M. Hauser, D. L. Featherman. New York: Academic

Featherman, D. L., Hogan, D. P., Sørensen, A. B. 1984. Entry into adulthood: Profiles of young men in the 1950's. See Baltes & Brim 1984, pp. 159–202.

Featherman, D. L., Lerner, R. M. 1985. *Ontogenesis and sociogenesis: Problematics for theory and research about development and socialization across the lifespan.* University of Wisconsin-Madison. Unpublished

Featherman, D. L., Sørensen, A. 1983. Societal transformation in Norway and change in the life course transition into adulthood. *Acta Sociol.* 26:105–26

Foner, A. 1982. Perspectives on changing age systems. See Riley et al 1981, pp. 217–28

Foner, A., Kertzer, D. L. 1978. Transitions over the life course: Lessons from age-set societies. *Am. J. Sociol.* 83:1081–1104

Foner, A., Kertzer, D. L. 1979. Intrinsic and extrinsic sources of change in life-course transitions. See Riley 1979, pp. 121–36

Fry, C. L., Keith, J. 1982. The life course as a cultural unit. See Riley & Abeles 1982, 2:51–70

Furstenberg, F. F. Jr., Nord, C. W., Peterson, J. L., Zill, N. 1983. The life course of children of divorce: Marital disruption and parental contact. *Am. Sociol. Rev.* 48:656–68

Furstenberg, F. F. Jr. 1976. *Unplanned Parenthood: The Social Consequences of Teenage Childbearing.* New York: Free Press

Gabriel, A., McAnarney, E. R. 1983. Parenthood in two subcultures: white middle-class couples and black, low income adolescents in Rochester, New York. *Adolescence* 18: 595–608

Garn, S. M. 1980. Continuities and change in maturational timing. In *Constancy and Change in Human Development,* ed. O. G. Brim, Jr., J. Kagan. Cambridge: Harvard Univ. Press

Gilligan, C. 1979. Woman's place in man's life cycle. *Harvard Educ. Rev.* 49:431–46

Goldscheider, F. K., DaVanzo, J. 1986. Semiautonomy and leaving home in early adulthood. *Soc. Forc.* In press

Greenberger, E., Steinberg, L. D. 1981. The workplace as a context for the socialization of youth. *J. Youth Adolesc.* 10:185–210

Hagestad, G. O., Neugarten, B. L. 1985. Age and the life course. See Binstock & Shanas 1985. In press

Haggstrom, G. W., and Associates. 1981. *Teenage Parents: Their Ambitions and Attainments.* Santa Monica: Rand

Haines, M. R. 1984. The life cycle, savings, and demographic adaptation: Some historical evidence for the United States and Europe. See Rossi 1984, pp. 43–63

Hannan, M. T., Tuma, N. B. 1979. Methods for temporal analysis. *Ann. Rev. Sociol.* 5:303–28

Hareven, T. K. 1978. Cycles, courses, and cohorts: Reflections on theoretical and methodological approaches to historical study of family development. *J. Soc. Hist.* 12:97–109

Hofferth, S. L., Moore, K. A. 1979. Early childbearing and later economic well-being. *Am. Sociol. Rev.* 44:784–815

Hogan, D. P. 1978. The variable order of events in the life course. *Am. Sociol. Rev.* 43:573–86

Hogan, D. P. 1980. The transition to adulthood as a career contingency. *Am. Sociol. Rev.* 45:261–76

Hogan, D. P. 1981. *Transitions and Social Change: The Early Lives of American Men.* New York: Academic

Hogan, D. P. 1984. The demography of lifespan transitions: Temporal and gender comparisons. See Rossi 1984, pp. 65–78

Hogan, D. P. 1985. Parental influences on the timing of early life transitions. *Current Perspectives on Aging and the Life Cycle,* Vol. 1, ed. Z. S. Blau. Greenwich: JAI. In press

Hogan, D. P., Kertzer, D. I. 1985. Longitudinal approaches to migration in social history. *Hist. Meth.* 18:20–30

Hogan, D. P., Kitagawa, E. M. 1985. The impact of social status, family structure, and neighborhood on the fertility of black adolescents. *Am. J. Sociol.* 90:825–55

Hogan, D. P., Mochizuki, T. 1985. *Demographic transitions and the life course: Lessons from Japanese and American comparisons.* Presented at the Ann. Meet. Am. Sociol. Assoc., New York

Hollingshead, A. B. 1961. *Elmtown's Youth.* New York: Wiley

Hout, M., Morgan, W. R. 1975. Race and sex variations in the causes of the expected attainments of high school seniors. *Am. J. Sociol.* 81:364–94

Johnson, C. L. 1974. Adolescent pregnancy: Intervention into the poverty cycle. *Adolescence* 9:391–406

Kaestle, C., Vinovskis, M. A. 1978. From fireside to factory: School entry and school learning in nineteenth-century Massachusetts. In *Transitions: The Family and the Life Course in Historical Perspective,* ed. T. K. Hareven. New York: Academic

Keating, D. 1980. Thinking processes in adolescence. See Adelson 1980, pp. 211–46

Kertzer, D. I., Keith, J., eds. 1984. *Age and Anthropological Theory.* Ithaca: Cornell Univ. Press

Liebow, E. 1967. *Tally's Corner: A Study of Negro Streetcorner Men.* Boston: Little, Brown

Lipman-Blumen, J., Tickamyer, A. R. 1974. Sex roles in transition: A ten-year perspective. *Ann. Rev. of Sociol.* 1:297–337

Marcia, J. E. 1980. Identity in adolescence. See Adelson 1980, pp. 159–87

Marini, M. M. 1978a. Sex differences in the determination of adolescent aspirations: A review of research. *Sex Roles* 4:723–53

Marini, M. M. 1978b. The transition to adulthood: Sex differences in educational attainment and age at marriage. *Am. Sociol. Rev.* 43:483–507

Marini, M. M. 1984a. Age and sequencing norms in the transition to adulthood. *Social Forc.* 63:229–44

Marini, M. M. 1984b. The order of events in the transition to adulthood. *Sociol. Educ.* 57:63–84

Marini, M. M. 1984c. Women's educational attainment and the timing of entry into parenthood. *Am. Sociol. Rev.* 49:491–511

McLaughlin, S. D., Micklin, M. 1983. The timing of the first birth and changes in personal efficacy. *J. Marriage Fam.* 45:47–57

Miller, J., Garrison, H. H. 1982. Sex roles: The division of labor at home and in the workplace. *Ann. Rev. Sociol.* 8:237–62

Miller, P. Y., Simon, W. 1980. The development of sexuality in adolescence. See Adelson 1980, pp. 383–407

Modell, J. 1980. Normative aspects of marriage timing since World War II. *J. Fam. Hist.* 5:210–34

Modell, J., Furstenberg, F. Jr., Hershberg, T. 1976. Social change and transitions to adulthood in historical perspective. *J. Fam. Hist.* 1:7–31

Moen, P. 1985. Continuities and discontinuities in women's labor force activity. See Elder 1985a, pp. 113–55

Moore, K. A., Caldwell, S. B. 1976. *Out of wedlock childbearing.* Work. Pap. 992-02. Washington, DC: Urban Inst.

Moore, K. A., Hofferth, S. L. 1978a. The consequences of age at first childbirth: Family size. Work. Pap. 1146-02. Washington, DC: Urban Inst.

Moore, K. A., Hofferth, S. L. 1978b. The consequences of age at first childbirth: Marriage, separation, and divorce. Work. Pap. 1146-03. Washington, DC: Urban Inst.

Moore, K. A., Hofferth, S. L. 1980. Factors affecting family formation: A path model. *Pop. Environ.* 3:78–98

Moore, K. A., Waite, L. J. 1977. Early childbearing and educational attainment. *Fam. Planning Perspec.* 9:220–25

Moore, K. A., Waite, L. J. 1981. Marital dissolution, early motherhood, and early marriage. *Social Forc.* 60:20–40

Morgan, S. P., Rindfuss, R. R., Parnell, A. 1984. Modern fertility patterns: Contrasts between the United States and Japan. *Pop. Dev. Rev.* 10:19–40

Murty, L. 1978. Transition for whom? Adolescence theories with androcentric bias. *Sex Roles* 4:369–373

Mussen, P., ed. 1970. Piaget's Theory. In *Carmichael's Manual of Child Psychology,* Vol. 1. New York: Wiley. 3rd ed.

Neugarten, B. L., Datan, N. 1973. Sociological perspectives on the life cycle. In *Life-Span Developmental Psychology: Personality and Socialization,* ed. P. B. Baltes, W. Schaie. New York: Academic

Neugarten, B. L., Hagestad, G. O. 1976. Age and the life course. See Binstock & Shanas 1976, pp. 35–55

Neugarten, B. L., Moore, J. W., Lowe, J. C. 1965. Age norms, age constraints, and adult socialization. *Am. J. Sociol.* 70:710–17

Ornstein, M. D. 1976. *Entry into the American Labor Force.* New York: Academic

Panel on Youth of the President's Science Advisory Committee. 1974. *Youth: The Transition to Adulthood.* Chicago: Univ. Chicago Press

Passuth, P. M., Maines, D. R., Neugarten, B. 1984. *Age norms and age constraints twenty years later.* Presented at the Ann. Meet. Midwest. Sociol. Soc., Chicago

Plath, D., Ikeda, K. 1976. After coming of age: Adult awareness of age norms. In *Socialization and Communication in Primary Groups,* ed. T. R. Williams, pp. 107–23. The Hague: Mouton

Presser, H. B. 1978. Age at menarche, sociosexual behavior, and fertility. *Soc. Biol.* 25:94–101

Protinsky, H., Sporakowski, M., Atkins, P. 1982. Identity formation: Pregnant and nonpregnant adolescents. *Adolescence* 17:73–80

Reskin, B., ed. 1984. *Sex Segregation in the Workplace: Trends, Explanations, Remedies.* Washington, DC: Natl. Acad.

Riley, M. W. 1973. Aging and cohort succession: Interpretations and misinterpretations. *Public Opin. Q.* 37:35–49

Riley, M. W., ed. 1979. *Aging from Birth to Death: Interdisciplinary Perspectives.* Boulder: Westview

Riley, M. W. 1985. Age strata in social systems. See Binstock & Shanas 1985. In press

Riley, M. W., Abeles, M. G., Teitelbaum, M. S., eds. 1982. *Aging from Birth to Death: Sociotemporal Perspectives.* Boulder, Colo: Westview. 2 vols.

Riley, M. W., Johnson, M., Foner, A. 1972. *Aging and Society, Vol. 3: A Sociology of Age Stratification.* New York: Sage

Riley, M. W., Waring, J. 1976. Age and aging. In *Contemporary Social Problems,* ed. R. K. Merton & R. Nisbet. New York: Harcourt, Brace & Jovanovich. 4th ed.

Rindfuss, R. R., Swicegood, C. G., Rosenfeld, R. A. 1985. *Disorder in the life course: How common and does it matter?* Presented at the Biennial Meet. Int. Soc. Study Behav. Develop.

Rossi, A. S. 1984. *Gender and the Life Course.* New York: Aldine

Ryder, N. B. 1965. The cohort as a concept in the study of social change. *Am. Sociol. Rev.* 30:843–61

Sewell, W. H., Hauser, R. M. 1975. *Education, Occupation, and Earnings: Achievement in the Early Career.* New York: Academic

Sewell, W. H., Hauser, R. M., Wolf, W. C. 1980. Sex, schooling and occupational status. *Am. J. Sociol.* 86:551–83

Shore, M. F. 1972. Youth and jobs: Educational, vocational and mental health aspects. *J. Youth Adolesc.* 1:315–23

Sørensen, A. B. 1980. Analysis of change in discrete variables. In *Historical Social Research,* ed. J. Clubb, E. Scheuch. Stuttgart: Klett-Cotta

Spanier, G. B., Glick, P. C. 1980. The life cycle of American families: An expanded analysis. *J. Fam. Hist.* 5:97–111

Spanier, G. B., Sauer, W., Larzelere, R. 1979. An empirical evaluation of the family life cycle. *J. Marriage Fam.* 41:27–38

Spenner, K. I., Otto, L. B., Call, V. R. A. 1982. *Career Lines and Career.* Lexington, Mass: Lexington

Stack, C. 1974. Sex roles and survival strategies in an urban black community. In *Woman, Culture, and Society,* ed. M. Zimbalist Rosaldo, L. Lamphere. Stanford: Stanford Univ. Press

Stack, C. 1975. *All Our Kin: Strategies for Survival in a Black Community.* New York: Harper & Row

Steinberg, L. D. 1982. Jumping off the work experience bandwagon. *J. Youth Adolesc.* 11:183–205

Stephenson, S. P. 1979. From school to work: A transition with job search implications. *Youth Soc.* 11:114–32

Stewart, M. W. 1981. Adolescent pregnancy: Status convergence for the well socialized female. *Youth Soc.* 12:443–64

Suttles, G. D. 1968. *The Social Order of the Slum.* Chicago: Univ. Chicago Press

Suttles, G. D. 1976. Urban ethnography: Situational and normative accounts. *Ann. Rev. Sociol.* 2:1–18

Teachman, J. D. 1982. Methodological issues in the analysis of family formation and dissolution. *J. Marriage Fam.* 44:1037–53

Tenhouten, W. D., Tzuen-jen, L., Kendall, F., Gordon, C. W. 1971. School and ethnic composition, social contexts, and educational plans of Mexican-American and Anglo high school students. *Am. J. Sociol.* 77:89–107

Thornton, A., Freedman, D. 1983. The changing American family. *Pop. Bull.* 38

Tittle, C. K. 1981. *Careers and Family Size: Sex Roles and Adolescent Life Plans.* Beverly Hills: Sage

Trussell, T. J. 1976. Economic consequences of teenage childbearing. *Fam. Planning Perspec.* 10:184–90

Trussell, T. J., Menken, J. 1978. Early childbearing and subsequent fertility. *Fam. Planning Perspec.* 10:209–18

Uhlenberg, P. 1978. Changing configurations

of the life course. In *Transitions: The Family and the Life Course in Historical Perspective,* ed. T. K. Hareven. New York: Academic

Voss, P. R. 1975. *Social determinants of age at first marriage in the United States.* Ph.D. thesis. Univ. Mich., Ann Arbor

Walters, J., Walters, L. H. 1980. Trends affecting adolescent views of sexuality, employment, marriage and childbearing. *Fam. Relat.* 29:191–203

Waring, J. M. 1975. Social replenishment and social change: the problem of disordered cohort flow. *Am. Behav. Sci.* 19:237–56

Wilson, W. J., Aponte, R. 1985. Urban poverty. *Ann. Rev. Sociol.* 11:231–58

Wilson, W. J., Neckerman, K. M. 1985. Poverty and family structure: The widening gap between evidence and public policy issues. Revision of paper presented at the 1984 US Dep. Health Hum. Serv. Conf., Williamsburg, Va.

Winsborough, H. H. 1978. Statistical histories of the life cycle of birth cohorts: The transition from school-boy to adult male. In *Social Demography,* ed. K. E. Taeuber, L. L. Bumpass, J. A. Sweet. New York: Academic

Winsborough, H. H. 1979. Changes in the transition to adulthood. See Riley 1979, pp. 137–52

Winship, C. 1986. Age dependence, heterogeneity, and the interdependence of life cycle transitions. In *Sociological Methodology, 1986,* ed. N. D. Tuma. New York: Jossey-Bass

Wolf, W. C., Rosenfeld, R. 1978. Sex structure of occupations and job mobility. *Soc. Forc.* 56:823–44

Zelnik, M., Kantner, J., Ford, K. 1981. *Sex and Pregnancy in Adolescence.* Beverly Hills: Sage

Ann. Rev. Sociol. 1986. 12:131–57

STATES AND SOCIAL POLICIES

Theda Skocpol and Edwin Amenta

Department of Sociology, The University of Chicago, Chicago, Illinois 60637

Abstract

Comparative social scientists have developed various arguments about the determinants of social policies, especially those connected with twentieth-century "welfare states." Structure-functionalists argue that the social policies of modern nations necessarily converge due to an underlying logic of industrialism, while neo-Marxists treat such policies as state responses to the social reproduction requirements of advanced capitalism. Yet most students of social policies are more attuned to history and politics. Concentrating on two dozen or fewer industrial capitalist democracies, many scholars have explored the alternative ways in which democratic political processes have helped to create programs and expand social expenditures. For a fuller range of nations past and present, scholars have also asked how ties to the world-economy, patterns of geopolitical competition, and processes of transnational cultural modelling have influenced social policies. Finally, there is now considerable interest in the independent impact of states on social policymaking. States may be sites of autonomous official initiatives, and their institutional structures may help to shape the political processes from which social policies emerge. In turn, social policies, once enacted and implemented, themselves transform politics. Consequently, the study over time of "policy feedbacks" has become one of the most fruitful current areas of research on states and social policies.

INTRODUCTION

States are organizations that extract resources through taxation and attempt to extend coercive control and political authority over particular territories and the people residing within them. "Policies" are lines of action pursued through states. Of necessity, all states have military and economic policies, for their territories must be defended and their revenues depend on the fortunes of

131

0360-0572/86/0815-0131$02.00

production and trade. If social policies are defined in the broadest possible terms as "state activities affecting the social status and life chances of groups, families, and individuals," then states have always had social policies as well. Military and economic measures in turn affect the status and life chances of individuals, and state-enforced property rules and judicial decisions help to define families and the rights of their members. More directly, the behavior of the poor or the socioeconomically dislocated has worried state authorities enough to inspire policies aimed at social control or amelioration. England's Poor Law from Tudor times was an example; so were the efforts of European monarchical authorities, or of Chinese Imperial officials, to control food supplies and prices in times of dearth.

Nevertheless, we rightly think of social policies as coming into prominence in the modern national states of the nineteenth and twentieth centuries. State organized or regulated mass education grew from the early nineteenth century, as did efforts to regulate industrial working conditions and environmental influences on people's health. Between the 1880s and 1920s, social insurance and pension programs were launched in Europe, the Americas, and Australasia to buffer workers in market economies against income losses due to disability, old age, ill health, unemployment, or loss of a family breadwinner (Flora & Alber 1981, Malloy 1979, Rimlinger 1971). After their inception, such programs spread to many additional countries and expanded in benefits and in coverage of the population. In the wake of World War II, moreover, most of the leading industrial-capitalist democracies became self-proclaimed "welfare states" (Flora & Heidenheimer 1981). By the mid-1970s, public expenditures for social-welfare purposes had burgeoned to an average of 20.7% of GDP in 13 European nations, and even in the United States such expenditures had increased from 10.3% to 15.7% of GDP between the early 1960s and the mid-1970s (Castles 1982b:51).

Sociologists and other social scientists have developed diverse arguments about the origins, expansion, and effects of social policies. Here we shall focus primarily on the policies associated with modern welfare states, with only occasional reference to other state activities that might be considered under the broad rubric of "social policy" as we have defined it. We shall survey the explanatory perspectives that have figured in recent cross-national research, with occasional glances at arguments about the United States alone. The discussion will be largely restricted to the *determinants* of social policies; we will not deal as fully with the much less clear-cut debates and findings about the redistributional *effects* that policies may—or may not—have had. Overall, our purpose is not only to indicate the current empirical standing of various arguments about policy determinants, but also to show the shifting orientations and methods of research of the last 10 to 15 years. In the social sciences, changing questions and ways of seeking answers are just as important as accumulations of research findings.

INDUSTRIALISM AND SOCIAL POLICY

Not long ago the view predominated among comparative social scientists that "economic growth is the ultimate cause of welfare state development" (Wilensky 1975:24, echoing Wilensky & Lebeaux 1958:230). All nations were thought to be caught up in a universal and evolutionist "logic of industrialism" through which technological imperatives would produce increasing convergence in social structures and basic policies as nations moved from traditional-agrarian to modern-industrial (Kerr et al 1964). Regardless of the forms of regimes or the dominant political ideologies, industrializing nations would institute similar sequences of social insurance or educational policies (Cutright 1965, Mishra 1973) and expand population-coverage and overall expenditures in tandem with economic development (Pryor 1968, Wilensky 1975). Industrialization and urbanization, it was argued, inherently require human capital development and make it difficult for families to care for the disabled, ill, elderly, or unemployed. An aging population accompanies economic development, creating especially strong needs and demands for public social spending (Wilensky 1975). At the same time, new resources become available for public authorities to respond to social needs and technological requisites. Attempting to put this argument on the strongest logical and empirical ground, some proponents (Coughlin 1979, Jackman 1975, Mishra 1973, Wilensky 1975, Williamson & Fleming 1977) have argued that convergence of social policies in industrializing nations may occur only up to a point, beyond which sociocultural variations persist among very rich countries.

Empirically, the logic-of-industrialism perspective fared well in cross-national studies based on data for the 1940s, 1950s, or 1960s, especially when large numbers of countries at all levels of economic development were included in cross-sectional designs and when the dependent variables were highly aggregated measures of "program experience" (Cutright 1965) or broad categories of social expenditure (Wilensky 1975). But once research became more longitudinal or sensitive to earlier or later time periods, and once the specific features of social policies were more closely examined, this perspective was undermined as a sufficient guide to causal processes.

For the origins of modern welfare state programs, Flora & Alber (1981) demonstrate that levels of industrialization fail to predict the timing of the adoption of a social insurance program by twelve European nations between the 1880s and 1920s; Orloff & Skocpol (1984) show that in the same period policy developments in Britain and Massachusetts cannot be differentiated according to logic-of-industrialism variables; and Collier & Messick (1975) find that neither levels nor significant thresholds of industrialization explain the timing of social insurance program adoptions in 59 nations between the 1880s and the 1960s. Examining the expansion of various categories of social public expenditures in 18 democratic capitalist nations during the 1960s and 1970s,

Castles (1982b:61–70) reinforces the conclusion of OECD (1978) that these nations have recently diverged rather than converged and that neither economic level nor economic growth can account for recent expenditure changes. Furthermore, both Stephens (1979, Ch. 4) and Myles (1984:94–97) adduce evidence against Wilensky's (1975) pivotal argument that national social welfare efforts are determined by the proportions of aged in the population.

Finally, Minkoff & Turgeon (1977) and Szelenyi (1983) both provide findings relevant to the crucial logic-of-industrialism proposition that capitalist and state-socialist nations converge during economic development toward similar social policies. Although this may be true if highly aggregated expenditure measures are used (Pryor 1968), a detailed look at programmatic profiles and particular policy provisions reveals that state-socialist authorities in centrally planned economies closely tailor social insurance and housing policies to the exigencies of labor discipline and control of migration. Moreover, while unemployment insurance is an important program in most developed capitalist nations, the state-socialist industrial societies do not have this kind of income-protection for the temporarily unemployed, not because they have no such people, but because these regimes officially guarantee (and require) employment for all workers.

CAPITALIST DEVELOPMENT AND SOCIAL POLICY

Logic-of-industrialism theorists have not been the only ones to use functionalist reasoning to predict converging patterns of social policy. Neo-Marxist theorists of "the capitalist state" have theorized in a similar manner, deriving understandings of what social policy does from their understandings of the overall logic of capitalist development. Neo-Marxist interest centers not on the transition from agrarianism to industrialism but on the transition within the capitalist mode of production from early "competitive" capitalism to advanced "monopoly" capitalism. As this transition occurs, the functional demands on capitalist states change and intensify, neo-Marxists agree. Yet those functional demands always remain contradictory—requiring the state both to promote capital accumulation and to retain democratic legitimacy—because capitalism is based on the wage relationship through which capital and labor both cooperate and conflict with one another.

Social policies tend to be specifically categorized by neo-Marxists as responses by states to the "social reproduction" needs of advanced capitalism (see discussions in Gough 1975, 1979: Ch. 3; O'Connor 1973; Offe 1984: Ch. 3, Marklund 1982:11–20; Mishra 1984: Ch. 3). These have both accumulation-promoting and legitimating aspects, for "social reproduction" includes the need to prepare appropriately motivated and skilled wage workers, the need to allow employees and their families to consume adequate goods and services for daily and generational renewal, and the need to preserve economic and political order in the face of possible discontent from (or about) the fate of the displaced, injured, sick, or elderly people who necessarily appear in market economies and who cannot be cared for by families alone. Despite different terminologies, there is considerable overlap between logic-of-industrialism and neo-Marxist understandings of the societal needs to which social policies putatively respond. The crucial difference lies in the greater stress placed by neo-Marxists on requisites of labor control.

Although all neo-Marxists treat social policies as responses to the contradictory functional requisites of advanced capitalism, there are a range of ways to develop this perspective. Some theorists rather exclusively stress the requirements of capital accumulation (e.g. the German "state derivationists" as discussed in Holloway & Picciotto 1978); others stress both the economic and the political systemic requirements of advanced capitalism (e.g. O'Connor 1973, Offe 1984); and still others stress systemic political requirements along with shifting conflicts and compromises within the capitalist class and between capital and labor [e.g. Poulantzas (1973), and the skillful "Poulantzian" case study of Weimar Germany by Abraham (1981)]. Despite such variations, however, all neo-Marxists agree that both initial expansions and eventual "crises" of welfare-state interventions should follow the rhythms of capital accumulation and related transformations in class relations.

How does one go from any variant of such an overarching theoretical perspective to empirically testable predictions about temporal and cross-national variations in concrete patterns of social policy? So far, neo-Marxist grand theorists have largely rested content with abstract conceptual elaborations tied to illustrative case materials for one nation at a time [e.g. the United States for O'Connor (1973), the United Kingdom for Gough (1979), and West Germany for Offe (1984)]. A very few attempts have been made to specify and test neo-Marxist hypotheses in cross-national research, and these have produced mixed results. On the tentatively positive side, Goran Therborn and others (Therborn et al 1978, Marklund 1982) are in the midst of research on Sweden in cross-national perspective, before and during the period of Social Democratic parliamentary ascendancy from 1932 onward. They take issue with some of the ideas we attribute below to "the Social Democratic model" of policy development and try to show that more fundamental and long-term patterns of economic transformation and class structure are associated with characteristics of public policies and social redistribution in Sweden and in other capitalist democracies. On the negative side of the ledger, Myles (1984:93–95) probes for causal effects attributable to capital centralization/concentration or to the size of the "surplus" population, but he finds neither of these variables, frequently invoked by neo-Marxists, to be effective in accounting for national variations in pension quality.

Neo-Marxist theorists face challenges not only in explaining national variations within advanced capitalism, but also in identifying the political actors that
initiate and shape public policies. Some neo-Marxists treat working class
organizations as key actors (e.g. Gough 1979, Marklund 1982), with the result
that their arguments and findings shade over into those of proponents of the
Social Democratic model. More often, neo-Marxists assert or imply that
"monopoly capitalists" are key political actors and that "capitalist states" act as
class-conscious directorates for the system as a whole. However, little systematic evidence has been produced for these formulations, and for the case of the
twentieth-century United States in particular, proponents of a "corporate liberal" approach (Berkowitz & McQuaid 1980, Quadagno 1984, Weinstein 1968),
which might be considered complementary to neo-Marxist theories, have come
up against strong criticisms from scholars who regard both the state and
democratic political forces as more causally significant than monopoly capitalists or state managers acting as executors for capitalists (see Block 1977a,b;
Skocpol 1980; Skocpol & Amenta 1985).

Finally, neo-Marxists also need to pinpoint which functional requisites arise
from wage-relations and market processes specific to capitalism as such. Aren't
many of them requisites faced by all industrial societies (Pryor 1968, Wilensky
1975) or experienced in parallel ways by the state managers of centrally planned
economies (Minkoff & Turgeon 1977)? To properly address this issue, we need
comparisons of policies in capitalist and state-socialist industrial nations,
pursued along the various lines that scholars such as Burawoy (1980), Lindblom (1977), Manchin & Szelenyi (forthcoming), Parkin (1972), Szelenyi
(1978), and Therborn (1978) have only begun to map out. Yet as such comparisons across "modes of production" are made, it will be difficult to control
for the effects of democracy on social policies, for there are as yet no socialist
nations that are also democratic.

HOW DOES DEMOCRATIC POLITICS MATTER?

Both logic-of-industrialism theorists and neo-Marxist functionalists have downplayed the significance of political struggles in industrial or capitalist democracies. But other clusters of scholars have argued that—especially within
the ranks of advanced capitalist democracies as such—politics outweighs
economic variables in determining national social policies. All researchers who
take democratic politics seriously share the basic assumption of Key (1949),
Lenski (1966), Marshall (1963), and Schumpeter (1942) that distributive outcomes in industrial/capitalist societies can be profoundly affected by governments, so that it matters whether there are representative-democratic structures, mass enfranchisement, competitive elections, or other less institutionalized means through which the populace can influence what its gov-

ernment does. For all theorists who argue that democracy matters, the social policies of modern welfare states are presumed to have at least some redistributive effects for the mass of people in their capacity as citizens. (In fact, it is never easy to sort out socioeconomic effects determined by state actions from those brought about by economic conditions or conjunctures. See the useful discussions in Keman & Braun 1984, Korpi 1980, Schmidt 1982, and Therborn et al 1978).

Representative Structures and Electoral Processes

Some scholars have left aside the issue of class divisions in the capitalist democracies and have explored whether formal democratic structures, mass electoral participation, or competitive elections seem related to the origins or growth of social policies across nations. As Hewitt (1977) and Myles (1984) have appropriately suggested, such hypotheses can be labelled "simple democratic" because they make no statements about either the class basis or the substantive ideological commitments of the political forces that bring about social policies. The idea is that something about Western-style liberal democracy as a set of institutions or processes is in itself sufficient to encourage the earlier or more extensive enactment of social policies.

The evidence about such simple democratic hypotheses is mixed, however. Although he primarily stresses the causal role of economic development, Cutright (1965) finds that, with economic development controlled, politically "representative" institutions led to earlier introductions of social insurance programs across 76 nations between 1934 and 1960. But looking at dependent variables having to do with government social expenditures, Jackman (1975) and Wilensky (1975) find no significant effects of representative institutions for similarly large and heterogeneous cross-national samples. Working with a smaller set of 17 "non-communist industrial countries" and using a historically sensitive measure of "democratic experience" (i.e. number of years of full democracy up to 1965, with universal suffrage, secret ballot, and elected executives all required for "full democracy"), Hewitt (1977) also fails to find positive effects of representative structures on "redistributive government spending." And Myles (1984:87–88) similarly finds that democratic political rights as such are not important predictors of pension quality across 15 capitalist democracies in 1975.

The picture for simple democratic arguments becomes a bit brighter when the participatory and electoral processes of such polities are probed more precisely. Through investigations into the relative timing of the adoption of several major types of social insurance policies, Flora & Alber (1981) find that the extension of the suffrage between 1880 and 1920 encouraged program adoptions in European parliamentary democracies (but not in bureaucratic monarchies). Schneider (1982) finds that "conventional political participation," measured as the number of votes cast in national elections on a per capita basis, strongly encouraged earlier adoptions of all types of programs in 18 Western nations between 1919 and 1975. In his aforementioned study of 15 capitalist democracies, Myles (1984:83, 86–89) finds that, even with working class power controlled for, relative approximations to perfectly competitive elections between 1945 and 1974 significantly affect pensions in 1975: "Faced with a high level of competition at the polls, it would appear that parties do indeed bid up the quality of pension entitlements in the pursuit of votes." This echoes cross-nationally the classic argument that V. O. Key (1949) made for social policymaking across states within the United States.

Finally, an "electoral-economic cycle" argument is a further kind of simple democratic hypothesis, one that links the *exact timing* of social benefit increases to the concerns of elected politicians competing for office. This approach has been applied to the United States, uncovering evidence of election-year timing of New Deal spending under Franklin Roosevelt (Wright 1974) and the election-year and precise monthly targeting of 9 out of 13 legislated Social Security increases between 1950 and 1976 (Tufte 1978: Ch. 2). For the US case, Tufte also reveals the administrative creation of gaps between pre-election benefit increases and post-election tax increases, and he offers models and a bit of suggestive evidence that could extend propositions about "electoral-economic cycles" to other nations with parliamentary governments (Tufte 1978:12, 100–101). Frey & Schneider (1978, 1982) slightly modify Tufte's argument by arguing that governments must be in a "popularity deficit" before they will manipulate social policies prior to elections; otherwise governing parties will act on their established ideological principles. These researchers find evidence in favor of such ideas in a study of the timing of transfer payments in West Germany, the United Kingdom, and the United States, but their results for the United Kingdom are countered by Alt & Chrystal (1983). Tufte's propositions also remain controversial for the US case itself (see the negative findings in Golden & Poterba 1980 and Griffin et al 1983).

The Effects of Popular Protest

Perhaps formal representative structures and conventional elections are not the only or the primary routes through which popular aspirations influence social policymaking in capitalist democracies. Two well-known students of American social policy, Frances Piven and Richard Cloward, have argued (1971, 1977) that new or increased welfare benefits (and other measures such as rules favoring union organization) have occurred as concessions by elites to protests by the poor and workers. Improved social policies have been conceded, say Piven & Cloward, only when economic and political crises render elites in a formal democracy unable simply to repress "disruptive" riots or strikes or demonstrations. The resulting social policies may truly benefit nonelites, Piven

& Cloward argue, but once popular disruptions cease, some benefits may be retracted and new bureaucratic controls will accompany any enhanced benefits that remain in force. Obviously, similar arguments might link programmatic innovations or increases in public social expenditure in many capitalist democratic nations to measures of industrial strike militancy and other kinds of "extra-institutional" popular action outside of orthodox economic or political routines. This mass disruption approach is certainly much more skeptical of the redistributive possibilities of capitalist democracy than are the simple democratic approaches, but it still posits possibilities for policy responses to popular demands.

Empirical evidence on "the Piven and Cloward thesis" and analogous arguments is at best weakly supportive for circumscribed applications. For the US case in particular, Achenbaum (1983), Massad (1980), Skocpol (1980), and Skocpol & Ikenberry (1983) all question the validity of Piven & Cloward's arguments for the 1930s. For the 1960s Albritton (1979) uses county-level AFDC data to reject Piven & Cloward's thesis. Others who have studied trends specifically in postwar US welfare transfer payments (Griffin et al 1983, Isaac & Kelley 1981, Jennings 1983) or welfare caseloads (Hicks & Swank 1983) have found greater empirical support for Piven & Cloward, especially for their arguments about the impact of racial insurgencies in the 1960s. Yet other causal variables downplayed by Piven & Cloward, such as unemployment rates and legal changes, have also been found to affect extensions of US welfare benefits.

Cross-nationally, Myles (1984) finds that civil protest from 1960 to 1970 had no significant magnitude of effect on the relative quality of public old-age pensions in 1975, but he finds that levels of strike activity by industrial workers had a small positive effect, when he controlled for the effects of working class political power exercised through institutional channels. Similarly, for the postwar United States, Griffin et al (1983) find that strikes had a slight impact on welfare outlays—but not on social insurance benefits, which have been expanded through regular institutional channels. Overall, we can tentatively conclude that mass disruption arguments are most applicable to times and places where working classes and other organized democratic forces lack access to regular institutional channels for affecting social policies. Even so, the effects of disruption may be slight and not in line with the demands posed, and analysts must probe for possible "backlash" effects against those who protest.

The Social Democratic Model of Welfare State Development

While authors of simple democratic arguments treat capitalist democracies as if they were classless, and advocates of the mass disruption thesis think in terms of dominant elites and occasionally protesting nonelites, a third group of analysts shares with neo-Marxists the view that the class division between capitalists and wage workers is the fundamental axis of power and of political struggles in industrialized capitalist democracies. Democracy matters for these proponents of the social democratic model of welfare state development, not because representative structures and electoral processes alone are thought to be very consequential, but because these arrangements make it *possible* for wage workers who become highly organized to displace class struggles from the industrial arena into the political arena and to use the democratic state as a nonmarket instrument for redistributing income and services away from the economically privileged (for basic discussions, see Hewitt 1977; Hollingsworth & Hanneman 1982; Korpi 1978: Chs. 1–2, 1980; Stephens 1979: Chs. 1–3). What is more, according to the logic of this social democratic model, when working class-based organizations gain direct control within the state, disruptive protests, including industrial strikes, become relatively unimportant means for workers to influence policy outcomes (and the volume of strike activity in capitalist democracies is, indeed, inversely correlated with measures of working class control of the state; see Hibbs 1978, Korpi & Shalev 1980).

The pure social democratic model of welfare state development entails an interlocked set of propositions that derive a comprehensive pattern of social and economic policies from prolonged working class control of the democratic capitalist state. The ideal-typical process works as follows: A high proportion of wage and, eventually, salaried workers become organized into centralized unions, and those unions financially nourish a social democratic or labor party supported by the same workers in their capacities as voters. Given such working class organizational strength in both the market and political arenas, the supposition is that the taxing, spending, and administrative powers of the state can be expanded, shifting class struggles into the political arena, where workers are favored in a democracy by their numbers. The model posits that the earlier and more fully the workers become organized into centralized unions and a social democratic party, and the more consistently over time the social democratic party controls the state, the earlier and more "completely" a modern welfare state develops.

What kinds of policies are considered to make up a comprehensive welfare state as envisaged in the social democratic model? According to the social democratic model, traditionally designated social policies—such as social insurance programs, welfare transfers, public housing, education, and health services—are to be closely coordinated with such economic policies as industrial regulations enforcing minimum wages, unionization, and workplace safety, and also coordinated with Keynesian-style macroeconomic management aimed at ensuring a full employment economy favorable to labor's bargaining power. Thus, Korpi (1980:297, 303) *defines* social policy to include "in principle, all of the ways in which the state enters into the distributive processes of the capitalist democracies," whether before or after the market allocates income, and he points to an ideal-typical array of policy characteristics that constitute an "institutional" pattern characteristic of full-fledged social democracy. This policy pattern includes an important role for programs designed to prevent social ills (such as unemployment or poverty or lack of skills) from arising in the first place; a predominance of universal and progressively tax-financed social benefits, rather than selective, contributory, or regressively financed benefits; programs offering better than minimal benefits to citizens; and a high degree of social provision directly through the state rather than through private organizations, yet without bureaucratic controls over individual conduct.

Clearly, Korpi's "institutional" policy pattern presumes that virtually all types of welfare state interventions should vary together (and that "all good things" can happen together!). Except where preventive policies (e.g. active labor market policies) can reduce the need for ameliorative policies (e.g. unemployment insurance), Korpi's conception does not seem to envisage the possibility of such systematic *trade-offs* between policies as, for example, Heidenheimer (1981) delineates in his contrast of the US emphasis on public education versus the European emphasis on social insurance, or as Schneider (1982) suggests in her contrast of countries emphasizing "social security" programs to those emphasizing "social equality" programs.

During the last 10 years (as Shalev 1983a,b elaborates), the social democratic model has dominated cross-national research on social policies and expenditures in the industrially most developed capitalist democracies. In many studies involving from 1 to 22 such nations, a great deal of empirical evidence has been amassed in support of the causal connections posited by the model (see Bjorn 1979; Cameron 1978; Castles 1978, 1982b; Esping-Andersen 1985; Furniss & Tilton 1977; Headey 1970, 1978; Hewitt 1977; Hibbs 1977; Kammerman & Kahn 1978; Korpi 1978, 1980, 1983; Korpi & Shalev 1980; Leibfried 1978; Martin 1973; Myles 1984, Ruggie 1984; Stephens 1979; Stephens & Stephens 1982; and Tufte 1978: Ch. 4).

A number of these studies examine particular kinds of social policies and compare from 1 to 14 other countries to Sweden—which is always taken as the social democratic prototype, because of the very high proportion of its labor force organized into centralized unions and because of the virtually continuous rule of the Swedish social democratic party after 1932. Thus Headey (1978) contrasts the greater achievement of redistributive "housing equity" under Sweden's social democratic policies with the failure to do as well of British Labor and US Democratic governments. Similarly, Kamerman & Kahn (1978) describe policies to help families in 14 nations, arrayed on a continuum from Sweden's "explicit and comprehensive" policies to the "implicit and reluctant" policies of the United States. Again with Sweden on the extreme social democratic end, Myles (1984: Ch. 4) finds "working class power"—

operationalized as union membership and centralization, and according to the number of years in the postwar period during which labor/social-democratic parties controlled the cabinet—to be the strongest predictor of the relative generosity, universality, and redistributiveness of old-age pensions across 15 nations in 1975. Ruggie (1984) argues that measures to help working women are better developed in Sweden as part of comprehensive pro–working-class policies than they are in Britian, where certain social policies have supposedly been more directly targeted at women's needs. Still further singing the praises of Swedish social democracy, Stephens & Stephens (1982) compare policies favoring workers' participation in industry in West Germany, France, Sweden and other large European countries; they find that such policies are best developed and work best where overall union and social-democratic party strength is greatest.

In addition, cross-national quantitative studies (including Bjorn 1979, Cameron 1978, Hewitt 1977) have focused on explaining postwar expansions of government social expenditures and have reached conclusions favorable to the social democratic model. Most notably, in a cross-sectional regression analysis of 17 capitalist democracies, Stephens (1979: Ch. 4) finds that the percentage of national income devoted to nonmilitary public spending in 1976 is significantly related to the number of years of social democratic rule and the degree of economy-wide bargaining by unions. And in a more disaggregated correlation analysis of the postwar expenditures of 18 capitalist democracies, Castles (1982b) finds that, from the early 1960s through the mid-1970s, cabinet seats held by Social Democratic parties had a stronger effect than competing variables on the share of public health expenditure in GDP in 1962, and on the share of general government expenditure minus total welfare.

Yet for all of the favorable evidence, the pure social democratic model has not been established beyond question as a sufficient guide to when, how, and why industrialized capitalist democracies create and expand social policies. Flora & Alber (1981) and Alber (1981) have shown that this model does not apply to the origins of European social insurance programs. Not unions and social democrats, but conservative monarchs or liberal politicians, were the agents of early European social insurance innovations. Moreover, for the 1930s watershed in which Scandinavian Social Democrats first assumed power, Castles (1978), Esping-Andersen (1985), and Weir & Skocpol (1985) all offer political analyses that underline the importance of social democratic–agrarian *coalitions* rather just the organizational strength of unions and social democratic parties themselves. Clearly, the social democratic model applies best to the relative expansion after World War II of national social expenditures. Yet on this safer postwar terrain, only Sweden really seems to fit the model unequivocally, and even such a close fit has not prevented scholars (such as Cameron 1978, Castles 1982b, Kelman 1981, Therborn et al 1978, and Weir &

Skocpol 1985) from respecifying the causal processes at work in that case. What is more, other countries such as the Netherlands have turned up as puzzling exceptions to the social democratic model, and efforts to handle anomalous cases have prompted scholars to formulate alternatives to the pure social democratic approach.

Party Systems and Party Organization

Among the alternatives have been perspectives that undertake further inquiry into the roles of political parties. Perhaps political parties other than social democratic parties have an impact upon social policies and expenditures. And perhaps the characteristics of entire systems of parties are more decisive than the orientations of particular types of parties studied in isolation from their competitors. These possibilities are at the heart of the latest research into "how politics has mattered" for the development of social policies in the capitalist democracies.

In a study of 19 nations during periods of democratic rule, Wilensky (1981) finds that "Catholic party power" from 1919 to 1976 positively affected social security efforts in 1965, in large part because such party power was associated with "corporatist" bargaining and with "invisible" taxes. Perhaps more important, Wilensky argues that the alternation in rule of Catholic and left-wing parties boosts social security effort. As a general explanation of social policy development, however, the Wilensky approach suffers from its heavy reliance on the cases of Belgium, Netherlands, Italy, Austria, and Germany. Like the Social Democratic model with its orientation to the Scandinavian cases, Wilensky's "Catholic party power" approach is most useful if it is taken as an analysis of one among alternative routes to recent welfare-state expansion.

The work of Castles (starting with Borg & Castles 1981) attempts to achieve greater generality by focusing on right-wing political parties as obstacles to welfare-state development. In a correlational analysis of many social spending programs in 18 OECD countries in the 1960s and 1970s, Castles (1982b) finds that the parliamentary and cabinet representation of right-wing parties discourages spending more than social-democratic representation promotes it. Castles also focuses on the precise *types* of spending promoted or tolerated by various sorts of parties. He argues (1982b:74–75) that "education is related to right-wing strength, health spending to social democratic strength and class politics, and public income maintenance seems unaffected by political considerations." Right-wing and center parties, Castles suggests, are least antagonistic to social transfer payments, because these are often based on insurance principles and interfere little with the operations of the market.

Like the social democratic model, a focus on right-wing or Catholic political parties assumes that parties will put into effect programs favored by their constituent groups. Other researchers, however, have begun to look into whether certain political parties are, instead, oriented toward patronage—the granting of "divisible," "distributive" benefits to particular business and popular constituencies (Shefter 1977). Thus, recent historical and comparative studies suggest that the patronage basis of US politics has had many consequences for the timing and contents of American social policies, in contrast to European policies (Katznelson 1985, Orloff & Skocpol 1984, Orloff 1985). Moreover, in a comparative study of five US states, Amenta et al (1984) find that the more patronage-oriented and factionalized a state's Democratic party, the longer it took to pass unemployment insurance in the 1930s, and the greater the concessions to business interests in the legislation that finally passed.

TRANSNATIONAL CONTEXTS AND SOCIAL POLICIES

Ironically, the narrowing of much recent cross-national research to less than two dozen advanced capitalist democracies has simultaneously opened new possibilities to take a more world-historical perspective for investigators of social policies in these and other nations. Scholars have begun to consider the ways in which changing transnational contexts—especially the world economy, geopolitics, and international cultural modelling—may have helped to shape national social policies before as well as during the twentieth century.

National Strategies in the World Economy

Students of "First World" industrial democracies and of Latin American "Third World" nations have all argued that social policies must be analyzed in relationship to overall government strategies for managing links to the international economy. Yet the economic strategies with which social policies are thought to be coordinated are not the same for the two sorts of countries.

In a pathbreaking examination of 18 developed capitalist countries, Cameron (1978) argues that the expansion of the "public economy" (defined as the increase of government revenues as a percent of GDP from 1960 to 1975) was best accounted for by exports plus imports of goods and services as a percent of GDP. Thus measured, "openness to the international economy" was even a better predictor than social democratic power (which Cameron believes is enhanced by openness). Because they need to adjust constantly to shifts in international markets, Cameron argues (1978:1260), "governments in small open economies have tended to provide a variety of income supplements in the form of social security schemes, health insurance, unemployment benefits, employment subsidies to firms and even job training." Katzenstein (1985) fleshes out this thesis, demonstrating that seven small trade-dependent European democracies use "democratic corporatist" bargains among unions, business, and government to coordinate economic and social policies. Labor movement involvement in the corporatist arrangements varies, however, and some national differences in social spending can be traced to that fact (Katzenstein 1985: Ch. 3).

Other scholars have skeptically reexamined Cameron's quantitative findings (see Castles 1981, 1982b; Schmidt 1982). According to Castles (1978: Ch. 3; 1982b:77–83), the historical effects of trade patterns are more important than economic openness after World War II. Castles looks to the original formation of political party systems with or without unified right-wing parties as the crucial arbiter of later welfare state expansion. He argues that various modes of national involvement in international trade in the nineteenth and early twentieth century were pivotal for determining whether conflicts within dominant classes would undermine the capacity of right-wing political forces to shape national politics in the democratic era.

For Latin American nations, meanwhile, scholarship on the development of social policies has largely ignored international trade as such and has suggested instead that social policies have been instituted or reshaped as explicit parts of state strategies to promote the economic development of nations situated in dependent positions in the world capitalist system. For example, Spalding (1980) links the launching of Mexican social security in the 1940s to the state's industrialization stategy. New social security taxes were to be used to help finance state investments, she argues, and key groups of workers had to be politically managed. Analogously, the use of social policies for the bureaucratic cooptation and control of strategic sectors of the working and middle classes during state-led development has also been highlighted in Stepan's (1978) work on Peru and in Malloy's (1979) study of Brazil as it compares to many other Latin American nations. Building on the same perspective, Malloy & Borzutzky (1982) explore the distributional and demographic consequences of Latin American social security policies.

Geopolitics and Social Policies

Modern national states have always been enmeshed in a world economy, but at the same time they have also been participants in a system of warring or potentially warring states. Several clusters of studies treat social policymaking as an adjunct of state-managed resource mobilization for international competition.

First, some research suggests that states have instituted social policies as part of their own organizational and territorial consolidation. Comparing England, France, Spain, and Brandenburg-Prussia, Tilly (1975) analyzes how the efforts of early modern European "statemakers" to extract revenues and build armies became variously intertwined with policies to stimulate the production of food and regulate its availability to officials and potentially rebellious peasants. Similarly, comparing nations in nineteenth-century Europe, Ramirez & Boli (1985) argue that state-sponsored mass schooling was instituted at moments of defeat and crisis as part of efforts by authorities to improve the competitive potential of their nations in the inter-state system.

A second cluster of studies takes note of the coincidence since the nineteenth century of modern "total warfare" with the growth of modern social insurance and welfare policies. According to a number of writers (Andreski 1968; Janowitz 1976: Ch. 3; and Titmuss 1958), mass citizen mobilization for modern warfare has encouraged more generous, universalistic, and egalitarian public social provision, especially when the line between soldiers and civilians becomes blurred, as it did in World-War-II Britain. Democratic politicians appealing for popular support in wartime can be seen as the agents of this welfare-warfare linkage, although systematic cross-national evidence is lacking. Another intervening mechanism has been suggested by Peacock & Wiseman (1961): Major wars, they suggest, require and allow governments to expand their fiscal base; after the war, much of the state's enhanced fiscal capacity remains, and new or expanded social expenditures may be instituted more easily than usual. Peacock & Wiseman document their thesis only for Britain, and efforts to extend the argument cross-nationally seem certain to reveal that state structures and domestic balances of political power mediate the impact of war on social policymaking in complex ways.

Finally, a third set of studies has explored whether modern social policies, once established, may be fiscally stunted by the need to compete with large or growing military establishments. In a cross-national look at 22 rich countries, Wilensky (1975: Ch. 4) finds support for his view that "little" wars and high military spending from 1950 to 1952 retarded, but did not halt, increases in national social spending. Other relevant time-series research on the US case alone has produced different results depending on the years covered. For 1939 to 1968, Russett (1970) found significant trade-offs between military spending and spending for education and health, but Russett (1982) and Griffin et al (1983) found no significant military versus social spending trade-offs for the periods 1947–1979 and 1949–1977, respectively. No doubt, short-term domestic political processes interact with fiscal constraints to determine whether state-provided "guns and butter" will be traded off or not.

International Cultural Modeling

The impacts of international contexts on national social policies need not be conceptualized solely in world-economic or geopolitical terms. According to John Meyer and others of what might be called the "cultural school" of world system analysis (see Bergesen 1980: Chs. 5–7; Meyer & Hannan 1979; and Thomas & Meyer 1984:475–78), the spread of a competitive state system from Europe to the entire globe has been accompanied and facilitated by the shared adherence of statemakers to world-wide cultural frames, including models of the types of institutional features thought to be necessary for any "modern" nation-state (or, for that matter, necessary even in their colonial dependencies; see Meyer et al 1979:51–53). According to this perspective, apparently similar *forms* of social policies—perhaps encouraged by internationally mobile professionals or by world organizations such as the United Nations or the International Labor Organization—may spread relatively quickly across nations, despite their varying world-economic situations or domestic characteristics. This offers an alternative to the logic of industrialism interpretation of the apparent convergence of many nations toward the same basic categories of social insurance, educational and health programs.

Most of the empirical work done so far by Meyer and his collaborators has not directly tested the notion that similar *forms* of social policies can be related to the international diffusion of common ideals or models. Yet Collier & Messick (1975) have been cited (by Thomas & Meyer 1984:476) in support of this perspective. This study shows that, after 1920, standard categories of social insurance programs spread rapidly from the early adopters in Europe and the Americas to many nations at all levels of development. Before 1920, however, Collier & Messick did not find diffusion from more to less developed European nations, and their notion that the opposite kind of diffusion might have occurred is called into question by Kuhnle's (1981) detailed demonstration that pioneering German social insurance policies of the 1880s did *not* straightforwardly serve as models for subsequent Scandinavian innovations. Moreover, sometimes nations avoid rather than imitate international models; thus Skocpol & Ikenberry (1983) show that European social insurance policies were positive models for US reformers before World War I, but became negative models afterwards. Future research on international modeling and diffusion needs to probe carefully the precise mechanisms of transmission from polity to polity, to consider different processes across time periods of world history, and to allow for negative as well as positive international modelling. Highly aggregated quantitative studies are unlikely to be sufficient to pin down these processes.

THE IMPACT OF STATES ON SOCIAL POLICYMAKING

Until recently, most work on the determinants of social policies has emphasized their socioeconomic roots and has treated states as if they were merely arenas of political conflict or passive administrative tools to be turned to the purposes of any social group that gains governmental power. Currently, however, scholars are exploring ways in which social policymaking may be shaped by the organizational structures and capacities of states and by the political effects of previously enacted policies. In short, states are being reconceptualized as partially autonomous actors and as consequential structures and sets of policies (see Skocpol 1985). "State-centered" work on social policy formation is at an early stage, however, so the emphasis in this final section is on emerging ideas rather than cumulations of research findings.

States as Actors and Structures

Not surprisingly, social policies have most often been traced to the autonomous initiatives of state authorities for capitalist nations in "lagging" or "dependent" international positions. (When the state-socialist nations are discussed, the ruling party authorities and technocrats are always treated as the initiators of social policies.) Many of the studies surveyed in the preceding section treat state authorities as the key actors. Moreover, the executive leaders of bureaucratic-authoritarian regimes have been identified as the ones most likely to initiate new social policies. Such authorities, the reasoning goes, already have strong administrative capacities at hand, and they have an interest in using social policies to faciliate economic development while deflecting popular discontent. This argument is to be found in Flora & Alber's explanation (1981) for the pioneering social insurance initiatives of "constitutional-dualist monarchies" in Bismarckian Germany and Hapsburg Austria, and in Malloy's (1979) parallel analysis for "patrimonial-bureaucratic" Brazil.

For liberal-democratic polities, autonomous state inputs into social policymaking have usually been conceptualized in terms of the contributions of civil bureaucrats to the creation or reworking of social policies (Heclo 1974a), or in terms of the putatively inherent tendency of strong state bureaucracies to expand social expenditures (see the reasoning and equivocal findings of De-Viney 1983). A few scholars are beginning to analyze state capacities to formulate and implement policies in more differentiated ways. Some have surveyed in general terms the alternative modes of intervention states can use to cope with either economic or social problems, ranging from direct state ownership or provision of services, through public expenditures, to the use of regulations or tax incentives to modify the actions of firms, families, and voluntary groups (e.g. Curtis 1983, Kramer 1981, Lowi 1972, Rainwater & Rein 1983:117–18). Others have focused much more specifically on the organizational and intellectual resources through which particular states have dealt— or failed to deal—with given kinds of problems (e.g. Davidson & Lowe 1981, Fainstein & Fainstein 1978, Headey 1978, Leman 1980: Ch. 6, Weir & Skocpol 1985).

Centralization of the state has also been examined, as well as bureaucratization. A number of studies provide some support for the hypothesis that administratively or fiscally centralized states are more conducive than decentralized states to generous and expanding social expenditures (Castles 1982b; DeViney 1983; Wilensky 1976, 1981). Yet in their time-series study of social expenditures in Britain, France, Italy, and Germany, Hage & Hanneman (1980) argue that centralized states can either promote or retard social expenditures. What is more, findings about "decentralized" state structures primarily refer to federal polities, and careful comparative studies make it clear that "federalisms" vary. Thus, Leman's (1977, 1980) work on Canada and the United States proposes that Canada's relatively centralized and parliamentary federalism has facilitated steady streams of social policy innovations and their diffusion across levels of government, whereas the highly decentralized federalism of the United States, combined with divisions of power among legislatures, courts, and executives, has forced major social policy innovations to come in "big bangs" at times of national economic or political crisis. Moreover, interesting arguments about the contrasting policy effects of German federalism amd US federalism appear in Heidenheimer et al (1983).

Beyond such examinations of state structures and capacities, comparative and historical scholars have also demonstrated that "state building" and the varying institutional structures of states affect social policymaking over the long run via their impact on political parties, class formation, and political culture. Thus Orloff & Skocpol (1984) and Orloff (1985) show how various sequences and forms of democratization and state bureaucratization affected both the capacities of civil administrations and the orientations of working-class groups and middle-class reformers toward social spending policies in Britain, Canada, and the United States from the nineteenth century through the 1930s. These works draw upon and complement the work of Katznelson (1981, 1985) and Shefter (1983; forthcoming) on the effects that varying national processes of state formation have had on the organization of political parties and on the political orientations and capacities of industrial workers. Analogously, Fainstein & Fainstein (1978), Skocpol (1980), Skowronek (1982), and Vogel (1978, 1981) all suggest ways in which the peculiar history of US state building has affected the political outlooks and capacities of American capitalists— encouraging their fierce opposition to many public social policies that, once instituted, might help (or at least not harm) the capitalist economy. And Kelman (1981) attributes to historical processes of state formation many differences in the styles of industrial safety regulation practiced in Sweden versus the United States since the 1960s.

Social Policies Reshape Politics

As we have just seen, states can be analyzed "architecturally," to find out how state building and state structures affect social policymaking through administrative and political processes. The effects of states can also be examined in a more fine grained and inherently dynamic way by *tracing the political consequences of already instituted policies or sets of policies.* For not only does politics create social policies; social policies also create politics. That is, once policies are enacted and implemented, they change the public agendas and the patterns of group conflict through which subsequent policy changes occur. Not surprisingly, scholars' sensitivity to such political feedback effects has emerged as public social provision matured in the West after the war.

"Policy feedbacks" (as we label the effects of social policies on politics) have been analyzed in a number of ways, depending upon the investigator's underlying model of the political process. For one example, Wilensky (1976, 1981) probes for possible "fiscal backlash" against high and growing social expenditures in the most industrially developed capitalist democracies (see also an alternative formulation in Rosenberry 1982). Wilensky maintains that "painfully visible taxes" (e.g. income and property taxes) arouse generalized public resistance to welfare state expansion, whereas democratic politicians who use "invisible taxes" (e.g., contributory-withholding or value-added taxes) can "tax, spend and yet stay cool." These ideas resemble those of economists who discuss "the fiscal illusion," referring to characteristics built into tax systems that lead voters to underestimate the cost of public goods (Borcherding 1977, Lowery & Berry 1983). There are, however, many disagreements over how to classify various kinds of taxes.

While Wilensky views politics as a dialectic between leaders and the public and analyzes policy feedbacks in those terms, Heclo (1974a) sees politics primarily as a process by which administrators, politicians, and reformist intellectuals "puzzle" about solutions to societal problems. But this "puzzling" does not occur in a vacuum. Rather it reacts to the perceived shortcomings of previous policies and asks how the governmental means at hand can be used to do better with adjusted or alternative policies. Heclo applies this "political learning" perspective to the long-term development of old-age and unemployment policies in Sweden and Britain from the nineteenth century through the 1960s, yet he does not offer explicit methods for analyzing the conditions under which administrators or intellectuals can actually influence policy developments. Amenta et al (1984) try to operationalize political learning variables more precisely in a comparative study of five US states; Weir & Skocpol (1985) analyze the varying relationships of economists to administrators and politicians in their comparative study of Sweden, Britain, and the United States.

Scholars who view social policy-making as wholly or partially grounded in sociopolitical conflicts and coalitions have also invoked policy feedbacks for explanatory purposes. Thus Orloff & Skocpol (1984) argue that reactions to Civil War pensions in the early twentieth-century United States undermined possibilities for cross-class coalitions in support of old-age pensions, and Weir & Skocpol (1985) argue that early New Deal interventions helped to undermine subsequent possibilities for farmer-worker coalitions in support of a "social-Keynesian" welfare state. In his comparative study of housing policies in Britain, Sweden, and the United States, Headey (1978: Ch. 9) shows how initial public programs in Sweden set in motion a "positive sequence of policy development" by creating new interest groups favoring further government interventions. In studies of the US case alone, Janowitz (1976, 1980) argues that the fragmentation and disorganization of American social policies has furthered political party decomposition and helped to prevent realigning elections. Piven & Cloward (1982) stress that US social policies since the New Deal have created new bureacratic and popular constituencies favoring expanded welfare programs; these include groups self-consciously oriented to the needs and values of women and children. Women, in fact, are a political constituency whose visibility has been enhanced by the operation of welfare-state programs (see Balbo 1982; Joffe forthcoming; Pearce 1978, 1983; Piven 1984).

Finally, perhaps the most thorough piece of research featuring an argument about policy feedbacks is a comparative study by Gösta Esping-Andersen (1978, 1985) of the long-term development of welfare states in Sweden and Denmark. Seeking to explain why the Danish Social Democratic party and welfare state are losing support, while their Swedish counterparts are proving more resilient in the face of fiscal stringencies, Esping-Andersen does detailed analyses of the political effects of major policies instituted in each country, including pensions, employment policies, and housing programs. He shows that the policy choices made by parties in power are crucial. Over time, policies affect various social groups in visible ways; the policies thus either undermine or help to consolidate and extend the electoral coalitions on which depend the future fortunes of the parties that authored the policies in the first place. This approach to analyzing policy feedbacks—through their effects on parties and electoral coalitions—can be applied far beyond the Danish and Swedish materials discussed by Esping-Andersen.

CONCLUSION

Since the mid-1970s, Western welfare states have apparently been in crisis, with fiscal stringencies brought on by international economic difficulties (Mishra 1984, Schmidt 1983). In the world of social science, however, the effect has merely been to heighten interest in the politics of social policy. Thus the theoretical and research tendencies that we have surveyed seem certain to undergo rapid development—and no doubt transformations—in the immediate future. All we can do is tentatively speculate about the likely directions for new work.

A point of diminishing returns seems to have been reached for highly aggregated quantitative analyses inspired by the logic-of-industrialism perspective or the social democratic model. The most informative quantitative studies are likely to be those that disaggregate, probing detailed program characteristics (e.g. Alber 1981, Steinberg 1982) or particular types of social spending (e.g. Castles 1982b, Coughlin & Armour 1983). Otherwise, we are likely to learn most in the near future from thorough comparative-historical studies of a few well-chosen cases at a time (e.g. Esping-Andersen 1985, Orloff 1985 Castles 1985). And this category should be considered to include studies of telling single cases, when such studies are explicitly informed by the hypotheses and findings of previous comparative research (e.g. Heclo 1974b, Pempel 1982, Quadagno 1982, Segalman 1982, Shalev 1984, Skocpol & Ikenberry 1983). Detailed historical studies of one or a few cases allow investigators to look for configurations of causes to explain social policies. As scholars move beyond single-factor hypotheses in this way, further insights can be expected about the effects of international contexts, and about the impact of states and parties, as well as social structures. And social policies can be analyzed in relationship to the totality of things states do—or refrain from doing—in various national and international situations.

As new research is designed, scholars should presume that the causes of policy origins are not necessarily the same as the causes of the subsequent development of policies, in part because policies themselves transform politics. Researchers should likewise be sensitive to precise time periods on national and world scales and attuned to processes unfolding over time. Analysts of states and social policies must, in short, become unequivocally *historical* in their orientation. That is the message that emerges most clearly from our brief overview of recent comparative research on the determinants of social policies. Both states and their policies are made and remade in a never-ending flow of politics, and social scientists must ask questions and seek answers in ways that respect such historicity.

Literature Cited

Abraham, D. 1981. Corporatist compromise and the re-emergence of labor/capital conflict in Weimar Germany. *Polit. Power Soc. Theory* 2:59–109

Achenbaum, W. A. 1983. The formative years of social security: A test case of the Piven and Cloward thesis. In *Social Welfare or Social Control: Some Historical Reflections on Regulating the Poor*, ed. W. I. Trattner, pp. 67–89. Knoxville, Tenn: Univ. Tenn. Press

Alber, J. 1981. Government responses to the challenge of unemployment: The development of unemployment insurance in Western Europe. See Flora & Heidenheimer 1981, pp. 151–83

Albritton, R. B. 1979. Social amelioration through mass insurgency? A reexamination of the Piven and Cloward thesis. *Am. Polit. Sci. Rev.* 73:1003–11

Alt, J., Chrystal, K. A. 1983. The criteria for choosing a politico-economic model, forecast results for British expenditures 1976–79: a reply to Frey and Schneider. *Eur. J. Polit. Res.* 11:115–23

Amenta, E., Clemens, E., Olsen, J., Parikh, S., Skocpol, T. 1984. Theories of social policy and the origins of unemployment insurance in five American states. Presented at the Ann. Meet. Soc. Sci. Hist. Assoc., Toronto, Canada

Andreski, S. 1968. *Military Organization and Society*. London: Routledge & Kegan Paul

Balbo, L. 1982. The servicing work of women and the capitalist state. *Polit. Power Soc. Theory* 3:251–70

Bergesen, A., ed. 1980. *Studies of the Modern World-System*. New York: Academic

Berkowitz, E., McQuaid, K. 1980. *Creating the Welfare State: The Political Economy of Twentieth-Century Reform*. New York: Praeger

Bjorn, L. 1979. Labor parties, economic growth and redistribution in five capitalist democracies. *Comp. Soc. Res.* 2:93–128

Block, F. 1977a. The ruling class does not rule. *Soc. Revolution* 33:6–28

Block, F. 1977b. Beyond corporate liberalism. *Soc. Probl.* 24:352–61

Borcherding, T. E., ed. 1977. *Budgets and Bureaucrats: The Sources of Government Growth*. Durham, NC: Duke Univ. Press

Borg, S. G., Castles, F. G. 1981. The influence of the political right on public income maintenance expenditure and equality. *Polit. Stud.* 29:604–21

Burawoy, M. 1980. The politics of production and the production of politics: A comparative analysis of piecework machine shops in the United States and Hungary. *Polit. Power Soc. Theory* 1:261–99

Cameron, D. 1978. The expansion of the public economy: A comparative analysis. *Am. Polit. Sci. Rev.* 72:1243–61

Castles, F. G. 1978. *The Social Democratic Image of Society.* London: Routledge & Kegan Paul

Castles, F. G. 1981. How does politics matter?: Structure or agency in the determination of public policy outcomes. *Eur. J. Polit. Res.* 9:119–32

Castles, F. G., ed. 1982a. *The Impact of Parties,* Beverly Hills, Calif: Sage

Castles, F. G. 1982b. The impact of parties on public expenditures. See Castles 1982a, pp. 21–96

Castles, F. G. 1985. *Working Class and Welfare: Reflections on the Political Development of the Welfare State in Australia and New Zealand, 1890–1980.* London: Allen & Unwin

Collier, D., Messick, R. 1975. Prerequisites versus diffusion: Testing alternative explanations of social security adoption. *Am. Polit. Sci. Rev.* 69:1299–1315

Coughlin, R. M. 1979. Social policy and ideology: Public opinion in eight rich nations. *Comp. Soc. Res.* 2:1–40

Coughlin, R. M., Armour, P. K. 1983. Sectoral differentiation in social security spending in the OECD nations. *Comp. Soc. Res.* 6:175–99

Curtis, J. L. 1983. The income tax as a policy tool: The contrasting cases of the United States and Britain. Presented Ann. Meet. Am. Polit. Sci. Assoc., Chicago

Cutright, P. 1965. "Political structure, economic development, and national social security programs." *Am. J. Sociol.* 70:537–50

Davidson, R., Lowe, R. 1981. Bureaucracy and innovation in British welfare policy 1870–1945. In *The Emergence of the Welfare State in Britain and Germany,* ed. W. J. Mommsen, pp. 263–95. London: Croom Helm

DeViney, S. 1983. Characteristics of the state and the expansion of public social expenditures. *Comp. Soc. Res.* 6:151–74

Esping-Anderson, G. 1978. Social class, social democracy, and the state: Party policy and party decomposition in Denmark and Sweden. *Comp. Polit.* 11:42–58

Esping-Anderson, G. 1985. *Politics Against Markets: The Social Democratic Road to Power.* Princeton, NJ: Princeton Univ. Press

Evans, P. B., Rueschemeyer, D., Skocpol, T.

1985. *Bringing the State Back In.* New York: Cambridge Univ. Press

Fainstein, S., Fainstein, N. 1978. National policy and urban development. *Soc. Probl.* 26:125–46

Flora, P., Alber, J. 1981. Modernization, democratization, and the development of welfare states in Western Europe. See Flora & Heidenheimer 1981, pp. 37–80

Flora, P., Heidenheimer, A. J., eds. 1981. *The Development of Welfare States in Europe and America.* New Brunswick, NJ: Transaction

Frey, B. S., Schneider, F. 1978. An empirical study of politico-economic interaction in the United States. *Rev. Econ. Stat.* 60:174–83

Frey, B. S., Schneider, F. 1982. "Politico-economic models in competition with alternative models: Which predict better? *Eur. J. Polit. Res.* 10:241–54

Furniss, N., Tilton, T. 1977. *The Case For the Welfare State: From Social Security to Social Equality.* Bloomington, Ind: Indiana Univ. Press

Golden, N. G., Poterba, J. M. 1980. The price of popularity: the political business cycle reexamined. *Am. J. Polit. Sci.* 24:696–714

Gough, I. 1975. State expenditure in advanced capitalism, *New Left Rev.* 72:3–29

Gough, I. 1979. *The Political Economy of the Welfare State.* London: Macmillan

Griffin, L. J., Devine, J. A., Wallace, M. 1982. Monopoly capital, organized labor, and military spending in the United States, 1949–1976. In *Marxist Inquiries,* ed. M. Burawoy, T. Skocpol, pp. 113–53. Supplement to *Am. J. Sociol.* 88: Chicago, Ill: Univ. of Chicago Press

Griffin, L. J., Devine, J. A., Wallace, M. 1983. On the economic and political determinants of welfare spending in the post-war era. *Polit. Soc.* 13:331–72

Hage, J., Hanneman, R. 1980. The growth of the welfare state in Britain, France, Germany, and Italy: A comparison of three paradigms. *Comp. Soc. Res.* 3:45–70

Headey, B. 1970. Trade unions and national wage policies. *J. Polit.* 32:407–39

Headey, B. 1978. *Housing Policy in the Developed Economy: The United Kingdom, Sweden and the United States.* London: Croom Helm

Heclo, H. 1974a. *Modern Social Politics in Britain and Sweden.* New Haven, Conn: Yale Univ. Press

Heclo, H. 1974b. The welfare state: The costs of American self-sufficiency. In *Lessons from America: An Exploration,* ed. R. Rose, pp. 253–77 New York: Wiley

Heidenheimer, A. J. 1981. "Education and social security entitlements in Europe and America." See Flora & Heidenheimer 1981, pp. 269–304

Heidenheimer, A. J., Heclo, H., Adams, C. T. 1983. *Comparative Public Policy: The Politics of Social Choice in Europe and America*. New York: St. Martin's Press. 2nd ed.

Hewitt, C. 1977. "The effect of political democracy and social democracy on equality in industrial societies: A cross-national comparison," *Am. Sociol. Rev.* 42:450–64

Hibbs, D. 1977. Political parties and macroeconomic policy. *Am. Polit. Sci. Rev.* 71:1467–87

Hibbs, D. 1978. On the political economy of long-run trends in strike activity. *Br. J. Polit. Sci.* 8:153–75

Hicks, A., Swank, D. H. 1983. Civil disorder, relief mobilization, and AFDC caseloads: A reexamination of the Piven and Cloward thesis. *Am. J. Polit. Sci.* 27:695–716

Hollingsworth, J. R., Hanneman, R. A. 1982. Working-class power and the political economy of western capitalist societies. *Comp. Soc. Res.* 5:61–80

Holloway, J., Picciotto, S. 1978. *State and Capital: A Marxist Debate*. London: Edward Arnold

Isaac, L., Kelly, W. 1981. Racial insurgency, the state, and welfare expansion: Local and national level evidence from the postwar United States. *Am. J. Sociol.* 86:1311–86

Jackman, R. W. 1975. *Politics and Social Equality: A Comparative Analysis*. New York: Wiley

Janowitz, M. 1976. *Social Control of the Welfare State*. Chicago: Phoenix

Janowitz, M. 1980. *The Last Half Century: Societal Change and Politics in America*. Chicago: Univ. Chicago Press

Jennings, E. T. Jr. 1983. Racial insurgency, the state, and welfare expansion: A critical comment and reanalysis. *Am. J. Sociol.* 88:1220–36

Joffe, C. 1986. *The Regulation of Sexuality*. Philadelphia, Penn: Temple Univ. Press. Forthcoming

Kamerman, S. B., Kahn, A. J., eds. 1978. *Family Policy: Government and Families in Fourteen Countries*. New York: Columbia Univ. Press

Katzenstein, P. 1985. *Small States in World Markets: Industrial Policy in Europe*. Ithaca, NY: Cornell Univ. Press

Katznelson, I. 1981. *City Trenches: Urban Politics and the Patterning of Class in the United States*. New York: Pantheon

Katznelson, I. 1985. Working-class formation and the state: Nineteenth-century England in American perspective. See Evans et al 1985, pp. 257–84

Kelman, S. 1981. *Regulating America, Regulating Sweden: A Comparative Study of Occupational Safety and Health Policy*. Cambridge, Mass: MIT Press

Keman, H., Braun, D. 1984. The limits of political control: A cross-national comparison of economic policy responses in eighteen capitalist democracies. *Eur. J. Polit. Res.* 12:101–8

Kerr, C., Dunlop, J. T., Harbison, F., Myers, C. A. 1964. *Industrialism and Industrial Man: The Problems of Labor and Management in Economic Growth*. New York: Oxford Univ. Press

Key, V. O. 1949. *Southern Politics in State and Nation*. New York: Knopf

Korpi, W. 1978. *The Working Class in Welfare Capitalism: Work, Unions and Politics in Sweden*. London: Routledge & Kegan Paul

Korpi, W. 1980. Social policy and distributional conflict in the capitalist democracies: A preliminary framework. *West Eur. Politics* 3:296–315

Korpi, W. 1983. *The Democratic Class Struggle* London: Routledge & Kegan Paul

Korpi, W., Shalev, M. 1980. Strikes, power and politics in the western nations, 1900–1976. *Polit. Power Soc. Theory* 1:301–34

Kramer, R. M. 1981. *Voluntary Agencies in the Welfare State*. Berkeley, Calif: Univ. Calif. Press

Kuhnle, S. 1981. The growth of social insurance programs in Scandinavia: Outside influences and internal forces. See Flora & Heidenheimer 1981, pp. 125–50

Leibfried, S. 1978. Public assistance in the United States and the Federal Republic of Germany: Does social democracy make a difference? *Comp. Politics* 11:59–76

Leman, C. 1977. Patterns of policy development: Social security in the United States and Canada. *Public Policy* 25:261–91

Leman, C. 1980. *The Collapse of Welfare Reform: Political Institutions, Policy, and the Poor in Canada and the United States*. Cambridge, Mass: MIT Press

Lenski, G. 1966. *Power and Privilege*. New York: McGraw-Hill

Lindblom, C. 1977. *Politics and Markets*. New York: Basic

Lowery, D., Berry, W. D. 1983. The growth of government in the United States: An empirical assessment of competing explanations. *Am. J. Polit. Sci.* 27:665–94

Lowi, T. 1972. Four systems of policy, politics, and choice. *Public Admin. Rev.* 32: 298–310

Malloy, J. M. 1979. *The Politics of Social Security in Brazil*. Pittsburgh, Penn: Univ. Pittsburgh Press

Malloy, J. M., Borzutzky, S. 1982. Politics, social policy, and the population problem in Latin America. *Int. J. Health Services* 12:77–98

Manchin, R., Szelenyi, I. 1986. Social policy under state socialism: Market, redistribution and social inequalities in East European socialist societies. In *Stagnation and Renewal in Social Policy*, G. Esping-Andersen, M. Rein, L. Rainwater, eds. White Plains, NY: M. E. Sharpe. Forthcoming

Marklund, S. 1982. *Capitalisms and collective income protection: A comparative study of the development of social security programs in Europe and the USA, 1930–1975.* Res. Rep., Dept. Sociol., University of Umea, Umea, Sweden

Marshall, T. H. 1963. *Class, Citizenship, and Social Development.* Chicago: Univ. Chicago Press

Martin, A. 1973. *The Politics of Economic Policy in the United States: A Tentative View From the Comparative Perspective.* Beverly Hills, Calif: Sage

Massad, T. 1980. Disruption, organization, and reform: A critique of Piven and Cloward. *Dissent* (Winter):81–90

Meyer, J. W., Hannan, M. T. eds. 1979. *National Development and the World System: Educational, Economic, and Political Change, 1950–1970.* Chicago: Univ. of Chicago Press

Meyer, J. W., Ramirez, F. O., Rubinson, R., Boli-Bennett, J. 1979. The world educational revolution, 1950–70. See Meyer & Hannan 1979, pp. 37–55

Minkoff, J., Turgeon, L. 1977. Income maintenance in the Soviet union in Eastern and Western perspective. In *Equity, Income, and Policy: Comparative Studies in Three Worlds of Development.* New York: Praeger

Mishra, R. 1973. Welfare and industrial man: A study of welfare in Western industrial societies in relation to a hypothesis of convergence. *Sociol. Rev.* 21:535–60

Mishra, R. 1984. *The Welfare State in Crisis: Social Thought and Social Change.* New York: St. Martin's

Myles, J. 1984. *Old Age in the Welfare State: The Political Economy of Public Pensions.* Boston: Little Brown

O'Connor, J. 1973. *The Fiscal Crisis of the State.* New York: St. Martin's

Offe, C. 1984. *Contradictions of the Welfare State.* Cambridge, Mass: MIT Press

OECD [Organization for Economic Cooperation and Development]. 1978. *Public Expenditure Trends.* Paris: OECD

Orloff, A. S. 1985. *The politics of pensions: A comparative analysis of the origins of pensions and old age insurance in Canada, Great Britain, and the United States.* PhD thesis. Princeton Univ.

Orloff, A. S., Skocpol, T. 1984. Why not equal protection? Explaining the politics of public social spending in Britain, 1900–1911, and the United States, 1880s–1920. *Am. Sociol. Rev.* 49:726–50

Parkin, F. 1972. *Class Inequality and Political Order.* New York: Praeger

Peacock, A. R., Wiseman, J. 1961. *The Growth of Public Expenditure in the United Kingdom.* Princeton, NJ: Princeton Univ. Press

Pearce, D. M. 1978. The feminization of poverty: Women, work and welfare. *Urban Soc. Change Rev.* 11:28–36

Pearce, D. M. 1983. The feminization of ghetto poverty. *Society* 21:70–74

Pempel, T. J. 1982. *Policy and Politics in Japan.* Philadelphia, Penn: Temple Univ. Press

Piven, F. F. 1984. Women and the state: Ideology, power, and the welfare state. In *Gender and the Life Course,* ed. Alice Rossi. New York: Aldine

Piven, F. F., Cloward, R. A. 1971. *Regulating the Poor.* New York: Vintage

Piven, F. F., Cloward, R. A. 1977. *Poor People's Movements: Why They Succeed, How They Fail.* New York: Pantheon

Piven, F. F., Cloward, R. A. 1982. *The New Class War: Reagan's Attack on the Welfare State.* New York: Pantheon

Poulantzas, N. 1973. *Political Power and Social Classes.* New York: New Left Books

Pryor, F. L. 1968. *Public Expenditures in Communist and Capitalist Nations.* London: George Allen & Unwin

Quadagno, J. S. 1982. *Aging in Early Industrial Society: Work, Family, and Social Policy in Nineteenth-Century England.* New York: Academic

Quadagno, J. S. 1984. Welfare capitalism and the Social Security Act of 1935. *Am. Sociol. Rev.* 49:632–47

Rainwater, L., Rein, M. 1983. The growing complexity of economic claims in welfare societies. See Spiro & Yuchtman-Yaar 1981, pp. 111–29

Ramirez, F., Boli, J. 1985. The political construction of mass education: European origins and worldwide institutionalization. Ann. Meet. Am. Sociol. Assoc., Washington DC

Rimlinger, G. 1971. *Welfare Policy and Industrialization in Europe, America, and Russia.* New York: Wiley

Rosenberry, S. A. 1982. Social insurance, distributive criteria and the welfare backlash: A comparative analysis. *Br. J. Polit. Sci.* 12:421–47

Ruggie, M. 1984. *The State and Working Women: A Comparative Study of Britain and Sweden.* Princeton, NJ: Princeton Univ. Press

Russett, B. M. 1970. *What Price Vigilance? The Burdens of National Defense.* New Haven, Conn: Yale Univ. Press

Russett, B. M. 1982. Defense expenditures and

national well-being. *Am. Polit. Sci. Rev.* 76:767–77

Schmidt, M. G. 1982. The role of the parties in shaping macroeconomic policy. See Castles 1982a, pp. 97–176

Schmidt, M. G. 1983. The welfare state and the economy in periods of economic crisis: A comparative study of twenty-three OECD nations. *Eur. J. Polit. Res.* 11:1–26

Schneider, S. K. 1982. The sequential development of social programs in eighteen welfare states. *Comp. Soc. Res.* 5:195–220

Schumpeter, J. 1942. *Capitalism, Socialism, and Democracy.* New York: Harper & Row

Segalman, R. 1982. Switzerland as welfare state. Presented at Ann. Meet. Am. Sociol. Assoc., San Francisco

Shalev, M. 1983a. The social democratic model and beyond: Two generations of comparative research on the welfare state. *Comp. Soc. Res.* 6:315–51

Shalev, M. 1983b. Class politics and the Western welfare state. See Spiro & Yuchtman-Yaar 1983, pp. 27–50

Shalev, M. 1984. Labor, state and crisis: An Israeli case study. *Indust. Rel.* 23:362–86

Shefter, M. 1977. Party and patronage: Germany, England, and Italy. *Polit. Soc.* 7:404–51

Shefter, M. 1983. Regional receptivity to reform; the legacy of the Progressive Era. *Polit. Sci. Q.* 98:459–83

Shefter, M. 1986. Trades unions and political machines: The organization and disorganization of the American working class in the late nineteenth century. In *Working Class Formation: Nineteenth Century Patterns in Europe and the United States.* Princeton, NJ: Princeton Univ. Press

Skocpol, T. 1980. Political response to capitalist crisis: Neo-Marxist theories of the state and the case of the New Deal. *Polit. Soc.* 10:155–201

Skocpol, T. 1985. Bringing the state back in: Strategies of analysis in current research. See Evans et al 1985, pp. 3–43

Skocpol, T., Amenta, E. 1985. Did capitalists shape social security? (A comment on Quadagno 1984.) *Am. Sociol. Rev.* 50:572–75

Skocpol, T., Ikenberry, J. 1983. The political formation of the American welfare state in historical and comparative perspective. *Comp. Soc. Res.* 6:87–147

Skowronek, S. 1982. *Building a New American State: The Expansion of National Administrative Capacities, 1877–1920.* New York: Cambridge Univ. Press

Spalding, R. J. 1980. Welfare policymaking: Theoretical implications of a Mexican case study. *Comp. Politics* 12:419–38

Spiro, S. E., Yuchtman-Yaar, E. 1983. *Evaluating the Welfare State: Social and*

Political Perspectives. New York: Academic

Steinberg, R. 1982. *Wages and Hours: Labor and Reform in Twentieth-Century America.* New Brunswick, NJ: Rutgers Univ. Press

Stepan, A. 1978. *The State and Society: Peru in Comparative Perspective.* Princeton, NJ: Princeton Univ. Press

Stephens, J. D. 1979. *The Transition from Capitalism to Socialism.* London: Macmillan

Stephens, E. H., Stephens, J. D. 1982. The labor movement, political power, and workers' participation in Western Europe. *Polit. Power Soc. Theory* 3:215–49

Szelenyi, I. 1978. Social inequalities under state socialist redistributive economies. *Int. J. Comp. Sociol.* 1–2:61–87

Szelenyi, I. 1983. *Urban Inequalities Under State Socialism.* Oxford: Oxford Univ. Press

Therborn, G. 1978. *What Does the Ruling Class Do When It Rules?* London: New Left Books

Therborn, G., Kjellberg, A., Marklund, S., Ohlund, U. 1978. Sweden before and after social democracy: a first overview. *Acta Sociologica,* (Suppl.):37–58

Thomas, G. M., Meyer, J. W. 1984. The expansion of the state. *Ann. Rev. Sociol.* 10:461–82

Tilly, C. 1975. Food supply and public order in modern Europe. In *The Formation of National States in Western Europe,* ed. C. Tilly, pp. 380–455. Princeton, NJ: Princeton Univ. Press

Titmuss, R. 1958. War and social policy. In *Essays on the Welfare State,* pp. 75–87. London: Allen & Unwin

Tufte, E. 1978. *Political Control of the Economy.* Princeton, NJ: Princeton Univ. Press

Vogel, D. 1978. Why businessmen distrust their state: The political consciousness of American corporate executives. *Brit. J. Polit. Soc.* 8:45–78

Vogel, D. 1981. The 'new' social regulation in historical and comparative perspective. In *Regulation in Perspective,* ed. T. McGraw, pp. 155–85. Cambridge, Mass: Harvard Univ. Press

Weinstein, J. 1968. *The Corporate Ideal in the Liberal State.* Boston: Beacon

Weir, M., Skocpol, T. 1985. State structures and the possibilities for 'Keynesian' responses to the great depression in Sweden, Britain, and the United States. See Evans, Rueschemeyer & Skocpol 1985, pp. 107–63

Wilensky, H. 1975. *The Welfare State and Equality: Structural and Ideological Roots of Public Expenditures.* Berkeley, Calif: Univ. Calif. Press

Wilensky, H. 1976. *The "New Corporatism",*

Centralization and the Welfare State. Beverly Hills, Calif: Sage

Wilensky, H. 1981. Leftism, Catholicism, and democratic corporatism: The role of political parties in recent welfare state development. See Flora & Heidenheimer 1981: 345–82

Wilensky, H., Lebeaux, C. N. 1958. *Industrial Society and Social Welfare*. New York: Russell Sage Foun.

Williamson, J. B., Fleming, J. J. 1977. Convergence theory and the social welfare sector: A cross-national analysis. *Int. J. Comp. Sociol*. 18:242–53

Wright, G. 1974. The political economy of New Deal spending: An econometric analysis. *Rev. Econ. Stat*. 56:30–38

Ann. Rev. Sociol. 1986. 12:159-80

CHILDHOOD IN SOCIODEMOGRAPHIC PERSPECTIVE[1]

Donald J. Hernandez

Marriage and Family Statistics Branch, Population Division, US Bureau of the Census, Washington, DC 20233, and Center for Population Research, Georgetown University, Washington, DC

Abstract

This article reviews the emerging sociodemographic literature on the relationships linking children and their families, by focusing on four topics: (*a*) the short-term implications for children of parents' family behavior, (*b*) the short-term implications for parents of the number and ages, or spacing, of their children, (*c*) the long-term implications of childhood family experiences for subsequent adult behavior, and (*d*) the probable family circumstances of children in the future.

Studies of how parents influence children found (*a*) that increases in illegitimate fertility and divorce led to a large rise in the proportion of children living in one-parent families, usually with the mother, and in stepfamilies, (*b*) that children in families maintained by mothers, but not in stepfamilies, experience numerous social, economic, and psychological disadvantages, (*c*) that, contrary to the popular stereotype, white children in families maintained by mothers are more likely than black children in such families either to be living with or to receive financial assistance from extended family members, and (*d*) declining fertility and birth cohort size may have led to reductions in the welfare of children compared to the welfare of the elderly during the last 20 years.

Studies of how children influence parents found that the presence of at least one child probably reduced marital satisfaction; the presence of a small number of children, especially preschool children, deters parental divorce; children reduce remarriage probabilities for young mothers, but increase them for older mothers; and at least the first and second child probably reduce family income and savings. Studies of how childhood experiences affect individuals in adult-

---

[1]The US Government has the right to retain a nonexclusive, royalty-free license in and to any copyright covering this paper.

hood find that divorce of one's parents reduces one's own marriage probabilities and increases one's own divorce probabilities; childhood stepfamilies have little effect on adult circumstances; contrary to the popular stereotype, children without siblings are not disadvantaged compared to other children; an increasing number of siblings leads to reduced educational attainments, and increasing educational mobility among men with small or medium numbers of siblings accounts for the increase observed for all men during this century. Recent projections suggest that 50–75% of the 1980 birth cohort may live in a one-parent family during childhood, with a range of 40–70% for whites and a range of 85–95% for blacks.

INTRODUCTION

Childhood marks the beginning of the life course, and the family provides the institutional basis for the care of most children. But only during the last decade has an emerging, yet substantial, sociodemographic literature begun to study a wide range of relationships linking children and their families. This literature concerns essentially four topics: (a) the short-term implications for children of parents' family behavior, (b) the short-term implications for parents of the number and ages, or spacing, of their children, (c) the long-term implications of childhood family experiences for subsequent adult behavior, and (d) the probable family circumstances of children in the future. This essay reviews major findings for each of these topics, focusing primarily upon published studies using nationally representative data, and concludes with a brief discussion of emerging research directions.[1]

IMPLICATIONS FOR CHILDREN OF PARENTS' FAMILY BEHAVIOR

Because the family provides the institutional basis for the care of children, it is by forming families that parents come to bear the primary and most immediate responsibility for the welfare of their children. The consequences for children of the family formation and dissolution behavior of parents, then, provide the natural starting point for this essay.

---

[1]Additional areas of sociological research on children, which are not reviewed here for lack of space or because they are less central or have been reviewed elsewhere recently, concern children's perceptions of the world (Bloom-Feshbach et al 1982); family interaction (Aldous 1977), neglected and abused children (no review known); the effect of mother's labor force participation upon children (Hayes & Kamerman 1983); the effects of day-care upon children (Belsky & Steinberg 1975; Silverstein 1981); delinquency, political socialization (Niemi & Sobieszek 1979); school achievement and educational and occupational attainments (Bielby forthcoming), adolescence, the transition to adulthood (Hogan 1986); the history of childhood, and family history (Cherlin 1983). Watts & Hernandez (1982) present a conceptual framework for child and family indicators, and an assessment of the availability of statistical data for a comprehensive set of child and family indicators.

The timing and sequencing of parents' marriages, divorces, and childbearing directly affect children in the short-term by determining their living arrangements, that is, the number of parents with whom they live and the nature of the family relationships linking them to their parents. Glick & Norton (1979; Glick 1979) characterize changes in the living arrangements of children between 1960 and 1978 with Decennial Census data and Current Population Survey data. The proportion of children living with two parents declined from 87.5 to 77.7%, that of children living with two natural parents, both married once, declined from 73.3 to 63.1%, that of children living with a natural parent and a stepparent rose from 8.6 to 10.2%, and of children living with one parent rose from 8.6 to 18.6%. Families of children living only with their mother account for 90% of the increase in the percentage of children living with one parent. The proportion living with a divorced mother rose from 1.9 to 6.9%, and the proportion living with a never-married mother rose from 0.3 to 2.6%.

The number of children living in mother-only families and stepfamilies increased, a result of increases in rates of out-of-wedlock births and of divorce and remarriage among parents. Numerous sociodemographic studies have focused on the consequences of these parental family behaviors for children. First, Berkov & Sklar (1976) report, using California data for the late 1960s and early 1970s, that infant mortality rates for children born out of wedlock are 1.6–1.7 times higher than for other children. They also report a sharp decline— from 30 to 12%—in the proportion of out-of-wedlock babies who were adopted by age three. Berkov & Sklar emphasize that increasing illegitimate fertility rates and declining adoption rates are leading to increases in the number of children exposed to the problems, including early death, and to handicaps, such as poor school performance, associated with being born out of wedlock.

The second major reason that children live in one-parent families is parental separation and divorce. Of children in one-parent families, 90% live with their mother. For those of such children who were 11–16 years old in 1981 and living in families maintained by their mothers, Furstenberg et al (1983) find, using National Survey of Children data, that the likelihood is greater that they will see their father if he provides financial support, but less if he, the mother, or both have remarried. Overall, two thirds of children who live in families maintained by their mother see their father less than once a month, and about one third had not seen him in the last five years. Only 16% of the children studied saw their father at least once a week.

The disruption of the parents' marriage might be expected to have rather immediate and serious psychological consequences for children. Summarizing results from a wide range of social and psychological studies, Longfellow (1979) reports on extensive research suggesting that the adjustment of children suffers from marital conflict, and that younger children are more likely than older children to suffer stress from a parental divorce. In a study of 60 families selected from participants in a six-week divorce counseling service, Wallerstein & Kelly (1980) report that many children and adolescents who are exposed to a parental separation and divorce find the experience to be fraught with fear, sadness, yearning, worry, feelings of rejection, loneliness, conflicted loyalties, and anger. During the five-year follow-up period, however, researchers find great variability in the extent to which different families succeed or fail in mastering the disruption, negotiating the transition successfully, and creating a stable and loving family arrangement.

More recently, Hetherington et al (1985) conclude from a six-year panel study of 60 white, middle-class children and their divorced parents that divorce is followed by a period during which personal and emotional adjustment deteriorates substantially. However, a process of restabilization and adjustment to the new situation follows, although some problems remain for at least six years. Peterson & Zill (1986) use data from the National Survey of Children to study several of these issues. They find that a parental marital disruption is associated with various negative psychological and behavioral outcomes for children, but postdivorce living arrangements and parental marital history are also important, as is parental marital conflict, even in an intact home. Furthermore, positive parent-child relationships can ameliorate to some extent the negative consequences of marital conflict or a marital disruption.

Beyond any psychological implications of a parental divorce, a reduction in the material standard of living often results when a father leaves a child's home due to separation or divorce, because the father's income is lost to the mother and children. Weiss (1984) uses data from the Panel Study of Income Dynamics to study this phenomenon for families that experienced marital disruptions during the period from 1969 to 1974. Classifying families by upper, middle, or lower income prior to marital disruption, he finds that women and children in disrupted households had family incomes that were only one-half as large five years later as the incomes for the corresponding groups who remained married. Studying sources of income for these groups, Weiss finds after five years that the proportion of disrupted households obtaining at least three fourths of their income from earnings of household members was 87%, 68%, and 25% for the original high, middle, and low income groups respectively. Much of the remaining income was obtained through welfare and food stamps for the latter two groups.

For children in families maintained by mothers, low income is only one of many difficulties. McLanahan (1983) uses Panel Study of Income Dynamics data for 1969–1972 to study differences between families maintained by two parents and families maintained by mothers, with regard to (a) income, education, and number of children, (b) changes in finances, employment, household composition, residence, and health, (c) neighbors known, relatives within walking distance, social club participation, and free household help received, and (d) self-esteem, feelings of efficacy, and hopefulness. Families maintained by mothers are found to experience more chronic distress not only because of low income, but also because of low levels of social support, a high frequency of major life changes, and a high likelihood that the mothers may experience negative self-images and negative views about the future. Families maintained by mothers are at an advantage only in receiving free household help. Children in such families experience numerous social, financial, and psychological disadvantages.

Black children in 1980 were much more likely than white children (44 vs 14%) to live with their mother only. Hofferth (1985a) uses Panel Study of Income Dynamics data for 1968–1979 to study racial differences for such children regarding help received from the extended family. She finds that black children in families maintained by mothers are more likely than corresponding white children to have members of their extended family in the home, but less likely to be receiving financial assistance from other households. Taken together, and contrary to the popular stereotype, black children in families maintained by mothers spend less time than do corresponding white children in families that either include extended family members or receive financial assistance from other households.

Of course, many families maintained by mothers become blended families with stepfathers when the mother (re)marries. Regarding the consequences for children, Cherlin (1981) argues that new family relationships in blended families, in the form of step-parents, -siblings, and -grandparents, can help to compensate for the effective loss of a parent and other kin through divorce. Furstenberg & Spanier (1984) suggest, based on a study in Centre County, Pennsylvania, that kin obtained through parental remarriage, particularly step-grandparents, may augment or enlarge the pool of relatives available as a support system for children. On the other hand, Cherlin (1981) also suggests that remarriages may yield complex family structures which lack in-stitutionalized solutions to the day-to-day problems that arise between adults and children in blended families.

Cherlin & McCarthy (1985) use 1980 June Current Population Survey data to characterize living arrangements of children with at least one divorced and remarried parent, estimating that about 10% of all children living with married parents are living with at least one stepparent. Bumpass (1984a) also uses these data to study family structures resulting from remarriage. He finds that many children live in families with relatively complicated or otherwise "non-traditional" structures; 11% of all children live with at least one remarried parent, 19% live in families maintained by mothers, 19% have one or more step-siblings.

Several studies document the consequences of remarriage and blended family living for children. For children aged 1–14 in 1972, Duncan (1984) finds with Panel Study of Income Dynamics data that, among children experiencing a parental divorce between 1971 and 1978, family income fell by a remarkable annual average of 8.7%, while the ratio of family income to family needs fell by an annual average of 5.8% where the ratio takes family size into account. On the other hand, the reverse occurred among children whose mother (re)married. Real family income increased by an annual average of 9.5%, and the ratio of family income to family needs rose by an annual average of 6.9%.

Numerous potential differences between high school sophomores reared by two natural parents and high school sophomores reared by a natural mother and stepfather were studied by Wilson et al (1975) using 1973 Youth in Transition Survey data. In 38 of their 39 comparisons, differences were quite small. Variables of the study included (a) educational and occupational aspirations, father's education, and family income, (b) discussing the future with their parents, (c) perceptions about their parents' feelings regarding the possibilities of their dropping out of high school, receiving bad grades, getting a high school diploma, or getting into behavioral difficulties in school, and (d) the total need for self-development and self-utilization, self-esteem, level of independence, and overall positive values attributed to social interactions of all sorts.

More recently, using data from the National Survey of Family Growth for 1976 to study natural, step, and adoptive children, Bachrach (1983) finds that children with a stepfather are more likely than those living with a natural father to have a mother who has not graduated from high school.

The results in preceding paragraphs suggest that entry into a stepfamily through the mother's (re)marriage increases the complexity of family relationships for many children and markedly increases their family income, but along a variety of additional dimensions the differences between children in natural and step families are relatively slight.

Preston (1984) adopts a more sweeping approach to studying the short-term implications for children of parental family behavior; he argues that during the past 20 years demographic factors have played an important role in producing declines in the welfare of children compared to the elderly. This is reflected in changes such as the following: (a) a slight decline in the proportion of all students graduating from high school between 1968–1980, (b) a 45 point drop in real SAT scores between 1970–1980, (c) an increase between 1970 and 1982 in poverty for children compared to the elderly, (d) an increase in suicide between 1960–1982, compared to the elderly, and (e) declines in expenditures on public programs for children compared to public programs for the elderly. Concerning how demographic factors produced these effects through action in the arenas of the family, politics, and industry, Preston's arguments can be summarized here only briefly.

First, increased divorce and illegitimate fertility led to difficulties for children but had little effect on the elderly. Second, declining fertility led to a smaller and less effective political constituency speaking for children, while increases in the number of elderly led to increases in the size and effectiveness of their political constituency. Third, declining fertility led to a smaller school-aged population, lower teachers' salaries, and a decline in teacher quality, while increases in the number of elderly led to a boom in the health care industry. Although these and more detailed causal arguments by Preston often are plausible, the ones which are supported best pertain to the economic consequences for children of parental divorce and birth out of wedlock, while other arguments about the negative consequences of declining fertility and cohort size are perhaps best viewed as intriguing hypotheses for future studies.

IMPLICATIONS FOR PARENTS OF THE NUMBER AND AGES OF CHILDREN

Since past research shows that the short-term circumstances and welfare of children are profoundly influenced by the family formation and dissolution behavior of their parents, and since children are the focus of considerable parental attention and resources in most marriages, it would be surprising if children did not, in turn, deeply affect their parents. Viewing the family as a social structure, we see that perhaps the most important facts about children in the family pertain to their number and their ages or spacing. Linking these facts, extensive research has described the consequences that the number, ages, and spacing of children have for the marital satisfaction of parents. This sociological literature is reviewed next, to be followed by discussion of studies addressing the effects of children upon parental family formation and dissolution behavior, family economic status, and family residential mobility.

How Children Affect Parents' Marital Satisfaction

As a surprising conclusion from a summary of marital research conducted in the 1960s (Hicks & Platt 1970), Spanier & Lewis (1980) highlight the discovery that children tend to detract from, rather than enhance, the quality of their parents' marital relationship. Spanier & Lewis report that studies during the 1970s confirm and specify the nature of this effect, finding that mothers experience more difficulty than fathers in adjusting to a new infant, that blacks experience greater difficulty than whites, and that the number and spacing of children may have smaller effects than previously appeared to be the case. Finally, many studies find a U-shaped pattern for marital quality over the course of the marital career, but the research is undermined by methodological difficulties (also see Hudson & Murphy 1980).

Marini (1980) addresses many of these issues using 15-year panel data from a study of 10 high schools in Illinois. Marini finds that marital satisfaction is not influenced by the number or spacing of children in the family, by the presence of at least one child, or by the age of the youngest child, but that a premarital pregnancy has a small negative effect on mother's, but not father's, marital satisfaction. The number of children has a negative effect on parental satisfaction, while premarital pregnancy has a negative effect for mothers but not fathers, and the age of the youngest child has a negative effect (which suggests that parental satisfaction declines as the child grows older); but the spacing of the children has no effect.

While Marini seeks to extend knowledge about the links between children and marital happiness through greater methodological rigor and more complete analysis of theoretically relevant variables, other recent studies adopt the strategy of focusing more precisely upon major subpopulations that appear to be relevant theoretically.

Glenn & McLanahan (1982) use General Social Survey data for 1973–1978 to study subpopulations distinguished by sex, race, educational attainment, religious preference, employment status, and stated ideal number of children. The results suggest that the presence of children and to a lesser extent the number of children have negative, but small, effects on marital happiness. Among white women, the negative effect of number of children may be greater for women who have full-time jobs outside the home than for other women. The evidence is equivocal for the differences between Catholics and non-Catholics, and the education effect is not statistically significant. Finally, for whites the negative effect for number of children is stronger for women whose ideal family size is small, but the first child reduces their marital happiness regardless of ideal family size.

Polonko et al (1982) seek to clarify the relationship between the presence of children and parents' marital satisfaction by distinguishing among three conceptually distinct subgroups of childless couples: those who are (a) voluntarily childless, (b) postponing childbearing, or (c) undecided about bearing any children. Data come from a stratified random sample, taken during 1969–1974 in a large Midwestern city, of marriage applicants who were white, married once, and married after the age of 21. Results suggest that different models of marital satisfaction are required for these three sets of women. Across these groups, however, women in each of the three childless categories report higher marital satisfaction than those who were mothers, but for those with at least one child, family size has no effect on marital satisfaction. Abbott & Brody (1985) focus on the effects not only of number of children, but also of their age and gender. Although the research uses a small convenience sample of 210 wives from Athens, Georgia, the intriguing results suggest that childless wives scored significantly higher on a marital adjustment scale than did those who were mothers, but the difference is accounted for by lower adjustment scores among mothers with preschool-aged children and/or two male children.

The possible reasons for any negative effect of children on marital satisfaction and adjustment are provided in a study by Gove & Geerken (1977) on the effect that children and employment have on the mental health of married men and women. Using data from a survey in Chicago designed to maximize variation between socioeconomic variables and household crowding, Gove & Geerken studied respondents aged 18–60 who were employed husbands, employed wives, and not-employed wives. The results indicate generally that husbands experience the fewest demands, the least desire to be alone, the fewest feelings of loneliness, and the fewest psychiatric symptoms (anxiety, fear, depression, irritability), while nonworking wives are at the other extreme, and working wives fall between. For each group these problems generally tend to increase with the number of children, and they tend generally to decrease as the age of the youngest child rises. Further analyses suggest that felt demands, desire to be alone, and loneliness act as intervening variables between number and ages of children and the experience of psychiatric symptoms. Perhaps similar mechanisms explain the negative relationships between children and marital satisfaction found in several recent studies reviewed here.

How Children Affect Parents' Family and Economic Behavior

If children influence marital satisfaction, it might be expected that they also would influence marital dissolution, remarriage, childbearing after remarriage, and other parental behaviors. Several studies have pursued these possibilities.

With 1970 National Fertility Survey data Thornton (1977) evaluates the impact over a four-year period that the cumulative number of children born has on marital stability. White women without a premarital pregnancy, who are mothers of small and medium numbers of children experience the lowest rates of marital dissolution, while those with large numbers of children are associated with only slightly higher dissolution rates. Childless women had the highest rates of dissolution. The pattern is the same for nonwhite women, except that the highest rates of dissolution are found among women with either no children or large numbers of children. Speculating on the mechanisms responsible for the U-shaped relationship, Thornton suggests that only one of the explanations proposed in earlier studies can account for the higher marital instability among women with a large number of children, namely that increasing numbers of children may lead to lower marital satisfaction, and hence higher rates of marital dissolution.

Taking another approach, Cherlin (1977) argues that the presence of pre-school-aged children in the family may deter marital disruption the most, because they require considerable parental attention or costly childcare services. Results based on the National Longitudinal Study of the Labor Market Experience for women aged 30–44 suggest that the presence of children 0–5 years old is a deterrent to separation or divorce during the four-year period of the study, when these children were, because of their young age, making particularly heavy demands upon parental time and effort. Moore & Waite (1981) also use data from the National Longitudinal Study of Labor Market Experience, but the data is for women aged 14–24. For these much younger women, married before age 19, the presence of young children (under age 3) has no effect on marital stability, but the presence of such children does inhibit marital dissolution among women first married at age 21 or older. They also find that births to teenagers who are black tend to increase their marital instability.

Koo & Suchindran (1980) moved beyond divorce to study remarriage; they sought to avoid the problems of earlier studies by applying sophisticated life-table techniques to June 1975 Current Population Survey data for white, once-divorced women. Koo & Suchindran argue that children may have different effects upon the remarriage probabilities of women in different age categories, for reasons related to the motivation both of mothers and of their prospective husbands. Koo & Suchindran found a strong negative relationship between mother's age at divorce and probability of remarrying. Children have a negative effect on remarriage for the youngest group of women, no effect for the next youngest group, and a positive effect for the oldest women; however, the number of children beyond one appears to have no effect. In other words, the presence of any children, not their number, appears to make the difference in remarriage probabilities.

Griffith, Koo, & Suchindran (1984) extend this line of research by studying the effect that the presence of children prior to a second marriage has on the chances of bearing a child in the second marriage and the chances that the second marriage will end in separation or divorce. Analyses conducted for both white and black women with data from the National Survey of Family Growth for 1973 show that the presence of a child for white women has no significant effect, but black women entering the second marriage with a child were significantly more likely than black or white childless women to bear a child in the second marriage. However, no significant differences were found between these groups in the probability of a second marital disruption.

The effect of children upon the economic situation of parents has been explored in several studies. Studying data for white women in the Detroit Area Study, Freedman & Coombs (1966) found that the more closely children are spaced, the lower the family's income is likely to be, and the smaller their accumulated assets. They also found that the husband's education and duration of marriage account for only part of the negative relationship between the spacing of children and the economic position of parents. More recently, Smith & Ward (1980) used panel data for 1967–1970 to study how children affect the accumulation and composition of assets and family income. They concluded that parents' consumption of market goods declines when a child is born, but in young families income falls by an even greater magnitude. In families where the wife does not work prior to the birth of the child, the study results suggest that the birth of a child may increase, rather than reduce, savings.

Finally, Hofferth (1983) used data from the Panel Study of Income Dynamics for 1968–1976 in a dynamic, sequential model of the socioeconomic causes and consequences of childbearing for changes in family income. She finds that the birth of the first child has the largest negative effect on family income, but the negative effect of the second child's birth is less than one half as large. Both effects, but especially the second, are due to reductions in number of hours the mother works for pay. The third child's birth is associated with increased family income, perhaps because couples decide to have a third child if they expect an increase in income. Finally, the birth of a fourth or higher order child has a negative, but not statistically significant, effect on income. These are the immediate or short-term effects, but Hofferth concludes that long-term effects cannot be identified in this study, because each couple was studied for only four years.

In the last study reviewed here concerning the effect of children on their parents, Long (1972) evaluates the influence of the number and ages of children upon residential mobility within and across counties; he used 1968–1970 Current Population Survey data. Long concludes that the age of children has a major effect on parents' mobility. Households with school-aged children are about one half as likely as other households to move. But the mechanisms remain to be specified, since families with school-aged children may tend to remain in the community "for the good of the children," or because once they have school-aged children, they develop friendships built around the children.

LONG-TERM EFFECTS OF CHILDHOOD FAMILY EXPERIENCES

A growing sociodemographic literature is devoted to studying the long-term effects of the experiences of children within the family upon their subsequent behavior in adulthood. I now turn to this literature, focusing first on the consequences that result from childhood experiences with different parental family behaviors and economic circumstances. Next, I take up studies concerned primarily with the influences on adult behavior and welfare of varying numbers of siblings in childhood.

Long-Term Effects of Parental Circumstances

Hogan (1978) uses data from the Occupational Changes in a Generation Supplement to the March 1973 Current Population Survey to study determinants of age at first marriage among ever-married men 20–65 years old. His model shows (a) whether respondent lived, at age 16, in an intact family, and with how many siblings, (b) the socioeconomic variables in childhood of father's education and occupational status, mother's education, whether the family head was in the labor force at age 16, family income, and farm origin, (c) demographic characteristics, and (d) socioeconomic characteristics. Hogan concludes that age at marriage is influenced by neither the childhood family variables nor the childhood socioeconomic variables. On the other hand, great changes in the age at marriage occur across birth cohorts, and regional differences in age at marriage have remained important. Furthermore, the only socioeconomic variables that influence age at marriage are college attendance and service in the military, presumably because they disrupt the normal life-cycle transition processes.

More recently, Kobrin & Waite (1984) studied age at marriage using panel data, encompassing 12 years, from the National Longitudinal Study of Labor Market Experience for women aged 14–24 in 1968 and men aged 14–24 in 1966. Variables in their model are similar to those in Hogan's, but Kobrin & Waite studied one recent birth cohort, instead of six cohorts spanning the first half of the twentieth century. They estimate separate models by single years of age, because earlier research (Waite & Spitze 1981) found that the first marriage process differs substantially by respondent's age. The results indicate that children who had not lived in a family with two natural parents through their early teens were less likely to marry between the ages of 18 and 29 than were children who did live with both natural parents. The likelihood of marriage in this time is reduced by 3 to 6 percentage points when a childhood family disruption has occurred.

Kobrin & Waite also found that differences between black and white children in their experiences with intact families do not account for the fact that blacks are considerably less likely than whites to marry. Finally, they find that extended parental education is associated with decreased likelihood of marriage of children to their middle 20s, but at older ages the direction is reversed; school enrollment of the child decreases the likelihood of marriage. Full-time employment for women has little effect, but full-time employment for men is the most important factor increasing the likelihood of marriage during the next year.

If childhood experience with parental marital disruption influences probabilities of marriage, does it also influence adult marital stability? In other words, is marital instability transmitted from one generation to the next? Reviewing six earlier studies on this topic, Mueller & Pope (1977) conclude that the intergenerational transmission hypothesis is supported empirically, but the magnitude of the effect is not large. Using 1970 National Fertility Study data, they sought to explain the 10.6% difference in the chances of a marital dissolution between women from disrupted families (25%) and women from intact families (14.4%). Mueller & Pope find that women from disrupted homes who have at least one sibling are more likely to experience a marital disruption of their own than are other women, because they marry younger and attain fewer years of education. Mueller & Pope propose research on two possible explanations of this effect: (a) parents with disrupted marriages are less able to exercise control over their children and (b) the mate selection process is hindered by limited economic resources in disrupted families.

Experience with marital disruption, with one-parent and blended families, also may have consequences during adulthood. Wilson et al (1975) used 1973 General Social Survey data to compare adults who lived with a stepfather at age 16 to adults who lived with a natural father. Studying numerous adult characteristics related to demography, religion, social stratification, politics, crime and delinquency, interpersonal relationships (general, marriage, and family), and personal evaluations of happiness and health, Wilson et al found few statistically significant differences between stepchildren and other children. They caution, however, that the results should be considered tentative, because the number of stepchildren in the sample is only 43, and many of the adult responses concern the family situation at age 16.

Nock (1982) also uses General Social Survey data, but for 1972–1977, to study the possible effects of parental separation, divorce, or death, and the differential effects of resulting family structures, on attitudes concerning (a) interpersonal trust and confidence, (b) estrangement and anomie, and (c) general satisfaction and happiness. The results indicate that nonwhite and female respondents tend to be less trusting and more anomic. The higher the education, the occupational prestige, and the age of the respondent the more trusting and less anomic the responses generally. Comparing nine family living arrangements, Nock finds few long-term effects associated with family disruption, and the few existing effects suggest the individual may be strengthened by the experience of a parental family disruption.

Card (1981) uses Project TALENT data to study a rather different phenomenon, namely, the consequences of having a teenage parent. Project TALENT data is based on a longitudinal national survey of persons in grades 9–12 in 1960. Card (1981) finds in the 11-year follow-up that children of teenage parents tend to have lower academic achievement, are more likely to live in a one-parent or stepparent home, and are slightly more likely to repeat the early marriage, early parenthood, and the higher fertility pattern of their parents.

Finally, this section closes by discussing a research effort which, though not based on nationally representative samples, merits attention both because it focuses on the long-term consequences for children of the dramatic economic disruptions associated with the Great Depression, and because it elaborates a promising conceptual framework for future sociodemographic research on childhood. From panel data spanning decades, developed by the Oakland Growth Study and the Berkeley Guidance Study, Elder (1974, 1981, 1985) draws many conclusions, including the following. First, the consequences for children of living through the Great Depression depended upon whether their own family income dropped sharply. If family income dropped by 35 percent or more, children tended to assume relatively early and large economic roles in the family, and the girls tended to assume greater domestic responsibilities. By the late 1950s, economic deprivation during childhood did not substantially influence men's occupational status, but it did lead to firmer vocational commitments during late adolescence and to earlier entry into stable careers. Among the economically deprived men, the perceived importance of marriage centered around the chance to bear and rear children, but for other men the marital relationship per se was of greater importance. Among women, the economically deprived placed greater emphasis during adulthood on the traditional domestic role of women. Elder finds in many additional areas that the impact of childhood experience both currently and in adulthood depends upon intervening factors in the life course.

For example, Elder et al (1985b) investigate the mutually reinforcing effects of (a) unstable (explosive or volatile) personalities within a family and (b) unstable marital and parent-child relations, as these develop over the life courses of various family members. They also investigate how such patterns are transmitted from one generation to the next. The results indicate that unstable parents tend to experience marital tensions and to act with arbitrariness as parents, and these lead to an increased likelihood that the children may be ill-tempered and difficult. This pattern tends to repeat itself in the next generation when the children grow to parenthood. Yet turning points and breaks exist in the intergenerational transmission cycle. For example, ill-tempered boys who achieve some control over their own adult lives in the domains of work, marriage, and parenting are more likely to break out of a cycle involving a troubled life course. In addition, the instability or resourcefulness of fathers acted to alter the consequences for children of the economic loss associated with the Depression.

From such studies, Elder (1985; Elder et al 1985a,b) argues for the potential value of studying persons as they are embedded in their families and as they experience change through time. He suggests that a full understanding of the long-term consequences for children of social and economic change requires attention to differences across individuals in their life courses and in their relationships to other family members within and across generations. This approach involves a balance between concepts of family disorganization and family adaptation and change, and it requires attention to conditions within the childhood family that may accentuate or ameliorate the effects of primary interest.

Since much of the research reviewed in the present essay can be seen as directing attention toward interrelated processes linking family members through time, the conceptual framework elaborated by Elder provides a potentially useful vehicle for interpreting the extant literature and for identifying promising directions for new sociodemographic research on childhood.

Long-Term Effects of Number of Siblings

From the perspective of a child, the immediate family usually consists not only of parents but also of siblings. Research discussed above has focused mainly on parents, but an equally prominent feature of childhood families is the number of siblings in these families. This section discusses, first, some consequences for subsequent adult behavior and circumstances of having no siblings in the family and, then, of variation in the number of siblings in the family. A brief summary of short-term effects provides the context for the extensive review of long-term effects in this section.[2]

Blake (1981a) draws upon prior research and new analyses to show that children without siblings, that is, "only children," are generally considered by Americans to be at a disadvantage compared to other children, because only children tend, it is believed, to be self-centered, domineering, anxious, quarrelsome, spoiled, overprotected, or lonely. In 1977, two thirds of Americans believed only children were disadvantaged. However, Blake observes that an earlier literature review of short-term effects finds no empirical support for the popular stereotype, and a recent study using data from the Project Talent Survey finds that, compared to children in two-child families, only children have better cognitive performance and are more mature, socially sensitive, and tidy. This research also finds no differences between only children and others with regard to calmness, impulsiveness, self-confidence, drive, vigor, leadership, and at age 29, with regard to life satisfaction.

Blake then uses General Social Survey data for 1972–1978 to study long-term differences along a large number of dimensions between adults who were only children and those who were not. She finds, regarding parent's background variables, that only children were as advantaged as children with one or two siblings with regard to parent's education, father's occupational prestige, and childhood family income. The only major difference is that fewer only children grew up through age 16 with both parents. Furthermore, adults with none or one sibling are less likely than others ever to have received public assistance. Adults with no siblings are equally or more likely to evaluate themselves as generally happy, satisfied with their health, hobbies, and jobs, and they are equally or more likely to be optimistic that other persons will be helpful and fair. Finally, small to negligible differences exist with regard to marital stability and with regard to support for major social, economic, and political institutions.

Glenn & Hoppe (1982) also use General Social Survey data, but for 1973–

---

[2]It should be noted that some results in studies reviewed here that are interpreted as long-term effects of number of siblings during childhood instead might actually be short-term effects of number of siblings during adulthood. This possibility merits attention in future research, but for present purposes I accept the interpretations, as presented in studies reviewed here, regarding the long-term nature of effects identified. See Heer (1985) for a review of additional related studies.

1978 and 1980, to focus especially upon the effects of number of siblings on several dimensions of psychological well-being among white adult males and females. They conclude that the overall negative effect of larger numbers of siblings on psychological well-being is stronger for males than females, that the negative relationship between number of siblings and self-rated happiness is greater for males than females. However, because differences between only children and children with large numbers of siblings never exceed seven percentage points, the negative effects should not be considered very substantial. Additional studies focus especially upon the effects of number of siblings upon educational attainments, at least partly because educational attainments play a critical role in determining subsequent occupational attainments and income during adulthood.

Blake (1981b) uses data for whites from the 1972–1980 General Social Survey, the 1970 National Fertility Study, the 1955 and 1960 Growth of American Families Studies, and the Youth in Transition Survey to analyze, as dependent variables, total years of education achieved by adults and college plans for tenth-grade boys. She addresses the dilution model, which suggests that in larger families parental resources are diluted because they must be divided among a larger number of children, leading to lower achievements and attainments among the children than would otherwise be the case. She also addresses the sibling tutoring (teaching) hypothesis which suggests that only children and last children will not achieve as highly as would be expected from a pure dilution model, because they do not have the advantage of having younger siblings to tutor in the home.

Blake finds that the tutoring hypothesis is not supported in previous research nor in the new analyses which she performs, except in one case, but the results in this case are an artifact resulting from the peculiarities of the sample used. Furthermore, Blake's results not only support the dilution model, they suggest that the negative impact of family size on educational attainment is an important one, rivaling father's socioeconomic status in magnitude.

Mott & Haurin (1982) use data from the National Longitudinal Study of Labor Market Experience, young men's and women's cohorts, to address the dilution model and tutoring hypothesis through age 24. Mott & Haurin conclude that in no instance for either men or women do only children have a statistically significant advantage over other sibling situations taken as a whole. On the other hand, small families are at an advantage, supporting the dilution theory, although the effect appears to be less powerful for men. In addition, for women but not for men, the tutoring model also is supported by results from several analyses. Alwin & Thornton (1984) use data from an 18-year longitudinal study of children and their families to study school achievement. They find evidence, supporting the dilution model, not only that the number of siblings has a negative effect upon educational attainment, but that increases in the number of siblings over the course of childhood also have a negative effect on educational attainment.

More recently, Blake (1985) explored more thoroughly the way in which the number of siblings interacts with father's education to influence a son's educational attainment. Using data from the Occupational Changes in a Generation Supplements to the 1962 and 1973 Current Population Survey and the 1972–1983 General Social Survey, Blake studies white males reared in intact families, controlling for several important variables. Highlighting the major conclusion of Featherman & Hauser (1978) that the influence of men's social origins on their own educational attainments has been declining during the twentieth century in America, Blake finds, where years of schooling through high school is the dependent variable, that increasing opportunities for social mobility occurred only among men with small and medium numbers of siblings. For men with seven or more siblings, no significant change has occurred in the magnitude of the effect of father's education on son's education.

These results indicate that the increase in upward educational mobility found by Featherman & Hauser is due almost entirely to the experience of men from small and medium-sized families. Although this review has not focused on the status attainment literature as such, Blake's research demonstrates the fundamental role that number of siblings plays in the attainment process by defining conditions under which social mobility has increased in the United States during the twentieth century.

FUTURE FAMILY CIRCUMSTANCES OF CHILDREN

Several studies projecting the probable family living arrangements of children have been conducted, because of growing interest in the short-term and long-term consequences for children of dramatic increases in the fertility and divorce of unmarried mothers. Extending Bane's (1976) approach, Glick (1979) develops projections based on the assumption of a continuation through 1990 of annual increases between 1960–1976 in the proportion of children whose parents ever had obtained a divorce. According to these projections the proportion of children living with two natural parents in their first marriage will decline from 63% to 56% between 1978 and 1990, the proportion in two-parent stepfamilies will rise from 10% to 11%, and the proportion in one-parent families will rise from 19% to 25%. Glick also projects that 45% of the children born in 1977 may live in a one-parent family before the age of 18, and if past trends continue the figure will reach 50% for the 1990 birth cohort.

Bumpass (1984b) uses life-table techniques with 1980 June Current Population Survey data to estimate childhood experiences regarding the incidence and duration of parental marital disruption. This study replicates and updates an earlier effort by Bumpass & Rindfuss (1979) and Furstenberg et al (1983). The new results are generally consistent with the earlier ones. For birth cohorts of 1977–1979, Bumpass (1984b) projects that about 41% of children born to married mothers will experience a parental marital disruption by age 16, and 49% of all children in the cohort will spend some time in a one-parent family. Bumpass also projects that the proportion of children who will experience a one-parent family by age 16 will be 68% if the mother dropped out of high school, 78% if the mother was a teenage mother, and 42% for white children compared to 86% for black children. Turning to projections of status durations, Bumpass finds that the majority of children experiencing a marital disruption will live in a family maintained by the mother for five years before she remarries, and about one half of children with remarried mothers will experience a second parental divorce.

Hofferth (1985b) uses 1968–1979 Panel Study of Income Dynamics data, June 1980 Current Population Survey data, vital rates for 1950–1958 compiled by the National Center for Health Statistics, and model life tables to develop multistate life-table models. These models pertain to (a) the proportion of children who ever experience each of 10 family types (living arrangements), (b) the length of time children remain in a particular family type, (c) the proportion of childhood spent in each family type, and (d) the impact on subsequent family type experience of the family type into which children are born. Hofferth (1985a,b) estimates that while 19% of white children born in 1950–1954 had lived in a one-parent family by age 18, the proportion will rise to 70% for those born in 1980. For black children the corresponding figures are 48 and 94%. She also estimates for the early cohort that the proportion of childhood spent in one-parent families was 8% for white children and 22% for black children, but the projected figures for the 1980 birth cohort are 31% for whites and 59% for blacks.

Bumpass (1985) has called into question Hofferth's new projections, however, arguing that they suggest such extensive childhood experience with one-parent families that they strain credibility. He notes that Hofferth's analysis is founded upon data that appear to involve (a) upward distortions in parental mortality, (b) claims that the vast majority of white never-married mothers will remain unmarried over the next 18 years (sharply contradicting recent estimates from the Current Population Survey), and (c) erroneous estimates of transition rates out of two-parent families with at least one remarried parent. Bumpass suggests that difficulties with Hofferth's projections arise either from the complicated procedures employed or from instability in the estimates of the many detailed transition probabilities.

Most recently, Norton & Glick (1986) derive projections based on assumptions involving: the proportion of births that are premarital where the mother remains unmarried for at least one year; the proportion of first marriages that may eventually end in divorce; the prevalence of long-term separations that either end in reconciliation or last indefinitely, and parental deaths. Their projections suggest that 59% of children born in 1983 may live in a one-parent family before reaching the age of 18. The components of this projection are 12% for premarital birth and no other reason, 40% for divorce, 5% for long-term separations, and 2% for parental death.

Although the pertinent ages and birth cohorts used in various projection studies differ somewhat, the empirical values projected by Norton & Glick (1986) appear to lie about halfway between the values implied by the projections of Bumpass (1984b) and those of Hofferth (1985b). Taken then as a whole, these various projections suggest that for children born in the late 1970s and early 1980s at least one out of two, and possibly three out of four, will spend at least one year in a one-parent family, with a range of 40–70% for whites and a range of 85–95% for blacks.

CONCLUSION

The last decade brought a rapid expansion in sociodemographic research on childhood using national data bases to study ways in which children and parents influence each other and ways in which childhood influences adulthood. Studies of how parents influence children found (a) that increasing illegitimate fertility and divorce led to a large rise in the proportion of children living in one-parent families, usually maintained by the mother, and stepfamilies, (b) that children in one-parent but not in stepfamilies experience numerous social, economic, and psychological disadvantages, (c) that, contrary to the popular stereotype, white children in families maintained by the mother are more likely than black children in such families either to be living with or to receive financial assistance from extended family members, and (d) that an intriguing possibility warranting future attention is that declining fertility and birth cohort size may have led to reductions in the welfare of children compared to the welfare of the elderly during the last 20 years.

Studies of how children influence parents found that (a) the presence of at least one child probably reduces marital satisfaction, (b) the presence of a small number of, especially preschool, children deters parental divorce, (c) children reduce remarriage probabilities for young mothers, but increase them for older mothers, and (d) at least the first and second child probably reduce family income and savings. Studies of how childhood experiences affect individuals in adulthood find that (a) parental divorce probably reduces one's own marriage probabilities and increases one's own divorce probabilities, (b) childhood stepfamilies have little effect on adult circumstances, (c) contrary to the popular stereotype, children without siblings are not disadvantaged compared to other children, (d) an increasing number of siblings leads to reduced educational attainments, and (e) increasing educational mobility among men with small or medium numbers of siblings accounts for the increase observed for all men during this century. Recent projections suggest that 50–75% of the 1980 birth cohort may live in a one-parent family during childhood, with a range of 40–70% for whites and a range of 85–95% for blacks.

Particularly intriguing are (a) Blake's (1981b, 1985) family-level conclusion that smaller numbers of siblings lead to higher educational attainments during adulthood, and (b) Preston's (1984) contrary societal-level suggestion that declining cohort size may have negative effects upon the current welfare of children, at least as compared to the elderly. As these and other topics are developed further, the application of the life-course perspective, particularly as suggested by Elder (1985; Elder et al 1985a,b), promises to yield valuable insights. The potentially critical importance of family and life-course influences which condition ongoing processes is well-represented in Blake's (1985) research showing that the number of siblings determines the nature of the relationship between father's and son's education. Projections concerning the extent to which children may, in the future, experience one-parent families suggest an emerging opportunity to apply the life-course framework to processes that fundamentally influence the well-being of children. The emerging sociodemographic study of childhood appears to have an exciting future.

Literature Cited

Abbott, D. A., Brody, G. H. 1985. The relation of child age, gender, and number of children to the marital adjustment of wives. *J. Marriage Fam.* 47:77–91

Aldous, J. 1977. Family interaction patterns. *Ann. Rev. Sociol.* 3:105–35

Alwin, D. F., Thornton, A. 1984. Family origins and the schooling process: Early versus late influence of parental characteristics. *Am. Sociol. Rev.* 49:784–802

Bachrach, C. A. 1983. Children in families: Characteristics of biological, step-, and adopted children. *J. Marriage Fam.* 45:171–79

Bane, M. J. 1976. Marital disruption and the lives of children. *J. Soc. Issues* 32:103–17

Belsky, J., Steinberg, L. 1975. The effects of day-care: A critical review, *Child Dev.* 49:929–49

Berkov, B., Sklar, J. 1976. Does illegitimacy make a difference? A study of the life chances of illegitimate children in California. *Pop. Dev. Rev.* 2:201–17

Blake, J. 1981a. The only child in America: Prejudice versus performance. *Pop. Dev. Rev.* 7:43–54

Blake, J. 1981b. Family size and the quality of children. *Demography* 18:421–42

Blake, J. 1985. Number of siblings and educational mobility. *Am. Sociol. Rev.* 50:84–94

Bloom-Feshbach, S., Bloom-Feshbach, J.,

Heller, K. A. 1982. Work, family, and children's perceptions of the world. In *Families That Work: Children in a Changing World,* ed. S. B. Kamerman, C. D. Hayes, pp. 268–307. Washington, DC: Natl. Acad.

Bumpass, L. L. 1984a. Some characteristics of children's second families. *Am. J. Sociol.* 90:608–23

Bumpass, L. L. 1984b. Children and marital disruption: A replication and update. *Demography* 21:71–82

Bumpass, L. L. 1985. Bigger isn't necessarily better: A comment on Hofferth's "updating children's life course." *J. Marriage Fam.* 47:797–98

Bumpass, L. L., Rindfuss, R. R. 1979. Children's experience of marital disruption. *Am. J. Sociol.* 85:49–65

Card, J. J. 1981. Long-term consequences for children of teenage parents. *Demography* 18:137–56

Cherlin, A. 1977. The effect of children on marital dissolution. *Demography* 14:265–72

Cherlin, A. J. 1981. *Marriage, Divorce, Remarriage.* Cambridge, Mass: Harvard Univ. Press

Cherlin, A. J. 1983. Changing family and household: Contemporary lessons from historical research. *Ann. Rev. Sociol.* 9:51–66

Cherlin, A. J., McCarthy, J. 1985. Remarried couple households: Data from the June 1980

Current Population Survey, *J. Marriage Fam.* 47:23–30

Duncan, G. J. 1984. *Years of Poverty, Years of Plenty.* Ann Arbor: Inst. Soc. Res., Univ. Mich.

Elder, G. H. Jr. 1974. *Children of the Great Depression: Social Change in Life Experience.* Chicago: Univ. Chicago Press

Elder, G. H. Jr. 1981. Scarcity and prosperity in postwar childbearing: Explorations from a life course perspective. *J. Fam. Hist.* 5:410–33

Elder, G. H. Jr., 1985. Household, kinship, and the life course: Perspectives on black families and children. In *Beginnings: The Social and Affective Development of Black Children,* eds. M. Spencer, G. Brookins, W. Allen, pp. 39–43. Hillsdale, NJ: Erlbaum

Elder, G. H. Jr., Caspi, A., van Nguyen, T. 1985a. Resourceful and vulnerable children: Family influences in stressful times. In *Development as Action in Context: Integrative Perspectives on Youth Development,* ed. R. K. Silbereisen, E. Eyferth. New York: Springer. In press

Elder, G. H. Jr., Caspi, A., Downey, G. 1985b. Problem behavior and family relationships. In *Human Development: Multidisciplinary Perspectives,* ed. A. Sorensen, F. Weinert, L. Sherrod. Hillsdale, NJ: Erlbaum. In press

Featherman, D. L., Hauser, R. M. 1978. *Opportunity and Change.* New York: Academic

Freedman, R., Coombs, L. 1966. Childspacing and family economic position. *Am. Sociol. Rev.* 31:631–48

Furstenberg, F. F. Jr., Nord, C. W., Peterson, J. L., Zill, N. 1983. The life course of children of divorce. *Am. Sociol. Rev.* 48:656–68

Furstenberg, F. F. Jr., Spanier, G. B. 1984. *Recycling the Family.* Beverly Hills: Sage

Glenn, N. D., Hoppe, S. K. 1982. Only children as adults: Psychological well-being. *J. Fam. Issues* 5:363–82

Glenn, N. D., McLanahan, S. 1982. Children and marital happiness: A further specification of the relationship. *J. Marriage Fam.* 44:63–72

Glick, P. C. 1979. Children of divorced parents in demographic perspective. *J. Soc. Issues* 35:170–82

Glick, P. C., Norton, A. J. 1979. Marrying, divorcing, and living together in the U.S. today. *Population Bulletin,* Vol. 32, No. 5. Pop. Ref. Bur. Washington, DC

Gove, W. R., Geerken, M. R. 1977. The effect of children and employment on the mental health of married men and women. *Soc. Forc.* 56:66–76

Griffith, J. D., Koo, H. P., Suchindran, C. M. 1984. Childlessness and marital stability in remarriages. *J. Marriage Fam.* 46:577–85

Hayes, C. D., Kamerman, S. B. eds. 1983. *Children of Working Parents: Experiences and Outcomes,* Washington, DC: Nat. Acad.

Heer, D. M. 1985. Effects of sibling number on child outcome. *Ann. Rev. Sociology.* 11:27–47

Hetherington, E. M., Cox, M., Cox, R. 1978. The aftermath of divorce. In *Mother-Child, Father-Child Relations,* ed. J. H. Stevens, Jr., M. Matthews. Washington, DC: Nat. Assoc. Educ. Young Children

Hetherington, E. M., Cox, M., Cox, R. 1985. Long-term effects of divorce and remarriage on the adjustment of children. *J. Am. Acad. Child Psychiatry* 24:518–30

Hicks, M., Platt, M. 1970. Marital happiness and stability: A review of the research in the sixties. *J. Marriage Fam.* 32:553–74

Hofferth, S. L. 1983. Childbearing decision making and family well-being. *Am. Sociol. Rev.* 48:533–45

Hofferth, S. L. 1985a. Children's life course: Family structure and living arrangements in cohort perspective. In *Life Course Dynamics: Trajectories and Transitions, 1968–1980,* ed. G. H. Elder, Jr., pp. 75–112. Ithaca: Cornell Univ. Press

Hofferth, S. L. 1985b. Updating children's life course. *J. Marriage Fam.* 47:93–115

Hogan, D. P. 1978. The effects of demographic factors, family background, and early job achievement on age at marriage. *Demography* 15:161–75

Hogan, D. P. 1986. The transition to adulthood. *Ann. Rev. Sociol.* 12:000–00

Hudson, W. W., Murphy, G. J. 1980. The non-linear relationship between marital satisfaction and stages of the family life cycle: An artifact of type I errors? *J. Marriage Fam.* 42:263–67

Kobrin, F. E., Waite, L. J. 1984. Effects of childhood family structure on the transition to marriage. *J. Marriage Fam.* 46:807–16

Koo, H. P., Suchindran, C. M. 1980. Effects of children on women's marriage prospects. *J. Fam. Issues* 1:497–515

Long, L. H. 1972. The influence of number and ages of children on residential mobility. *Demography* 9:371–82

Longfellow, C. 1979. Divorce in context: Its impact on children. In *Divorce and Separation: Context, Causes, and Consequences,* eds. G. Levinger, O. C. Moles, pp. 287–306. New York: Basic

Marini, M. M. 1980. Effects of the number and spacing of children on marital and parental satisfaction. *Demography* 17:225–42

McLanahan, S. S. 1983. Family structure and stress: A longitudinal comparison of two-parent and female-headed families. *J. Marriage Fam.* 45:347–57

Moore, K. A., Waite, L. J. 1981. Marital dissolution, early motherhood, and early marriage. *Soc. Forc.* 60:20–40

Mott, F. L., Haurin, R. J. 1982. Being an only child: Effects on educational progression and career orientation. *J. Fam. Issues* 3:575–93

Mueller, C. W., Pope, H. 1977. Marital instability: A study of its transmission between generations. *J. Marriage Fam.* 39:83–93

Niemi, R. G., Sobieszek, B. I. 1977. Political socialization. *Ann. Rev. Sociol.* 3:209–33

Nock, S. L. 1982. Enduring effects of marital disruption and subsequent living arrangements. *J. Fam. Issues* 3:25–40

Norton, A. J., Glick, P. C. 1986. One-parent families: A social and economic profile. *J. Fam. Relat.* 35:9–17

Peterson, J. L., Zill, N. 1986. Marital disruption, parent-child relationships, and behavioral problems in children. *J. Marriage Family* 48: In press

Polonko, K. A., Scanzoni, J., Teachman, J. D. 1982. Childlessness and marital satisfaction. *J. Fam. Issues* 3:545–73

Preston, S. H. 1984. Children and the elderly: Divergent paths for America's dependents. *Demography* 21:435–57

Silverstein, L. 1981. A critical review of current research on infant day care. In *Child Care, Family Benefits and Working Parents,* ed. S. B. Kamerman, A. J. Kahn. New York: Columbia Univ. Press

Smith, J. P., Ward, M. P. 1980. Asset accumulation and family size. *Demography* 17:243–60

Spanier, G. B., Lewis, R. A. 1980. Marital quality: A review of the seventies. *J. Marriage Fam.* 42:825–39

Thornton, A. 1977. Children and marital stability. *J. Marriage Fam.* 39:531–38

Waite, L. J., Spitze, G. D. 1981. Young women's transition to marriage. *Demography* 18:681–94

Wallerstein, J. S., Kelly, J. B. 1980. *Surviving the Breakup: How Children and Parents Cope with Divorce.* New York: Basic

Watts, H. W., Hernandez, D. J., eds. 1982. *Child and Family Indicators: A Report with Recommendations.* New York: Soc. Sci. Res. Council

Weiss, R. S. 1984. The impact of marital dissolution on income and consumption in single-parent households. *J. Marriage Fam.* 46:115–27

Wilson, K. L., Zurcher, L. A., McAdams, D. C., Curtis, R. L. 1975. Stepfathers and stepchildren: An exploratory analysis from two national surveys. *J. Marriage Fam.* 37:526–36

Ann. Rev. Sociol. 1986. 12:181–204

FEMALE LABOR FORCE BEHAVIOR AND FERTILITY IN THE UNITED STATES

Evelyn Lehrer

Department of Economics, University of Illinois at Chicago, Chicago, Illinois 60680

Marc Nerlove

Department of Economics, University of Pennsylvania, 3718 Locust Walk CR, Philadelphia, Pennsylvania 19104

Abstract

This article critically reviews the literature on fertility and female labor force behavior in the United States, with particular emphasis on recent quantitative research by economists, demographers, and sociologists. We first examine the empirical evidence regarding the influence on fertility and female employment of certain key variables: the value of female time, husband's income, and relative economic status. Then the issue of whether there is direct causality between fertility and female labor supply is addressed. We review simultaneous equations models and a new approach to the study of causality. Sequential decision-making models are also discussed.

Factors that may mediate the fertility–labor supply nexus are examined. These include childcare arrangements, husband's income, wife's education, and the convenience of employment. Differentials in the relationship between fertility and labor supply among racial and religious groups are noted. The article concludes with a discussion of changes over time in the association between fertility and female employment.

181

0360-0572/86/0815-0181$02.00

INTRODUCTION

Why are fertility and female employment associated? The key to the answer lies in the centrality of the mother's role in our society: The primary responsibility for childcare lies with her. Two complementary hypotheses have been offered in the demographic and sociological literature: (*a*) The demands of working are in conflict with the demands of childcare, i.e. there is a strain between the mother and worker roles. In Weller's words (1977:44): "Given the separation of home and gainful employment that is present in an industrialized society such as our own and the relatively inflexible hours connected with most forms of employment, an incompatibility between the roles of mother and worker may be said to exist." (*b*) Associated with each of these roles, there is a particular set of rewards, in the emotional, social, and cultural dimensions. To some extent, there are possibilities of substitution between these two sets. As Blake puts it (1970:342), "employment will often entail satisfactions alternative to children (companionship, recreation, stimulation, and creative activity), or the means to such satisfactions in the form of financial remuneration." This might be called the *substitution hypothesis*.

Similar concepts are found in the economics literature (e.g. see articles in Schultz 1974). Parents are assumed to derive utility from various "commodities" produced with time and market goods inputs. Among these commodities is a highly time intensive one: "child services." Various "market baskets" representing different combinations of commodities may yield the same level of utility. This is the counterpart to the substitution hypothesis. The mother is viewed as having to decide how to best allocate her time among employment (which increases the family's command over market goods), child services, and other home activities. A trade-off between child care services and market work arises because of the mother's time constraint (i.e. the scarcity of her time resources), coupled with the fact that jobs in our economy typically cannot be performed jointly with childcare tasks. This is the counterpart to the role incompatibility hypothesis. Economic theory also emphasizes the importance of fixed time and money costs associated with labor-market entry: "The existence of costs of participation imparts a discontinuity in the labor supply function, reflecting the fact that women will not be willing to work below some minimum number of hours. . . . Preschool children appear to be the most important source of work costs" (Cogan 1980:328).

In addition, economic theory suggests that for those mothers with greater stocks of human capital, the opportunity cost (in terms of market goods foregone) associated with bearing and rearing children is higher; these women are thus expected to display lower fertility and greater labor-market attachment.

As noted by Groat et al (1976:115), "Although the existence of an inverse association between fertility and employment histories has been documented in many studies, the causal directions of this association are complex and not very well understood." Indeed, there is a substantial amount of confusion surrounding the causality issue. For example, Weller (1977:43) lists four possibilities:

1. Family size affects labor force participation;
2. Labor force participation affects family size;
3. Both family size and labor force participation affect each other; and
4. The observed negative relationship is spurious and is caused by common antecedents of both variables.

The role incompatibility hypothesis is then discussed under the second category. Yet fertility and female employment occupy symmetric positions in the role incompatibility hypothesis—nothing in that hypothesis suggests causality in one direction rather than the other.

Mincer (1963:78) has written in support of the hypothesis of common antecedents: "The economic analyses of fertility and labor-force participation presented here suggest that the choices of labor and family size are not causally related to one another. Rather, these choices are simultaneously determined by the same basic economic variables. The higher the female wage rate and the lower the husband's earning power, the higher the labor-force rate and the smaller the fertility rate."

While many researchers would not go so far as to assert that all of the female labor supply–fertility nexus can be traced to the influence of exogenous factors on each, undoubtedly at least part of the relationship may be explained in this way. The first section of this article examines the empirical evidence regarding the impact on fertility and female work of certain key variables—the value of female time, income, and relative economic status.

The issue of whether there is direct causation from fertility to female labor supply and vice-versa is addressed in the second major section. In one type of theory, couples are envisioned as making fertility and female work decisions simultaneously, at one point in time—usually at the outset of marriage. Statistically, these interdependent decisions are analyzed within the context of simultaneous equations models. Results obtained using this approach are reviewed, and difficulties noted by several investigators are discussed. A promising recent approach is also presented.

Another, very different, view is that fertility and female labor supply decisions are made sequentially. Decisions regarding female employment in the current period and whether or not to advance to the next parity are made in light of perceived benefits and costs associated with children and with market activities; these, in turn, are influenced by past fertility and time-allocation choices. Models based on this perspective are reviewed.

The fact that the fertility–female labor supply nexus is, in general, much weaker in less developed countries than in the United States has been attributed in part to differences in the extent to which surrogates for the mother are readily and inexpensively available (Stycos & Weller 1967). Several authors have advanced the hypothesis that within the United States, variations among households in the availability and price of childcare arrangements may influence the fertility–labor supply linkage. It has also been suggested that the nature of the mother's market activities may play an important role: Women whose jobs allow them to work close to home and on a part-time basis may experience less conflict between the mother and worker roles. The third major section reviews these and other factors that may affect the nature of the fertility–labor supply relationship.

The fourth section examines evidence suggesting that the association between fertility and maternal employment varies among racial and religious groups. Changes in the labor supply–fertility nexus over time, and their implications, are discussed in the closing section.

THE IMPACT OF EXOGENOUS FACTORS ON FERTILITY AND LABOR SUPPLY

This section reviews findings on the impact of exogenous variables on fertility and female labor supply. Because the influences of interest for the present purposes are total effects, attention is focused mostly on results from studies based on fertility and labor-supply equations with no endogenous variables in the right-hand side. From a policy perspective also, the main interest is on total effects, rather than on short-run responses conditioned on either fertility or labor supply.

Value of Female Time

Economic theory suggests that an increase in the opportunity cost of children should be associated with a decrease in family size. For the United States, the fact that mother's education and other measures of the value of female time have a negative impact on fertility has been interpreted in this way and confirmed with many bodies of data (Cain & Weininger 1973; Lehrer & Nerlove 1981, 1982; Dooley[1] 1982; Carliner et al 1984; Moffitt 1984a; Rosenzweig & Schultz 1984).

Most studies find also that indicators of the value of female time affect

---

[1]Dooley finds this result for both blacks and whites using individual Census data. His analyses of published SMSA data, however, yield significant negative coefficients for the wage variable only for blacks. In addition to the difficulties associated with the use of aggregate data described by Dooley, it might be noted that the regressions include *two* variables closely correlated with the value of female time: education and wage. Other studies have found that due to high collinearity between these variables, inclusion of both in the model may be problematic (e.g. Mohan 1984).

employment positively.[2] In his life-cycle analysis, Moffitt (1984a) shows that increases in the level of the female wage profile increase the profile of labor supply. Examining participation in two different years and in the interval between those years, Rosenzweig & Schultz (1984) find that education has a significant positive impact. Carliner et al (1984) report that an increase in wife's educational attainment is associated with a significant increase in lifetime labor supply. Based on a sample of women less than 45 years of age, Lehrer & Nerlove (1981, 1982) show that the positive effect of education is more pronounced in the period before the first child—a finding that may reflect in part the fact that the wife's education raises the productivity of time spent on childcare.[3] Schultz's (1980) labor force participation equations, stratified by age and race, suggest a similar pattern for whites: female wage elasticities for the 14–24, 25–34, 35–44, 45–54, and 55–64 age categories are, respectively, 1.5, 1.0, 0.2, 0.8, and 1.7. For blacks, the figures are 0.9, 0.9, 0.4, 0.4, and 0.7.

DeVaney's (1983) analysis of US time-series data for the period 1947–1977 shows that, consistent with the studies reviewed above, changes in female wages affect fertility and employment in opposite directions.

Husband's Income

Coefficients associated with measures of husband's income in fertility equations range from significantly negative (Lehrer & Nerlove 1981, 1982) to insignificant (Carliner et al 1984), and significantly positive (e.g. in some of the regressions reported by Cain & Weininger 1973, by Dooley 1982, and by Rosenzweig & Schultz 1984). As the theory of child quantity-quality interactions shows, negative coefficients do not imply that parents regard children as inferior goods[4] (Becker & Lewis 1974). The essence of the argument is that, ceteris paribus, a positive relationship between the availability of resources and fertility would be expected. But other things are not held constant: As income rises, the desired "quality" of children rises, and having an additional child becomes more expensive.

[2]An exception is Cramer (1979). Commenting on a regression of hours of employment in 1971 on wife's wage, husband's wage, *hours of employment in 1967,* and several other variables, the author states: "The small effect of husband's wage rate on wife's employment trend, the much larger negative effect of her own potential wage rate, and the persistently large effect of fertility status are inconsistent with the strongly human-capital oriented versions of microeconomic theory. . . ." (p. 186). If husband's and wife's wages affect employment in 1971, as postulated, they surely affect employment in 1967. Thus, much of their effect on employment in 1971 is included in the coefficient on the 1967 employment variable. This coefficient also captures unmeasured factors, such as preferences for market activities, that are persistent through time.

[3]Leibowitz (1977) suggests two ways in which maternal education may influence the childrearing process and the production of child quality: the "worker effect" and the "allocative effect."

[4]A good is said to be "inferior" if quantity demanded decreases in response to an increase in income.

There is more agreement among studies regarding the impact of income on female employment. Carliner et al (1984) find a significantly negative effect of husband's earnings on wife's lifetime labor supply; Rosenzweig & Schultz (1984) report negative and generally significant effects on labor force participation in two years and in the interval between those years. Schultz (1980) notes that the depressing impact of husband's income on labor force participation is less pronounced for the youngest age cohort (14–24 years). Along similar lines, Lehrer & Nerlove (1981, 1982) report that husband's income has a significant effect only after the onset of childbearing.

Relative Economic Status

Easterlin (1968, 1973) has emphasized the importance for demographic behavior of relative economic status, i.e. the comparative earnings experience of young adults and their parents. The material aspirations of young people are viewed as a function of the standard of living they experienced during childhood and adolescence. Those growing up in affluent households develop high standards of consumption. If, as adults, they find that labor-market conditions make it difficult to support the desired style of living, then "the resulting economic stress will lead to deferment of marriage and, for those already married, to the use of contraceptive techniques to avoid childbearing, and perhaps also to the entry of wives into the labor market" (Easterlin 1973:181).

Moffitt (1982) finds that, indeed, the lifetime wealth of the parental generation has a negative influence on the age-fertility profile, and a positive effect on the age–female labor supply profile, own generation wealth held constant. DeVaney (1983) provides further evidence in support of the hypothesis that relative economic status affects fertility and female work in opposite directions.

Oppenheimer (1982) argues persuasively that an individual's aspirations, or preferences for consumption, are shaped not only by conditions in the parental household, but also by contemporaneous occupational reference groups. The author develops the theory of a "lower white-collar squeeze": Men in lower white-collar occupations often have high educational levels and correspondingly high aspirations for consumption and for the schooling of their children; at the same time, their earnings are not too different from those of many blue-collar workers. The wife's market work is used as a way to alleviate the imbalance between the desired standard of living and the husband's earning capacity. This explains the fact that, ceteris paribus, wives of lower white-collar men work not only more than wives of higher white-collar men, but also more than wives of men in blue-collar occupations with lower earnings. Although the possibility of an additional response in the form of reduced fertility is suggested, this is not investigated in detail.

Schultz (1981:159) has noted that attempts to test Easterlin's hypothesis or variations of it with cross-sectional data are subject to an important difficulty: "In the aggregate context, a cohort's size is truly exogenous from the individual's point of view, and imposes what may therefore be construed as an unanticipated income effect on the standard of living of all members of that birth cohort." However, "the entire research strategy of constructing a ratio of intergenerational incomes in the cross-section in order to determine if it is positively correlated with the second generation's fertility is marred. Since the second generation's income status (relative to almost anything) is partly an endogenous choice variable, it is likely to reflect other unobserved conditions, tastes, and stochastic events that probably also influence fertility decisions."

Summary, Qualifications, and Suggestions for Future Research

The evidence reviewed above suggests that at least part of the negative relationship between fertility and female employment may be traced to the fact that these variables are influenced in opposite directions by changes in the value of female time and relative economic status. Whether changes in husband's income contribute to the negative association is less clear at the present time.

Nerlove (1974) has noted that the coefficient on female education in a fertility equation may overstate the impact associated with the opportunity cost of time. Positive assortative mating by education in the marriage market leads men with higher-than-average levels of education to marry women who also have higher-than-average levels of schooling. Differences in tastes are not likely to be reflected in the educational attainment of men; however, it is very plausible that women with limited interest in market activities and high preferences for children will, in general, seek less formal education than women with opposite preferences. If, as is likely, there is positive assortative mating by preferences for children, then men with a given educational attainment with strong preferences for children will tend to marry women with less schooling than the average associated with the level these men have achieved. If the husband's schooling level is associated primarily with an income effect, while his wife's education is associated mostly with the opportunity cost of time, it follows that the negative impact of the opportunity cost of time as measured this way on fertility will tend to be exaggerated, holding male educational attainment constant, since the difference between the two across couples partly reflects differences in preferences that are unobservable and not included in the statistical analysis. By a similar argument, the coefficient on wife's education in a female labor-supply equation is likely to be biased upwards.

While most economic studies view wife's education as a proxy for the value of her time and husband's education as an indicator of the household's permanent income, with the qualifications noted above, other channels through which male and female education may operate have been suggested (e.g. Cochrane 1979).

Future research on the total effects of various explanatory factors on fertility and female labor supply might pay particular attention to the discrete nature of some of the decisions involved. For instance, one might attempt to measure the total impact of wife's education, husband's income, and other variables on (*a*) the wife's current intentions regarding whether or not to have a (another) child, and (*b*) her current employment status. Procedures for estimating these types of influences, taking into account the fact that the fertility and employment decisions are made jointly, are discussed by Nerlove & Press (1973, 1976) and Lehrer (1985), among others.

Due in part to data limitations, the studies reviewed in this section treat the mother's human capital stock as exogenous. In fact, at any given point in time, this stock reflects not only factors beyond her control (e.g. inherited ability), but also past decisions regarding investments in formal education and other forms of human capital—decisions that are influenced by expected fertility and labor supply. Those women who at a young age foresee low fertility and a strong attachment to the labor force are more likely to make investments in human capital specific to the labor market than are their counterparts with weaker commitment to market activities. Some quantitative estimates of these relationships have been made (e.g. Lehrer & Stokes 1985). The exogeneity of the female human capital stock has also been questioned in the growing literature on the timing of entry into motherhood and educational attainment (e.g. Rindfuss et al 1980, Lehrer 1985).

DO FERTILITY AND FEMALE LABOR SUPPLY CAUSALLY AFFECT EACH OTHER?

Simultaneous-Equations Models

One of the first empirical studies to emphasize the simultaneous nature of fertility and female labor supply decisions is Nerlove & Schultz's (1970) analysis of Census data from Puerto Rico. Many nonrecursive models have been estimated since then with US data.

Postulating that fertility and employment plans are made jointly, Waite & Stolzenberg (1976) estimate a simultaneous equations model with two dependent variables: fertility expectations and labor force participation plans. The authors find that "the number of children a woman plans to bear has only a small effect on the probability that she plans to participate in the labor force when she is 35 years old. However, . . . a woman's plans to participate in the labor force when she is 35 have a substantial effect on the total number of children she plans to bear in her lifetime" (p. 235). On the basis of a measure of period fertility[5]

---

[5]"Period" fertility refers to births that occur within a specified short interval of time. Alternatively, fertility can be viewed longitudinally, as the number of births that women have over their lifetimes.

(number of children under age 2) and current labor force participation as dependent variables, Hout (1978) arrives at a different conclusion: "Fertility affects employment strongly at each parity, but employment does not affect fertility at any parity." Noting the differences in specification of the key variables (actual period fertility versus planned fertility; actual current labor force behavior versus expected employment), Hout proposes the following reconciliation: "in the short run, the discomforts of pregnancy and the demands of newborns decrease labor force participation and thereby account for the negative association between fertility and employment while, in the long run, fertility is curtailed to accommodate career commitments" (p. 151).

Inspection of results from other nonrecursive models, however, reveals that the estimated labor supply–fertility relationship does not follow this pattern in a systematic way. Using measures of cumulative fertility and long-run labor supply (labor force participation after marriage or after leaving school), Smith-Lovin & Tickamyer (1978) find a negative coefficient on fertility in the labor-supply equation, but Fleisher & Rhodes (1979) report an insignificant coefficient for whites, and a significantly positive coefficient for blacks and whites combined. Discrepancies are also found among studies using measures of cumulative fertility and current labor supply: Link & Settle (1981) find an insignificant coefficient on fertility in the labor-supply equation; Cain & Dooley (1976) report insignificant coefficients for some age groups and significantly positive coefficients for others; Schultz (1978) finds negative coefficients. Schultz also finds that expected fertility has a negative impact on labor supply for whites; the effect is insignificant for blacks. DeFronzo (1980) examines the relationship between the number of children ever born per 1000 ever-married women aged 20–24 (CEBM) and the percentage of these women in the labor force (LFPM). The coefficients on fertility in the labor-supply equations are negative but not significant; the same is true when changes over time in CEBM and LFPM are examined. As can be seen from Tables 1 and 2, the coefficients on labor supply in the fertility equations are negative in most cases, but not always significant.

Most of these articles use two-stage least squares or other instrumental variables techniques. Reviewing some of the earlier studies, Cramer (1980) emphasizes the following problems: (a) The adequacy of the instruments used for fertility and female market activity has a major impact on the nature of the resulting estimates. Weak instruments lead to multicollinearity and estimates that are unstable and imprecise. (b) The identifying restrictions used are generally arbitrary, and the results may be sensitive to the restrictions chosen.[6]

The essential characteristic of the identification problem is that it is a

---

[6]Procedures to examine the sensitivity of results to identifying restrictions are outlined by Land & Felson (1978).

Table 1 Simultaneous Equations Models: Micro Data

Author(s)	Definition of fertility (F)	Definition of labor supply (L)	Data	Identifying Restrictions		Results		Observations
				Omitted from L equation	Omitted from F equation	Coefficient on F in L equation	Coefficient on L in F equation	
Waite & Stolzenberg 1976	Number of children respondent plans to have	Plans for labor force participation at age 35	National Longitudinal Surveys, Young Women	Ideal family size; respondent's number of siblings	Work attitudes, mother's labor force participation	Negative; significant in some specifications	Significantly negative	Coefficient on F in L equation quantitatively small
Schultz 1978	Children ever born	Hours worked during the year	Survey of Economic Opportunity 1967	Wife's residential origins, her age, schooling of both spouses	NA*	Significantly negative	NA	Only labor supply equations are estimated
	Number of additional children expected	Same	Same	Same	NA	Significantly negative for whites. Insignificant for blacks		Same

Hout 1978	Number of children under age 2	Labor force participation in period 1968-1970	1970 Census	Duration of marriage	Previous employment	Significantly negative (for most values of previous parity) for whites. Insignificant for blacks	Generally insignificant	—
Smith-Lovin & Tickamyer 1978	Number of children at the time of survey	Number of years in labor force since marriage	1970 Explorations in Equality of Opportunity Survey	Respondent's number of siblings, fecundity, religion variables	Work before marriage, mother's labor force participation	Significantly negative	Positive, not significant	Another model is estimated with sex role attitudes as a third endogenous variable
Fleisher & Rhodes 1979	Number of children ever born	Proportion of years in labor force since leaving school	National Longitudinal Surveys, Young and Mature Women	Father's schooling, interaction terms	Mother's schooling, interaction terms	Not significant for whites; significantly positive for blacks and whites combined	L not included in F equation	Wage and child quality equations

NA, not applicable

Table 2 Simultaneous Equations Models: Aggregate Data

Author(s)	Definition of fertility (F)	Definition of labor supply (L)	Data	Identifying Restrictions — Omitted from L equation	Identifying Restrictions — Omitted from F equation	Results — Coefficient on F in L equation	Results — Coefficient on L in F equation	Observations
Cain and Dooley 1976	Number of children ever born per 1000 ever-married women	Proportion of married females in the labor force during census week	1970 Census and other aggregate data; 124 SMSAs	Religion variable, rural residence, industrial structure	Male unemployment rate; rate of female disabilities, industrial structure	Insignificant in most equations; positive where significant	Significantly negative for whites; negative for blacks but not always significant	Equation for female wage also estimated
De Fronzo 1980	Number of children ever born per 1000 ever-married women aged 20–24 (CEBM)	Percentage of 20–24 year old married women in the labor force (LFPM)	1960 and 1970 Census, and other aggregate data; 48 states	Land area per person	Female income	Negative, but not significant	Significantly negative	

	Change in CEBM from 1960 to 1970	Change in LFPM from 1960 to 1970	Same	Land area per person, 1960	Change in female income	Negative, but not significant	Negative, but not significant	—
Link & Settle 1981	Number of children ever born per 1000 married registered nurses (RN)	Percentage of married registered nurses in the labor force during census week	1970 Census and other aggregate data; 88 SMSAs	Births/1,000 in 1969; religion; deaths/1,000, physicians and beds/100,000; crime rate; index of monopsony; vocational training; average age of RNs; unionization; industrial structure; percentage of RNs employed by Federal government; potential labor market experience	Education; total unemployment rate; RN disability; deaths/1,000; physicians and beds/100,000; crime rate; index of monopsony; vocational training; unionization; industrial structure; percentage of RNs employed by Federal government; potential labor market experience	Negative, but not significant	Significantly negative	Equation for female wage also estimated

theoretical one. Thus, it is not possible to test empirically (as DeFronzo 1980:267 attempts to do) the restrictions which permit identification.[7]

A third problem might be added to Cramer's list: The instruments chosen are often variables likely to be endogenous, such as ideal family size (Waite & Stolzenberg 1976) or past labor supply (Hout 1978). To the extent that these variables are jointly determined with fertility and current employment, the objective of the two-stage-least-squares procedure, namely, purging the right-hand variables of their correlation with the residuals, remains unaccomplished.

Recent studies reflect some disillusionment with simultaneous equations systems. Commenting on Harman's (1970) work, Rosenzweig (1978:334) notes:

> In that study, attempts were made to estimate the direct impact of some of the endogenous decision variables (the children's labor force participation, for example) on fertility using simultaneous equations techniques. To do this, however, requires imposing restrictions on the sets of variables assumed to influence each household decision which are not only *ad hoc* but are inconsistent with the household time-allocative model in which all household decisions are influenced by the same set of circumstances. Thus, while a positive correlation may be observed between the employment of children and family size . . . this does not imply that decreasing child employment will actually reduce fertility since both may simply reflect other exogenous factors.

Similar concerns have been expressed by Nerlove & Razin (1981), Lehrer & Nerlove (1981), and Carliner et al (1984), among others. Building on the work of Rosenzweig & Wolpin (1980), the latter authors develop a model which emphasizes the fact that the coefficients associated with endogenous variables in structural equations depend crucially on the identifying restrictions chosen: "The fact that the coefficient on fertility in a labor supply equation may be zero does not . . . mean that fertility and labor supply are unrelated or that an *exogenous* increase in fertility would not affect labor supply" (p. 7).

The Impact of Exogenous Changes in Fertility

A different way to study causality running from fertility to labor supply has been recently proposed. Rosenzweig & Wolpin (1980) rely on a natural experiment, the birth of twins, to measure the impact of an exogenous fertility change. Women who have twins in their first pregnancy are found to respond by reducing the level of market activity; later in the life cycle, however, there is a compensatory increase in labor supply.

Using information on contraceptive behavior and actual fertility over a five-year period, Rosenzweig & Schultz (1984) isolate the supply component of fertility and divide it into two parts: one representing fecundity, which is a fixed or permanent component, and another indicating random fertility shocks.

---

[7]Overidentifying restrictions can be tested, e.g. Theil (1971:507–08). One of the papers cited above (Cain & Dooley 1976) reports such a test.

The authors find that variations in fecundity among women have a significant effect on labor supply in the expected direction (i.e. more fecund respondents work less)—an effect that increases over the life cycle. In contrast, a transitory, exogenous increase in the supply of births results in a compensatory pattern of labor-supply response, similar to that uncovered by Rosenzweig & Wolpin (1980). Further research in this direction would appear to hold considerable promise.

Sequential Decision-Making: Dynamic Models

A number of authors have expressed objections to the one-period model of family decision-making. Namboodiri (1972) has argued against focusing on completed family size as the key decision in fertility analyses:

> While any couple may even at the time of marriage have some idea about how many children to have altogether, it is unlikely that a firm decision will be made once and for all immediately after marriage. It seems more logical to assume that decisions would be made sequentially, each step dealing with the addition of a (another) child to the family (p. 198).

Turchi (1975) has argued that while couples must make their fertility decisions early in the life cycle for biological reasons, the same is not true of labor force participation. The asymmetry between fertility and labor-supply decisions is also emphasized by Oppenheimer (1982:23):

> . . . once children are born, couples are no longer entirely free to rethink their decisions about fertility. But it is still possible to modify the couple's decision about the wife's labor-force behavior—both her total labor supply over the life-cycle and how it will be distributed. Since young children are an impediment to mothers' working and older children involve expenditure commitments (including previously unanticipated ones), then at this point in the revamping of the utility-maximization plans, number and ages of children become exogenous to wives' labor-force behavior.

Cramer (1980) develops a model where fertility and employment decisions made in past years are taken as exogenous to decisions made in the current period. Using data from the Panel Study of Income Dynamics, 1968–1973, he postulates the following model:

$$E_1 = f(X)$$

$$F = g(E_1, X)$$

$$E_2 = h(E_1, F, X),$$

where E_1 represents initial employment status (hours worked), F is a dichotomous variable indicating whether or not a child was born during the 1968–1973 interval, E_2 represents employment status in the year following the birth (or in 1971 if there were no births), and X is a vector of exogenous variables. This model, and similar ones by Cramer (1979) and Gurak & Kritz

(1982), are estimated using ordinary least squares procedures. As Cramer (1980:175–76) notes, the objective is "to estimate whether prior employment determined who had a baby (called 'fertility status'), whether fertility status determined subsequent employment, and what effects the exogenous variables had on both behavioral sequences."

Use of ordinary least squares, however, is problematic. Individuals differ in their preferences for market versus nonmarket activities, and if, as is likely, these unobserved characteristics are persistent through time, the estimated coefficients will reflect this heterogeneity, in addition to any "real" effects of past employment and fertility.

Panel studies and surveys with retrospective data provide the opportunity to study each individual's past behavior. Procedures for using this information to isolate person-specific characteristics are suggested by Balestra & Nerlove (1966) and Nerlove (1971). Heckman & Willis (1975) estimate a dynamic fertility model which confirms the presence of persistent variations in fecundity and other unobserved characteristics among couples. Estimates of the effects associated with exogenous variables are seen to be sensitive to whether or not this heterogeneity is taken into account. Heckman's (1979) dynamic model of female labor supply suggests that women differ also in their propensity to engage in market activities and that these differences are persistent through time.

A vast number of studies are based on ordinary-least-squares analyses which neglect heterogeneity and treat the number and ages of children, as well as past female employment, as exogenous determinants of current fertility and labor-supply behavior. Pragmatic considerations often underlie this approach. Many data sets lack enough information to estimate person-specific effects. In addition, studies to date have not been very successful in predicting family size—much less the timing and spacing of children. For some purposes, the problems arising from excluding the number and ages of children, or relying on predicted values based on instrumental regressions with very low R^2s, may overwhelm the difficulties arising from treating these variables as exogenous. Most of the studies reviewed in the following sections implicitly take this view.

FACTORS THAT MAY MEDIATE THE FERTILITY–LABOR SUPPLY NEXUS

Factors that have been hypothesized to influence the nature of the association between fertility and labor supply are reviewed below.

Childcare Arrangements

MARKET ARRANGEMENTS   Using a two-step procedure that combines aggregate and micro data, Stolzenberg & Waite (1984) examine whether the strength of the influence of children on maternal employment varies with the availability and price of market care. The finding that a relatively large number of childcare workers per female labor force participant (as measured by Census data) is associated with a small depressing impact of children on mother's labor supply is interpreted as lending support to the hypothesis that availability of market care influences the extent to which children constrain mother's employment.

Two considerations suggest that this result must be interpreted with caution since it may reflect, at least in part, causality running in the opposite direction, i.e. from the level of constraint to the number of workers that are attracted to the formal childcare market. (a) Childcare needs are, to a very large degree, met by relatives, friends, neighbors, and unlicensed babysitters. Most of these informal childcare workers do not appear in Census figures and thus are not considered in the childcare worker per labor force participant ratio. (b) Areas where mothers of young children have high participation rates are likely to be those where female wages are relatively high. They are also likely to be areas where those women who engage in market activity, do so more hours per year. These two characteristics—high wages and high level of labor supply—are associated with increased reliance on market forms of care (Lehrer & Kawasaki 1985).

These observations suggest that, rather than measuring the ease with which childcare can be arranged, the number of (reported) childcare workers per labor force participant may reflect the extent to which workers have been attracted to the formal childcare sector.

AVAILABILITY OF RELATIVES   Using data from the 1960 and 1970 censuses, Weller (1977) examined how the correlation between children ever born and employment status is affected by the presence of a relative in the household. The data sets are divided into several subsamples according to race, years married, education, and presence of relatives. For some subsets the results lend support to the hypothesis that the fertility–labor supply relationship is weaker in families where a relative is available; for other subsets, no clear pattern is discerned.

The presence of young children constrains the labor-force participation of black mothers to a lesser extent than that of their white counterparts (Bell 1974, Lehrer & Nerlove 1984). It has been suggested that the greater prevalence of extended family arrangements among black households may be one factor accounting for this racial difference (e.g. see Clifford & Tobin 1977).

RELATIONSHIP BETWEEN TYPE OF CHILDCARE ARRANGEMENT USED AND INTENDED FERTILITY   Due to data limitations, the studies reviewed above focus on the availability of either market or nonmarket arrangements. Using data from the 1976 National Survey of Family Growth, Lehrer & Kawasaki (1985) find that, ceteris paribus, among two-earner households with infants or preschoolers, reliance on a relative for childcare (as opposed to a babysitter or an organized facility) is positively associated with intentions to have further children. Two possible explanations are suggested. (a) The availability of relatives may have a pronatalist effect because it reduces the economic burden of raising children. The monetary cost associated with care by a relative is not only substantially lower than that associated with other forms of care, it is also unlikely to increase significantly as further children are added to the household. This is in sharp contrast to care in organized facilities, where few or no discounts on the price per child are made when more than one child per family is enrolled. (b) There may be differences among modes in terms of compatibility between the mother and worker roles. Perhaps the activities of raising children and working are most compatible when a relative is available to take care of the children, especially in the first three or four years.

Husband's Income

Bean et al (1982) hypothesized that "as husband's income decreases, 'role incompatibility' becomes less and less relevant to decisions about whether and how much to work. Hence, fertility is less likely to constrain labor force participation among women whose husbands have low income, holding constant the market opportunities of the wife" (p. 6). Using samples of Mexican American, Puerto Rican, and Cuban women drawn from the 1976 Survey of Income and Education, the authors regress number of weeks worked in 1975 on education, fertility, husband's income, and an interaction term between husband's income and fertility. The results are mixed. Some support for the hypothesis emerges for Mexican Americans but not for other groups.

Wife's Education

Leibowitz (1975) reports that better-educated mothers have higher participation rates than their less educated counterparts, *except* during the childrearing years. Regressions run separately for each of three major education groups show that the depressing impact of the presence of young children on mother's labor supply is more pronounced among the better educated women. An explanation in terms of substitution of other factors of production for mother's time in child care is offered: ". . . other workers (baby-sitters, grandmothers, other children over six) are more similar in education and ability to the mothers with little schooling and are therefore good substitutes for them. However, if education increases the productivity of time spent in childcare, better-educated women would find these other workers relatively unsatisfactory substitutes" (p. 193). Other factors discussed are high income elasticity for childcare and increased productivity of time spent in childcare activities with increased education. Fleisher (1977) has suggested that, in fact, education increases a mother's productivity in childrearing *more* than in the labor market.

Supporting Leibowitz' results, Hill & Stafford (1974) find that women in high socioeconomic status families, who are disproportionately college educated, make a greater reduction in their labor-market activities per child in the 0–2.9 age range than do other women. Interestingly, however, analysis of more recent data shows a *smaller* per-child reduction in labor-market time in the presence of babies for college-educated mothers than for mothers with only high school education, suggesting that new patterns may be emerging (Hill & Stafford 1980).

Convenience of Employment

The "convenience" of employment may affect the extent to which the roles of mother and worker are incompatible. Using data from the 1960 Census and three indicators of convenience (availability of work at home, close proximity to work, and short working hours), Darian (1975) finds some support for this hypothesis. Additional evidence suggesting that the convenience of employment (measured by distance to work and mode of transportation used) may play a role is provided by Stolzenberg & Waite (1984).

DIFFERENTIALS BY RACE AND RELIGION

Sweet (1973), Bell (1974), and others have documented the fact that the presence of children has a greater depressing impact on the employment of white mothers than on that of their black counterparts. Emphasizing that this difference should not be interpreted as evidence that black women "care less" about their children, Bell suggests an explanation based on the long-term inadequacy of the husband's earning power in black households: "The black wife is more likely to be *locked into* market work in order to maintain the basic expenditures of the family" (p. 477). Sweet (1973) suggests three additional explanations: (*a*) Black families may have easier access to childcare, paid or unpaid; (*b*) black women who wish to work may encounter less resistance from their husbands; and (*c*) the employment of black women is more likely to be part-time and more likely to involve evening hours.

The literature on black-white *fertility* differentials suggests the presence of an important race by education interaction effect: The tendency for blacks to have higher fertility than whites is less accentuated at higher than at lower levels of schooling. For example, based on data from the 1970 National Fertility Study, Johnson (1979) reports that among mothers with an elementary school education, on average blacks had 1.42 more children than whites; the gap narrows to only 0.087 children among mothers with four or more years of college. Is the labor-supply response to the presence of small children by these high status black mothers also more similar to that of white mothers? To the best of our knowledge, this question has not been investigated.

Regarding religion, a recent study by Chiswick (1986) shows that the depressing impact on labor supply of school age and smaller children is more pronounced for Jewish women; at the same time, Jewish mothers are more likely to work when the children are older and more "goods-intensive." The author concludes that if these behavioral patterns of Jewish mothers have continued from generation to generation, "the greater investments in child quality may contribute to the higher earnings and greater returns from schooling and on-the-job training observed among adult Jewish men."

Along similar lines, Hill & Stafford (1977) examine the role of religious affiliation on female labor supply and on the quantity of time inputs to child-care. The authors cite evidence that Catholics have higher earnings than Protestants for a given level of formal schooling, and present regressions suggesting that Catholic mothers work less in the market and spend more time in housework when their children are small than do their Protestant counter-parts. "Hopefully," the authors say, these and other results they report, will "lead to an interpretation of the background variables which are usually in-cluded in earnings functions in a manner which is consistent with their relation-ship to preschool investments in human capital" (p. 539).

Research on racial and religious differentials in the female labor supply—fertility linkage has begun only recently and further work on this issue would be desirable. For at least three reasons, as richer bodies of data become available, attention should be focused on both measures of maternal employment and direct indicators of quantity and quality of time spent on childcare. First, recent work by Hill & Stafford (1980) shows that while there is a smaller per child reduction in labor-market time for college-educated than for high-school edu-cated women in the presence of babies, the former group spends more time on childcare. This result suggests that more time spent in the labor force does not necessarily imply less time for childcare—it may mean less leisure for the mother or less time for other home activities.

Second, Lindert (1978:199) shows that "for given family composition, children of working mothers receive more total time in childcare from all persons. That is, the estimated deficit in mother's time is more than made up by extra (nonschool) time inputs by the husband and others." Once it is recognized that if the mother works, others will, in general, assume some of the childcare responsibilities, it becomes apparent that the relative education of mother and potential substitute caretakers is an important parameter. Based on data for children from a low socioeconomic status, Wolfe (1982) reports that the mother's "absence has no significant effects in any of the regressions (IQ is the dependent variable) and, in fact most signs are positive. One might argue that a mother's absence could raise the quality of time inputs to child care by providing substitute caretakers who are, on average, better teachers" (p. 224). Different results would probably emerge if the impact of maternal employment were analyzed using data on households with better educated mothers.

And third, there is some evidence that there are differences among racial and religious groups in the nature of the childcare arrangements made by working mothers (Duncan & Hill 1975, Lehrer & Kawasaki 1985).

These considerations have implications not only for future research on differences in fertility and female time-allocation patterns by race and religion, but also for the question of how maternal employment and time allocation decisions may influence the child.

CHANGES OVER TIME

In 1950, the labor force participation rate for married women with children under 6 years of age was 11.9%; for those with children 6–17 years of age, it was 28.3%. The figures had risen, respectively, to 18.6% and 39.0% by 1960, and to 49.9% and 63.8% by 1983 (Waldman 1983). Clearly, women with young children are working in the market much more today then they did in the past. The traditional pattern of post-school work, interruption of employment, and possibly a subsequent return to the labor force, has been eroding, with women remaining more closely attached to the labor force during the childrearing years (e.g. see Shapiro & Mott 1979, Mott & Shapiro 1983). If, as is likely, this trend continues, we may expect to see in the future a move towards convergence in the male and female occupational distributions and a narrowing in the wage differential between the sexes (Mincer & Polachek 1974, Lehrer & Stokes 1985). The implications that women's increased commitment to market activities may have in terms of (a) income distribution among families, and (b) the quantity and quality of time spent on childcare are less clear at the present time and warrant close attention.

As Ryder (1980) documents, changes in the timing of births have come to be the main driving force behind movements of period fertility in the United States. This development underscores the importance of improving our understanding of the complex relationships between the timing of births, completed family size, and female employment. Research on this issue has already begun (Razin 1980, Nerlove & Razin 1981, Moffitt 1984b). Efforts in this direction will continue in the years ahead.

ACKNOWLEDGMENT

Anonymous referees for the *Annual Review of Sociology* provided useful comments on an earlier draft of this paper.

Literature Cited

Balestra, P., Nerlove, M. 1966. Pooling cross-section and time series data in the estimation of a dynamic model: The demand for natural gas. *Econometrica.* 34(4):585–612

Bean, F. D., Swicegood, G., King, A. G. 1982. Fertility and labor supply among Hispanic American women. Paper No. 3.017, Tex. Popul. Res. Ctr., Austin

Becker, G. S., Lewis, H. G. 1974. Interaction between quantity and quality of children. In *Economics of the Family*, ed. T. W. Schultz, pp. 81–90. Chicago: Univ. Chicago Press

Bell, D. 1974. Why participation rates of black and white wives differ. *J. Hum. Resour.* 9(4):465–479

Blake, J. 1970. Demographic science and the redirection of population policy. In *Social Demography*, eds. T. R. Ford, G. F. De-Jong, pp. 326–56. Englewood Cliffs, NJ: Prentice-Hall

Cain, G. G., Dooley, M. D. 1976. Estimation of a model of labor supply, fertility, and wages of married women. *J. Polit. Econ.* 84(4)(2):S179–S199

Cain, G. G., Weininger, A. 1973. Economic determinants of fertility: Results from cross-sectional aggregate data. *Demography* 10 (2):205–21

Carliner, G., Robinson, C., Tomes, N. 1984. Lifetime models of female labor supply, wage rates, and fertility. *Res. Pop. Econ.* 5:1–27

Chiswick, B. 1986. Labor supply and investment in child quality: A study of Jewish and Non-Jewish women. *Rev. Econ. Statist.* In press

Clifford, W. B., Tobin, P. L. 1977. Labor force participation of working mothers and family formation: Some further evidence. *Demography* 14(3):273–84

Cochrane, S. H. 1979. *Fertility and Education. What Do We Really Know?* Baltimore & London: The Johns Hopkins Univ. Press

Cogan, J. 1980. Labor supply with costs of labor market entry. In *Labor Market Supply: Theory and Estimation*, ed. J. P. Smith, pp. 327–64. Princeton: Princeton Univ. Press

Cramer, J. C. 1979. Employment trends of young mothers and the opportunity cost of babies in the United States. *Demography* 16(2):177–97

Cramer, J. C. 1980. Fertility and female employment: Problems of causal direction. *Am. Sociol. Rev.* 45:167–90

Darian, J. C. 1975. Convenience of work and the job constraint of children. *Demography* 12(2):245–58

DeFronzo, J. 1980. Female labor force participation and fertility in 48 states: Cross sectional and change analyses for the 1960–1970 decade. *Sociol. Soc. Res.* 64(2):263–78

DeVaney, B. 1983. An analysis of variations in U.S. fertility and female labor force participation trends. *Demography* 20(2):147–61

Dooley, M. D. 1982. Labor supply and fertility of married women: An analysis with grouped and individual data from the 1970 U.S. Census. *J. Hum. Resour.* 17(4):499–532

Duncan, G., Hill, C. R. 1975. Modal choice in child care arrangements. In *Five Thousand American Families—Patterns of Economic Progress*, eds. G. Duncan, J. N. Morgan, 3:235–58. Ann Arbor: Institute Soc. Res.

Easterlin, R. A. 1968. *Population, Labor Force, and Long Swings in Economic Growth: The American Experience.* New York: Columbia Univ. Press

Easterlin, R. A. 1973. Relative economic status and the American fertility swing. In *Family Economic Behavior*, ed. E. B. Sheldon, pp. 170–223. Philadelphia: Lippincott

Fleisher, B. M. 1977. Mother's home time and the production of child quality. *Demography* 14(2):197–212

Fleisher, B. M., Rhodes, G. F. 1979. Fertility, women's wage rates, and labor supply. *Am. Econ. Rev.* 69(1):14–24

Groat, H. T., Workman, R. L., Neal, A. G. 1976. Labor force participation and family formation: A study of working mothers. *Demography* 13(1):115–125

Gurak, D. T., Kritz, M. M. 1982. Female employment and fertility in the Dominican Republic: A dynamic perspective. *Am. Sociol. Rev.* 47(6):810–18

Harman, A. M. 1970. *Fertility and Economic Behavior of Families in the Philippines*. Santa Monica: The Rand Corp.

Heckman, J. J. 1979. New evidence on the dynamics of female labor supply. In *Women in the Labor Market*, ed. C. B. Lloyd, E. S. Andrews, C. L. Gilroy, pp. 66–97. New York: Columbia Univ. Press

Heckman, J. J., Willis, R. J. 1975. Estimation of a stochastic model of reproduction: An econometric approach. In *Household Production and Consumption*, ed. N. E. Terleckyj, pp. 99–138. New York: Columbia Univ. Press

Hill, C. R., Stafford, F. P. 1974. Allocation of time to preschool children and educational opportunity. *J. Hum. Resour.* 9(3):323–41

Hill, C. R., Stafford, F. P. 1977. Family background and lifetime earnings. In *The Distribution of Economic Well-Being*, ed. F. T. Juster, pp. 511–49. Cambridge, Mass: Ballinger

Hill, C. R., Stafford, F. P. 1980. Parental care

of children: Time diary estimates of quantity, predictability and variety. *J. Hum. Resour.* 15(2):219–39

Hout, M. 1978. The determinants of marital fertility in the United States: 1968–1970: Inferences from a dynamic model. *Demography* 15(2):139–59

Johnson, E. N. 1979. Minority-group status and the fertility of black Americans, 1970: A new look. *Am. J. Sociol.* 8(6):1386–1400

Land, K. C., Felson, M. 1978. Sensitivity analysis of arbitrarily identified simultaneous-equations models. *Sociol. Methods Res.*, 6(3):283–307

Lehrer, E. 1985. Log-linear probability models: An application to the analysis of timing of first birth. *Appl. Econ.* 17(3):477–89

Lehrer, E., Kawasaki, S. 1985. Child care arrangements and fertility: An analysis of two earner households. *Demography* 22 (4):499–513

Lehrer, E., Nerlove, M. 1981. The labor supply and fertility behavior of married women. In *Research in Population Economics*, ed. J. L. Simon, 3:123–45. Greenwich: JAI

Lehrer, E., Nerlove, M. 1982. An econometric analysis of the fertility and labor supply of unmarried women. In *Research in Population Economics*, ed. J. L. Simon, P. H. Lindert, 4:217–35 Greenwich: JAI

Lehrer, E., Nerlove, M. 1984. A life-cycle analysis of family income distribution. *Econ. Inq.* 22(3):360–73

Lehrer, E., Stokes, H. 1985. Determinants of the female occupational distribution: A log-linear probability analysis. *Rev. Econ. Statist.* 67(3):395–404

Leibowitz, A. 1975. Education and the allocation of women's time. In *Education, Income and Human Behavior*, ed. F. T. Juster, pp. 171–97. New York: McGraw Hill

Leibowitz, A. 1977. Parental inputs and children's achievement. *J. Hum. Resour.* 12 (2):242–51

Lindert, P. H. 1978. *Fertility and Scarcity in America.* Princeton, NJ: Princeton Univ. Press

Link, C. R., Settle, R. F. 1981. A simultaneous equation model of labor supply, fertility and earnings of married women: The case of registered nurses. *Southern Econ. J.* 47(4):977–89

Mincer, J. 1963. Market prices, opportunity costs, and income effects. In *Measurement in Economics. Studies in Mathematical Economics and Econometrics in Memory of Yehuda Grunfeld*, ed. C. F. Christ, M. Friedman, L. A. Goodman, Z. Griliches, A. C. Harberger et al, pp. 67–82. Stanford: Stanford Univ. Press

Mincer, J., Polachek, S. 1974. Family investments in human capital: Earnings of women. *J. Polit. Econ.*, 82(2/2):76–108

Moffitt, R. 1982. Postwar fertility cycles and the Easterlin hypothesis: A life-cycle approach. In *Research in Population Economics*, ed. J. L. Simon, P. H. Lindert, 4:237–52. Greenwich: JAI

Moffitt, R. 1984a. Profiles of fertility, labour supply and wages of married women: A complete life-cycle model. *Rev. Econ. Stud.* 51(2):263–78

Moffitt, R. 1984b. Optimal life-cycle profiles of fertility and labor supply. In *Research in Population Economics*, ed. T. P. Schultz, 5:29–50 Greenwich, Conn: JAI

Mohan, R. 1984. Labor force participation in a developing metropolis: Does sex matter? Unpublished manuscript. Washington, DC: The World Bank

Mott, F. L., Shapiro, D. 1983. Complementarity of work and fertility among young American mothers. *Pop. Stud.* 37(2):239–52

Namboodiri, N. K. 1972. Some observations on the economic framework for fertility analyses. *Pop. Stud.* 26(2):185–206

Nerlove, M. 1971. Further evidence on the estimation of dynamic economic relations from a time series of cross sections. *Econometrica* 39(2):359–81

Nerlove, M. 1974. Toward a new theory of population and economic growth. *J. Polit. Econ.* 84:S200–S216

Nerlove, M., Press, J. 1973. *Univariate and Multivariate Log-Linear and Logistic Models.* Santa Monica: The Rand Corp.

Nerlove, M., Press, J. 1976. *Multivariate log-linear probability models for the analysis of qualitative data.* Northwestern Univ., Ctr. Statist. Probability. Discussion paper #1

Nerlove, M., Razin, A. 1981. Child spacing and numbers: An empirical analysis. In *Essays in the Theory and Measurement of Consumer Behavior in Honour of Sir Richard Stone*, ed. A. Deaton, pp. 297–324. Cambridge Univ. Press

Nerlove, M., Schultz, T. P. 1970. *Love and Life Between the Censuses: A Model of Family Decision-Making in Puerto Rico.* Santa Monica: The Rand Corp.

Oppenheimer, V. K. 1982. *Work and the Family: A Study in Social Demography.* New York: Academic

Razin, A. 1980. Number, birth spacing and quality of children: A microeconomic view. In *Research in Population Economics*, ed. J. Simon and J. DaVanzo, 2:279–93. Greenwich, Conn: JAI

Rindfuss, R. R., Bumpass, L., St. John, C. 1980. Education and fertility: Implications for the roles women occupy. *Am. Sociol. Rev.* 45:431–47

Rosenzweig, M. R. 1978. The value of children's time, family size and non-household child activities in a developing country: Evidence from household data. In *Research in*

Population Economics, ed. J. Simon, 1:331–47. Greenwich, Conn: JAI

Rosenzweig, M. R., Schultz, T. P. 1984. The demand for and supply of births: Fertility and its life cycle consequences. Discussion paper #462, Economic Growth Ctr. Yale Univ.

Rosenzweig, M. R., Wolpin, K. I. 1980. Life-cycle labor supply and fertility: Causal inferences from household models. *J. Polit. Econ.* 88(2):328–48

Ryder, N. B. 1980. Components of temporal variations in American fertility. In *Demographic Patterns in Developed Societies*, ed. R. W. Hiorns, pp. 15–54. London: Taylor & Francis

Schultz, T. P. 1978. The influence of fertility on labor supply of married women: Simultaneous equation estimates. *Res. Labor Econ.* 2:273–351

Schultz, T. P. 1980. Estimating labor supply functions for married women. In *Female Labor Supply: Theory and Estimation*, ed. J. P. Smith, pp. 25–89. Princeton, NJ: Princeton Univ. Press

Schultz, T. P. 1981. *Economics of Population*. Reading, Mass: Addison-Wesley

Schultz, T. W. 1974. *Economics of the Family. Marriage, Children and Human Capital*. Chicago & London: Univ. Chicago Press

Shapiro, D., Mott, F. L. 1979. Labor supply behaviour of prospective and new mothers. *Demography* 16(2):199–208

Smith-Lovin, L., Tickamyer, A. R. 1978. Non recursive models of labor force participation, fertility behavior and sex role attitudes. *Am. Sociol. Rev.* 43(4):541–57

Stolzenberg, R. M., Waite, L. J. 1984. Local labor markets, children and labor force participation of wives. *Demography* 21(2):157–70

Stycos, J. M., Weller, R. H. 1967. Female working roles and fertility. *Demography* 4(1):210–17

Sweet, J. A. 1973. *Women in the Labor Force*. New York & London: Seminar

Theil, H. 1971. *Principles of Econometrics*. New York: Wiley

Turchi, B. A. 1975. *The Demand for Children: The Economics of Fertility in the United States*. Cambridge, Mass: Ballinger

Waite, L. J., Stolzenberg, R. M. 1976. Intended childbearing and labor force participation of young women: Insights from non-recursive models. *Am. Sociol. Rev.* 41(2):235–52

Waldman, E. 1983. Labor force statistics from a family perspective. *Monthly Labor Rev.* 106(12):16–20

Weller, R. H. 1977. Wife's employment and cumulative family size in the United States, 1970 and 1960. *Demography* 14(1):43–65

Wolfe, J. R. 1982. The impact of family resources on childhood IQ. *J. Hum. Resour.* 17(2):213–35

Ann. Rev. Sociol. 1986. 12:205–31
Copyright © 1986 by Annual Reviews Inc. All rights reserved

LIFE-COURSE AND GENERATIONAL POLITICS

Richard G. Braungart

Department of Sociology, Syracuse University, Syracuse, New York 13210

Margaret M. Braungart

Arts and Sciences, CHRP, SUNY at Upstate Medical Center, Syracuse, New York 13210

Abstract

This essay first reviews the literature on life-course politics and generational politics. The major contributions and problems inherent in each perspective are identified, and an interactive approach to life-course and generational politics is suggested. Second, the methodological designs employed to study life-course and generational politics are outlined, including the cross-sectional, time-series, longitudinal, and aging-cohort-period designs. An evaluation is made of the major shortcomings and suitability of the various research strategies to studying life-course and generational politics.

HISTORICAL AND THEORETICAL ORIGINS

Explaining political behavior has intrigued Western scholars for centuries, and one of the most enduring explanations has been age. "The truest community to which one can belong," observed Wohl (1979:203), "is that defined by age and experience." Age is one of the most basic social categories of human existence and a primary factor in all societies for assigning roles and granting prestige and power. However, age is not a unitary concept and may be used in reference to life-cycle development (young, middle-aged, and old) or in a generational sense (lineage descent or a particular age group in history). Those born around the same period in time share a similarity in both life-cycle development and

205

0360-0572/86/0815-0205$02.00

historical experiences. The entrance of successive age groups into society has been a constant feature of human history, but each group has "come into existence" within a certain historical and political setting, and this sociohistorical process provides an important force for political stability and change.

The ancient Greeks were well aware of the significance of age for understanding human behavior and politics. To the Greeks, life was divided into different stages having unique characteristics and interests. Youth overdo everything, it was noted, and require the steady direction of their elders; thus, relations between the age groups are seldom harmonious, and this has important consequences for society and politics. Plato identified generational strife as a significant force for social change, while Aristotle commented that political revolutions are due not only to the struggle between rich and poor but to the conflict between fathers and sons (McKeon 1941; Feuer 1969; Esler 1974, 1979, 1982; Nash 1978). Generational descent was recognized in ancient literature as an important factor in the transmission of values from one generation to the next in the family. As Ptahhotep observed in the twenty-seventh century B.C. in his Maxims for right conduct: "A son who hearkens . . . reaches old age; he attains reverence. He speaks likewise to his own children, receiving the instruction of his father" (Feuer 1969:30).

During the Middle Ages, however, the understanding of human development and age-based behavior was minimal. Little distinction was made between childhood and adolescence, and youngsters were viewed as adults, only smaller. Since creation was thought to be instantaneous, the child did not develop; he was preformed: a tiny fully formed little person or homunculus was found in the sperm; when implanted in the uterus it simply grew larger in size for nine months (Muuss 1968). Medieval artists portrayed children as miniature adults, and the Latin term for child *(puer)* and adolescence *(adolescens)* were used interchangeably until the eighteenth century (Gillis 1974). With industrialization, however, discontinuity between child and adult statuses became more apparent, and the implications of human development and generational placement gained interest. Goethe observed that every person's fundamental world view is determined by the experiences of youth, with members of the same generation linked throughout life by bonds of mutual understanding that set them apart from others (Esler 1974).

In the nineteenth century, the discussion took a more scientific and theoretical form, and two perspectives emerged on age and sociopolitical change. The positivists stressed the importance of life-course development, contending that the distinct ages of life act as conditioning forces for human experiences, with social change and historical development seen as firmly rooted in the human life cycle (Marias 1970, Jansen 1975). Emphasizing the importance of generations, those from the romantic-historical school argued that biological age is not so important in understanding societal stability and change as are significant cultural and historical factors that structure the mentality of a generation, bind its members together, and separate them from older and younger generations. Generations thus were defined on the basis of historical differences and social change (Jansen 1975; Esler 1982, 1984; Braungart & Braungart 1984a).

These two, somewhat different, analytic approaches to understanding age, age-group relations, and sociopolitical change continue to be represented in contemporary theory and research. Although age is the fundamental component of both perspectives, it is given a slightly different temporal focus in each model. Many of the assumptions of the positivists are evident in a life-course approach to politics which views age from a lifetime or maturational perspective. The romantic-historical interpretation is represented in the generational approach to understanding politics, which emphasizes the social and historical influences on, and political consequences of, age-group membership (Jansen 1975). In contemporary discussions and research, however, the term "generation" has several different meanings and uses: (a) generational descent, or lineage-age groups, such as parent generation and offspring generation; (b) cohort, or an age group born around the same time in history, such as the 1920s cohort and 1950s cohort; and (c) political generation, or a special age group in history that becomes aware of its uniqueness and joins together to work for social and political change, such as the Great Depression Generation and the 1960s Generation (Troll 1970; Elder 1975, 1985; Bengtson & Cutler 1976; Braungart & Braungart 1984a, 1985a; Bengtson et al 1985).

While the life-course approach and the generational approach to explaining political behavior are not mutually exclusive, they often are treated as separate in political discussions and research, which tend to emphasize one perspective while ignoring the other. Yet both approaches are concerned with age-group differences in politics, the question of whether political views change or remain stable over the life course and why political generations take form. In this essay these two approaches to politics are examined along with some of their problems. In order to better describe and understand the relationship between age, time, and politics, we suggest that the two perspectives be combined into a life-course and generational approach to politics. In the latter section of the essay, the major methodological designs used to investigate age and politics are outlined and evaluated.

The study of life-course and generational politics has not attained the status of a formal field of inquiry, but in pulling together the theoretical discussion and empirical research concerned with the age and politics—as we have been doing for a number of years—we find a unity of purpose apparent in the diverse scholarly efforts of sociologists, psychologists, anthropologists, psychiatrists, historians, and political scientists. The importance of age to understanding human behavior and the structure of societies in general has been given explicit theoretical focus in life-span developmental psychology (Goulet & Baltes 1970, Baltes & Brim 1979–1984), aging and gerontology (Binstock & Shanas 1976, Birren & Schaie 1977, Huyck & Hoyer 1982), and age stratification theory (Eisenstadt 1956, Parsons 1963, Riley 1978, Streib & Bourg 1984). These theoretical and empirical perspectives on age are applicable to a number of behaviors, and in this essay the focus is on politics. Age, of course, is only one of many orientations in understanding politics—and certainly not a dominant one at this time (Braungart & Braungart 1984b, 1985a). However, in many societies some of the traditional explanations for political behavior, such as social class, political party, and personality, are losing their potency, while age may become increasingly important in understanding politics, especially with rising youth populations in developing nations and rapidly expanding aged populations in advanced societies (United Nations 1981, Braungart & Braungart 1986).

Perhaps one reason age has not received much direct focus in relation to politics is that the literature on the subject is widely scattered among a number of disciplines and needs to be synthesized into some kind of framework (Hudson & Binstock 1976). Theoretical discussions and research related to age and politics come from a number of directions and include a variety of topics and levels of analysis. The purpose of this essay is to pull together the diverse perspectives and findings concerning age and politics. The theoretical dimensions of life-course and generational politics are outlined, the principal findings reviewed and illustrated by different types of empirical studies, and the major methodological strategies used in the study of life-course and generational politics are evaluated. The treatment of the subject is not exhaustive; it is merely selective and illustrative.

LIFE-COURSE POLITICS

The life-course approach to explaining political behavior is based largely on life-cycle interpretations of human behavior. The assumptions of the life-course approach are that as individuals grow older, they undergo certain qualitative changes in physiology, cognitive functioning, emotional patterns, and needs. These biopsychological changes occur over the life span and are considered to be sequential, irreversible, and for the most part universal. The maturational unfolding process occurs as individuals of similar age levels move in a sequential direction toward certain characteristic growth patterns. Because each stage of life is associated with its own orientations, needs, and interests, relations between age groups are not likely to be smooth, and this sets the stage for generational conflict. Although the life-course theory tends to emphasize biopsychological growth and changes over the life course, social factors influence how the life cycle is played out. Thus, biopsychological development occurs within the social and historical context (Goulet & Baltes 1970, Featherman 1983, Dannefer 1984).

Several different types of political studies reflect the assumptions of life-course developmental theory. The focus on age-related patterns of human behavior has prompted some researchers to identify characteristic ways of political thinking and behavior at various stages of life. The emphasis in life-course theory on the different needs, crises, and orientations of each stage has resulted in a number of political investigations into the extent of age-group differences in politics. The life-course approach also indicates that individuals undergo changes in their patterns of growth and interests, although whether individuals change or remain relatively stable in their political orientations has been widely debated (Hudson & Binstock 1976, Braungart & Braungart 1985a). Much of the information on the life-course approach to politics can be organized around the major stages of life, revealing certain identifiable patterns of political thought and behavior for each stage and marked age-group differences and changes over the life course.

Politics in Childhood

A major contribution of life-course politics studies has been to further knowledge about age-related patterns of political behavior. Some of the most interesting work here concerns the development of political thought in children, based largely on Piaget's theory of cognitive development and child development research. For example, interviews of children and adolescents have indicated that: (a) There are clear limits to the child's ability to conceptualize and understand politics, depending on the particular stage of cognitive development; and (b) the child's ability to become aware of and to comprehend the political world occurs gradually over the course of childhood and adolescence. More specifically, while children as young as 3–6 years of age have some awareness of politics and an affective identification with political symbols such as the President, flag, and country, the ability to grasp the meaning of political concepts such as government and law does not begin until late childhood. Even at this stage political thought is concrete and simplistic, and it is not until mid and late adolescence that political awareness may become strong and political thinking more complex. Research has also indicated that the quality of political thought is modified by factors such as intelligence, family background, gender and ethnic differences, and social class, while the direction of political orientation is influenced by socialization agents such as family, friends, teachers, and media (Erikson 1963, Greenstein 1965, Hess & Torney 1967, Adelson 1971, Stacey 1977, Adelson & Hall 1980, Gallatin 1980).

Politics in Youth

The stage of youth is of particular interest from a political perspective, since it appears to be an important time in life for the development of political attitudes and behavior. The cognitive changes that occur during youth apparently set the stage for greater political awareness and heightened critical ability. Consequently, what is happening politically as the young person comes of age has much to do with the kinds of political attitudes the individual forms during these early years. Moreover, youth is the time to strive for independence, to form an identity, to search for fidelity, and to find the relationship between the self and society (Adelson 1980). These developmental characteristics are likely to make youth critical of their elders, society, and politics, and this has been interpreted by some to indicate that youth have a "predisposition" to generational conflict, rebellion, and revolution (Bettelheim 1963, Erikson 1968, Feuer 1969, Keniston 1971).

In piecing together studies of youth politics, we find many of the assumptions of life-course theory are supported. For example, large-scale national and cross-national surveys of young people from the 1960s to the 1980s indicate that youth (around the ages of 15–24) are apt to be critical of society and politics, especially adults' handling of social problems (Yankelovich 1974; Braungart 1975, 1980; Barnes & Kaase 1979; Klineberg et al 1979; Braungart & Braungart 1985b). These studies also have reported that youth tend to be center or left of center in their political identification, and in research comparing the responses of different age groups, young people are more likely to be politically liberal than older age groups. Although these surveys do not indicate that young people as a group are especially interested or active in politics, a few are deeply concerned, and some have made a significant mark in the political arena (Flacks 1971, Braungart & Braungart 1985b). An examination of 64 revolutionary leaders over a 300-year period indicated that one of their most common characteristics was their young age—36% had participated in revolutionary activity before age 20 and 84% by age 35 (Rejai & Phillips 1979, Braungart 1981). It is the young who have provided the cadre for social and political revolutions throughout history, and since the 1830s the young people have been responsible for periods of volatile political unrest and social movements (Braungart 1984a, 1984b, 1984c).

Politics in Middle Age

Not much attention has been given to identifying characteristic modes of political behavior in middle age. Surveys of age differences in political attitudes and behavior seldom have focused directly on the middle-age group; primarily the middle-aged have been employed as a base against which to compare the political attitudes of youth or those of the elderly. An examination of these studies, however, indicates that consistently the middle-aged are the least alienated of all age groups; they tend to be less liberal than the young but not as conservative as the old; and they are more likely to vote and participate in mainstream politics (Martin et al 1974, Milbrath & Goel 1977, Braungart, M. M. & Braungart, R. G. 1982). These findings have been interpreted as due to the superior power position of the middle-aged and their strong developmental stake in society and politics (Martin et al 1974, Braungart, M. M. & Braungart, R. G. 1982, Bengtson et al 1985).

When the middle-aged have been examined from a case-study or psychobiographical perspective, much of the analysis rests on life-course interpretations. The bulk of the work here involves examinations of the mentor-protege relationship and the effect of the mid-life crisis on certain political leaders. Levinson's (1978) developmental studies of middle-aged men, some of whom reported a mentor-protege relationship, prompted several investigations into the importance of a mentor-protege relationship in the lives of certain politicians (Kellerman 1978, Kearney 1984). Mentor relationships not only teach young politicians much about politics but also provide opportunities for career advancement. The effect of a mid-life crisis on political leaders has been the subject of several psychobiographical accounts of politicians, with age-related crises at mid-life resulting in major changes in their political policies and personal behavior (Shore 1972; Post 1980, 1984; Crosby 1984). Though these case studies are fascinating, the question remains how extensive these patterns are among political leaders as a group.

Politics in Older Adulthood

The growing interest in gerontology has directed some attention to understanding the political attitudes and behavior characteristic of older adulthood. Aggregate surveys of age-group differences in politics have generally found that older persons are more conservative than the young or middle-aged, and although the explanation has been put forth that the biopsychological slowdowns of old age may promote a more politically conservative orientation, this life-course interpretation has not been widely accepted (Hudson & Binstock 1976, Braungart, M. M. 1984). Conclusions about voting participation are less clear. Some studies have reported that the likelihood of voting declines after middle age, while other studies have found that voting turnout is higher for older persons. In either case, the voting participation of older adults almost always surpasses that of young adults (Campbell 1971, Brotman 1977, Braungart, M. M. & Braungart, R. G. 1982, Rollenhagen 1984).

In addition to political surveys of older adults, an occasional case study of political leaders has been undertaken to determine the effects of the aging and disease processes on political behavior and decisions. Aging research has indicated there is wide variation in physiological and psychological declines with age: while some older persons may experience rapid declines and become more negative as they age, others suffer little decline, become highly positive in their outlooks, and perform in a highly competent manner (Butler & Lewis 1982). Psychobiographical studies of aging political leaders support this generalization (Post 1980, 1983, 1984; Crosby & Crosby 1981). As Post (1980) pointed out, Stalin's basically distrustful personality became paranoia in later life; Mao Tse-tung's perception of "little time left" may have accelerated the pace of the Great Leap Forward and Cultural Revolution; while Chou En-lai, despite the devastating effects of cancer, was able to maintain his good judgment, balance, and intelligence until his death at age 78.

Problems with the Life-Course Approach to Politics

Although these studies indicate that age and life-cycle development are important in understanding politics and political behavior, a number of concerns need to be raised. One issue involves whether the identification of age-group differences in political attitudes and behavior can be automatically interpreted as resulting from changes in life-cycle development. Are older persons more conservative than the young because of the biological and psychological slowdowns with age, or have the political attitudes developed in their youth not changed much and thus appear conservative in a rapidly changing society?

Another problem is that the assumptions of life-course theory indicate the need both to identify normative patterns of behavior and to track changes within individuals over time. Group studies attempt to define normative political behavior based on age-group characteristics, but, as Dannefer (1984) notes, such studies tend to consider those who do not conform to the model as deviant, when in fact their responses have implications for politics. On the other hand, while psychobiographical studies provide information about changes in an individual's political behavior over time, they leave unanswered the question of how characteristic the political behavior is for the population at large. The lack of large-scale longitudinal studies of political behavior over the life course is surprising.

A major criticism of life-cycle research in general and life-course politics studies in particular is the tendency in both the design and analysis of research to neglect social factors and the historical context (Brim 1976, Featherman 1983, Dannefer 1984). The emphasis on the unfolding nature of life-course development implies that change in political attitudes and behavior is more likely to result from biopsychological processes within the individual than from any response to external events. For example, student protest against the Vietnam war in the 1960s was interpreted from a life-course perspective as due largely to the high energy levels and rebellious nature of youth, but this explanation neglected the particular political and historical issue of the Vietnam war itself (Bettelheim 1963, Feuer 1969, Duncan 1980).

Some of the other difficulties of research on life-course politics have plagued many types of life-cycle studies. First is the issue of the meaningfulness of the concept of age to understanding behavior, much less to deciding on cut-off points that sort respondents into the conventionally accepted categories of youth, middle age, and old age (Wohlwill 1970, Streib 1976). That is, if one knows an individual is 21, 45, or 68 years of age, does this really indicate what kinds of political behavior to expect of him or her? Second, while there are clear descriptions of qualitative differences in political attitudes and behavior based on age, there is little understanding how the process of political learning occurs and what triggers the changes from one stage to the next (Brim 1976, Gallatin 1980). Some of these issues, especially the influence of sociohistorical factors, are addressed in the generational politics literature.

GENERATIONAL POLITICS

For the purposes of this analysis, generational politics is considered from three different perspectives: (a) generational descent or lineage politics, (b) cohort politics, and (c) political generations. The lineage perspective refers to generations in a kinship sense and is evident in the political socialization literature that examines how offspring learn political attitudes from their parents, while the focus in cohort and generational political research is on the social and historical conditions that influence the formation of political attitudes and behavior. In the aging and politics literature, the terms "cohort" and "generation" have often been used interchangeably, but for the sake of clarity, it is suggested that a distinction be made between the two terms. A cohort is a group of "persons born in the same time interval and aging together" (Ryder 1965:844), while a generation shares not only cohort membership but also develops an age-group consciousness as a unique age group with a distinct set of attitudes and behavior at odds with those of other age groups in society; in addition, a generation is directed toward influencing change (Braungart & Braungart 1985a). Thus, a cohort represents a social category "in itself," while a generation acts as a social group "for itself" (Mannheim 1952; Ortega y Gasset 1961; Esler 1982, 1984). The key interests within the generational politics perspective include determining the extent of age-group similarities and differences in politics, describing the politics of cohorts or political generations, identifying the antecedent conditions and mobilization of political generations, and assessing the stability of political views learned during youth, especially for members of an active political generation. The theory and research related to each of these aspects of generational politics are reviewed next.

Lineage Politics

One of the oldest meanings of the term generation refers to generational descent, such as grandfather, parent, offspring generations. In political research, the transmission of political values, attitudes, and behavior from one generation to the next within the family has been a major topic of interest. A number of sociological and psychological theories stress the importance of socialization experiences as the younger generation learns about politics from the parent generation. Behaviorist, social learning, and symbolic interactionist theories all emphasize that much of human behavior has to do with what has been learned from significant others, either through direct instruction and reward/punishment/nonreinforcement experiences or through observation and modeling. Offspring listen to political discussions in the family and observe the political behavior of their parents, while parents tend to reward offspring expressions of political attitudes and behavior that correspond to their political beliefs, and perhaps they act to extinguish contrary political views in their children. The political socialization efforts of the parent generation are not necessarily direct or intensive, but nonetheless have a significant influence on the political orientations of offspring (Bengtson & Cutler 1976, Cutler 1977, Stacey 1977, Gallatin 1980, Jennings & Niemi 1981, Bengtson et al 1985).

Much of the research within the lineage politics perspective has focused on the extent of political agreement between parents and their high school or college-age offspring, particularly since psychoanalytic theory predicts that the youthful stage is a time for young people to exert their independence and rebel against the parent generation. Interest in whether young people adhered to or turned against the politics learned in the home was a key topic in the 1960s when students throughout the United States protested over the Vietnam war, civil rights, and in loco parentis policies of universities (Braungart & Braungart 1972). While one group of scholars argued that this was life-course generational conflict par excellence, as young people rejected the adult generation and acted out a host of deep-seated emotional conflicts in the political arena (Feuer 1969, Hendin 1975, Duncan 1980), other scholars contended that activist youth were not rebelling against parents and their politics but were merely carrying out the political values learned in the home (Flacks 1967, 1971; Keniston 1968, 1971; Braungart 1979). Much of the research on student activists in the 1960s confirmed the socialization explanation of generational transmission of political values from parent to offspring (Flacks 1967; Keniston 1968; Haan 1971; Wood 1974; Braungart 1979, 1980).

Most studies that have focused on the extent of political agreement between parents and offspring in the general population have concluded that the correlation is a moderate one (Cutler 1977, Stacey 1977, Jennings & Neimi 1981). This finding might be interpreted as supportive of political stability or as leaving some room for political change in the politics of the young. In an eight-year panel study of parent-offspring politics by Jennings & Niemi (1981), the modest correlation between parent and offspring political views when youngsters were in high school tended to decline following high school. After leaving home, other political socialization forces come into play. Newcomb's (1943) classic study of Bennington College students demonstrated that the college experience may be one factor weakening parent-offpring political agreement, since a number of freshmen from Republican homes changed their political views in keeping with the liberal orientation of Bennington College. In addition, research also has indicated that the transmission of parents' political values to offspring is itself affected by a number of factors such as the rate of social change, social mobility, the extent of cultural integration, the nature of the parent-offspring relationship, and the child's level of cognitive development (Bengtson & Black 1973, Davies 1977, Gallatin 1980).

Cohort Politics

The effect of social and historical factors on the political attitudes and behavior of age groups is given strong focus in the literature related to cohort politics. The term cohort here refers to a birth cohort, or a group of persons born around the same time who share a particular set of social and historical experiences. The political significance of belonging to a cohort is that those born at a similar time in history are destined to experience a particular set of meaningful events at the same stage of life-cycle development. As Ryder (1965) pointed out, each cohort has a distinctive demographic composition and characteristics and thus grows up with a particular set of age norms, expectations, and opportunities that help condition the attitudes and behavior of its members throughout life. Social and political events may well have differential effects on the various age cohorts in society, depending on each cohort's stage in life-cycle development and its previous experiences. Dramatic historical events, such as economic depression, war, immigration, technological innovation, and cultural change affect all members of society but are considered to have an especially strong impact on the political attitudes of youth who are in their formative stage of political learning. When society changes rapidly and cohorts come of age under different conditions, the members of each cohort are likely to develop their own perception and style of politics which, if substantially different from the experiences of others, may provoke generational conflict. However, while life cycle theorists predict some significant changes in political orientations over the life course, one of the key assumptions of the cohort interpretation is that the political attitudes and behavior formed during a cohort's youth provide the foundation for interpreting subsequent political events; thus attitudes and behavior do not change appreciably with age (Heberle 1951; Mannheim 1952;

Ortega y Gasset 1961; Ryder 1965; Marias 1968; Rintala 1968, 1979; Braungart & Braungart 1984a, 1985a).

One approach to studying cohort politics has been to focus on the politics of a particular age cohort. For example, Loewenberg (1983) combined elements of psychoanalysis with a cohort interpretation to explain the rise of Nazism after World War I. He contended that the relatively large birth cohort of 1900–1914 grew up during World War I and shared a number of dramatic experiences such as fathers away at war, hunger and deprivation during the War, fathers coming home defeated to a humiliated imperial Germany, high unemployment, and bitter disappointment with government. It is these experiences during their formative years that made this particular cohort so receptive to the simplistic, brutal solutions offered by the Nazis. An indication of the cohort effect was reflected in the age-group composition of German political parties in the early 1930s. The Social Democratic Party, the most democratic of the German political parties, had a membership only 19.3% of which was between the ages of 18–30, and only 8% under age 25, while in the Nationalist Socialist Party, the Nazis, the proportion of membership between ages 18–30 rose from 37.6% in 1931 to 42.2% by 1932 (Loewenberg 1983:251).

Most of the large-scale surveys involving age and politics have focused on explaining age differences in political party identification, liberal versus conservative political identification, and alienation (Hudson & Binstock 1976, Hendricks & Hendricks 1977). For example, a number of studies have reported that older age groups are more conservative and likely to support the Republican Party when compared to younger age groups, and while life cycle theorists have contended that the increasing conservatism with age is based on aging slowdowns and the length of time the older age groups have had to identify with society (Crittenden 1962), stronger support has been given to a cohort explanation. That is, aging cohorts do not necessarily become more conservative, and the cohort that entered the electorate during the Depression–New Deal years has maintained a strong identification with the Democratic Party throughout life (Campbell et al 1960, Glenn & Hefner 1972). Several large-scale, cross-national surveys of Western Europeans over the last 20 years have also been interpreted from a cohort perspective: Cohorts that grew up during the economic depressions of the 1930s and experienced World War II hold different value orientations than the cohorts that came of age during the relatively affluent post–World War II years (Inglehart 1977, 1979, 1981, 1986; Mushaben 1983, 1984; Szabo 1983). Older cohorts appear more concerned with economic and national security; younger cohorts support expressive values and life styles, but not the NATO Alliance or defense expenditures, and are suspicious of the United States and the Soviet Union. These findings have important implications for foreign policy and European-American relations in the future.

Political Generations

A cohort becomes transformed into a political generation when many of its members become aware that they are bound together by a shared age-group consciousness and mobilize as an active force for political change (Braungart & Braungart 1984a, 1985a). Wilhelm Dilthey in the 1860s was one of the early developers of the idea that a generation is influenced by cultural trends in ways different from other age groups in society and that it acts to promote social change. The concept of a generation continued to be discussed in the 1920s and 1930s and was given its most powerful theoretical statement by Mannheim (1952), who distinguished biological generations from social generations, drawing a parallel between belonging to a generation and membership in a social class. Rapid social change sets one generation apart from the next and increases the probability that each new generation of youth will develop its own unique mentality and style. Mannheim (1952:304) also pointed out that within a generation may exist any number of "generation units" who "work up the material of their common experience in different ways." The formation of competing generation units is largely based on the diverse social locations of the members of a generation. The concept of social generation was extended in Heberle's (1951) discussion of political generations, Eisenstadt's (1956) examination of age groups within the social structure and their political impact, Rintala's (1968) focus on the importance of historical events in influencing the formation of a political generation, and Esler's (1984) emphasis on the collective mentality of a generation.

The study of age-group differences in politics becomes especially important from a political standpoint when political attitudes divide along age-group lines, indicating that a political generation may be taking form. A political generation is said to come into existence when an age group rejects the existing order, joins together, and attempts to redirect the course of politics as its generational mission (Ortega y Gasset 1961, Braungart & Braungart 1984a, Esler 1984). Four important youthful political generations have been identified in history: Young Europe, Post–Victorian, Great Depression, and 1960s Generation (Braungart 1984a,b,c). The question of why political generations arise during certain periods in history but not in others has not been answered clearly by life-course explanations. In the generational politics literature it has generally been addressed from two perspectives: those explanations emphasizing antecedent historical circumstances and social discontinuities (Smelser 1968, Lipset & Altbach 1969, Gurr 1970, Hamilton & Wright 1975, Eckstein 1976, Eisenstadt 1978, Gusfield 1979), and those explanations stressing the importance of mobilization opportunities (Etzioni 1968, Oberschall 1973, Tilly 1975, Zald & McCarthy 1979). From a generational perspective, the dynamics of the formation of political generations appear to be that historical circumstances (especially population growth, urbanization, industrialization, economic depression, unemployment, technological change, nationalism, and cultural change) and mobilization forces (organized networks, solidarity, charismatic leadership, intergroup competition, and conflict over political goals) have combined during certain periods in history to form active political generations (Braungart 1984a,c).

Problems with the Generational Approach to Politics

A number of problems arise in studying generational politics, not the least of which is the ambiguity surrounding the term generation itself. Generation has been used loosely to refer to an age-group in terms of life-cycle stage, family descent, cohort placement, and as a decisive political force for change. When the term itself is unclear, problems of operationalization are exacerbated (Kertzner 1983; Braungart & Braungart 1984a, 1985a). It has been argued that the term generation should be limited to mean an active generation such as a political generation, since the major element in the definition of a generation is the heightened age-group consciousness and collective mentality that unites its members (Esler 1984); the lack of such age-group consciousness indicates the existence of a cohort rather than a generation. In addition, although generation has been used in a kinship sense to refer to generational descent, the use of parent generation is nebulous with respect to age-group membership, since, for example, the parents of high school seniors may represent a wide range of ages (with some in their late 30s and others in their 60s). Thus, in lineage socialization studies of politics, few inferences can be made about either life-course influences or the effect of historical cohort experiences on parents' political beliefs.

Determining boundaries and cut-off points is another issue in generational politics research. While there has been considerable quibbling over the duration of a generation—whether it lasts 15 or 30 years (Mannheim 1952, Ortega y Gasset 1961)—it has been argued that since the pace of social change has accelerated, the time between generations is lessening (Berger 1960). However-er, from a life-course perspective, the reverse could also be argued: the time between generations is lengthening, since young people in Western societies are delaying adult responsibilities such as working and establishing a family. In dealing with demographic cohorts or dynamic political generations, separating one birth group from another is no easy task (Spitzer 1973, Cutler 1977, Rosow 1978). Part of the problem is deciding what criteria to use in making age or generational divisions. Although quantitative criteria are often employed— such as groupings by decade of birth, election years, or a fixed interval of time—it has been suggested that generations be divided according to qualitative criteria such as distinct historical events or experiences (Rosow 1978, Rintala 1979, Kertzner 1983). However, when qualitative criteria are used to identify a generation, the data may no longer meet the assumptions of equal intervals necessary to perform certain mathematical operations (Knoke 1984). Yet, careful and imaginative attempts at defining age groups and generations may well enhance the understanding of the dynamic relationship between cohorts, generations, and politics.

Another issue concerns determining at what point a cohort becomes a full-fledged political generation. While "awareness," "uniqueness," "solidarity," and "mobilizing" for social and political change are the characteristics distinguishing a generation from a cohort, it is not always clear when a political generation is taking form, nor is it a simple matter to operationalize and measure "generational awareness" or "collective mentality." Little is known about the development of shared collective mentalities and how these become activated into a genuine force for political change, nor is there much understanding of the interplay between competing political generation units, the maintenance of of a political generation's activity, why a political generation comes to an end, and the direct and indirect consequences of a political generation's efforts for change. Thus far, empirical examinations of political generations have been post hoc; it is difficult to predict when and where a political generation will emerge. Throughout the world today the historical circumstances appear highly conducive to the formation of political generations, and presently there is a political-generational war being fought in South Africa. Although young people are politically active in a number of other countries over issues such as nature protection, ecology, anti-nuclear power, anti-nuclear weapons, racism, governmental repression, national liberation, religious struggles, and youthful rowdyism, such activity has not yet attained the status that suggests a political generation (Mushaben 1983, 1984; Braungart 1984b; Braungart & Braungart 1985b).

One of the major weaknesses of age-based political studies in general is their somewhat limited focus, with a tendency to consider either life-cycle factors or cohort-generational forces in explaining political behavior. What is needed is a more comprehensive approach to studying age-based patterns of political behavior, age differences and changes in politics, and the formation of decisive political generations in history.

LIFE-COURSE AND GENERATIONAL POLITICS

A division between life-course politics and generational politics is clearly evident in the theoretical and empirical literature from the nineteenth century onward. The classification of a study as representing a life-course perspective or a generational interpretation depends primarily on its emphasis. The life-course perspective is most apparent in those studies focusing on age-related patterns and changes in political behavior without much attention to historical and social factors. On the other hand, generational political studies stress the impact of parental socialization and important historical events without much consideration of personal growth and life-course development. However, the study of the relationship between age and politics demands a broad approach that includes aspects of life-course development *and* historical influences within the context of the sociopolitical period. A major contention in this essay is that a more fruitful approach to understanding political behavior is to weave together elements of life-course and generational politics.

Although considerable research effort has been devoted to determining whether life-cycle forces or cohort effects have a stronger impact on political behavior, we suggest an interactive approach, which reflects much of the current discussion in the life-span developmental literature that calls for greater consideration of historical and social factors in the study of life-course development (Brim 1976; Elder 1981, 1985; Featherman 1983; Dannefer 1984). The use of the term "interactive" here implies that the combined effects of life cycle and cohort factors are more than additive (Riley 1973). Thus, the young and old may react differently to the same political event due to their particular stage in life-cycle development and unique cohort experiences. The life-course and generational politics approach necessitates an understanding of life-course development and sociohistorical change, as well as the interplay between these two forces in influencing political attitudes and behavior and the way these relationships may change over time. Such interaction not only involves life-course and cohort-generational factors but also consideration of the sociopolitical period during which empirical studies are conducted. The dimensions of analysis are the same as those employed in the aging-cohort-period design but, instead of viewing the dimensions in their traditional additive sense, these effects are considered jointly, with the expectation that they may combine in different ways for various age groups or segments of age groups and that any observed relationships may change with changes in the political situation.

The difference between the additive kinds of explanations for youth movements and an interactive life-course and generational politics approach is demonstrated as follows. From a life-course perspective, youth protest represents one possible outcome for the emotional expression and release of youthful developmental tensions. From a generational perspective, youth unrest occurs when a large-size birth cohort comes of age under a particular set of historical experiences, social structural conditions, and opportunities for mobilization. However, the appearance of youth movements is more than the result of either life-course forces or cohort experiences; it represents instead an interaction between life-course development, cohort/generation experiences, and sociopolitical trends. More specifically, an examination of four extraordinary periods of generational activity indicates that during each period, the life-cycle characteristics of youth (high energy levels, increased cognitive awareness, the search for identity, and the relationship between self and society) in combination with a particular set of cohort experiences (sharing a large birth cohort with high levels of education, growing up under specific global, societal, and family conditions) have interacted with certain historical trends (a disappointing set of social conditions, social discontinuities, and mobilization forces) to produce political generations of youth and competing generational units (Braungart 1984a,b,c).

There are several research studies available that include a life course–generational type of political analysis. The life-course and generational approach to understanding political behavior has been used successfully in several case studies of single individuals (Marschak 1980, Shelton 1982, Rintala 1984). For example, Rintala (1984) provided a historical account of Vera Brittain, a British middle-class woman who came of age during World War I and regarded herself as both a chronicler of her generation and a political activist. Rintala's careful descriptive account shows how history influenced Brittain's political orientations and behavior over her life course; it supports the thesis that political consciousness is largely the product of personal and historical experiences in a changing society.

At the group level of analysis, several studies representing a life-course and generational approach to politics have focused on student activists from the 1960s generation. A critical question in this research was whether the politics of these activists changed and mellowed with age or whether in their adult years they adhered to the political orientations developed during their youth. A comparison of follow-up surveys of former activists and an examination of the personal lives of 1960s activist leaders indicated that, with few exceptions and contrary to some reports in the media, these left-wing protesters did not join the Establishment and pursue careers in business; they chose careers that were in keeping with their youthful social and political values, and many continued to maintain political commitment and interest throughout their adulthood. However, the generational effect was not the only factor accounting for adult political behavior. Life-cycle effects and period effects interacted with generational effects in the adult lives of these former 1960s activists. Interviews with former activist leaders indicated that while many held similar political values and orientations consistent with their younger years, their tactics and strategies for attempting to implement their politics had mellowed considerably (Braungart & Braungart 1980). Whether this political "mellowing" was due to aging or to the changing political climate, or both, is uncertain, but for individuals and groups there are elements of stability and change in political orientations and behavior over time.

A more informative approach is to provide a comparative type of analysis. Using life-history interviews Whalen & Flacks (1980, 1984) conducted follow-up studies of the life-course development of a group of former student protesters and tracked their life patterns from 1970, when they were involved in a bank-burning incident in California, into their adulthood years in the 1980s. The study focused on both commonalities and differences in life patterns and revealed that activists experienced shifts in their careers and politics as they reacted to changing sociopolitical and personal situations. Yet the experience of being part of the protest generation carried with them into adulthood and strongly affected their political values and perceptions. Whalen & Flacks also interviewed a group of adults who had been members of fraternities and sororities in college at the same time as the protesters and found a marked contrast in adult life patterns between the two groups. The study clearly demonstrated that the former activists did not pursue conventional life styles nor abandon politics in adulthood, and it highlighted the interplay between life-cycle development, the generational effect, and the way in which two different segments of the same age group responded differently to politics over time.

METHODOLOGICAL STRATEGIES

Understanding life-course and generational politics involves the study of age, time, and politics. The principal types of methodological designs employed by researchers concerned with various aspects of age and politics include cross-sectional, longitudinal, time-series, and aging-cohort-period designs. The choice of which design to use depends partially on the research question, but the choice is an important one since the outcome and contribution of research rest heavily on the methodology employed. Researchers have used quantitative and qualitative techniques in their investigations of life-course politics and generational politics; however, certain methodological procedures are more appropriate than others in addressing the central issues involved in life-course and generational politics. We outline some of the strengths and weaknesses of the designs and indicate which strategies are most suitable, given the present state of knowledge in these areas.

The *cross-sectional design* is the simplest type, since it involves measuring individuals of different ages at only one point in time. However, because cross-sectional studies are not conducted over time, information cannot be gained about some of the central issues in life-course and generational politics analysis. The studies do not reveal age-group and intraindividual changes in politics over time or whether age differences in political behavior are due to life course or cohort effects, because life-course development and cohort effects are confounded in the cross-sectional design. For example, if older adults in a cross-sectional study are found to be more politically conservative than young people, it is still uncertain whether the observed age differences are due to the effects of aging or to cohort experiences (Baltes et al 1977, Braungart & Braungart 1985a). Thus, the cross-sectional design is not particularly useful to the purposes of research in life-course politics, generational politics, or the interactive approach.

Some of the shortcomings of the cross-sectional design are addressed in the *time-series design* where different samples, assumed to be equivalent in their characteristics, are drawn and measured at various points in time. Such a design is useful for tracking public opinion within a changing society. Although the time-series design provides more information than the cross-sectional design and avoids some of the logistical problems of the longitudinal design, intraindividual change in politics cannot be assessed nor can cohort effects be separated from period effects (Baltes et al 1977, Huyck & Hoyer 1982). Serious consideration must be given in the time-series design to standardizing data sets so that they are comparable, to determining how often measurements should be taken, and to recognizing that the rate of change may fluctuate (because this could affect standard measurement and research results) (Hyman 1972, Hage et al 1980).

Most appropriate to the study of life-course and generational politics is the *longitudinal design* in which an individual, group, or several groups are measured at various points in time. The observation may be prospective or—although somewhat less desirable—retrospective. The longitudinal design provides information about age differences, age changes, and intraindividual change in politics over time. However, if age changes are observed, the question remains whether shifts in political behavior occurred because of life-course development or because society changed (Baltes et al 1977, Goldstein 1979, Clubb & Scheuch 1980, Reuband 1980). There are also a number of other difficulties inherent in the longitudinal design: high cost, sample attrition, the subjects' familiarity with measurement instruments, and the social psychological effects of being part of an ongoing research project (Goldstein 1979). Despite these difficulties, the longitudinal design is best suited to the goals of life-course and generational political research, since it is the only design that allows some assessment of changes in political views both within and between individuals over time.

Two of the most widely used types of longitudinal designs in life-course and generational political research are the *panel design* and *life-history analysis*. Panel designs involve remeasurement of the same sample(s) over time. The panel design provides aggregate information as well as information about intraindividual change over time and has been used effectively in political research. One panel study identified short-term fluctuations in shifting political attitudes and voter intentions over the course of an election (Lazarsfeld et al

1944); another eight-year panel study focused on the stability and change in political orientations of a group of parents and their offspring (Jennings & Niemi 1981). However, the duration of a panel study is relatively short compared to a life-course perspective, where the interest is in life-long changes in politics from youth through older adulthood. Life-history analysis is a longitudinal technique that focuses on the life experiences, perceptions, and interpretations of events by one person or group (Erikson 1975, Bertaux 1981, Elder 1985). The political biography has been a popular form of life-history analysis that examines the life course of a single political leader (Erikson 1969, 1974, 1975; Post 1980, 1984; Crosby 1984; Rintala 1984). However, criticisms have been leveled at some political biographies for being too psychoanalytic—for dwelling on the effects of early childhood experiences rather than giving sufficient focus to the importance of cohort effects or analyzing adult political behavior within the context of the historical moment (Crosby & Crosby 1981).

Life-history accounts also have been conducted at the group level of analysis, which gives a better indication of age-group patterns of political behavior than is possible with the political biography approach. Life-history analysis when applied to groups also enables the researcher to keep track of each individual over time, thereby providing information about those whose behavior is more nearly unique. For example, there has been a group life-history study of several members of the "generation of 1914" (Wohl 1979), a comparison of the life patterns of former activists of the 1960s with fraternity and sorority members (Whalen & Flacks 1984), and a study of a group of American Indian veterans of the Vietnam war and their three-generation families (Holm 1984). The selective and subjective nature of the life-history technique, creative as it may be, may affect both researchers and subjects and thereby threaten the study's reliability and validity.

The cross-sectional, time-series, and longitudinal designs are the basic research strategies used to study the relationships between age and politics. However, the findings of a study based on a cross-sectional design may differ from those based on a longitudinal design (Baltes et al 1977). A key interest in political research has been to move beyond mere descriptions of age-group differences to attempts to determine the relative effects of aging, cohort experiences, and period effects on political attitudes and behavior. The aging-cohort-period (sometimes termed life cycle–generational–time of measurement) design has received considerable attention in this regard. The design requires a large data set collected over time—most often using the cross-sectional sequence (a series of equivalent samples measured at various points in time), rather than the longitudinal sequence (repeated measurements conducted for cohorts over time). Despite the popularity of the design for investigating political party identification, political trust, feelings of political efficacy and alienation, the results are not always clear, and it is not unusual to find a combination of effects for a particular political attribute (Bengtson & Cutler 1976, Rodgers 1982, Abramson 1983, Knoke 1984).

The most serious problem with the aging-cohort-period design is identification—that is, given the values of two of the parameters, such as aging and cohort, the third value, in this case the period effect, is determined automatically (Knoke 1984). The problem of identification can be handled if the researcher is able to assume one of the parameters is not operating, but in many cases such an assumption is unrealistic or unwarranted. However, even small amounts of measurement error or errors in specifying constraints for any of the three parameters can result in inaccurate estimates (Rodgers 1982). One suggestion is to conduct a series of both longitudinal and cross-sequential studies, to allow clearer specification of aging, cohort, and period effects. Deciding how to organize the data in such a case is a challenge (see Baltes et al 1977). Another proposal is to supplement the aging-cohort-period design with multivariate correlation-regression techniques, such as path analysis or structural equation models (Baltes et al 1977). However, the major consideration here is that while the design is based on additive assumptions, in many cases, aging, cohort, and period effects are likely to be interactive (Riley 1973; Braungart & Braungart 1985a).

In this study we suggest that life course and generational politics be combined into an interactive approach. The inclusion of the life-course dimension indicates the need for a longitudinal methodology that encourages research at both the individual and group levels of analysis. However, a quantitative type of analysis may not be especially appropriate to the purposes of life-course and generational politics research at this time for several reasons: (a) Individual differences tend to be obscured in aggregate data analysis; (b) highly quantitative procedures that provide for a clear analysis of interaction effects and meet the assumptions of the data are not readily available; and, most important, (c) the concepts inherent in life-course and generational analysis are theoretically ambiguous and not well understood at this point, so quantifying nebulous concepts is a meaningless exercise.

The use of qualitative comparative procedures may be more helpful in clarifying some of the theoretical concepts and identifying the dynamics and processes involved in life-course and generational analysis. For example, one strategy might be to conduct a combined qualitative analysis of historical period effects, cohort-generational effects, and aging effects for individuals and groups over time; this approach would allow the researcher to link life-course development to historical experiences within the context of societal and larger global cycles. As an illustration, in the analysis of political generations, careful attention needs to be given to the unique *period effects* (e.g. Young Europe) during which time nonrandom clusters of political generations take form, come into conflict with other age groups in society, and mobilize into competing intragenerational units to change the course of politics. At the same time, specification should be given to *cohort-generational effects* (e.g. Young Russia, Young Ireland) and *life-cycle effects* of individual members within a generation unit (e.g. the life-course development of a Narodnik or Fenian). Comparisons might also be made with other political generations in history (Post Victorian, Great Depression, 1960s Generation) to identify the patterns of similarity and differences in the formation, activity, demise, and impact of political generations (Braungart 1984a,b,c; Braungart & Braungart 1984a, 1985a). Another strategy might be to take a more personal focus, such as using comparative life-history analysis (Elder 1974, Wohl 1979, Marschak 1980, Whalen & Flacks 1984). Once there is more information about the dynamics and processes involved in life-course and generational politics, then more precise quantitative types of analysis may make a contribution to theory building especially if better interactive methodologies and statistical techniques become available for gathering and analyzing social science data.

CONCLUSION

In this essay, the relationship between age and politics has been discussed and explored from two theoretical perspectives: life-course politics and generational politics. A third approach has been suggested that involves the interaction of life-course and generational politics. Each of these three conceptual approaches makes certain assumptions about the relationship between age and politics and offers a slightly different explanation for age-group differences in politics, age-group changes in politics, and the formation of political generations in history. In addition, each conceptual approach favors certain methodological strategies over others. See Table 1 for a summary of the basic concepts and methodological strategies used in the three approaches to studying life-course and generational politics.

The study of life-course and generational politics is complex and requires an understanding of biopsychological life-course processes, of the effect of cohorts and generations, and of the influence of unique historical periods on political behavior. In order to assess age-group political patterns, variations, differences, and changes in politics, we need to conduct longitudinal studies and to make comparisons between and within cohorts or generations over time, that use both the group and individual levels of analysis. Such an undertaking requires interdisciplinary conceptual understanding and solid methodological skills. Even as information accumulates and generalizations are made about life-course and generational politics, associations must be tracked over time since they may well change with fluctuations in the dynamic relationship between age and politics.

Table 1 Basic Concepts and Methodological Strategies for Studying Life-Course and Generational Politics

Concepts and Strategies	Life-Course Politics	Generational Politics	Life-Course and Generational Politics
General Assumptions	Focus on age-related biopsychological characteristics of each stage in the life course that may influence political attitudes and behavior.	Generational politics results from the clash of political attitudes and behavior that are learned through socialization and the historical conditioning experiences of youth which last throughout life.	Emphasis on the interaction between life-course development, social mobilization, and historical experiences as these affect political attitudes and behavior.
Age-Group Differences over Politics	Since age groups are in different stages of life-course development, with different needs, interests, and orientations, political conflicts may result.	Since different generations (age-conscious cohorts) have different historical experiences, especially in rapidly changing societies, they tend to disagree over politics.	Political differences are the result of life-course development in combination with cohort/generational experiences, which may be more evident during certain periods than others.
Age-Group Changes in Politics	Changes in biopsychological development in the life course promote age-group changes in political attitudes and behavior.	Changes in political outlooks are minimal; the political attitudes and behavior learned within a youth cohort/generation endure throughout life.	Changes in political views may occur due to life cycle and period effects, but there is a strong element of stability in the cohort/generational experiences of youth.
Political Generations	Political generations result from mobilized developmental needs and interests of individual members.	Political generations result from the historical circumstances and dynamics of mobilization that produce intergenerational and intragenerational conflict.	Political generations are due to the interaction between life-course forces as age-conscious cohorts grow up under unique historical circumstances and react to disappointing societies by mobilizing for change.
Methodological Strategies	Longitudinal and aging-cohort-period (longitudinal sequence) designs are suitable; must track individual over time.	Time-series, longitudinal, and aging-cohort-period designs are suitable; comparative studies of cohorts and political generations are useful.	Longitudinal, aging-cohort-period (longitudinal sequence) designs are suitable; track and compare individuals, political generations, and historical periods over time.

Literature Cited

Abramson, P. R. 1983. *Political Attitudes in America: Formation and Change.* San Francisco: Freeman

Adelson, J. 1971. The political imagination of the young adolescent. *Daedalus* 100:1013–50

Adelson, J., ed. 1980. *Handbook of Adolescent Psychology.* New York: Wiley

Adelson, J., Hall, E. 1980. Children and other political naifs. *Psychol. Today* November:56–69

Baltes, P. B., Brim, O. Jr., eds. 1979–1984. *Life-Span Development and Behavior.* Vols. 1–6. New York: Academic

Baltes, P. B., Reese, H. W., Nesselroade, J. R. 1977. *Life-Span Developmental Psychology: Introduction to Research Methods.* Monterey, Calif: Brooks/Cole

Barnes, S. H., Kaase, M. eds. 1979. *Political Action: Mass Participation in Five Western Democracies.* Beverly Hills, Calif: Sage

Bengtson, V. L., Black, K. D. 1973. Intergenerational relations and continuities in socialization. In *Life-Span Developmental Psychology: Personality and Socialization,* ed. P. B. Baltes, K. W. Schaie, pp. 207–34. New York: Academic

Bengtson, V. L., Cutler, N. E. 1976. Generations and intergenerational relations: Perspectives on age groups and social change. See Binstock & Shanas 1976:130–59

Bengtson, V. I., Cutler, N. E., Mangen, D. J., Marshall, V. W. 1985. Generations, cohorts, and relations between age groups. In *Handbook of Aging and the Social Sciences,* ed. R. H. Binstock, E. Shanas, pp. 304–38. New York: Van Nostrand Reinhold

Berger, B. M. 1960. How long is a generation? *Br. J. Sociol.* 11:10–23

Bertaux, D., ed. 1981. *Biography and Society: The Life History Approach in the Social Sciences.* Beverly Hills, Calif: Sage

Bettelheim, B. 1963. The problem of generations. See Erikson 1963:64–92

Binstock, R. H., Shanas, E., eds. 1976. *Handbook of Aging and the Social Sciences.* New York: Van Nostrand, Reinhold

Birren, J. E., Schaie, K. W. eds. 1977. *Handbook of the Psychology of Aging.* New York: Van Nostrand, Reinhold

Braungart, M. M. 1984. Aging and politics. *J. Polit. Milit. Sociol.* 12:79–98

Braungart, M. M., Braungart, R. G. 1982. The alienation and politics of older, middle-aged, and young adults: An inter- and intra-age group analysis. *Micropolitics* 2:219–55

Braungart, R. G. 1975. Youth and social movements. In *Adolescence in the Life Cycle,* ed. S. E. Dragastin, G. H. Elder, Jr., pp. 255–89. New York: Wiley

Braungart, R. G. 1979. *Family Status, Socialization and Student Politics.* Ann Arbor, Mich: University Microfilms International

Braungart, R. G. 1980. Youth movements. See Adelson 1980:560–97

Braungart, R. G. 1981. Mini reviews: Political sociology. *J. Polit. Milit. Sociol.* 9:136

Braungart, R. G. 1984a. Historical and generational patterns of youth movements: A global perspective. See Tomasson 1984:3–62

Braungart, R. G. 1984b. Historical generations and generation units: A global perspective. *J. Polit. Milit. Sociol.* 12:113–35

Braungart, R. G. 1984c. Historical generations and youth movements: A theoretical perspective. In *Research in Social Movements, Conflict and Change,* ed. R. E. Ratcliff, 6:95–141. Greenwich, Conn.: JAI

Braungart, R. G., Braungart, M. M. 1972. Administration, faculty and student reaction to campus unrest. *J. College Stud. Per.* 13:112–19

Braungart, R. G., Braungart, M. M. 1980. Political career patterns of radical activists in the 1960s and 1970s: Some historical comparisons. *Sociol. Focus* 13:237–54

Braungart, R. G., Braungart, M. M. 1984a. Generational politics. *Micropolitics* 3:349–415

Braungart, R. G., Braungart, M. M., eds. 1984b. Special issue on "Life-course and generational politics." *J. Polit. Milit. Sociol.* 12:1–212

Braungart, R. G., Braungart, M. M. 1985a. Conceptual and methodological approaches to studying life course and generational politics. In *Research in Political Sociology,* ed. R. G. Braungart, 1:269–304. Greenwich, Conn: JAI

Braungart, R. G., Braungart, M. M. 1985b. *Youth problems and politics in the 1980s: Some multinational comparisons.* Presented at Int. Sociol. Assoc. Res. Comm. 34 Conf. on Youth, Primorsko, Bulgaria

Braungart, R. G., Braungart, M. M. 1986. Youth dependency and national development: The global status of youth in the 1980s. Unpublished manuscript, Dep. Sociol., Syracuse Univ.

Brim, O. G. Jr. 1976. Theories of the male mid-life crisis. In *Counseling Adults,* ed. N. K. Schlossberg, A. D. Entive, pp. 1–18. Monterey, Calif: Brooks/Cole

Brotman, H. B. 1977. Voter participation in November, 1976. *Gerontologist* 17:157–159

Butler, R. N., Lewis, M. I. 1982. *Aging and Mental Health.* St. Louis, Mo: Mosby

Campbell, A. 1971. Politics through the life cycle. *Gerontologist* 11:112–17

Campbell, A., Converse, P., Miller, W., Stokes, D. 1960. *The American Voter*. New York: Wiley

Clubb, J. M., Scheuch, E. K., eds. 1980. *Historical Social Research: The Use of Historical and Process-Produced Data*. Stuttgart: Klett-Cotta

Crittenden, J. A. 1962. Aging and party affiliation. *Publ. Opinion Q*. 26:648–57

Crosby, F., Crosby, T. L. 1981. Psychobiography and psychohistory. In *Handbook of Political Behavior*, ed. S. Long, 1:195–254. New York: Plenum

Crosby, T. L. 1984. Gladstone's decade of crisis: Biography and the life course approach. *J. Polit. Milit. Sociol*. 12:9–22

Cutler, N. E. 1977. Political socialization research as generational analysis. See Renshon 1977:294–326

Dannefer, D. 1984. Adult development and social theory: A paradigmatic reappraisal. *Am. Sociol. Rev*. 49:100–16

Davies, J. C. 1977. Political socialization: From womb to childhood. See Renshon 1977:142–71

Duncan, M. 1980. Radical activism and the defense against despair. *Sociol. Focus* 13: 255–63

Eckstein, H. 1976. A theory of stable democracy. In *Society and Politics*, ed. R. G. Braungart, pp. 142–50. Englewood Cliffs, NJ: Prentice-Hall

Eisenstadt, S. N. 1956. *From Generation to Generation: Age Groups and Social Structure*. New York: Free Press

Eisenstadt, S. N. 1978. *Revolution and the Transformation of Societies*. New York: Free Press

Elder, G. H. Jr. 1974. *Children of the Great Depression*. Chicago: Univ. Chicago Press

Elder, G. H. Jr. 1975. Age differentiation and the life course. *Ann. Rev. Sociol*. 1:165–90

Elder, G. H. Jr. 1981. History and the life course. See Bertaux 1981:77–115

Elder, G. H. Jr., ed. 1985. *Life Course Dynamics*. Ithaca, NY: Cornell Univ. Press

Erikson, E. H., ed. 1963. *Youth: Change and Challenge*. New York: Basic Books

Erikson, E. H. 1968. *Identity: Youth and Crisis*. New York: Norton

Erikson, E. H. 1969. *Gandhi's Truth*. New York: Norton

Erikson, E. H. 1974. *Dimensions of a New Identity*. New York: Norton

Erikson, E. H. 1975. *Life History and the Historical Moment*. New York: Norton

Esler, A., ed. 1974. *The Youth Revolution*. Lexington, Mass: Heath

Esler, A. 1979. *Generational Studies: A Basic Bibliography*. Williamsburg, Va: Esler

Esler, A. 1982. *Generations in History: An Introduction to the Concept*. Williamsburg, Va: Esler

Esler, A. 1984. "The truest community": Social generations as collective mentalities. *J. Polit. Milit. Sociol*. 12:99–112

Etzioni, A. 1968. *The Active Society*. New York: Free Press

Featherman, D. L. 1983. Life-span perspectives in social science research. In *Life-Span Development and Behavior*, ed. P. B. Baltes, O. Brim, Jr., 5:1–57. New York: Academic

Feuer, L. S. 1969. *The Conflict of Generations*. New York: Basic

Flacks, R. 1967. The liberated generation: An exploration of the roots of student protest. *J. Soc. Issues* 23:52–75

Flacks, R. 1971. *Youth and Social Change*. Chicago: Rand McNally

Gallatin, J. 1980. Political thinking in adolescence. See Adelson 1980:344–82

Gillis, J. R. 1974. *Youth and History*. New York: Academic

Glenn, N. D., Hefner, T. 1972. Further evidence on aging and party identification. *Publ. Opinion Q*. 36:31–47

Goldstein, H. 1979. *The Design and Analysis of Longitudinal Studies*. New York: Academic

Goulet, L. R., Baltes, P. B., eds. 1970. *Life-Span Developmental Psychology: Research and Theory*. New York: Academic

Greenstein, F. I. 1965. *Children and Politics*. New Haven, Conn: Yale Univ. Press

Gurr, T. R. 1970. *Why Men Rebel*. Princeton, NJ: Princeton Univ. Press

Gusfield, J. 1979. The modernity of social movements: Public roles and private parts. In *Societal Growth*, ed. A. H. Hawley, pp. 290–307. New York: Free Press

Haan, N. 1971. Moral redefinition in families as a critical aspect of the generational gap. *Youth and Soc*. 2:259–83

Hage, J., Gargan, E. T., Hanneman, R. 1980. Procedures for periodizing history: Determining eras in the histories of Britain, France, Germany and Italy. See Clubb & Scheuch, 1980:267–83

Hamilton, R. F., Wright, J. 1975. *New Directions in Political Sociology*. Indianapolis: Bobbs-Merrill

Heberle, R. 1951. *Social Movements*. New York: Appleton-Century-Crofts

Hendin, H. 1975. *The Age of Sensation*. New York: Norton

Hendricks, J., Hendricks, C. D. 1977. *Aging in Mass Society*. Cambridge, Mass: Winthrop

Hess, R. D., Torney, J. V. 1967. *The Development of Political Attitudes in Children*. Garden City, NY: Doubleday

Holm, T. 1984. Intragenerational rapprochement among American Indians: A study of thirty-five Indian veterans of the Vietnam war. *J. Polit. Milit. Sociol*. 12:161–70

Hudson, R. B., Binstock, R. H. 1976. Political

systems and aging. See Binstock & Shanas 1976:369–400

Huyck, M. H., Hoyer, W. J. 1982. *Adult Development and Aging*. Belmont, Calif: Wadsworth

Hyman, H. H. 1972. *Secondary Analysis of Sample Surveys: Principles, Procedures and Potentialities*. New York: Wiley

Inglehart, R. 1977. *The Silent Revolution: Changing Values and Political Styles among Western Publics*. Princeton, NJ: Princeton Univ. Press

Inglehart, R. 1979. Political action: The impact of values, cognitive level, and social background. See Barnes & Kaase 1979:343–80

Inglehart, R. 1981. Post-materialism in an environment of insecurity. *Am. Polit. Sci. Rev.* 75:880–900

Inglehart, R. 1986. Intergenerational changes in politics and culture: The shift from materialist to postmaterialist value priorities. In *Research in Political Sociology*, Vol. 2, ed. R. G. Braungart. Greenwich, Conn: JAI. In press

Jansen, N. 1975. *Generation Theory*. Johannesburg: McGraw-Hill

Jennings, M. K., Niemi, R. G. 1981. *Generations and Politics: A Panel Study of Young Adults and Their Parents*. Princeton, NJ: Princeton Univ. Press

Kearney, R. N. 1984. The mentor in the commencement of a political career: The case of Subhas Chandra Bose and C. R. Das. *J. Polit. Milit. Sociol.* 12:37–47

Kellerman, B. 1978. Mentoring in political life: The case of Willy Brandt. *Am. Polit. Sci. Rev.* 72:422–33

Keniston, K. 1968. *Young Radicals*. New York: Harcourt, Brace & World

Keniston, K. 1971. *Youth and Dissent*. New York: Harcourt Brace Jovanovich

Kertzner, D. I. 1983. Generation as a sociological problem. *Ann. Rev. Sociol.* 9:125–49

Klineberg, O., Zavalloni, M., Louis-Guerin, C., BenBrika, J. 1979. *Students, Values, and Politics: A Crosscultural Comparison*. New York: Free Press

Knoke, D. 1984. Conceptual and measurement aspects of the study of political generations. *J. Polit. Milit. Sociol.* 12:191–201

Lazarsfeld, P. F., Berelson, B., Gaudet, H. 1944. *The People's Choice*. New York: Duell, Sloan & Pearce

Levinson, D. J. 1978. *The Seasons of a Man's Life*. New York: Ballantine

Lipset, S. M., Altbach, P. G., eds. 1969. *Students in Revolt*. Boston: Houghton Mifflin

Loewenberg, P. 1983. *Decoding the Past: The Psychohistorical Approach*. New York: Knopf

Mannheim, K. 1952. The problem of genera-

tions. In *Essays on the Sociology of Knowledge*. K. Mannheim, pp. 276–320. London: Routledge & Kegan Paul

Marias, J. 1968. Generations: The concept. See Sills 1968:88–92

Marias, J. 1970. *Generations: A Historical Method*. University, Ala: Univ. Ala. Press

Marschak, M. 1980. *Parent-Child Interaction and Youth Rebellion*. New York: Gardner

Martin, W. C., Bengtson, V. L., Acock, A. C. 1974. Alienation and age: A context-specific approach. *Soc. Forc.* 53:266–82

McKeon, R., ed. 1941. *The Basic Works of Aristotle*. New York: Random House

Milbrath, L. W., Goel, M. L. 1977. *Political Participation*. Chicago: Rand McNally

Mushaben, J. M. 1983. The forum: New dimensions of youth protest in Western Europe. *J. Polit. Milit. Sociol.* 11:123–44

Mushaben, J. M. 1984. Anti-politics and successor generations: The role of youth in the West and East German peace movements. *J. Polit. Milit. Sociol.* 12:171–90

Muuss, R. E. 1968. *Theories of Adolescence*. New York: Random House

Nash, L. L. 1978. Concepts of existence: Greek origins of generational thought. *Daedalus* 107:1–21

Newcomb, T. M. 1943. *Personality and Social Change*. New York: Dryden

Oberschall, A. 1973. *Social Conflict and Social Movements*. Englewood Cliffs, NJ: Prentice-Hall

Ortega y Gasset, J. 1961. *The Modern Theme*. New York: Harper & Row

Parsons, T. 1963. Youth in the context of American society. See Erikson 1963:93–119

Post, J. M. 1980. The seasons of a leader's life: Influences of the life cycle on political behavior. *Polit. Psychol.* 2:35–49

Post, J. M. 1983. Woodrow Wilson reexamined: The mind-body controversy redux and other disputations. *Polit. Psychol.* 4:289–306

Post, J. M. 1984. Dreams of glory and the life cycle: Reflections on the life course of narcissistic leaders. *J. Polit. Milit. Sociol.* 12:49–60

Rejai, M., Phillips, K. 1979. *Leaders of Revolution*. Beverly Hills, Calif: Sage

Renshon, S. A., ed. 1977. *Handbook of Political Socialization: Theory and Research*. New York: Free Press

Reuband, K. H. 1980. Life histories: Problems and prospects of longitudinal designs. See Clubb & Scheuch, 1980:135–63

Riley, M. W. 1973. Aging and cohort succession: Interpretations and misinterpretations. *Publ. Opinion Q.* 37:35–49

Riley, M. W. 1978. Aging, social change, and the power of ideas. *Daedalus* 107:39–52

Rintala, M. 1968. Generations, political. See Sills 1968:92–95

Rintala, M. 1979. *The Constitution of Silence: Essays on Generational Themes.* Westport, Conn: Greenwood

Rintala, M. 1984. Chronicler of a generation: Vera Brittain's testament. *J. Polit. Milit. Sociol.* 12:23–35

Rodgers, W. L. 1982. Estimable functions of age, period, and cohort effects. *Am. Sociol. Rev.* 47:774–87

Rollenhagen, R. E. 1984. Age-related changing levels of voting turnout across time. *Gerontologist* 24:205–07

Rosow, I. 1978. What is a cohort and why? *Hum. Dev.* 21:65–75

Ryder, N. B. 1965. The cohort as a concept in the study of social change. *Am. Sociol. Rev.* 30:843–61

Shelton, R. M. 1982. *To Lose a War: Memories of a German Girl.* Carbondale, Ill: Southern Ill. Univ. Press

Shore, M. 1972. Henry VIII and the crisis of generativity. *J. Interdis. Hist.* 2:359–90

Sills, D., ed. 1968. *Encyclopedia of the Social Sciences.* Vol. 6. New York: Macmillan

Smelser, N. J. 1968. *Essays in Sociological Explanation.* Englewood Cliffs, NJ: Prentice-Hall

Spitzer, A. B. 1973. The historical problem of generations. *Am. Hist. Rev.* 78:1353–85

Stacey, B. 1977. *Political Socialization in Western Society: An Analysis from a Life-Span Perspective.* New York: St. Martin's

Streib, G. F. 1976. Social stratification and aging. See Binstock & Shanas, 1976:160–85

Streib, G. F., Bourg, C. J. 1984. Age stratification theory, inequality, and social change. See Tomasson 1984:63–77

Szabo, S. F. 1983. *The Successor Generation: International Perspectives of Postwar Europeans.* Woburn, Mass.: Butterworths

Tilly, C. 1975. Revolutions and collective violence. In *Handbook of Political Science,* ed. F. I. Greenstein, N. W. Polsby, 3:483–555. Reading, Mass: Addison-Wesley

Tomasson, R. F., ed. 1984. *Comparative Social Research.* Vol. 7. Greenwich, Conn: JAI

Troll, L. E. 1970. Issues in the study of generations. *Aging Hum. Devel.* 1:199–218

United Nations. 1981. *International Youth Year: Participation, Development, Peace.* New York: United Nations

Whalen, J., Flacks, R. 1980. The Isla Vista "bank burners" ten years later: Notes on the fate of student activists. *Sociol. Focus* 13:215–36

Whalen, J., Flacks, R. 1984. Echoes of rebellion: The liberated generation grows up. *J. Polit. Milit. Sociol.* 12:61–78

Wohl, R. 1979. *The Generation of 1914.* Cambridge, Mass: Harvard Univ. Press

Wohlwill, J. F. 1970. Methodology and research strategy in the study of developmental change. See Goulet & Baltes 1970:149–91

Wood, J. L. 1974. *The Sources of Student Activism.* Lexington, Mass: Heath

Yankelovich, D. 1974. *The New Morality: A Profile of American Youth in the 70's.* New York: McGraw-Hill

Zald, M. N., McCarthy, J. D., eds. 1979. *The Dynamics of Social Movements.* Cambridge, Mass: Winthrop

Ann. Rev. Sociol. 1986. 12:233–53

EFFICIENCY AND SOCIAL INSTITUTIONS: Uses and Misuses of Economic Reasoning in Sociology

Anthony Oberschall and Eric M. Leifer*

Department of Sociology, University of North Carolina, Chapel Hill,
North Carolina 27514

Abstract

We review recent applications of the "new institutional economics" to a variety of social institutions. The applications use the idea of efficiency to account for the emergence and persistence of institutions such as the family, sharing groups, private property, discrimination, and the norm of reciprocity. Efficiency entails eliminating costly externalities with the least possible transaction costs (i.e. costs involved in negotiating, writing, and enforcing agreements). Our critique of efficiency shows how power relations, goal ambiguity, and the institutional relativism of choice render efficiency problematic. The sociological criterion of reproducibility may be more relevant where these features hold. If efficiency analysis is used, the sociologist should insist that it allow the identification of inefficiencies and that institutional participants welcome suggested improvements in efficiency.

INTRODUCTION

The last two decades have seen the spread of economic reasoning into sociological topics. The "free rider" problem, popularized by Olson (1965), has become a key concern of collective action theorists (Oberschall 1973, Oliver 1980, Hechter 1983). Rational choice theory has influenced the study of the family, crime and punishment, discrimination, and other fields (Becker 1976,

---

*Order of authorship was randomly determined.

0360-0572/86/0815-0233$02.00

1981; Becker et al 1977; Scanzoni 1981, Hirschleifer 1985). The new institutional economics (Williamson 1975, 1981) has had an impact on organization theory (Francis et al 1983) and the study of labor markets (Granovetter 1983), as well as the study of nonwork institutions (Ben-Porath 1980, Pollack 1985).

Economists were motivated to move outside of their traditional concerns as the limitations of General Equilibrium Theory (GET) became apparent. In GET, for example, the family or household was assumed to be a single entity making production and consumption decisions. Intrahousehold behavior, such as the decision to marry, to bear and educate children, to divorce, and the like, were arbitrarily ignored though they had a direct bearing on the size and composition of the population, the number of households, the labor force and human capital production, consumption, and other mainline economic topics (Sawhill 1977). Becker (1976, 1981) took rational choice theory into the family and other previously "noneconomic" areas, insisting that human behavior had a round-the-clock consistency economists had long been willing to ignore (see Leibenstein 1979).[1]

Adequate reviews of Becker's approach are available—Hannan (1982), Ben-Porath (1982), Sawhill (1977), MacRae (1978), and Berk & Berk (1983). Here we focus on a literature spawned by another limitation of GET. In the world of GET, there is only one kind of institution—the market (see Arrow & Hahn 1971).[2] GET markets produce allocations of resources where, given initial endowments, no individual could be made better off without making at

[1]Becker's approach treats preferences over the "fundamental aspects of life" (e.g. health, prestige, sensual pleasures) as stable givens and postulates the existence of a "production function" that links goods and services to the fundamental sources of utility. Marginalist predictions are then possible, relating changes in the use production inputs to changes in market prices and incomes. In practice, predictions are applied to aggregate behavioral tendencies rather than individual actions (e.g. the greater the cost of raising children, the lower the expected fertility rate). Individuals themselves need not explicitly maximize over stable preferences, as long as the tendencies make it appear "as if" individuals were making rational choices.

Because sociologists have been more interested in the diversity and distribution of values than in marginalist predictions derived on the basis of given values, Barry (1970) argued that this approach complements rather than substitutes for sociological analysis. In any case, sociologists are likely to insist on a convincing story about the nature and stability of the givens (i.e. preferences, production functions) on which Becker's brand of explanations are based. The economist Hirschleifer's (1977) search for an answer takes him out of economics altogether and into evolutionary biology. Hirshleifer has a difficult task ahead of him: "Preferences . . . are scientifically analyzable and even in principle predictable in terms of the inheritance of past genetic and cultural adaptations together with the new adjustments called for by current environmental circumstances" (p. 26).

[2]There is also an implicit enforcer of contracts (i.e. the State) which without cost ensures that all contracts are executed. The enforcer allows self-interested individuals to enter into contractually ensured, mutually advantageous relationships; it thus allows the economist to ignore cheating, "bad faith," and costly, drawn-out litigation.

least one individual worse off (i.e. markets are "Pareto efficient" institutions). This desireable property, however, renders nonmarket institutions anomalous as they could not surpass markets in realizing possible gains from voluntary exchange.

Nonmarket institutions did not attract the attention of economists so long as they were viewed as noneconomic. Commons (1934) was a pioneer in recognizing the importance of political and legal institutions in shaping economic transactions. Collective actions and legal decisions led to regulations and conceptions of property that made markets possible or impossible. Common's "institutional economics" was made more compelling by Coase's (1937) insight that the firm itself was a nonmarket institution, where authority replaced markets in resolving distributional issues. Firms "made" instead of "bought" not only needed components, but also non-entry-level employees, through internal labor markets. If GET was the whole story, distributional issues should be resolved by markets—not politicians, lawyers, or managers, and their respective constituencies.

Recently, a "new institutional economics" has arisen that adds to the version, developed by Commons and Coase, with assumptions about explicit individual choice and about human nature in general.[3] The new institutional economics looks for the efficiency of nonmarket institutions (analogous to the way in which Becker and associates look for rationality in "noneconomic" individual behavior). Nonmarket institutions may be efficient where the assumptions of GET are not met in real settings. These stringent assumptions include no information asymmetries, no uncertainty, unbounded rationality, no transaction costs, and extensive private property rights that rule out the possibility of externalities (i.e. no public goods). Where these assumptions are violated, nonmarket institutions may be more efficient than markets and hence can be explained in terms of efficiency.

The next section provides an overview of the new institutional economics and discusses a variety of applications to economic, social, and political institutions. This task, however, is not sufficient to explain the spread of economic reasoning into sociology. Here we must look at the receiving side of sociology and assess the needs this reasoning satisfies and the questions it leaves unanswered.

The most general sociological explanation of social institutions is functionalist. Institutions fulfill societal needs, or "functional prerequisites." Society must *reproduce* itself in and through individual behavior and relies on in-

---

[3]These assumptions are given by Williamson (1975). Choice is driven by "bounded rationality," which limits a corporate unit's ability to anticipate future contingencies in market contracts. Human nature is based on "self interest with guile" (i.e. opportunism), which creates the need for close monitoring in situations of uncertainty and few alternatives.

stitutions for this purpose. Resources must be allocated and cooperation enacted to maintain stratification systems. In reproducing themselves and the social system of which they are part, institutions train the young in the ways of the old and compel potential deviants to conform.

The functionalist mode of explanation is the reverse of the economist's. The functionalist starts at the societal or aggregate level and ends up analyzing individual behavior as it conforms to institutions; this in turn confers a stable and distinct reality to the societal level. The economist starts with individual wants and ends up analyzing institutions that produce social welfare and satisfy individual wants. As Duesenberry (1960) quipped, "Economics is all about why people make choices, while sociology is all about why they don't have any choices to make."

Dissatisfaction with functionalism focuses on its neglect of the wants and choices of individuals. The "oversocialized conception of man" (Wrong 1961) renders social change problematic and does not help explain why a particular institution comes to serve a function instead of one of a variety of alternative institutions. The dissatisfaction with functionalism has made sociologists receptive to economic reasoning, which promises to bring a choice-making individual back into the study of social institutions.

Following the applications of economic reasoning in the next section, we assess the limits of this reasoning in the section on Uses, Misuses, and Alternatives. Efficiency analysis, we suggest, glosses over power considerations, ignores the ambiguity of institutional goals, and underestimates the institutional relativism of choice. We concur that sociologists err in emphasizing conformity over choice, but note that economists fail to recognize the importance of conformity *in* choice. The wants and perceived opportunities of individuals are often shaped through social processes; conformity is a considerable challenge for the individual making choices in complex settings. In light of the interdependencies between conformity and choice, we reexamine the criterion of "reproducibility" and contrast it with the efficiency criterion of economists.

THE EMERGENCE AND PERSISTENCE OF INSTITUTIONS: APPLICATIONS OF THE NEW INSTITUTIONAL ECONOMICS

The new institutional economics seeks to account for the emergence and persistence of institutions on the basis of their efficiency. It recognizes that rational behavior may produce negative externalities in a collectivity. In the well-known "Prisoner's Dilemma," each side has an incentive to spurn cooperation and defect, but if *both* defect they would regret not having cooperated. Likewise, in the "tragedy of the commons," each villager is motivated to increase their own usage of the commons, yet if all do so the commons will be exhausted (e.g. overgrazed), to the detriment of all villagers (Hardin 1968). In such situations, institutions that reduce the externalities are likely to arise and persist. Investing in a trust relationship (or exchanging hostages), for example, may facilitate cooperation and hence resolve a prisoner's dilemma, while the institution of private property rights eliminates the tragedy of the commons. The new institutional economics holds that institutions arise and persist when the benefits they confer are greater than the transaction costs (e.g. negotiating, writing, and enforcing norms or rules) involved in creating and sustaining them.[4]

Transactions are the basic unit of the new institutional economics. Features of transactions dictate the type of institutionalized relationship that forms between transactors—the "governance structure," in Williamson's (1975) terminology. Market relations, for example, might be quite adequate where the quality of items traded is easy to assess and a large number of potential trading partners exist. If these features don't exist, however, the market may be an inefficient institution.

Williamson (1981, 1984) has identified three key dimensions on which transactions differ. *Uncertainty* comes about to the degree that it is costly to meter the quantity and/or quality of the good or service that is exchanged. The *frequency* of a transaction (when high) may motivate institution building or (when low) may prohibit investment in an institution. Finally, *asset specificity* is high whenever the value of what is exchanged depends heavily on the specific identities of the transactors. The investments people make in pleasing particular others may have little value outside their relationship, just as car-carrying railcars have only a scrap value outside their use in shipping particular makes of automobiles. High uncertainty, frequency, and asset specificity motivate investment in nonmarket institutions.

Informal Institutions: Stereotypes, Relationships, and Networks

Buying and selling a used auto between two parties is a nonrecurring transaction. Both parties can buy and sell a variety of used autos from a variety of competitors without any asset-specific investment in each other. Uncertainty is high because the condition of the car is expensive to ascertain, beyond what a short test drive and checking for dents will allow. An important consequence

---

[4]This issue of how institutions arise is not fully resolved. Williamson (1984) invokes an "institutional designer," imputing considerable intelligence to the process of institutional evolution. Nelson & Winters (1982) reject microeconomic choice assumptions altogether in opting for an evolutionary approach. Here efficiency is the end result of blind variety, selection, and retention, rather than individual foresight. This is much too radical a departure from microeconomics for the new institutional economists. The centrality of individual choice in microeconomics must be rejected if the evolutionary mechanism is to be a determining force.

follows: The seller's incentive to pass off a "lemon" on the buyer makes the buyer leary about paying a premium for an apparent "peach," but this in turn inclines any seller to continue driving a peach until it becomes a lemon (Akerlof 1970). In equilibrium, buyers only get the lemons they pay for. Though nobody is "cheated" here, both sides would clearly prefer the option of being able to buy and sell well-maintained used cars (i.e. the market for lemons is a "second-best" solution). The infrequency of transactions, however, means the losses to the transactors will not be sufficient to justify the transaction costs involved in building alternative institutional arrangements.

The result above may yield insight into stereotyping and discrimination. Within the same group, metering cost and uncertainty is low as a result of information the parties have about each other directly or by way of third-party sources. Consider, however, a majority-group member who infrequently interacts with a minority member. High uncertainty may attend the infrequent encounters, as the majority member lacks information on particular minority members. Facing high costs in discovering the "true" characteristics of a minority group member, the transactor resorts to readily available stereotypes, as a low-cost information source.

One now has the making of a "lemon" market. Acting on the basis of stereotypes, the majority will discriminate against the minority, either through avoidance or by asking a higher price (or offering a lower one) to compensate for the greater uncertainty. Note also that since minority members collectively bear the brunt of negative stereotyping and discrimination, each has no incentive to put much effort into actively countering the stereotype by "exemplary" behavior. The stereotype becomes self-fulling in the absence of exogeneous factors, and resulting discrimination is likely to continue.

The consequences of introducing high frequency can be seen in Popkin's (1981) comparison of rice and rubber markets. The quality of dried rice can be easily measured by sampling from rice sacks. Impersonal sales in an auction market among many interchangeable and changing buyers and sellers is the rule. Not so in rubber. The quality of rubber cannot be ascertained until several months after its sale when further processing of the unsmoked raw rubber has taken place. The sales transaction between rubber producers and wholesalers is thus fraught with considerable uncertainty, not found in rice sales. A high-quality producer could not realize a higher price in an auction market because the buyer cannot distinguish quality variation at the time of sale. In an auction market for rubber, quality would drop to the lowest common denominator.

On the other hand, if a producer builds a reputation for high quality over time, which can be done best in an ongoing, long-term relationship with the same buyers, he can realize a higher price for his rubber than a low-quality producer. In fact, according to Popkin (1981), the rubber trade is dominated by customer markets with long-term agent-client relationships. Such an institutional arrangement makes it possible to reduce the uncertainty about quality, a reduction in the information costs associated with the transaction.

Palay (1983) focuses on asset specificity in his analysis of rail carrier-shipper relations for a variety of commodities. Where no special railcars are needed and a number of rail and truck alternatives exist, both carrier and shipper put a heavy emphasis on "exit" (see Hirschman 1970) as a response to an inability or unwillingness to live up to the terms of a contract. In the much different situation of shipping finished automobiles, where special railcars are needed and there are few viable alternatives for either shipping automobiles or using the special railcars, both shipper and carrier are willing to invest heavily in establishing a "businesslike" relationship. A carrier invested between $1.5 to $2 million in special railcars on the basis of an informal agreement, while one shipper reimbursed a carrier more than $1 million for the unamortized portion of such an investment when the shipper altered the design of its automobiles, thus rendering the carrier's special railcars obsolete. The shipper made this reimbursement outside of any contractual obligation, because it was in the shipper's "best interest" to keep the carrier "healthy, viable and happy to guarantee that we will get the equipment we need, when we need it" (Paley 1983:15).

Axelrod (1984) used an ingenious approach for learning about cooperation among egoists. He sponsored a computer tournament where leading theorists from a variety of fields were asked to submit strategies in fortran programs for playing an iterated Prisoner's Dilemma game. Each entrant's program was matched against each other program for 100 trials in a round-robin tournament format. The lure of defecting in a single trial had to be weighed against the high cost of possible mutual defection over many trials. The great variety of submitted programs reflected the lack of an analytical solution to this problem. The programs ranged from a simple 4-line program to a complex 75-line program incorporating the intricacies of Bayesian decision theory. Entrants, in short, faced considerable uncertainty over the strategy of the opposition.

Much to everyone's surprise, the highest score was achieved by Anatol Rappoport's 4-line TIT FOR TAT program. TIT FOR TAT cooperates on the first trial, and then mimics its opponent's response on the (now) prior trial. Thus TIT FOR TAT cooperates as long as its opponent does, punishes defection with subsequent defection, but resumes cooperation promptly when the opponent once more cooperates.

To check the robustness of TIT FOR TAT'S adaptibility, Axelrod distributed the tournament results to a larger set of potential entrants and asked them to submit a new program. Rappoport entered TIT FOR TAT again and, amazingly, won again. Analysis revealed why this should be so. Entrants with cooperating strategies locked in on cooperation with each other and accumulated high payoffs for each other. Other entrants used primarily defecting strategies that sought to take advantage of a cooperator's trust and took precautions against being exploited by another defector; they, however, locked in on damaging mutual defection and thus accumulated low payoffs with each other. A defector was unable, however, to exploit TIT FOR TAT beyond an initial move. It would have to resume cooperation with TIT FOR TAT before it had another chance to exploit TIT FOR TAT, and at that point TIT FOR TAT would first balance accounts before in turn resuming cooperation. This being so, TIT FOR TAT was not vulnerable to exploitation by scheming egoists.

Axelrod's concern is with the evolutionary implications of the tournament's results. He shows, via additional simulations, that a small group of TIT FOR TAT "cooperators" can survive and even prosper in a larger population of defectors. For present purposes, it is crucial to recognize the importance of high transaction frequency in producing these results. In a single trial, a defector would exploit a cooperator and quickly exit. With multiple trials, however, defection carries the substantial risk of being dragged into mutual destruction. In the real world, people should invest in building a relationship of cooperation and "trust" when the prospects are strong for subsequent interaction.

In a particularly telling example from World War One, Axelrod shows how a "Live and Let Live" understanding developed between allied and German troops in frontline trenches—each side refrained from shooting to kill the other, despite the orders of the high commands. This real-world example also indicates how an advantageous behavioral rule has the tendency to become a norm (see Opp 1983). New recruits and units get taught the rule by old timers, are rewarded for conforming and punished for deviance.

The topic can be broadened to include the persistence of personal, diffuse social relationships and transactions that lead to cliques and networks operating within the interstices of the major organizations and institutions of a complex society, and which are used to get things done when the formal system fails. Such instances are reported in bureaucratized and centralized social systems, such as France, and even more commonly in economies of scarcity, as in mainland China, where some scarce goods and services are virtually unobtainable in the planned sector. The parallel, informal system consisting of personal relationships and cliques is called by various names: "systeme D" in France, and "back-door" *(guangxi)* in China. Under conditions of extreme economic uncertainty and political instability, as experienced by one of the authors in Zaire, the informal system can gain ascendancy to such a degree that the offices and resources of the major bureaucracies are captured by cliques and patrons for their private use, i.e. public resources are privatized. A similar line of thought led Eric Wolf (1966:19) to write that ". . . complex societies in the modern world differ less in the formal organization of their economic and legal and political system than in the character of their supplementary interpersonal sets," by which he meant kinship, friendship, patronage, and the like.

Viewed in a transaction cost framework, impersonal bureaucratic social institutions and the market provide substitutes for family, clique, and small group transactions, and vice versa. Which is the more advantageous (least costly) depends once more on the dimensions of transactions: frequency, uncertainty, and asset specificity. The beginning of a theory has been outlined by Ben-Porath (1980) and Ouchi (1980). The guiding idea is that investment in resources specific to a relationship between identified parties, called "specialization by identity", can save on transaction costs, compared to alternative modes of impersonal transacting in the market or in bureaucracies.[5]

Formal Institutions: Property Rights and Sharing Groups

Demsetz (1967) has argued that the least costly solution to the "tragedy of the commons" is private property rights, as opposed to shared land ownership with restrictions on use. He discusses the interesting case of the emergence of private property among Labrador Indians in the eighteenth century, a period that saw the rise of a lucrative beaver fur market. Originally, every family hunted only beavers used for their own consumption, and there were enough beavers in the forest streams to satisfy the needs of all families. The external costs imposed by hunters on each other were very small; consequently no restrictions on land and on beavers limited hunting among the Indians.

With the spread of the fur trade, these costs increased. As the demand and price for beaver fur increased, the scale of hunting also increased. The Indians killed beaver faster than they reproduced, and the search for additional beavers extended over an ever-widening area. Gradually over a period of some decades, and starting in the districts that were the first centers of the fur trade, a system of private property rights was instituted. The system was simple and cheap to operate, as, for instance, marking off a family's property by blazing the trees with crests. Each family or band became responsible for husbanding its furbearing animals. It was no longer in a family's interest to overexploit its privately owned resource. Private property internalized the earlier external costs, i.e. the costs of each family's hunting practices would be borne by themselves alone, not by other families.

Demsetz further argued that an important reason for low transaction costs in private property rights among Labrador Indians was that beavers and other

---

[5]According to Ben-Porath (1980), the family can be viewed as a set of interrelated contracts (husband-wife, parent-child, . . .) with the following attributes: transactions are between specific persons, nontransferable to third parties; they extend over a long period of time without a specific duration; they encompass a large number of activities; the terms of contract are open-ended, diffuse obligations that are backed by social norms and exist as a nonseparable bundle; large, outstanding balances are tolerated for an indefinite period of time; enforcement of the contracts is mostly internal to the group; and a collective identity shared by all family members affects each member's transactions with those outside.

forest animals confine their territory to small areas, while their fur had a high value. Thus, only a small territory had to be marked and policed by each family for a high value resource to be managed.

On the other hand, Indians in the Southwest plains failed to institute property rights in buffalo and other game. There the commercial importance of game was much less than for furbearing forest animals. Also, because the grazing plains animals roamed over a vast territory, "the value of establishing boundaries to private hunting territories is . . . reduced by the relatively high cost of preventing animals from moving to adjacent parcels." The transaction costs of establishing and enforcing private property rights remained high compared to the external costs that plains hunters imposed on each other. Not until the introduction of cheap barbed wire would these costs be greatly reduced.

The California Gold Rush offers a closer look at the emergence of property rights [as analyzed by Umbeck (1977, 1981) and Oberschall (1985)]. At the time gold was discovered (1848), California was sparsely settled and unencumbered by prior property claims. As in the Labrador Indian case, the earliest arrivals simply occupied ground not yet worked by others; this action imposed no external costs on others. When the gold rush swelled and the crowding ensued, fights broke out as miners encroached on neighbors' claims, a sign that external costs were increasing.

Spontaneously, miners in a particular area would call a meeting at which they would constitute themselves into a sovereign mining district and decide on the allocation of mining claims, membership rules, and enforcement machinery, i.e. they would decide on property rights and governance institutions. The most prominent feature of the miners' institutions was their egalitarian character: equal division of land; one claim per miner; one miner, one vote in the assembly. These are fairness norms of the "wait your turn" and "first come, first served" variety that often are the assumed rules of interaction among strangers in a variety of collective settings. Schelling (1963:111–13) has pointed out the importance of such focal point solutions in bargaining, that is solutions with a feature that distinguishes them qualitatively from alternative solutions.

Consider any other principle for allocation, for example, "to each according to his need,"—that is, a larger lot to those who had dependents back home, or a larger lot to those who hadn't yet struck any gold. Some would be disadvantaged and oppose it, and suggest some alternative principle that others would find objectionable in turn. Further, whatever the principle, false claims by miners on the criterion (the number of dependents) would be costly or impossible to check. These problems did not develop with the simple equal-division rules.

Umbeck (1977) points out that within the framework of fairness norms, not the land but the gold could be equally divided. Miners might decide to work as a team and split the proceeds evenly, or more likely in shares proportional to labor input. From an incentive- and transaction-cost point of view, the gold division scheme has several drawbacks compared to land division. Land division takes place but once at the start, in a simple operation with low transaction costs. Equal plots of fixed size are laid out; marker stakes are driven into the ground; plots are assigned by lot. Thereafter, every miner works as long and as hard as he pleases and is capable of. The amount of gold he gets is directly linked to his effort, which is a powerful incentive for productivity, and to his luck (how much gold is located in his lot).

As for social control costs, each miner or small partnership polices the claim against encroachers at low cost. By virtue of a residency rule, which required miners to be physically present on their claim most of the time, most monitoring and enforcement costs were absorbed in work routines. Should disputes nonetheless arise, the officers arbitrated or organized a trial on the spot.

In the gold division scheme there exists an incentive problem and continuous metering and enforcement costs that are not internalized by each miner. Because gold is unevenly distributed in the area, labor input and effort cannot be metered by the amount of gold mined. Lest shirking and free riding be encouraged, close supervision of the miners is needed, as is an accounting system recording the hours and days worked. Miners have to be further monitored lest they dishonestly keep some of the gold that is to be surrendered to the common pot for equal division. Finally, the gold accumulated has to be periodically divided, adding yet another transaction cost to the gold division scheme. Overall then, land division is more efficient than gold division on both incentives and transaction costs criteria.

Among the near 500 mining districts created, Umbeck (1981) reports that the rules and form of governance just described were adopted by all districts for which records survive, and that they worked satisfactorily. Despite gambling, drinking and high living associated with the search for adventure and riches by mostly young and middle-aged males, homicide rates were lower in the mining camps than in the rest of California.

The privatization of property clearly resolves negative externality problems and can often be sustained with low transaction costs. In many situations, however, privatization is limited by technological or economic constraints. Public goods such as radio signals or national security cannot readily be privatized. The "free rider" problem (i.e. the rationality of shirking in the provision of public goods) necessitates considerable transaction costs in terms of implementing selective incentive systems to provide public goods (Olson 1965). In other cases, privatization may be impeded by economic constraints. An individual may not be able to afford a swimming pool but may be able to combine his or her resources with others to purchase a swimming pool.

This problem is central to the theory of sharing groups, which Lindenberg (1982) takes up as an extension of Buchanan's (1965) theory of clubs. Sharing is advantageous because it lowers the cost for each, allowing some to use products or services that could not be purchased privately. But it is inconvenient compared to individual ownership, because others' access rights limit one's own use opportunities. Though cost declines with number of shares, so does benefit. More benefit, though with more cost, can be obtained with more of the shared good. Any sharing arrangement, furthermore, has transaction costs. Rules must be negotiated, written, and enforced. For a small group this can be done informally; for a large group it might entail the creation of a specialized social unit and roles. Transaction costs are usually assumed to increase with group size and heterogeneity.

If people seek to maximize the net benefit from sharing, given budget constraints, what amount of the good will they share and what size will be the sharing groups? Further, how does amount and size vary with some important variables such as the sharers' incomes and the heterogeneity of the population? To solve the problem analytically, Lindenberg made the usual assumptions about benefit and cost functions (e.g. costs decrease with group size and increase with quantity of the good).

Lindenberg shows, among other things, that prosperity makes sharing groups smaller and more numerous until most goods become completely privatized in single-member groups. Though the inconvenience of sharing is eliminated with growing affluence and privatization, an important basis for group formation and bonding has also been undermined. There is a tendency for all goods to follow the trend observed in US transportation. Public transportation gives way to the family automobile, which in turn gives way to each family member driving their own car. Looking at the family as a social unit for sharing consumption, sharing group theory predicts the ultimate differentiation of the family into "single member sharing groups," i.e. the loss of an important function, which (ceteris paribus) weakens the institution of the family in an affluent society.

For a complete analysis, the transaction costs involved in implementing a sharing arrangement must be considered. For example, Popkin (1981) notes the low incidence of cooperative ownership of plough animals in Southeast Asia, such as plough teams shared among several peasant families, or even of instances where plough animals can be rented without a driver. The lack of both can be explained with reference to high information costs created by uncertainty. Beyond obvious external signs of cuts from whipping, it is difficult to tell whether the animals were overworked, inadequately fed, or internally injured. These consequences of abuse may not become evident for several days, by which time it is possible other users of the plough team may have been responsible for the damage. Not some cultural attribute of the peasantry, but the difficulty of collecting timely information about the proper care of animals, a most important part of the transaction, might explain the absence of cooperative institutions in plough animals.

USES, MISUSES, AND ALTERNATIVES

The previous section provided instances of economic reasoning for explaining a variety of institutions. In this section we point to missing components and hidden assumptions in these explanations that may trouble the sociologist, and we offer a sociological critique to stimulate debate. Whether accepted or rejected, economic reasoning forces sociologists to clarify their own thoughts on the emergence and persistence of institutions.

What About Power?

Power is an elusive concept, yet one most sociologists are reluctant to abandon. Power considerations are conspicuously absent from the economic reasoning in the first section. This stems from the marginalist orientation of economics, where the *freedom* of choice at the margins is neatly separated from the *constraints* reflected in the "given" distributional setting where choice occurs.

Consider stereotyping and the resulting discrimination. Stereotyping was viewed as a cheap way to avoid the high costs of obtaining accurate information. Thus, if the individual qualities of a minority group member could be known without cost, stereotyping—and hence discrimination—would cease to exist. This ignores, however, why a particular group was singled out in the first place for special status as a stereotyped minority. It also ignores the lengths to which some people go in maintaining stereotypes even when they are barraged by costfree information. Finally, the theory depicts the stereotype as a "second best" solution when minority aspirations have been so discouraged that the minority gives the majority no more than it believes it can get. The convenience of a stereotype at the margin does not appear sufficient to account for why particular groups get targeted and tied down by negative stereotypes.

The marginalist orientation is carried to the institutional level in the new institutional economics. The efficiency of institutions was assessed at the level of aggregate performance. Institutional change or evolution was attributed to incremental improvements at the aggregate level. No attention was given to the variances of benefits and costs across participants, and how these change with the emergence of a new institution.

Consider the emergence of private property rights. Their spontaneous emergence and egalitarian character in the California Gold Rush was an exceptional case, dependent on a very peculiar social context. Even here, some miners stood to lose by the emergent institutions and may have needed more than aggregate efficiency arguments to be convinced. In settings with more entrenched social structures, preexisting power relations may make efficiency justifications superfluous in rationalizing an institution. The medieval open-held system and the commons were not replaced by private ownership of land in Britain as a consequence of decisions about efficiency in which all had an equal voice (Polanyi 1944), just as socialized property in the Soviet Union and Eastern Union did not get instituted because of externalities and transaction costs.

The anthropologist Monica Wilson (1963) recognized the importance of power for the emergence of property rights among the Xhosa in Eastern Cape Province:

> ". . . the choice has yet to be made whether the common will continue to be used by the village as a unit or divided into individual holdings . . . the difficulty about a common is to reach agreement on the principle by which the stock is to be limited. If a maximum number of cattle which every villager may graze is fixed, the rich object; they lose more than the poor. If, on the other hand, each man is allowed a proportion of his present holding the poor may lose all the rights they have . . ."

Individual holdings would remove the costs of agreeing over usage rights but would not make the evidently vexing concern that the poor "may lose everything they have" go away. "Efficiency" can easily be used as a gloss for power in the redistribution of rights and privileges.

Perrow (1985) questions the importance of efficiency considerations in the firm, Williamson's (1975, 1981) home turf. Williamson argues a firm will subsume a supplier into its structure when internal transactions involving authority are less costly than market transactions. Perrow notes that an internal division can give the parent firm more headaches than an external supplier; he argues that mergers and takeovers are motivated by the power struggles among firms within and across markets. Large size confers advantages that may have little to do with "efficiency." For more on this argument, see Francis et al (1983).

What About Goal Ambiguity?

Efficiency can be defined where the goals of actors and corporate units are clearcut. Costs and benefits are then amenable to a clear separation. The profit maximizing firm, for example, draws its benefits (i.e. profits) from the sale of finished products and incurs its costs in the process of production. The beneficial public good is provided through the costly activities of volunteers and contributors. The efficient institution produces benefits at the least possible cost.

In many situations, however, it is not clear that activities and transactions in the pursuit of an ostensible goal are costs alone. Benefits may be derived from participation in a "costly" activity. Hirschman (1979) makes this point in questioning Olson's (1965) treatment of the "free rider" problem. Many people find participation a source of satisfaction regardless of the outcome. The free rider misses the fun of participation. This would have been obvious to Tocqueville, viewing the endless political debate among nineteenth century Americans, or to an onlooker to the New Left activities of the late 1960s, viewing the frustration of those unable to devote *more* time to collective pursuits.

Eccles (1985) carried this reasoning onto economic turf in his study of transfer pricing in multidivisional firms. Divisions in a firm are sometimes each other's customers. Since the divisions operate within a common authority structure, a wide range of nonmarket mechanisms exist to regulate exchange between them. In firms that emphasize division autonomy (and hence performance responsibility) but which have substantial input-output interdependencies between divisions, Eccles observed a very peculiar transfer policy. The firm mandated internal transfers (i.e. compelled a division to buy from another of its divisions rather than an outside supplier), but left the transfer price to be determined by the division managers. Since the transfer price directly affected division profits (but not firm profits), division managers had a zero-sum conflict to resolve in determining the transfer price. Eccles, indeed, observed a good deal of conflict between division managers. When Eccles asked the firms' CEOs what they intended to do about the high "transaction costs" incurred in arriving at a price agreement, the CEOs consistently said they intended to do nothing. What was going on?

Eccles conjectured that the conflict was serving two functions. First, when brought before the CEO, the conflict provided valuable information about the operating conditions of the divisions. Division managers would offer this information in the course of developing their argument for a favorable transfer price. Second, the conflict resolution process afforded a valuable display of the division managers' style—information useful in the promotion process. To become candidates for promotion, managers were expected to balance tenacity in the pursuit of division goals with the ability to take on a larger corporate perspective. In this way, the top level's broad viewpoint gets reproduced across generations of CEOs.

Eccles' work illustrates the difficulty of separating costs and benefits in ongoing institutions. A transfer price has no direct consequence on firm profits, and thus one might expect the CEO who wants to minimize the transaction costs to fix a price that eliminates the "costly" conflict. Transfer pricing, however, is deeply intertwined in the ongoing concerns of the firm. To understand transfer pricing conflict, the hidden benefits of some of the "costs" have to be recognized.

In itself, this presents no insuperable obstacles for the economist. "Costs" and "benefits" are ultimately given data for the economist. Most economists concede that corporate units may have multiple goals. It is common, for example, to place managerial security alongside profit maximization as goals of the firm. This creates often complex trade-offs but does not undermine the relevance of efficiency as long as the goals and trade-offs can be specified.

Sociologists often avoid the intentionality implied in "goals" and use instead the term "functions" for designating the purposes institutions are meant to accomplish. Among them are some that individuals are only dimly aware of. Merton (1968) called these "latent" functions. Even among "manifest" functions, there may exist contradictions that generate confusion and conflict. This view of functions makes them tentative hypotheses that are never exhausted with certainty. When there is ambiguity over the functions of institutions, or goals of corporate units, efficiency analysis is problematic.

Consider the treatment of trust relationships in the new institutional economics. Trust in a relationship minimizes transaction costs under conditions of uncertainty, high frequency, and asset specificity. The prospect of transacting into an indefinite future discourages each side from exploiting the other's trust, as the short-term gains are outweighed by the long-term losses. Benefits accrue from the goods and services exchanged, and costs consist of the investments required to build trust through an adherence to the norm of reciprocity (which must be less than writing and enforcing explicit contracts). In this scenario, costs, benefits, goals, and efficiency are transparent.

A close look at trust relationships, however, might reveal that the long-term must be built from the short-term, rather than vice versa. *A lot of effort is required before there is an indefinite transaction future ahead to constrain exploitative behavior.* Asset specificity and even some behavioral uncertainty can grow out of this effort (rather than being present from the start) and can motivate the trust relationship. The actor cannot behave opportunistically precisely when the opportunist should do so, yet the actor also cannot behave too nonopportunistically, lest the opportunist in others is encouraged. In the process of building an indefinite future (which may run the whole course of this future!), costs, benefits, goals, and hence "efficiency" may be ambiguous. The ambiguity, furthermore, can be self-reproducing—adapting to ambiguity may generate more ambiguity (Leifer 1986).

The ambiguity of costs, benefits, and goals suggests a reversal of the economist's logic. Instead of explaining institutions on the basis of transaction cost minimization, one might try explaining what comes to be regarded as "costly" and "beneficial" in terms of institutions. Bargaining, monitoring, and enforcement elicit varying enthusiasms in the modern factory, the fruit market, and the family. Institutions that regulate shared resources create attachments and tastes for egalitarianism and sharing of risk that are offended when resources are divided into private property. In a cross-cultural study of Japan, South Korea, and Taiwan, Hamilton & Biggart (1985) illustrate the difficulties transaction cost analysis encounters. In Taiwan, for example, firms remain small, relying on market over authority relations precisely where the new institutional economics predicts the opposite.

Even without reversing the economist's logic, any interdependence between institutions and individual goals or preferences creates obstacles for efficiency analysis. If, say, the transition from a commons to individual holdings changes what individuals value, then the elimination of a "cost" within the commons framework does not imply this elimination will be looked on as a savings from the individual holdings framework. An ordering of institutions on the efficiency criterion is problematic if the framework for the ordering, i.e. the preferences of the individuals, is itself derived from the institution.

What About Choice?

Economists assume stable goals, or basic values, allow stable and consistent preference orderings over alternatives (Becker 1976). Their theory of choice depends on consistent preference orderings to generate predictions, and stable orderings to render the predictions falsifiable. The economic actor is never disappointed (Hirschman 1979) or surprised (Cohen & Axelrod 1982) in executing a chosen alternative. In the new institutional economics, this affective foresight carries across institutional change.

Sociologists make values and norms relative to institutional settings. Individuals internalize the values and "voluntaristically" obey the norms of particular institutional settings. Instead of making choices, individuals conform to norms. If there is a choice, it is between the alternatives of conformity and deviance. Why norms are internalized, and hence deviance minimized, is not clear. Why particular institutional frameworks will emerge and persist is also not clear. If economists err in ignoring the effects of institutional setting on individual values, sociologists may err in the opposite direction by not giving the individual more leeway in shaping institutional arrangements.

Sociologists, we suggest, need to recognize that conformity often requires considerable choice. The most "intendedly conformist" individual must confront a steady barrage of choices in social situations. Diverse and conflicting norms are often available. And the guidance provided by "given" norms has been greatly overestimated. Reciprocity, for example, instructs us that social relationships involve a balance of give and take. To someone whose tastes and dispositions are not fully predictable, the questions of what and how much should be given and when, to avoid coming off as a giver or taker, are not a trivial matter. The popularity of advice columns is testimony that social norms do not provide sufficient guidance in specific situations. Conforming poses difficult choices. The ability of individuals to confront these choices stands behind the survival of any norm.

Conversely, economists should recognize that choice-making often entails considerable conformity. The challenge for choice in complex and differentiated social settings may be how and where to fit in. Consider the "choice" of a firm entering or operating in a typical market setting where there are a handful of firms, each making a branded product that has a well-established reputation and a unique price. The intendedly rational firm would like to select a product design, an advertising strategy, distribution channels, a plant location, and a pricing policy that maximize profits. But how is it supposed to go about doing this? Most likely, its "choice" will involve searching for a niche that conforms to the existing "shape" of the market (see White 1981, Leifer 1985a). White (1981) shows how the simultaneous efforts of firms to find their place in a market terms-of-trade schedule can lead to a schedule that is continuously *reproduced* through these efforts. Conformity, in differentiated settings, is a challenging goal for one who must attempt to choose.

Neither conformity nor choice are simple matters in social settings. Instead of being antithetical, they are intertwined. Individuals seek guidance in choice from the experiences and fates of others in what they must deem as comparable situations. Their focus of choice is funneled onto the traces from an operating institution, blending diachronic and synchronic elements (see Granovetter 1985). A choice *between* institutions seems remote where an institution is needed to give shape to choices.

CONCLUSION: WHAT ABOUT EFFICIENCY?

Power relations, goal ambiguity, and the institutional relativism of choice pose serious obstacles for efficiency analysis. They produce settings where efficiency is not well defined. For these settings, we suggest the alternative criteria of reproducibility. This criterion, however, should be detached from the functionalist view of individuals mechanically conforming to norms. Institutional reproduction may depend on the intertwining of diachronic conformity and synchronic choice.

The question becomes, what criteria is driving the central tendencies? In the first section, we looked for efficiency and claimed some successes; in the second section, we looked for obstacles and also claimed some successes. A litmus test is needed to help us avoid finding only what we are looking for. The normative aspect of efficiency provides the basis for a litmus test. We offer it to potential users of economic reasoning.

The following test should be applied at the moment efficiency is discovered. First, ask yourself if your discovery allows you to identify any real world inefficiencies. Inefficiency is, after all, as much a part of the efficiency driven world as efficiency, whether one attributes efficiency to a "designer" or to evolution. Designers must be allowed to make mistakes, while nature must have variety to select from. There is no point to efficiency analysis if it does not aid in the discovery of inefficiency. The lifetime Dr. Pangloss spent in discovering this was the best of all possible worlds hardly needs repeating.

Inefficiency, of course, will have multiple interpretations. An incorrect identification of goals, and hence what are viewed as costs and benefits, may lead to the mistaken appearance of inefficiency. The user of economic reasoning will have varying degrees of confidence in the "givens" he or she used to discover efficiency. Hence the second component of the litmus test is to test your identification out on institutional participants. *Participants should welcome an improvement in efficiency.* If you meet with strong resistance, there is something wrong with your analysis. It could be that a hidden goal (or function) was excluded, and its inclusion would lead to acceptable efficiency recommendations.

Unfortunately, in the process of (*a*) finding inefficiency and (*b*) convincing participants, there is no discrete point at which we can say efficiency analysis is inapplicable. The litmus test is subjective: Are you confident about the prospects of clearly recognizing inefficiency and convincing participants to alter their inefficient ways? When confidence flags, the framework in which efficiency is defined should be questioned.

The reason for this litmus test is that *economic reasoning can be misused.* The flexibility which has allowed its extensions into sociological terrain also has allowed for its misuse. March & Olsen (1983) found "efficiency" was invoked to support competing proposals within organizational politics. Over the course of antitrust history, "efficiency" arguments have been used both to restrain mergers and to defend them (Armentano 1982, Brozen 1982). Efficiency can be imposed by manipulating the specification of transaction costs in ways remote from the transactors' perceptions. The test hinders these ex post exercises by insisting that, if efficiency is a salient ideal, some institutions should fall short of them, and few should resist being brought closer to the ideal.

There is some irony in the fact that economics is a normative science, yet in practice often ignores the individual it purports to help. Choice models are used for predicting aggregate tendencies, where individuals are treated only "as if" they made a rational choice. The new institutional economics acknowledges constraints to rational choice, yet still encourages us to view institutions "as if" they were designed by an efficiency expert (Williamson 1984). It is unlikely that sociologists will ignore the concerns of flesh and blood human beings to the degree that economists sometimes have. The final test of efficiency's applicability to institutional analysis hinges on the grassroots support it generates. This support will come only if efficiency analysis helps us understand and improve social institutions, rather than merely rationalize them.

ACKNOWLEDGMENTS

The authors benefitted from the comments of Howard Aldrich and Francois Neilson.

Literature Cited

Akerlof, G. 1970. The market for lemons: Quality uncertainty and the market mechanism. *Q. J. Econ.* 84:488–500

Armentano, D. T. 1982. *Antitrust and Monopoly: Anatomy of a Policy Failure.* New York: Wiley

Arrow, K., Hahn, F. 1971. *General Competitive Analysis.* San Francisco: Holden-Day

Axelrod, R. 1984. *The Evolution of Cooperation.* New York: Basic

Barry, B. 1970. *Sociologists, Economists and Democracy.* London: Collier-MacMillan

Becker, G. S. 1976. *The Economic Approach to Human Behavior.* Chicago: Univ. Chicago Press

Becker, G. S. 1981. *A Treatise on the Family.* Cambridge: Harvard Univ. Press

Becker, G. S., Landes, E. M., Michael, R. T. 1977. An economic analysis of marital instability. *J. Polit. Econ.* 85:1141–87

Ben-Porath, Y. 1980. The F-connection: Families, friends, and firms and the organization of exchange. *Pop. Dev. Rev.* 6:1–29

Ben-Porath, Y. 1982. Economics and the family—match or mismatch? a review of Becker's "Treatise on the Family." *J. Econ. Lit.* 20:56–62

Berk, R. A., Berk, S. F. 1983. Supply-side sociology of the family: The challenge of the new home economics. *Ann. Rev. Sociol.* 9:375–95

Brozen, Y. 1982. *Mergers in Perspective.* Washington: Am. Enterprise Inst.

Buchanan, J. 1965 An economic theory of clubs. *Economics* 32:1–13

Coase, R. H. 1937. The nature of the firm. *Econometrica* 4:386–405

Cohen, M., Axelrod, R. 1982. Coping with complexity: The adaptive value of changing utility. Inst. Public Policy Stud., Univ. Mich.

Commons, J. R. 1934. *Institutional Economics.* New York: MacMillan

DeAlessi, L. 1980. The economics of property rights: A review of the evidence. *Res. Law Econ.* 2:1–47

Demsetz, H. 1967. Toward a theory of property rights. *Am. Econ. Rev.* 57:347–59

Duesenberry, J. 1960. Comments on 'An economic analysis of fertility', by Gary S. Becker. In *Demography and Economic Change in Developed Countries.* Princeton: Universities Natl. Bur. Conf. Ser., II, pp. 231–40

Eccles, R. 1985. *The Transfer Pricing Problem: A Theory for Practice.* Lexington, Mass: Lexington

Francis, A., Turk, J., Willman, P. 1983. *Power, Efficiency and Institutions: A Critical Appraisal of the 'Markets and Hierarchies' Paradigm.* London: Heinemann

Granovetter, M. 1983. *Labor mobility, internal markets and job-matching: A comparison of the sociological and economic approaches.* Dep. Sociol., State Univ. NY, Stony Brook. Mimeo

Granovetter, M. 1985. Economic action and social structure: A theory of imbeddedness. *Am. J. Sociol.* 91(3):481–510

Hamilton, G. G., Biggart, N. W. 1985. Market, culture, and authority: A comparative analysis of management and organization in the Pacific Basin. Work. Pap. 85-04. Univ. Calif., Davis

Hannan, M. T. 1982. Families, markets, and social structures: An essay on Becker's "A Treatise on the Family." *J. Econ. Lit.* 20:65–72

Hardin, G. 1968. The tragedy of the commons. *Science* 62:1243–48

Hechter, M., ed. 1983. *The Microfoundations of Macrosociology.* Philadelphia: Temple Univ. Press

Hirschleifer, J. 1977. Economics from a biological viewpoint. *J. Law Econ.* 20:1–52

Hirschleifer, J. 1985. The expanding domain of economics. *Am. Econ. Rev.* 75:53–68

Hirschman, A. O. 1970. *Exit, Voice and Loyalty.* Cambridge: Harvard Univ. Press

Hirschman, A. O. 1979. *Shifting Involvements: Private Interest and Public Action.* Princeton, NJ: Princeton Univ. Press

Leibenstein, H. 1979. The missing link—micro-micro theory. *J. Econ. Lit.* 17:493–96

Leifer, E. M. 1985a. Markets as mechanisms: Using a role structure. *Soc. Forc.* 64:442–72

Leifer, E. M. 1986. *Equality through involvement and ambiguity.* Unpublished. Dept. Sociol. Univ. NC, Chapel Hill

Leifer, E. M., White, H. 1986. A structural approach to markets. In *Structural Analysis of Business,* ed. M. Mizruchi, M. Schwartz. Cambridge: Cambridge Univ. Press Forthcoming

Lindenberg, S. 1982. Sharing groups: Theory and suggested applications. *J. Math. Sociol.* 9:33–62

MacRae, D. 1983. Review essay: The Sociological economics of Gary S. Becker. *Am. J. Sociol.* 83(5):1244–58

March, J. G., Olsen, J. P. 1976. *Ambiguity and Choice in Organizations.* Bergen, Norway: Universitetsforlaget

March, J. G., Olsen, J. P. 1983. Organizing political life: What administrative reorganization tells us about government. *Am. Polit. Sci. Rev.* 77:281–96

Merton, R. 1968. *Social Theory and Social Structure*. New York: Free Press

Nelson, R. R., Winters, S. A. 1982. *An Evolutionary Theory of Economic Change*. Cambridge: Harvard Univ. Press

Oberschall, A. 1973. *Social Conflict and Social Movements*. Englewood Cliffs, NJ: Prentice-Hall

Oberschall, A. 1985. *The California Gold Rush*. Presented at Meet. Am. Sociol. Assoc., Washington, DC

Oliver, P. 1980. Rewards and punishments as selective incentives for collective action: Theoretical investigations. *Am. J. Sociol.* 85:1356–75

Olson, M. 1965. *The Logic of Collective Action*. Cambridge: Harvard Univ. Press

Opp, K. 1983. *Die Entstehung sozialer Normen*. Tubingen: Mohr

Ouchi, W. G. 1980. Markets, bureaucracies and clans. *Admin. Sci. Q.* 25:129–40

Palay, T. M. 1983. *Comparative institutional economics: The governance of rail freight contracting*. Law School, Univ. Wisc., Madison. Unpublished paper.

Perrow, C. 1985. *Complex Organizations: A Critical Essay*. New York: Random House. 3rd ed.

Polanyi, K. 1944. *The Great Transformation*. Boston: Beacon

Pollack, R. A. 1985. A transaction cost approach to families and households. *J. Econ. Lit.* 23:581–608

Popkin, S. 1981. Public choice and rural development—free riders, lemons, and institutional design." In *Public Choice and Rural Development*, ed. C. Russell, N. Nicholson. Washington, DC: Resources for the Future, Inc.

Sawhill, I. V. 1977. Economic perspectives on the family. In *The Family,* ed. A. Rossi et al. New York: Norton

Scanzoni, J. 1981. *Sexual Bargaining: Power Politics in the American Marriage*. Chicago: Univ. Chicago Press

Schelling, T. 1963. *The Strategy of Conflict*. New York: Oxford Univ. Press

Umbeck, J. 1977. Theory of contract choice and the California Gold Rush. *J. Law Econ.* 20:421–36

Umbeck, J. 1981. *A Theory of Property Rights*. Ames, Iowa: Iowa Univ. Press

Weick, K. 1979. *The Social Psychology of Organizing*. Reading, Mass: Addison-Wesley

White, H. C. 1981. Where Do Markets Come From? *Am. J. Sociol.* 87:517–47

Williamson, O. E. 1975. *Markets and Hierarchies: Analysis and Antitrust Implications*. New York: Free Press

Williamson, O. E. 1981. The economics of organization: The transaction cost approach. *Am. J. Sociol.* 87:548–77

Williamson, O. E. 1984. The economics of governance: Framework and implications, *J. Inst. Theoret. Econ.* 140:195–223

Wilson, M. 1963. Effects on the Xhosa and Nyakyusa of scarcity in land. In *African Agrarian Systems,* ed. D. Biebuyck. London: Oxford Univ. Press

Wolf, E. 1966. Kinship, friendship, and patron-client relations in complex societies. in *The Social Anthropology of Complex Societies,* ed. M. Banton. New York: Praeger

Wrong, D. 1961. The oversocialized conception of man in modern sociology. *Am. Sociol. Rev.* 26:184–93

Ann. Rev. Sociol. 1986. 12:255–75

GENDER DIFFERENCES IN ROLE DIFFERENTIATION AND ORGANIZATIONAL TASK PERFORMANCE

Henry A. Walker

Department of Sociology, Stanford University, Stanford, California 94305

Mary L. Fennell

Department of Sociology, University of Illinois at Chicago, Box 4348, Chicago, Illinois 60680

Abstract

The review begins with a discussion of research on both gender differences in behavior and role differentiation. Next, the article examines predictions made by four theoretical perspectives (functional, sex-role, status-effects, and legitimation theories) which have been brought to bear on the issue of gender differences in role differentiation. The findings of small-group, organizational, and labor market studies are reviewed in the next section. The review concludes with a summary of the empirical findings and suggestions for further theoretical work.

INTRODUCTION

We review recent theory and research on gender differences in role differentiation and in organizational task performance. We discuss these issues together for two reasons: First, much of the literature on gender differences assumes that there are typical "female" and "male" behaviors. The broad spectrum of behaviors assumed to vary with gender includes the organization of functional

255

0360-0572/86/0815-0255$02.00

roles in all-male and all-female groups (cf Marrett 1972, Giele 1978). Second, functional role differentiation is assumed to have important effects on task performance. One of the classic sociological arguments suggests that role differentiation permits more efficient expenditures of collective resources and more effective attainment of collective goals (Durkheim 1964).

Much of the work on gender differences in role differentiation has focused on either individual or small group behavior (Lipman-Blumen & Tickamyer 1975, Miller & Garrison 1982). However, significant changes in women's participation in the paid labor force have made it increasingly important to understand the nature of gender differences in work organizations. The modern work force is highly segregated by gender (Baron & Bielby 1980, 1982; Bridges 1982); males and females enter different industries and occupations and generally perform different tasks within broad occupational categories. Considerable evidence also suggests that gender-based divisions of labor and reward allocations are commonplace within firms (Kanter 1977, Stewart & Gudykunst 1982, Baron 1984). Hence, this review includes research on role differentiation and task performance in organizations and labor markets, as well as in small-groups.

The review begins with an overview of research on gender differences in role differentiation and the theoretical explanations that have been brought to bear on the issue. The next section of the article summarizes recent empirical findings. It includes research on gender differences in role differentiation, role assignment, and task performance. The review concludes with suggestions for further empirical and theoretical work.

GENDER AND ROLE DIFFERENTIATION

The study of gender differences in role differentiation combines research on role differentiation with studies of gender differences in behavior. The two research programs have developed independently, and there are important differences in their central concepts, research procedures, and explanatory schemas. Indeed, the relevant empirical phenomena occur at different levels of analysis.

Role differentiation is a characteristic of groups and may take either of two general forms: A group is differentiated along strictly *functional* lines when its members perform different roles and the roles are not differentiated on the basis of status or on the basis of their contributions to the collective process, e.g. as measured by overall rates of participation or influence on decisions. *Hierarchical* differentiation exists when the roles that group members occupy receive different status evaluations and have varying amounts of influence on collective outcomes or on the actions of other group members. Groups exhibit varying degrees of both functional and hierarchical differentiation.

It is generally believed that there are extensive gender differences in social behavior. The evidence for a systematic relation between gender and social behavior is sketchy (Maccoby & Jacklin 1974) and is more often anecdotal or ideological than rigorously scientific. Research on gender differences typically explores the extent to which individual males and females, or homogeneous groups of males and females, exhibit similar or different behavioral tendencies.

Investigations of gender differences in role differentiation have borrowed from both group-level and individual research. First, group-level studies have been expanded to include gender composition as a factor in the emergence of patterns of role differentiation. Two issues are of fundamental importance: (a) Is role differentiation equally likely to emerge in all-male as in all-female groups? (b) Given the emergence of role differentiation, are the patterns of role differentiation in homogeneous groups of males and females similar, e.g. do they share similar forms of functional and/or hierarchical differentiation?

Similarly, researchers who are concerned with gender differences in individual behavior have investigated (a) the importance of gender as a criterion for role assignment in mixed-gender groups, (b) the question, whether role performance varies with the gender of role occupants and, (c) the question, whether the gender of role occupants influences the responses of others to their actions.

THEORETICAL EXPLANATIONS

Two general types of theories have been proposed as explanations of gender differences in role differentiation, and they parallel the empirical emphases noted above. First, theories of role differentiation have been extended to the problem of gender differences in role assignment, and second, theories of gender differences have been applied to the study of role differentiation. We discuss two traditional approaches (functional and sex-role theories), and two more recent formulations (status-effects and legitimation theories.

Traditional Formulations

FUNCTIONAL THEORY   The theory of functional role differentiation (Bales 1953, Bales & Slater 1955) has been used to explain role differentiation in families (Zelditch 1955) and organizations (Etzioni 1965), as well as in small task groups. The theory implies a direct relationship between role differentiation and collective task performance: Functional role differentiation is assumed to emerge as a response to incompatible task contingencies, e.g. the need to solve collective problems and the need to maintain group cohesion. When such incompatibilities arise, groups are assumed to develop separation of functions in order to facilitate the resolution of each problem. Hierarchical role differentiation is explained as a result of differences in the survival value of role behaviors and of the skills required to perform them (cf Davis & Moore 1945). Hierarchical role differentiation is expected when social roles have differential importance for the survival of the group and/or there are differences in the skills or training required to perform them.

Functional theories generally assume that the process of differentiation is similar across groups (Davis & Moore 1945, Parsons 1964). Competence is assumed to be the principal criterion for assignment of actors to particular roles. However, Parsons (1964) has argued that *qualities* (like race or gender) are often linked to competence by the expectations for performance held by group members. As a result, gender can become an important criterion for role assignment through its association with perceptions of competence, even if there is no demonstrable association between gender and either past per-formances or the skills necessary for successful performance. Hence, although functional theories imply an absence of gender differences in the likelihood of role differentiation in all-male and all-female groups, they predict gender differences in role assignment in mixed-gender groups. Expectation states theory (Berger et al 1974) offers a more formal—but entirely consistent—explanation for the emergence of functional and hierarchical differentiation in initially undifferentiated groups.

Sex-role theories   Sex-role socialization theories are among the oldest expla-nations for gender differences in role assignment, and a number of explanations are subsumed under that rubric. They include arguments with strong biological or physiological components (Freud 1933, Horney 1967), as well as more social and psychological formulations (Bandura & Walters 1963, Kohlberg 1966, Mischel 1966). The principal argument of sex-role theories is that gender-appropriate behaviors are acquired through social learning. Individuals internalize the role-appropriate behaviors and enact them. Behavioral tenden-cies acquired in this manner are assumed to be highly resistant to change and not situationally specific, although there is disagreement on the latter issue (cf Duncan & Duncan 1978). Sex-role theories imply that patterns of role differen-tiation in all-female groups will be different than those in all-male groups and that gender differences in role assignment will occur in mixed-gender groups.

Recent Advances

STATUS-EFFECTS THEORIES   Status-effects theories (Berger et al 1977, Kan-ter 1977, Ridgeway 1978) have been applied to the problem of gender differ-ences in role assignment with increasing frequency over the past decade. The most highly-developed and thoroughly tested of such arguments, that of Berger et al, suggests that group members use status information to create performance expectations for themselves and other group members. In turn, differences in expectations for performance determine the nature of actual performances. Berger et al (1980) argue that gender is a status characteristic and demonstrate that gender organizes interaction in the manner suggested by the theory.

Similarly, Kanter (1976, 1977) argues that the structure of a group (e.g. the proportion of low- and high-status members) or of society has important implications for the behavior of females and males. Women (and other minorities) are perceived as tokens in settings in which they comprise less than 35% of the population (skewed groups). Token status evokes three responses that can be detrimental to the performances of tokens—heightened visibility, increased isolation, and role entrapment (the attribution of stereotypical roles to tokens). As skewness is reduced (minorities become more numerous), detrimental responses are assumed to decline. Kanter's arguments are intuitively appealing, but attempts to validate them empirically have been either methodologically problematic [cf Spangler et al (1978) and comments by Kuzloski (1979) and by Walker (1980), as well as the reply by Pipkin et al (1980)] or nonsupportive (Finigan 1982, Scott et al 1982, Izraeli 1983).

Status-effects theories predict gender differences in role assignment in mixed-gender settings, with males assigned to and accepting the more important (higher status) roles. In addition, the theory implies differences in the responses which others make to male and female occupants of similar roles. But since differences in gender-status are assumed to be the principal source of gender differences in behavior, comparisons of homogeneous groups of males and females should indicate similar patterns of functional and hierarchical role differentiation.

LEGITIMATION THEORIES   Recently, several investigators have suggested that gender differences in role assignment are due to the effects of variations in legitimacy (Eskilson & Wiley 1976, Meeker & Weitzel-O'Neill 1977). The relationship of legitimacy to role differentiation was initially specified by Verba (1961) who argued that the likelihood of role differentiation increased as the legitimacy of task activity and of persons engaged in task leadership decreased.

Fennell et al (1978, and McMahon et al 1976) argue that the legitimacy of task activity is gender-specific: Instrumental and other "leadership" behaviors are legitimate for males (but not for females), while expressive actions are legitimate for females. The theory assumes that group members will behave legitimately. Hence, gender differences in role assignment are expected in heterogeneous groups, with females occupying the less-valued, less influential, expressive roles. The theory also leads to predictions of gender differences in role differentiation in homogeneous groups. Because instrumental behavior is legitimate for males but illegitimate for females, members of all-male groups are expected to exhibit high levels of task activity, intense competition for task leadership, and relatively low levels of expressive behavior. That pattern of interaction is assumed to result in both functional and hierarchical differentiation.

On the other hand, groups of females (for whom instrumental behavior is illegitimate) are expected to exhibit lower levels of task activity but higher levels of expressive behavior. That pattern should result less often in either functional or hierarchical differentiation in all-female task groups. The differences in patterns of role differentiation should also be associated with differences in task performance, with the less differentiated, all-female groups exhibiting lower levels of task performance than all-male groups.

ROLE DIFFERENTIATION: EMPIRICAL FINDINGS

Small Group Research

INSTRUMENTAL AND EXPRESSIVE DIFFERENTIATION   Instrumental and expressive actions are the categories of behavior most often examined in studies of role differentiation. The functional theory of differentiation implies that all-female and all-male groups are equally likely to develop functional and hierarchical differentiation. In contrast, sex-role and legitimation theories predict gender differences in the likelihood of both functional and hierarchical role differentiation. Status-effects theories do not offer predictions on role differentiation in homogeneous groups, but the general argument implies an absence of differences.

Sex-role, status-effects and legitimation theories all predict gender differences in role assignment in mixed-gender groups. Each theory suggests that males are more likely to be assigned (and to accept) instrumental roles and that females are more likely to occupy expressive roles. However, variations in perceptions of competence and in the gender-specific legitimacy of actions condition the predictions of status-effects and legitimation arguments. Competence is also assumed to be the primary criterion for role assignment in the functional theories of differentiation. But gender is assumed to be an important secondary criterion for role assignment (Parsons 1964). Hence, functionalist arguments suggest gender differences in role assignment in groups that exhibit functional or hierarchical role differentiation.[1]

[1]The predictions of legitimation arguments and sex-role socialization theories are very similar on first inspection. There are important differences in the underlying mechanisms which point to fundamental differences in the implications of the two arguments. Theories of sex-role socialization generally ignore situational differences, and variants of the argument which do suggest that sex-role behavior is situationally specific do not generally specify the conditions under which such behavior is expected. Legitimation arguments assume that the relation of gender to patterns of role differentiation varies with situationally specific definitions of legitimacy. That is, groups may exhibit traditional gender differences, no gender differences, or nontraditional gender differences, e.g. task-oriented females and expressive males. Furthermore, to the extent that collective definitions of legitimacy influence individual actions (cf Zelditch & Walker 1984), the role behavior of males and females is expected to vary with the gender composition of groups, as Kanter has argued. Sex-role theories do not generally imply effects of gender composition on role behavior.

Bass (1967) concluded, after an extensive review of studies, that males are more task oriented than females (who are generally more interaction oriented). However, orientation varies with other status variables (e.g. occupation and age) and is not always consistent with behavior. The pattern of role assignment in mixed-gender groups is unambiguous and consistent with Bass's conclusions on orientation: Females more often engage in expressive actions than males, who are more likely to behave instrumentally (the extensiveness of this pattern is documented in Lockheed & Hall 1976, Meeker & Weitzel-O'Neill 1977, Fennell et al 1978, Berger et al 1980).

There are few systematic findings of gender differences in the patterns of role differentiation exhibited by homogeneous groups. Eskilson & Wiley (1976) found no evidence of gender differences in rates of participation. Similar findings are reported by Thompson (1981), and Lamb (1981) reports no gender differences in initial speaking order or time consumed while speaking in same-sex triads.

Several investigations have examined differentiation of participation or functional differentiation. Gray & Mayhew (1972) examined differentiation of participation in all-male and all-female groups and found no gender differences. Yamada et al (1983) report no gender differences in participation patterns among all-male and all-female groups in a study of cooperation and interaction styles. Feldman (1973) concluded that power (an instrumental behavior) was more evenly distributed among groups of girls at a summer camp than among similar groups of boys. However, the differences were not significant, and there was no evidence of gender differences in functional role differentiation.

Piliavin & Martin (1978) studied homogeneous and mixed-gender groups and found gender differences between all-female and all-male groups in rates and types of role activity. Females and males were more likely to engage in task than socioemotional activities in all groups. The distribution of task and socioemotional acts in homogeneous groups was consistent with predictions based on sex-role and legitimation theories: All-male groups had higher levels of task activity than did all-female groups. These differences remain when data from mixed-gender groups are analyzed. However, females in mixed-gender groups had higher levels of task acts than did females in homogeneous groups. There were no statistically significant differences in the behaviors of males in mixed and homogeneous groups. This last finding is inconsistent with sex-role theories but is consistent with legitimation theory, if it is assumed that mixed-gender groups are male domains and if expectations for task performances are higher in "male" than in "female" groups.

Finally, Wentworth & Anderson (1984) studied emergent leadership in mixed-gender groups and found that the relationship between leadership and gender varied with sex-typing of the task. Male emergent leaders were more numerous than female leaders when groups worked at a "male" task. More of the emergent leaders were female than male when groups worked at "neutral" or "female tasks, but the differences were not statistically significant.

Recent work on perceptions and expectations about the behavior of females in leader or supervisory roles appears to contradict Bass's general conclusion. Sussman et al (1980) simulated role-playing in an organizational setting, varying sex composition and the gender of the person in the supervisory role. Both male and female subjects were more likely to believe that socially facilitative strategies (agreeing, supporting, releasing tension) were important to their chances for advancement when their supervisor was female rather than male, but this result was not statistically significant. However, female subjects were significantly more likely than male subjects to feel that *task* facilitative strategies (asking for opinions or suggestions, seeking and providing information) were most important.

Work by Deutsch & Leong (1983) shows that the validity of assumptions about gender differences in the occupation of stereotypic instrumental/ expressive roles is more problematic when perceptions of competence are considered. In general, male subjects were less satisfied with their performances when they interacted with a highly competent, rather than less competent, coworker. They were also more likely to evaluate their experience as interesting (regardless of the coworker's gender). However, subjects responded more favorably to competent females than to equally competent males when they were required to work in a *cooperative* (rather than competitive) manner. The authors invoked sex-role stereotypes regarding competitive/ supportive behavior to explain this result. Finally, Thompson (1981) analyzed the behavior of two subordinates and one leader working on a collective task. Males and females did not differ in participation rates, but females were more supportive of other subordinates.

DOMINANCE AND INFLUENCE   Leaders are clearly important to the smooth functioning of group life. The empirical evidence on gender differences in the assumption of leadership roles, the behavior of persons in leadership roles, and the responses of subordinates to leaders is contradictory. Lamb (1981) found no gender differences in patterns of dominance as measured by eye-gaze. Eskilson & Wiley's (1976) study of leadership in three-person groups reports no gender differences in performance outputs among leaders.

A number of studies indicate that females are more compliant than males (Endler et al 1973, Geller et al 1973, Endler et al 1975, Adams & Landers 1978). Those findings are countered by studies that fail to find gender differences in compliance (Newton & Schulman 1977, Son & Schmitt 1983, Morelock 1980, Klopfer & Moran 1978). Similarly, Kollock et al (1985), using data on interaction among couples (both single and mixed-gender), found that dominance in conversation is primarily linked to power within the relationship, regardless of the gender of the actor.

There are also no systematic gender differences in patterns of cooperation. Meeker (1977) found that gender differences in cooperative responses varied with the nature of payoffs and members' responsibility (whether equal and alternating or shared) in a study of same-sex dyads. There were no gender differences in behavior when partners were conditioned on equal payoffs and shared responsibility, but females were more cooperative than males when payoffs were unequal and the partners had equal but alternating (by trial) responsibility. Several other studies report no gender differences in cooperative behavior (Wiley 1973, Yamada et al 1983). Ridgeway's (1981, 1982) work on perceived motivation toward the group and ability to exert influence in the group is particularly interesting. She found that females expect more cooperation from other females than from males. Further, females tend to question the legitimacy of anyone attempting to seize the initiative in all-female groups. Yamada et al (1983) studied cooperation in dyads and found that males anticipated less cooperation from their partners than did females. Furthermore, male (but not female) expectancies varied with the partner's gender: Less cooperation was expected of male than of female partners.

Each of the theories considered above predicts gender differences in role assignment in mixed-gender groups and, in general, findings from studies of small groups are supportive. However, situational variation in behavior (e.g. as in Piliavin & Martin 1978, Kollock et al 1985) favors a legitimation interpretation. Comparisons of all-female and all-male groups indicate few differences in the distribution of participation among group members, in patterns of role differentiation, or in the behavior of female and male occupants of particular roles. Some studies of dominance and influence suggest that females are more compliant than males, but dominance appears to vary more with differences in power or competence than with differences in gender. The findings are generally supportive of functional and status-effects arguments.

Organizational Research

We review organizational research on gender-based role differentiation in this section. A more general review of the organizational bases of inequality and stratification has been conducted by Baron (1984). We concentrate on three major questions: (a) Are there gender differences in assignment or promotion to positions and especially to leadership or supervisory roles in organizations? (b) Is there differential hiring of men and women by certain types of firms or for certain types of jobs across organizations? And finally, (c) Are there distinctive features of women's organizations, e.g. voluntary associations, trade unions, or trade associations? In general, there is much more research on the first of these three questions, and much of it is experimental.

GENDER-BASED ROLE DIFFERENTIATION WITHIN FIRMS   Role differentiation within firms can take the form either of hierarchical differentiation (assignment or promotion to positions of authority) or of functional differentiation (assignment to particular types of jobs or tasks). Wolf & Fligstein (1979) used survey data to investigate hierarchical differentiation, and they reported clear gender-based differences in promotion: Women do not move into supervisory positions at the same rate as men. They explained these results in terms of employer practices and human capital theory, i.e. women fail to advance due to decrements in qualifications. Those conclusions were questioned by Bridges & Miller (1981; see also the reply by Fligstein et al 1981), who suggested that work experience and tenure have a greater effect for men than for women, and that women are severely handicapped by childcare demands. However, the basic finding that males are more likely to gain promotion than females was confirmed with a larger, more nationally representative sample.

Using experimental data, Stewart & Gudykunst (1982) also report gender differences in promotions: When age, education, and tenure are controlled, women receive more promotions than men, but they occupy significantly lower positions in the organizational hierarchy. Taylor & Ilgen (1981) report gender differences in assignment in functionally differentiated groups. Female employees are more likely to be rated as suitable for low challenge tasks than equally qualified males. However, assignment to dull or challenging tasks may be affected by the gender of the task allocator: Mai-Dalton & Sullivan (1981) report that both women and men express same-sex preferences when assigning personnel to challenging tasks.

Although evidence seems to affirm that role assignment is based on gender, it is not clear that there are differences in the extent to which males and females possess "leadership characteristics" or exhibit different strategies or styles of leadership. Brown (1979) reviewed research on sex differences in leadership and concluded that the results depend on the nature of the study: Studies which examine traits, e.g. dominance or passivity, or utilize responses of students, generally support the view that women lack the leadership characteristics possessed by males. On the other hand, studies which focus on styles of leadership, e.g. autocratic or democratic, are about evenly split on the issue of gender differences. But studies which report actual managers' perceptions of other managers generally fail to support the argument that there are gender differences in the possession of leadership skills.

Two recent studies indicate that men and women in comparable positions of authority use similar strategies or styles of leadership. Instone et al (1983) suggest that women and men supervise similarly when they have equal access to power resources. Furthermore, Bruning & Snyder (1983) report no evidence of pervasive sex differences in their survey data on leadership behavior or organizational commitment.

Lastly, do subordinates react differently to men and to women with comparable leadership styles in positions of authority? One organizational simulation and two survey studies report no differences in the manner in which subordinates react to female and male managers. Arnett et al (1980) found no significant differences in subordinate "liking" scores or responsiveness to male and female managers. Terborg & Shingledecker (1983) collected attitudinal data from 463 employees of a Fortune 500 firm on subordinate assessments of general supervision, understanding of their performance evaluation processes, self-ratings of performance, and fairness of supervision. The only significant differences were found on "evaluation understanding." Male subordinates working for male managers were least likely to understand how their performances were evaluated. Finally, Petty & Bruning (1980) investigated subordinate job satisfaction and perceptions of supervisory behavior. They found comparable correlations between subordinate job satisfaction and perception of a "considerate" leadership style whether the supervisor was male or female.

GENDER-BASED HIRING   Szafran (1982) conducted an extensive review of research on the effects of both global and conceptual organizational characteristics on hiring of women and blacks. Several organizational variables were found to be positively associated with female participation. They include formalization, proportion of secondary occupations within the firm (e.g. clerical or service workers), and community support for equal opportunity. He concludes that not all types of firms are equally likely to hire women. Similarly, equally qualified men and women are not equally likely to be hired for certain types of jobs. Gerdes & Garber (1983) report that female applicants with competence comparable to male applicants were rated less suitable for technical-managerial jobs. Further, higher competence did not mitigate discrimination against women for technical-managerial positions. Firth (1982) reports similar findings from a study of the job market for accountants. Finally, Levinson (1975) examined the responses of prospective employers to telephone inquiries concerning position openings. Of all sex-inappropriate inquiries, 35% were met with unambiguous gender discrimination. Interestingly, male callers experienced higher rates of discrimination than female callers.

WOMEN'S ORGANIZATIONS   Research on role differentiation in women's organizations is sketchy and is often only indirectly related to the issue of distinctive organizational features. Giele (1978:337) suggests that implementation of a feminist vision of social organization (which she infers from feminist critiques of organized religion) would result in organizations structured "in terms of networks rather than hierarchies" (Bentley & Randall 1974). Neal (1976) uses a 'circle' image rather than a 'pyramid' to suggest the model of social organization that would prevail in the future." (See French, 1985, who argues that the "female," i.e. nonhierarchical, pattern of organization is histor- ically antecedent to the hierarchical pattern commonly observed in contempo- rary societies and institutions.) Others have argued that women's organizations should be more highly centralized, but actual empirical analyses of such female structures are hard to find (cf review by Marrett 1972).

McPherson & Smith-Lovin (1982) examined the types and sizes of voluntary organizations to which men and women belong. They found that men tend to belong to much larger organizations than women and that men are more likely to hold memberships in business-related, labor, and veterans' organizations. Women tend to join social, church, or community groups. Although interest- ing, this analysis does not shed light on the structural features of women's (or men's) voluntary associations.

Social histories of women's trade unions and trade associations are in- creasingly available and more detailed (cf Foner 1980). Similarly, several descriptions of women's political organizations exist, many in the form of case histories of organizations in the women's movement, such as Daniels' (1979) description of the Women's Equity Action League, Clusen's (1979) account of the League of Women Voters, Seifer & Wertheimer's (1979) comparison of four working women's organizations, and Feit's (1979) history of the National Women's Political Caucus. These rich case histories could perhaps serve as a basis for analyses of the distinctive structural features of women's organiza- tions.

A particularly interesting case is described in Mansbridge's (1983) analysis of "decision by accretion" (Weiss 1980) by the pro-ERA forces prior to the defeat of the Equal Rights Amendment. Decision by accretion refers to a fairly common form of organizational decision-making: Decisions are made passive- ly, almost through default, rather than through any active, rational decision- making process. The pattern is reminiscent of Cohen et al's (1972) garbage can model of organizational choice. It seems important to develop and test hypoth- eses concerning the extent to which decision-making by accretion is characteristic of women's organizations, and whether it is associated with organizational failure or less than satisfactory performance.

Findings on gender differences in role assignment in work organizations generally indicate that females and males are assigned to different classes of organizations and that they hold different types of positions within organiza- tions. The evidence appears to suggest that differential assignment is due in large part to gender-typing of work activities. These findings are consistent with predictions of functional, status-effects, sex-role, and legitimation theo- ries. However, the general finding that leaders do not differentially attribute leadership characteristics to women and men is not explained by any of the arguments. Similarly, the general failure to find differences in responses to male and female leaders is more consistent with functional and legitimation arguments than with either sex-role or status-effects theories. Finally, although there is relatively little evidence on the issue, the apparent absence of gender differences in the organization of women's and men's organizations is consistent with functional and status-effects arguments.

Role Differentiation in Labor Markets

There is an extensive literature on gender stratification within industries or sectoral labor markets (Gross 1968, England 1981, Bridges 1982). We do not attempt to review that literature here, but we are interested in the extent to which gender stratification in labor markets can be used as evidence for any of the theories of role differentiation reviewed earlier. Specifically, is role differentiation at the market level the result of sex role socialization, or is it tied to more structural processes of control (legitimation) or situational status norms?

Sex-role socialization theories would explain gender stratification in markets as the result of gender-typed occupational choices: Women and men are assumed to sort themselves into jobs that best reflect their differential tendencies to assume expressive or instrumental roles. Women in nontraditional jobs are defined as anomalies and are expected to have poorer performances than men, and different work values and attitudes. However, Gomez-Mejia (1983) used survey data from a national sample of employees to show that the work-related attitudes of men and women with similar occupational experiences tend to converge over time. Furthermore, women in nontraditional fields tend to view men and women as equally competent to enter nontraditional fields (Tawil & Costello 1983).

The assumptions underlying sex-role socialization theories are consistent with the arguments of human capital theory. Human capital theories treat income and job status as rewards for personal investments in education and job experience. Ornstein (1983) points out the inadequacies of human capital models and their failure to explain the unequal earnings of men and women in identical fields with identical "investments," as well as the fact that women receive smaller returns than men for each year of education and experience. Rosenfeld's (1980) study of sex differences in trajectories of career rewards also demonstrates that men tend to receive greater returns in both status and wages than women over their employment careers. Such gender-based differences in reward structures seem to suggest that more is at work than simple self-selection into lower paying jobs, or differential investment in training or job skills (see review by Bielby & Baron 1983).

A number of authors have suggested recently that role differentiation in labor markets (and its translation into gender-based occupational segregation and income differences) can be explained as the result of features of the social structure, e.g. industrial structure (Bridges 1982), or the use of women's labor to establish control over labor processes (Thomas 1982). Bridges (1982) found that market power (the extent to which an industry is able to limit competition) is positively related to sex segregation, but an industry's capitalist organization (massed labor organized around repetitive labor processes) was unrelated to segregation. Borrowing from class-based analyses of the labor process (Braverman 1974, Burawoy 1979, Edwards 1979), Thomas (1982) argues that *management* of migrant farm labor uses family and status distinctions between men and women to create and preserve distinctions between ground crews (labor which is generally skilled and male) and wrap crews (unskilled labor comprised of females and older workers). But Thomas' example is also consistent with the application of status-effects and legitimation theories to labor market processes.

The findings from studies of labor market processes are generally consistent with research on small groups and work organizations. Women and men are sorted into different occupations and receive different reward allocations, even when they have similar attitudes and values concerning work or similar training and skills. The findings are not generally consistent with sex-role explanations, i.e. that these differences are produced by the differential socialization of males and females. However, they are consistent with functional, status-effects, and legitimation arguments.

TASK PERFORMANCE: EMPIRICAL FINDINGS

Small Group Research

A few small group investigations have examined gender differences in task performance, but the findings do not form a systematic pattern. Some studies report differences, others report no differences, and the findings of some investigations are self-contradictory. Rosenthal (1978) reports that female subjects spent more time on math problems than did male subjects. Gray & Mayhew (1972) report that, among homogeneous groups playing a Yahtzee-like game, males complete more games than do females. However, gender differences are reduced significantly when interaction is not highly structured and is permitted to proceed spontaneously.

The findings of Bell et al (1972) are ambiguous: Among groups working at Leavitt's common-symbols task, females made more errors and sent more messages than did males. But the investigators failed to find gender differences in the time required to complete the task. Rosenthal (1978) found no gender differences in the amount of time required on a sentence completion task, and Stitt et al (1983) report no gender differences in time required to produce paper airplanes. Finally, Spoelders-Claes (1973) reports that females and males had equivalent performance times and qualities when they worked at a card-sorting task.

Organizational Research

Examinations of gender differences in task performance have been conducted infrequently at the organizational level and are difficult to summarize. Studies in this area tend to focus most often on evaluations of men and women as leaders or supervisors. As a result, "task performance" is translated as evaluations of the effectiveness of persons in management or leadership roles. The studies can be divided into two categories: (*a*) evaluations of the effectiveness of men and women as leaders and evaluations of different leadership styles, and (*b*) examinations of the existence and extent of performance evaluation bias against women in organizations.

The results of Wiley & Eskilson's (1982) survey of male managers are not straightforward. They varied sex of leader and type of power used (either expert power or reward power) and found no main effects for the type of power used in the leadership role, nor was there any interaction between sex of leader and type of power. A laboratory study by Brown & Geis (1984) varied both sex of leader and legitimacy of leader, considering both legitimacy through authorization and legitimacy through endorsement. They found no pro-male bias in evaluations of leader performance, but they did find significant effects of the presence or absence of both types of legitimation—leaders of either sex were rated more highly if they were either endorsed or authorized.

Stevens & DeNisi (1980) used the Women as Managers Scale to assess sex role stereotypes in attributions of gender to performances of hypothetical managers. The investigators found evidence of bias against women as managers and report that clear descriptions of the success or failure of women had no effect on attitudes toward them as managers. It appears that evaluations are biased by preexisting attitudes and attributions. Tsui & Gutek (1984) conducted a field study of middle managers to investigate the existence of performance evaluation bias against women. Unlike Stevens & Denisi, they found no evidence of pro-male bias. Similarly, Mobley's (1982) investigation of nonmanagement, nonprofessional employees also failed to find pro-male bias in performance evaluations.

In contrast to research on role differentiation and role assignment, there is relatively little research on gender differences in performance. A few studies report that males perform better than females, but those findings are offset by a larger number of studies that report no gender differences in performance. Organizational research has generally focused on performance evaluations rather than actual performances and the majority of studies report no differences in the performance evaluations of males and females. If performance evaluations are taken as an indicator of actual evaluations, the small-group and organizational findings are generally consistent with functional and status-effects arguments. Those arguments suggest an association between role differentiation and task performances. As we report above, there are few differences in patterns of role differentiation in all-female and all-male groups.

SUMMARY AND DISCUSSION

We began this review by suggesting that the study of gender differences in role differentiation is concerned with both individual and group differences. Our findings demonstrate the importance of that distinction. The findings of investigations that examine individual differences, i.e. behavior in mixed-gender groups, are highly systematic. The roles to which males and females are assigned, come to occupy or enact are very different. The general pattern is consistent across small task groups, organizations, and labor markets: The roles males occupy are generally more instrumental, more influential, and more highly rewarded than those that females occupy. Females are more often found in expressive, passive, and cooperative roles. Functional and sex-role theories, as well as status-effects and legitimation theories, predict such differences. But the findings do not provide definitive support for any single theory. Gender, rank, and gender-composition covary in mixed groups, and it is not possible to disaggregate their separate effects on the behavior of individual males and females in most studies of mixed-gender groups.

Studies concerned with group-level differences, i.e. comparisons of all-male and all-female groups, present a somewhat more perplexing puzzle. A number of studies report group level differences, but they are counterbalanced by a large number of investigations which find no differences. The lack of systematic findings makes the task of explaining group-level differences more difficult. However, as we discuss below, commonalities in the findings suggest a basis for future theoretical work.

Toward Theoretical Synthesis

Competence appears to play an important role in much of the work reviewed here. The findings of several investigations are directly influenced or mediated by variations in competence, and variations in competence are implied by other findings (e.g. Piliavin & Martin 1978, Wentworth & Anderson 1984). It is relatively clear that gender-based competence evaluations vary with the nature of the task, i.e. whether the task is perceived to be "female" or "male."

Finally, competence (or perceptions of competence) plays an important role in the theoretical formulations we have reviewed. Functional theories of role differentiation (Davis & Moore 1945, Parsons 1964) and status-effects theories (Berger et al 1980, Ridgeway 1981) point to the importance of competence as a basis for role assignment. Status-effects theories (Berger et al 1974) also suggest that perceptions and evaluations of differences in competence are important conditions for role differentiation regardless of actual differences.

Theories of sex-role socialization imply that males and females will possess different levels of competence for a variety of tasks. In addition, task characteristics are assumed to play a role in the creation or activation of competence evaluations in status-effects, legitimation, and some versions of sex-role theories.

The extension of legitimation theory to the problem of gender differences in role differentiation is one of the most promising developments of the last decade. The formulation uses key concepts and assumptions from several of the other theories discussed in this review. First, the argument is situational: Theories of legitimation presume that the likelihood of an action's occurrence varies with its legitimacy. In turn, the legitimacy of an act is assumed to vary with the legitimacy of the actor who performs it and of the role that he or she occupies (Zelditch & Walker 1984). Fennell et al (1978) have suggested that the gender-based legitimacy of a task is an important factor in determining the presence or absence of role differentiation. Hence, legitimation theory incorporates Bales's basic idea—that task contingencies are important to the development of role differentiation—with Berger et al's (1977) most recent formulation of status-effects theory. Berger et al argue that processes which lead to role differentiation are activated when there is a link between task characteristics and status characteristics.

Second, the argument posits both individual and social causes of gender differences in behavior. An individual's beliefs about the legitimacy of an action are most probably acquired and internalized through some social learning process. As such, they can be expected to vary across actors and situations. But Zelditch & Walker (1984; Walker et al 1986) demonstrate that definitions of legitimacy are also based in the collectivity and that collective definitions of legitimacy have independent effects on individual actions. Legitimation theories suggest an explanation for the seemingly unsystematic variation in the behavior of males and females in homogeneous groups under *objectively* similar conditions: Situational variations in the collective definitions of task-legitimacy can have important effects on patterns of role differentiation.

The most important contribution of legitimation theory may lie in its potential applicability to both heterogeneous and homogeneous settings. The possibility of a unified theory of role differentiation that can explain gender differences (or their absence) in role differentiation, as well as gender differences in role assignment, is exciting. But such developments await more intensive research which documents the relationships that exist among task characteristics, perceptions of competence, gender, and social behavior.

ACKNOWLEDGMENTS

The authors are grateful to Terri Fain Anderton for her assistance in abstracting various materials used in this review.

Literature Cited

Adams, K. A., Landers, A. D. 1978. Sex differences in dominance behavior. *Sex Roles* 4:215–23

Arnett, M. D., Higgins, R. B., Priem, A. P. 1980. Sex and least preferred co-worker score effects in leadership behavior. *Sex Roles* 6:139–52

Bales, R. F. 1950. *Interaction Process Analysis: A Method for the Study of Small Groups.* Reading, Mass: Addison-Wesley

Bales, R. F. 1953. The equilibrium problem in small groups. In *Working Papers in the Theory of Action,* ed. T. Parsons, R. F. Bales, E. A. Shils, pp. 111–61. Glencoe, Ill: Free Press

Bales, R. F., Slater, P. 1955. Role differentiation in small decision-making groups. In *Family, Socialization and Interaction Processes,* ed. T. Parsons, R. F. Bales, pp. 259–306. Glencoe, Ill: Free Press

Bandura, A., Walters, R. H. 1963. *Social Learning and Personality Development.* New York: Holt, Rinehart & Winston

Baron, J. N. 1984. Organizational perspectives on stratification. *Ann. Rev. Sociol.* 10:37–69

Baron, J. N., Bielby, W. T. 1980. Bringing the firms back in: Stratification, segmentation, and the organization of work. *Am. Sociol. Rev.* 45:737–65

Baron, J. N., Bielby, W. T. 1982. Workers and machines: Dimensions and determinants of technical relations in the workplace. *Am. Sociol. Rev.* 47:175–88

Bass, B. M. 1967. Social behavior and the orientation inventory: A review. *Psychol. Bull.* 68:260–92

Bell, C., Cheyney, J., Mayo, C. 1972. Structural and subject variation in communication networks. *Hum. Relat.* 25:1–8

Bentley, S., Randall, C. 1974. The spirit moving: A new approach to theologizing. *Christ. Crisis* Feb:3–7

Berger, J., Conner, T. L., Fisek, M. H. 1974. *Expectation States Theory: A Theoretical Research Program.* Cambridge, Mass: Winthrop

Berger, J., Fisek, M. H., Norman, R. Z., Zelditch, M. Jr. 1977 *Status Characteristics and Social Interaction: An Expectation States Approach.* New York: Elsevier

Berger, J., Rosenholtz, S. J., Zelditch, M. Jr. 1980. Status organizing processes. *Ann. Rev. Sociol.* 6:479–508

Bielby, W. T., Baron, J. N. 1983. Organizations, technology, and worker attachment to the firm. In *Research in Social Stratification and Mobility,* ed. D. J. Treiman, R. V. Robinson, 2:77–113. Greenwich, Conn: JAI

Braverman, H. 1974. *Labor and Monopoly Capital: The Degradation of Work in the Twentieth Century.* New York: Monthly Rev.

Bridges, W. P. 1982. The sexual segregation of occupations: Theories of labor stratification in industry. *Am. J. Sociol.* 88:270–95

Bridges, W. P., Miller, B. 1981. Sex and authority in the workplace: A replication and critique. *Am. Sociol. Rev.* 46:677–83

Brown, S. M. 1979. Male versus female leaders: A comparison of empirical studies. *Sex Roles* 5:595–611

Brown, V., Geis, F. 1984. Turning lead into gold: Evaluations of men and women leaders and the alchemy of consensus. *J. Pers. Soc. Psychol.* 46:811–24

Bruning, N. S., Snyder, R. 1983. Sex and position as predictors of organizational commitment. *Acad. Mgmt. J.* 26:485–91

Burawoy, M. 1979. *Manufacturing Consent: Changes in the Labor Process Under Monopoly Capital.* Chicago: Univ. Chicago Press

Clusen, R. C. 1979. The League of Women Voters and political power. See Cummings & Schuck 1979, pp. 112–32

Cohen, M. D., March, J. G., Olsen, J. P. 1972. A garbage can model of organizational choice. *Admin. Sci. Q.* 17:1–25

Cummings, R., Schuck, V., eds. 1979. *Women Organizing.* Metuchen, NJ: Scarecrow. 410 pp.

Daniels, A. 1979. W.E.A.L.: The growth of a feminist organization. See Cummings & Schuck 1979, pp. 133–51

Davis, K., Moore, W. E. 1945. Some principles of stratification. *Am. Sociol. Rev.* 10:242–49

Deutsch, F. M., Leong, F. T. L. 1983. Male response to female competence. *Sex Roles* 9:79–91

Duncan, B., Duncan, O. D. 1978. *Sex Typing and Social Roles: A Research Report.* New York: Academic

Durkheim, E. 1964. *The Division of Labor in Society.* New York: Free Press

Edwards, R. C. 1979. *Contested Terrain.* New York: Basic

Endler, N. S., Minden, H. A., North, C. 1973. The effects of reinforcement and social approval on conforming behaviour. *Eur. J. Soc. Psychol.* 3:297–310

Endler, N. S., Wiesenthal, D. L., Coward, T., Edwards, J., Geller, S. H. 1975. Generalization of relative competence mediating conformity across differing tasks. *Eur. J. Soc. Psychol.* 5:281–87

England, P. 1981. Assessing trends in occupational sex segregation, 1900–1976. In *Sociological Perspectives on Labor Mar-*

kets, ed. I. Berg, pp. 273–95. New York: Academic Press

Eskilson, A., Wiley, M. G. 1976. Sex composition and leadership in small groups. *Sociometry* 39:183–94

Etzioni, A. 1965. Dual leadership in complex organizations. *Am. Sociol. Rev.* 30:688–98

Feit, R. F. 1979. Organizing for political power: The National Women's Political Caucus. See Cummings & Schuck 1979, pp. 184–208

Feldman, R. A. 1973. Power distribution, integration, and conformity in small groups. *Am. J. Sociol.* 79:639–64

Fennell, M. L., Barchas, P., Cohen, E. G., McMahon, A. M., Hildebrand, P. 1978. An alternative perspective on sex differences in organizational settings: The process of legitimation. *Sex Roles* 4:589–604

Finigan, M. 1982. The effects of token representation in participation in small decision-making groups. *Econ. Ind. Democr.* 3: 531–50

Firth, M. 1982. Sex discrimination in job opportunities for women. *Sex Roles* 8:891–913

Fligstein, N., Sobel, M., Wolf, W. C. 1981. Response to Bridges and Miller. *Am. Sociol. Rev.* 46:685–88

Foner, P. S. 1980. *Women and the American Labor Movement.* New York: Free Press

French, M. 1985. *Beyond Power: On Women, Men and Morals.* New York: Summit

Freud, S. 1933. *New Introductory Lectures on Psycho-Analysis.* New York: Norton

Geller, S. H., Endler, N. S., Wiesenthal, D. L. 1973. Conformity as a function of task generalization and relative competence. *Eur. J. Soc. Psychol.* 3:53–62

Gerdes, E. P., Garber, D. M. 1983. Sex bias in hiring: Effects of job demands and applicant competence. *Sex Roles* 9:307–19

Giele, J. Z. 1978. *Women and the Future.* New York: Free Press

Gomez-Mejia, L. R. 1983. Sex differences during occupational socialization. *Acad. Mgmt. Rev.* 26:492–99

Gray, L. N., Mayhew, B. H. Jr. 1972. Proactive differentiation, sequence restraint, and the asymmetry of power: A multidimensional analysis. *Hum. Relat.* 25: 199–214

Gross, E. 1968. *Plus ca change . . .?* The sexual structure of occupations over time. *Soc. Probl.* 16:198–208

Horney, K. 1967. *Feminine Psychology.* New York: Norton

Instone, D., Major, B., Bunker, B. B. 1983. Gender, self confidence, and social influence strategies: An organizational simulation. *J. Pers. Soc. Psychol.* 44:322–33

Izraeli, D. N. 1983. Sex effects or structural effects? An empirical test of Kanter's theory of proportions. *Soc. Forc.* 62:153–65

Kanter, R. M. 1976. The impact of hierarchical structure on the work behavior of women and men. *Soc. Probl.* 23:415–30

Kanter, R. M. 1977. *Men and Women of the Corporation.* New York: Basic

Klopfer, F. J., Moran, T. 1978. Influences of sex composition, decision rule, and decision consequences in small group policy making. *Sex Roles* 4:907–15

Kohlberg, L. 1966. A cognitive-developmental analysis of children's sex-role concepts and attitudes. In *The Development of Sex Differences,* ed. E. E. Maccoby, pp. 82–173. Stanford: Stanford Univ. Press

Kollock, P., Blumstein, P., Schwartz, P. 1985. Sex and power in interaction: Conversational privileges and duties. *Am. Sociol. Rev.* 50:34–46

Kuzloski, J. 1979. Token women: Comment on Spangler, Gordon and Pipkin. *Am. J. Sociol.* 84:1438–39

Lamb, T. A. 1981. Nonverbal and paraverbal control in dyads and triads: Sex or power differences? *Soc. Psychol. Q.* 44:49–53

Levinson, R. M. 1975. Sex discrimination and employment practices: An experiment with unconventional job inquiries. *Soc. Probl.* 22:533–43

Lipman-Blumen, J., Tickamyer, A. R. 1975. Sex roles in transition: A ten-year perspective. *Ann. Rev. Sociol.* 1:297–338

Lockheed, M. E., Hall, K. P. 1976. Conceptualizing sex as a status characteristic: Applications to leadership training strategies. *J. Soc. Issues* 32:111–24

Maccoby, E. E., Jacklin, C. N. 1974. *The Psychology of Sex Differences.* Stanford: Stanford Univ. Press

Mai-Dalton, R. R., Sullivan, J. 1981. The effects of manager's sex on the assignment to a challenging or a dull task and reasons for the choice. *Acad. Mgmt. J.* 24:603–12

Mansbridge, J. 1983. *Organizing for the ERA: A case study in decision by accretion.* Presented at Ann. Meet. Conf. Group Polit. Econ., Chicago

Marrett, C. B. 1972. Centralization in female organizations: reassessing the evidence. *Soc. Probs.* 19:348–57

McMahon, A. M., Barchas, P., Cohen, E. G., Hildebrand, P., Fennell, M. L. 1976. *Organizational task performance in male and female groups.* Tech. Rep. No. 58, Lab. Soc. Res., Stanford Univ.

McPherson, J. M., Smith-Lovin, L. 1982. Women and weak ties: Differences by sex in the size of voluntary organizations. *Am. J. Sociol.* 87:883–904

Meeker, B. F. 1977. Interaction in a cooperative game. *Pac. Sociol. Rev.* 20:475–91

Meeker, B. F., Weitzel-O'Neill, P. A. 1977. Sex roles and interpersonal behavior in task oriented groups. *Am. Sociol. Rev.* 42:91–105

Miller, J., Garrison, H. H. 1982. Sex roles: The division of labor at home and in the workplace. *Ann. Rev. Sociol.* 8:237–62

Mischel, W. 1966. A social learning view of sex differences in behavior. In *The Development of Sex Differences*, ed. E. E. Maccoby, pp. 56–81. Stanford: Stanford Univ. Press

Mobley, W. H. 1982. Supervisor and employee race and sex effects on performance appraisals: a field study of adverse impact and generalizability. *Acad. Mgmt. J.* 25: 598–606

Morelock, J. C. 1980. Sex differences in susceptibility to social influence. *Sex Roles* 6:537–48

Neal, S. M. A. 1976. A sociological perspective on the moral issues of sexuality today. In *Sexuality and Contemporary Catholicism*, ed. F. Bockle, J. M. Pohier, pp. 61–70. New York: Seabury

Newton, R. R., Schulman, G. I. 1977. Sex and conformity: A new view. *Sex Roles* 3: 511–21

Ornstein, M. D. 1983. Class, gender, and job income in Canada. In *Research in Social Stratification and Mobility*, ed. D. J. Treiman, R. V. Robinson, 2:41–75. Greenwich, Conn: JAI

Parsons, T. 1964. A revised analytical approach to the theory of social stratification. In *Essays in Sociological Theory*, ed. T. Parsons, pp. 386–439. New York: Free Press. Rev. ed.

Petty, M. M., Bruning, N. S. 1980. A comparison of relationships between subordinates' perceptions of supervisory behavior and measures of subordinates' job satisfaction for male and female leaders. *Acad. Mgmt. J.* 23:717–25

Piliavin, J. A., Martin, R. R. 1978. The effects of the sex composition of groups on style of social interaction. *Sex Roles* 4:281–96

Pipkin, R. M., Spangler, E., Gordon, M. A. 1980. Reply to Walker. *Am. J. Sociol.* 85:1229–32

Ridgeway, C. L. 1978. Conformity, group-oriented motivation, and status attainment in small groups. *Soc. Psychol.* 41:175–88

Ridgeway, C. L. 1981. Nonconformity, competence, and influence in groups: a test of two theories. *Am. Sociol. Rev.* 46:333–47

Ridgeway, C. L. 1982. Status in groups: The importance of motivation. *Am. Sociol. Rev.* 47:76–88

Rosenfeld, R. A. 1980. Race and sex differences in career dynamics. *Am. Sociol. Rev.* 45:583–609

Rosenthal, S. F. 1978. The relationship of attraction and sex composition to performance and nonperformance experimental outcomes in dyads. *Sex Roles* 4:887–98

Scott, J. S., Bonjean, C. M., Markham, W. T., Corder, J. 1982. Social structures and intergroup interactions: Men and women of the federal bureaucracy. *Am. Sociol. Rev.* 47:587–99

Seifer, N., Wertheimer, B. 1979. New approaches to collective power: Four working women's organizations. See Cummings & Schuck 1979, pp. 152–83

Son, L., Schmitt, N. 1983. The influence of sex bias upon compliance with expert power. *Sex Roles* 9:233–46

Spangler, E., Gordon, M. A., Pipkin, R. M. 1978. Token women: An empirical test of Kanter's hypothesis. *Am. J. Sociol.* 84: 160–70

Spoelders-Claes, R. 1973. Small-group effectiveness on an administrative task as influenced by knowledge of results and sex composition of the group. *Eur. J. Soc. Psychol.* 3:389–401

Stevens, G., DeNisi, A. S. 1980. Women as managers: Attitudes and attributions of performance by men and women. *Acad. Mgmt. J.* 23:355–61

Stewart, L. P., Gudykunst, W. B. 1982. Differential factors influencing the hierarchical level and number of promotions of male and females within an organization. *Acad. Mgmt. J.* 25:586–97

Stitt, C., Schmidt, S., Price, K., Kipnis, D. 1983. Sex of leader, leader behavior, and subordinate satisfaction. *Sex Roles* 9:31–42

Sussman, L., Pickett, T. A., Berzinski, I. A., Pearce, F. W. 1980. Sex and sycophancy: Communication strategies for ascendence in same-sex and mixed-sex superior-subordinate dyads. *Sex Roles* 6:113–27

Szafran, R. F. 1982. What kinds of firms hire and promote women and blacks? A review of the literature. *Sociol. Q.* 23:171–90

Tawil, L., Costello, C. 1983. The perceived competence of women in traditional and nontraditional fields as a function of sex-role orientation and age. *Sex Roles* 9:1197–1203

Taylor, S. M., Ilgen, D. R. 1981. Sex discrimination against women in initial placement decisions: A laboratory investigation. *Acad. Mgmt. J.* 24:859–65

Terborg, J. R., Shingledecker, P. 1983. Employee reactions to supervision and work evaluation as a function of subordinate and manager sex. *Sex Roles* 9:813–24

Thomas, R. J. 1982. Citizenship and gender in work organizations: Some considerations for theories of the labor process. *Am. J. Sociol.* 88:86–112 (Suppl.)

Thompson, M. E. 1981. Sex differences: Differential access to power or sex role socialization? *Sex Roles* 7:413–24

Tsui, A. S., Gutek, B. A. 1984. A role set analysis of gender differences in performance, affective relationships, and career success of industrial middle managers. *Acad. Mgmt. J.* 27:619–35

Verba, S. 1961. *Small Groups and Political Behavior.* Princeton, NJ: Princeton Univ. Press

Walker, H. A. 1980. A reevaluation of a test of Kanter's hypothesis. *Am. J. Sociol.* 85:1226–29

Walker, H. A., Thomas, G. M., Zelditch, M. Jr. 1986. Legitimation, endorsement and stability. *Soc. Forc.* 64:620–43

Weiss, C. H. 1980. Knowledge creep and decision accretion. *Knowledge* 1:381–404

Wentworth, D. K., Anderson, L. R. 1984. Emergent leadership as a function of sex and task type. *Sex Roles* 11:513–24

Wiesenthal, D. L., Endler, N. S., Geller, S. H. 1973. Effects of prior group agreement and task correctness on relative competence mediating conformity. *Eur. J. Soc. Psychol.* 3:193–203

Wiley, M. G. 1973. Sex roles in games. *Sociometry* 36:526–41

Wiley, M. G., Eskilson, A. 1982. The interactions of sex and power base on perceptions of managerial effectiveness. *Acad. Mgmt. J.* 25:671–77

Wolf, W. C., Fligstein, N. D. 1979. Sex and authority in the workplace: The causes of sexual inequality. *Am. Sociol. Rev.* 44:235–52

Yamada, E. M., Tjosvold, D., Draguns, J. G. 1983. Effects of sex-linked situations and sex composition on cooperation and style of interaction. *Sex Roles* 9:541–53

Zelditch, M. Jr. 1955. Role differentiation in the nuclear family: A comparative study. In *Family, Socialization and Interaction Processes,* ed. T. Parsons, R. F. Bales, pp. 307–52. Glencoe, Ill: Free Press

Zelditch, M. Jr., Walker, H. A. 1984. Legitimacy and the stability of authority. In *Advances in Group Processes,* ed. E. J. Lawler, 1:1–25. Greenwich, Conn: JAI

Ann. Rev. Sociol. 1986. 12:277–306
Copyright © 1986 by Annual Reviews Inc. All rights reserved

THE SHIFTING SOCIAL AND ECONOMIC TIDES OF BLACK AMERICA, 1950–1980

Walter R. Allen

Department of Sociology, University of Michigan, Ann Arbor, Michigan 48109

Reynolds Farley

Department of Sociology, University of Michigan, Ann Arbor, Michigan 48109

Abstract

This article examines significant demographic trends that illustrate the advances of many black Americans from 1954 to 1984. We also examine trends which indicate deterioration in the socioeconomic circumstances and life chances of a significant portion of the black population. The two competing trends in the status of black Americans (at one extreme an emerging black elite, at the other a growing black underclass) have been central in provocative debates about economics and race over the past decade. This article locates the debate in historical context, summarizing the work of early theorists on this issue. The article then uses US Census data to document changes from 1950–1980 in occupational distribution, labor force participation, educational attainment, income and earnings, fertility and mortality rates, and family organizational patterns for black and whites. Using the political economy perspective, we argue that race and economic status are inexorably linked in this society. Shifts in the society's economic base coupled with historical (and contemporary) patterns of racial oppression explain the disproportionate concentration of blacks in the underclass. Sociologists are challenged to analyze the nexus of race and economics in America using early theoretical models and rigorous modern methodologies.

277

0360-0572/86/0815-0277$02.00

INTRODUCTION

The past 30 years have been momentous in the history of black America. In 1950, black Americans experienced life under the severe restrictions imposed by racial discrimination. In much of the country, blacks could not attend the same schools, eat at the same restaurants, or stay at the same hotels as whites. Black Americans were also denied opportunities in education and employment and, in southern states, their voting rights. They lagged far behind whites in terms of earnings, health status, and occupational achievement. The year 1954 brought a critical shift in the legal status of black Americans, a shift many thought equal in importance to the Emancipation Proclamation. On May 17, 1954, the Supreme Court declared racial segregation in the public schools to be illegal. This pivotal decision was a beacon of promise in a long history of struggle, providing black Americans the prospect of a new future filled with greater opportunity.

Over the next three decades, a great transition occurred in the political, economic, and social fortunes of black America. In 1984, black America saw its first viable candidate for the presidency of the United States. In relatively short succession, black Americans also saw the first black Miss America and the first US black in space. These "firsts" were exclamation points to a pattern of increased black access in areas of the society that were previously restricted. Blacks were visible as directors of large foundations, as mayors of major urban centers, as superstars of the stage, screen, and playing fields, and as owners of thriving business enterprises. The social and economic tides of black America had shifted profoundly, ushering in a level of prosperity and accomplishment unrivalled in the history of this country.

This article describes these changes. We examine significant demographic trends that illustrate the advances of many black Americans from 1950 to 1984. Yet, we also examine trends from this period which indicate a deterioration in the socioeconomic circumstances and life chances of a significant portion of the black population. These two competing realities in the black community represent profound counterpoints for attempts to assess the changing status of black Americans. At one extreme is an emerging black elite. At the other is a black underclass mired in poverty and possibly at risk of permanent exclusion from full participation in the society.

These two competing trends in the status of black Americans have been at the center of provocative debates about economics and race over the past decade (Sowell 1975, Wilson 1978, Willie 1979, Lieberson 1980, Marable 1983, Farley 1984, Fusfeld & Bates 1984, Murray 1984, Wilson & Aponte 1985). The debate can be summarized by the following concerns:

1. To what extent has the relative social and economic position of blacks in America improved since the 1960s civil rights movement?

2. To what extent have social and economic cleavages among black Americans been heightened and are they now growing even larger?
3. To what extent has the government's obligation to provide equal opportunities to black Americans been fulfilled?

These concerns orient contemporary debate over race and economics in black America. Has there been substantial economic progress? Has this economic progress been widely distributed across the black community? What is the proper role for government to play at this point?

We first review the literature on race and economics as factors in the lives of black Americans, divided into pre–civil rights era and post–civil rights era. We then provide a brief empirical synopsis of important social and economic trends among black Americans from 1950 to 1980. We summarize census data that compare income distributions, occupational classification, educational attainment, and family organization for blacks and whites. Finally, we point to the need for and the directions of further study of the race-economics nexus in American life.

ECONOMICS AND RACE IN THE BLACK COMMUNITY: ORIGINS OF THE DEBATE

Social scientists who describe black Americans have long debated the relative importance of economics and race. In the earliest sociological study of black Americans, W. E. B. DuBois raised questions pertaining to these issues. His massive project, *The Philadelphia Negro: A Social Study,* was devoted to an examination of how racial identity and economic status jointly shaped the realities of blacks living in Philadelphia in the late nineteenth century (DuBois 1967). In painstaking detail, DuBois sought first to show how a system of racial discrimination limited educational attainment, occupations, housing, family organization, and the quality of life experienced by the 9000 blacks living in the city's fifth ward. Second, he documented the factors, most often economic, educational, and cultural in nature, which explained differences among blacks.

In *The Philadelphia Negro,* DuBois demonstrated that the health status, illiteracy rates, crime patterns, housing, and family life of blacks were conditioned not only by race discrimination but specifically by economics. Indeed, DuBois concluded that the denial of economic opportunities caused the problems experienced by blacks: "There is no doubt that in Philadelphia the centre and kernel of the Negro problem so far as the white people are concerned is the narrow opportunities afforded Negroes for earning a decent living" (DuBois 1967:394).

E. Franklin Frazier conducted investigations during the 1930s which were explicit in their examination of the relationships between race and economics.

In the first, a 1931 study of black family life in Chicago, Frazier examined the hypothesis that " . . . family disorganization among Negroes was an aspect of the selective and segregative process of the urban community" (Frazier 1964:416). Frazier argued that clear-cut economic differences existed within Chicago's black population. These were so significant and distinctive that Frazier used them to partition the black community into five well-defined socioeconomic zones. As one moved outward from the black community's center (the most economically depressed zone), the social and economic standing of the black community improved. At the same time, the overall quality of life experienced by blacks improved.

In 1937, Frazier replicated his Chicago study in "Negro Harlem: An ecological study" (Frazier 1937). Once again, Frazier sought empirical support for his theory of how economics and race combined to influence the lives of black Americans. His data supported the view of black community life as internally differentiated. Economic status was granted primary importance as the cause of these divisions within the black community. Thus, in New York as in Chicago, his data showed the link between economic status in the black community and the observed levels of marital disruption, illegitimacy, and crime. The prevalence of such problems declined in direct proportion to increases in a neighborhood's overall socioeconomic status. Although Frazier concedes the importance of both racial status and economic conditions, he concluded that socioeconomic factors are ultimately more important (Frazier 1937, Allen & Farrell 1982).

Two other landmark studies of the interaction of race and economics in black America were conducted during the 1930s; they focused on the southern experience. In *Shadow of the Plantation,* Charles S. Johnson conducted an intensive examination of over 2400 blacks living in rural Macon County, Alabama (Johnson 1934). The stated purpose of his research was to understand the customs and institutions of Negro peasants as representatives of an authentic folk culture. After examining family life, social relations, religious beliefs, health status, and educational patterns, Johnson concluded,

> It has been impossible to escape the force of tradition, as represented in the customs established under the institution of slavery and adhered to, by the white population in their relation to the Negroes, and by the Negroes in relation to themselves. (Johnson 1934:208)

Under the enduring influence of a plantation economy, rural southern blacks were characterized by extreme cultural isolation, high rates of illiteracy, low social mobility, and limited opportunities for schooling. Due to the twin historical forces of economic and racial subjugation, the life circumstances and life chances of blacks in Johnson's study were greatly restricted. Where rural blacks in other areas of the South were able to avoid or temper negative conditions in their lives, it was because they possessed more economic resources. To demonstrate this point, Johnson compared rural blacks in Gibson

County, Tennessee, to those in Macon County, Alabama. "In Gibson County there is greater and longer-range migration, a more pronounced interest in education, more property ownership, and more clearly recognizable affectional ties within families. . . . Differences in customs follow closely these statistical differences, and suggest very clearly the different standards and codes under which the two types of rural areas operate" (Johnson 1934:211).

Deep South: A Social Anthropological Study of Caste and Class described economics and race in a small southern city located in the heart of the "Black Belt" (Davis et al 1941). The city was a trade center for surrounding cotton counties which were 80% black; over 50% of the city's population was also black. Thus, in many respects, this city represented a halfway point between the northern urban and southern rural settings discussed to this point. The researchers, a black married couple and a white married couple (all were trained social anthropologists), lived in "Old City" for two years observing the system of race and economic relations.

The researchers concluded that life in "Old City" was directed by an elaborate set of rules based on racial and economic group membership. Of the two, race far exceeded economics in defining the boundaries of life.

> The 'caste line' defines a social gulf across which Negroes may not pass, either through marriage or those other intimacies which "Old City" calls 'social equality'. A ritual reminder is omnipresent in all relationships that there are two separate castes—a superordinate white group and a subordinate Negro group. (Davis et al 1941:59)

Since race discrimination was located in the context of the total society, race influenced—and was influenced by—other factors in the society. The researchers concluded that "One of the most important factors in modifying caste behavior is the class structure of both the Negro and white castes (Davis et al 1941).

Shortly after publication of *Deep South,* another important study of race and class appeared. This book, *Black Metropolis: A Study of Negro Life in a Northern City,* provided an assessment of black-white relations in Chicago, the social organization of the black community, and how these factors influenced the personalities and institutions of blacks in Chicago. *Black Metropolis* reveals important and distinct differences between the lives of black Americans living in a large northern city and those living in a small southern city. Nevertheless, there was a disturbing consistency across these two settings. Despite more plentiful economic, educational, and political opportunities in the north,

> . . . the *type* of status relations controlling Negroes and whites remains the same and continues to keep the Negro in an inferior and restricted position. He cannot climb into the higher group although he can climb higher in his own group. (Drake & Cayton 1945:781)

Finally, two major studies from the 1940s looked at questions of race and economics among black Americans in broader historical and theoretical relief. Gunnar Myrdal's *An American Dilemma: The Negro Problem and American*

Democracy was published in 1944 (Myrdal 1962). This study was the most detailed and encompassing ever done on black Americans. Myrdal concluded that the chronic economic underdevelopment of black Americans resulted from an established tradition of subordinate relations with whites. Myrdal observed:

> There is a cultural and institutional tradition that white people exploit Negroes. . . . Within this framework of adverse tradition, the Negro in every generation has had a most disadvantageous start. Discrimination against Negroes is thus rooted in this tradition of economic exploitation. (Myrdal 1962:208)

The second major study of broader historical and theoretical questions about the interaction of economics and race in the lives of black Americans was *Caste, Class and Race* by Oliver C. Cox. Cox attempted to clarify the concepts of caste, class, and race. He selected black-white relations in the United States as his setting for the consideration of these issues. Like the others before him, Cox found a close correspondence between race and economics in the lives of black Americans. However, unlike those who preceded him, Cox is more explicit in his recognition of this correspondence. In his estimation, class was more important than race; thus he saw racial exploitation and antipathy as instruments in the perpetuation of an exploitative economic system. Cox argues, " . . . Negroes must learn that their interest is primarily bound up with that of the white common people in a struggle for power and not essentially in a climb for social status" (Cox 1948:534).

RACE AND ECONOMICS IN CONTEMPORARY AMERICA: HAS THE SIGNIFICANCE OF RACE DECLINED?

The civil rights movement was a watershed event in the history of black Americans (Morris 1984, Jones 1985); this mass-based social movement changed the fundamental structure of racial relations in the United States. The variety of strategies employed during the civil rights movement included mass civil disobedience, court litigation, economic boycotts, urban rebellion, voter registration, and mobilization of the mass media—to name but a few. Concerted political action during the civil rights movement resulted in the enactment of new legislation, the issuance of Presidential executive orders, and changed public opinion, so that the social status of black Americans was drastically redefined.

It is important to stress that in many respects, the civil rights movement represented the culmination of trends set in motion by the Emancipation Proclamation and earlier events in American history. Thus, the changes evident by 1980 in the social, political, and economic status of black Americans were products of factors both contemporary and historical. William J. Wilson's

(1978) argument to this effect spurred lively debate over the relationship of race and economics in contemporary America.

In *The Declining Significance of Race,* Wilson argued that "Race relations in America have undergone fundamental changes in recent years, so much so that now the life chances of individual blacks have more to do with their economic class position than with their day-to-day encounters with whites (Wilson 1981:1). According to Wilson, traditional patterns of interaction between blacks and whites, characterized by systematic racial oppression, had been basically altered. This came about because of changes in the system of production; that is, structural shifts in the national economy. More specifically, Wilson argues that the shift from a plantation-based or preindustrial economy to a manufacturing-based or industrialized economy fundamentally changed the relation of blacks to the national economy and to whites.

Wilson goes on to argue that "As race declined in importance in the economic sector, the Negro class structure became more differentiated and black life chances became increasingly a consequence of class affiliation" (Wilson 1978:153). Once the artificial cap on black social mobility, represented by strict segregation, was removed, greater income and occupational and educational differentiation were observed within the black community. Two countervailing trends resulted. Black Americans with resources or "access to the means of production," as Wilson puts it, experienced unprecedented job opportunities and upward social mobility. At the same time, black Americans who lacked education and job skills experienced soaring unemployment rates, declining labor force participation rates, increasing restriction to low-wage occupations, and a growing reliance on welfare. This is attributable, in part, to structural changes in the economy which eliminated many jobs in agriculture and manufacturing once filled by blacks. Due to historical factors, therefore, only a small percentage of the total black population was able to take full advantage of the expanded opportunities (i.e. largely middle- and upper-income blacks).

In 1978, C. Eric Lincoln presented an essay at the University of Mississippi's Symposium on Southern History which supported Wilson's basic assertions. Lincoln suggested that the Supreme Court ruling outlawing segregation in the nation's schools was both the impetus for further change and a reflection of changes that had already occurred in the black American identity and in black community unity. Lincoln saw the emergence of a sizeable black middle class as a positive sign. The old caste system had finally been broken; economics rather than race was now the primary factor in the lives of black Americans. However, he noted troubling developments as a consequence of this change:

. . . for the black masses appear to be in steady decline even as the black elite search for their niche in the American dream. The gulf widens; the old bonds are ravelling under the tension of new opportunities, new privileges, new interests, and new horizons—*for some.* (Lincoln 1979:28)

Among the many voices raised to contest Wilson's thesis of "a declining significance of race" was that of Charles V. Willie. In *The Caste and Class Controversy*, he brought together numerous critiques of Wilson's book (Willie 1979). These rejected the book's central premise that economic class, more than race, explains the limited mobility opportunities of poor blacks. Thus, Robert Hill cautioned against overstatement of the actual economic gains of blacks in the 1960s and 1970s; Thomas Pettigrew pointed to the persistence of significant race differences within class groups; and Dorothy Newman implicated the international flight of capital and industry in the creation of a black underclass in the United States. Of all the critics, Willie was most explicit in rejection of the Wilson thesis. His counter-hypothesis suggests:

> . . . that the significance of race is increasing and that it is increasing especially for middle-class blacks who, because of school desegregation and affirmative action and other integration programs, are coming into direct contact with whites for the first time for extended interaction. (Willie 1979:157)

Wilson's thesis is also criticized by Oliver & Glick (1982) who call it the "new orthodoxy on Black mobility." This doctrine assumes that: (*a*) occupational opportunities and social mobility increased dramatically for blacks in the 1960s, (*b*) any remaining race discrimination in securing jobs or social mobility is an artifact of past rather than present forces, and (*c*) social policy should focus on the class system rather than on race or other group characteristics. These authors conclude:

> The ultimate error of the new orthodoxy is its failure to acknowledge that the gains that blacks made during the 1960's came in an atypical era. It was an era which witnessed the greatest effort at government intervention in U.S. history, an era of economic abundance and social and political turmoil. (Oliver & Glick 1982:522)

They also criticize the tendency to overstate black gains, the persistence of drastic black-white differences in occupational equality and the clear tenuousness of much of the black progress.

Sharon Collin's critique of Wilson's position argues that the demand for black middle-class workers was largely *created* by federal government programs. Moreover, she sees the black middle-class work force as concentrated in segregated areas of the labor force. As a disproportionately public-sector work force, blacks " . . . are most likely to be found in federal, state, and local government functions that legitimize and subsidize black underclass dependency. Blacks employed in the private sector remain concentrated in economically underdeveloped areas, or in intermediary positions . . ." (Collins 1983:379). The end result is instability in black employment opportunities and limited social mobility.

Farley also criticized Wilson's thesis when he questioned whether the social and economic gap between blacks and whites had indeed narrowed (Farley

1984). The data show considerable reduction in race differences by educational attainment, and the occupations and earnings of employed workers. There was little improvement in relative unemployment rates or in rates of labor force participation. Progress in the areas of school integration, family income, poverty, and residential segregation was, at best, mixed. Adopting what he refers to as the "optimistic view", Farley concludes that racial differences in key areas of social and economic status will continue to diminish in the future.

In a later study, he and Bianchi specifically addressed the question of social class polarization among blacks. Here, as in the earlier study, he concludes that the premise of polarization in the black community is doubtful. "The pattern is not one where . . . a growing share of all income is obtained by the rich" (Farley & Bianchi, 1985:25). On the other hand, the relative employability of blacks with limited educations is worsening compared to better-educated blacks.

BLACK AMERICA, 1950–1980

Our review of the debate on race and economics reveals areas of both consensus and disagreement. Authors agree that race relations in the United States have changed fundamentally over the period, evolving from a strictly-enforced caste system, characterized by the absolute, unequivocal subordination of blacks to whites, to a system of power relations incorporating elements of social status, economics, and race. The issue for debate is not whether race relations have changed. Most scholars concede this point. Rather, the question is: What combination of economic and racial factors now characterize black-white relations in American society?

The second question emerging from our review is more empirical. Authors have debated the extent to which the social and economic characteristics of black Americans changed over this critical period. What improvements in the occupational, educational, and income status of blacks resulted from the redefinition of black-white relations? At this point, we begin the empirical analysis of selected social and economic trends.

Our empirical assessment of selected social and economic changes in the status of black Americans will be limited. More detailed and systematic examination is provided in our forthcoming book, *The Color Line and the Quality of Life: The Problem of the Twentieth Century*. For this article, we restrict ourselves to examination of the following areas of black American life: occupational distribution, labor force participation, median income, levels of schooling, family organization, fertility rates, and mortality rates. Taken together, these statistics provide an accurate summary of the current socioeconomic status of black Americans; in addition, the statistics lend insight to important historical patterns. Caution is advised in attempts to generalize these statistics since only aggregate patterns are summarized. No reliable information is provided about local areas or the values, behaviors, and attitudes of individuals.

Occupational Distribution

The changing occupational distribution of the black and white populations from 1940 to 1980 is presented in Table 1. In 1940, two fifths of all black men worked on farms, another one third worked as machine operators or industrial laborers. The most significant change over the next four decades was the exodus from agriculture. During World War II, black men increased their representation in the blue-collar occupations, becoming laborers, operatives, or crafts workers. The 1960s and 1970s brought increasing representation of black men in the higher occupational categories: professional, managerial, and clerical positions. As might be expected, over the entire period there was an upgrading of the occupations held by white men, especially in the years prior to 1960. White men shifted from the factories to office work; however, occupational change among white men has been much less than for black men, largely because whites were never so highly concentrated in farming and laboring jobs.

Employment changes among black women can best be understood by examining declines in domestic service. On the eve of World War II, six out of ten employed black women worked as domestics: cleaning, cooking, and washing clothes in white homes. The war presented opportunities for black women to move into other service jobs or to operate machines in factories. In the 1950s, black women moved into clerical positions and during the 1960s and 1970s, black women continued their movement into clerical jobs, but also entered the sales and professional ranks. Once again, the occupational changes that occurred during this period were much greater for blacks than whites. This difference in magnitude of occupational change is related to the concentration of black women in domestic service at an earlier point.

Duncan's socioeconomic index scores provide a summary of the comparative occupational prestige of jobs held by blacks and whites. The index was developed in 1950 and updated in 1970. Scores at the upper end of the scale signify highly-prestigious positions, while those at the lower end signify low-prestige occupations. Thus, occupations in the professional category are awarded scores of 74 or higher, while some occupations in the manual labor category receive scores of 10 or lower.

The examination of socioeconomic scores reveals the upgrading of occupations that has occurred for blacks, as well as the large remaining differences between the races. For black men, the average socioeconomic score rose from 16 points in 1940 to 31 in 1980. Nevertheless, in 1980 the average status of a nonwhite man's job was equivalent to that of the typical white man forty years earlier. A substantial lag in occupational prestige is also apparent for black women; the average socioeconomic score for black women in 1980 also equalled that of white women in 1940.

Table 1 Occupational distributions by race and sex, 1940–1980[b]

Occupation	Black or nonwhite males (%)[a]					White males (%)				
	1940	1950	1960	1970	1980	1940	1950	1960	1970	1980
Professional	1.8	2.2	3.8	7.8	10.7	5.9	7.9	11.4	14.6	16.1
Proprietors, managers, officials	1.3	2.0	3.0	4.7	6.7	10.7	11.7	14.5	15.3	15.3
Clerical	1.1	3.1	5.8	7.4	8.4	7.1	6.8	7.2	7.1	6.2
Sales	1.0	1.1	1.2	1.8	2.7	6.8	7.0	6.5	6.1	6.4
Craftsmen	4.4	7.8	9.5	13.8	17.1	15.7	20.0	19.8	20.7	21.4
Operatives	12.6	21.4	24.3	28.3	23.4	19.0	20.3	19.0	18.6	16.1
Domestic service	2.9	1.0	0.4	0.3	0.2	0.2	0.1	0.1	0.1	<0.1
Other service	12.4	13.5	14.9	12.8	15.8	5.9	5.2	5.6	6.0	7.9
Farmers, farm managers	21.2	13.5	4.8	1.7	0.6	14.1	10.1	6.1	3.6	2.6
Farm laborers	19.9	10.4	9.5	3.9	2.4	7.0	4.2	3.3	1.7	1.5
Non-farm laborers	21.4	24.0	22.8	17.5	12.0	7.6	6.7	6.5	6.2	6.5
Total	100.0	100.0	100.0	100.0	100.0	100.0	100.0	100.0	100.0	100.0
Mean socioeconomic index	16	18	21	27	31	30	33	36	39	40

Table 1 (Continued)

	Black or nonwhite females (%)					White females (%)				
	1940	1950	1960	1970	1980	1940	1950	1960	1970	1980
Professional	4.3	5.7	6.0	10.8	14.8	14.9	13.5	13.1	15.0	17.0
Proprietors, managers, officials	0.7	1.4	1.8	1.9	3.7	4.4	4.8	5.4	4.8	7.4
Clerical	0.9	4.0	9.3	20.9	29.3	25.0	31.1	32.9	36.3	36.0
Sales	0.5	1.4	1.5	2.5	3.1	8.2	9.6	8.5	7.7	7.3
Craftsmen	0.1	0.7	0.5	0.8	1.4	1.1	1.6	1.1	1.2	1.9
Operatives	6.2	14.9	14.1	17.6	14.9	20.5	20.3	15.1	14.1	10.1
Domestic service	60.0	42.0	35.2	17.5	6.5	11.1	4.1	6.1	3.4	1.9
Other service	10.5	19.1	21.4	25.7	24.3	11.6	11.5	13.7	15.3	16.0
Farmers, farm managers	3.0	1.7	0.6	0.1	0.1	1.1	0.6	0.5	0.3	0.4
Farm laborers	13.0	7.6	9.0	1.5	0.5	1.2	2.2	3.3	1.5	0.8
Nonfarm laborers	0.8	1.5	0.6	0.7	1.4	0.9	0.7	0.3	0.4	1.2
Total	100.0	100.0	100.0	100.0	100.0	100.0	100.0	100.0	100.0	100.0
Mean socioeconomic index	13	18	21	29	36	36	39	39	40	43

[a]Data for 1940 and 1950 are from decennial censuses. Data for other years are from the *Current Population Survey*. They are estimates of annual averages rather than a specific month. Data for 1940 and 1950 refer to blacks; for the other years, nonwhite.

[b]Source: US Bureau of the Census, *Sixteenth Census of the United States: 1940, Population*, III(1) Table 63; *Census of Population 1950*, P-C1, Table 128; US Bureau of Labor Statistics *Employment and Earnings*, Vol. 7(7) (Jan. 1961) Table A-17; Vol. 17(7) (Jan. 1971) Table A-17; Vol. 28(1) (Jan. 1981), Table 22.

The index of occupational dissimilarity (Table 2) provides a comparison of the black and white occupational distributions. Since these measures were calculated on broad occupational categories, racial differences are understated. Nevertheless, the measures report sharp declines in occupational segregation by race. At the end of the Great Depression, the index value was 43 for men and 63 for women. These figures meant that in order to achieve a racial parity in the occupational distributions, 43% of the black or white males and 63% of females would have to be redistributed or placed in different jobs. In 1980, the index values had fallen to 24 for men and 17 for women. The decades of greatest change were the 1960s and 1970s, a period when blacks moved into higher-ranking occupations. These measures indicate a clear trend: Blacks and whites are becoming more similar in terms of the jobs that they hold; yet the racial difference remains quite large.

Labor Force Participation

Two indicators commonly used to gauge the employment situation of a population are unemployment rates and labor force participation rates. Many analysts believe that a third measure, the proportion of population actually holding a job, may provide more useful information. This measure is sometimes referred to as the employment-population ratio. Figure 1 presents age-standardized information about the proportion of total population at work for six age-race groups. In 1950, 70% of men aged 16 to 24 held jobs. The trend toward longer school attendance in the intervening years delayed entry into the labor force, and by 1983, a much lower proportion of young men were at work. The drop-off in employment was greater among black men, partly because whites were more likely to combine work and school. Just after the Korean War, the racial difference in proportion employed among men 16 to 24 was only 2 percentage points. This difference increased to 14 points by 1973, jumped to 20 points during the recession of the mid-1970s, and then remained stable.

Table 2   Indexes of occupational dissimilarity by race[a]

	Men	Women
1940	43	63
1950	37	53
1960	37	43
1970	31	28
1980	24	18

[a]Source: See Table 1.

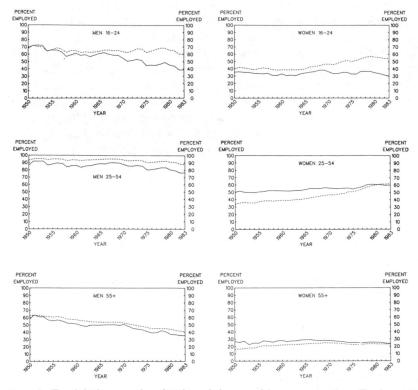

Figure 1 Trends in the proportion of total population at work by race, sex, and age (Employment-population ratios), 1950–1983. Data have been standardized for age within group. Source: US Bureau of Labor Statistics, *Handbook of Labor Statistics,* December, 1983: Table 15; *Employment and Earnings,* 31(1): Table 3.

Although racial differences are much smaller among men 25 to 54, trends are similar: a gradual increase in the racial disparity until 1973–1975, a sharper increase in the racial disparity during that recession, and no contraction thereafter. In 1983, only 77% of black men in this group held jobs compared to 88% of white men. Stated differently, despite the economic recovery, about one adult black man in four is either unemployed or not in the labor force. Among men 55 and over, there has been a decline in employment, but the racial gap has not grown larger. Older men of both races are now retiring rather than working.

Throughout the post–World War II era, there has been a persistent increase in the employment of young (aged 16–24) white women but very little change among blacks; thus, the racial difference has grown much larger. In 1950, 40% of the white and 35% of the black women aged 16–24 were at work; in 1983, the racial disparity was 24 points. The proportion of adult women at work was previously higher for blacks than for whites. Due to the greater employment of white women, this has changed, and in the early 1980s, for the first time the proportion of women aged 25–54 at work was greater for whites than blacks.

Educational Attainment

Educational attainment is another important area for the comparison of the races. In 1940, blacks 25–34 were three-and-a-half years behind whites of similar age in median years of school completed (Table 3). Outside the South, the race difference in median years of school for this age group was 2 years. By 1960, these respective figures had declined to 2 and 1 years, and in 1981, the races were virtually indistinguishable as regards median years of school completed for people 25–34 years old.

Over the four decades that encompassed World War II, the mass migration of blacks out of the South, and the Civil Rights era, blacks managed to eliminate almost all of the difference in median school years completed. At the same time, there was a general change in education patterns such that 75% or more of the age group 25–34 had graduated from high school. Significantly, the black disadvantage in the proportion of population completing 4 years or more of high school in 1940 was 28 percentage points; by 1981, this was reduced to 9 percentage points. However, a reverse pattern was evident for the proportion of population completing college from 1940 to 1981. The black-white difference in the proportion graduating from college actually increased from 5% in 1940 to 12% in 1981. Rates of college enrollment have gone up some for blacks, but even more rapidly among whites. Undoubtedly, the declining role of traditionally black colleges over the 40-year period partly explains this pattern. Support for this interpretation is provided by the fact that 1981 race differences in the proportions graduating from college were much lower in the South (10 percentage points), an area where traditionally black colleges are still abundant, as compared with the North and West (15 percentage points). A related factor is the tendency for black students, who now more often attend predominantly white colleges, to have higher attrition rates than their white peers—or than black peers on black campuses (Blackwell 1981).

Income and Earnings

Changes in income patterns may occur on either a cohort or a period basis. In the case of cohort change, race differences in educational attainment and aspirations are expected to lessen over time, thus reducing race differences in income for each new cohort. Period change is associated with dramatic shifts in a particular decade because of significant changes in the economic, political, or social sphere (such as those taking place during the 1960s). Table 4 presents changes on a period basis for specific age groups. Among men, there is clear evidence of a *period* pattern of change (amounts are shown in constant 1983 dollars). Black incomes—as a percent of whites—went up more across the

Table 3 Racial differences in the educational attainment of persons 25–34: 1940–1980[a]

	High school graduates (%)				Four years of college completed (%)				Median school years completed			
	1940	1960	1970	1981	1940	1960	1970	1981	1940	1960	1970	1981
Total United States												
Blacks	11	33	52	76	2	4	6	12	6.9	10.3	12.0	12.6
Whites	39	61	74	87	7	12	17	24	10.4	12.3	12.6	12.9
Racial difference	28	28	22	9	5	8	11	12	3.5	2.0	.6	.3
South												
Blacks	8	27	45	74	1	5	6	13	6.2	9.3	11.5	12.6
Whites	32	55	68	84	6	11	15	23	9.6	12.1	12.5	12.8
Racial difference	24	28	23	10	5	6	9	10	3.4	2.8	1.0	.2
North and west												
Blacks	20	41	58	79	2	4	6	10	8.7	11.2	12.2	12.7
Whites	41	64	76	88	7	12	17	25	10.7	12.3	12.6	13.0
Racial difference	21	23	18	9	5	8	11	15	2.0	1.1	.4	.3

[a]Source: US Bureau of the Census, *Current Population Reports*, P-23, No. 80, "The Social and Economic Status of the Black Population in the U.S.: An Historical View, 1790–1978," and P-20, No. 390, "Educational Attainment in the U.S.: March 1981 and 1980."

Table 4 Median income in constant 1983 dollars by age for black and white men and women, 1949–1983[c]

	Men					Women				
	1949[a]	1959[a]	1969	1979	1983	1949	1959	1968	1979	1983
Ages 15 to 24										
Black median	$3,300	$3,600	$4,900	$5,000	$2,800	$1,800	$2,600	$4,000	$4,000	$2,600
White median	5,000	5,100	5,400	6,700	4,600	3,900	3,300	4,200	4,700	3,600
Racial gap	−1,700	−1,500	−500	−1,700	−1,800	−2,100	−700	−200	−700	−1,000
Black as % of white	66	71	91	75	61	45	79	95	85	72
Ages 25 to 34										
Black median	$6,800	$9,900	$15,300	$13,900	$11,300	$3,100	$4,400	$8,600	$9,700	$8,200
White median	12,000	17,200	22,300	20,600	17,500	6,100	6,800	9,100	10,400	8,600
Racial gap	−5,200	−7,300	−7,000	−6,700	−6,200	−3,000	−2,400	−500	−700	−400
Black as % of white	57	58	68	69	65	52	65	94	93	95
Ages 35 to 44										
Black median	$7,100	$11,000	$16,000	$17,300	$15,300	$3,100	$4,500	$8,300	$10,200	$9,600
White median	13,400	19,400	25,800	26,900	23,200	6,300	7,500	9,400	10,000	8,700
Racial gap	−6,300	−8,400	−9,800	−9,600	−7,900	−3,200	−3,000	−1,100	+200	+900
Black as % of white	53	57	62	65	66	49	60	89	103	110

Table 4 *(Continued)*

	Men					Women				
	1949[a]	1959[a]	1969	1979	1983	1949	1959	1968	1979	1983
Ages 45 to 54										
Black median	$ 6,700	$ 9,600	$14,600	$16,100	$15,000	$2,700	$3,500	$ 6,800	$ 8,200	$8,000
White median	13,100	18,200	25,000	27,400	24,200	6,100	8,100	10,200	10,400	8,200
Racial gap	−6,400	−8,600	−10,400	−11,300	−9,200	−3,400	−4,600	−3,400	−2,200	−200
Black as % of white	51	53	59	59	62	44	43	67	80	97
Ages 55 to 64										
Black median	$ 5,300	$ 7,700	$11,100	$11,900	$10,200	$2,100	$2,800	$ 4,500	$ 5,500	$5,200
White median	11,200	15,700	20,700	22,100	19,700	4,600	6,000	8,400	8,400	6,300
Racial gap	−5,900	−8,000	−9,600	−10,200	−9,500	−2,500	−3,200	−3,900	−2,900	−1,100
Black as % of white	47	49	53	54	52	46	47	54	65	82
Ages 65 and over										
Black median	$ 2,500	$ 3,300	$ 4,700	$ 5,600	$ 5,800	$1,600	$2,100	$2,900	$ 3,900	$4,100
White median	5,100	6,300	8,100	10,200	10,200	2,600	2,700	4,000	5,300	5,800
Racial gap	−2,600	−3,000	−3,400	−4,600	−4,400	−1,000	−600	−1,100	−1,400	−1,700
Black as % of white	49	53	57	56	57	62	78	73	73	71

[a]Data for 1949 and 1959 refer to whites and nonwhites.

[b]Data for 1949 and 1969 refer to persons 14 to 24 who reported income. Data for 1982 were obtained from the *Current Population Survey*. For other years, data are from decennial censuses.

[c]Source: U.S. Bureau of the Census, *Census of Population: 1950*, P-C1: Table 139; *Census of Population: 1960*, PC(1)-1D: Table 219; *Census of Population: 1970*, PC(1)-D1: Table 245; *Census of Population: 1980*, PC80-1-D1A: Table 293; *Current Population Reports*, Series P-60, No. 146, Table 46.

range of ages during the 1960s than in the previous decade. Following 1970, there were no more than small gains for black men in any age group. Judged by income data, the 1960s were the years of greatest improvement for black men.

When differences in the annual median incomes of men are considered, black progress is much less impressive. The racial gap in income actually increased in the 1950s and the 1960s for men age 35 and over. Since the recession of the mid-1970s, income levels have fallen at similar rates for both races. However, since whites began the period with more income, the racial gap declined slightly. Among young men in 1983, blacks had incomes 61% of whites, a slight decline from 1949 when the figure was 66%.

For black women, the 1960s was a prosperous decade that brought improvements in their relative income and decreases in the gap that separated their purchasing power from that of white women. However, black women also made progress relative to whites in the 1950s and 1970s. By 1980, black women aged 35–44 had achieved an income advantage over their white peers. This difference in median income is explained by several factors, such as the longer tenure of black women in the labor force relative to their peers and the greater tendency for white women to be employed part-time.

Fertility and Mortality Rates

To describe race trends in fertility for married and unmarried women, we used birth rates calculated for the 1940–1983 period. Table 5 shows births per thousand women classified by age and marital status. The rates for married women 15–19 are extremely high because marriages for these young women are often hastened by pregnancies. We see in Table 4 that for black women, marital fertility rates peaked in 1960 and then fell rapidly; indeed, the age-specific fertility rates were cut by nearly half. Among unmarried black teenagers, the peak birth rates were recorded in 1970, but for older unmarried black women, the peak came in 1960. Fertility has definitely fallen in the recent period and by 1983, unmarried black women were bearing children much less frequently than in the past. In other words, the rate at which unmarried black women bear children has been declining for two decades.

Trends among married white women resemble those among married blacks—a peak in fertility rates in 1960 and an uninterrupted decline thereafter. Unmarried white women, however, differ from blacks in that their fertility rates have risen since 1960, perhaps a result of the increasing tendency for white women to cohabit and then bear children before marriage. In short, the frequency with which unmarried women bear children has been *declining* among blacks but *rising* among whites. Racial differences in the fertility of unmarried women are slowly decreasing; however, unmarried black women are still three to four times as likely as whites to become mothers.

Turning to death rates, we find that at the end of the Depression the

Table 5 Birth rates for married and unmarried women by race: 1940–1983

Ages	Births per thousand married women					Births per thousand unmarried women				
	1940	1950	1960	1970	1983	1940	1950	1960	1970	1983
Black* women										
15–19	340	475	713	533	492	43	69	77	97	86
20–24	264	292	364	263	227	46	105	167	131	110
25–29	150	180	224	148	127	33	94	172	101	82
30–34	105	114	142	81	70	23	64	104	72	45
35–44	56	47	54	29	17	9	20	36	22	13
White women										
15–19	401	399	532	432	346	3	5	7	11	19
20–24	263	281	355	244	200	6	10	18	23	26
25–29	168	193	219	165	146	4	9	18	21	23
30–34	103	116	121	78	78	3	6	11	14	15
35–44	34	39	39	20	15	1	2	4	4	5

*Data for 1940 and 1960 refer to nonwhites.
Sources: US National Center for Health Statistics, *Monthly Vital Statistics Report*, Vol. 34, No. 6 (Supplement); Stephanie J. Ventura, *Trends and Differentials in Births to Unmarried Women*; US National Center for Health Statistics, *Vital and Health Statistics*, Series 21, No. 36; Robert D. Grove and Alice M. Hetzel, *Vital Statistics Rates in the United States: 1940–1960*, Public Health Series Publication No. 1677.

age-adjusted mortality rate for black men was 53% greater than that for white men (1,764 vs 1,373 deaths per 100,000). In 1983 the race difference in mortality rates was 46% (1,025 vs 702 deaths). Despite urbanization, improvements in economic status, and the expansion of government spending for health, the ratio of black to white deaths for men changed only a little over the past four decades. The largest racial gaps were at ages 25–44 where mortality rates for black men in *both* 1940 and 1983 were two to two-and-one-half times higher. At the very oldest ages, black death rates fell below those of whites (15,386 vs 18,797). This may be due to a tendency for blacks to exaggerate age, although selective mortality at earlier ages may produce an elderly black population less at risk of disease than the comparable white population.

During the 1940s, there were substantial declines in the death rates of black and white women at all ages. Especially large declines in mortality occurred for black women under age 35, as deaths due to childbirth and contagious disease were reduced. During the 1950s and 1960s, there was a slow-down in the shift toward lower mortality rates for women but, unlike the rates for men, they continued to fall. The 1970s witnessed the resumption of a fast-paced decline in mortality with unusually large improvements among older women. Unlike the situation among men, there has been a gradual racial convergence of death rates among women. In 1940, the age-adjusted rate for black women was 71% higher (1,505 vs 879 deaths per 100,000); by 1983, the difference had dropped to 46% (572 vs 392 deaths).

For most age groups of men, there has been little racial convergence in death rates, while the racial disparity has gradually declined among women. When mortality rates by cause are examined, we find a complicated picture of racial similarities and differences (see Table 6) (US Department of Health and Human Services 1985). For most causes, black rates of mortality exceed those of whites by a wide margin. In 1950, they had much higher death rates from homicides, tuberculosis, influenza, and stroke (cerebrovascular diseases). In the two decades following 1950, mortality rates among black men rose for some causes—cancer, diabetes, motor vehicle accidents, and suicide—but declined for others, including heart disease and cerebrovascular causes. The era since 1970 is very different from the previous period. Those death rates that had been slowly declining in the 1950s and 1960s fell much more rapidly. For other causes—cirrhosis, diabetes, accidents, homicide and suicide—the death rates for black men began to decline.

Despite these changes, there is little evidence of a racial convergence of death rates by cause. The advantages black men enjoyed in 1950 with regard to cancer and cirrhosis disappeared, and death rates from those causes are now considerably higher among blacks. Homicide is the leading cause of death among black men 15 to 34 and second to heart disease among black men 35 to 44. In spite of a recent decline, homicide is now the fourth leading killer of

Table 6 Death rates by cause for blacks and whites by sex, average annual changes in death rates, and black rate as a percent of white, 1950–1983

	Age-adjusted deaths per 100,000 men			Annual change in death rates for men (%)		Black male rate as per-cent of white	
	1950	1970	1983	1950-1970	1970-1983	1950	1983
Deaths from all causes							
Black	1,373	1,319	1,020	−0.2	−2.0	143	146
White	963	893	698	−0.4	−1.9		
Diseases of the heart							
Black	416	376	308	−0.5	−1.5	109	119
White	381	348	257	−0.5	−2.3		
Cerebrovascular diseases							
Black	146	124	64	−0.8	−5.1	168	183
White	87	69	35	−1.2	−5.2		
Malignant neoplasms							
Black	126	198	232	+2.3	+1.2	96	147
White	131	154	158	+1.3	+0.2		
Influenza and pneumonia							
Black	64	54	24	−0.8	−6.2	237	160
White	27	26	15	−0.2	−3.6		
Tuberculosis							
Black	81	11	4	−10.0	−8.8	352	700
White	23	3	<1	−10.2	−13.8		
Cirrhosis							
Black	9	33	23	+6.5	−2.8	75	177
White	12	19	13	+2.3	−2.9		
Diabetes							
Black	12	21	18	+2.8	−1.2	109	200
White	11	13	9	+0.8	−2.8		
Motor vehicle accidents							
Black	40	50	26	+1.1	−5.0	111	93
White	36	40	28	+0.3	−2.7		
All other accidents							
Black	66	69	40	+0.2	−4.2	147	167
White	45	36	24	−1.1	−3.1		
Suicide							
Black	7	10	11	+1.8	+0.7	39	58
White	18	18	19	0.0	+0.4		
Homicide							
Black	51	82	54	+2.4	−3.2	1275	675
White	4	7	8	+5.6	+1.0		

Table 6   (*continued*)

	Age-adjusted deaths per 100,000 women			Annual change in death rates for women (%)		Black female rate as per-cent of white	
				1950-1970	1970-1983		
	1950	1970	1983	1950-1970	1970-1983	1950	1983
Deaths from all causes							
Black	1,107	814	590	−1.5	−2.5	172	150
White	645	502	393	−1.3	−1.9		
Diseases of the heart							
Black	350	252	192	−1.6	−2.1	156	151
White	224	168	127	−1.4	−2.2		
Cerebrovascular diseases							
Black	156	108	54	−1.8	−5.3	195	180
White	80	56	30	−1.8	−4.5		
Malignant neoplasms							
Black	132	124	130	−0.3	+0.4	111	119
White	119	108	109	−0.5	+0.1		
Influenza and pneumonia							
Black	50	29	10	−2.7	−8.2	263	111
White	19	15	9	−1.2	−3.9		
Tuberculosis							
Black	51	4	1	−12.7	−10.7	510	500
White	10	1	<1	−11.5	−12.3		
Cirrhosis							
Black	6	18	11	+5.5	−3.8	100	183
White	6	9	6	+2.1	−3.1		
Diabetes							
Black	23	31	21	+1.5	−3.0	144	233
White	16	13	9	−1.0	−2.8		
Motor vehicle accidents							
Black	10	14	8	−1.7	−4.3	91	80
White	11	14	10	+1.2	−2.6		
All other accidents							
Black	28	22	14	−1.2	−3.5	140	175
White	20	13	8	−2.2	−3.7		
Suicide							
Black	2	3	2	+2.0	−3.1	40	33
White	5	7	6	+1.7	−1.2		
Homicide							
Black	12	15	11	+1.1	−2.4	1200	366
White	1	2	3	+3.5	+3.1		

SOURCES: U.S. Department of Health and Human Services, *Health United States, 1981*: Table 14; U.S. National Center for Health Statistics, *Monthly Vital Statistics Report*, Vol. 33, No. 4, Supplement (December 20, 1984): Table 9.

black men; the age-adjusted rate for blacks is nearly seven times that for white men.

Throughout the 1950 to 1983 period, there were declines in the mortality rates of women from most causes of death, with the rates of improvement greater after 1970 than before. Death rates for both black and white women from all major causes have been declining with one important exception. Since 1970, the malignant neoplasm death rate has changed very little among women of either race.

When we examine the panel of data for women in Table 5, we find evidence in both the total death rate and the cause-specific rates of a racial convergence in causes of death among women. In 1950, the age-adjusted death rate for black women exceeded that of white women by 72%; in 1983, this difference was 50%.

Family Organizational Patterns

Our final comparison of the races is in terms of family organizational patterns. As Table 7 shows, patterns of family organization have changed significantly since 1960 among blacks, while these patterns have remained relatively stable for whites. In the 20 years from 1940 to 1960, the proportion of all black families with both the husband and wife present was stable at around 75%. Between 1960 and 1970, this proportion dropped to 68%, and by 1984 the proportion was down to 52%, a precipitous decline of nearly 25 percentage points in a 25-year period. At the same time, the trend was toward an increasing number of families headed by women who did not have a husband present; from 1960 to 1984, this category of families nearly doubled among blacks (22% to 43%).

Paradoxically, this period of rapid change in black family structure roughly parallelled the modern Civil Rights Movement era. The result has been the creation, at least for this period, of a new modal organizational pattern in lower-income black family life: single female family heads living with their children. We emphasize lower income here because our findings show race differences in the proportion of husband-wife families to be fewer than 10 percentage points for families earning $25,000 or more annually in 1980 (Farley & Allen, in press). The rapid expansion in the number of female-headed families among the urban poor has been attributed to shifts in the economy that had the effect of putting black men out of work (Norton 1985; Wilson & Aponte 1984).

THE DILEMMA PERSISTS: ECONOMICS AND COLOR IN AMERICA

In this paper, we have briefly examined the nexus of race and economics in contemporary black America. We began by reviewing the historical research

Table 7 Distribution (by %) of families by type and race: 1940–1984

Year and race	All families (Thousands)	Percent of all families			
		Total	Husband-wife	Male head, no wife present	Female head, no husband present*
Black					
1940**	2,699	100.0	77.1	5.0	17.9
1950***	3,432	100.0	77.7	4.7	17.6
1960	3,950	100.0	74.1	4.1	21.7
1970	4,774	100.0	68.1	3.7	28.3
1975	5,498	100.0	63.9	3.7	32.4
1980	6,042	100.0	55.5	4.3	40.2
1984	6,675	100.0	51.6	5.3	43.1
White					
1940**	28,740	100.0	85.5	4.4	10.1
1950	35,021	100.0	88.0	3.5	8.5
1960	40,873	100.0	89.2	2.7	8.1
1970	46,022	100.0	88.7	2.3	9.1
1975	49,451	100.0	86.9	2.6	10.5
1980	51,389	100.0	85.6	2.8	11.6
1984	53,934	100.0	84.4	3.0	12.6

*Includes widowed, divorced, and single women, women whose husbands are in the Armed Forces or otherwise away from home involuntarily, as well as those separated from their husbands through marital discord.
**Data revised to exclude one-person families.
***Data include families of "other" races.

SOURCE: US Bureau of the Census, *Current Population Reports*, Series P-23, No. 80, "The Social and Economic Status of the Black Population in the U.S.: An Historical View, 1790–1978," and Series P-20, Nos. 276, 282, 307, 326, 340, 352, 366, 371, 381, 388, 398.

record, and we then considered selected demographic patterns for the years 1950–1980. The contemporary debate over "the declining significance of race' has provided an orienting framework throughout. We asked the question, "What is the relative power of economics and color in the lives of black Americans?"

Early studies demonstrate the undeniable power of race over the lives of black Americans. The caste barrier in our society once defined the least white person as more significant than the greatest black person. While the force of this prescription was, to an extent, modifiable by related social factors (e.g. region, occupational class, biological lineage), the essential elements of our race-based caste system remained intact. It is critical to note, however, the importance attributed to economic factors in such calculations. Even when slavery (the purest expression of this country's caste system) was at its height, free Negroes of economic means were able to use their resources to buffer the effects of the caste system on their lives (Fields 1985).

The racial caste system in the United States has had a heavy economic emphasis from its inception (Fusfeld & Bates 1984; Marable 1983). The system's origins, definitions, and justifications were bound up in this country's efforts to develop its agricultural, industrial, and economic capacities. Blacks were instrumental in this equation, first as a seemingly limitless supply of slave labor, then as a source of peons and inexpensive proletariat labor, and finally as a reserve labor force. The historical redefinition of the racial caste system has placed greater emphasis on economic factors—there is consensus on this point. Disagreement persists, however, around questions of the extent to which race played a part in the emergence and solidification of economic inequalities.

The empirical record presents a picture of substantial progress by black Americans since 1950. Evidence presented here and elsewhere (Reid 1982) shows that there has been significant improvement in black social and economic status. The legal basis of segregation and race discrimination has been all but eliminated. Relative to the World War II era, black Americans have increased their earnings, educational attainment, occupational status, and political power. Black Americans continue, however, to lag significantly behind whites on various measures of social and economic well-being. Of special concern is the group of black Americans who not only lag significantly behind whites, but behind other blacks as well, in terms of their social and economic well-being.

The black "underclass" represents the subgroup of black Americans characterized by: chronic unemployment, lack of real opportunities to succeed, prospects of intergenerational poverty, and angry despair (Glasgow 1980). In this sense, the underclass is trapped. Their lack of resources may sentence them to life on the society's periphery. The processes that culminated in the creation and maintenance of a black underclass are broad and historical, having to do with the society's changing economic base and with changes in the significance of race. Therefore, simplistic explanations are problematic; it is not sufficient to attribute sole causality for current patterns to the workings of racism or capitalism, government social policy, or individual values: All had a part to play. There are multiple sources of causation at work.

The black underclass in America is a reflection of the nature of racial and economic relationships in post-industrial society. A political economy perspective is useful, therefore, because it recognizes the complex interconnections of these questions. It is important for us to explicitly recognize that economic relations shape (and are shaped by) the social setting.

> Today's urban racial ghettos are the result of the same forces that created modern America, and one of the byproducts of American affluence is a ghettoized racial underclass. . . . Racism is more than a psychological problem of whites; it has roots in white-black economic relationships. Poverty is not simply the result of poor education, skills and work habits of the poor. It is one outcome of the structure and functioning of the economy. (Fusfeld & Bates 1984:xiii–xiv)

Approaching the question of "caste or class" from a political economy perspective elevates the debate and offers a reasonable prospect of solution.

Many commentators have addressed the system of historical, economic, social, and political factors that account for the persistence of racial inequality in the United States (Carmichael & Hamilton 1967, Allen 1969, Baron 1969, Tabb 1970, Swan 1981, Fusfeld & Bates 1984). These scholars describe a system of relations that oppresses the overwhelming majority of black Americans, a system that limits their choices and futures, largely because they are of black ancestry. In the past, race definitely provided the most significant basis for this oppression. Equally certain is the fact that race is not without substantial significance in the present—the increased significance of economic factors notwithstanding.

> Given the fundamental racism of American society, what we find is that even though racial exploitation is no longer an essential element in terms of sustaining a sector of a ruling class, racial dominance has become so socially diffused that it has become an inextricable part of the mediating processes through which much of the basic economic and political controls for the whole society are exercised. In other words, the mechanisms for subjugating black people have become interlaced with the complex of mechanisms by which power is exercised over both white and black. (Baron 1969:171).

The political economy perspective is useful to focus on the structural elements of racial inequality. This is vitally important since personal expressions of racism are far less common now than before. Social mores no longer openly support the denial of black rights or encourage visceral expressions of racist behavior (e.g. name-calling, physical attacks, etc). Racial discrimination in this era is more often impersonal in its expression, resulting from routine organizational patterns and procedures. Thus, racial inequality is perpetuated through the "normal" operation of the society's key institutions. The initial disadvantages of the black urban poor in educational attainment, economic standing, family structure, and upward social mobility are compounded and exacerbated over time. As a result, members of the black underclass are prime candidates for failure. In postindustrial America, they are expendable, lacking both marketable skills and exploitable resources (Wilson & Aponte 1985, Lieberson 1980).

In postindustrial America, members of the black underclass represent appendages of questionable—if not outright nonexistent—utility. The black underclass is characterized by high unemployment, educational failure, marital disruption, and disproportionate imprisonment. The concentration of problems in the ranks of the black urban poor results from shifts in the country's economic and social organization since World War II. Thousands of jobs in the black community were eliminated as the economy moved from a labor-intensive, industrial base to a capital-intensive, service industry base (Wilson & Aponte 1984). As the black community itself became more diverse and dispersed in social terms, a deterioration in community cohesion, stability, and cultural identification resulted.

The disproportionate concentration of blacks in the underclass results from the combined forces of social change and historical (and contemporary) patterns of racial oppression. Shifts in the economic base of the society exacerbated already existent racial inequities. Race provided a fundamental basis for the stratification of opportunities and rewards, thus black economic disadvantage became institutionalized. At the same time, a racist ideology justifying these inequities evolved, was validated, and became woven into the very cultural fabric of this society. In this manner, the social and political disadvantage of blacks was institutionalized. The momentum of systematic economic inequities and systemic race discrimination has had its effect on the contemporary scene. The black underclass is a creation of the societal forces that crystallized urban poverty (Wilson & Aponte 1984).

Although social scientists have seen fit to debate the significance of race in the lives of black Americans, black people themselves display little confusion over this point. Data from ethnographic research (Gwaltney 1980), from social survey research studies (Hatchett 1982, 1983), and from public opinion polls (Clark & Harris 1985) are consistent. These data sources reveal that the rank and file of black Americans continue to see race as a significant factor in their lives. More often than not, respondents cite race discrimination (past and present) as a primary basis for the denial of equal educational, employment, and housing opportunities to black people. Moreover, as recently as 1980 and 1983, urban rebellions in the Liberty City/Miami area were explicitly linked to continuing racial tensions and racial inequality (Ball-Rokeach & Short 1985; Porter & Dunn 1984).

American sociology has been slow to move beyond an emphasis on individual psychology and behavior in the examination of racial inequality. The current debate over "caste and class" in black America offers an opportunity for expanding our horizons, for engaging in the joint consideration of systemic and individual factors as determinants of black life chances. It is ironic to note in this connection the long history of speculations about the emergence of an underclass in modern society. Marx foresaw the creation and perpetuation of a *lumpen proletariat* in postindustrial societies (*Das Capital*); Cox anticipated a future for blacks as " . . . exploited and exploitable workers, . . . more highly urbanized than any other native-born population group in the country" (Cox 1948:xxxiii); and C. Wright Mills concluded, "The bottom of this society is politically fragmented, and even as a passive fact, increasingly powerless; at the bottom there is emerging a mass society" (Mills 1956:324). The challenge confronting the discipline at this point is to look deeply and perceptively into the nexus of race and economics in America. Early theoretical formulations need to be merged with rigorous modern methodologies in an attempt to better understand how economics influences race and how race influences economics in the postindustrial United States.

ACKNOWLEDGMENT

This manuscript is an outgrowth of a recently completed monograph entitled *The Color Line and the Quality of Life: Problem of the Twentieth Century*. That monograph was sponsored by the National Committee for Research on the 1980 Census, which received support from the Social Science Research Council, the Russell Sage Foundation, and the Alfred P. Sloan Foundation, in collaboration with the US Bureau of the Census. The article was also supported by the Cornerhouse Fund. Important critiques of earlier drafts were provided by Michael Dawson, Walter Farrell, Nesha Haniff, Aldon Morris, Ernest Wilson, and an unidentified reviewer for the *Annual Review of Sociology*.

Literature Cited

Allen, R. 1969. *Black Awakening in Capitalist America: An Analytical History*. Garden City, NY: Anchor Books

Allen, W. R., Farrell, W. C. Jr. 1982. Black Harlem revisited: Patterns of ecological and social organizational change, 1940–1970. In *Urban Patterns: Studies in Human Ecology*, ed. G. Theodorson, pp. 188–93. University Park: Penn. State Univ. Press

Ball-Rokeach, S. J., Short, J. F. Jr. 1985. Collective violence: The redress of grievance and public policy. In *American Violence and Public Policy: An Update of the National Commission on the Causes and Prevention of Violence*, ed. L. Curtis, pp. 155–80. New Haven: Yale Univ. Press

Baron, H. M. 1969. The web of urban racism. In *Institutional Racism in America*, ed. L. Knowles, K. Prewitt, pp. 134–76. Englewood Cliffs, NJ: Prentice-Hall

Blackwell, J. E. 1981. *Mainstreaming Outsiders: The Production of Black Professionals*. Bayside, NY: General Hall

Carmichael, S., Hamilton, C. 1967. *Black Power: The Politics of Liberation in America*. New York: Vintage

Clark, K. B., Harris, K. C. 1985. What do Blacks really want? *Ebony Mag*. XL (Jan.):108–115

Collins, S. 1983. The making of the Black middle class. *Soc. Probl*. 30(April):369–81

Cox, O. C. 1948. *Caste, Class and Race: A Study in Social Dynamics*. New York: Doubleday

Davis, A., Gardner, B., Gardner, M. 1941. *Deep South: A Social Anthropological Study of Caste and Class*. Chicago: Univ. Chicago Press

Drake, St. C., Cayton, H. 1945. *Black Metropolis: A Study of Negro Life in a Northern City*. New York: Harcourt, Brace

DuBois, W. E. B. 1967. *The Philadelphia Negro: A Social Study*. New York: Schocken. (First publ. 1899)

Farley, R. 1984. *Blacks and Whites: Narrowing the Gap?* Cambridge, Mass: Harvard Univ. Press

Farley, R., Allen, W. 1985. *The Color Line and the Quality of Life: The Problem of the Twentieth Century*. New York: Russell Sage Found. Forthcoming

Farley, R., Bianchi, S. 1985. Social class polarization: Is it occurring among Blacks? *Res. Race Ethnic Relat*. 4:1–31

Fields, B. J. 1985. *Slavery and Freedom on the Middle Ground: Maryland During the Nineteenth Century*. New Haven, Conn: Yale Univ. Press

Frazier, E. F. 1937. Negro Harlem: An ecological study. *Amer. J. Sociol*. 43(July):72–88

Frazier, E. F. 1964. The Negro family in Chicago. In *Contributions to Urban Sociology*, ed. E. W. Burgess, D. J. Bogue, pp. 404–18. Chicago: Univ. Chicago Press

Fusfeld, D., Bates, T. 1984. *The Political Economy of the Urban Ghetto*. Carbondale: S. Ill. Univ. Press

Glasgow, D. 1980. *The Black Underclass: Poverty, Unemployment and Entrapment of Ghetto Youth*. San Francisco: Jossey-Bass

Gwaltney, J. L. 1980. *Drylongso: A Self-Portrait of Black America*. New York: Vintage

Hatchett, S. 1982. Black racial attitude change in Detroit, 1968–1976. PhD thesis. Univ. Mich. Dep. Sociol., Ann Arbor

Hatchett, S. 1983. Black Americans surveyed: Two unique ISR studies explore the experiences and perspectives of Black America," Univ. Mich., Ann Arbor: Inst. Soc. Res. *Newslet*. (Spring/Summer):3, 7

Johnson, C. S. 1934. *Shadow of the Plantation*. Chicago: Univ. Chicago Press

Jones, J. 1985. *Labor of Love, Labor of Sorrow.* New York: Basic

Lieberson, S. 1980. *A Piece of the Pie: Black and White Immigrants Since 1880.* Berkeley: Univ. California Press

Lincoln, C. E. 1979. The new black estate: The coming of age of black America, In *Have We Overcome? Race Relations Since Brown,* ed. M. Namorato, pp. 1–30. Jackson: Univ. Press Miss.

Marable, M. 1983. *How Capitalism Underdeveloped Black America: Problems in Race, Political Economy and Society.* Boston: South End

Mills, C. W. 1956. *Power Elite.* New York: Oxford Univ. Press

Morris, A. 1984. *Origins of the Civil Rights Movement.* New York: Free Press

Murray, C. 1984. *Losing Ground: American Social Policy, 1950–1980.* New York: Basic

Myrdal, G. 1962. *An American Dilemma: The Negro Problem and Modern Democracy.* Vols. I, II. New York: Pantheon. (Orig. publ. 1944).

Norton, E. H. 1985. Restoring the Traditional Black Family. *NY Times Mag.* June 2:42–25

Oliver, M., Glick, M. 1982. An Analysis of the New Orthodoxy on Black Mobility. *Soc. Probl.* 29 (June):511–23

Porter, B., Dunn, M. 1985. *The Miami Riot of 1980.* Lexington, Mass: Heath

Reid, J. 1982. Black America in the 1980's. *Popul. Bull.* 37(4):1–38

Sowell, T. 1975. *Race and Economics.* New York: McKay

Swan, L. A. 1981. *Survival and Progress: The Afro-American Experience.* Westport, Conn: Greenwood

Tabb, W. 1970. *The Political Economy of the Urban Ghetto.* New York: Norton

US Department of Health and Human Services 1985. *Black and Minority Health.* Washington, DC: GPO

Willie, C. V. 1979. *Caste and Class Controversy.* Bayside, NY: General Hall

Wilson, W. J. 1978. *The Declining Significance of Race: Blacks and Changing American Institutions.* Chicago: Univ. Chicago Press

Wilson, W. J. 1981. Shifts in the analysis of race and ethnic relations, In *The State of Sociology: Problems and Prospects,* ed. J. F. Short, Jr., pp. 101–18. Beverly Hills, Calif: Sage

Wilson, W. J., Aponte, R. 1985. Urban Poverty. *Ann. Rev. Sociol.* 11:231–58

Ann. Rev. Sociol. 1986. 12:307–28

ALTERNATIVES TO BUREAUCRACY:
Democratic Participation In The Economy

Joyce Rothschild

Department of Sociology, University of Toledo, Toledo, Ohio 43606

Raymond Russell

Department of Sociology, University of California, Riverside, California 92521

Abstract

This article critically reviews and integrates the social science literature on "alternatives to bureaucracy," focusing particularly on democratic participation in the economy. First, it looks at the social forces and public attitudes that support worker ownership and worker control efforts in the contemporary United States, and it examines the state's involvement in those reforms. It summarizes the research with respect to four challenges to democracy that these alternative organizations face in their dual need to get work tasks accomplished and to still retain their democratic form. First, how do size, technology, and the division of labor affect an organization's ability to maintain active participation and democracy? Second, how does organizational democracy affect individual participants' satisfaction with their work? Third, how does democratization of work processes affect the economic performance of these firms? Finally, obstacles to the stability, retention, and spread of these organizational innovations are discussed.

INTRODUCTION

The past century and especially the past 50 years have witnessed the ascent of bureaucracy that Max Weber predicted. Large formalized bureaucracies have come to control an increasing share of economic assets in the private sphere, just as they have come to administer public decisions and not-for-profit activity. In fact, the master trend of the twentieth century may be toward growing concentration and increasing size of organization both in the economy and in

307

0360-0572/86/0815-0307$02.00

governmental institutions; this trend leaves fewer organizational units in control of ever larger spheres of activity and renders the individual ever more remote from the centers of power. Trends of this magnitude, however, often set into motion social forces that oppose them, countertrends that eddy against the main current. The movement against bureaucracy and toward greater autonomy and participation in the workplace is such a countertrend.

A number of movements have gained momentum in the United States that promise to give people more voice in their work lives. Although there are three separate movements struggling to create functioning "alternatives to bureaucracy" within the economy, they are perhaps united by the same *zeitgeist* that would recreate modern organizations on a human scale, giving people at all ranks greater power over the organization's process and product (Schumaker 1973, Sale 1980).

The first effort to develop more participatory, indeed self-managing, work organizations took place at the grassroots. Without any material assistance from the state to speak of, thousands of worker cooperatives and collectives have been created in communities all around the United States (Case & Taylor, 1979). As functioning examples of an alternative model of organization that is internally cohesive and built on the logic of substantive rationality (in contrast to the formal rationality of bureaucracy) these grassroots co-ops are important (Rosner & Blasi 1985, Rothschild-Whitt 1979b). In Weberian terms, they replace bureaucratic authority, inasmuch as it is based upon incumbency in office, with consensual, democratic authority that resides in the collectivity as a whole. In Marxian terms, they replace production for exchange value in a market with production for social utility value. Either way, these grassroots collectives encompass organizational practices and aspirations that are a radical departure from those that are available in their capitalist-bureaucratic context, and this cooperative-democratic model has its own characteristics and dilemmas (Rothschild & Whitt 1986).

Were these grassroots collectives isolated in their attempts to develop organizational democracy, their significance would diminish, but in recent years they have been joined, perhaps unwittingly, by two even larger movements in other parts of the economy to create democratic organizational forms, albeit of a more moderate scope.

The first of these efforts to develop more responsive and participatory organizations took place within the large corporation. As many as one third of the Fortune 500 have apparently initiated some form of worker participation in Quality of Work Life (QWL) projects (Walton 1979), and a recent survey by the New York Stock Exchange (1982) indicates that only 3% of corporate managers believe that this trend toward worker participation will prove to be a fad. Conceptually, these QWL programs create alternative, "parallel" niches within the bureaucratic structure, such as problem-solving groups that report directly to the top of the organization, thereby freeing employees somewhat from the intimidation of rank and allowing the organization to tap the contributions of all on a more nearly equal basis (Kanter et al 1982).

Another far-reaching movement within the economy has sought to increase employee involvement in the ownership (rather than in the governance) of their firms. In the United States, these efforts have largely taken the form of Employee Stock Ownership Plans, or "ESOPs." The American ESOPs have proliferated rapidly since they received their initial authorization from the federal government in 1974. By 1985, over 6000 American corporations were estimated to have established ESOPs, covering a total workforce of more than 10 million employees (*Business Week* April 15, 1985, p. 102), but the amount of stock that is worker-owned in many of these cases may be small. The number of cases where employees actually own a *majority* of the voting stock (at least 51%) is approximately 500, with a mean size of 680 workers per company (National Center for Employee Ownership, personal communication, 1984).

In sum, all three movements are seeking to democratize work organizations, though QWL concentrates on involving workers in the decision-making process and ESOPs concentrate on worker ownership of equity stakes, while the cooperative movement encompasses both ownership and control issues.

The recent spread of all of these organizational innovations has given rise to a great deal of social scientific research. The aim of this article is to review this recent research. It will begin by taking a closer look at the social forces and public attitudes that have supported these reforms.

Why Alternative Organizations Are Proliferating

Some perspectives on worker participation have emphasized the role in inspiring reform of employees and specifically, of the "new worker"—more highly educated and autonomous. However, aggregate levels of job satisfaction have remained stable for decades (Katzell 1979, Weaver 1980, Chelte et al 1982), and studies of alienation have reported lower levels in bureaucratic organizations than in other kinds of workplaces (Kohn 1971, 1976). While there is thus little evidence of any wholesale disaffection with bureaucratic life, there is still a good deal of evidence that American workers prefer more democratic forms of organization when they are given a choice. Perhaps the most celebrated finding that points toward this conclusion comes from a poll of 1237 adult Americans conducted by Peter Hart, Inc., in 1975. That study asked respondents whether they would prefer to work for a company that was owned and controlled by "outside investors," by "the employees," or by "the government." Fully 66% of those polled chose to work in the employee-owned firm (Rifkin 1977:176).

Other evidence indicates that the desire for democratic forms of work is held more strongly by some portions of the labor force than by others. In their recent reanalysis of the Hart poll data, Zipp et al (1984) found that female workers and those under 35 are significantly more likely than others to endorse a variety of democratic reforms. However, they found no significant effect by race, party identification, or union membership. Overall, the researchers found that the social base of support for workplace democracy includes nearly all segments of society, especially blue-collar workers and professional/technical workers; only managers and owners are not in general support.

Like that of Zipp et al, a recent reanalysis of the 1977 Quality of Employment Survey national probability sample of working Americans indicates that support for workplace participation is stronger among women than among men and that it is stronger among younger workers (Fenwick & Olson 1984). Somewhat at odds with the Zipp findings, however, Fenwick & Olson find that support for workplace participation increases with education, but declines with increased occupational status and income (1984:17–18).

In comparing a sample of workers in Indianapolis to a sample in Sweden, Haas (1980) found both groups to be extremely supportive of workplace democracy, but only the Swedes favor having a "final say" in work-related decisions. Other sociologists have suggested that aspirations for more workplace autonomy are highest among educated white collar workers who already enjoy a relatively high degree of autonomy in their work (Kohn & Schooler 1969, Gouldner 1979).

In the early 1970s, a countercultural movement that drew much of its strength from educated youth stimulated interest in alternative organizations. In little more than a decade, this movement led to the creation of more than a thousand producer cooperatives (Jackall & Crain 1984), at least 1,300 alternative schools (Case & Taylor 1979:293), between 5,000 and 10,000 food cooperatives (Case & Taylor 1979:90), and an even greater number of rural and urban communes (Case & Taylor 1979:285; Zablocki 1980; Berger 1981). These organizational achievements of the counterculture, however, have tended to remain in special niches of the economy, such as custom and craft production and services, where they are not in direct competition with capitalist enterprises, or in relatively labor intensive fields where the costs of entry are low (Rothschild & Whitt 1986). Some have been involved in the provision of not-for-profit, individualized services such as rape crisis centers, feminist health collectives, free schools, and so forth (Swidler 1979, Schlesinger & Bart 1982).

These collectivist organizations arose from a fundamental ideological commitment to autonomy and self-determination coupled with a sense of opposition to hierarchical authority systems and the inequality that accompanies them. Many participants, especially in the workplace collectives, also were motivated by a desire to earn a livelihood in a manner consistent with these expressed values.

In contrast, most of the QWL cases and many (although not all) of the ESOP cases, have arisen on the initiative of owners and managers. Why would capital be interested in sponsoring the extension of ownership or participation to workers? Braverman (1974) and others have argued that capitalists will continue to prefer forms of work organization that degrade skills, thereby cheapening labor, making it more easily replaceable, and depriving employees of control over their work. However, recent Marxist works have faulted Braverman for ignoring the costs to employers of neglecting workers' consciousness; such works demonstrated empirically that capitalist businesses take very seriously their need to "manufacture consent" (Burawoy 1978, 1979; Stark 1980; Littler & Salaman 1982). Edwards (1979) interprets bureaucracy itself as a response to this need, but he also attributes a number of flaws to bureaucratic organization that create pressures for more participatory forms of work organization. These works have in turn stimulated essays that view the current experimentation with worker participation and employee ownership as part of capitalism's enduring search for more effective strategies of control (Ramsey 1977, 1983; Derber & Schwartz 1983; Russell 1984b).

Another recent literature links the choice of different forms of work organization to various "transaction costs" (Williamson 1975, 1981; Ouchi 1980; Jones 1983; Butler 1983a,b; Russell 1985b). These authors grant that when employees are low in skill and relatively easy to supervise, employers are unlikely to make serious investments to increase employees' involvement in their jobs or their firms. Employee voice and participation can be expected, however, when employees perform idiosyncratic tasks that are difficult to supervise and that cause them to acquire unique or intuitive skills in the course of their work. These circumstances make employers vulnerable to losses from employee turnover or from inadequately motivated employees, and therefore it is especially advantageous to encourage employees to identify more closely with their jobs and their firms. Ouchi (1980) argues that where these features are salient, bureaucracies tend to be displaced by "clans." For Ouchi, clan structures receive exceptionally high loyalty from their employees and therefore rely more heavily on informal than formal mechanisms of control. As examples of clan organization, Ouchi points to the nineteenth-century utopian communities described by Kanter (1972) and to the high-tech manufacturing firms of the contemporary United States and Japan.

In recent years, growing international competition for markets has put new pressures on organizations to improve their labor productivity. While this can lead to downward pressure on wages, union busting, and in general more repressive labor discipline, a *shortage* of workers with special, needed skills and knowledge may move organizations in the opposite direction (Naisbitt & Aburdene 1985). Broadened participation by workers has sometimes improved labor motivation and productivity (Blumberg 1973, Frieden 1980). Thus, many American firms have sought more cooperative relations with their employees through the use of such innovations as quality circles, labor-management committee systems, and profit-sharing agreements (Simmons & Mares 1983; New York Stock Exchange 1982).

In other cases, firms hard pressed by their competition have turned to employee ownership. Sometimes the worker ownership option is chosen in the start-up of new firms expected to be quite profitable, such as People's Express, because managers see the labor motivation and productivity advantages inherent in the idea and also the tax advantages of recent capital formation laws passed by Congress. At other times, ESOPs are utilized by retiring owners, eager to sell their long-standing and often highly profitable firms to their employees as a group rather than to an outside conglomerate buyer. The ESOP provides an internal market, allowing the original family owners to cash out their position, while still maintaining the family name and integrity of the firm; this would not be possible in a sale to a conglomerate. Employee ownership has sometimes been the option of last resort to avert a plant shutdown following capital disinvestment. In these cases it is often in the mutual interest of local management, the workers, the union, and community leaders alike to work together to "save" the plant. Firms under pressure—such as a number of the airlines—have asked for wage concessions, and the unions have countered by insisting upon stock in exchange for wage and benefit reductions that would have been exacted anyway. Thus, worker ownership in the United States has come about through many routes and as a result of the initiative of many parties.

In the United States and even more in Europe, efforts to promote more democratic forms of work organization have also been actively encouraged by the state. In socialist Yugoslavia, for example, the right of workers to manage their own workplaces has been written into the constitution of the state. In many Western European countries, a variety of forms of workers' participation in management, including the establishment of workers' councils and worker representatives on Boards of Directors, are a matter of law (IDE 1983). The political processes that have given rise to worker participation legislation in Western Europe have been reviewed by Esping-Andersen & Friedland (1982) and by Stephens & Stephens (1982). All seem to agree that the passage of this legislation reflects the strength of labor unions and socialist parties within these countries; but whether these reforms constitute a real victory for European workers or a mere sign of their co-optation remains a matter of debate.

In the United States, the federal government has remained indifferent to appeals for worker participation, but it has supported the spread of Employee Stock Ownership Plans (ESOPs) by passing 16 laws since 1974 that grant a number of tax advantages both to employee-owned companies and to the banks that are willing to make loans to such companies. At the state level, 13 states have passed laws encouraging employee ownership through the use of technical assistance efforts and industrial revenue bonds (Rosen et al 1986:2).

The reasons for the government's involvement in ESOP development in the

United States reveal the complexity and ambiguity of this phenomenon in a capitalist society. National legislation favorable to worker ownership in the United States has garnered the support of some of the most liberal members of Congress, along with some of the most conservative. Examination of the actual participants in worker buy-outs reveals that leadership has come variously from managers, owners, unions, workers, city and state officials, and even sometimes social scientists (Whyte et al 1983). Apparently, different groups read different meanings into this phenomenon. Some who have advanced worker ownership in Congress have seen it as a way to reinvigorate capitalism, while others have seen in it a way to bring economic justice to the system. Some bring to their efforts no conscious ideology at all, seeing worker buy-out merely as a financing mechanism available to save businesses and jobs. It can be argued that worker ownership via the ESOP model is inherently ambiguous regarding which class interests it serves. It can be altered in specific ways to benefit different class interests, depending upon who is involved in the planning and design, and its ideological justifications can be shifted accordingly (Rothschild-Whitt 1984).

Challenges to Democracy in Alternative Organizations

Although efforts to promote democracy in the economy thus take a diversity of forms and are advocated for a wide variety of reasons, many of them have a common set of problems. The burden of social science has been to study the many problems or challenges that these organizations must resolve in order to get organizational tasks accomplished, while still surviving as democracies. In the following review, we examine four major challenges to democracy in alternative organizations that we see the research literature as addressing.

First, how do size, technology, and the division of labor affect an organization's ability to maintain participation and democracy? These variables can influence the gulf that may come to exist between the order-givers and order-takers, even in what are ostensibly democratic organizations.

Second, what impact, if any, do these changes in organizational structure have on individual participants' attitudes and behavior? Much research on these experiments has attempted to document their impact on such variables as individual motivation, satisfaction, and allegiance to a firm.

Third, what effect does democratization have on the economic performance of these firms? Whether or not improvements in productivity and economic performance are the explicit goal of the new organizational form, these organizations must all achieve at least some measure of economic viability, simply in order to survive.

A final challenge faced by all of these innovators is whether they will be able to stabilize and institutionalize successful reforms. Workplace innovations, even where they have been quite meaningful to their participants and fully viable in an economic sense, still need to demonstrate that they can spread and be long-lived. Some obstacles to the retention and spread of organizational cooperation, and possible means of overcoming them, will be discussed in the final section.

Size, Technology, and the Division of Labor

There has been considerable debate among scholars of the sociology of organizations over whether "size" or "technology" is the more important determinant of bureaucratic organization. In attempts to establish alternatives to bureaucracy, both large size and routine technologies appear to hinder democratic forms of workplace organization. Both factors have frequently contributed to a division of labor that draws sharp distinctions between leaders and followers, and between mental and manual employees.

In an empirical study on the effects of industrial plant size, Ingham (1970) finds that increasing size is associated with lowered cohesion of the work group, less worker satisfaction, and reduced worker identification with the firm. In a study of kibbutzim Rosner (1981:32–35) discovers that participation in both the plant and the community declines as the assembly size increases.

Evidence that the contemporary cooperatives in the United States have indeed tended to be quite small comes from a survey of American worker cooperatives reported by Jackall & Crain in 1984: The 95 cooperatives surveyed show a median size of only 6.5 employees per firm. While the small size of these organizations may be due in large part to their relative youth and economic marginality, the literature has also described a number of instances of successful democratic businesses that chose to spin-off new enterprises rather than allow themselves to grow beyond a certain point (Rothschild-Whitt 1979a:222–4). The cooperatives of Mondragón, Spain, also make it a policy to spin off subsidiaries in order to keep down their size (Johnson & Whyte 1977:23).

Mansbridge (1980) has argued that organizational democracy works best with relatively small groups, although Rothschild & Whitt (1986) point out that the data do not provide a single cut-off point beyond which democratic control yields to oligarchic control. Optimal size, while strictly limited, seems to depend upon the structure and function of the organization.

Researchers of cooperatives in communist societies have come to similar conclusions. Kowalak (1981) examined 30 years of post-war experience with worker cooperatives in Poland and concluded that "democracy is inversely proportional to the size of the cooperative, and it seems to be a rule in spite of several experiments being made to avoid the consequences of that rule." He therefore urges that cooperatives not exceed a size compatible with a general meeting of all the members, not simply their representatives. Limits to cooperative size seem also to be acknowledged in China, where the mean cooperative firm size is 78, while the average size of state-owned firms is 850 (Lockett 1981).

Beyond this issue of organizational size, several authors have also argued that alternative organizations are most likely to arise and to succeed in industries and occupations in which skills and responsibilities can be widely shared, thereby minimizing the incidence of inequalities rooted in the nature of work (Rothschild-Whitt 1979b, Ouchi 1980, Russell 1985b).

Other evidence indicates that without small size and an egalitarian division of labor, nonbureaucratic forms of organization are difficult to establish and maintain. In large corporations that have tried "quality of work life" (QWL) experiments, for example, lower and middle managers have often shown little sympathy for workplace reforms that require them to share power with their subordinates (Walton 1975, Berg et al 1978; Yanovitch 1978), and rank-and-file workers have sometimes been ill equipped to take advantage of the rare participation opportunities that they do receive (Witte 1980). In conventional firms that shift to employee ownership, managers often retain the same decision-making rights that they had before the change in ownership (Hammer & Stern 1980, Hammer et al 1982, Russell 1984b). Researchers have often found that, even when employees do obtain formal authority for governing their firms, managerial personnel continue to exercise a disproportionate influence in assemblies of the membership (Rus 1970, Tannenbaum et al 1974, Zupanov 1975, Obradovic 1975, Obradovic & Dunn 1978, Verba & Shabad 1978, Russell et al 1979, IDE 1981).

While they present formidable obstacles to the democratization of a firm, large size and division of labor do not completely rule out workplace reform. Kanter (1983) has shown, for example, that many large firms have been among the most persistent sponsors of broader worker participation in working-life decisions, in part because the top managers of these firms have seen these changes as crucial to their organizations' continued success. Employee-owned firms and worker cooperatives have also shown a good deal of ingenuity in coping with the problems presented by the division of labor and large organizational size. For example, programs of shopfloor-level job redesign have been attempted in Israeli kibbutzim (Cherns 1980, Leviatan & Rosner 1980) and in the cooperatives of Mondragón, Spain (Johnson & Whyte 1977). Other organizations have encouraged the development of work teams, committees, and other intermediate bodies that promise to help decentralize their structures (Mansbridge 1980, Sacks 1983, Gunn 1984:138–9). Other common strategies have been to accept a given division of labor, but to minimize its consequence by rotating a large proportion of the membership into and out of various leadership positions (Rosner & Cohen 1983, Leviatan 1983, Rothschild-Whitt 1979b:516–7), or by reserving rights of membership or seats on boards of directors solely for nonmanagerial employees (Russell 1985a:61).

Member Satisfaction and Motivation

Alternative work organizations generally have a positive effect upon workers' satisfaction with their jobs and identification with their firms. Such findings have been reported both for worker participation in conventional firms (Blumberg 1969, Cummings & Molloy 1977, Locke & Schweiger 1979) and for a large variety of cooperatives, collectives, and employee-owned firms (Long 1978a,b, 1979; Russell et al 1979; Greenberg 1980; Russell 1982; Schlesinger & Bart 1982; Rosen et al 1985; Rothschild & Whitt 1986: Ch. 6). Less autocratic work environments are also associated with less alienation and superior mental health among workers (Kohn & Schooler 1973, Tannenbaum et al 1974, Kohn 1976, Leviatan & Rosner 1980).

However, within this general picture of favorable psychological outcomes, some noteworthy exceptions and qualifications have emerged. For example, of the two studies that have attempted to measure the impact of worker-ownership on absenteeism, both found higher rates of absence in the worker-owned firms. One of these studies (Rhodes & Steers 1981) compared a plywood cooperative in the Pacific Northwest to a matched conventional firm; the other (Hammer et al 1981) used before-and-after data from a furniture manufacturing firm that had recently been purchased by its employees. The authors of both studies argue that worker-owners seemed to feel that their status as owners gave them the right to stay home when their health was below par, whereas nonowners were more fearful that even justifiable absences would arouse the suspicion and displeasure of superiors.

This evidence of higher absences among worker-owners may be linked to other recent studies that indicate that workplace democracy can actually add to the worry and strain of work. Cooperatives and collectives, for example, often evoke high levels of loyalty and involvement from their participants, but stress and burnout may result from intense engagement (Mansbridge 1980; Rothschild & Whitt 1986: Ch. 6; Swidler 1979). In a 1977 survey of California's worker-owned scavenger firms, worker-owners also registered higher levels of anxiety and hostility than nonowners who did the same work. At that time it was unclear whether this finding reflected a long-term consequence of cooperative ownership in these firms or was due to the more immediate circumstance that many of these worker-owners were being sued by their nonowning employees while that study was being done (Russell 1982).

In addition to these occasional suggestions of negative consequences, worker ownership has sometimes appeared to have little or no impact on the attitudes or behavior of employees. Particularly where employee stock ownership arrangements have been superimposed on a conventional firm and the organization has remained unchanged in other respects, the worker ownership has had little effect on attitudes or satisfaction (Long 1979, 1982; French & Rosenstein 1981;

Kruse 1981). Researchers have concluded from these and other studies that employee ownership is unlikely to bring about much change in workers' attitudes, motivations, or allegiances to the firm, unless it is accompanied by a significant expansion in workers' participation in decision-making as well (Whyte et al 1983).

This conclusion, however, has recently been challenged by the research of Rosen et al (1986), who surveyed employee attitudes in 37 companies with Employee Stock Ownership Plans. These authors found that job satisfaction and organizational commitment had little to do with whether or not employees received the right to vote their stock, but these feelings were enhanced by the dollar value of the stock they received. While this research includes the largest number of ESOPs studied to date, its results need further analysis. For example, we need to know whether employees' favorable responses to ESOPs are actually a response to stock ownership per se or to the fact that compensation is being increased by the employer's gift of stock. Might employees have been even happier to have received the gift in cash instead of stock? As Rosen et al note, the right to vote stock may not be an especially meaningful form of worker participation.

Long (1978b) describes a case in which substantial forms of worker owner-ship and worker participation were present within the same firm. The firm was a Canadian trucking company that had recently been bought by its employees. Long found that both workers' ownership of stock and their participation in decision-making had independently significant and favorable effects on em-ployees' attitudes.

Within the United States, at least four efforts to establish "democratic ESOPs" have been developed since 1980. The structure of these firms has provided for greater worker control on the shop floor, more access to corporate information, and worker representatives on Boards of Directors. These cases have utilized the cooperative principle of "one worker-one vote;" unlike earlier cases, all these were brought into being with active union involvement. It is too early to report results from these "democratic ESOPs," but for a description of how they have parted company from the earlier ESOP examples, and for what salutory effects upon workers they might be expected to have, see Midwest Center for Labor Research (1985).

Empirical studies of the actual motives of participants come to varying conclusions. A case study of a mid-1970s worker buy-out found that job-saving motives were foremost among both blue-collar and white-collar employees (Hammer & Stern 1980). In an examination of historical materials on coopera-tives in the United States from 1880 to 1935, Shirom (1972) concludes that the cooperatives were formed by members chiefly as a defensive measure to save jobs or to avoid downward mobility, and secondarily, to achieve entrepreneur-ial ambitions. Totally lacking in America, he argues, were collectivist ideals, although such ideals were sometimes found among European cooperators. In a recent study of the plywood co-ops in the Pacific Northwest (started in the 1920s), Greenberg (1981) argues that the members of the co-ops joined the firms for economistic reasons. In a 1974 comparison of American, Austrian, Italian, Yugoslav, and kibbutz workers, for example, Tannenbaum et al found that the Yugoslav and kibbutz samples reported the highest levels of actual participation by rank-and-file employees, but these groups also recorded the highest levels of desire for participation among rank-and-file employees. As a result, discrepancies between "ideal" and "real" participation were lowest among the American employees, and this may help to explain why job satisfaction was also highest within the American group (Tannenbaum et al 1974).

This finding contrasts markedly with the collectivist values and desire for autonomy apparent in contemporary collectives. Rothschild & Whitt (1986) see participation in the contemporary collectivist organizations as motivated by a "coalescence of material and ideal interests," i.e. participation in the cooperatives provides a means of livelihood that is consistent with members' values. Similar conclusions emerge from a study of the new "O & O" (meaning worker Owned and Operated) cooperative grocery stores spun-off from A & P through a unique contract with the United Food and Commercial Workers Union. The researchers found that those workers who choose to pledge money for worker ownership (a worker must pledge $5000 to become a co-op member of an O & O) are more interested in avoiding unemployment, and they are more entrepreneurial than nonpledgers. However, they also have stronger collectivist/participatory values than do nonpledgers (Hochner & Granrose 1986). The strength of the latter factor was contrary to the initial hypotheses of the researchers. Hochner & Granrose (1986) conclude ". . . the level of collective idealism expressed by these workers (former A & P employees) points to a greater interest in workplace reform than is generally recognized among American workers."

Economic Performance

The economic behavior of labor-managed workplaces has been a topic of increasing interest to neoclassical economic theorists and social science researchers alike. Pioneering theoretical works by Ward (1958), Vanek (1970, 1977), and Meade (1972) have given rise to a voluminous literature and to several valuable literature reviews and efforts at synthesis, such as those of Ireland & Law (1982), Pryor (1983), and Stephen (1984).

Within the theoretical literature, attention has gradually shifted away from the question of whether labor-managed firms could under any circumstances be competitive with conventional capitalist firms, toward a more detailed exploration of a number of cooperative models that could at least hypothetically be expected to perform as well as or better than conventional firms. A major limitation of these modeling efforts, however, is that they have tended to race far ahead of our actual empirical experience with worker-managed firms. And at the level of models alone, Pryor (1983:152) has complained that "almost anything can be shown to happen," depending on the assumptions that are made about the structures and goals of both labor-managed and conventional firms. Pryor therefore concludes his review of this theoretical literature by remarking that:

> Theoretical analyses have given us too many conflicting theories of behavior of production cooperatives. If we are to be able to say anything definite about such organizations, it is imperative to leave our armchairs and empirically to investigate how these cooperatives actually work (1983:164).

For more empirically minded investigators, the major problem until recently has been finding enough instances of labor-managed firms to write about. One set of intensive studies has documented the success of three unusually dynamic populations of cooperative firms: the Israeli kibbutzim (Barkai 1977, Don 1977); the plywood cooperatives of the American Pacific Northwest (Berman 1967, 1982; Bellas 1972); and the producer cooperatives of Mondragón, Spain (Thomas & Logan 1982, Bradley & Gelb 1983a). Jones (1976, 1979, 1980, 1984) has also attempted surveys of the past and present economic performance of producer cooperatives both in Western Europe and in the United States. These efforts have recently been supplemented by research symposia edited by Stephen (1982) and Jones & Svejnar (1982), and by literature reviews reported by Abell (1983), Cornforth (1983), and Stephen (1984).

Despite this progress, several problems continue to stand in the way of our ability to generalize about the comparative economic performance of cooperative versus conventional enterprises. First, researchers have been able to dredge up only sketchy economic data from small numbers of cooperative firms. In those rare instances when reliable information on cooperatives has been found, data on comparable sets of conventional firms have generally been lacking. Second, direct comparisons between labor-managed and conventional firms are problematic because of their different goals. Thus, while the studies cited above have made it clear that some cooperative firms have done well and others have not, the question of whether cooperative firms are any more or less prone to failure than conventional firms remains difficult to answer.

Within the United States, recent research has focused less on the labor-managed firm than on the consequences of employee ownership. As indicated earlier, employee ownership in the American context has occasionally been accompanied by some form of worker control, but more frequently it has produced little or no change in the preexisting patterns of decision-making for a firm. Economic analyses of employee ownership in the United States have concentrated on such recent innovations as worker buy-outs of closing firms and the spread of Employee Stock Ownership Plans to otherwise healthy firms. Studies of worker buyouts generally find significant reductions in labor costs and improvements in labor productivity, although in some cases these economies have not been sufficient to save the firms involved (Whyte et al 1983; Bradley & Gelb 1983b; Gunn 1984: Ch. 5; Russell 1984b).

Although worker buyouts of firms in distress are still relatively rare, other forms of employee ownership have been more common, making possible quantitative studies of the economic performance of employee-owned vs conventional firms (Conte & Tannenbaum 1978, Livingston & Henry 1980, Marsh & McAllister 1981, Brooks et al 1982, Rosen & Klein 1983, Tannenbaum et al 1984). All of these studies have employed an essentially similar design. In each instance, the authors gathered economic data from a sample of firms with some degree of employee ownership; they then compared the performance of those firms to that of a matched set of conventionally owned firms. Most of these studies have taken profitability as their dependent variable, with the exception of Marsh & McAllister (1981) who looked at labor productivity, and Rosen & Klein (1983) who chose employment growth as their criterion. Conte & Tannenbaum (1978), Marsh & McAllister (1981), and Rosen & Klein (1983) all report a favorable impact for employee ownership on the economic performance of a firm. Tannenbaum et al (1984) found no difference in profitability between employee-owned and nonemployee-owned firms, while Livingston & Henry (1980) and Brooks et al (1982) found firms with employee ownership to be less profitable than conventional firms.

In attempting to reconcile these conflicting findings, several aspects of the design of these studies are worthy of note. First, in addition to differences in the dependent variables they used, these studies also differed substantially in the populations of worker-owned firms from which they drew their samples. Conte & Tannenbaum (1978) and Tannenbaum et al (1984) drew general samples of "employee-owned firms," including firms with and without Employee Stock Ownership Plans (ESOPs). Rosen & Klein (1983) also looked at both ESOP and non-ESOP firms, but confined themselves to firms that were majority employee-owned (i.e. at least 51% owned by the workers). Marsh & McAllister (1981) sampled only firms with ESOPs; while the research of Livingston & Henry (1980) and Brooks et al (1982) is based on a sample of firms with employee stock purchase plans established prior to 1974 and is therefore not a study of ESOPs at all.

Even more important than these differences in the populations of organizations sampled due to some common limitations on the generalizability of the studies with low response rates and nonrandom sampling frames. A fundamental problem affecting all of this research is that, as of this writing, there is no means available for drawing a random sample of employee-owned firms. Even the federal government, which called forth the ESOPs, cannot provide an accurate listing of ESOP firms or do more than estimate the total number of firms that have these plans. The US General Accounting Office has recently been asked by Congress to identify and survey a sample of firms with ESOPs and to make a new effort to compare the economic performance of ESOP and nonESOP firms, but the results of that study will not be available until the latter half of 1986.

The literature on the economic consequences of workers' participation in decision-making and of efforts to improve the quality of working life (QWL) are in many ways parallel to the literature on the economic performance of worker-owned and -managed firms. While successful QWL cases have frequently been reported (for reviews, see Blumberg 1969, Cummings & Molloy 1977, Katzell et al 1977, Guzzo & Bondy 1983, Katzell & Guzzo 1983), hard-nosed critiques of these studies have often faulted many aspects of their designs and concluded that the economic merits of these QWL innovations remain unproved (Katzell et al 1977, Locke & Schweiger 1979, Levitan & Johnson 1982, Levitan & Werneke 1984).

Degeneration or Institutionalization?

Beyond the difficulties inherent in efforts to create alternative work environments that are both economically viable and meaningful to their participants, workplace reformers have had to face one additional and possibly even greater challenge: the problem of making their innovations last. Researchers have often noted that even economically successful workplace reforms tend to be short-lived. Walton (1975) and Levitan & Johnson (1982) have made this observation about demonstration projects in job redesign, and it has been made even more frequently about communes, cooperatives, and other varieties of worker-owned firms. Of these latter organizations, it is sometimes suggested that the more they succeed as businesses, the more they tend to lose their democratic character, to "degenerate" back into conventional organizational forms.

The idea that democracy yields to oligarchy goes back to the compelling thesis of Michels (1962). The more specific notion that worker-managed workplaces inevitably degenerate is usually attributed to the Fabian socialists Sidney and Beatrice Webb. In 1920 they asserted categorically that "All such association of producers that start as alternatives to the capitalist system either fail or cease to be democracies of producers" (Webb & Webb 1920:29). For the Webbs and later writers on this subject, evidence of degeneration has taken such specific forms as an increasing reliance on hired, nonmember labor; increasingly oligarchical patterns of decision-making; the accumulation of ownership shares in fewer and fewer hands; and the sale of the firm entirely to conventional owners.

The causes to which these degenerative tendencies have been attributed are as diverse as the phenomenon of degeneration itself. In recent years, degeneration has received considerable attention from economists. In the eyes of Vanek (1977) and Ellerman (1982), degeneration results from the way in which the founders of democratic workplaces obtain capital for their firms. When these firms are financed through member contributions or retained earnings, members often have no other means to recoup these investments than by employing hired labor or by auctioning off their membership shares. Vanek and Ellerman therefore predict that degenerative pressures will be minimized if labor-managed firms obtain their capital through loans, either from external sources or in the form of interest-bearing loans from individual members that are automatically returned to departing members without in any way altering the structure of the firm.

Other works have identified causes of degeneration that have nothing to do with the accumulation of capital by a firm. In the work of Ben-Ner (1984) and Miyazaki (1984), degenerative pressures originate simply in the availability of cheap nonmember labor outside a labor-managed firm. Ben-Ner notes that these firms will always be tempted to employ this cheaper hired labor, even in cases in which nonmember labor is clearly less productive than the labor of members. This is because when the firm adds a new member, its income increases, but the number of people who share in that income will also increase; assuming that scale economies have been exhausted, the net income per member will remain unchanged. However, if the firm hires nonmember labor, its income may not increase as fast, but whatever profits result will become additions to the incomes of the existing members (Ben-Ner 1984).

In addition to these economic accounts, the degeneration of labor-managed firms has also been attributed to a variety of other organizational and normative processes. One tradition emphasizes the inevitability of elite formation (Shirom 1972), or Michels' "iron law of oligarchy" (Hartmann 1979). Others have associated degeneration with a gradual erosion of the unique consciousness, division of labor, consensual decision-making, and other characteristics that originally defined these enterprises, under the impact of routinization, contact with the outside world, and the importation of inappropriate technologies (Niv 1980, Berger 1981, Russell 1984b, 1985a). Sometimes work groups are able to maintain a closely knit and consensual "clan" structure, but only by excluding other ethnic groups and cultures that they consider "outsiders" (Ouchi 1980, Russell 1984a).

Thus, potential causes of the degeneration phenomenon have not been hard to find. Taken together, these explanations do much to support pessimistic assertions about the inevitable demise of democratic enterprises. The degeneration issue, however, is another area in which theorizing about the nature of worker-managed firms has outstripped our empirical knowledge about the actual behavior of these firms. Most discussions of degeneration have been based on impressionistic evidence, and they have offered few opportunities to generalize about how widespread these processes really are, how rapidly they operate, which causal factors are most important in prompting them, or under what circumstances they can be held in check.

To date, the most detailed empirical study of the long-term dynamics of alternative workplaces dealt with nineteenth-century American communes (Kanter 1972). This study indicates that tendencies to revert to more conventional, bureaucratic structures have indeed shown up, but alternative workplaces are *not* inevitably doomed to succumb to these tendencies. Rosner (1982), for example, has identified sources of stability in the contemporary kibbutz movement, and Batstone (1983) in his study of the French cooperatives draws the optimistic conclusion that oligarchical degeneration has often led to the establishment of new forms of representation for rank-and-file members. By analyzing the dynamics of the American grassroots cooperatives, Rothschild & Whitt (1986) are able to identify specific strategic choices that members may make at critical junctures in the organization's life, that sustain and renew democracy, as opposed to undermining it.

In addition, specific techniques for financing the creation of labor-managed firms may put them on a more secure footing. These financing methods are best illustrated by the cooperatives of Mondragón, Spain. At the heart of this cluster of cooperatives lies a bank, the *Caja Laboral Popular,* which was created specifically to help finance the development of cooperative firms (Johnson & Whyte 1977). The *Caja* is itself a cooperative and makes the adoption of democratic cooperative structures a precondition for its loans. The Mondragón cooperatives also obtain capital from member contributions and from retained earnings, but most of these funds are accounted for as loans from the individual members and are returned to those individuals as they retire. These financial arrangements appear to have made the Mondragón cooperatives unusually resistant to some of the most common economic sources of degeneration, and similar arrangements have recently been advanced by nonprofit funding agencies located in the United States. (The Industrial Cooperatives Association (ICA) of Somerville, Massachusetts, and the Philadelphia Association for Cooperative Enterprise (PACE) are two examples.)

Alternative workplaces are also likely to show greater stability where they enjoy the active sponsorship of the state. Yugoslavia's self-managed workplaces do not employ nonmember labor, for example, because the laws of that country do not permit it. In many Western European countries, workers' representation at various levels of decision-making, including the Boardroom, is now required by law.

In the United States we already have some relevant but little known legislation that promotes worker ownership. For example, members of the plywood cooperatives have been advised by their attorneys that they should limit the use of nonmember labor within their firms, because they might otherwise lose the favorable tax status that cooperatives enjoy in the tax code. Of even greater significance for the United States is the current federal sponsorship of Employee Stock Ownership Plans (ESOPs). Federal laws governing ESOPs have evolved since 1974, and today the federal provisions require these plans to be open to incoming employees and to include procedures through which departing employees can receive their accumulated capital without in any way altering the structure of the plans. These laws may thus help to make the ESOPs a form of worker ownership that is more resistant to degeneration. The ESOP laws also stipulate circumstances under which the voting rights over ESOP stock must be "passed through" to the employees; and although voting rights are usually tied to number of shares owned, which is usually quite unequal in the ESOPs, there are a few post-1980 ESOP cases that have found ways within the law to ensure the cooperative principle of "one worker-one vote" (Midwest Center for Labor Research 1985).

Alternative forms of work organization are constantly being developed, and the specific forms that they take and who benefits from them depend upon which constituent groups remain involved in their development. We have seen that QWL, ESOPs, and direct worker cooperatives are all examples of workplace democratization, but the specific forms they have taken have varied greatly, and their outcomes are by no means predetermined. Several types of democratic participation in the economy that have emerged within the past decade show greater promise than predictions such as the Webbs' "demise of democracy," or Braverman's "degradation of work," or Michels' "iron law of oligarchy" would lead us to expect.

Literature Cited

Abell, P. 1983. The viability of industrial producer co-operation. In *International Yearbook of Organizational Democracy*, ed. C. Crouch, F. A. Heller, 1:73–103. Chichester: Wiley

Barkai, H. 1977. *Growth Patterns of the Kibbutz Economy*. Amsterdam: North-Holland

Batstone, E. 1983. Organization and orientation: A life cycle model of French cooperatives. *Econ. Ind. Democ.* 4:139–61

Bellas, C. 1972. *Industrial Democracy and the Worker-Owned Firm*. New York: Praeger

Ben-Ner, A. 1982. Changing values and preferences in communal organizations: Econometric evidence from the experience of the Israeli kibbutz. In *Participatory and Self-Managed Firms: Evaluating Economic Performance*, ed. D. C. Jones, J. Svejnar, pp. 255–86. Lexington, Mass: Lexington

Ben-Ner, A. 1984. On the stability of the cooperative type of organization. *J. Comp. Econ.* 8:247–60

Berg, I., Freedman, M., Freeman, M. 1978. *Managers and Work Reform: A Limited Engagement*. New York: Free Press. 316 pp.

Berger, B. M. 1981. *The Survival of a Counterculture: Ideological Work and Everyday Life Among Rural Communards*. Berkeley: Univ. Calif. Press

Berman, K. V. 1967. *Worker-Owned Plywood Companies: An Economic Analysis*. Pullman: Wash. State Univ. Press

Berman, K. V. 1982. The worker-owned plywood cooperatives. See Lindenfeld & Rothschild-Whitt 1982, pp.

Blumberg, P. 1968. *Industrial Democracy: The Sociology of Participation*. New York: Schocken

Bradley, K., Gelb, A. 1983a. *Cooperation at Work: The Mondrágon Experience*. London: Heinemann

Bradley, K., Gelb, A. 1983b. *Worker Capitalism: The New Industrial Relations*. Cambridge: MIT Press

Braverman, H. 1974. *Labor and Monopoly Capital: The Degradation of Work in the Twentieth Century.* NY: Mon. Rev.

Brooks, L. D., Henry, J. B., Livingston, D. T. 1982. How profitable are employee stock ownership plans? *Fin. Exec.* (May):32–40

Burawoy, M. 1978. Toward a Marxist theory of the labor process: Braverman and beyond. *Polit. Soc.* 8:247–312

Burawoy, M. 1979. *Manufacturing Consent: Changes in the Labor Process under Monopoly Capitalism.* Chicago: Univ. Chicago Press

Butler, R. 1983a. Control of workflow in organizations: Perspectives from markets, hierarchies, and collecties. *Hum. Relat.* 36:421–40

Butler, R. 1983b. A transactional approach to organizing efficiency: Perspectives from markets, hierarchies, and collectives. *Admin. Soc.* 15:323–62

Case, J., Taylor, R. C. R., eds. 1979. *Co-ops, Communes & Collectives: Experiments in Social Change in the 1960s and 1970s.* New York: Pantheon

Chelte, A. F., Wright, J., Tausky, C. 1982. Did job satisfaction really drop during the 1970's? *Mon. Labor Rev.* 105(11):33–36

Cherns, A., ed. 1980. *Quality of Working Life and the Kibbutz Experience.* Norwood, Penn: Norwood

Conte, M., Tannenbaum, A. S. 1978. Employee owned companies: Is the difference measurable? *Mon. Labor Rev.* 101:23–28

Cornforth, C. 1983. Some factors affecting the success or failure of worker cooperatives: A review of empirical research in the United Kingdom. *Econ. Ind. Democ.* 4:163–190

Cummings, T. G., Molloy, E. S. 1977. *Improving Productivity and the Quality of Work Life.* New York: Praeger

Derber, C., Schwartz, W. 1983. Toward a theory of worker participation. *Soc. Inquiry* 53:61–78

Don, Y. 1977. Dynamics of development in the Israeli kibbutz. In *Cooperative and Commune: Group Farming in the Economic Development of Agriculture,* ed. P. Dorner. Madison: Univ. Wisc. Press

Edwards, R. 1979. *Contested Terrain.* New York: Basic

Ellerman, D. 1982. On the legal structure of workers' cooperatives. See Lindenfeld & Rothschild-Whitt 1982. pp. 299–313

Esping-Andersen, G., Friedland, R. 1982. Class coalitions in the making of West European economies. In *Political Power and Social Theory,* 3:1–52. Greenwich, Conn: JAI

Fenwick, R., Olson, J. 1984. *Contested terrain or created consensus: Why workers want participation in workplace decision-making.* Presented at the Ann. Meet. Am. Sociol. Assoc., San Antonio, Tex.

French, J. L., Rosenstein, J. 1981. *Employee stock ownership and managerial authority: A case study in Texas.* Presented at the Ann. Meet. Southwestern Sociol. Assoc., March

Frieden, K. 1980. Workplace Democracy and Productivity. Washington, DC: Natl. Center Econ. Alternatives

Gouldner, A. W. 1979. *The Future of Intellectuals and the Rise of the New Class.* New York: Oxford Univ. Press

Greenberg, F. S. 1980. Participation in industrial decision making and work satisfaction: The case of producer cooperatives. *Polit. Sci. Q.* 60:551–69

Greenberg, F. S. 1981. Industrial self-management and political attitudes. *Am. Polit. Sci. Rev.* 75(March):29–42

Gunn, C. E. 1984. *Workers' Self-Management in the United States.* Ithaca: Cornell Univ. Press. 251 pp.

Guzzo, R. A., Bondy, J. A. 1983. *A Guide to Worker Productivity Experiments in the United States 1976–81.* New York: Pergamon

Haas, A. 1980. Workers' views on self-management: A comparative study of the U.S. and Sweden. In *Classes, Class Conflict, and the State,* ed. M. Zeitlin, pp. 276–95. Cambridge, Mass: Winthrop

Hammer, T. H., Landau, J. C., Stern, R. N. 1981. Absenteeism when workers have a voice: The case of employee ownership. J. Appl. Psychol. 66:561–73

Hammer, T. H., Stern, R. N. 1980. Employee ownership: Implications for the organizational distribution of power. *Acad. Mgmt. J.* 23:78–100

Hammer, T. H., Stern, R. N., Gurdon, M. A. 1982. Worker ownership and attitudes toward participation. See Lindenfeld & Rothschild-Whitt 1982, pp. 87–108

Hartmann, H. 1979. Works councils and the iron law of oligarchy. *Br. J. Indust. Rel.* 17:70–82

Hochner, A., Granrose, C. 1986. Sources of motivation to choose employee ownership as an alternative to job loss. *Acad. Mgmt. J.* 28:860–75

Industrial Democracy in Europe International Research Group. 1981. *Industrial Democracy in Europe.* New York: Oxford Univ. Press

Ingham, G. K. 1970. *Size of Industrial Organization and Worker Behavior.* Cambridge: Cambridge Univ. Press

Ireland, N. J., Law, P. J. 1982. *The Economics*

of Labour-Managed Enterprises. London: Croom Helm

Jackall, R., Crain, J. 1984. The shape of the small worker cooperative movement. See Jackall & Levin 1984, pp. 88–108

Jackall, R., Levin, H. M., eds. 1984. *Worker Cooperatives in America.* Berkeley: Univ. Calif. Press

Johnson, A. G., Whyte, W. F. 1977. The Mondragon system of worker production cooperatives. *Ind. Labor Relat. Rev.* 31:18–30

Jones, D. 1976. British producer cooperatives. In *The New Worker Co-operatives,* ed. K. Coates, Nottingham: Spokesman

Jones, D. 1979. U.S. producer cooperatives: The record to date. *Ind. Relat.* 181:342–57

Jones, D. 1980. Producer co-operatives in industrialized Western economies. *Br. J. Ind. Relat.* 16:141–54

Jones, D. 1984. American producer cooperatives and employee-owned firms: A historical perspective. See Jackall & Levin 1984, pp. 37–56

Jones, D., Svejnar, J., eds. 1982. *Participatory and Self-Managed Firms: Evaluating Economic Performance.* Lexington, Mass: Lexington

Jones, G. R. 1983. Transaction costs, property rights, and organizational culture: An exchange perspective. *Admin. Sci. Q.* 28:454–67

Kanter, R. M. 1972. *Commitment and Community: Communes and Utopias in Sociological Perspective.* Cambridge, Mass: Harvard Univ. Press

Kanter, R. M. 1983. *The Change Masters: Innovations for Productivity in the American Corporation.* New York: Simon & Schuster

Kanter, R. M., Stein, B., Brinkerhoff, D. 1982. Building participatory democracy within a conventional corporation. See Lindenfeld & Rothschild-Whitt 1982, pp. 371–382

Katzell, R. A., Bienstock, P., Faerstein, P. H. 1977. *A Guide to Worker Productivity Experiments in the United States 1971–1975.* New York: New York Univ. Press

Katzell, R. A., Guzzo, R. A. 1983. Psychological approaches to productivity improvement. *Am. Psychol.* 38:468–72

Katzell, R. A. 1979. Changing attitudes toward work. In *Work in America: The Decade Ahead,* ed. C. Kerr, J. Rosow, pp. 35–57. New York: Van Nostrand

Kohn, M. L. 1971. Bureaucratic man: A portrait and an interpretation. *Am. Sociol. Rev.* 36:461–74

Kohn, M. L. 1976. Occupational structure and alienation. *Am. J. Sociol.* 82:111–30

Kohn, M. L., Schooler, C. 1969. Class, occupation, and orientation. *Am. Sociol. Rev.* 34:659–78

Kohn, M. L., Schooler, C. 1973. Occupational experience and psychological functioning: An assessment of reciprocal effects. *Am. Sociol. Rev.* 38:97–118

Kowalak, T. 1981. *Work Co-operatives in Poland.* Paper presented at the First Int. Conf. Producer Cooperatives, Copenhagen, June

Krauz, E., ed. 1983. *The Sociology of the Kibbutz.* New Brunswick: Transaction

Kruse, D. 1981. *The effects of worker ownership upon participation desire: An ESOP case study,* Honors B.A. thesis. Harvard College, Cambridge, Mass.

Leviatan, U. 1983. Organizational effects of managerial turnover in kibbutz production branches. In *The Sociology of the Kibbutz,* ed. E. Krauz, pp. 385–402. New Brunswick: Transaction

Leviatan, U., Rosner, M. 1980. *Work and Organization in Kibbutz Industry.* Norwood, Penn: Norwood

Levitan, S. A., Johnson, C. M. 1982. *Second Thoughts on Work.* Kalamazoo, Mich: Upjohn

Levitan, S. A., Werneke, D. 1984. Worker participation and productivity change. *Mon. Labor Rev.* 107:28–33

Lindenfeld, J., Rothschild-Whitt, J., eds. 1982. *Workplace Democracy and Social Change.* Boston: Porter Sargent

Littler, C. R., Salaman, G. 1982. Bravermania and beyond: Recent theories of the labour process. *Sociology* 16:251–69

Livingston, D. T., Henry, J. B. 1980. The effects of employee stock ownership plans on corporate profits. *J. Risk. Ins.* 47:491–505

Locke, E. A., Schweiger, D. M. 1979. Participation in decision-making: One more look. *Res. Organ. Behav.* 1:265–339

Lockett, M. 1981. *Producer cooperatives in China: 1919–1981.* Paper presented at the First Int. Conf. Producer Cooperatives, Copenhagen, Denmark, June

Long, R. J. 1978a. The effects of employee ownership on organizational identification, employee job attitudes, and organizational performance: A tentative framework and empirical findings. *Hum. Relat.* 31:29–48

Long, R. J. 1978b. The relative effects of share ownership vs. control on job attitudes in an employee-owned company. *Hum. Relat.* 31:753–63

Long, R. J. 1979. Desires for and patterns of worker participation after conversion to employee ownership. *Acad. Mgmt. J.* 22 (3):611–617

Long, R. J. 1982. Worker ownership and job attitudes: A field study. *Ind. Relat.* 21:196–215

Mansbridge, J. J. 1980. *Beyond Adversary Democracy.* New York: Basic. 398 pp.

Marsh, T. R., McAllister, D. E. 1981. ESOPs tables: A survey of companies with Employee Stock Ownership Plans. *J. Corp. Law* 6:551–623

Meade, J. E. 1972. The theory of labour-managed firms and of profit sharing. *Econ. J.* 82:402–28

Michels, R. 1962. *Political Parties.* New York: Free Press

Midwest Center for Labor Research. 1985. Workers as Owners. Special issue of *Labor Res. Rev.* 6 (Spring): pp. 1–114

Miyazaki, H. 1984. On success and dissolution of the labor-managed firm in the capitalist economy. *J. Polit. Econ.* 92:909–31

Naisbitt, J., Aburdene, P. 1985. *Re-inventing the Corporation.* New York: Warner

New York Stock Exchange, Office of Economic Research. 1982. *People and Productivity: A Challenge to Corporate America.* NY Stock Exchange

Niv, A. 1980. Organizational disintegration: Roots, processes, and types. In *The Organizational Life Cycle: Issues in the Creation, Transformation, and Decline of Organizations,* ed. J. R. Kimberly, R. H. Miles, pp. 375–94. San Francisco: Jossey-Bass

Obradovic, J. 1975. Workers' participation: Who participates? *Ind. Relat.* 14:32–44

Obradovic, J., Dunn, W. N., eds. 1975. *Workers Self-Management and Organizational Power in Yugoslavia.* Pittsburg: Univ. Ctr. Int. Stud., Univ. Pittsburg

Ouchi, W. G. 1980. Markets, bureaucracies, and clans. *Admin. Sci. Q.* 25:129–41

Pryor, F. L. 1983. The economics of production cooperatives: A reader's guide. *Annals Pub. Co-op. Econ.* 5:133–72

Ramsay, H. 1977. Cycles of control: Worker participation in sociological and historical perspective. *Sociology* 11:481–506

Ramsay, H. 1983. Evolution or cycle? Worker participation in the 1970s and 1980s. In *International Yearbook of Organization Democracy,* ed. C. Crouch, F. A. Heller, 1:203–25. Chichester/New York: Wiley

Rhodes, S. R., Steers, R. M. 1981. Conventional vs. worker-owned organizations. *Hum. Relat.* 34:1013–35

Rifkin, J. 1977. *Own Your Own Job.* New York: Bantam

Rosen, C., Klein, K. 1983. Job-creating performance of employee-owned firms. *Mon. Labor Rev.* 106:15–19

Rosen, C., Klein, K., Young, K. 1986. *Employee Ownership in America: The Equity Solution.* Lexington, Mass: Lexington Books

Rosner, M. 1981. *Participatory political and organizational democracy and the experience of the Israeli kibbutz.* Paper presented at the First Int. Conf. on Producer Cooperatives, Copenhagen, Denmark, June

Rosner, M. 1982. *Democracy, Equality, and Change: The Kibbutz and Social Theory.* Darby, Penn: Norwood

Rosner, M., Blasi, J. 1985. Theories of Participatory Democracy and the Kibbutz. In *Social Dynamics: Essays in Honor of S. N. Eisenstadt,* ed. E. Cohen, et al pp. 295–314. Boulder, Colo.: Westview

Rosner, M., Cohen, N. 1983. Is direct democracy feasible in modern society?: The lesson of the kibbutz experience. In *The Sociology of the Kibbutz,* ed. E. Krauz, pp. 209–35. New Brunswick: Transaction

Rothschild-Whitt, J. 1979a. Conditions for democracy: Making participatory organizations work. See Case & Taylor 1979, pp. 215–44.

Rothschild-Whitt, J. 1979b. The collectivist organization: An alternative to rational-bureaucratic models. *Am. Sociol. Rev.* 44:509–27

Rothschild-Whitt, J. 1984. Worker ownership: Collective response to an elite-generated crisis. In *Research on Social Movements, Conflict and Change,* ed. (6):167–194. Greenwich, Conn: JAI

Rothschild, J., Whitt, A. 1986. *The Cooperative Workplace: Potentials and Dilemmas of Organizational Democracy and Participation.* New York: Cambridge Univ. Press. In press

Rus, V. 1970. Influence structure in Yugoslav enterprise. *Ind. Relat.* 9:148–60

Russell, R. 1982. The rewards of participation in the worker-owned firm. See Lindenfeld & Rothschild-Whitt 1982, pp. 109–24

Russell, R. 1984a. The role of culture and ethnicity in the degeneration of democratic firms. *Econ. Ind. Democ.* 5:73–96

Russell, R. 1984b. Using ownership to control: Making workers owners in the contemporary United States. *Polit. Soc.* 13:253–94

Russell, R. 1985a. *Sharing Ownership in the Workplace.* Albany: State Univ. NY Press

Russell, R. 1985b. Employee ownership and internal governance. *J. Econ. Behav. Organ.* 6:217–41

Russell, R., Hochner, A., Perry, S. E. 1979. Participation, influence, and worker ownership. *Ind. Relat.* 18:330–41

Sacks, S. R. 1983. *Self-Management and Efficiency: Large Corporations in Yugoslavia.* London: Allen & Unwin

Sale, K. 1980. *Human Scale.* New York: Coward, McCann, Geoghegan

Schlesinger, M., Bart, P. 1982. Collective work and self-identity: Working in a feminist illegal Abortion Collective. See Lindenfeld & Rothschild-Whitt 1982, pp. 139–53

Shirom, A. 1972. The industrial relations systems of industrial cooperatives in the United States, 1880–1935. *Labor Hist.* 13:533–51

Shumacher, E. F. 1973. *Small Is Beautiful: Economics As If People Mattered.* New York: Harper & Row

Simmons, J., Mares, W. 1983. *Working Together: Participation from the Shop Floor to the Boardroom.* New York: Knopf

Stark, D. 1980. Class struggle and the transformation of the labor process. *Theory Soc.* 9:89–130

Stephen, F. H., ed. 1982. *The Performance of Labour-Managed Firms.* London: MacMillan

Stephen, F. H. 1984. *The Economic Analysis of Producers' Cooperatives.* New York: St. Martin's

Stephens, E. H., Stephens, J. D. 1982. The labor movement, political power, and workers' participation in Western Europe. In *Political Power and Social Theory,* 3:215–49. Greenwich, Conn: JAI

Swidler, A. 1979. *Organization without Authority: Dilemmas of Social Control in Free Schools.* Cambridge, Mass: Harvard Univ. Press

Tannenbaum, A. S., Cook, H., Lohmann, J. 1984. *The Relationship of Employee Ownership to the Technological Adaptiveness and Performance of Companies.* NSF Res. Rep. Ann Arbor, Mich: Inst. Soc. Res.

Tannenbaum, A. S., Kavcic, B., Rosner, M., Vianello, M., Wieser, G. 1974. *Hierarchy in Organizations.* San Francisco: Jossey-Bass

Thomas, H., Logan, C. 1982. *Mondragon: An Economic Analysis.* London: Allen & Unwin

Vanek, J. 1970. *The General Theory of Labor-Managed Market Economies.* Ithaca: Cornell Univ. Press

Vanek, J. 1977. *The Labor-Managed Economy.* New York: Cornell Univ. Press

Verba, S., Shabad, G. 1978. Workers' council and political stratification: The Yugoslav experience. *Am. Polit. Sci. Rev.* 72:80–95

Walton, R. E. 1975. The diffusion of new work structures: Explaining why success didn't take. *Organ. Dynam.* 3(3) (Winter):3–21

Walton, R. E. 1979. Work innovations in the U.S. *Harvard Bus. Rev.* 57(4) (July–August):88–98

Ward, B. 1958. The firm in Illyria: Market syndicalism. *Am. Econ. Rev.* 48:566–89

Weaver, C. N. 1980. Job satisfaction in the United States in the 1970s. *J. Appl. Psychol.* 65:364–67

Webb, S., Webb, C. 1920. *A Constitution for the Socialist Commonwealth of Great Britain.* London: Longmans

Wells, M. J. 1981. Alienation, work structure, and the quality of life: Can cooperatives make a difference? *Soc. Probl.* 28:548–62

Whyte, W. F., Hammer, T. H., Meek, C. B., Nelson, R., Stern, R. H. 1983. *Worker Participation and Ownership: Cooperative Strategies for Strengthening Local Economies.* Ithaca, NY: ILR

Williamson, O. E. 1975. *Markets and Hierarchies: Analysis and Antitrust Implications.* New York: Free Press

Williamson, O. E. 1981. The economics of organization: The transaction cost approach. *Am. J. Sociol.* 87:548–77

Witte, John F. 1980. *Democracy, Authority and Alienation in Work.* Chicago: Univ. Chicago Press

Yanowitch, M. 1978. Pressures for more 'participatory' forms of economic organization in the Soviet Union. *Econ. Anal. Workers' Mgmt.* 12:403–17

Zablocki, B. 1980. *Alienation and Charisma: A Study of Contemporary American Communes.* New York: Free Press

Zipp, J. F., Luebke, P., Landerman, R. 1984. The social bases of support for workplace democracy. *Perspectives* 27:395–425

Zupanov, J. 1975. Participation and influence. In *Self-Governing Socialism,* ed. B. Horvat, M. Markovic, R. Supek, 2:76–87. White Plains, NY: Int. Arts & Sciences Press

Ann. Rev. Sociol. 1986. 12:329–46

RELIGIOUS MOVEMENTS: CULT AND ANTICULT SINCE JONESTOWN

Eileen Barker

Dean of Undergraduate Studies, London School of Economics and Political Science, Houghton Street, London WC2A 2AE, England

Abstract

The article contains an overview of theoretical and empirical work carried out by sociologists of religion in the study of new religious movements and the anticult movement since 1978; it pays special attention to the aftereffects of the mass suicide/murder of followers of Jim Jones in Guyana. The different theories as to why people join the movement are discussed—whether they are 'brainwashed,' what influences (pushes and/or pulls) the wider society has on the membership. Mention is made of the role of sociologists themselves as witnesses in court cases and as participant observers at conferences organized by the movements. Bibliographic details are supplied of writings about particular movements, in particular countries, and concerning particular problems (finances, family life, legal issues, conversion, 'deprogramming,' etc) It is suggested that the differences between the movements are considerably greater than is often recognized and that there is a need for further comparative research and more refined classificatory systems before our theoretical knowledge can develop and be tested satisfactorily. Various changes (such as the demographic variables of an aging membership, the death of charismatic leaders, and the socialization of second-generation membership; changing relationships with the 'host' society; and the growth—or demise—of the movements) provide much more of interest for the sociologist to study in the future.

INTRODUCTION

In November 1978 nearly the whole of the Western world had the "cult problem" brought starkly and vividly to its attention. US Congressman Leo

329

0360-0572/86/0815-0329$02.00

Ryan was shot dead at a jungle airport following an investigative visit to Jonestown, a community in Guyana built by members of the People's Temple. A religious group founded in 1953, the People's Temple was led by an ordained minister of the Disciples of Christ, the Reverend Jim Jones. A few hours after the murder of Ryan and 4 of his companions, Jones and over 900 of his followers were dead. First, the babies had cyanide squirted down their throats by syringe, and then the older children, followed by the adults, lined up to drink from cups of Kool-Aid laced with cyanide—it was a suicide ritual that the community had rehearsed on several previous occasions. It is not certain, however, that all of Jones' followers had been entirely willing to make this final gesture. Several had been shot as they tried to escape into the jungle. Nearly 300 of the victims had not reached their seventeenth birthday; a further 200 were over 65 (Wooden 1981).

These tragic events were to have two sorts of consequences for sociologists studying the new religious movements that had emerged in the West during the previous decade or so. First, it was clear that much more had to be learned about the movements and their potential consequences, both for the individuals most closely involved and for society as a whole. Secondly, the data themselves were to undergo a significant change. No new religion would be regarded in quite the same light or treated in quite the same way after Jonestown.

Prior to 1978, the People's Temple was not to be found featured in the anticult literature; for the rest of the 1970s and well into the 1980s, it was difficult to find a page, let alone an issue, of a magazine or newsletter published by the anticult lobby that did not contain at least one (frequently several) references to the mass suicide/murder. Merely a matter of days after the event, books written by journalists were selling like hot cakes (Kilduff & Javers 1978, Krause 1978).[1] Early in December 1978, a Gallup Poll found that 98% of the US public had heard or read about the People's Temple and the Guyana massacre—a level of awareness matched in the pollsters' experience only by the attack on Pearl Harbor and the explosion of the atom bomb. In a public opinion survey carried out by Albert Gollin in January, 1979, a nonexistent "spoof cult" was included in a list of religious movements about which residents of Washington, DC were asked their opinion. While it was not altogether unexpected that most respondents had heard of and reacted unfavorably to movements such as the Unification Church and the Hare Krishna, it was interesting that one in ten claimed to have heard of the spoof cult, and over a

[1]Countless articles and a score or more books have since been written about the People's Temple; some of the more interesting sociological information and/or insights can be gained from Coser & Coser (1979), Hall (1981), D. P. Johnson (1980), Lincoln & Mamiya (1980), Lindt (1981, 1982), E. W. Mills (1982), Reston (1981), and J. Richardson (1980).

quarter expressed an unfavorable attitude towards it. Almost one third of the respondents reported that they would be willing to see cult members forced to rejoin their families (Lindt & Gollin, unpublished paper presented at the Ann. Meet. Am. Assoc. Publ. Opinion Res., June 1979, p. 18).

The horror of Jonestown was compounded by its apparent incomprehensibility. How, it was repeatedly asked, was it possible for adult men and women, at least some of whom were reasonably well educated, to agree to take their own lives at the behest of a man who, in the eyes of most people, was surely nothing but a raving lunatic? And could it happen again? One answer to the "how" question seemed to emerge: It must have been some kind of mind control which was responsible. Accusations of brainwashing had certainly been levelled at new religions before Jonestown (Delgado 1977, Enroth 1977, Stoner & Parke 1977), and the practice of "deprogramming" (forcibly kidnapping members of the movements and holding them against their will until they renounce their faith) had been introduced in the early 1970s (Bryant 1979, Patrick 1976, H. Richardson 1977). After Jonestown, descriptions by media and anticultist pressure groups of conversion as brainwashing, and consequent arguments for the necessity of deprogramming, were heard with considerably more sympathy than had previously been the case.

During the next few years, reports were commissioned by various government and other official agencies throughout North America and Western Europe (e.g. Berger & Hexel 1981, Cottrell 1984, Derks 1983, Hill 1980, Vivien 1985). Constant attempts were made to pass legislation controlling the practices of the movements and/or giving the courts the right to grant parents custody of their adult children (Kelley 1982; H. Richardson 1980:20–36). Although the clamor for legislation that would allow parents to obtain "conservatorship orders" and/or to hospitalize their adult children has died down, it certainly has not died away. Many other legal issues have arisen: The new religions have fought for custody of their infant children, immigration rights, tax relief, definition as a religion, charitable status, and redress against deprogramming. They have defended themselves against charges of brainwashing, fraudulent practices, breaking-up of families, violations of by-laws, obstruction, tax evasion and so on. . . . Some of these disputes reach right to the heart of complicated constitutional principles; they explore the limits of the rights of groups whose actions (possibly as a direct consequence of their beliefs) are at variance with the perceived interests of the rest of society. Here we find the new religions testing boundaries of permissible behaviour, the balance between belief and action, and, for the United States, the interpretation of the First Amendment (Delgado 1979/1980 invokes the Thirteenth Amendment). Much work is still to be done on the effect of the law on the new religions—and of the new religions on the law—but some of the groundwork has been laid

(Barker 1984c, Beckford 1985, Kelley 1982, New York University 1979/1980, Robbins 1984a, Robbins et al 1986, Shepherd 1982).

This hive of legal activity has resulted in academics testifying in court or serving as "expert witnesses" on one side or the other. A further, potentially divisive, way in which students of the new religions have found themselves becoming part of their own data results from the sponsorship of conferences (and subsequent publications of proceedings) by some of the movements—most notably the Unification Church, but also ISKCON, Sekai Kyusei Kyo, the Soka Gakkai, the Brahma Kumaris, the Divine Light Emissaries, and the Church of Scientology. The debate came into the open with the publication in 1978 of Horowitz's edited volume, *Science, Sin, and Scholarship,* and was continued during the Cincinnati meeting of the Society for the Scientific Study of Religion in 1980. As a result, a special edition of *Sociological Analysis* was devoted to the subject, with Beckford (1983a), Horowitz (1983a,b), and Robbins (1983a) arguing, for different reasons, against scholars attending Unification-sponsored conferences, and Barker (1983b), Wallis (1983), and Wilson (1983), defending their attendance. The debate continues (Robbins 1985, Robertson 1985) and will no doubt do so as long as academics accept the hospitality offered them by the movements.

It would, of course, be ridiculous to assume that the Jonestown tragedy was directly, or even indirectly, responsible for all the social activity that has surrounded the new religions since the end of the 1970s. An as yet unpublished longitudinal study by van Driel and J. Richardson reveals that coverage of the new religious movements was higher in the period between October 1976 and April 1977 than at any other time (at least in the newspapers and newsweeklies analyzed, and so long as references to the People's Temple itself were excluded). It is, however, safe to say that the tragedy provided a significant focal point of reference for the public. Furthermore, van Driel and Richardson's research suggests that there were several changes in the content of the reports after Jonestown. While the movements had previously been treated individually (the Unification Church was mentioned most frequently), after Jonestown they tended to be all lumped together under the now highly derogatory label "cult." Despite pleas from the movements themselves (e.g. Subhananda 1978), all the new religions were contaminated by association, the worst (most "sinister" and "bizarre") features of each belonging, by implication, to them all. It has, however, been demonstrated by J. Richardson (1980) and others that the People's Temple was, in a number of important respects, markedly different from other new religions. Indeed, one of the clearest conclusions to have emerged from sociological research is that a very considerable diversity exists among the movements.

It is, indeed, difficult to decide which movements are most usefully classified as new religions and/or cults. Sociologists have found it helpful, at least for comparative purposes, to work with a fairly wide definition, including a variety of "alternatives" to mainline religions. The most commonly drawn distinction is that between the more obviously religious groups (which, like ISKCON, the Unification Church, the Children of God or Ananda Marga, are likely to expect total commitment—the members living together in a commune and working full-time for the movement) and the "para-religions" of the Human Potential movement (which, like *est,* TM, the Emin or Exegesis, have a clientele seeking enlightenment or self-development in one form or another). This is not a clear distinction, however, and too many movements (Church of Scientology, Rajneeshism, Divine Light Mission) straddle the boundaries or may fall on either side, according to which characteristic is being stressed (Barker 1982a). Unfortunately, there still is not a classificatory system as helpful for distinguishing the new religions as that which Wilson (1970) devised for the previous generation of sects. Wallis's (1984) categories of world-affirming, world-rejecting, and world-accommodating movements are probably the most useful ones available, but they are too crude for detailed comparative analysis; more refined distinctions still need to be developed.

Perhaps the most noticeable feature of sociological studies of the new religions is their sheer quantity[2]—something that is clearly indicated by even a cursory glance at the articles and reviews in journals such as *Sociological Analysis, Social Compass,* or *The Review of Religious Research.* An editorial comment in the December 1984 issue of the *Journal for the Scientific Study of Religion* notes that the new religions comprised one of the three most popular topics among the articles submitted for publication during the year. Although most of the research has been conducted in the United States, there is a growing

---

[2]General books on the new religions include Beckford (1985), Bromley & Shupe (1981), Melton & Moore (1982), Pavlos (1982), Shupe (1981), Westley (1983), and, concentrating on Eastern influences, Ellwood (1979). Several dictionaries and encyclopedias are now including entries on the new religions (e.g. Eliade 1986, Hinnells 1984). Brief descriptions of several of the movements are to be found in the appendices of Barker (1982b) and Melton & Moore (1982), and somewhat fuller accounts appear in Melton (1979, 2nd ed., forthcoming). Two book-length annotated bibliographies—one by D. Choquette, the other by M. Mickler (for literature on the Unification Church)—and a dictionary of minority religions compiled by B. Wilson are in preparation. Currently available bibliographic sources include Hackett (1981), Robbins (1981b, 1983b), Robbins & Anthony (1979), Robbins et al (1978), Beckford & Richardson (1983), and Barker (1985b). Rambo (1982) and Snow & Machalek (1984) provide bibliographies on conversion.

Readers of a general nature: Barker 1984b, Coleman & Baum 1983, Fichter 1983, Robbins & Anthony 1981, Stark 1986a, Wilson 1981a. Readers with a particular focus: conversion (J. Richardson 1978), the deprogramming/brainwashing controversy (Bromley & Richardson 1983), mental health (H. Richardson 1980), evangelizing (Clarke 1986b), millenialism and charisma (Wallis 1982a), the family (James 1983, Kaslow & Sussman 1982), and what we might learn about society from the study of the new religions (Barker 1982b).

body of knowledge about the movements in other countries,[3] and several resource centers have been instituted for the study and/or collection of data and literature about the new religions throughout the world.[4]

The two movements that have received the most systematic attention from sociologists are the Unification Church and the International Society of Krishna Consciousness (ISKCON). Lofland's (1977) enlarged edition of his original (1966) study of the "Moonies" (although he does not identify them as such) and Judah's (1974) study of the Hare Krishna still provide invaluable reference points of comparison for post-Jonestown researchers of both these and an ever increasing number of other movements.[5] Mention has already been made of a further movement that has caught the attention of sociologists, sharing as it does more than a few characteristics of certain of the new religions: the anticult

[3]For introductory information for specific countries or ethnic groups, see: United States (Melton 1979, J. Richardson 1983, Robbins 1983b, Stark & Bainbridge 1981a), North American Indians (Turner 1978), North American blacks (Simpson 1978), Canada (Bibby 1983, Bird 1979, Bird & Reimer 1982), Britain (Barker 1983a, Beckford 1983c), Finland (Holm, 1981, Sundback 1980), Sweden (Nordquist 1982), Holland (van der Lans & Derks 1983, Köllen 1980, Kranenborg 1982), Belgium (Dobbelaere et al 1985), France (Baffoy 1978, Séguy 1980), Germany (Berger & Hexel 1981, Hardin 1983), Africa and other Third World Societies (Jules-Rosette 1979, 1985; Turner 1977, 1979), Japan, whose *Rush Hour of the Gods* (McFarland 1967) was earlier than that of the West (Arai 1972; Earhart 1970, 1982).

[4]In the United States, the Center for the Study of New Religious Movements was set up under the direction of Jacob Needleman at the Graduate Theological Union, Berkeley, in 1977. It had to close in 1983, but the GTU library continues to house a very useful section devoted to the new religions. Gordon Melton's Institute for the Study of American Religion, with its vast collection of publications by and about the new religions, has recently moved from Chicago to the University of California at Santa Barbara. In Birmingham, England, Harold Turner directs a Study Centre for New Religious Movements in Primal Societies. A Centre for New Religious Movements has been collecting information at King's College, London, while its Research Fellow, Peter Clarke, edits a "journal of contemporary religions", *Religion Today*. Another journal devoted to the new religions, *Update*, is published quarterly by the well-stocked Dialog Center at Aarhus, Denmark.

[5]Descriptions and analyses of specific movements: Ananda Cooperative Village (Nordquist 1978), Children of God, now known as the Family of Love (Van Zandt 1985; Wallis (1979, 1981), Divine Light Mission (Downton 1979, 1980), Eastern groups (Ellwood 1979; Preston 1981; Volinn 1982, 1985), Hare Krishna (Daner 1976; Burr 1984; Carey 1983; Gelberg 1983; Knott 1986; Rochford 1982, 1985; Shinn 1983), Human Potential movement (Heelas 1982; Stone 1981; Wallis 1984), *est* and Zen Buddhism (Tipton 1981, 1982), the Jesus movement (J. Richardson et al 1979), the Manson Family (Nielson 1984), occultism, paganism, witchcraft and magic (Benassi et al 1980, Melton 1982), The Process (Bainbridge 1978), Rajneeshism (Coney & Heelas 1986; Mullan 1983; Wallis & Bruce 1985: Ch. 8), Rastafarianism (Cashmore 1983; Clarke 1986a), the Renaissance movement (Borowski 1984), Sekai Kyusei Kyo (Derrett 1984), Scientology (Wallis 1976; Bainbridge & Stark 1980), Soka Gakkai/Nichiren Shoshu (Snow 1976, 1979; Snow & Phillips 1980), Synanon (Gerstel 1982; Mitchell et al 1980; Ofshe 1980), transcendental meditation (Bainbridge & Jackson 1981; Johnston 1980), Metaphysical Movement (Wagner 1983), UFO cults (Balch 1980, 1982), Unification Church (Barker 1981, 1983c,d, 1984a, 1985a; Beckford 1981, 1985; Bromley & Shupe 1979b; Fichter 1985; Galanter 1980, 1983; Galanter et al 1979; Horowitz 1978; James 1983; Kehrer 1981; Taylor 1982).

movement (Shupe, Bromley & Oliver 1984). The term is a generic one, used to cover a wide range of groups formed with the specific purpose of disseminating information, offering advice and counselling, and/or lobbying those in authority to take action to curb the activities of cults. The most comprehensive studies of anticult activities are reported in two books, one on the movement in America by Shupe & Bromley (1980), and the other by Beckford (1985) on the anticultists of Britain, France, and West Germany. A comparative overview of the data has led to the interesting observation that different societies reveal quite a lot about their own internal structures, assumptions, and values through their reactions to the new religions (Barker 1982b: section V; Beckford 1979, 1983b; Shupe & Bromley 1985; Hardin & Kehrer 1982; Miller 1983; Shupe & Bromley 1981). Whatever their particular concerns, anticultists throughout the world are, however, well-nigh unanimous in their opinion that the new religions procure their membership through the employment of techniques of mind control or brainwashing.

Providing support for the anticultist position, those who [generally following Lifton (1961, Ch. 22)] interpret cult membership as the result of something being done to a helpless victim, have tended to be psychologists or psychiatrists (Clark 1979; Clark et al 1981; Conway & Siegelman 1978, 1982; Singer 1979; Verdier 1980; West 1982). Sociologists, on the other hand, have tended to dismiss the brainwashing thesis. When, for example, Barker (1981, 1984a) found that 90% of those attending a Unification workshop did not join, and that the majority of those who did join left within two years, she concluded that mind control could hardly be accepted as an adequate explanation for Unification membership. There are, however, a few sociologists who support the brainwashing thesis (Levine 1980a,b; Enroth 1977) and some psychologists who argue strongly against it (Coleman 1982, Kilbourne 1983, Kilbourne & Richardson 1984).[6]

Those who favor the brainwashing thesis have rarely themselves conducted any empirical research into the current membership of the movements; they tend, instead, to rely mainly on information from exmembers, and, in particular, exmembers who have been "deprogrammed." Research on defectors has repeatedly shown, however, that there is a significant difference between the accounts of the movements given by those who have been "deprogrammed" and those who left of their own accord, the latter tending to be considerably less condemnatory (Barker 1984a; Beckford 1985; Solomon 1981; Skonovd 1981,

---

[6]Further critiques of the brainwashing thesis and reductionist approaches which "medicalize" conversion are to be found in Barker (1985a), Beckford (1985), Bromley & Shupe (1979b, 1981), Bromley & Richardson (1983), H. Richardson (1980), J. Richardson (1978, 1985a,b), Robbins (1981a,b, 1984b), Robbins & Anthony (1980a,b, 1982), Shupe (1981), Snow & Machalek 1982, 1983, 1984), Snow & Phillips (1980), Strauss (1979) and Wallis (1982c, 1984).

1983; Wright 1983, 1984). It has, furthermore, been observed that most people tend to produce increasingly selective accounts of conversions (and deconversions) with the passage of time (Barker 1983d; Beckford 1978, 1985).

An alternative hypothesis, favored by anticultists, that concentrates on the individual rather than a manipulative social context, but still excludes much in the way of choice, suggests that people who join the new religions are, in some way, abnormally pathetic or weak. Psychological tests that incorporate a comparison with the "normal" population have, however, tended to produce little evidence in support of this notion with respect to either converts or sometime members (Galanter 1980, 1983; Galanter et al 1979; Kilbourne 1983; Kuner 1984; Ungerleider & Wellisch 1983). However, these results have been severely questioned by clinical psychologists, such as Ash (1983, 1985), who believe that there is a recognizable "cult-induced psychopathology."

Lofland & Stark's seminal essay on "becoming a world-saver" (1965) continues [despite the fact that it was "revisited" by Lofland (1978)] to provide a springboard from which others eagerly jump. Among the more provocative jumpers of late are Long & Hadden (1983), who ask whether what they call the "social drift" model of Lofland & Stark and others is really all that different from the brainwashing model, or whether their apparent contradictions cannot be resolved with a revised concept of socialization. In addition, J. Richardson (1985a,b) insists that the convert ought to be seen as an active agent who chooses, not a passive subject who responds to external powers. Focussing on diversity, Lofland & Skonovd (1981) have distinguished six conversion "motifs," and Barker (1984a) has constructed a model which, rather than prejudging the active/passive issue on a priori grounds in any particular instance, makes use of control groups to test empirically the extent to which a number of variables, both "internal" and "external" to the actor, influence the outcome of a recruitment process.

It is not altogether surprising that the majority of sociologists incorporate at least some reference to the state of contemporary society in their explanations of the existence of the new religions. For some, the movements are *reflections* or microcosms of society (Long 1979). B. Johnson (1981), for example, believes that the movements "mirror the concern with self." More frequently, however, it is argued that the movements can be explained as *reactions* to the wider society; the emphasis is on a "push" from outside; any "pull" from the movements is perceived in their promise to compensate for the shortcomings of the wider society. It would, however, be a mistake to believe that it is the materially oppressed who flock to the current wave of new religions. The People's Temple was an exception in that it was one of the few instances (Rastafarianism is another) in which a significant proportion of the membership has consisted of the socially disadvantaged. If the middle-class members of the majority of movements complain about deprivation, it is likely to be spiritual, community, or "real-relationship" deprivation to which they are referring. Several commentators have suggested that, in a secular society in which neither social concepts nor a social context is readily available for religious expression, several of the new religions give people permission to explore religious and spiritual dimensions to life (Barker 1979, 1984a). Wilson (1981b, 1982a,b,) suggests that those who join the movements are, like others in the past who have found themselves facing the bureaucratic institutionalization of the established churches, seeking a surer, swifter path to salvation. Stark & Bainbridge (1979, 1981a,b; Bainbridge & Stark 1979; Stark 1981), who have long insisted on a distinction being drawn between "sects" (schisms from mainline churches) and "cults" (innovations), argue that secularization is a self-limiting process in that it stimulates the growth of cults where the conventional churches are weakest, and sects where the churches are stronger and that many cults and sects which originated in the United States actually flourish better in the more secularized climate of western Europe (Stark 1985b).

The concept of rationalization is frequently related to that of secularization. Wallis (1982c, 1984) suggests that some of the movements provide the sense of community which has been lost in the modern, rationalized society. Campbell (1982), on the other hand, argues that one kind of rationalization to be found in modern society leads not to secularization but to a systematization that subsumes symbols under higher principles; there may, he argues, have been a major shift away from belief, but it has been to "seekership" rather than to unbelief. Anthony & Robbins (1982a) have considered some of the movements as a vestigial expression of American civil religion and, following Glock & Bellah (1976), they see an ambiguity in moral values that has resulted in movements that both celebrate moral relativism as instrumental in achieving "self-realization" and provide absolute standards of right and wrong (1982b). Tipton (1981, 1982) in his account of how three different kinds of movements supply three different ethical systems for their followers, also focuses on the moral order—or the lack of moral order—available in post-countercultural society. He suggests that movements such as *est* provide a justification for the drop-outs of the 1960s who want to drop back into middle-class life.

Perhaps the most trenchant criticism that can be made about the research that has been conducted to date is that few empirical studies have made use of control groups for comparison. There are exceptions, as when, for example, a team researches several movements (Wuthnow 1978 in the San Francisco Bay Area, Bird & Reimer 1982 in Montreal); and some interesting comparisons have been made with new religions of other times and places (Hampshire & Beckford 1983, Miller 1983, Pritchard 1976, Werblowsky 1982). But all too often descriptions of a new religion are presented without any indication of whether the characteristics ascribed to it are peculiar to that particular movement or whether they might be equally typical of either other new religions or more conventional institutions. While those who have not read sociological accounts of the new religions might still be at a loss to understand why anyone joins the movements, those who have read some of the sociological literature could well be at a loss to understand why *all* young adults are not members, so all-encompassing are some of the explanations. Take, for example, the report of research by a sociologist-psychotherapist team which, we are told, explains how young adults join cults (*a*) to find a family, (*b*) as a spiritual search (*c*) for security, (*d*) to differentiate themselves from their parents (*e*) as adolescent rebellion, (*f*) seeking adventure, (*g*) for attention, (*h*) because of their idealism, (*i*) because of underemployment and dead-end jobs (Doress & Porter 1981).

While most of the generalizations that have been made about the new religions have been concerned with explanations of (and social responses to) their existence, there are now a sufficient number of reliable monographs to enable some interesting comparative analyses to be undertaken from a number of different perspectives. Bromley & Shupe's use of a resource mobilization model is, for example, particularly rewarding when applied to the means the movements use to finance their various activities—the methods varying from peddling wares in the street to charging thousands of dollars for self-development courses, and from tithing to the running of multinational businesses (Bird & Westley 1985, Bromley 1985, Bromley & Shupe 1980, J. Richardson 1982). Other areas of comparative interest include those of family life and the socialization that occurs within the movements (Kaslow & Sussman 1982). Numerous tensions between ideals and practical contingencies have been observed. Members of the Unification Church, for example, find themselves having to part from their parents, their spouses, and even their children in pursuit of the ideal of establishing the kingdom of heaven on earth—a kingdom in which the basic unit is a closely united nuclear family (Barker 1983c).

Mention has already been made of changes in the data that could, at least in part, be attributed to the Jonestown tragedy, but, of course, plenty of other changes have taken place in the cultural milieu that have affected the membership and the practices (and, to some extent, the beliefs) of the new religions. The economic recession and the rise of the new political right are but two obvious examples. The movements have, furthermore, accommodated, assimilated, or become more intensely sectarian as a direct result of societal reaction to them. Moreover, societal reaction is itself changing, not merely in intensity, but also in its major concerns (for example, there now seems to be less in the North American media about the Unification Church's alleged practices of brainwashing and/or breaking up of families, and more concern over its economic and political activities). And, of course, the rather obvious fact that many of the movements are no longer quite as "new" as they were means that their internal composition is undergoing a number of changes, most of which are, as yet, uncharted. First, there are various effects of a purely demographic nature. Most of those who joined the movements in the early 1970s are now approaching their late thirties, are married, and have children. (It should be noted that the mean age does not rise by twelve months annually as there is usually a high turnover rate and new members tend to be younger than average). Members of the more demanding movements, who were quite happy to lead "sacrificial" lives thousands of miles away from home, have become less prepared to carry out "missions" that affect their relationships with their partners and their own children. The adventurous youth often wants a more settled career in middle-age; the devotee who was once prepared to submit to the will of the leader may now resist demands for unquestioning obedience. In both ISKCON and the Unification Church, the mid-1980s are witnessing the vocal discontent of second-level leadership—several Moonies are now openly circulating critical "underground" broadsheets.

Turning to another demographic variable, sociologists of religion have long recognized the difference between the "born into" and the "born again," but little work has yet been done on the challenges that a second generation membership is bringing to the movements. A further, inevitable happening is that several of the movements' founders have died (Meher Baba 1969, Swami Prabhupāda 1977, Bob Marley 1981, Victor Weirville 1985, and Ron Hubbard in 1986), and although some interesting work has been done on the effect of charismatic leadership (D. Johnson 1980, Wallis 1982a,b, 1984), further research is required on its routinization.

The bureaucratization that occurs to even the most democratic and "congregationalist" of new religions, and the growth of authoritarian power structures that prosper within movements promising individuals absolute freedom, have often been noted in the past. Wallis (1976, 1984) has described the transition from the cultic techniques of Dianetics to the religiously underpinned Church of Scientology. During the next decade or so, the new religions will offer sociologists ample opportunity to understand more about how and under what circumstances such processes occur and, in the case of the more millenarian movements, about the changes that take place when prophecies fail.

Finally, it should be noted that there is no evidence that the new religions are continuing to grow—not, indeed, that their numerical significance has ever been as great as their social and sociological interest. Although it is possible that the number of cults (very widely defined) that have emerged since World War II could reach four figures, the actual membership of individual movements has seldom been more than a few thousand—many will not have secured as many as one hundred followers at any one time. (Even an eminently visible movement such as the Unification Church has never had more than ten thousand full-time members in the West, although it is possible that 30,000 or more may have passed through during the 1970s.) So far as can be estimated (and there is still a great deal of simple head-counting to be done), membership figures have either stabilized or dropped since Jonestown. Of course, the 1980s may witness the rise of "newer" religious movements, while others fade away. It is to be hoped that, in the wake of Jonestown, sociologists will chart the failures as assiduously as they chart the successes.

Literature Cited

Anthony, D., Robbins, T. 1982a. Spiritual innovation and the crisis of American civil religion. *Daedalus* Winter:215–34

Anthony, D., Robbins, T. 1982b. Contemporary religious ferment and moral ambiguity. See Barker 1982b:243–63

Arai, K. 1972. New religious movements. In *Japanese Religion: A Survey by the Agency for Cultural Affairs,* ed. I. Hori (Transl. by Y. Abe, D. Reid), pp. 89–104. Tokyo: Kodansha Int.

Ash, S. M. 1983. *Cult induced psychopathology: A critical review of presuppositions, conversion, clinical picture, and treatment.* PhD thesis. Rosemead School Psych., Biola Univ.

Ash, S. M. 1985. Cult-induced psychopathology, Part I: Clinical picture. *Cultic Stud. J.* 2:31–90

Baffoy, T. 1978. Les sectes totalitaires. *Esprit* Jan.:53–9

Bainbridge, W. S. 1978. *Satan's Power: A Deviant Psychotherapy Cult.* Berkeley: Univ. Calif. Press

Bainbridge, W. S., Jackson, D. H. 1981. The rise and decline of transcendental meditation. See Wilson 1981a:135–58

Bainbridge, W. S., Stark, R. 1979. Cult formation: Three compatible models. *Sociol. Anal.* 40:283–95

Bainbridge, W. S., Stark, R. 1980. Scientology: To be perfectly clear. *Sociol. Anal.* 41:128–36

Balch, R. W. 1980. Looking behind the scenes in a religious cult: Implications for the study of conversion. *Social. Anal.* 41:137–43

Balch, R. W. 1982. Bo and Peep: A case study of the origins of messianic leadership. See Wallis 1982a:13–72

Barker, E. V. 1979. Whose service is perfect freedom: The concept of spiritual well-being in relation to the Reverend Sun Myung Moon's Unification Church in Britain. In *Spiritual Well-Being,* ed. D. Moberg, Washington DC: Univ. Press Am.

Barker, E. V. 1981. Who'd be a Moonie? A comparative study of those who join the Unification Church in Britain. See Wilson 1981a:59–96

Barker, E. V. 1982a. From sects to society: A methodological programme. See Barker 1982b:3–15

Barker, E. V., ed. 1982b. *New Religious Movements: A Perspective for Understanding Society.* New York: Edwin Mellen

Barker, E. V. 1983a. New religious movements in Britain: The context and the membership. *Soc. Compass* XXX/1:33–48

Barker, E. V. 1983b. Supping with the devil: How long a spoon does the sociologist need? *Sociol. Anal.* 44:197–207

Barker, E. V. 1983c. Doing love: Tensions in the ideal family. See James 1983:35–52

Barker, E. V. 1983d. With enemies like that . . .: Some functions of deprogramming as an aid to sectarian membership. See Bromley & Richardson 1983:329–44

Barker, E. V. 1984a. *The Making of a Moonie: Brainwashing or Choice?* Oxford: Blackwell

Barker, E. V., ed. 1984b. *Of Gods and Men: New Religious Movements in the West.* Macon, Ga: Mercer Univ. Press

Barker, E. V. 1984c. The British right to discriminate. *Society.* 21:35–41

Barker, E. V. 1985a. The conversion of conversion: A sociological anti-reductionist perspective. In *Reductionism in Academic Disciplines,* ed. A. Peacocke, pp. 58–75. Guildford: Univ. Surrey SRHE & NFER Nelson

Barker, E. V. 1985b. New religious movements: Yet another great awakening? See Hammond 1985:36–57

Beckford, J. A. 1978. Accounting for conversion. *Br. J. Sociol.* 29:249–62

Beckford, J. A. 1979. Politics and the anti-cult movement. *Ann. Rev. Soc. Sci. Relig.* 3: 169–90

Beckford, J. A. 1981. A typology of family responses to a new religious movement. *Marriage Fam. Rev.* 4:41–5

Beckford, J. A. 1983a. Some questions about the relationship between scholars and the new religious movements. *Sociol. Anal.* 44:189–96

Beckford, J. A. 1983b. "Brainwashing" and "deprogramming" in Britain: The social sources of anti-cult sentiment. See Bromley & Richardson 1983:122–38

Beckford, J. A., 1983c. The public response to new religious movements in Britain. *Soc. Compass* XXX:49–62

Beckford, J. A. 1985. *Cult Controversies: The Societal Response to the New Religious Movements.* London: Tavistock

Beckford, J. A., Richardson, J. T. 1983. A bibliography of social scientific studies of new religious movements. *Soc. Compass* XXX:111–35

Benassi, V. A., Singer, B., Reynolds, C. B. 1980. Occult belief: Seeing is believing. *J. Sci. Study Relig.* 19:337–49

Berger, H., Hexel, P. 1981. *Ursachen und Wirkungen gessellschäftlicher Verweigerung junger Menschen unter besonderer Berücksichtigung der 'Jungendreligionen'*. Mimeo. Vienna: Eur. Ctr. Soc. Welfare Training Res.

Bibby, R. W. 1983: Searching for the invisible thread: Meaning systems in contemporary Canada. *J. Sci. Study Relig.* 22:101–09

Bird, F. B. 1979. The pursuit of innocence: New religious movements and moral accountability. *Sociol. Anal.* 40:335–46

Bird, F. B., Reimer, W. 1982. Participation rates in new religious and para-religious movements. *J. Sci. Study Relig.* 21:1–14. See also Barker 1984b:215–38

Bird, F. B., Westley, F. 1985. The economic strategies of new religious movements. *Sociol. Anal.* 46:157–70

Borowski, K. 1984. *Attempting an Alternative Society: A Sociological Study of a Selected Communal-Revitalization Movement in the United States*. Norwood, Penn: Weiman

Bromley, D. G. 1985. Financing the millenium: The economic structure of the Unificationist movement. *J. Sci. Study Relig.* 24:253–274

Bromley, D. G., Richardson, J. T. eds. 1983. *The Brainwashing/Deprogramming Controversy: Sociological, Psychological, Legal and Historical Perspectives*. New York: Edwin Mellen

Bromley, D. G., Shupe, A. D. 1979a. *"Moonies" in America: Cult, Church, and Crusade*. Beverly Hills: Sage

Bromley, D. G., Shupe, A. D. 1979b. "Just a few years seem like a lifetime": A role theory approach to participation in religious movements. In *Research in Social Movements, Conflict and Change*, ed. L. Kriesberg, pp. 159–85. Greenwich, Conn: JAI

Bromley, D. G., Shupe, A. D. 1980. Financing the new religions: A resource mobilization approach. *J. Sci. Study Relig.* 19: 227–39

Bromley, D. G., Shupe, A. D. 1981. *Strange Gods: The Great American Cult Scare*. Boston: Beacon

Bryant, M. D., ed. 1979. *Religious Liberty in Canada: Deprogramming and Media Coverage of New Religions*. Toronto: Canadians for the Protection of Civil Liberty

Burr, A. 1984. *I Am Not My Body: A Study of the International Hare Krishna Sect*. New Delhi: Vikas

Campbell, C. B. 1982. The new religious movements: The new spirituality and post-industrial society. See Barker 1982b:232–42

Carey, S. 1983. The Hare Krishna Movement and Hindus in Britain. *New Community* 10:477–86

Cashmore, E. E. H. 1983. *Rastaman: the Rastafarian Movement in England*. London: Unwin.

Clark, J. G. 1979. Cults. *J. Am. Med. Assoc.* 24:281–99

Clark, J. G., Langone, M., Schechter, R., Daly, R. 1981. *Destructive Cult Conversion: Theory, Research and Treatment*. Weston, Mass: Am. Fam. Found.

Clarke, P. B. 1986a. *Black Paradise: The Rastafarian Movement*. Wellingborough, Northants: Aquarian.

Clarke, P. B., ed. 1986b. *The New Evangelists: The New Religious Movements, Their Methods and Aims*. London: Ethnographica. In press

Coleman, J., Baum, G., eds. 1983. *New Religious Movements*. New York: Seabury

Coleman, L. 1982. *Psychiatry the Faithbreaker: How Psychiatry is Promoting Bigotry in America*. Sacramento, Calif: Printing Dynamics

Coney, J., Heelas, P. L. F. 1986. *Bhagwan: The Way of the Heart*. Wellingborough, Northants: Aquarian. In press

Conway, F., Siegelman, J. 1978. *Snapping: America's Epidemic of Sudden Personality Change*. Philadelphia: Lippincott

Conway, F., Siegelman, J. 1982. Information disease: Have the cults created a new mental illness? *Sci. Dig.* 90:86–92

Coser, R. L., Coser, L. 1979. Jonestown as a perverse utopia. *Dissent* 26/2:158–62

Cottrell, R. 1984. *Report on the Activity of Certain New Religious Movements within the European Community*. European Parliament, Committee on Youth, Culture, Education, Information and Sport. PE 82.322/fin.

Daner, F. 1976. *The American Children of Krsna: A Study of the Hare Krsna Movement*. New York: Holt, Rinehart & Winston

Delgado, R. 1977. Religious totalism: Gentle and ungentle persuasion under the First Amendment. *S. Calif. Law Rev.* 51:1–98

Delgado, R. 1979/1980. Religious totalism as slavery. See New York University 1979/1980; 51–67

Derks, F. 1983. *Uittreding Uit Nieuwe Religieuze Bewegingen: Ideniteitsverwarring Bij Ex-Sekteleden*. Nijmegen: Katholieke Univ. (English-language summary available from author)

Derrett, E. M. A. 1984. Sekai Kyusei Kyo: A Japanese 'new' religion in Britain. *Relig. Today* 1/2&3:12–3

Dobbelaere, K., Voisin, M. 1985. Sects and new religious movements. In *België en zijn*

Goden, ed. K. Dobbelaere, L. Voye, J. Billiet, J. Remy. Leuven, Cabay:395–437

Doress, I., Porter, J. N. 1981. Kids in cults. See Robbins & Anthony 1981:297–302

Downton, J. V. 1979. *Sacred Journeys: The Conversion of Young Americans to Divine Light Mission.* New York: Colombia Univ. Press

Downton, J. V. 1980. An evolutionary theory of spiritual conversion and commitment: The case of Divine Light Mission. *J. Sci. Study Relig.* 19:381–96

Earhart, H. B. 1970. *The New Religions of Japan: A Bibliography of Western-Language Materials.* Tokyo: Sophia Univ. 2nd ed.

Earhart, H. B. 1982. *Japanese Religion: Unity and Diversity.* Belmont, Calif: Wadsworth. 3rd ed.

Eliade, M. 1986. *The Encyclopedia of Religion.* New York: Macmillan. In press

Ellwood, R. S. 1979. *Alternative Altars: Unconventional and Eastern Spirituality in America.* Chicago: Univ. Chicago Press

Enroth, R. 1977. *Youth, Brainwashing, and the Extremist Cults.* Grand Rapids, Mich: Zondervan

Fichter, J. H., ed. 1983. *Alternatives to American Mainline Churches.* Barrytown, NY: Unification Theological Seminary

Fichter, J. H. 1985. *The Holy Family of Father Moon.* Kansas City, Mo: Leaven

Galanter, M. 1980. Psychological induction into the large-group: Findings from a modern religious sect. *Am. J. Psychiatry.* 137:1574–1579. See also Bromley & Richardson 1983:183–204

Galanter, M. 1983. Unification Church ("Moonie") dropouts: Psychological readjustment after leaving a charismatic religious group. *Am. J. Psychiatry* 140:984–89

Galanter, M., Rabkin, R., Rabkin, J., Deutsch, A. 1979. The "Moonies": A psychological study of conversion and membership in a contemporary religious sect. *Am. J. Psychiatry* 136:165–79

Gelberg, S. J., ed. 1983. *Hare Krishna, Hare Krishna.* New York: Grove

Gerstel, D. A. 1982. *Paradise Incorporated: Synanon.* Novato, Calif: Presidio

Glock, C. Y., Bellah, R. N., eds. 1976. *The New Religious Consciousness.* Berkeley: Univ. Calif. Press

Hackett, D. G. 1981. *The New Religions: An Annotated Introductory Bibliography.* Berkeley: Ctr. Study. New Relig. Movements

Hall, J. 1981. The apocalypse at Jonestown. See Robbins & Anthony 1981: 171–90; see also Levi 1982:35–54

Hammond, P. E., ed. 1985. *The Sacred in a Secular Age.* Berkeley: Univ. Calif. Press

Hampshire, A. P., Beckford, J. A. 1983. Religious sects and the concept of deviance: The Moonies and the Mormons. *Br. J. Sociol.* 34:208–29

Hardin, B. 1983. Quelques aspects du phénomène des nouveaux mouvements religieux en République Fédérale d'Allemagne. *Soc. Compass* XXX:13–32

Hardin, B., Kehrer, G. 1982. Some social factors affecting the rejection of new belief systems. See Barker 1982b:267–83

Heelas, P. 1982. Californian self religions and socializing the subjective. See Barker 1982b:69–85

Hill, D. G. 1980. *Study of Mind Development Groups, Sects and Cults in Ontario.* Rep. Ontario Govt. Toronto

Hinnells, J. R., ed. 1984. *The Penguin Dictionary of Religions.* Harmondsworth: Penguin

Holm, N., ed. 1981. *Aktuella religiösa rörelser i Finland (Religious Movements in Finland Today).* Abo: Abo Academy Found.

Horowitz, I. L., ed. 1978. *Science, Sin, and Scholarship: The Politics of Reverend Moon and the Unification Church.* Cambridge: MIT Press

Horowitz, I. L. 1983a. Universal standards, not uniform beliefs: Further reflections on scientific method and religious sponsors. *Sociol. Anal.* 44:179–82

Horowitz, I. L. 1983b. A reply to critics and crusaders. *Sociol. Anal.* 44:221–26

James, G. G., ed. 1983. *The Family and the Unification Church.* Barrytown, NY: Unification Theological Seminary

Johnson, B. 1981. A sociological perspective on new religion. See Robbins & Anthony 1981:51–66

Johnson, D. P. 1980. Dilemmas of charismatic leadership: The case of People's Temple. *Sociol. Anal.* 40:315–23

Johnston, H. 1980. The marketed social movement: A case study of the rapid growth of TM. *Pac. Sociol. Rev.* 23:333–54

Judah, J. S. 1974. *Hare Krishna and the Counterculture.* New York: Wiley

Jules-Rosette, B., ed. 1979. *The New Religions of Africa.* Norwood, NJ: Ablex

Jules-Rosette, B., 1985. The sacred and Third World societies. See Hammond 1985: 215–33

Kaslow, F., Sussman, M., eds. 1982. *Cults and the Family.* New York: Haworth

Kehrer, G., ed. 1981 *Das Entstehen einer neuen Religion.* Munich: Kösel-Verlag

Kelley, D. M., ed. 1982. *Government Intervention in Religious Affairs.* New York: Pilgrim

Kilbourne, B. K. 1983. The Conway and Siegelman claims against religious cults: An assessment of their data. *J. Sci. Study Relig.* 22:380–85

Kilbourne, B. K., Richardson, J. T. 1984. Psychotherapy and new religions in a pluralist society. *Am. Psychol.* 39:237–51

Kilduff, M., Javers, R. 1978. *The Suicide Cult: The Inside Story of the Peoples Temple Sect and the Massacre in Guyana.* New York: Bantam

Knott, K. 1986. *My Sweet Lord: The Hare Krishna Movement.* Wellingborough, Northants: Aquarian.

Köllen, K. 1980. *Jeugdsekten in Nederland.* Amersterdam: Allert de Lange

Kranenborg, R. 1982. *Oosterse geloofsbewegingen in het Westen.* Ede: Zome & Keuning

Krause, C. A. 1978. *Guyana Massacre: The Eyewitness Account.* New York: Berkeley

Kuner, W. 1984. New religious movements and mental health. See Barker 1984:255–64

Levi, K., ed. 1982. *Violence and Religious Commitment: Implications of Jim Jones' People's Temple Movement.* University Park: Penn. State Univ. Press

Levine, E. M. 1980a. The case for deprogramming religious cult members. *Society* March/Apr:34–38

Levine, E. M. 1980b. Rural communes and religious cults: Refuges for middle class youth. *Adolesc. Psychiatry* 8:138–53

Lifton, R. J. 1961. *Thought Reform and the Psychology of Totalism: A Study of "Brainwashing" in China.* London: Gollancz

Lincoln, C. E., Mamiya, L. M. 1980. Daddy Jones and Father Divine: The cult as political religion. *Relig. Life* 49/Spring:6–23

Lindt, G. 1981–1982. Journeys to Jonestown: Accounts and interpretations of the rise and demise of the People's Temple. *Union Seminary Q. Rev.* XXXVII:159–74

Lofland, J. 1977. *Doomsday Cult: A Study of Conversion, Proselytization, and Maintainance of Faith.* New York: Irvington. Enlarged Ed. (Orig. ed. 1966)

Lofland, J. 1978. Becoming a world saver revisited. See Richardson 1978:805–18

Lofland, J., Skonovd, N. 1981. Conversion Motifs. *J. Sci. Study Relig.* 20:373–85. For elaborated version, see Barker 1984b:1–24

Lofland, J., Stark, R. 1965. Becoming a world-saver: A theory of conversion to a deviant perspective. *Am. Sociol. Rev.* 20:862–74

Long, T. E. 1979. Cult culture cultivation: Three different tillings of a common plot. *J. Sci. Study Relig.* 18:419–23

Long, T. E., Hadden, J. K. 1983. Religious conversion and the concept of socialisation: Integrating the brainwashing and drift models. *J. Sci. Study Relig.* 22:1–14

McFarland, H. N. 1967. *The Rush Hour of the Gods: A Study of the New Religious Movements in Japan.* New York: Macmillan

Melton, J. G. 1979. *The Encyclopedia of American Religions,* 2 vols. Wilmington, NC: McGrath

Melton, J. G. 1982. *Magic, Witchcraft, and Paganism in America: A Bibliography.* New York: Garland

Melton, J. G., Moore, R. L. 1982. *The Cult Experience: Responding to the New Religious Pluralism.* New York: Pilgrim

Miller, D. E. 1983. Deprogramming in historical perspective. See Bromley & Richardson 1983:15–28

Mills, E. W. 1982. Cult extremism: The reduction of normative dissonance. See Levi 1982:75–87

Mills, J. 1979. *Six Years with God: Life Inside Rev. Jim Jones' People's Temple.* New York: A & W

Mitchell, D., Mitchell, C., Ofshe, R. 1980. *The Light on Synanon.* New York: Seaview

Mullan, B. 1983. *Life as Laughter: Following Bhagwan Shree Rajneesh.* London: Routledge & Kegan Paul

Needleman, J., Baker, G., eds. 1978. *Understanding the New Religions.* New York: Seabury

New York University 1979/1980. Alternative Religions: Government Control and the First Amendment. *New York University Rev. Law Soc. Change.* 9:1

Nielson, D. A. 1984. Charles Manson's family of love: A case study of anomism, puerilism and transmoral consciousness in civilizational perspective. *Sociol. Anal.* 45:315–37

Nordquist, T. A. 1978. *Ananda Cooperative Village.* Uppsala Univ.: Religionshistoriska Inst.

Nordquist, T. A. 1982. New religious movements in Sweden. See Barker 1982b:173–88

Ofshe, R. 1980. The social development of the Synanon Cult: The managerial strategy of organizational transformation. *Sociol. Anal.* 41:109–27

Patrick, T., with Dulack, T. 1976. *Let Our Children Go!* New York: Dutton

Pavlos, A. J. 1982. *The Cult Experience.* Westport/London: Greenwood

Preston, D. L. 1981. Becoming a Zen practitioner. *Sociol. Anal.* 42:47–55

Pritchard, L. K. 1976. Religious change in nineteenth-century America. See Glock & Bellah 1976:297–330

Rambo, L. R. 1982. Current research on religious conversion: A bibliography. *Relig. Stud. Rev.* 8:146–59

Reston, J. Jr. 1981. *Our Father Who Art in Hell.* New York: Times Books

Richardson, H., ed. 1977. *Deprogramming: Documenting the Issue.* New York: Am. Civil Libert. Union

Richardson, H., ed. 1980. *New Religions and Mental Health: Understanding the Issues.* Lewiston, NY: Edwin Mellen Press

Richardson, J. T. ed. 1978. *Conversion Careers: In and Out of the New Religions.* London: Sage

Richardson, J. T. 1980. People's Temple and Jonestown: A corrective comparison and critique. *J. Sci. Study Relig.* 19:239–55. Also published in a slightly different form as "A comparison between Jonestown and other cults." See Levi 1982:21–34

Richardson, J. T. 1982. Financing the new religious movements. *J. Sci. Study Relig.* 21:255–68. See also Barker 1984b:65–88

Richardson, J. T. 1983. New religious movements in the United States: A review. *Social Compass.* XXX:85–110

Richardson, J. T. 1985a. The active vs. passive convert: Paradigm conflict in conversion/recruitment research. *J. Sci. Study Relig.* 24:163–79

Richardson, J. T. 1985b. Studies of conversion: Secularization or re-enchantment? See Hammond 1985:104–21

Richardson, J. T., Stewart, M. W., Simmonds, R. B. 1979. *Organized Miracles: A Study of a Contemporary, Youth, Communal, Fundamentalist Organization.* New Brunswick NJ: Transaction

Robbins, T. 1981a. Church, state and cult. *Sociol. Anal.* 42:209–26

Robbins, T. 1981b. *Civil Liberties, "Brainwashing" and "Cults": A Select Annotated Bibliography.* Berkeley: Ctr. Study New Relig. Movements

Robbins, T. 1983a. The beach is washing away: Controversial religion and the sociology of religion. *Sociol. Anal.* 44:207–14

Robbins, T. 1983b. Sociological studies of new religious movements: A selective review. *Relig. Stud. Rev.* 9:233–39

Robbins, T. 1984a. Marginal movements. *Society* 21:47–52

Robbins, T. 1984b. Constructing cultist "mind control". *Sociol. Anal.* 45:241–56

Robbins, T. 1985. Nuts, sluts, and converts: Studying religious groups as social problems: A comment. *Sociol. Anal.* 46:157–70

Robbins, T., Anthony, D. 1979. The sociology of contemporary religious movements. *Ann. Rev. Sociol.* 5:75–89

Robbins, T., Anthony, D. 1980a. Brainwashing and the persecution of cults. *J. Relig. Health* 19:66–9

Robbins, T., Anthony, D. 1980b. The limits of coercive persuasion as an explanation of conversion to authoritarian sects. *Polit. Psychol.* 2:22–37

Robbins, T., Anthony, D., eds. 1981. *In Gods We Trust: New Patterns of Religious Pluralism in America.* New Brunswick, NJ: Transaction

Robbins, T., Anthony, D. 1982. Deprogramming, brainwashing and the medicalization of deviant religious groups. *Soc. Probl.* 39:283–97

Robbins, T., Anthony, D., Richardson, R.

1978. Theory and research on today's 'new religions.' *Sociol. Anal.* 39:95–122

Robbins, T., Shepherd, W., McBride, J., eds. 1986. *Cults, Culture and the Law: Perspectives on New Religious Movements.* Chico, Calif. Scholars. In press

Robertson, R. 1985. Scholarship, partisanship, sponsorship and "The Moonie Problem": A comment. *Sociol. Anal.* 46:179–84

Rochford, R. 1982. Recruitment strategies, ideology and organization in the Hare Krishna movement. *Soc. Probl.* 29:399–410. See also Barker 1984b:283–302

Rochford, R. 1985. *Hare Krishna!* New Brunswick, NJ: Rutgers Univ.

Séguy, J. 1980. La socialisation utopique aux valeurs. *Arch. Sci. Social. Relig.* 50:7–21

Shepherd, W. C. 1982. The prosecutor's reach: Legal issues stemming from the new religious movements. *J. Am. Acad. Relig.* 50:187–214

Shinn, L. D. 1983. The many faces of Krishna. See Fichter 1983:113–35

Shupe, A. D. 1981. *Six Perspectives on New Religions: A Case Study Approach.* New York: Edwin Mellen

Shupe, A. D., Bromley, D. G. 1980. *The New Vigilantes: Deprogrammers, Anti-Cultists, and the New Religions.* Beverly Hills: Sage

Shupe, A. D., Bromley, D. G. 1981. Apostates and atrocity stories: Some parameters in the dynamics of deprogramming. See Wilson 1981a:179–216

Shupe, A. D., Bromley, D. G. 1985. Social responses to the cults. See Hammond 1985:58–72

Shupe, A. D. Jr., Bromley, D. G., Oliver, D. L. 1984. *The Anti-Cult Movement in America: A Bibliography and Historical Survey.* New York: Garland

Simpson, G. E. 1978. *Black Religions in the New World.* New York: Columbia Univ. Press

Singer, M. T. 1979. Coming out of the cults. *Psychol. Today* Dec 8:72–82

Skonovd, L. N. 1981. *Apostasy: The process of defection from religious totalism.* PhD thesis. Univ. Calif., Davis

Skonovd, L. N. 1983. Leaving the 'cultic' religious milieu. See Bromley & Richardson 1983:91–105

Snow, D. A. 1976. *The Nichiren Shoshu Buddhist movement in America: A sociological examination of its value orientations, recruitment effort, and spread.* PhD thesis. Univ. Calif., Los Angeles

Snow, D. A. 1979. A dramaturgical analysis of movement accomodation: Building idiosyncrasy credit as a movement mobilization stategy. *Symb. Interact.* 2:23–44

Snow, D. A., Machalek, R. 1982. On the presumed fragility of unconventional beliefs. *J.*

Sci. Study Relig. 21:15–26 See also Barker 1984b:25–44

Snow, D. A., Machalek, R. 1983. The convert as a social type. In *Sociological Theory 1983*, ed. R. Collins, pp. 259–89. San Francisco: Jossey-Bass

Snow, D. A., Machalek, R. 1984. The sociology of conversion. *Ann. Rev. Sociol.* 10: 167–90

Snow, D. A., Phillips, C. L. 1980. The Lofland-Stark conversion model: A critical reassessment. *Soc. Probl.* 27:430–47

Snow, D. A., Zurcher, L. A., 1980. Ekland-Olsen, S. 1980. Social networks and social movements: A microstructural approach to differential recruitment. *Am. Sociol. Rev.* 45:787–801

Solomon, T. 1981. Integrating the 'Moonie' experience: A Survey of ex-members of the Unification Church. See Robbins & Anthony 1981:275–94

Stark, R. 1981. Must all religions be supernatural? See Wilson 1981a:159–78

Stark, R., ed. 1986a. *Religious Movements: Genesis, Exodus, and Numbers.* Barrytown, NY: Unification Theological Seminary. In press

Stark, R. 1986b. Europe's receptivity to religious movements. See Stark 1985a. In press

Stark, R., Bainbridge, W. S. 1979. Of churches, sects and cults: Preliminary concepts for a theory of religious movements. *J. Sci. Study Relig.* 18:117–33

Stark, R., Bainbridge, W. S. 1981a. American-born sects: Initial findings. *J. Sci. Study Relig.* 20:130–149

Stark, R., Bainbridge, W. S. 1981b. Secularization and cult formation in the Jazz Age. *J. Sci. Study Relig.* 20:360–373

Stark, R., Bainbridge, W. B., Doyle, D. 1979. Cults of America: A reconnaisance in time and space. *Sociol. Anal.* 40:347–59

Stone, D. 1981. The social consciousness of the human potential movement. See Robbins & Anthony 1981:215–28

Stoner, C., Parke, J. A. 1977. *All God's Children: The Cult Experience—Salvation or Slavery?* Radnor, Penn: Chilton

Strauss, R. 1979. Religious conversion as a personal and collective accomplishment. *Sociol. Anal.* 40:158–65

Subhananda das. 1978. *Please Don't Lump Us In: A Request to the Media.* Los Angeles: Int. Soc. Krishna Consciousness

Sundback, S. 1980. New religious movements in Finland. *Temeros.* 16:132–9

Taylor, D. 1982. Becoming new people: The recruitment of young Americans into the Unification Church. See Wallis 1982a:177–230

Tipton, S. M. 1981. *Getting Saved in the Sixties: Moral Meaning in Conversion and Cultural Change.* Berkeley: Univ. Calif. Press

Tipton, S. M. 1982. The moral logic of alternative religions. *Daedalus* III/1:185–214

Turner, H. W. 1977. *Bibliography of New Religious Movements in Primal Societies.* Vol. I: *Black Africa.* Boston: Hall

Turner, H. W. 1978. *Bibliography of New Religious Movements in Primal Societies.* Vol. II: *North America.* Boston: Hall

Turner, H. W. 1979. *Religious Innovation in Africa: Collected Essays on New Religious Movements.* Boston: Hall

Ungerleider, J. T., Wellisch, D. K. 1983. The programming (brainwashing)/deprogramming religious controversy. See Bromley & Richardson 1983:200–14

van der Lans, J. M., Derks, F. 1983. Les nouvelles religions aux Pays-Bas: Contexte, appartenance, réactions. *Soc. Compass* XXX:63–84

Van Zandt, D. E. 1985. *Ideology and structure in the Children of God: A study of a new sect.* PhD thesis. Univ London, Lon. Sch. Econ.

Verdier, P. A. 1980. *Brainwashing and the Cults: An Exposé on Capturing the Human Mind.* North Hollywood: Wilshire

Vivien, A. 1985. *Les Sectes en France: Expressions de la liberté morale ou facteurs de manipulations?* Rapport au Premier Ministre. Paris: La Documentation Française

Volinn, E. 1982. *Lead us from darkness: The allure of a religious sect and its charismatic Leader.* PhD thesis. Columbia Univ., New York

Volinn, E. 1985. Eastern meditation groups: Why join? *Sociol. Anal.* 46:147–56

Wagner, M. B. 1983. *Metaphysics in Midwestern America.* Columbus: Ohio State Univ. Press

Wallis, R. 1976. *The Road to Total Freedom: A Sociological Analysis of Scientology.* London: Heinemann

Wallis, R. 1979. *Salvation and Protest.* London: Francis Pinter

Wallis, R. 1981. Yesterday's children: Cultural and structural change in a new religious movement. See Wilson 1981a:97–134

Wallis, R., ed. 1982a. *Millenialism and Charisma.* Belfast: Queen's Univ. Press

Wallis, R. 1982b. The social construction of charisma. *Soc. Compass* 29:25–31

Wallis, R. 1982c. The new religions as social indicators. See Barker 1982b:216–31

Wallis, R. 1983. Religion, reason and responsibility: A reply to Professor Horowitz. *Sociol. Anal.* 44:215–20

Wallis, R. 1984. *The Elementary Forms of the New Religious Life.* London: Routledge & Kegan Paul

Wallis, R., Bruce, S. 1986. *Sociological*

Theory, Religion and Collective Action. Belfast, Queen's Univ. In press

Werblowsky, Z. 1982. Religions new and not so new: Fragments of an agenda. See Barker 1982b:32–46

West, L. J. 1982. Contemporary cults: Utopian image, infernal reality. *Ctr. Mag.* 15:10–3

Westley, F. 1983. *The Complex Forms of the Religious Life: A Durkheimian View of New Religious Movements.* Chico, Calif: Scholars

Wilson, B. R. 1970. *Religious Sects.* London: Weidenfeld & Nicolson

Wilson, B. R., ed. 1981a. *The Social Impact of New Religious Movements.* Barrytown, NY: Unification Theological Seminary

Wilson, B. R. 1981b. Time, generations, and sectarianism. See Wilson 1981a:217–34

Wilson, B. R. 1982a. *Religion in Sociological Perspective.* Oxford: Oxford Univ. Press

Wilson, B. R. 1982b. The new religions: Some preliminary considerations. See Barker 1982b:16–31

Wilson, B. R. 1983. Sympathetic detachment and disinterested involvement: A note on academic integrity. *Sociol. Anal.* 44:183–8

Wooden, K. 1981. *The Children of Jonestown.* New York: McGraw Hill

Wright, S. A. 1983. *A sociological study of defection from controversial new religious movements.* PhD thesis. Univ. Connecticut, Storrs

Wright, S. A. 1984. Post-involvement attitudes of voluntary defectors from controversial new religious movements. *J. Sci. Study Relig.* 23:172–82

Wuthnow, R. 1978. *Experimentation in American Religion: The New Mysticisms and their Implications for the Churches.* Berkeley: Univ. Calif. Press

Wuthnow, R. 1982. World order and religious movements. See Barker 1982b:47–65

Ann. Rev. Sociol. 1986. 12:347–71

RURAL COMMUNITY DEVELOPMENT

Gene F. Summers

Department of Rural Sociology, University of Wisconsin, Madison, Wisconsin 53706

Abstract

The author discusses rural community development in the United States by tracing its historical origins, reviewing its status within sociology, contrasting development of the community with development in the community, and reviewing three basic strategies of rural community development: authoritative intervention, client-centered intervention, and radical reform. The author concludes that federal intervention policies have created elaborate and complex interdependencies among state and federal governments, the private sector, and communities, and that rural community development requires a sociology that maps these relationships and provides explanations for changes in them.

INTRODUCTION

To appreciate and understand contemporary issues in rural community development,[1] it is helpful to step back to the 1880s. As industrial capitalism

---

[1]There is a closely related literature on rural development in the United States, of which rural sociologists are major architects. Some recent contributions include Copp (1972), Nolan & Heffernan (1974), Stanfield (1975), Hammill (1975), LeVeen (1979), Hobbs (1980), Lovejoy & Krannich (1981), Dillman & Hobbs (1982), Hobbs (1983), Dillman (1983), Wilkinson, Hobbs & Christenson (1983), Hardy (1983), Bradshaw & Blakely (1983) and Wilkinson (1984). *Community* is absent from the titles of articles and books in this literature, which seems appropriate since community as a form of social organization is generally tangential or subordinated to the main focus of their content. The boundary between rural development and rural community development is not sharply delimited since conditions of human existence in rural areas involve both; e.g. housing, health services, local government, jobs, income (Carter Administration 1979, Block et al. 1983). Moreover, many rural sociologists contribute to both sets of literature and this leads understandably to some blurring of boundaries. However, rural development is considerably broader in scope than rural community development; the former covers national policy and development strategies for the entire rural segment of society. In the review here, an attempt has been made to maintain a focus on rural *community* development which is more circumscribed than rural development, albeit embedded in it. See Wilkinson (1984, 1985a, b, 1986) for useful discussions of the interface of these two foci of development.

347

0360-0572/86/0815-0347$02.00

made its great surge, urban America was on the move, quickly surpassing earlier achievements of European nations. To many urbanites the evidence clearly supported their undaunted optimism and faith in evolutionary social progress. Yet in the midst of obviously rising affluence there existed the paradoxical injustice of poverty and inequality. Muckrackers, social reformers, and an occasional sociologist were documenting the argument that America was not entirely a good and just society for all.

In 1900 the nation held a vivid recollection of the radical agrarian mood of the Populist Party; that mood had grown increasingly ugly in response to the farm crisis that had escalated during the last quarter of the nineteenth century (Goodwyn 1978). Although William Jennings Bryan was defeated in 1896 as the Populist candidate for the Presidency, the political unrest in the countryside continued to be a serious concern of urban industrial interests which depended upon farmers to supply cheap food for the growing army of industrial workers. At the same time, projections of agricultural output fell far short of expected population growth. Thus, there was a sense that something had to be done about the "farm problem."

The Country Life Movement emerged as an urban sponsored alternative to the radical economic proposals of the Populists (Bowers 1974; Swanson 1972; Danbom 1979, Phifer et al 1980). It was a social, cultural, and moral reform movement that "embraced a program calling for the revolutionary modification of rural America" (Danbom 1979: vii). President Theodore Roosevelt's 1908 Commission on Country Life gave it legitimacy and called national attention to the need to improve rural life. The Commission concluded that the major sources of the problems of rural people were lack of organization, failures of rural social institutions, and inadequate infrastructures, rather than the failure of the industrial capitalist system, as the Populists claimed.

Spurred by the Commission on Country Life and the Country Life Movement, Congress passed the Smith-Lever Act of 1914 and created the Cooperative Extension Service; the act called for the presence of "at least one trained demonstrator or itinerant teacher for each agricultural county. . . . He is to assume leadership in every movement, whatever it may be, the aim of which is better planning, better living, more happiness, more education, and better citizenship" (US House of Representatives 1915). Throughout the Commission report (Commission on Country Life 1911), a constant theme was the need for thorough analysis of conditions in rural America, and one might argue reasonably that rural sociology, as well as rural community development, was a progeny of the Country Life Movement (Smith 1957, Newby 1980, Hooks & Flinn 1981, Booth & Fear 1985, Fear & Schwarzweller 1985).

To improve the efficiency of American agriculture, science and technology had to be brought to bear on farming practices, and that meant farmers needed a better basic education. Clearly, by 1900 the industrial revolution had come to America, and the millions of rural residents represented a potentially huge market for industrial products. However, their ability to consume was seriously hampered by their poverty and their isolation from centers of production. Thus, it was argued by the Country Life Movement that improvements in communication, transportation, and the economic well-being of rural people were needed.

In the sociological terminology of today, rural America at the turn of the century was viewed by the Commission and Country-Lifers as an underdeveloped region. A program of change was proposed that was intended to raise rural America to twentieth-century standards of urban social and economic organization and efficiency (Bailey 1911, Brazil 1981, Fiske 1912, Foght 1910, Gillette 1913).

Rural community development was a major component of the proposed program of rural progress. For nearly a half-century, there followed a lively and productive sociological concern with rural communities. But the social forces that came in the wake of World War II swept rural community development off center stage, at least momentarily.

RURAL COMMUNITY IN SOCIOLOGY

For several years sociology virtually abandoned the rural community as an object of study, on the assumption that it had been eclipsed by the great changes of mass society (Vidich & Bensman 1958, Stein 1960, Warren 1963, Martindale & Hanson 1969, Gallaher & Padfield 1980). These authors and others claimed that the increased presence of extra-local forces in the community (vertical integration) had destroyed the horizontal integration and rendered small rural communities powerless in the face of broad and powerful forces of urbanization, industrialization, bureaucratization, and centralization. The basic argument was that social organizational changes wrought by these macro processes had robbed rural communities of local autonomy in their decision-making and had absorbed them into mass society. In recent years there has been a growing sense that the pronounced impotence of rural communities has been somewhat exaggerated.

Critique of the Mass Society Thesis[2]

In a very thoughtful analysis of the urbanization of rural areas, Richards (1978) questions the two basic postulates of the mass society thesis: (1) "that American

[2]Albert Hunter (1978) argues convincingly that the belief that there has been a loss of local community sentiments in mass society has two empirical origins: (a) the Chicago School of the 1920s and 1930s which emphasized the disorganization of social relations in Chicago's neighborhoods, and (b) the transformation of small town life as a result of the increasing scale of social organization. He then presents a strong empirical basis for concluding that local sentiments of community persist. Virtually all the evidence presented is drawn from studies in urban and metropolitan settings and therefore is not included in this review, even though they provide corroboration of the position taken here.

rural towns are being absorbed into the larger culture through the development of vertical ties between individual institutions of the local community and mass society along with (2) the simultaneous deterioration of horizontal ties among local institutions" (Richards 1978:569). The first postulate is not supported by American community history concerning rural settlements; the second fails on both logical and empirical grounds, according to Richards.

Richards claims that the history of community social organization portrays vertical integration as a significant factor from the beginning of American settlement, despite the celebration of an earlier small-town autonomy that appears in the mass society literature. In the development of America, especially of its interior, symbiotic relationships always existed between the growth of urban and rural America. Frontier towns and villages were linked to commercial, industrial, and port cities, and their exports were dependent upon national and international commodity markets. Ghost towns (some long forgotten) and centennial celebrations (in which earlier histories are well remembered) attest to the historical reality of the vertical integration of rural communities. Far from being superimposed on autonomous rural communities, vertical integration provided the genesis of the American rural community. On this basis Richards speculates that continued or even increased vertical linkage to urban society may assure communities greater latitude in decision-making, especially if they entail a diversity of agricultural, industrial, and governmental ties. Fuguitt's recent review (1985) concludes unequivocally that this is the pattern of change in nonmetropolitan areas.

Richards also argues that there is no logical imperative that requires abandonment of local autonomy to be the inevitable consequence of vertical integration. Such reasoning is a clear example of the *post hoc, ergo propter hoc* logical fallacy. However, there is empirical evidence to support the notion that a dual structure of local decision-making may emerge, a bifurcation of power in which local groups or individuals are influential on some issues and external actors on others.

Schulze (1958) found that national firms had become economically dominant in the small city he studied, but the firms did not participate in community decision-making. Seiler & Summers (1979) report that establishing a very large steel mill with over 1000 employees in a rural Illinois county with only 5000 residents had little impact on the pattern of local decision-making, although the mill clearly was a dominant economic force in the rural area. A more recent review of the increased presence of the Federal government and multinational energy corporations in Western rural communities shows a similar pattern of bifurcation in decision-making (Summers & Bloomquist 1983). Agents of these external forces intervene in decision-making when their economic interests are at stake, but in other arenas of local decision-making, established patterns tend to persist.

Such evidence clearly supports the argument that increased vertical integration does not necessarily destroy horizontal integration. It does not, however, support an inference that the horizontal pattern is unaffected or unchanged. Rather, it is more consistent with the empirical data to view local autonomy as a relative phenomenon and the impact of changes in vertical integration as varying according to a complex matrix of variables characterizing the external agent and the local community. An initial effort to develop a theory along this line of reasoning may be found in the work of Branch et al (1984). The model was prepared to assist those concerned with social change in western-US communities facing a likelihood of energy development. It is a social organization model of local communities which was developed with increased vertical integration as an explicit factor, presumed to be significant. Most of the defining data for the model were drawn from experiences of energy resource communities and industrializing rural American communities (Summers et al 1976; Summers & Branch 1984; Summers & Selvik 1979, 1982; Detomasi & Gartrell 1984; Murdock & Leistritz 1979; Bowles 1981; Chalmers et al 1982; Leistritz & Murdock 1981; Summers 1983.)

Relative Autonomy

Investigation of the impact of vertical integration on the relative autonomy of rural communities requires comparative analysis. Although such studies are infrequent in the literature, several exist and generally lend support to the notion that effects are conditioned by community characteristics, especially the attitudes of local leaders. From his study of six Wisconsin and Missouri towns, Adams (1969) concluded that willingness of leaders to compete with neighboring communities was the most significant attribute of growing communities. Simon & Gagnon (1967) studied three southern Illinois towns and explicitly challenged the notion that vertical integration leads to loss of local autonomy. They concluded that whether a small town succeeds depends on the organizational structure of community decision-making and the values of decisionmakers. Hirschl & Summers (1983) found that the presence of citizen groups, organized for local economic development, was the single most significant determinant of job growth in 44 rural Wisconsin communities. Hickey (1982) studied the technical assistance needs and uses of local governments in eight Virginia small towns and found evidence that this form of vertical integration encourages horizontal networking as well as active manipulation of the larger bureaucratic structure by locals. Moxley (1985) studied community programs and projects and other citizen actions in two small North Carolina communities over a ten-year period. He concludes that Federal and state government support for programs "does not mean that local social action is futile or that local initiative, cooperation and decision making is of any less importance in reducing dependency" (p. 72). As a locality gains in complexity, sophistication, and competence, it is less dependent on other communities in its hinterland, or as Clark asserts, "the greater the resources available to the local community, the greater its autonomy" (Clark 1973). Such optimism may be misplaced if it ignores the matter of who controls the resources or the conditions under which they are made available.

Control of essential resources is critical to the relative autonomy of any social organization. Shaffer & Summers (1984) argue that communities compete for resources and markets in much the same manner as private firms in a market economy, and it is the local state which represents the "community interest" in such competition. To execute its responsibility, the local state must possess at least two crucial criteria of independence: (*a*) its right to raise revenue and determine its use and (*b*) its right to control its personnel—who shall be hired and fired, and what shall be the conditions of work. In the United States, local governments retain these rights and in doing so guarantee a significant degree of influence on the community's future (Peterson 1981). Shaffer & Summers (1984) also argue that what is most important is how well the local state exercises its power in creating and maintaining local institutions to shape and guide the efficient use of economic resources, the maintenance of resources, and adaptability to changing conditions.

Private Troubles, Public Issues, Mobilization

There is yet another, more psychosocial, explanation for the persistence of local, territorially focused communities in the face of macro political, economic, and social forces. As long as there are human beings confronting a harsh physical and social environment, there will be community as a form of collective action because mobilization has its roots in the private troubles of individuals (Summers 1985). Maslow's (1954) hierarchy of needs captures the essence of this truth, as Wilkinson (1979) and Rubin (1969) have noted. At the base are needs for material goods necessary for biological survival and security from physical harm. As these are secured, social needs begin to predominate. Virtually every utopian vision is a blueprint for a community that includes the freedom from threats to individual well-being and the liberty to explore and develop.

Threats to such felt needs are experienced as private troubles, as personal burdens. They are integral elements of existential being, lived largely in proximal space. Many, perhaps most, of the threats to the fulfillment of perceived needs have their origin in the proximal life space of individuals. As individuals share their private troubles with others who share a common space, they quickly discover they are not alone in their misery and need. Thus, private troubles become public issues around which people are able and sometimes willing to mobilize for collective action.

Warren (1978) notes that it is not necessary to view the community as a

Parsonian concrete collectivity (Parsons 1951) or formal organization in order to understand locality oriented mobilization. Rather one may view the community as an interactional field (Long 1958, Kaufman 1959, Wilkinson 1970) consisting of clustered interactions of people and organizations, occupying a restricted geographic area and revealing extensive systemic interconnections. The community, per se, may not act, but the parts do (Young 1970, Tilly 1973). Moreover, the extent to which collective actions have a specific local focus varies among communities. Thus, unified and single public-interest collective action is not a defining characteristic of communities but rather a variable attribute, and the isolation of conditions that lead to this variation is an important research need.

Mobilization for collective action can generate a sense of communion among those actively involved in pursuing a common cause. Of course, the organizational focus of mobilization need not always be a locality or territory. It may be a religious, political, labor, ethnic, racial, or gender organization, or the national state (Rubin 1969).

Recognition that some public issues transcend the proximal environment sometimes leads to collective actions on a broader stage. For example, many community groups have turned to the national state as the appropriate organizational instrument to intervene in society and provide solutions to public issues which they believe they cannot develop for themselves. But when the nation state, or other extra-local instruments of intervention, fails to perform in accordance with expectations, there will almost certainly be a resurgent interest in local efforts. Thus, it is precisely at those moments in history when private troubles are most severe and widely shared, and when extra-local organizations are least responsive, that community as communion will manifest its strongest territorial expression (Summers 1985). Following a similar line of reasoning, Ravitz (1982) concludes that community development has potential for being most effective in periods of social and economic crisis and when distrust of extra-local entities is high. There is some evidence such conditions currently prevail.

A recent study of over 9000 Pennsylvania residents, urban and rural, found that across a spectrum of 35 welfare programs and activities rural residents were less inclined to turn to extra-local solutions than were urban residents (Camasso & Moore 1985). Lest there be misunderstanding: On 30 of the 37 issues, a majority of both urban and rural residents favored greater extra-local effort, but rural residents consistently less so than the urban. This finding is particularly relevant for local collective mobilization in rural communities because it leads one to the work of Fischer (1981) regarding rural-urban differences in public response and to Granovetter (1973) and Craven & Wellman (1973) concerning "strong and weak ties" in networks of social relationships. According to Fischer, urbanites have gained a capacity to deal publicly with nonsignificant others without sacrificing intimate ties and traditional values. Granovetter documented the existence of "strong ties" and "weak ties" in social networks. The former refer to repetitive social relationships with high emotional intensity and intimacy. Weak ties involve less intense social relationships which often occur in large, loosely knit organizations and associations. Granovetter argues it is the "weak ties" that build bridges between people of differing backgrounds and interests. Craven & Wellman (1973) report evidence that urban settings provide more opportunities for individuals to participate in "weak tie" networks. Thus, for rural community development to realize its potential of facilitating local collective action, it may be necessary to encourage the formation of more "weak tie" networks. This point is consistent with Richards (1984) characterization of an effective Iowa farm community as one with shared values, conflict resolution mechanisms, local issues, and healthy indigenous social networks; it also corroborates Young's discussion of "reactive subsystems" (Young 1970).

In the second edition of *The Community in America* (1972) Warren added a noteworthy epilogue in which he states his belief that "The death of the community has been highly exaggerated. Transformed, si—muerto, no!" (Warren 1972: 408). In the third edition (1978) Warren added two chapters in which he explains more fully the horizontal and vertical patterns of contemporary communities. He asserts that "although the macrosystem exercises its powerful influence, it does not by any means completely determine what happens locally. Much local structure and behavior are determined primarily at the local level" (Warren 1978: 435). In the last sentence of the book he explicitly rejects the allegation "that attention to the macrosystem necessarily means 'writing off' local communities as unimportant" (Warren 1978).

Perhaps the shifting views regarding the loss of local autonomy tell us more about the fads and foibles of sociologists than about the changing realities of rural communities. In any event, the literature reviewed in this section makes a rather strong case that rural communities have not been swept away or made meaningless by the forces of mass society and when this survey is added to Hunter's (1978) review of urban experience, the persistence of local community sentiments and locality based systems is undeniable.

DEVELOPMENT *OF* OR *IN* THE COMMUNITY?

A basic tension exists in rural community development between those who view community as the causal factor in the well-being (social, political, economic) of residents of a locality and those who view it as a denotative term referring to the stratification system, the power structure, or the human ecology that prevails in a locality. These four views are the traditional paradigms of community sociology which Bernard (1973) analyzed at length, concluding that they are no longer capable of accommodating contemporary realities. Nevertheless, the notion persists that community is a qualitative field of social interaction with the capacity to influence and shape the well-being of participants; this notion continues to have strong proponents in the rural community development field.

Development of Community

This view is stated eloquently by Wilkinson (1972, 1979, 1986). He begins by describing social well-being in humanist terms following the works of Gordon Allport, Abram Maslow, Carl Rogers, and others. Self-actualization, the central concept elaborated by Maslow (1954) refers to a growth motive which emerges when motives for survival, security, and esteem are satisfied. Social well-being, according to Wilkinson, refers to social conditions that foster self-actualization. "Community refers to certain social relationships in the life space of the person, which, it is argued, serve both as a means of achieving social well-being and as a definition, or end, of its realization" (Wilkinson 1979: 7). Circularity notwithstanding, community clearly is posited as a prime causal factor in personal growth. Wilkinson also offers several reasons why community is an important causal factor. It is the setting for the individual's contact with society; it is global (i.e. complete) in an institutional sense (see also Hillery 1968); it is the primary realm of social experience beyond the family; it is a significant aspect of the self-concept of an individual; it is an arena for immediate expression of the fundamental human disposition toward association; and it can foster particular attitudes of collective responsibility (Wilkinson 1979: 8).

Community development is seen as a purposive activity by people to strengthen a "community field." It consists, according to Wilkinson, of acts by people that open and maintain channels of communication and cooperation among local groups.

A similar view of development was expressed by a leading urban community organizer, Saul Alinsky. Although he used a radical vocabulary (Alinsky 1969, 1971), his organizing strategy emphasized democratic citizen participation and community cohesion. His analysis of power and the use of conflict were tools for achieving these goals (Silberman 1964, Meenagan 1972, Fish 1973, Gleb & Sardell 1974, Reitzes & Reitzes 1980).

Greisman (1980) also argues that community is essential to the satisfaction of human needs, especially the need not to feel alienated from society. Durkheim made the same argument much earlier in the *Division of Labor in Society*. A variety of intermediate structures between the state and the individual are regarded as essential in bridging the gap between them. Community is one of a "whole series of secondary groups near enough to the individuals to attract them strongly in their sphere of action and drag them in this way, into the general torrent of social life" (Durkheim 1964: 28). Although Rubin (1969) follows the same line of reasoning and goes on to argue that community may have a nonterritorial locus, he does not exclude the territorial community.

From this point of view the creation and maintenance of social structures, territorial and nonterritorial, which mediate between individuals and society, are essential to the well-being of humans. Development of the community requires attention to these integrative structures.

Development in the Community

In sharp contrast are those who argue for efforts to bring about development *in* the community—economic growth, modernization, improved social services—rather than development *of* the community; a distinction noted several years ago by Kaufman (1959). Treated in this way, community is essentially a territorial setting where social processes take place which may enhance the lives of at least some of the people who reside there or which may improve a locality's standing relative to other localities. However, it is altogether possible that the process of achieving development *in* the community may produce development *of* the community. The circularity of Wilkinson's definition is therefore very understandable (Wilkinson 1979).

Community economic development[3] provides a good example of the orientation to development *in* the community. The emphasis is on creating jobs and raising the real incomes of residents. The local economy is treated very much as if it were a business firm, and attention is given to efficient use and maintenance of productive resources and to changes in the external environment, both markets and the supply of materials for production (Harmston 1983; Pulver 1979; Isard 1956, 1975; Thompson 1965; Shaffer 1985; Tiebout 1962).

The community is seen as a collection of micro units, including households, that have common economic interests. These units, their interactions, and their relationships with external units make up the community economic system (Harmston 1983:4). People are seen as consumers and as suppliers of labor; this makes community economic analysis and demography comfortable partners. Similarly, the centrality of competition and spatial factors in the dynamics of the community economic system makes human ecology a natural ally. Together these three partners (community economics, demography, and human ecology) constitute a very potent force in academe and thus currently dominate the field of rural community development. It is also the case that economic development concerns top the list of local officials' perceived needs, and thus there is a

---

[3]Portions of this discussion of community economic development are taken from a longer, unpublished essay by Shaffer & Summers (1984). Other examples of development *in* the community could have been chosen, but community economic development is used because, in my opinion, it occupies a dominant position in the activities of professionals engaged in rural community development.

"strong market" for this approach to development (Camasso & Moore 1985, Reinhard & Summers 1985).

We are accustomed to thinking about private sector firms operating in a market characterized by competition, but we are frequently oblivious to the fact that communities also compete. And it is the local state which represents the "community interest" in such competition (Peterson 1981). There are conflicting interest groups in every community based on class, ethnicity, race, age, religion, education, occupation, or other social categories. Superimposed on them is the local state whose authority and power coincide with the territorial perimeter of a local system. The future well-being of the community depends on actions of the local state, although not exclusively so. At times local state politics and actions may coincide with other corporate interest groups, but that occurrence is coincidental because the ultimate interest of the local state must be the continued existence of the social system that occupies its territory.

In competition with other local states, there are at least three significant dimensions of comparisons: economic, social, and political (Peterson 1981). They are not empirically independent but they are analytically separable, and the following discussion dwells on the economic competition among communities. Firms compete in the private economy and their managers only incidentally consider the interests of the community or the community's stake in the competition among local states. The private sector is only marginally interested in the territorial or spatial dimensions of the competition among communities. This distinction between local state and private sector goals is crucial because it allows one to recognize the basis for the sometimes apparent lack of common interests between local officials and local business owners and managers.

Community economic development is the capacity of the local state to continue generating income and employment in order to maintain, if not to improve, its relative economic position. Observations of growing, stable, and declining communities lead to the conclusion that the institutional apparatus is critical. Vital communities possess social constructions, with underlying assumptions, which encourage and permit the orderly and efficient use of economic resources, ensure their maintenance, and allow adaptation to changes in the environment.

Perhaps in the short run, say, in less than five years, community economic development depends largely on the existing export base and the mechanisms in place that enable the locality to capture the money generated by it. But markets for products and services come and go. Consumer demand today is vastly different than 50 years ago, or even 10. Therefore, the longevity of any community ultimately depends on its ability to renew its export base; the capacity to invent, to innovate, or to acquire new exports. Community economic development requires a local network of services and facilities which insure the continued availability of factors of production—especially land, labor, and capital (Tiebout 1956, 1962; Thompson 1965; Peterson 1981).

LAND   Land is the economic resource most amenable to control by the community. All production occurs somewhere; it must have a spatial location. Communities also occupy space, and because of the prerogatives of the modern state, they have a great deal of control over their territories. Since land is an essential economic resource, its control gives the community, operating through the local state, a substantial ability to direct the economic vitality of the community.

It is the case, of course, that the local state today has less control over its territory than was the case in the historical period of the city state. Likewise, the land use powers of the local state vary noticeably from one nation-state to another and therefore constitute an important dimension of cross-national comparisons. The local state powers in Canada are much less than those of local states in the United States for example. Consequently, specific policy options that are workable and wise in the United States may be weak or not feasible in Canada. Nevertheless, local institutions exercise land-use controls in virtually every society.

Land varies in its economic potential and therefore in its value. Because it does so, its potential dictates to a large extent the economic vitality of the community. Historically, great cities emerged where land had great economic potential. The need to change modes of transportation made land in the immediate vicinity valuable. It was needed for the freight transfer activity, as a site for housing workers, and as a resource for provisioning their needs. Breaks in transportation gave us harbor cities, railroad junction cities, river cities. Today, air transportation and motorways have diminished the power of the transportation break to determine land value in these cities. Where other uses have been found for the land and the value has remained high, the city economy has retained its vitality. In some instances, once thriving transportation-break cities have declined and shrunk to near extinction. Communities whose birth was sired by immobile natural resources face a similar threat once the resource is depleted. But every local state must take steps to ensure the continued economic value of its land.

The cases of transportation and natural resource extraction imply that changes beyond community control determine local land values. To some extent that is true, since no community is totally autonomous. But communities can exercise considerable control over future land uses and therefore land values. The local state can determine land uses to a great extent through planning future land-use patterns, exercising the power of eminent domain, regulating the size, type, and use of construction, as well as through discretionary provision of public services. The location of roads, streets, highways, sewers, gas lines, bridges, tunnels, parks, and schools all impinge on future land uses and land values.

The public investments that shape future land uses and land values are immobile. They cannot migrate to another community as other factors of production can. Rather they create a magnet for attracting and retaining labor and capital needed for production. Many students of community politics note that land is the focal point of local politics—e.g. Molotch 1976. It cannot be otherwise because land is the economic resource over which the local state exercises greatest control.

LABOR   Skilled workers are relatively scarce in the labor force, a situation which allows them to demand higher wages. They also are concentrated in firms and industries where innovation is occurring through research and development. This gives the firm monopoly power of the early lead in a new industry, and the higher profit margins are passed on, in part to labor.

Skilled labor is not only better educated but generally more intellectually agile and constitutes a resource to the community in noneconomic arenas.

There are options local states can use to enhance their ability to retain and attract a skilled labor force. Through zoning laws they can ensure adequate land for middle-class residences. They can build and maintain parks, recreation facilities, high quality schools, and adult education programs. Provision of public services seldom used by middle-class residents can be kept to a minimum or eliminated and thereby the tax burden to skilled labor can be reduced. Lowered taxes can be translated into a higher benefit/tax ratio for skilled workers (e.g. their real wages can be increased), which thereby increases the competitive position of the community in attracting and retaining them.

This strategy of public investment is rational from the perspective of the local state's interest in community economic vitality, i.e. in maintaining or improving its economic position. It also coincides with the economic interests of middle-class workers. However, this market-based strategy largely ignores the interests of unskilled and semiskilled workers.

To maintain equity among classes under the conditions of a market-oriented public economy, it is necessary for the national state to assume responsibility for the redistributive function. For the local state, operating in a market economy, it is irrational to adopt policies that increase the benefit-to-tax ratio of taxpayers who already are above the average ratio; the poor, the handicapped, the dropouts (Peterson 1981). To a degree, equity becomes a function of both the national and local states, but the national state is the dominant partner. It sets the rules for competition among local states which have considerable flexibility in responding to those rules or pushing them further. The constraint for the local state is that it cannot exceed the 'national norm' of equity without making itself less competitive relative to other communities. Local attempts to redress inequitable outcomes of the market enter the realm of intercommunity competition when they exceed the limits of the national state's rules.

CAPITAL   Unlike nation states, local states have very limited tools with which to control the flow of capital into and out of their territories. Tariffs, price and wage controls, monetary policies, and deficit spending are mechanisms reserved to the national state. Therefore, communities are left largely to the use of devices that minimize the local cost of capital investment to enterprises within their territories or that create investment opportunities and thereby generate a competitive advantage.

Cost reduction is the strategy most often pursued by local states, and there are several tactical tools available. They may reduce the tax burden for firms by minimizing public services, especially to taxpayers with above average benefit/tax ratios and to nontaxpayers. They may offer public land at a discount price or perhaps free of charge. They may provide tax holidays where law allows such practice. They may exempt or discount the assessment of real property; land, buildings, machinery, equipment. They may reduce or ignore regulations such as safety and pollution codes. Such public subsidies may attract capital to the community, but the extent to which the local state can reduce costs to capital without jeopardizing its economic vitality in the long run is a matter of considerable debate.

STRATEGIES OF DEVELOPMENT

Rural community development is planned intervention to stimulate social change for the explicit purpose of the "betterment of the people." This global desire to improve the conditions of human existence appears to enjoy a virtual consensus. The adjective "rural," of course, draws a boundary around the arena of action. The focus of rural community development is on the quality of life, or well-being, of people residing in sparsely settled areas; in the United States, this is generally taken to mean small cities, towns, and villages in nonmetropolitan areas.

As a special case of planned social change, rural community development shares many basic assumptions with other types of deliberate intervention. Development goals are based on a vision of what might be or ought to be and therefore are normative and not necessarily shared by all concerned. Development as planned change "is putting a particular ideological orientation into action to restructure the social, normative and economic order for desired ends" (Christenson & Robinson 1980:7). It entails the execution of deliberate policies, often by those in power (Portes 1976).

Rural community development is derived from a vision of society which stresses the utilization of knowledge, particularly science and technology, to solve problems. This notion that, by applying systematic and appropriate knowledge, social systems can be changed deliberately for the betterment of all is sharply contrasted with the belief that if left alone homeostatic forces will evolve a system providing the maximum good. The latter is clearly the laissez-faire doctrine of social Darwinism, and while its popularity among sociologists has declined, it is by no means extinct in society. The field is thus properly viewed as an integral element in the reform-oriented tradition of intellectual liberalism. Its heritage has the same roots and its history follows the same patterns of waxing and waning popularity (Phifer et al 1980).

Although social scientists involved in rural community development accept the interventionist philosophy, they have fundamental disagreements about how best to intervene. The differing views reflect much more pervasive debates among sociologists and other social scientists concerned with the planning of change. The reform vs revolution debate centers on the question of whether the desired improvements in the human condition can be achieved by revisions of the existing system or only by revolutionary action. The populist vs elitist debate, focuses on who should control the decisions regarding goals and methods of intervention. Should control be in the hands of the people whose lives would be most directly affected; or should it reside with scientists, technicians, and other planners with specialized knowledge, or with persons who own scarce resources and therefore have a powerful vested interest in system changes? The structural vs individualistic debate concerns the appropriate target for intervention. Should efforts be focused on improving institutional or individual capacities? And the outcome vs process debate emphasizes the time perspective of development. Should intervention be directed toward producing immediate improvements in material well-being or toward developing new social, economic, and political processes presumed necessary to sustain well-being in the long run?

Several writers have analyzed positions taken in these debates, and the associated assumptions; they attempted to organize them into descriptive models of planned intervention (Sanders 1958, Rothman 1974, Crowfoot & Chesler 1974, Chin & Benne 1976, Christenson & Robinson 1980). Chin & Benne's general strategies for effecting changes in human systems is the most encompassing of these models, since their analysis is not limited to community development. They identify three types or groups of strategies—empirical/rational, normative/re-educative, and power/coercive. Christenson & Robinson discuss three "themes of community development" that closely parallel the more generalized strategies of Chin & Benne. These three themes are labeled, (a) technical intervention, planning or assistance, (b) self-help, nondirective or cooperative, and (c) conflict or confrontation. It is useful to note that these models of intervention are derived from writings of social scientists and other members of academe, many of whom work also as change agents but are outsiders to the communities where they serve. Thus, the "folk wisdom" or indigenous social thought schemes of various client or target group members is excluded, unless it is incorporated into the writing of professionals. In the review that follows attention is directed to assumptions, goals, and preferred modes of intervention; it follows the analyses of Chin & Benne (1976), and Christenson & Robinson (1980).

Authoritative Intervention

In following an authoritative intervention strategy, an agent (usually external to the community) introduces a change in the belief that the project will improve the community and that it is in line with the self-interest of the community. People are assumed to be rational and therefore willing to adopt the proposed change if it can be rationally justified and if it can be shown by the change agent that the community will gain by the proposed change.

The fundamental article of faith in this approach is the belief that ignorance, superstition, and incorrect information are the chief foes of improvements in the human condition. Scientific research will expand the knowledge base, and education will free humans from ignorance and superstition. When confronted with an unmet need, basic scientific researchers, it is presumed, can *and will* discover the causal factors and engineer a solution. People in the target community will then follow their rational self-interest and adopt the recommended solution.

This development approach also implies certain conditions about the provider-recipient relationship. First, someone decides the recipient needs assistance. Often this is the provider or the project sponsor; seldom is it the recipient. Second, the provider's knowledge is superior to the recipient's. Third, there exists a social and political climate in which a provider-recipient relationship can be established.

Authoritative intervention has its origin in the life sciences and physical sciences and has led to the belief that problems afflicting the human condition are *primarily* biological or physical, not cultural, social, political, economic, or demographic. Thus, application of biological and physical sciences is believed to offer the greatest hope. Social sciences play a secondary role; often their task is to find ways to speed the adoption and diffusion of new technologies intended to improve the well-being of citizens.

A great many achievements have been made as a result of authoritative intervention which introduces "new and improved" technologies. This is particularly true where the root problem is biological or physical. Improvements in health, nutrition, sanitation, safety, air and water quality, food production, and other consumer product developments have profoundly affected human welfare over the past 50 years.

Without denying the value of the technical intervention, protagonists of client-centered intervention and radical reform argue against its universality and exclusive superiority. Criticism centers largely on the locus of control in the development process. Who decides there is a problem in need of solution and the best course of action? Who decides on the availability of resources? Critics argue that the answers to these questions are always the same in the elitist-derived, authoritative intervention strategy. The deciding voice is an external agent, who may be an absentee landlord, a Federal or state government official, managers in a business firm with headquarters elsewhere, or representatives of a national association or church. The notion that authoritative intervention threatens local autonomy and a sense of community is quite prevalent in the criticism.

By contrast the protagonists of client-centered intervention and radical reform believe that most people want to control their own lives and should. They share the elitist' view of humans as rational beings, capable of learning, and guided by self-interest. They also accept science as a valid method in the search for truth, i.e. empirically verifiable knowledge. They disagree sharply with authoritative interventionists as to who should control the development process.

Client-Centered Intervention

Client-centered intervention, with its populist-based ideology (Canovan 1981), places great emphasis on political equality and popular sovereignty as the means by which citizens control their own lives. In this view, a primary function of the state is to guarantee every citizen's right to freedom of expression. While these concepts are ancient in the history of democratic theory and are crucial to modern liberalism, contemporary statements of the populist ideology derive major support from behavioral and social sciences. This is in sharp contrast to authoritative interventionists whose ideology is closely integrated with the biological and physical sciences.

What is perhaps most distinctive about the populist-based intervention strategy is the emphasis placed on the individual citizen; it is client-centered. All people are believed to be inherently active in searching for ways to satisfy their needs. Their behavior is purposive, and experiences in their daily lives are continually and consciously evaluated for usefulness in satisfying their needs. People learn from their experiences and evolve workable systems of beliefs, values, and behaviors. Thus, their experiential learning is a method of truth seeking and reality testing not unlike the scientists' experimentation. Preserving citizens' rights to engage in experimentation and to incorporate what is learned into everyday living is the ultimate guarantee of freedom and civilization, the long-term improvement in the human condition.

While there are many variations on the populist ideology when translated into development approaches, all emphasize the client system and the necessity of active client involvement in working out programs of change. The change agent must learn to work in partnership with the client, who actively participates in defining the problem, considering alternative solutions, assessing availability of resources, and choosing a course of action. The problem is not assumed *a priori* to be one which can or must be solved by more technical knowledge, although that possibility is not ruled out. Indigenous knowledge is treated as having equal value with scientific knowledge, and the possibility is maintained that a workable solution to the problem may be a combination of the two. Moreover, the methods and concepts of the social and behavioral sciences, as well as those of physical and biological sciences, are accepted as resources for the client and the change agent.

Radical Reform

Among the strategies of rural community development in the United States, radical reform is the most unusual, in several respects. First, rural community development projects and programs rarely have been guided by the radical reform strategy, especially by Marxist ideologies. They are more commonly guided by a mixture of authoritative and client-centered intervention strategies. Second, the fundamental premise of radical reform is that only through major reformation of the structure of the local system, and ultimately of society, can the objectives of development be realized. This idea is rather foreign to the American polity, which leads one to the third peculiarity. Radical reform is a strategy based on ideologies which have considerable popularity among the intelligentsia, especially those with an urban orientation, but which have very few practiners in rural communities of the United States. This lack of widespread citizen mobilization to achieve the goals of radical reform is a continuing source of puzzlement and debate among its intellectual architects. Finally, the strategy of radical reform incorporates a very wide range of tactical styles, from the nonviolent civil disobedience of Ghandi and Martin Luther King to the extremely violent terrorism of activists of both right and left political persuasions.

What holds these divergent groups together analytically is a common set of assumptions. They all believe that the existing system incorporates injustices and inequities which those in power perpetuate for their benefit. They also share an assumption that persons in power will not accept meaningful reforms willingly. Changes that are necessary for truly significant improvements in the human condition can be achieved only by using power to alter the existing system fundamentally. It is in their choice of instruments of power that radical reformists diverge.

The advocates of nonviolent, civil disobedience rely heavily on the moral "rightness" of their plan of reform to garner mass support for mobilization. It would appear that the approach has its greatest potential when a widely held moral principle is being violated by holders of power or can be shown to be threatened by institutionalized practices within the system. The successes of Ghandi, King, and Alinsky are illustrative cases. While moral persuasion is the centerpiece of this tactical style, it often is combined with economic and political sanctions such as consumer boycotts or worker strikes which assume that ultimately power is in the hands of the governed. Partisans of this style accept democratic principles and advocate radical reform as a strategy for achieving their vision of what community, and society, ought to be.

The basic premise of marxist-derived development is that barriers to improvements in the human condition are determined by the predominant manner in which people are organized for production purposes. While the precise form of these relations may vary, in capitalist societies a ruling class always controls the means of production—land and other natural resources, capital, labor, and knowledge. Because of the power of the ruling class, its ideology pervades the centers of education, religion, and government. All who work in and for these institutions are "tools" of the power elite. Exploitation of productive workers is the basis of the power of the ruling class. The elite will occasionally accommodate minor demands, creating an illusion of reform, while in fact retaining its power. Thus, a radical removal of the ruling class is the only hope the proletarian class has of successfully bringing in the changes they desire. Only through a revolutionary social movement can the dispossessed proletarian class replace the ruling elite.

Change agents committed to this theory believe that the basis of contemporary revolutionary movements lies in a proletarian class consciousness. Thus, worker mobilization is the first task of marxist radical reform. When the oppressed are made aware of the true source of their discomfort and misfortune, they can be mobilized to challenge the power elite. It is not necessary for all workers to be mobilized; some may play a supportive role. The objective of the movement is to seize control of production and replace existing managers with members of the proletarian class who will establish a nonexploitive system of social relations. Tactics for gaining control may range from electing a favorable government to violent military action. In all cases, however, the ultimate goal is to replace the ruling elite, as a necessary condition for correcting major social injustices.

CONCLUSIONS

Many of the social facts addressed by the Smith-Lever Act of 1914 and Roosevelt's New Deal legislation still existed in midcentury America. During the period of the New Deal, efforts of the federal government to cope with the problems of rural communities reached a new zenith, but these programs were given low priority during the war years. Even though Truman served notice that he intended to extend the reform programs of the New Deal, his efforts produced few tangible results in Congress. The "Cold War," the Korean war, and a coalition of Southern Democrats and conservative Republicans blocked federal efforts until the 1960s.

By 1960 there was a heightened public and governmental concern with issues of civil rights, poverty, environmental quality, and urban congestion. The big-city racial riots of the mid-1960s made plain to everyone the obvious causal connection between the decaying central cities and the problems of rural America, specifically, the circumstances stimulating the rural-urban migration of poorly educated persons, black and white. Thus, in 1961 Congress passed the Area Redevelopment Act to provide capital to problem areas in the form of low-cost loans to industry, and loans and grants to communities for upgrading infrastructural support for new industry. This was followed in 1964 by the Economic Opportunity Act designed to attack poverty. The Appalachian Regional Commission was established in 1965, and the Economic Development Act of 1965 created several additional regional commissions and funded a variety of economic development efforts in the rural areas that were coping with high rates of poverty and unemployment. The Rural Development Act of 1972 and the Rural Development Policy Act of 1980 provided still further assistance to small communities.

Throughout this period of legislative activity it appears the underlying assumption was that rural poverty and the urban crisis were the product of a spatial mismatch of labor supply and demand (Hansen 1970). Earlier efforts to deal with the labor market disjuncture by encouraging rural-urban migration apparently had only exacerbated the problem. The obvious alternative, within the limits of a market-oriented economy, was to encourage capital mobility to rural areas where it could be put to work creating jobs, raising incomes, and strengthening the fiscal base of local government. The implementation of this federal intervention strategy generated a decade of rural industrialization, an associated growth in the service sector of rural America, and a "population turnaround" (Summers & Branch 1984, Fuguitt 1985). It also created an elaborate and extremely complex matrix of interdependencies among state and federal governments, the private sector and communities.

Today, rural community development needs a sociology that maps these relationships and which provides explanations for changes in them over time and across societies. Sociologists have a crucial role to play in constructing a proper sociology of community.

Following World War II many sociologists with an interest in community turned their attention to the cities, calling themselves urbanists, while many rural sociologists concerned with rural communities and their development engaged in the task of "modernizing" the Third World. But the waning of sociologists' attention to rural community development in the United States has not meant that communities ceased to exist in rural America, that local community sentiments have become extinct, that locality-oriented decision-making has been rendered meaningless by the large-scale organization of mass society, or that the rural standard of living has achieved parity with urban industrial America.

There are strong pressures upon many sociologists, especially rural sociologists, to become more involved in the *practice* of rural community development. University administrators, colleagues, and potential clients urge them to provide more assistance to local public officials, to citizen groups, to private developers and consultants, to special interest groups, and to county faculty in the Cooperative Extension Service. These pressures are likely to increase as Federal budget cuts deepen in response to the huge deficit and as universities are encouraged by state legislators to become more responsive to the practical problems of society, especially those related to a lagging economy.

While most sociologists appear personally to hold improvement in human conditions as an ultimate motivating force, or at least a legitimation for the disciplinary enterprise, few accept the implementation of intervention strategies as a proper role for sociologists *qua* sociologists. No matter how significant rural community development may be, its practice is not accepted as sociology. Thus, most sociologists, including rural sociologists, resist the pressures to become more involved in the *practice* of rural community development.

Although these two endeavors are understandably separate, a partnership between sociologists and rural community development practitioners is essential. A proper sociology of community would facilitate the work of practitioners who lack the time, the resources, the opportunities, and often the necessary training and skills to research these underlying forces and the context within which intervention is planned.

In the absence of a viable sociology of community, practitioners are left to depend upon conventional wisdom, which too often turns out to be based on myths. Caught up in the local situation where they are attempting to assist development efforts, practitioners are prone to ignore extra-local forces, to their own peril. Conversely, sociologists who ignore the work of practitioners put themselves at risk also. Ignorance of local realities encourages acceptance of urban and macro biases in sociology, as well as intellectual and ideological received wisdom, which also often turn out to be based on myths.

Rural community development needs a sociology that maps state, economic, and community relationships and provides explanations for changes in them. There are a great many areas of interrelationship, and much of the literature comprising rural community studies prior to 1950 is of limited value for understanding rural communities today. Bernard has argued that the sociology of community is in need of a new paradigm (1973). The task is an enormous and worthy challenge to sociologists concerned with rural community development.

ACKNOWLEDGMENTS

Preparation of this manuscript was supported by the College of Agricultural and Life Sciences, University of Wisconsin-Madison, and the North Central Regional Center for Rural Development. The review benefited from the helpful comments of E. M. Beck, Leonard Bloomquist, James Christenson, Glenn Fuguitt, Jess Gilbert, Tom Hirschl, Ron Hustedde, Don Johnson, Lorna C. Miller, Robert Moxley, Glen C. Pulver, Ron E. Shaffer, Matthew Snipp, W. Keith Warner, E. A. Wilkening, Ken Wilkinson, Franklin Wilson, and an anonymous reviewer for the *Annual Review of Sociology*.

Readers will find reason to claim that some important issues in rural community development are not covered in this review, and I wish to acknowledge that fact a priori. Limitations of space force choices which inevitably result in omissions that are regrettable. Fortunately, some of them are dealt with in previous issues of the *Annual Review of Sociology* (Clark 1975, Sanders & Lewis 1976, Newby 1983, Summers & Branch 1984, Fuguitt 1985), are planned for future issues, or appear in other summary volumes (Bell & Newby 1971, Bernard 1973, Whiting 1974, Summers et al 1976, Clemente 1977, Blakely 1979, Bradshaw & Blakely 1979, Lonsdale & Seyler 1979, Murdock & Leistritz 1979, Summers & Selvik 1979, Christenson & Robinson 1980, Sofranko & Williams 1980, Bowles 1981, Hawley & Mazie 1981, Leistritz & Murdock 1981, Summers & Selvik 1982, Detomasi & Gartrell 1984, Lonsdale & Enyedi 1984, Fear & Schwarzweller 1985, Johnson et al 1986).

Literature Cited

Adams, B. 1969. The small trade center: Processes and perceptions of growth and decline. In *The Community*, ed. R. French, pp. 471–84. Itaska, Ill: Peacock

Alinsky, S. D. 1969. *Reveille for Radicals.* Chicago: Univ. Chicago Press

Alinsky, S. D. 1971. *Rules for Radicals.* New York: Random

Bailey, L. H. 1911. *The Country-Life Movement in the United States.* New York: MacMillan

Bell, C., Newby, H. 1971. *Community Studies.* London: Allen & Unwin

Bernard, J. 1973. *The Sociology of Community.* Glenview, Ill: Scott, Foresman

Blakely, E. J. ed. 1979. *Community Development Research: Concepts, Issues, and Strategies.* New York: Human Sciences

Block, J. R., Naylor, F. W. Jr., Phillips, W. 1983. *Better Country: A Strategy for Rural Development in the 1980s.* Washington, DC: US Dep. Agric., Office Rural Devel. Policy

Booth, N., Fear, F. A. 1985. *Community Development: An Old Idea Comes of Age.* East Lansing, Mich: Mich. State Univ. Dep. Resource Devel. Unpublished manuscript

Bowers, W. L. 1974. *The Country Life Movement in America, 1900–1920.* Port Washington, NY: Kennikat

Bowles, R. T. 1981. *Social Impact Assessment in Small Communities.* Toronto: Buttersworth

Bradshaw, T. K., Blakely, E. J. 1979. *Rural Communities in Advanced Industrial Society: Development and Developers.* New York: Praeger

Bradshaw, T. K., Blakely, E. J. 1983. National, state, and local roles in rural policy development. *The Rural Sociol.* 3(July): 212–19

Branch, K., Hooper, D. A., Thompson, J., Creighton, J. 1984. *Guide to Social Assessment: A Framework for Assessing Social Change.* Boulder, Colo: Westview

Brazil, W. D. 1981. Notes on the Country Life Commission. *The Rural Sociol.* 1(March):92–94

Camasso, M. J., Moore, D. E. 1985. Rurality and the residual social welfare response. *Rural Sociol.* 50:397–408

Canovan, M. 1981. *Populism.* New York: Harcourt Brace Jovanovich

Carter Administration. 1979. *Small Community and Rural Development Policy.* Washington, DC: The White House

Chalmers, J., Pijawka, D., Branch, K., Bergmann, P., Flynn, J., Flynn, C. 1982. *Socioeconomic Impacts of Nuclear Generating Stations: Summary Report on the NRC Post-Licensing Studies.* Washington, DC: US GPO for the US Nuclear Regulatory Commis.

Chin, R., Benne, K. 1976. General strategies for effecting change in human systems. In *The Planning of Change*, eds., W. Bennis, S. K. Benne, R. Chin, K. Corey, pp. 13–21. New York: Holt, Rinehart, Winston. 3rd ed.

Christenson, J. A., Robinson, J. W. Jr., eds. 1980. *Community Development in America.* Ames: Iowa State Univ. Press

Clark, T. N. 1973. Community autonomy in the national system: Federalism, localism and decentralization. *Soc. Sci. Info.* 12:101–28

Clark, T. N. 1975. Community power. *Ann. Rev. Sociol.* 1:271–95

Clemente, F. ed. 1977. *The New Rural America. The Annals* 429(January):1–144

Commission on Country Life. 1911. *Report of the Commission on Country Life.* New York: Sturgis & Walton

Copp, J. H. 1972. Rural sociology and rural development. *Rural Sociol.* 37 (December):515–34

Craven, P., Wellman, B. 1973. The network city. *Sociol. Inq.* 43:57–88

Crowfoot, J. E., Chesler, M. A. 1974. Contemporary perspectives on planned social change: A comparison. *J. Appl. Behav. Sci.* 10:278–303

Danbom, D. B. 1979. *The Resisted Revolution: Urban America and the Industrialization of Agriculture, 1900–1930.* Ames: Iowa State Univ. Press

Detomasi, D. D., Gartrell, J. W., eds. 1984. *Resource Communities: A Decade of Disruption.* Boulder, Colo: Westview

Dillman, D. A. 1983. How a national rural policy can help resolve rural problems. *The Rural Sociol.* 3(November):379–83

Dillman, D. A., Hobbs, D. J., eds. 1982. *Rural Society in the U.S.: Issues for the 1980s.* Boulder, Colo: Westview

Durkheim, E. 1964. *Division of Labor in Society.* Transl. G. Simpson. Glencoe, Ill: Free Press

Fear, F. A., Schwarzweller, H. K. 1985. Introduction: rural sociology, community, and community development. In *Research In Rural Sociology and Development*, Vol. 2, *Focus on Community*, eds. F. A. Fear, H. K. Schwarzweller, pp. xi–xxxvi. Greenwich, Conn: JAI

Fear, F. A., Schwarzweller, H. K. eds. 1985. *Research in Rural Sociology and Development: Focus on Community.* Greenwich, Conn: JAI

Fischer, C. S. 1981. The public and private worlds of city life. *Am. Sociol. Rev.* 46: 306–16

Fish, J. H. 1973. *Black Power/White Control.* Princeton, NJ: Princeton Univ. Press

Fiske, G. W. 1912. *The Challenge of the Country: A Study of Country Life Opportunity.* New York: Association

Foght, H. W. 1910. *The American Rural School: Its Characteristics, Its Future, and Its Problems.* New York: Macmillan

Fuguitt, G. V. 1985. The nonmetropolitan population turnaround. *Ann. Rev. Sociol.* 11:259–80

Gallaher, A. Jr., Padfield, H., eds. 1980. *The Dying Community.* Albuquerque, NM: Univ. NM Press

Gillette, J. M. 1913. *Constructive Rural Sociology.* New York: Sturgis & Walton

Gleb, J., Sardell, A. 1974. Strategies for the powerless. *Am. Behav. Sci.* 17:507–30

Goodwyn, L. 1978. *The Populist Movement: A Short History of the Agrarian Revolt in America.* New York: Oxford Univ. Press

Granovetter, M. S. 1973. The strength of weak ties. *Am. J. Sociol.* 78:1360–80

Greisman, H. C. 1980. Community cohesion and social change. *J. Community Dev. Soc.* 11:1–17

Hammill, A. E. 1975. A rounding of perspective on the Rural Development Act of 1972. *Rural Sociol.* 40(Spring):80–82

Hansen, N. 1970. *Rural Poverty and the Urban Crisis.* Bloomington: Ind. Univ. Press

Hardy, D. F. II. 1983. Federal assistance for rural development. *The Rural Sociol.* 3(November):392–98

Harmston, F. K. 1983. *The Community as an Economic System.* Ames: Iowa State Univ. Press

Hawley, A. H., Mazie, S. M. 1981. *Nonmetropolitan America In Transition.* Chapel Hill: Univ. NC Press

Hickey, A. A. 1982. The network of assistance: A vertical pattern of the community. *J. Community Dev. Soc.* 13(1):59–67

Hillery, G. A. Jr. 1968. *Communal Organizations: A Study of Local Societies.* Chicago: Univ. Chicago Press

Hirschl, T. A., Summers, G. F. 1983. Economic development improves employment in Wisconsin. *Small Town* 13:22–24

Hobbs, D. J. 1980. Rural development: Intentions and consequences. *Rural Sociol.* 45(Spring):7–25

Hobbs, D. J. 1983. Rural America in the 1980s: Problems and prospects. *The Rural Sociologist* 3(March):62–66

Hooks, G. M., Flinn, W. L. 1981. "The Country Life Commission and early Rural Sociology." *The Rural Sociol.* 1(March):95–100

Hunter, A. 1978. Persistence of local sentiments in mass society. In *Handbook of Contemporary Urban Life*, ed. D. Street and Assoc., pp. 133–62. San Francisco: Jossey-Bass

Isard, W. 1956. *Location and Space Economy.* New York: Wiley

Isard, W. 1975. *Introduction to Regional Science.* Englewood Cliffs, NJ: Prentice-Hall

Johnson, D. E., Meiller, L., Miller, L., Summers, G. F. eds. 1986. *Building A Responsive Society: Needs Assessment Theory and Practice.* Ames: Iowa State Univ. Press

Kaufman, H. F. 1959. Toward an interactional conception of community. *Soc. Forc.* 38:8–17

Leistritz, F. L., Murdock, S. H. 1981. *The Socioeconomic Impact of Resource Development: Methods for Assessment.* Boulder, Colo: Westview

LeVeen, E. P. 1979. Enforcing the Reclamation Act and rural development in California. *Rural Sociol.* 44(Winter):667–90

Long, N. 1958. The local community as an ecology of games. *Am. J. Sociol.* 64 (November):251–61

Lonsdale, R. E., Seyler, H. L. eds. 1979. *Nonmetropolitan Industrialization.* New York: Wiley

Lonsdale, R. E., Enyedi eds. 1984. *Rural Public Services: International Comparisons.* Boulder, Colo: Westview

Lovejoy, S. B., Krannich, R. S. 1981. Rural development: A critical perspective. *The Rural Sociol.* 1(March):84–91

Martindale, D., Hanson, R. G. 1969. *Small Town and Nation.* Westport, Conn: Greenwood

Maslow, A. H. 1954. *Motivation and Personality.* New York: Harper

Meenagan, T. M. 1972. Community delineation: Alternative methods and problems. *Sociol. Soc. Res.* 56:345–55

Molotch, H. 1976. The city as a growth machine: Toward a political economy of place. *A. J. Sociol.* 82(September):309–32

Moxley, R. L. 1985. Vertical assistance, population size and growth in the context and results of community civic action. *J. Community Dev. Soc.* 16(1):57–74

Murdock, S. H., Leistritz, F. L. 1979. *Energy Development in the Western United States: Impacts on Rural Areas.* New York: Praeger

Newby, H. 1980. Rural sociology—A trend report. *Current Sociol.* 28(1):1–141

Newby, H. 1983. The sociology of agriculture: Toward a new rural sociology. *Ann. Rev. Sociol.* 9:67–81

Nolan, M. F., Heffernan, W. D. 1974. The Rural Development Act of 1972: A skeptical view. *Rural Sociol.* 39(Winter):536–45

Parsons, T. 1951. *The Social System.* New York: Free Press

Peterson, P. E. 1981. *City Limits.* Chicago: Univ. Chicago Press

Phifer, B. M., List, E. F., Faulkner, B. 1980. History of community development in America. In *Community Development in America*, ed. J. A. Christenson, J. W. Robinson, Jr., pp. 18–37. Ames: Iowa State Univ. Press

Portes, A. 1976. On the sociology of national development: Theories and issues. *Am. J. Sociol.* 82:55–85

Pulver, G. C. 1979. A theoretical framework for the analysis of community economic development policy options. In *Nonmetropolitan Industrial Growth and Community Change*, ed. G. F. Summers, A. Selvik, pp. 105–117. Lexington, Mass: Heath

Ravitz, M. 1982. Community development: Challenge of the eighties. *J. Community Dev. Soc.* 13(1):1–10

Reinhard, K., Summers, G. F. 1985. Community concerns of local officials in Wisconsin. *Small Town* 15(March–April):27–29

Reitzes, D. C., Reitzes, D. C. 1980. Saul D. Alinsky's contribution to community development. *J. Community Dev. Soc.* 11(2):39–52

Richards, R. O. 1978. Urbanization of rural areas. In *Handbook of Contemporary Urban Life*, ed. David Street and Assoc., pp. 551–91. San Fransisco: Jossey Bass

Richards, R. O. 1984. When even bad news is not so bad: Local control over outside forces in community development. *J. Community Dev. Soc.* 15(1):75–85

Rothman, J. 1974. Three models of community organization practice. In *Strategies of Community Organization*, ed. F. Cox, J. Erlich, J. Rothman, J. Tropman, pp. 22–39. Itasca, Ill: Peacock. 2nd ed.

Rubin, I. 1969. Function and structure of community: Conceptual and theoretical analysis. *Int. Rev. Community Dev.* 21–22:111–119. Reprinted in *New Perspectives on the American Community*, ed. R. Warren, pp. 108–118. Chicago: Rand McNally. 3rd. ed.

Sanders, I. 1958. Theories of community development. *Rural Sociol.* 23:1–12

Sanders, I., Lewis, G. F. 1976. Rural community studies in the United States: A decade in review. *Ann. Rev. Sociol.* 2:35–53

Schulze, R. O. 1958. The role of economic

dominants in community power structure. *Am. Sociol. Rev.* 23(February):3–9

Seiler, L. H., Summers, G. F. 1979. Corporate involvement in community affairs. *Sociol. Q.* 20:375–86

Shaffer, R. E. 1985. *Community Economic Analysis.* Madison: Univ. Wisc., Dep. Agric. Econ. Unpubl. manuscript

Shaffer, R. E., Summers, G. F. 1984. *Community Economic Vitality.* Paper presented to the Four Nations Conference, Aberdeen, Scotland, August, 1984. Madison: Univ. Wisc., Dep. Agric. Econ.

Silberman, C. E. 1964. *Crisis in Black and White.* New York: Random

Simon, W., Gagnon, J. H. 1967. Decline and fall of the small town. *Trans-Action* 4(April):42–51

Smith, T. L. 1957. Rural sociology in the United States and Canada: A trend report. *Curr. Sociol.* 6(1):1–18

Sofranko, A. J., Williams, J. D. 1980. *Rebirth of Rural America: Rural Migration in the Midwest.* Ames, Ia: North Central Regional Ctr. Rural Dev.

Stanfield, G. G. 1975. A recritique and reanalysis of the Rural Development Act of 1972. *Rural Sociology* 40(Spring):75–79

Stein, M. 1960. *The Eclipse of Community: An Interpretation of American Studies.* Princeton, NJ: Princeton Univ. Press

Summers, G. F. ed. 1983. *Technology and Social Change in Rural Areas.* Boulder, Colo: Westview

Summers, G. F. 1985. *Sociology and Rural Community Development.* Plenary address at the Rural Sociol. Soc. ann. meet. in Blacksburg, Va., August, 1985. Madison: Univ. Wis., Dep. Rural Sociol.

Summers, G. F., Bloomquist, L. E. 1983. *Votes Count, But Resources Decide.* Madison: Univ. Wisconsin, Dep. Rural Sociol. Unpubl. manuscript

Summers, G. F., Branch, K. 1984. Economic development and community social change. *Ann. Rev. Sociol.* 10:141–66

Summers, G. F., Evans, S. D., Clemente, F., Beck, E. M., Minkoff, J. 1976. *Industrial Invasion of Nonmetropolitan America: A Quarter Century of Experience.* New York: Praeger

Summers, G. F., Selvik, A. eds. 1979. *Nonmetropolitan Industrial Growth and Community Change.* Lexington, Mass: Heath

Summers, G. F., Selvik, A. eds. 1982. *Energy Resource Communities.* Madison, Wisc: MJM

Swanson, R. M. 1972. *The Country Life Movement, 1900–1940.* PhD thesis. Minneapolis: Univ. Minn.

Thompson, W. R. 1965. *A Preface to Urban Economics.* Baltimore: The Johns Hopkins Univ. Press

Tiebout, C. M. 1956. A pure theory of local expenditures. *J. Polit. Econ.* 64:416–24

Tiebout, C. M. 1962. *The Community Economic Base Study.* Paper No. 16. Washington, DC: Committee Econ. Dev.

Tilly, C. 1973. Do communities act? *Sociol. Inq.* 43(December):209–240

US House of Representatives. 1915. *Cooperative Agricultural Extension Work: Report to Accompany H. R. 7951.* 63rd Congress, 2nd Session, House Rep. 110, Committee Agric.

Vidich, A. J., Bensman, J. 1958. *Small Town in Mass Society: Class Power and Religion in a Rural Community.* Princeton, NJ: Princeton Univ. Press

Warren, R. 1963. *The Community in America.* Chicago: Rand McNally

Warren, R. 1972. *The Community in America.* Chicago: Rand McNally. 2nd ed.

Warren, R. 1978. *The Community in America.* Chicago: Rand McNally. 3rd ed.

Whiting, L. R. ed. 1974. *Communities Left Behind.* Ames: Iowa State Univ. Press

Wilkinson, K. P. 1970. The community as a social field. *Soc. Forc.* 48(March):311–22

Wilkinson, K. P. 1972. A field theory perspective for community development research. *Rural Sociol.* 37:43–52

Wilkinson, K. P. 1979. Social well-being and community. *J. Community Dev. Soc.* 10(1):5–16

Wilkinson, K. P. 1984. Implementing a national strategy of rural development. *The Rural Sociol.* 4(September):348–53

Wilkinson, K. P. 1985. Rural community development: A deceptively controversial theme in rural sociology. *The Rural Sociol.* 5(March):119–24

Wilkinson, K. P. 1985a. Community development in rural America: Sociological issues in national policy. Paper presented at the ann. meet. Southern Assoc. Agric. Scientists in Biloxi, Miss., February, 1985. University Park, Penn: Penn. State Univ. Dep. Agric. Econ. Rural Sociol.

Wilkinson, K. P. 1985b. *In search of the community in the changing countryside.* Presidential address at the Rural Sociol. Soc. meet., August 22, 1985, Blacksburg, Va. University Park: Penn. State Univ. Dep. Agric. Econ. Rural Sociol.

Wilkinson, K. P. 1986. In search of the community in the changing countryside. *Rural Sociol.* 51(Winter):1–17

Wilkinson, K. P., Hobbs, D. J., Christenson, J. A. 1983. An analysis of the national rural development strategy. *The Rural Sociol.* 3(November):384–91

Young, F. W. 1970. Reactive subsystems. *Am. Sociol. Rev.* 35(April):297–307

Ann. Rev. Sociol. 1986. 12:373–99

ARAB SOCIOLOGY TODAY: A VIEW FROM WITHIN

Georges Sabagh and Iman Ghazalla

Von Grunebaum Center for Near Eastern Studies and Department of Sociology, University of California, Los Angeles, California 90024

Abstract

Some of the accomplishments and shortcomings of Arab sociology during the last few years are assessed from the perspective of Arab sociologists. This assessment of Arab sociology from the insiders' perspective involves (*a*) reviewing selected papers presented at one of the most recent Arab sociology conferences, (*b*) analyzing the results of a survey of 36 Arab sociologists, and (*c*) describing in detail the major contributions of Arab sociologists and social scientists to the study of Islam, with particular reference to Islamic social movements. Recent socioeconomic changes and political events in the Arab world help explain the rising interest in sociology. Arab sociologists view their discipline as still in process of becoming and in a state of crisis. The sociopolitical and disciplinary aspects of this crisis and the solution suggested to remedy it are described. Arab sociological studies of Islamic social movements have the following features: (*a*) an emphasis on the diversity, complexity, and historical specificity of these movements, (*b*) a recognition of the need for an interdisciplinary approach, (*c*) a focus on the sociological characteristics of leaders and followers, (*d*) analyses of the origin of the movements, and (*e*) an emphasis on the need for a methodology more personal and subjective than the one used in the West. This research, as well as the survey of Arab sociologists, indicates that there is a noticeable trend toward the substantive indigenization of Arab sociology and that Arab sociologists are aware of the need to be innovative and flexible in their selection and use of research methods. These also show that there has been little theoretical indigenization of Arab sociology. This may explain, in part, the sense of crisis felt by Arab sociologists.

373

0360-0572/86/0815-0373$02.00

INTRODUCTION

This review presents an assessment of some of the accomplishments and shortcomings of Arab sociology during the last few years. Such an assessment can be done either from an "outsider" or an "insider" perspective. There are, of course, advantages in looking at both perspectives. In the words of Hamnett et al (1984:85), "Insider's research can provide insights, inner meanings, and subjective dimensions that are likely to be overlooked by outsiders. The outsider can bring a comparably detached perspective to the problems he investigates." While Western sociologists, particularly in France and the United States, have made important contributions to the sociological study of the Arab World, most of them are obviously "outsiders." The most compelling reasons for focusing on the "insiders' " views of Arab sociology is the Arab sociologists' call for the "indigenization" of their discipline. Hamnett et al identified as follows the two major components of the indigenization of social sciences, widely advocated in the Third World:

> Theoretical indigenization is a condition in which social scientists of a nation are involved in constructing distinctive conceptual frameworks and metatheories that reflect their own world views, social and cultural experiences, and perceived goals. . . . . Substantive indigenization is concerned with the content focus of the social sciences. The essential argument for substantive indigenization is that the main thrust of research and teaching in a country should be toward its own society and people and their economic and political institutions (1984:78).

The thrust to indigenization means that Arab sociologists would tend to assess the state of their discipline in different ways than would Western sociologists. To be sure, as we shall see from the results of our survey, many Arab sociologists have been trained in the United States or Europe, and often their own theoretical and research work may reflect that training. Nevertheless, they see indigenization as an important goal for their discipline. Indeed, contributing to Arab scholarly journals and publishing the results of their work in Arabic is one way of stressing the importance of indigenization. Ideally, one should make a comparative analysis of both insiders' and outsiders' views of and contributions to Arab sociology, but this is beyond the scope of this paper.

The evaluation of the state of Arab sociology from the insiders' perspectives is accomplished in three ways. First, we review in detail selected papers presented at a recent conference of Arab sociologists assessing the status of sociology in the Arab world. Secondly, we analyze the results of a survey of the opinions of a small sample of Arab sociologists on their own work and on priorities for their discipline. Thirdly, we describe major contributions of Arab sociologists to the study of Islam, with particular reference to Islamic social movements. Since these movements are committed to authenticity and indigenization, their study by Arab sociologists should provide a distinctively insider's perspective.

THE RISING IMPORTANCE OF SOCIOLOGY IN THE ARAB WORLD

The 1980s have witnessed an upsurge of interest in the critical appraisal of the status of sociology in the Arab world not only by sociologists but also by other Arab social scientists and intellectuals. Thus, the issue transcends the discipline itself and has implications for the future of critical social thought in Arab countries. In the last three years alone, the following six specialized conferences took place, all attempting to evaluate the state of Arab sociology and Arab social sciences in general (Nasr 1985:168):

(a) The problem of methodology in social science research (Cairo, January 1983)
(b) The problematic of social sciences in the Arab world (Cairo, February 1983)
(c) Toward an Arab Sociology (Abu-Dabi, April 1983)
(d) The policy of social sciences in the Arab World (Tunis, February 1984)
(e) Sociology and the issue of the Arab individual (Kuwait, April 1984)
(f) The status of Sociology in the Arab World (Tunis, January 1985), which culminated in the founding of an Arab Sociological Association.

To this list should be added an international conference on "The Evaluation and Application of Survey Research in the Arab World" (Bellagio, 1983), in which both Arab and non-Arab social scientists participated (Tessler et al 1986).

Why has there been such a growth of interest in evaluations of the state of Arab sociology and social sciences in general? Answers to this difficult question must be sought not only in the rapid social and economic changes experienced by Arab countries in recent years, but also in terms of the development of sociology in the Arab world and its response to the dominating theoretical and methodological influences of Western sociology.

Recent Socioeconomic Changes in the Arab World

The 1970s were marked by important political developments and economic events that were to have a lasting impact in the Arab world and that help explain the rising importance of Arab sociology.

The 1973 Arab-Israeli war challenged the presumed invincibility of the Israeli armed forces. In the same year and as a result of this war, oil prices rose dramatically with far-reaching social, economic, and demographic consequences not only in the Gulf States but also in the whole Arab world. There was an increase in the gap between "poor" and "rich" Arab countries and a rising tide of international migration from the former to the latter countries.

As can be seen in Table 1, there was in 1983 an enormous range in the GNP per capita, from a high of around $20,000 in Kuwait, Qatar, and the United Arab Emirates to a low of around $400–$500 in the Sudan, Mauritania, Yemen AR, and Yemen PDR. The highest incomes are in the smallest Arab countries, and the most populous Arab countries (Sudan, Egypt, Morocco) have among the lowest incomes. This income differential is in part responsible for a massive labor migration from the poor Arab countries, particularly Egypt and the Yemens, to the rich Arab countries (Amin & Awny 1985). One measure of the importance of this migration is provided by the figures on the share of workers' remittances in the GNP of the smaller labor-exporting countries: such remittances constituted 43.4%, 37.8%, and 21.2% of the GNP of Yemen PDR, Yemen AR, and Jordan respectively (see Table 1). Estimates

Table 1 Per capita income and worker remittances for Arab countries

Arab countries by income levels	Population in millions 1983	GNP per capita ($) 1983	Average annual growth of GNP per capita 1965–1983	Remittances as per cent of GNP 1983
High income oil exporters				
United Arab Emirates	1.2	23,870	NA	—[b]
Qatar	.3	21,210	−7.0[a]	—[b]
Kuwait	1.6	17,880	.2	—[b]
Saudi Arabia	10.4	12,230	6.7	—[b]
Bahrain	.4	10,510	NA	—[b]
Lybian Arab Jamhariya	3.4	8,480	−.9	—[b]
Oman	1.1	6,250	6.5	.6
Other Arab Countries				
Iraq	14.7	NA	NA	NA
Algeria	20.6	2,320	3.6	.8
Jordan	3.2	1,640	6.9[a]	21.2
Syrian Arab Rep.	9.6	1,760	4.9	2.7
Tunisia	6.9	1,290	5.0	4.0
Morocco	20.8	760	2.9	5.8
Egypt Arab Rep.	45.2	700	4.2	10.4
Yemen Arab Rep.	7.6	550	5.7	37.8
Yemen People D. R.	2.0	520	NA	43.4
Mauritania	1.6	480	.3	.1
Sudan	20.8	400	1.3	.3
Somalia	5.1	250	−.8	1.7

[a]For periods other than 1965–1983
[b]These countries have a net negative workers' remittances
Source: The World Bank (1985), pp. 174–75, 200–01, and 232

of the size of the Arab labor migration streams vary widely (Amin & Awny 1985, Ibrahim 1982b), but there is no doubt that it was substantial in 1980 and increased rapidly in the 1970s. For Egypt alone, one estimate places the number of workers abroad at over 1,000,000 in 1980 as compared to around 400,000 in 1975 (Amin & Awny 1985).

The sudden increase in the wealth of some Arab countries is part of what Saad Eddin Ibrahim (1982b) has called the "New Arab Social Order," which involves the appearance of new social forces and new values and behavior patterns. This has resulted in a great deal of social chaos and the emergence of new social problems.

There has been an increase in the military, economic, and sociocultural penetration of Arab countries by the United States and other Western countries. This penetration, which the ruling elites have been unable to counteract, is further exacerbated by the consolidation of Israel in the occupied territories of the West Bank, which no wars or diplomatic maneuvers appear to thwart.

There is increasing social fragmentation within several Arab countries which is based on legitimate and semilegitimate claims of diversity and particularism (Ibrahim 1985).

Arab Sociology in Process

With few exceptions, an Arab sociology with its own theories and methods has not yet emerged (Irabi 1982). On the whole, Arab sociology is dependent on copying and translating Western sociological works. The training of early generations of sociologists in the United States, France, or Germany resulted in almost slavish adherence to Western concepts and models, even when these were often irrelevant to the Arab context. The first stage of the development of Arab sociology largely grew out of cultural interchange with the West brought about by colonialism. It is not surprising that many Arab sociologists, particularly in North Africa, have emphasized the importance of the "decolonization" of sociology in the Arab World (Ben Jelloun 1977, Karoui & Zghal 1975, Khatibi 1985).

Even though the proliferation of Western schools of social theory resulted in the substantial theoretical eclecticism of Arab sociology (Ben Salem 1982, Stambouli 1977), there are no distinctive theoretical perspectives in sociology that address the major issues faced by Arab society (Bassiouni 1979). While some Arab sociologists (el-Kordy 1980) have adopted and applied "dependency theory," this paradigm emerged out of the Latin American and not the Arab experience. There is nothing comparable to this paradigm, except the reference back to Ibn Khaldun, which had already been noted in the assessment of trends in the early 1970s (Sabagh 1976; see also Al-Qazzaz 1975; el-Saaty 1977). But the Khaldunian model is hardly adequate for the analysis of current social changes in the Arab world. Thus Arab sociology is still "in process," which explains the title, "Toward an Arab Sociology," of a recent conference of Arab sociologists in Tunis. In Irabi's view, "it is imperative for Arab sociology to develop an independent theory in which the particularisms of Arab development and society stand at the center of socio- logical interest" (1982:183). Sari echoes the opinions of many Arab sociolog- ists when he states that "it is ironic that Arab sociologists acknowledge the limitations of Western theories, but continue to depend on them—often entirely—in their research and studies" (1983:52).

One of us completed an assessment of the state of sociology in the Arab world, Iran, and Turkey in the 1960s and the early 1970s (Sabagh 1976). While it was noted that much had already been accomplished, much more research and theoretical work was needed to shed light on the key problems of the region, including the consequences of rapid urbanization, social inequal- ity, and such major social issues as the role of Islam in society. Where does Arab sociology stand now? The general picture that emerges from the papers presented at a conference in Tunis, January 1985, is one of "sociology in crisis." In the words of Hegazy (1985:75), "A critical appraisal of the state of sociology in the Arab world shows that it is in a state of crisis theoretically and methodologically, in addition to being isolated and alienated from actual social reality." Since the Tunis conference constitutes the most recent and most extensive assessment of the state of the field by the major Arab sociolo- gists, we shall focus on some of the themes that emerged: the current status of the field, reasons for the current "crisis," reasons for the discontent of the Arab sociologists with their discipline, and solutions suggested to remedy the present situation.

ARAB SOCIOLOGY IN CRISIS

The 1985 Tunis conference, as well as the other conferences held in the early 1980s, indicates why leading Arab sociologists consider their discipline to be in crisis. Two major reasons are given. One pertains to the fundamental sociopolitical conditions faced by Arab sociologists, and the other refers more specifically to the state of the discipline itself.

Sociopolitical Aspects of the Crisis

A recurrent theme has been the *negative impact of the political climate in Arab countries* on the growth of critical sociological work. According to Hegazy (1985), sociology originated and developed in relation to ruling institutions. Consequently, it confined itself to the imitation of Western models, searching for solutions to social problems from an abstract point of view within the confines of the status quo. Thus, certain topics were defined as "politically forbidden" and sociologically sensitive, including, for example, the lack of democracy and the resultant political apathy, the ideological and economic dependency on the West, the Arab-Israeli conflict, and the deepening of social inequality (Sari 1985). An even more pessimistic view is expressed by the Algerian sociologist el-Kanz (Nasr 1985:171), who argues that "sociology is disfigured by the political institution . . . society is the monopoly of the government and not a subject for research . . . there is no legitimacy whatsoever for a rational discourse about the social structure of any Arab country." Consequently, Arab sociology is "an impossible practice, a superficial endeavor in universities;" its only chance to develop is "either in exile or in secret." A somewhat less pessimistic view is offered by the Egyptian sociologist Abdel Moty (Nasr 1985:170).

While few Arab sociologists have criticized the status quo in their writings, there is some indication of change with the emergence of neo-Marxists and groups favoring *turath* (neocultural heritage). They agree on the critical issues in sociology but are in theoretical conflict. Hegazy and Abdel Moty see the beginning of a critical Arab sociology. Participants at the Tunis 1985 conference disagreed about the extent to which Arab sociologists are free to express their views and investigate crucial topics such as political authority, class conflict, and other important issues pertaining to religion, sex, and minorities. They also disagreed about the extent to which sociologists have to make ideological choices. By contrast, there was consensus that the political climate in Arab countries places serious restraints on sociological theory and research.

The oppressive political climate has a number of negative personal and professional consequences for Arab sociologists. According to Abdel Moty, it tends to foster the emergence of a class of "compradorial" research sociologists who are dependent on foreign countries "intellectually, financially, and behaviorally" (Nasr 1985:171). A bleak picture is painted of Arab sociologists who submit to authority, are opportunistic, and supervise foreign-funded research that involves the exploitation of younger scholars and graduate students. Furthermore, they are uselessly engaged in "tribal" conflicts between Marxists, functionalists, and followers of the French, American, English, and Soviet schools. Ibrahim (1985) has concluded that this "tribalism" has become the opiate of Arab sociology.

Most prominent Arab sociologists deplore the dependence of their discipline on Western sociology, and some view this dependence as a form of apology for colonialism and neocolonialism and a justification of the status quo. The most radical critique is provided by Sari (1985). In his view, the intellectual effort of Arab sociologists is dominated by Western analytic frameworks such as structural-functionalism. Most Arab research produced from the 1950s to the mid-1970s is based on positivism in its old and revised forms, and this has led to the neglect of the development of dialectical analysis and the critical-historical mode of analysis. Thus for Sari, it is only in the 1980s that some Arab sociologists have liberated themselves from dependence on Western analytic schemes and research orientations. He has high praise for al-Bitar's (1979) study of Arab unity, Ibrahim's (1980b) survey of Arab public opinion on Arab unity, El Sayed Yassin's (1980) analysis of the content of Arab national thought, and Halim Barakat's (1984) comprehensive analysis of the major issues facing Arab society.

Disciplinary Aspects of the Crisis

The two major disciplinary aspects of this crisis are the discrepancy between the quantitative and qualitative growth of Arab sociology, and the discontent with the present state of theory, methodology, and research in Arab sociology. The arguments presented on this aspect of the crisis are briefly summarized.

While numbers have rapidly increased of sociology departments, research centers, sociology Phds, and sociological publications, it is rare to find an Arab sociologist giving a comprehensive and objective analysis of Arab social reality. But even in quantitative terms, there are differences among Arab countries. While the quantitative growth of sociology has been considerable in Egypt, Tunisia, and Lebanon, sociology still occupies a weak and peripheral position in most other Arab countries. Sari (1985) asserts that Arab sociology cannot grow qualitatively without developing its own theoretical framework and methodological tools. Only then can the contradictions of Arab society be confronted and eliminated.

There was consensus in Tunis about the paucity of empirical sociological research and the inadequacy of research tools. For Ibrahim (1985), the few field studies about aspects of Arab social reality are still fragmented and incomplete. There is very little integration of related studies or accumulation of sociological knowledge about Arab society. Other Arab sociologists attribute this situation to the lack of research topics relevant to the major concerns of Arabs, to the inadequacy of the research model, and to improper execution of research plans. Despite the abundance of major social problems, research studies focus repeatedly on traditional, and presumably "safe," topics such as divorce, adultery, and problems of adolescents. The main issues that Arab sociologists should be dealing with include social, intellectual, and economic backwardness, the fragmentation of the Arab world, and the dependency on the new colonial centers. Serious efforts are lacking in the important fields of the sociology of religion, social stratification, social history, and the sociology of social movements and revolutions. Research designs are isolated from the social process as well as from historical circumstances. For example, studies of religious movements fail "to answer the important question of what these movements are responding to" (Hegazy 1985).

While Arab sociologists paint a bleak picture of the state of their discipline and of their intellectual and social ineffectiveness, their self-appraisal is a necessary step to remedy the inadequacies of Arab sociology. On the more positive side, in the selection of research topics the Arab sociologist is on his own ground. For example, the many studies of the social, economic, and political impact of the massive Arab international migration emerge out of recent Arab experience (e.g. Ali 1983, Amin & Awny 1985, Abdel Moty 1983, Bouhdiba 1979, Fergany 1983, Saad el-din & Abdel Fadil 1983, Serageldin 1983, al-Tamimi 1982). They indicate that this migration will have far-reaching consequences for the Arab world.

It is illuminating to consider Ibrahim's (1985) delineation of the sociological studies needed to better understand Arab social reality and the future of Arab society. His suggestions, however, cover the whole range of the sociological enterprise and are so comprehensive as to lead one to think that Arab sociology has progressed very little beyond what was described in the early 1970s. Unfortunately, his discussion does not differentiate between topics that have been fairly well studied, such as population structure and trends and urbanization, and those that have been relatively neglected, such as the sociology of the state. His suggestions may be summarized as follows.

Demographic studies are needed to assess the growth, distribution, movement, and characteristics of the population of the Arab world. Of particular importance are the rates of economic participation, the structure of the available labor force, and its effects on rural-urban migration and international migration between Arab countries. Basic demographic data are already available, but they need to be fully analyzed in order to provide a general picture of the demographic base of the Arab world.

Ecological studies are needed to deal with the main patterns of livelihood resulting from the interaction between man and his natural environment in the Arab world. The most important of these are the beduin tribal patterns and the process of urbanization. The aim of these studies should be to evaluate the effects of development and alternative population distribution policies on these ecological interrelations. Special attention should be paid to the influence of the size and social structure of cities on contemporary and future political stability.

Studies of *class structure* are needed to delineate the class system and its degree of crystallization in each Arab country and in the Arab world as a whole. Such studies should also evaluate the effect of class structure on the productive process, sociopolitical stability, and the process of social change.

Ethnic social formations should be described and analyzed, particularly in relation to class structure and the effects of majority—minority relationship on the level of internal conflict.

The present and future roles of *organized occupational groups* (unions, syndicates, etc) in political activity and development have to be assessed.

Major institutions such as the army; security; the religious, educational, and scientific establishments; and the media have to be studied in terms of the degree of their independence and their influence on value patterns, legitimacy, and sociopolitical control.

Studies are needed of *values and behavioral patterns,* with special attention given to the role of religion, especially Islam, the colonial heritage, and to major value conflicts. Examples of such conflicts are authenticity versus modernization and nationalism versus local patriotism.

Of particular importance are *sociological analyses of the Arab state.* Such analyses should include the following topics: the division and fragmentation caused by Western colonialism and its impact on Arab unity and disunity; the origins of the present patterns of local states and the differences between these states in wealth, population, production patterns, and social solidarity; styles of nation building before and after independence and the relative role played by religion and secular ideologies, power, oppression, and political participation; the translation of legitimacy into laws, constitutions, and political discourses; the nature of the influence (direct or indirect, legitimate or illegitimate) of different groups on political decision-making.

Studies are needed not only of *ruling elites in the Arab World* but also of *alternate elites.* Issues to be addressed include the class origins of ruling elites, the degree to which they are representative of their own society, and the mechanisms for exerting authority and insuring elite continuity. Studies of alternate elites should map the different parties, forces, and political elements in the Arab world aspiring to be in power and the degree of their legitimacy or recognition by ruling elites. Research should focus on the rise and influence of these groups and on their programs and ideologies with respect to the issues of Arab unity, development, distributive justice, national independence, the Arab-Israeli conflict, religion, and democracy. Ibrahim (1985) recommends that special attention should be given to contemporary religious movements. Other Arab sociologists agree with him on the importance of focusing on *contemporary Islamic movements* and their alternative ideologies. It has been suggested that such movements should be studied from the perspective of an *Islamic sociology.* An Islamic sociology would provide an alternative ideological choice, competing with Marxist and functionalist ideologies. Since this issue is likely to become increasingly important in the next few years, we need to consider the probable nature of Islamic sociology.

Arab or Islamic Sociology? While these terms have increasingly been used in the Arab and the non-Arab Muslim worlds, is there *really* an Arab sociology or an Islamic sociology as compared, for example, to an Egyptian, Tunisian, or Lebanese sociology? Many of the participants in the Tunis conference are sympathetic to the idea of Arab nationalism and Arab unity, and they emphasize the need for an Arab sociology. Most of them are also believers in secularism and the secular outlook of Western sociology even while they try to transcend the latter. They represent a major sociological current in the Arab world, but by no means the only existing one. According to Adel Hussein, "Renewal starts with refusing the principle of secularism and going back to Islamic values; any theoretical base must reflect the indigenous environment" (Hegazy 1985:79). Thus, the call for an Arab or an Islamic sociology is in reality a call for the indigenization of sociology in terms of theoretical perspective, methodology, and priorities of topics for study. The need for the indigenization of sociology has also been stressed by sociologists in Africa and the Third World in general (e.g Akiwowo 1980). In the Arab world, this need focuses on an Arabic or Islamic orientation depending on the ideological preference of those involved.

The Iranian revolution and the creation of an Islamic Republic, as well as the emergence of Islamic fundamentalist social movements both in and outside the Arab world, have stimulated a real wave of scholarly interest in these movements, the sociopolitical aspects of Islam, and more generally of Islam as a system of values and as a social system. While an understanding of these aspects of Islam will require a multidisciplinary approach, there is no doubt that sociology has much to contribute. It can provide an important departure from the usual exegetic analysis of Islam and move toward an analysis of the sociology of Muslims and of societies organized on a Muslim basis. The sociological study of Islam not only addresses important social issues in Arab countries, but also provides a vehicle for attempts at the indigenization of Arab sociology. This is no argument, however, on whether the sociological study of Islam should be from the perspective of an indigenous Arab sociology or from that of Islamic sociology with its own distinctive theories, methods, and research priorities.

Before we turn to a description of the contributions of Arab sociologists to the sociological study of Islam, particularly contemporary Islamic social movements, we present a more "quantitative" assessment of Arab sociology today. This evaluation is based on a survey of Arab sociologists.

A SURVEY OF ARAB SOCIOLOGISTS

During 1983–1984 a survey of Arab sociologists was designed and carried out in collaboration with Professor Salah Bassiouni of Ain Shams University in Cairo. A brief questionnaire was mailed to 84 Arab sociologists, of whom 16 resided in the United States, Canada, and France at the time. Questionnaires were also sent to five non-Arab sociologists who had done extensive research on the Arab world, but they are not included in the present analysis. The purpose of the questionnaire was to obtain information on the following items:

current and prior position, university where highest degree was obtained, theoretical orientation, research methods used and reasons for using methods, sources of funding of research, areas of specialization in sociology, list of publications, and "the highest priorities for sociological research in the Arab world."

The list of names was drawn from those who were members of the American Sociological Association and other professional associations or who were known to Bassiouni or to the senior author. The distribution of the questionnaires sent and received by country is listed in Table 2.

In addition, letters were sent in 1984 to heads of departments of sociology at the University of Baghdad and the University of Khartoum. As a result, three questionnaires were received from sociology professors at the University of Baghdad, including the head of the Department, and one questionnaire came from Khartoum. There were English, French, and Arabic versions of the questionnaire, and about half of all those that were completed were in Arabic.

The fact that Egypt heads the list of sociologists to whom questionnaires were sent is not surprising and reflects the quantitative growth of sociology in Egypt noted above. (See also Akiwowo 1980, Bassiouni 1979, el-Saaty 1977.) According to a survey carried out in 1976 by the Organization for the Promotion of Social Science in the Middle East, 40 of the 80 Arab sociologists who responded to the survey were from Egypt (Rentz 1977). In another study in 1980, Egyptians constituted 85% of 46 Arab sociologist respondents (al-Isa & al-Husseini 1982). The same study indicates that these sociologists had a predominantly middle-class origin.

Table 2 Results of questionnaire sent to Arab sociologists

Country	Questionnaires	
	Sent	Received
Egypt	28	13
USA, Canada	14	4
Tunisia	11	5
Saudi Arabia	7	2
Qatar	7	3
Kuwait	5	0
Libya	4	2
Morocco	3	1
France	2	0
Lebanon	1	1
Jordan	1	1
Yemen AR	1	0
Total	84	32

About 48% of those with a PhD in sociology had received this degree from a university in the United States and only 21% from an Arab university, most of which were in Egypt. In the 1976 survey, comparable figures were: 47% had a Ph.D. in sociology from a US school, and only 30% from an Arab university (mostly in Egypt). The Arab sociologists' feeling of a "crisis" in their discipline may be traced, in part, to a conflict or tension that may exist between their predominantly Western training and their desire for indigenization. It should be kept in mind in interpreting the results of the survey that proportionately fewer Arab sociologists with Arab graduate training responded to our questionnaire.

Social conflict theory was mentioned in almost 40% of the responses as the preferred theoretical perspective. Functionalist theory came next with 23%. The preference for functionalist theory was much lower among US or Arab-trained sociologists than among those trained in England. Unfortunately, the questionnaire did not distinguish between types of conflict theories. Reflecting a pessimistic view of conditions in the Arab world, the vast majority of those who espoused a conflict theory stated that they did so because it provides a "better interpretation of the Arab countries' situation." The preference of Arab sociologists for "structural theories" was also noted by al-Issa & al-Husseini (1982) in their 1982 survey of Arab sociologists.

When it comes to research methods utilized by the Arab sociologists in our sample, the following methods appeared to be the most popular:

Interviews	83%
Surveys	70%
Observations	70%
Questionnaires	63%
Statistical analysis	63%
Document study	50%

Many sociologists used more than one research procedure. In answer to an openended question about the reasons for utilizing the particular methods, many respondents indicated the importance of versatility and innovativeness in the use of these various methods and the need for adapting them to the particular social groups they are studying. For example, Saad Eddin Ibrahim (American University in Cairo) states that "In a diverse and fairly inhospitable area vis a vis social research, a sociologist has to be flexible and amenable to use all techniques possible." This point will be elaborated in our review of Ibrahim's work on Islamic militant groups. Samir Khalaf (American University in Beirut) agrees with Ibrahim when he states that "For the analysis of contemporary problems, surveys, questionnaires and interviews, along with nonparticipant observations, are useful, effective, illuminating means for generating data and documenting theoretical hunches and propositions." Khalil Omar (University of Baghdad) indicated a preference for "observation" as a research method because "our people still don't trust the objectivity of questionnaires, surveys, and interviews." Musa Abdul Jalil (University of Khartoum) suggests that "qualitative research methods" are more appropriate for the rural population he studies.

Even given such views on theoretical perspectives, there is no indication that total methodological indigenization would be advocated even by those Arab sociologists who have modified existing research procedures extensively to facilitate their use in Arab countries. While there are many obstacles to field research in the Arab world, there appears to be less sense of a "crisis" in sociological methodology than in sociological theory.

Responses to the question on sponsorship of the research partly confirm the views cited above about the dependence of many Arab sociologists on foreign sources of funding: The two categories with the highest response rate (of about 43%) were "foreign organizations" and "the researcher himself." However, the fact that such a high percentage indicated sole dependence on their own resources partly belies the accusation of "compradorial sociologists" leveled at Arab sociologists.

Answers to the following questions allow us to delineate the most important substantive topics/areas in Arab sociology: (a) topics/areas in the respondent's work, (b) the highest priorities for sociological research on the Arab World, and (c) current research projects. The distribution of replies is summarized in Table 3.

Surprisingly, not one sociologist mentioned the study of Islam as a "high" priority and only two mentioned "religious behavior/religion as a dynamic factor." Nevertheless, a number of specific topics/areas mentioned are closely related to the sociopolitical situation in the Arab world. Apart from the Arab-Israeli conflict, the following are high priority areas: "the social and economic effects of migration on the social structure of the Arab Gulf states; social aspects and impact of disunity in the Arab world; hindrances to development in the Arab World; social realities in the Arab World; the Arabs and imperialism; the

Table 3 Proportion of substantive areas and/or topics mentioned by Arab sociologists as priorities or as topics of their own work

Substantive areas and/or topics	Priorities(%)	Own work (%)
Social change	54	68
Social class, inequality	24	20
Migration, population	33	31
Socioeconomic development, planning/underdevelopment	21	54
Women, women and development, women's emancipation, youth	33	43
Rural society, villages, peasants	15	23
Arab-Israeli conflict	15	14
Social conflict in general, social conflict in Middle East	6	43

social impact of oil on the Arab countries." On the other hand, Arab sociologists share with sociologists in many parts of the world an interest in the study of change and social class. The interest in "development" was also noted by al-Issa & al-Husseini (1982) in their survey.

Compared to priorities, current research projects deal more with substantive issues that are immediately relevant to the Arab world or a particular Arab country. They also show that Arab sociologists do not shy away from politically or sociologically sensitive topics. The following is a partial list of current research projects as described in the questionnaires: "Minorities and political integration in the Arab World; the Arab world in the year 2,000; social reality in the Arab novel; the sociology of Ibn Khaldun; interpersonal relations in Islamic society; social control in the Islamic context; Islamism in Tunisia; effects of legal reforms in Tunisia; kinship and patrimony in Tunisia; the dialectic of traditional modernity in Lebanon; the impact of the civil war in Lebanon; social and political orientation of some members of the educated class in Egypt; democracy in Egypt; poverty in some Egyptian groups; population and family planning in Egypt; cost of dowries; indicators of change in Saudi Arabia; social configuration of a region in Qatar; the situation and needs of children in the Gulf."

The survey thus indicates a strong trend toward substantive indigenization of Arab sociology. On the other hand, there appears to be no similar trend with respect to theoretical indigenization. However, the latter finding may be partly a consequence of the nature of the questions asked as well as the particular sample of those Arab sociologists who responded to the questionnaire.

THE CONTRIBUTIONS OF ARAB SOCIOLOGISTS TO THE SOCIOLOGY OF ISLAM

A Western sociologist, Bryan Turner (1974), makes the most critical assessment of the present state of the sociology of Islam, as perceived by an outsider. According to him, the systematic study of Islam has been a neglected field in sociology, with hardly any major sociological studies of Islam and Islamic society. Marx and Durkheim had little or nothing to say about Islam, although some peripheral members of the Durkheim school were interested in the role of Islam in North Africa (Valensi 1984). Weber died before his Religionssoziologie was completed by a full study of Islam, and there are no other major sociological theorists who have been concerned with Islam and Islamic society. Although a few orientalist scholars have claimed a sociological approach to Islam, it has had no impact on mainstream sociology (cf Burke 1980). Bryan Turner (1974:7) argues that there is "a strong case to be made for the theoretically crucial importance of Islam: as a prophetic, this-wordly, salvation religion with strong connections with the other Abrahamic religions, Islam is a potential test case of Weber's thesis on religion and capitalism." Arab sociologists would agree with the importance of sociological studies of Islam, but from a perspective clearly different from that of Turner. In our view, the indigenization of the sociology of the Arab world lies precisely in reversing Turner's priority. Instead of using Islam as a test case for Western theories, its study can become the basis for the theoretical indigenization of Arab sociology. The sociology of Islam as the center of the cultural heritage of the Arab world lies at the core of an overall comprehensive alternative sociocultural enterprise of which sociological theory and methodology are only one aspect.

The present emphasis on the contributions of Arab social scientists to the sociological study of Islam is not meant to minimize the contributions of Western social scientists. In recent years an increasing number of Western social scientists have provided important theoretical and comparative insights in the sociological study of Islam and more particularly Islamic social movements (e.g. Davis 1874, Snow & Marshall 1984). For example, to Snow & Marshall the important question is "how this resurgence of Islamic militancy informs our understanding of social movements and change in the Third World" (1984:145). This comes close to Jansen's (1980) argument that "militant Islam today is part of the much wider Third World problem of how to come to terms with the Western way of life that is rapidly becoming the global way of life." Few Arab sociologists would disagree with Snow & Marshall's (1984:146) conclusion that "Islamic movements of today are in part a consequence of the cultural degradation and desecration that seems to be an inevitable concomitant of the imperialism associated with the market-expanding efforts of Western multinational corporations." While Snow & Marshall (1984) appropriately emphasize the political aspects of Islamic social movements, they do not point out that this is precisely what Arab social scientists are focusing on.

Western social scientists who contribute to the sociological study of Islam have to be aware of the need to avoid the pitfalls of either the orientalist or the modernization views. According to Ibrahim (1980a), the "orientalist" view treated Islam "ideationally" and insulated it from a changing social structure while "modernization" theorists believed Islam to be a polar opposite of secularism, science, and technology, and that as Arab countries modernize, Islam is destined to weaken. The Islamic revolution in Iran and the dramatic emergence of Islamic fundamentalist groups provided a real challenge to this view. As a consequence, Islam was "rediscovered" by Western scholars. Thus, in 1980 alone, 27 symposia and conferences on different aspects of Islam were held in universities and research centers in the United States. Saad Eddin Ibrahim warns us of the creeping danger of neo-orientalism and the tendency to mystify Islamic militancy. This view is shared by Dessouki who argues that "it is conceptually inadequate and factually problematic to aggregate the many diverse contemporary movements and ideas and come up with a general interpretation or cause for all of them" (1982:8). Western scholarship is criticized for often portraying Islamic groups as extremist, with dogmatic reactions to modernity, the scholarship thus representing a retrogressive development. In contrast, Arab sociological writings on the phenomenon emphasize its diversity, complexity, and historical specificity. The most adequate approach has to be interdisciplinary and has to relate the contemporary movements to previous ones; it must allow for diversity and contradictions between Islamic groups, and between them and the political regimes. The analysis of Islamic groups has to be in terms of the specific process of social change, such as the changing position of social classes and groups, political participation, identity crisis, the stability of regimes and distributive justice. Finally, we cannot ignore the transnational nature of Islam and the appeal to Islam, and we therefore must investigate the interaction of internal and external factors. While some of these promises have been met, others have yet to be fulfilled.

What Needs To Be Known About Islamic Social Movements?

The study of Islamic social movements is a prime example of the kind of contributions that Arab sociologists and social scientists can make to an understanding of the role of Islam in the contemporary Arab world. These movements have been variously called Islamic revivalism, revitalization, reassertion, renewal, awakening, fundamentalism, and neo-fundamentalism, as well as militant or political Islam (Dessouki 1982). These movements seek to build "a new social order based on Islam" (Ibrahim 1980a:429). As is suggested by Dessouki and others, they all use political means to achieve this goal and are thus engaged in the mobilization, organization, and possibly the seizure of political authority. Their political activism is in the name of Islam and involves the growing use of Islamic symbolism and legitimation. Dessouki also indicates that the following questions from a sociological perspective need to be asked about these groups:

> Why does a ruling class feel the need to resort to Islamic ideology as a legitimizing device? Why do opposition Islamic movements emerge? What are the ideological and structural, internal or external, factors that create the milieu conducive to their emergence? Who are the potential, and actual, members of these groups and to what social class or strata of society do they belong? Why do these movements have more appeal to certain classes and strata than to others? What do these groups understand of Islam, and which aspects of religion do they emphasize? And what impact do these Islamic resurgent groups have on social and political change? (1982:6)

Answers to these questions are difficult to obtain, partly because Islamic groups have emerged recently and are still evolving, and partly because there is a scarcity of firsthand information based on observations, intensive interviews, or surveys. The fact that these groups are often engaged in clandestine activities makes knowledge of them very hard except through government-controlled media coverage of arrests and trials, coverage specifically geared toward projecting a negative image. Nevertheless, different Arab sociologists and other Arab social scientists have already started to give us valuable answers to Dessouki's questions. Most existing studies are indeed interdisciplinary, comparative, and historical.

There are at least three systematic empirical studies about the membership, structure, and dynamics of specific Islamic movements; these studies are based on interviews and observations carried out in the natural setting of these groups. The first is a recent unpublished study sponsored by the National Center for Sociological and Criminological Research in Cairo and focused on two Islamic groups whose members were arrested for militant activity and violence and whose leaders were executed. Lengthy interviews were conducted with members of these groups after they were imprisoned (Ibrahim 1980a). The second study is by Elbaki Hermassi (1984), a Tunisian sociologist, and is based on interviews with about 50 jailed leaders of the Islamic Movement and a national sample survey in Tunisia. The third study is by Fadwa el-Guindi (1982), an Egyptian anthropologist and was based on field work among university students. In addition, there are numerous other studies of Islamic movements in different parts of the Arab world, mostly based on historical material and secondary sources (e.g. Aly & Wenner 1982, Ayubi 1980, Al-Thakeb & Scott 1982, Ansari 1984, Belhassen 1981, Ben Achour 1981, Zghal 1981).

Methodological Issues in Field Studies of Islamic Movements

Sociological field studies of Islamic social movements provide crucial material for an understanding of these movements. There are, however, many methodological issues and great obstacles in the design and execution of such studies. In most Arab countries no field study or survey can be carried out without permission from the appropriate governmental agency (Tessler et al 1986). Thus, when a team from the National Center for Sociological and Criminological Research in Cairo applied for the government's permission to interview the leaders of the two most prominent militant groups, they were turned down because these groups were called "revivalist movements" in the study design. After prolonged negotiations, a compromise was reached by stating that the study would focus on "religious violence." This conformed to the government policy of labelling members of Islamic militant groups as deviants, abnormals, and heretics and treating them as common criminals. Thus, sociological studies of these groups in the Arab world raise many political, ethical, and practical problems. Both the protagonists and antagonists may be tempted to use research projects for their own purposes. There is an overall inhospitability to field studies, even when initial goodwill is established and a great deal of suspicion concerning the motives of the social scientist. The militants initially refused to see the research team which, in their view, was defined either as part of a corrupt society or as working for the government. The research team had to promise them neutrality and objectivity. The militants requested to be allowed to read everything the members of the research team had ever published, and they discussed some of the material with the team. In Ibrahim's words:

> Some of the interviews were more like graduate seminar sessions, with lively and hot-tempered exchanges. In other words, they refused to play the conventional role of research subjects. They interviewed us as much as we interviewed them. At times they asked us to react to their views, something that goes against the grammar of social research (1980a:428).

This kind of interaction between the researchers and research subjects led Ibrahim to argue, in a special seminar held in Kuwait in 1985, that the qualitative advancement of Arab sociology rests on modifying Western methods to fit Arab reality. In a difficult research environment, it is often necessary to have more extensive interaction with the research subjects than is usually the case. In particular, when studying social movements whose members inquire about the scope of the research and who pose questions themselves, there is a real need to devise new interviewing methods adapted to the particular Arab sociopolitical environment. The Cairo research team ended up spending an average of more than 10 hours per interview for the 33 militants interviewed. Thus, the kind of methodology needed for field studies in the Arab world is one that is more personal and subjective than that used in the West; it can thus reflect the more personalized social interaction. This is clearly described as follows by Ibrahim:

> A human bond developed between the research team and the Muslim militants. They became not only open but quite eager to talk . . . .. So deeply did they become committed to our research objective that when the government withdrew our research permit, their leaders tried to reach us through secret channels, bypassing the prison authorities altogether (1980a:428).

In February 1977 the Egyptian authorities put an end to prison interviewing without giving any official reasons. The permit to resume interviewing was never granted; thus the research is incomplete.

Sociological Characteristics of Selected Islamic Movements

The diversity and multiplicity of Islamic movements and the contradictions between them and secular Arab regimes are apparent in the studies and writings of leading Arab social scientists. According to Hanna Batatu (1982), an Iraqi political scientist, the Muslim Brethren in Syria represent a response to distinguishable conditions and to the interests of clearly identifiable social groups. They put themselves forward as the natural spokesmen of the Islamic Sunni community and define their conflict with Syria's Alawi rulers as a conflict between Sunnis and Alawis. They argue that the Alawis who represent about

9–10% of the population cannot indefinitely dominate the Sunni majority in Syria. In Batatu's view, the conflict is plainly not about religion. What has been at stake since the Ba'athist takeover in 1963 are the social interests of the upper- and middle elements of the landed, mercantile, and manufacturing classes. While the conflict between Sunnis and Alawis is specific to Syria, the Muslim Brethren in Syria share in common with other opposition groups in the Arab world the emphasis on political emancipation and democratic rights of the common citizens. The fascinating aspect of the Islamic movement is that it responds both to very specific sociopolitical circumstances and to very general sociopolitical aspirations for basic political freedom.

One important sociological question pertains to the social origin of the Muslim Brethren of Syria, compared to that of Islamic groups in other Arab countries. In the last few years, the militants have carried out attacks on government buildings, police stations, and Ba'ath party headquarters and have provoked demonstrations and large-scale shutdowns of shops and schools. According to Batatu, these militants were university students and professional men in their 20s and 30s, as is evident from the occupational distribution of the activists who were arrested between 1976 and May 1981. Out of a total of 1324, no fewer than 28% were students, 8% school teachers, and 13% members of the professions, including engineers, physicians, lawyers, and pharmacists.

While the movement of Muslim Brethren in Syria was essentially based in cities and defended the interests of landed, mercantile, and manufacturing classes, the Islamic movement in Tunisia, according to Hermassi (1984), has its greatest strength in small towns. It is primarily a movement of the educated youth (see also Belhassen 1981, Ben Achour 1981, Zghal 1981). The general sample of members has a median age of 25 years and is constituted mainly of university students. Even the jailed leaders of the movement at the time of the study were young, with a median age of 30 years. Other important characteristics mentioned by Hermassi are the strong concentration of student members in science faculties (compared to their weaker presence in the humanities and the social sciences) and the massive participation of women. The findings with respect to the socioeconomic origins of jailed leaders of the movement in Tunisia contrast with those reported by Saad Eddin Ibrahim (1980a) for Egypt. While the members of militant Islamic groups in Egypt are mostly of middle- or lower-middle-class origin, Tunisian activists are mainly from poor and un-educated families, and, in spite of their rapid educational mobility, they are blocked socioeconomically. With no chance of being "in" they identify with those that are "out" and are in permanent and obsessive search for an alterna-tive. The same search for an alternative also characterizes the Islamic move-ment in Egypt.

According to Hanafi (1982:67), the Islamic alternative in Egypt is the only real one because it is "the only organizational form expressing the deep-rooted traditional stream." As suggested by Hanafi, there are many different ways that this Islamic alternative has been expressed in Egypt. Those that do not question the social or political system of the country, as the fundamentalist groups do, are allowed to multiply without any obstacles. Some examples are the construction of mosques, the multiplication of Islamic publishers, the growing sale of religious books (some of which have become best-sellers), the broadcasting of prayers through loudspeakers in the streets, and the slogan calling for the application of the Shari'a (Islamic law)—increasingly used by all parties. Some Muslim preachers have become as popular as movie stars. The preaching of Sheikh Metuwalli on television attracts millions of viewers and is widely used by the ruling elite to persuade the masses to support public policy. It is precisely because these elites are frightened by the possibility of a Khomeni-type Islamic revolution that they encourage these various and nonthreatening expressions of the Islamic alternative.

Ibrahim (1982a) also examines the possibilities of an Islamic alternative in Egypt. Some Islamic groups such as the Moslem Brothers demonstrate a clear historical continuity which dispels the current Western views that see Islamic movements everywhere as if they sprang from nowhere. The Moslem Brothers in Egypt are oriented toward a total change of society; they see no separation between religion and state, and they seek maximum involvement in wordly affairs. A grass roots movement, they appeal to the lower middle class, the fastest growing class in Egypt in recent years. Only after the 1967 defeat did the Moslem Brothers begin to win back the support of an increasing segment of Egypt's middle classes. The movement emerged as the most vocal critic of the Sadat's socioeconomic policies. They openly attacked the regime's failure to deal effectively with Egypt's problems of education, housing, transportation, and inflation. The dramatic food riots of January 1977 gave them the opportunity to launch a sharp attack on Sadat's regime. They mocked the government for blaming the widespread riots on communists and asserted that the riots were merely normal symptoms of more profound and prevalent problems affecting various sectors of the population.

It is interesting to note that the Moslem Brothers' attack on Sadat's socioeconomic policies was nearly identical with that of the secular left. The necessity of looking at contradictions among different Islamic groups is clearly spelled out by Ibrahim (1982a). He points out that the leadership of the Moslem Brothers has detached itself from other Islamic groups, which engage in violent confrontations with the regime. The Moslem Brothers opted for nonviolence instead. But Ibrahim's assessment is that the condemnation of the violent fringes of the Islamic movement is only tactical and provisional until the movement rebuilds and consolidates itself. Because of the historical continuity of the movement, its leaders have learned from past premature confrontations with the regime, for example, with Nasser's regime. They have also learned to engage in alliances and coalition formation with the other secular groups—including secular liberals and leftists.

This contrasts sharply with the tactics and policies of the more militant Islamic groups in Egypt also studied by Ibrahim. The bloody confrontation of July 1977 between the regime and members of a militant islamic group labeled by the media as "Repentance and Holy Flight" (RHF) reflected the growing despair of the most volatile elements of the population—youth of the lower middle and working class who sought salvation in Islamic militancy. The size of the group came as a surprise to both the government and the public. Interrogations revealed a sizable movement of between 3000 and 5000 active members who are highly organized and quite widely spread horizontally and vertically throughout Egyptian society. This violent confrontation was not the first of its kind against the Sadat regime. Earlier, in April 1974, another militant Islamic group, the Islamic Liberation Organization, attempted to stage a coup d'etat which was spectacular in scope, planning, and timing. In addition, scattered confrontations occurred between the authorities and other militant Islamic elements which, however, attracted much less publicity than the one mentioned above. From 1975 to 1979, Muslim groups achieved landslide victories in university student unions. This prompted the government to dissolve these unions by presidential decree in the summer of 1979. According to Ibrahim, the use of violence by some militant groups gives the regime a legitimate excuse to go all-out against all Islamic groups. Government counterattacks, however, do not seem to have stemmed the tide of the militant groups. For every group that is liquidated, two or three new organizations emerge.

The analyses by Ibrahim and Hermassi of militant Islamic groups indicate that Arab sociologists studying such groups are interested in the same aspects of movements as their Western colleagues: the general societal conditions giving rise to a movement, its ideology, leadership, mode of recruitment of members, social origins of members, internal organization, and strategy and tactics. According to Ibrahim (1980a), the members interviewed believed that the righteous Muslim cannot exist individually and must strive to build and maintain a community of the faithful. It is his religious duty to see to it that a truly Muslim social order comes about. Ibrahim suggests that such a belief sooner or later takes on an organizational form that leads to an inevitable confrontation with the ruling elite. They perceive Egypt's present economic problems as the outcome of mismanagement of resources, the application of imported policies, the corruption of top officials, conspicuous consumerism, and low productivity. An important component of the militants' economic thinking is condemnation of excessive wealth differentials both between and within Muslim countries. Social differentiation and stratification, however, are accepted pillars of the Muslim order, but it is man's labor that is the only acceptable mechanism of differentiation. They believe that it is the duty of every true Muslim to remove injustice.

The founding leaders of the two militant groups studied had been hanged, and information about them was obtained from their followers. They were said to have great charisma, to be extremely eloquent, and to be highly knowledge-able not only about religion but also about national and international affairs. Both leaders recruited followers from among students who were recent univer-sity graduates. The three recruitment methods employed were kinship, friend-ship, and worship. Those recruited in turn enlisted their close friends and relatives. What Ibrahim found most significant sociologically is the social selectivity of members. The typical member is young, from rural or small-town background, from the upwardly mobile middle or lower middle class, with high achievement and motivation, and from a normally cohesive family. Ibrahim indicates that this profile poses some perplexing theoretical problems, "since it is sometimes assumed in social sciences that members of 'radical movements' must be alienated, marginal, anomic, or must possess some other abnormal characteristics" (1980a:440). On the basis of observations and interviews of militant Islamic women, Fadaw el-Guindi, an Arab anthropologist, agrees with Ibrahim that members of militant Islamic groups are definitely not alienated, marginal, or anomic individuals. In her words, "they are not dropouts from society to a primitive commune, or from college to find themselves, nor from this world to other-wordly asceticism" (1982:482–83).

What Accounts for the Spread of Islamic Militant Movements?

In search of an explanation for the rising tide of Islamic militant movements, Batatu, Ibrahim, Dessouki, Tibi, and others have suggested placing the phe-nomenon in its historical and comparative perspective and in the process of social change taking place in the Arab countries. In modern Arab history, militant Islamic movements have sprung up in several countries, and many of them have used violence to challenge the status quo. They are to be dis-tinguished from Sufi movements oriented toward the individual rather than toward changing a social or political system. All Islamic militant movements of the last ten centuries share the common objective of total change in the individual and society and a willingness to use violence to bring about this change. In modern times, several ideological and organizational similarities exist between the two militant groups studied by Ibrahim and the Muslim Brotherhood in Egypt and the Mujahideen in Iran. A comparative historical analysis of these four groups would help to find answers to the following questions: What are the common underlying structural factors between past and present Islamic movements? Since militant Islamic groups are not the only ones whose ideology and actions challenge the present social order, why have other leftist opposition groups not been as successful? If, as Ibrahim (1980a) sug-gests, the social profile of those who join radical leftist or Marxist groups is quite similar to Islamic militants, why is it that in recent years the balance has tilted in favor of Islamic groups? Ibrahim (1980a) indicates that the following four factors may account for the failure of leftist movements: (*a*) the ability of Arab ruling elites to dismiss Marxist opposition as atheist agents of a foreign power; (*b*) recent setbacks suffered by quasi-socialist experiments in Egypt and elsewhere in the Arab world; (*c*) the sense of communion provided by Muslim groups with their emphasis on brotherhood and mutual sharing; and (*d*) the deep rootedness of Islam. The deep-rootedness of Islam and the use of Islam by both the ruling elites and opposition groups are points that appear in most sociological writings on Islamic movements. Among the masses, Islam provides a frame of reference for their collective identity, a symbol of self-assertion, and a consciousness that is rooted in their own history and tradition, not derived from foreign penetration and cultural domination. This is recurrently referred to by Arab scholars and intellectuals as the question of authenticity versus modernization. A return to Islam is a return to authenticity *(asala)*, an assertion of national pride and independence of thought (Dessouki 1981:7). It should be emphasized, however, that Islamic resurgence is not a reaction to modernization per se, but to a kind of Westernization that not only overlooks but often despises national traditions and cultural symbols. Dessouki insists that Islamic resurgence reflects a "society in crisis." Some Arab social scientists have actually analyzed Islamic social movements in terms of modernization and authenticity. Thus, el-Guindi (1982) argues that Islamic movements are very much "in" and "are aggressively building models based on an already established, recently legitimized indigenous cultural theory of Islam."

In view of the complexity of the questions pertaining to the rise of Islamic movements, we would have to agree with Tibi (1983:12) who stated that "the general assumptions about the relations between Islam and social change must be broken down to specific and detailed hypotheses." In our view, some of these hypotheses would have to come from the theoretical literature on social movements. One example is Ralph Turner's (1981) hypothesis that "a movement grows in number because it attracts and holds adherents with diverse motives, goals and conceptions of the movement." Deukmejian (1985:4) in a recent analysis of Islamic fundamentalist groups provides an elaboration of this hypothesis when he states that "both in its militant and passive forms, contemporary Islamic fundamentalism possesses the three general attributes of pervasiveness, polycentrism, and persistence." It is pervasive in the sense that it is not limited to any individual country or social class. It is polycentric since it appears "to possess no single revolutionary leadership or organizational epicenter . . . but to the extent that the crisis situations in different societies are similar, the Islamic movement could eventually assume a truly transnational character." Thirdly, Islamic movements have "persisted" in the recent history of the Arab Muslim world.

CONCLUSION

It is significant that a whole conference was held in 1985 on the issue of "Authenticity and Modernization," to discuss its intellectual, political, social, and legal aspects. The argument here is that social science and intellectual discourse on authenticity and indigenization is another aspect of the same search for authenticity and indigenization by Islamic movements. Before this authenticity and indigenization of Arab sociology, and of Arab social sciences in general, can be achieved, a number of complex methodological and theoretical problems have to be resolved. To paraphrase Hanafi (1982), the Arab social scientist is not an impartial spectator but someone who is trying to perceive a trend of which he is a part. The social scientist is at once the subject and object trying to analyze his own society. Thus, the pessimistic review of the state of Arab sociology by Arab sociologists is understandable. But solutions are being and will be found within the Arab world for some of the complex problems posed by the indigenization of Arab social sciences. In our view, there is already a trend toward the substantive indigenization of Arab sociology. This is suggested not only by the results of our survey, but also by our review of sociological studies of Islamic social movements. Furthermore, many Arab sociologists are keenly aware of the need to be flexible and innovative in their selection and use of research procedures. The stumbling block remains the theoretical indigenization of Arab sociology, and this is the main source of the pessimism of Arab sociologists. But, there can be little or no indigenization of theory until there have been ample systematic studies and analyses of various facets of Arab society. For some time to come, such studies will have to be guided by a number of specific hypotheses and theoretical hunches that emerge out of the experience of Arab sociologists. It could be argued, however, that theoretical indigenization is a necessary but not a sufficient condition for the establishment and the growth of an Arab sociology. When Arab sociologists do construct their own theoretical models, they will have to relate them to sociological theories developed in other parts of the world, or face the risk of theoretical provincialism. Such a task will have to be accomplished in collaboration with sociologists from different regions of the world, and on the basis of equality and mutual understanding.

Literature Cited

Abdel Moty, A. B. 1983. Effects of foreign labor on social harmony. (In Arabic). In *Foreign Labor in the Arab Gulf States,* ed. N. Fergany, pp. 211–49. Beirut: Ctr. for Arab Unity Stud.

Akiwowo, A. A. 1980. Sociology in Africa today. *Curr. Sociol.* 28:1–126

Ali, L. 1983. Migration and problems of Arab unity: A study of Arabs in Oil Societies (In Arabic). *Al-Siyasah Al-Dawliya* 19:69–86

Al-Qazzaz, A. 1975. Impressions of sociology in Iraq. *Int. Soc. Sci. J.* 27:781–86

Aly, A. M. S., Wenner, M. W. 1982. Modern Islamic reform movements: the Muslim Brotherhood in Contemporary Egypt. *The Middle East J.* 36:336–61

Amin, G. A., E. Awny. 1985. *International Migration of Egyptian Labour. A Review of the State of the Arts.* Ottawa: Int. Dev. Res. Cent.

Ansari, H. 1984. The Islamic militant in Egyptian politics. *Int. J. Middle East Stud.* 16:123–44

Ayubi, N. M. 1980. The political revival of Islam: the case of Egypt. *Int. J. Middle East Stud.* 12:481–99

Barakat, H. 1984. *Contemporary Arab Society: An Exploratory Sociological Study* (In Arabic). Beirut: Ctr. Arab Unity Stud.

Bassiouni, S. 1979. *The Present State of Sociology in Egypt*. (In Arabic) Cairo: Ain Shams Univ.

Batatu, H. 1982. Syria's Muslim Brethren. *MERIP Rep.* 12(9):12–20

Belhassen, S. 1981. Femmes Tunisiennes Islamistes. See Souriau 1981, pp. 77–94

Ben Achour, Y. 1981. Islam perdu. Islam retrouve. See Souriau 1981, pp. 65–76

Ben Jelloun, T. 1977. Decolonizing sociology in the Maghreb. In *Arab Society in Transition*, eds. S. E. Ibrahim, N. S. Hopkins, pp. 685–12. Cairo: Am. Univ. Cairo

Ben Salem, L. 1982. Interet des analyses en termes de segmentarite pour l'etude des societes du Maghreb. *R. l'Occident Musulman Mediterranee* 33:113–35

al-Bitar, N. 1979. *From Division to Unity: Basic Laws of the Historical Experiences of Unification* (In Arabic). Beirut: Cent. Arab Unity Stud.

Bouhdiba, A. 1979. Arab migrations. In *Arab Industrialization and Economic Integration*, ed. R. Aliboni, pp. 134–87. London: Croom Helm

Burke, E. III. 1980. The sociology of Islam: The French tradition. In *Islamic Studies: A Tradition and Its Problems*, ed. M. H. Kerr, Malibu, Calif: Undena Publications

Davis, E. 1984. Ideology, social class and Islamic radicalism in modern Egypt. In *From Nationalism to Revolutionary Islam*, ed. S. A. Arjomand, pp. 134–57. Albany: State Univ. NY Press

Dessouki, A. E. H. 1981. The resurgence of Islamic organization in Egypt: An interpretation. In *Islam and Power*, eds. A. S. Cudsi, A. E. H. Dessouki, pp. 107–18. Baltimore: The John Hopkins Univ. Press

Dessouki, A. E. H. 1982. The Islamic resurgence: Sources, dynamics, implications. In *Islamic Resurgence in the Arab World*, ed. A. E. H. Dessouki, pp. 3–31. New York: Praeger

Deukmejian, R. H. 1985. *Islam in Revolution: Fundamentalism in the Arab World*. Syracuse, NY: Syracuse Univ. Press

Fergany, N., ed. 1983. *Foreign Labor in the Arab Gulf States*. (In Arabic) Beirut: Cent. Arab Unity Studies

el-Guindi, F. 1982. Veiling Infitah with Muslim ethic: Egypt's contemporary Islamic Movement. *Soc. Probl.* 28:456–85

Hamnett, M. P., Porter, D. J., Singh, A., Kumar, K. 1984. *Ethics, Politics, and International Social Science Research*. Honolulu: Univ. Hawaii Press

Hanafi, H. 1982. The relevance of the Islamic alternative in Egypt. *Arab Stud. Q.* 4:54–74

Hegazy, M. E. 1985. The present crisis in sociology in the Arab World (In Arabic). *Al-Mustaqbal Al-Arabi* 75:60–84

Hermassi, E. 1984. La societe tunisienne au miroir islamiste. *Monde Arabe-Maghreb-Machrek* 103:39–56

Ibrahim, S. E. 1980a. Anatomy of Egypt's militant Islamic groups: Methodological notes and preliminary findings. *Int. J. Middle East Stud.* 12:423–53

Ibrahim, S. E. 1980b. *Trends of Arab Public Opinion Toward the Issue of Unity* (In Arabic). Beirut: Cent. Arab Unity Stud.

Ibrahim, S. E. 1982a. An Islamic alternative in Egypt: The Muslim Brotherhood and Sadat. *Arab Stud. Q.* 4:75–93

Ibrahim, S. E. 1982b. *The New Arab Social Order: A Study of the Social Impact of the Oil Wealth*. Boulder, Colo: Westview

Ibrahim, S. E. 1985. Contemplating the future of Arab sociology: From proving existence to realizing promises. (In Arabic) *Al-Mustaqbal Al-Arabi* 77:129–39

Irabi, A. 1982. Zum Stand der gegenwartigen arabischen Soziologie. *Zeitschr. Soziol.* 11: 167–82

al-Issa, J. S. and al-Husseini, S. 1982. Sociology and Arab reality: A study of the views of Arab sociologists (In Arabic). *Al-Mustaqbal Al-Arabi* 41:28–51

Jansen, 1980.

Karoui, H. and A. Zghal. 1975. La decolonisation et la recherche en Sciences Sociales: le cas de la Tunisie. *Dritte Welt* 4:171–91

Khatibi, A. 1985. Double criticism: The decolonization of Arab Sociology. In *Contemporary North Africa: Issues of Development*, ed. H. Barakat, pp. 9–19. Washington, DC: Georgetown Univ.

el-Kordy. 1980. Underdevelopment and development in sociology: A critical analysis. (In Arabic) *Al Kitab Al-Sanawi Li-Ilm Al-Ijitma* 1:19–45

Jansen, G. H. 1980. *Militant Islam*. New York: Harper & Row

Nasr, S. 1985. A conference: toward an Arab Sociology. (In Arabic) *Al-Mustaqbal Al-Arabi* 77:168–74

Rentz, S. B. 1977. *Directory of Social Scientists*. Cairo: Org. Promotion Soc. Sci. in Middle East

Saad, D. I., Abdel Fadil, M. 1983. *The Movement of Arab Workers: Problems, Effects, and Policies*. Beirut: Cent. Arab Unity Stud.

el-Saaty, H. 1977. Sociology and contemporary development in Egypt. *Die Dritte Welt* 5:242–55

Sabagh, G. 1976. Sociology. In *The Study of the Middle East*, ed. L. Binder, pp. 511–64. New York: John Wiley.

Sari, S. 1983. Sociology and Arab sociological problems: Concerns and interests. (In Arabic) *Al-Mustaqbal Al-Arabi* 58:52–69

Sari, S. 1985. Arab Sociologists and the study

of Arab social issues: A critical appraisal. (In Arabic) *Al-Mustaqbal Al-Arabi* 75:85–95

Serageldin, I. 1983. International labor migration in the Arab world. (In Arabic) *Al Mustaqbal Al-Arabi* 47:66–88

Snow, D. A., Marshall S. 1984. Cultural imperialism, social movements, and Islamic Revival. In *Research in Social Movements, Conflict and Change* ed. R. Ratcliff, pp. 131–52. Greenwich, Conn: JAI

Souriau, C. ed. 1981. *Le Maghreb Musulman en 1979*. Paris: Ctr. natl. recherche sci.

Stambouli, F. 1977. Remarques épistémologiques sur sciences sociales et développement. *Dritte Welt* 5:307–11

al-Tamimi, A. M. K. 1983. Political consequences of foreign migration. (In Arabic) *Al-Mustaqbal Al-Arabi* 50:86–103

al-Thakeb, F., Scott, J. S. 1982. Islamic fundamentalism: A profile of its supporters. *Int. R. Modern Sociol.* 12:175–95

Tessler, M., Palmer M., Ibrahim S. E. Farah T., Lesch, A. Ibrahim B. 1986. *The Evaluation and Application of Survey Research in the Arab World*. Boulder, Colo: Westview

Tibi, B. 1983. The renewed role of Islam in the political and social development of the Middle East. *Middle East J.* 37:3–13

Turner, B. S. 1974. *Weber and Islam: a Critical Study*. London: Routledge & Kegan Paul

Turner, R. S. 1981. Collective behavior and resource mobilizations as approaches to social movements: Issues and continuities. In *Research in Social Movements, Conflicts and Change*. ed. L. Kreisberg, pp. 1–23. Greenwich Conn: JAI

Valensi, L. 1984. Le Maghreb vu du Centre: sa place dans l'école sociologique française. In *Connaissance du Maghreb*. ed. J. C. Vatin Paris: Cent. natl. recherche sci.

World Bank. 1985. *World Development Report 1985*. New York: Oxford Univ. Press

Yassin, S. 1980. *Analysis of the Content of Arab National Thought: An Exploratory Study* (In Arabic). Beirut: Cent. Arab Unity Stud.

Zghal, A. 1981. Le retour du Sacré et la nouvelle demande idéologique des jeunes scolarisés. Le cas de la Tunisie. See Souriau 1981, pp. 41–64

Ann. Rev. Sociol. 1986. 12:401–29
Copyright © 1986 by Annual Reviews Inc. All rights reserved

NEW DEVELOPMENTS IN THE SAMPLING OF SPECIAL POPULATIONS

Seymour Sudman

Survey Research Laboratory, University of Illinois, 1005 Nevada Street, Urbana, Illinois 61801

Graham Kalton

Survey Research Center, Institute for Social Research, University of Michigan, Ann Arbor, Michigan 48106–1248

Abstract

This paper describes alternative methods for careful sampling of special populations. It discusses the use of single or multiple lists, even when incomplete, along with supplementary measures using telephone and mail techniques. If the special populations are clustered there are several alternatives for reducing costs substantially. These involve telephone or mail screenings to eliminate zero segments with a single contact, use of two or three contacts to eliminate zero segments if face-to-face screening is required, use of lists to identify nonzero segments, use of combined screening, and reducing the sampling rate in nonzero areas that have low densities.

For some populations the use of network sampling can be very effective. Some populations can be defined by their activities and sampled at locations where they participate. These careful methods should be used if one is trying to generalize to a total special population.

INTRODUCTION

A special population is defined as a small subgroup of a population of interest to a researcher. What is meant by small is fairly arbitrary. The usefulness of most

401

of the procedures discussed in this paper increases as subgroups become smaller. In recent years many surveys of special populations have been conducted including, for example, surveys of:

1. Racial and ethnic groups such as blacks, Hispanics, Cubans, Vietnamese, and guest workers in Europe;
2. Households or individuals in special types of housing such as very large apartments, trailers, or substandard housing;
3. Persons with incomes above or below a given amount;
4. Employees in specific occupations and industries;
5. Persons with an illness such as heart disease or cancer; and
6. Users of a given service or product.

Such populations are often difficult and costly to identify. If no lists are available, screening methods will need to be used, although with rare populations the screening costs can equal or far exceed the actual cost of interviewing. It is also possible that substantial numbers of members of special populations will be missed because they are incorrectly identified during screening.

Researchers with limited resources may be inclined to throw up their hands in dismay when faced with a rare special population and to use ad hoc convenience samples. While these convenience samples may be adequate for an exploratory stage of research, they are totally inadequate for making careful estimates about the special population.

In this paper we discuss efficient probability methods of sampling that produce useful estimates, either unbiased or only slightly biased, at substantial reductions in cost over previous methods. We believe that these methods should generally be preferred for careful samples of special populations. The paper is divided into three main sections: The first discusses general procedures that may apply to all special populations; the second discusses efficient methods for reducing costs when the special populations are geographically clustered; and the final section discusses methods for sampling special populations defined by their activities (e.g. fishing) at the locations of those activities.

While there was some earlier interest in sampling special populations, much of the work has been done since 1970 and has not yet found its way into standard textbooks on sampling. For the sake of completeness, we also include some earlier references.

GENERAL PROCEDURES

Use of Lists

If a complete list of the special population exists then obviously it should be used, and the other techniques described in this paper are then unnecessary. In many situations, a list exists, but it is incomplete. As we shall show, even incomplete lists may be very useful in selecting efficient samples of special populations. In many cases, lists contain very large fractions of the population, and the question then becomes whether it is necessary or worthwhile to supplement the list with other far more expensive methods.

One simple way to consider this issue is to examine the relative bias of omitting nonlist cases under different assumptions. Suppose the rate of behavior for population members on the list is X while that for population members not on the list is rX, and let W be the proportion of the population not on the list. The relative bias caused by omitting nonlist members is $W(r - 1)/[W(r - 1) + 1]$.

The relative bias is small for small W and r, but rises as W and r increase. It must also be remembered, however, that for special populations the cost of locating nonlist members is very large, while the list charges are generally well below a dollar a name. Denoting the screening cost as $\$c$/contact and π as the proportion that the special population is of the total population, the cost of the screening calls needed to identify each nonlist member is $c/W\pi$. Results on the percentage relative bias and the screening costs for different values of r and W with $c = \$2$ and $\pi = 0.1$ are summarized in Table 1.

When the cost of sampling nonlist members is high, it is often reasonable to exclude them from the sample and to accept the resultant bias. Whether this is appropriate depends on the size of the sample: The relative contribution of the bias term to the mean square error of a survey estimate is greater the larger the sample, so that while it may be appropriate to accept the bias with a small sample, it would not be appropriate to do so with a larger one. To illustrate this point let us compare two sampling schemes for estimating the proportion of members of the special population with a certain attribute. One scheme is to select a stratified sample, with list members in one stratum and nonlist members in the other; simple random samples are selected within each stratum, and an optimum allocation is used to divide the sample between the strata. The second

Table 1 Relative biases and costs by proportion missing from list and differences in behavior rates

	Relative bias with varying proportion missing from list				
	Proportion missing (W)				
Rate of behavior in nonlist group (rX)	.05	.10	.20	.30	.40
1.25×	1.2	2.4	4.8	7.0	9.1
1.5×	2.4	4.8	9.1	13.0	16.7
2×	4.8	9.1	16.7	23.1	28.6
3×	9.1	16.7	28.6	27.5	44.4
Cost (assumes $c = \$2$, $\pi = .1$)	$400	$200	$100	$67	$50

scheme is to select a simple random sample from the list. Let the budget available be sufficient to collect data from n members of the list frame, and let the relative cost of collecting data from the nonlist sample members (i.e. location and interviewing costs) to that for the list sample members (interviewing costs only) be t. With the first scheme, the relvariance of the unbiased estimator of the population proportion P is:

$$RV \doteq [(1 - W)(P_1Q_1)^{1/2} + W(P_2Q_2)^{1/2}]^2/nP^2,$$

where P_1 is the proportion with the attribute among list members, $Q_1 = 1 - P_1$; P_2 is the proportion with the attribute among nonlist members; and $Q_2 = 1 - P_2$. Provided P_1 and P_2 are neither close to 0 nor close to 1, P_1Q_1 and P_2Q_2 may be approximated by PQ, so that RV reduces to

$$RV \doteq \frac{Q[1 + W(\sqrt{t} - 1)]^2}{nP}.$$

The second scheme produces a biased estimate. Again approximating P_1Q_1 by PQ, the relative mean square error of this estimate is:

$$RMSE \doteq \frac{Q}{nP} + \left[\frac{W(r - 1)}{W(r - 1) + 1}\right]^2.$$

If $RMSE < RV$, the second scheme is preferable, while if $RV > RMSE$, the first scheme is preferable.

An Example

Suppose one wishes to select a sample of academic sociologists and has to decide whether to sample only from the directory of the American Sociological Association or whether also to sample from lists of university faculty members to cover sociologists who are not members of the ASA.

Assume 10% of sociologists are not on the ASA list, so $W = 0.1$. Since location costs are substantial, it costs \$20 to locate and interview a sociologist using university lists. Using the ASA list, it costs only \$5; thus $t = 4$. If $P = 0.5$ and $r = 1.25$, then $RV = 1.21/n$ and $RMSE = (1/n) + (1/1681)$. Thus $RV = RMSE$ at $n = 353$. For larger n, $RV < RMSE$, so that the stratified scheme is preferable, whereas for smaller n, $RMSE < RV$. Thus, the sample from the ASA list only is preferable.

If one had a limited budget of, say, $1500, sampling 300 names only from the ASA list would yield the smallest error. If, however, one had $3000, the stratified sample would be preferred.

Multiple Frames

Even though no complete list of a rare population is available, there may exist one or more partial lists. Thus, for instance, the membership lists of the various engineering societies may serve as partial lists for a survey of qualified engineers. Sometimes the combination of several partial lists covers the population under study, but often a screening sample is also needed to give representation to those on none of the lists.

When multiple frames are used, it is likely that some members of the special population will be included on more than one frame; For instance, an engineer may be a member of more than one engineering society. When the frames are combined, the problem arises that some members will have more than one listing. This is the well-known frame problem of duplicates, for which there are several standard solutions (Kish 1965; Sudman 1976).

One obvious solution is to remove the duplicate listings from the combined frame, but this is often difficult. Moreover, the process can be error-prone, with the risk that some listings will be incorrectly eliminated because they have been falsely matched with other listings, while some duplicate listings may remain because of a failure to identify their duplications (for instance, because the spelling of a name or a description of an address is different).

A second solution is to identify each member of the population uniquely with one of his or her listings and to treat his or her other listings as blanks on the sampling frame. The engineering societies could, for example, be placed in order, and the engineers could then be identified with the listings for the first of the societies of which they are members. This solution works well when one can readily determine from the lists whether the selected listings represent members of the population or are blanks. It is less useful when this determination has to be made by contacting the members of the population whose listings are selected, because of the costs involved. Contact with these members once made, it is often economic to collect the full survey responses from them.

The third solution is to take a routine sample of the listings and then to make weighting adjustments in the analysis to compensate for the duplicates. Sample members are given weights that are inversely proportional to their expected number of selections. The use of these weighting adjustments will as a rule lead to an increase in sampling errors, so that for a given sample size the survey estimates will not be as precise as they would have been for the equal probability sample that would have been obtained with either of the first two solutions. However, if the information on duplication has to be collected from the respondents, this is often the economic solution to the problem.

An alternative form of weighting adjustment employs the multiple frame methodology introduced by Hartley (1962, 1974). Discussion of that methodology falls outside the scope of this paper. The reader is referred to the discussion by Kalton & Anderson (1986) and the references given in that paper.

The Use of Previously Collected Samples

Previously conducted sample surveys can sometimes be used to generate a list for a sample of a special population (Sudman 1967). Thus, if a previous general population survey had determined religion and ethnicity, a sample of Jews or Hispanics could be selected from that sample for a new study. An early example of such a use is by Greeley & Rossi in their study of Catholic Americans (1966). Several issues relate to the quality of the data and privacy concerns of respondents.

In using an earlier study a researcher must ask how much time has elapsed since that study was conducted. The longer the time, the more respondents will have moved and the greater the number of outdated addresses. People who have moved can, of course, be traced, but this tracing operation can often be more expensive than simple screening. While there is no single time span appropriate for all studies, we would suggest that samples from studies conducted more than two years earlier would usually have many outdated addresses, and their use would be inefficient. Samples drawn from more recent studies would contain fewer households who had moved, and these could be traced at less cost. Although almost all persons can be traced if one is willing to spend sufficient resources, it is likely that a researcher would be satisfied if 90% or more of the sample from the earlier study could be located.

The discussion thus far has assumed that the previous study was carefully conducted with a probability sample and that it elicited reasonable cooperation from its respondents. If the initial sample was of poor quality, any subsample from it would necessarily also be of poor quality. Assuming the initial sample was well designed, one would need to assess the cooperation rate on that study and compare it to the cooperation rate that could be achieved on a new screening study. Normally on a screening survey, cooperation is higher than on a complete interview because the screener interview is shorter and information can be obtained from any adult in a household. However, if the cooperation rate on the previous study is not substantially lower than that which could be obtained with a new screening interview, the cost differences will make the use of the previous study a desirable alternative.

The question arises: Is it an invasion of respondent privacy to use a name obtained in one survey to select the sample for a new study? This is clearly not the case if the respondent has been advised of the possibility of being selected for another study and has given permission to be recontacted. In other situations the position is not so clearcut. An approach sometimes used is to contact those respondents identified as members of the special population to ask their permission to be contacted for the new study. Those agreeing are then included in the sample for the new study. This approach of course suffers the disadvantage of the additional cost of obtaining the permission. It has been found that mail methods are not very effective in obtaining permission; many respondents who agree when asked personally will not return mail requests.

Use of Current or Future Surveys of the General Population for Screening

One way to avoid outdated addresses is to add the screening questions to one or more sample surveys that will be conducted in the near and in the more distant future. Sometimes one survey with a large sample will produce a sample of the special population sufficiently large to be useful, or sometimes a group of researchers, each interested in a different special population, can pool their resources to mount a large-scale multipurpose screening survey. On other occasions, the screener questions can be added to several surveys conducted by one or more survey organizations. These organizations will need to be compensated for their location efforts, but costs may be lower than direct screening costs because they are shared with the existing surveys. Again, the researcher needs to ensure that the sample designs and response rates are satisfactory for the purposes of the special population survey.

The major problem with prospective screening is that it may take a long time before sufficient members of the special population are located. If the researcher has planned for a lengthy interviewing period and is not faced with major time constraints, the cost savings of the prospective screening may exceed the additional costs that are incurred from an extended interviewing period.

An example of the use of prospective screening is the British survey of victims of serious accidents by the Center for Socio-Legal Studies (Harris et al 1982). A question on accidents was added to a large number of omnibus type surveys and used until a sufficient sample was located.

Mail Screening

A relatively cheap way to screen for a special population is a mail questionnaire. This method has been widely used in some European countries, particularly Great Britain, where name-and-address registers exist. Response rates to the mail screening are often quite good, probably because of the simplicity of the questionnaire. Hunt (1978), for example, reports a response rate of 80% to a mail questionnaire collecting demographic details for the occupants of 11,500 households; the questionnaire was used to identify a sample of the elderly. In the United States there are no such registers, so the questionnaire has to be addressed to the "Resident" or "Occupant." Usually the response rates to questionnaires addressed in this way have been too low to make this method useful in careful sampling.

In some cases mail methods may be feasible in the United States, for example, when the study of a special population is limited to a single state or a small number of states or cities. In these cases, there may be city directories that can be used or other lists obtained from state records. The most widely used such lists are of licensed drivers or vehicle owners. These are not always available, and when they are, they still omit nonowners or non-drivers. However, in some areas these omissions are not large. As the cost of such lists increases, their use for screening becomes problematic.

The Use of Mail Panels

Mail panels are groups of households recruited to respond to mail questionnaires sent to them periodically by a survey organization. These panels have been widely used in commercial marketing research to test new products. Because they often contain over 100,000 households, such panels have sometimes been used to screen for special populations. Thus, for instance, mail panels were used in one study by the Federal Trade Commission to locate the purchasers of hearing aids and in another study to locate purchasers of house trailers.

Although 80% to 90% of panel households cooperate on a study, the major problem with mail panels is that the initial cooperation rate of households invited to participate in a panel is often 10% or less. Mail panels are usually balanced by major demographic variables to remove the most obvious selection biases, but other biases may still remain. These unknown selection biases may distort the survey results, and the researcher will not be able to assess the possible distortion unless some independent checks can be made.

The Use of Telephone Screening

The conduct of surveys by telephone interviewing has increased markedly in the United States in recent years. This mode of data collection is cheaper than face-to-face interviewing, especially when the object is screening interviews. In view of the high proportion of telephone numbers not listed in directories, sampling for telephone surveys of the general population is generally carried out by some form of random digit dialing (RDD) procedure. Telephone screening surveys that use such methods produce samples less clustered than are area probability samples. This is a disadvantage when the subsequent interviews with members of the special population must be conducted face-to-face. However, Sudman (1978) has shown that it is still usually far more efficient to screen by phone then by face-to-face interview.

The overall proportion of households with telephones in the United States now exceeds 94%, but there are segments of the population where the proportion is appreciably lower. These segments include, for instance, low income rural groups and Hispanics. Of course, telephone screening, unless supplemented, is not appropriate where telephone ownership by the special population is low.

Use of Large Clusters in Screening

When a special population that is fairly evenly scattered throughout the general population is to be identified by face-to-face screening, it is often efficient to screen large areas, such as complete city blocks or entire villages. As Kish (1965:405) points out, even large clusters of the general population will yield only small clusters of the special population. In clusters containing no members of the special population, however, all the screening interviews will be wasted; methods for eliminating zero clusters are discussed below.

It is not always necessary to determine the status of household members by contacting the household. Sometimes the information needed to determine whether they are members of the special population can be obtained from neighbors, although such information may be subject to error. Collecting information from other informants works best when the characteristics determining the special population are highly visible such as skin color or blindness. We discuss the use of neighborhood informants later.

Field Procedures for Screening

Since screening is expensive, researchers naturally desire to make the screening interview as short and simple as possible. One approach is to design the series of screening questions in such a way that the first "no" answer ends the interview. Thus, for a special population consisting of employed black men under 25 with living parents, the first screening question might be used to determine race, with the interview terminating there unless the answer is "black;" the next question might ask age, with the interview terminating if the informant is over 24; etc. The major drawback to this approach is that the informant may quickly recognize that a very specific type of respondent is sought. He or she may then simply give a "no" answer to avoid what may be perceived as the bother of the interview.

The solution to this problem involves a longer screening interview in which the interviewer obtains a complete listing of household members and collects the requisite screening information for each. Sometimes the interviewer is not told what the desired characteristics are, so that neither the informant not interviewer can deliberately misclassify the household members to avoid the subsequent interviews.

Unfortunately, even when deliberate distortions of responses are avoided, the problem of misclassification remains serious. Misclassification errors may either classify nonmembers of the special population as members (false positives) or classify members as nonmembers (false negatives). False positives are not so serious since there is the opportunity to detect them at the subsequent interview. On the other hand, respondents who give false negatives cause greater concern because they are missed from the survey. Unfortunately, false negatives are usually more prevalent than false positives because classification errors tend to reduce the variability in the population: When informants are incorrect, their answers will tend to move toward the more common responses and away from the rare responses that define the special population.

The magnitude of misclassification errors may easily be underestimated. Previous studies have shown misclassification errors of 5%–10% on many variables looked at singly. These errors multiply, however, when the special population is defined by many characteristics. Thus, for some complex populations as many as one third to one half of eligible respondents could be missed. These errors can be reduced by making the screening questions more detailed, but this adds to the length and cost of the screening interview. Although misclassification cannot be avoided, it can be minimized by careful, thorough screening. The more complete the screening, the greater the likelihood that future studies of special populations can use the screening sample.

Sometimes an accurate determination of whether individuals are members of the special population requires expensive tests, while at the same time a cheap but imperfect screening test exists. Thus, for example, expensive medical tests may be needed to determine with certainty whether an individual has a particular disease, while the responses to some questions about symptoms may provide a good indication. In such cases, the cheap but imperfect test may be used as an initial screening device to separate a large sample into strata according to the likelihood that they are in the special population. Then a subsample may be drawn from the large sample, and the strata with the greater likelihoods can be sampled at higher rates. To be effective, this two-phase sampling procedure requires that the screening test be many times cheaper than the final test. Deming (1977) suggests that it needs to be at most one sixth of the cost and preferably much less. Of course, the screening test needs to have a reasonably high power to discriminate between members of the special population and others. The major requirement is that it be effective in identifying members of the special population correctly; It is far more important to avoid false negatives than false positives. An approach that can sometimes be useful is to relax the criteria for the positive classification by the screening test, thereby deliberately erring in favor of false positives in order to reduce the level of false negatives.

In general, as well as sampling from those classified as positive on the screener, a sample needs to be drawn from those classified as negative to ensure that the false negatives are represented in the final sample. However, when the false negatives are a negligible proportion of the special population, the need for a sample from the stratum of those classified as negative by the screener disappears. The second-phase sample can then be restricted, with appreciable savings in cost, to the stratum of those classified as positive by the screener. Before adopting this procedure, however, the researcher needs to be highly confident that the proportion of false negatives is negligible.

Sequential Sampling Methods for Determining Screening Rates

In many cases the size of the special population will be known only vaguely, and hence the appropriate screening rate to produce a sample of the desired size cannot be specified precisely. This will apply especially when there are no (or only limited) census data on the special population. While preliminary estimates may be made on the basis of expert judgment or of extrapolation from small pilot studies, or from census or survey data, these estimates are generally too unreliable for use in budgeting or in determining the true work load.

In this situation it is often useful to build up the sample sequentially. Thus, for instance, the initial sample might be one half of that thought likely to be needed. The information collected from this sample and the experience gained about the costs of data collection can then be used to revise the estimates of the additional sample and budget needed to complete the study. Although this sequential procedure slightly increases the time and cost of the study, it is well worth it to reduce the uncertainties involved in locating a special population.

Multiplicity Sampling

The aim of multiplicity, or network, sampling is to spread the identification of members of the special population more broadly over the total population; thereby the number of screening contacts needed is reduced (Sirken 1970, 1972). The procedure may be best described with an example. Suppose that a sample of male Vietnam veterans is required. A conventional screening approach would select a sample of households and include all the male Vietnam veterans in the selected households in the sample. A large initial sample would be required since Vietnam veterans comprise only a small fraction of the total population. With a multiplicity sample, a veteran would be identified for the sample not only because he was a member of a selected household, but also because he was linked in a clearly specified way to one of the selected households. The linkage might be, for instance, that the veteran is the father or son of a member of a selected household. This spreading of the selection of the veterans over a network of reporting units reduces the number of screening contacts needed but creates a multiplicity of ways in which any veteran can be selected. These multiplicities correspond to duplicate listings on the sampling frame, and weighting adjustments are needed in the analyses to compensate for them.

Multiplicity samples may be used either to estimate the prevalence of the special population in the total population or to identify members of the special population for inclusion in a survey of that special population. The latter is of interest here. The researcher's major concerns in choice of linkages are then whether sampled informants will know if those linked to them are members of the special population and whether informants will be able to provide the information necessary so that linked special population members can be contacted for the survey. In addition, special population members need to be able to identify those who, if sampled, would lead to their own inclusion in the sample, since this information is needed for determining the weights to be used in the analysis.

Linkages to close relatives have been used in multiplicity samples for several surveys of rare illnesses (e.g. Czaja et al 1984, Sirken et al 1978, Sirken et al 1980), for a survey of births and deaths (Nathan 1976), and for a survey of Vietnam era veterans (Rothbart et al 1982). Linkages to neighboring households have been used in a survey of ethnic minorities (Brown & Ritchie 1981) and in a pilot survey of home vegetable gardeners using sewage sludge (Bergsten & Pierson 1982). The last of these surveys was conducted by telephone, and Bergsten & Pierson report that efforts based on the information provided by the initial informants resulted in contact with only 70% of neighbors. On the other hand, Rothbart et al (1982) and Czaja et al (1984) found that the use of networks of relatives almost always made it possible to locate the members of the special population. Even if an informant does not have the complete address or telephone number, he or she can give the names of other relatives who will know how to locate the member of the special population.

Other networks such as more distant relatives, coworkers, or members of the same church or other social organization may also be considered for use in locating members of special populations. Sudman (1985b) has shown that for visible characteristics, such as physical handicaps, reports from coworkers and members of the same church or social group are reasonably accurate. As the group becomes larger, however, the accuracy of reports of network members decreases, so that one usually gets better results with smaller networks.

The utility of multiplicity sampling depends upon a balancing of its advantages against its disadvantages. Its prime advantage is the reduction of the total sample size needed to identify a given sample size of members of the special population. This reduction is, however, achieved at the cost of unequal selection probabilities, resulting in the need for weights in the analysis with a consequent increase in sampling error. In addition, failures by informants to identify members of the special population, failures to trace identified members of the special population, and errors by sampled members of the special population in identifying the potential informants linked to them can all result in biases. There is a cost involved in identifying the potential informants—extra questions need to be asked to find out about them, and nonresponse to any of these questions can cause problems (Sirken et al 1978). Moreover, the costs of tracing and contacting members of the special population need to be taken into account, since they can be substantial. Multiplicity sampling is a valuable technique in the right circumstances, but it is not always appropriate.

Snowballing

The basic idea underlying snowballing and snowball sampling is that members of a special population often know each other, and the technique is applicable only with populations for which this is the case. When one or more members of the special population are located, they are asked to name other members of the special population who are then asked to name others, and so on.

A widely used application of snowballing is in the study of local elites. Starting with a list of persons in certain key positions, each is asked to name the other leaders in the community, whether or not they hold official positions. It is generally found that after talking with the first dozen or so persons, no new names are generated and all the community leaders have been located. The number of members of a local elite is fairly small and all those identified are usually interviewed for the study (Rossi & Crain 1968). In other applications, the size of the special population may be larger, in which cases a probability sample may be selected from the list that has been compiled.

The use of snowballing described above is for creating a sampling frame. The quality of the resultant sample depends on the completeness of the frame that is constructed. If some members of the special population are missed, they are likely to be the socially isolated. In many surveys social isolation may be associated with the survey variables, in which case incompleteness in the sampling frame will result in a bias in the survey estimates. It is therefore important to take due care to compile as complete a frame as possible.

A looser application of snowball sampling is to stop the snowballing process as soon as the desired sample size has been reached, interviewing those named as members of the special population as soon as they are contacted. Such a sample is clearly biased towards those with many contacts with other members of the special population. This procedure does not yield a probability sample, and the results obtained with its use should be treated with due caution. Descriptions of snowball samples of this type are provided by Snow et al (1981) for a sample of Hispanics in Atlanta, Georgia; by Welch (1975) for a sample of

Mexican Americans in Omaha, Nebraska; and by Biernacki & Waldorf (1981) for a sample of ex-heroin addicts.

GEOGRAPHICALLY CLUSTERED SAMPLES

Many geographically clustered special populations are located in a limited number of geographic areas. Conversely, there are a large fraction of total geographic segments in which *no* members of the special population are located. The standard procedure in this case often leads to large numbers of screening calls in these zero segments and to no eligible respondents.

If the zero segments are known in advance from Census data or some other source such as expert judgment, substantial cost savings are possible by eliminating the screening of these zero segments. In this case, the optimum

Table 2 Notation used

Notation	Definition
M	Number of geographic segments in the sampling frame
m	Number of segments selected for screening
P_i	Number of special population units in segment i
K_i	Total number of units in segment i
π_i	Proportion of special population in segment i
$k + 1$	Cluster size in any segment
n	$m(k + 1)$, total sample size of special population
N	ΣK_i, size of total population
S	ΣP_i, size of special population
π	S/N, proportion of special population to total population
t	$\Sigma K_i/N$, proportion of units in zero segments, i.e. all i where $P_i = 0$
ρ	Homogeneity (intraclass correlation) of the special population within the geographic segments
ρ'	Homogeneity between blocks within segment
j	Expected number of blocks contacted within segment for face-to-face screening
$k' + 1$	Cluster size per block for face-to-face screening
$j(k' + 1)$	Cluster size per segment for face-to-face screening
C_S	Unit cost of screening a contact
C_{SP}	Unit cost of screening a contact by telephone
C_I	Cost of data collection from an eligible unit of the special population
C_P	Total expected costs of telephone methods in all segments
C_U	Total expected cost for a nonclustered sample with equivalent variance
C_T	Travel costs for one trip for face-to-face screening and interviewing of a segment
C_F	Total expected costs of face-to-face screening and interviewing in all segments
C_L	Cost per unit on a list
C_M	Total expected costs of using lists and clustering
C_{ME}	Total expected costs of using lists and not clustering for a sample with equivalent variance

procedures for screening and data collection using mail or telephone procedures involve no clustering, while the optimum procedures for face-to-face interviewing would utilize the standard optimum cluster procedures developed by Hansen et al (1953). Frequently, however, zero segments are not known in advance. Sudman (1972, 1985a) has discussed optimum procedures when this is the case.

The rapid elimination of zero segments through use of one (or a few) screening contacts can substantially reduce screening costs, particularly if the proportion of zero segments is high. The widely used method for improving the efficiency of random digit dialing procedures described by Waksberg (1978) may be adapted for special populations with even greater cost savings than for general populations.

The procedure, as used in either mail or telephone screening, requires that initially a single unit be sampled within a geographic segment. If that unit is a member of the special population, additional screenings are conducted in the segment until the desired cluster size is reached. In telephone sampling, banks of numbers are all the same size and are selected with equal probabilities. For geographic sampling, initial segments will vary in size, and these segments will be selected by the standard procedure of sampling with probabilities proportionate to size (PPS). Once the segments are selected, sampling within segments will be at a rate inversely proportional to size so that each selected unit will have an equal probability of selection. To facilitate the discussion in this section, the notations used are given in Table 2.

Sampling of geographic segments is done with replacement, so that a segment may be selected multiple times. Sampling of households or individuals at the final stage is without replacement.

A geographic segment is selected with probability K_i/N. The probability that a unit selected within that segment is a member of the special population is P_i/K_i. Thus, the overall probability of a segment being selected and retained is:

$$\left(\frac{K_i}{N}\right)\left(\frac{P_i}{K_i}\right) = \frac{P_i}{N}. \qquad\qquad 1.$$

Among nonzero clusters only, the probabilities of selection are P_i/S. To obtain a self-weighting sample, the second-stage sample size is set at $k + 1$. The overall probability of selection of a member of the special population in a cluster is:

$$\left(\frac{P_i}{S}\right)\left(\frac{k+1}{P_i}\right) = \frac{k+1}{S}. \qquad\qquad 2.$$

Waksberg shows that the expected screening costs for this procedure are:

$$\frac{m}{\pi}[1 + (1 - t)k]C_S. \qquad 3.$$

Total expected costs for screening and interviewing are:

$$C_P = m(k + 1)C_I + \frac{m}{\pi}[1 + (1 - t)k]C_S$$

$$= m(k + 1)\left[C_I + C_S \frac{(1 - t)}{\pi}\right] + \frac{mt}{\pi}C_S. \qquad 4.$$

It, therefore, follows immediately from Hansen et al (1953, Ch. 6) that:

$$(k + 1)_{\text{optimum}} = \left\{\frac{tC_S}{\pi\left[C_I + \frac{(1 - t)}{\pi}C_S\right]}\left(\frac{1 - \rho}{\rho}\right)\right\}^{1/2} \qquad 5.$$

The cost for a sample of size n under this optimum allocation is found by substituting the value of $k + 1$ from Formula 5 into Formula 4. The cost for a nonclustered sample with the equivalent variance is:

$$C_U = \frac{m(k + 1)}{1 + k\rho}\left(C_I + \frac{C_S}{\pi}\right). \qquad 6.$$

The ratio of costs from formulas 4 and 6 is:

$$\frac{C_P}{C_U} = (1 + k\rho)\frac{C_I\pi + C_S(1 - t) + tC_S/(k + 1)}{C_I\pi + C_S}. \qquad 7.$$

Very substantial cost savings of about 70% or more are possible when t, the proportion of units in zero segments, is around 0.9, π is correspondingly low, and ρ is around 0.01. On the other hand, there is no advantage to these clustered screening methods where t is less than 0.5 or 0.6, π is greater than 0.2, and ρ is about 0.10.

An example here illustrates the effectiveness of geographic screening. It is assumed that telephone sampling and interviewing are used and that virtually all eligible households have telephones.

Telephone Screening of Black Households Using Random Digit Dialing.

Suppose one wishes to select a national sample of 1200 black households, as did Blair & Czaja (1982) who used this method. Black households are approximately 3% of all working U.S. telephone numbers, according to the results of Blair & Czaja, as well as other independent estimates. Also, from an analysis of census block statistics it is estimated that about 70% of all working banks of 100 telephone numbers have no black households. Groves & Kahn (1979) estimate that 65% of all telephone banks consist solely of nonworking numbers. Thus:

$$t = 1 - (0.35)(0.30) = 0.9$$

and

$$\pi = 0.03.$$

The interviewing cost C_I is estimated to be $10, and the screening cost C_S is estimated as $2. We shall assume that ρ, the estimate of homogeneity, is 0.05. This is a realistic value for a broad range of consumer and household variables, although larger and smaller values of ρ are also likely.

Using Formula 5,

$$(k + 1)_{opt} = \frac{0.9}{(0.03)5 + 0.1} \left(\frac{0.95}{0.05}\right)^{1/2} = 8.$$

From Formula 2, the cost of this method using the optimum cluster design is:

$$C_P = 1200 \left[10 + \frac{2(0.1)}{0.03}\right] + \frac{150}{0.03} (0.9) (2) = \$29,004.$$

The actual cost for an unclustered sample with an equivalent variance is:

$$C_U = \frac{1200}{1 + 7 (0.05)} \left(10 + \frac{2}{0.03}\right) = \$68,151,$$

and the ratio C_P/C_U equals 0.43.

Clusters with Too Few Eligible Households

Optimum cluster sizes may be fairly large for relatively rare population screening. The procedure becomes biased if a selected cluster contains fewer than $k + 1$ members of the special population. Two alternative procedures can prevent this bias:

1. Increase the size of the cluster from banks of 100 to banks of several hundred or more.
2. Weight the data in a cluster by the ratio $(k + 1)/r$ where r is the number of eligible households within the cluster. Optimum procedures would usually involve weighting.

It must be recognized, however, that either of these procedures reduces the efficiency of the screening. Increasing the size of the cluster reduces the number of zero clusters, whereas weighting the data increases sample variances (Waksberg 1983).

Face-to-Face Screening Required

For some purposes, such as determining the condition of housing units and interviewing in those that meet, or fail to meet, prespecified criteria, or in ethnic groups with low telephone coverage, it may be necessary to conduct face-to-face screening. The cost function for this process is strongly affected by the cost of listing and of travel to and from the segment. Thus, the procedure used for mail and telephone surveys of selecting nonzero segments on the basis of the characteristics of a *single* unit may no longer be optimum. Rather, it may be more efficient to conduct *multiple* screening calls before deciding whether to include or exclude a cluster.

Using the notation in Table 1, let C_T equal travel costs for one trip to an average segment. It is assumed that the segments have been listed previously, so that no additional listing costs are required. We use the same cost function as previously, adding, however, the term C_T for travel to screen the cluster. Let C_F be the expected total costs for this face-to-face procedure.

Then,

$$C_F = m(k + 1)\left[C_I + C_S\left(\frac{1 - t}{\pi}\right)\right] + m\left[\frac{t}{\pi}C_S + C_T\left(\frac{\pi + 1}{\pi}\right)\right].\qquad 8.$$

The optimum size for a single cluster is:

$$(k + 1)_{\text{opt}} = \left[\frac{tC_S + C_T(\pi + 1)}{C_I\pi + (1 - t)C_S}\left(\frac{1 - \rho}{\rho}\right)\right]^{1/2}.\qquad 9.$$

The value of multiple starts depends on the fact that the homogeniety between elements in a cluster typically declines as the cluster increases in geographic size. If this is not the case, then the new cost function merely means an increase in optimum cluster size. This is immediately evident, since the numerator in Formula 9 has a C_T term but is otherwise identical to the telephone optimum in Formula 5.

Consider the following design. Clusters are selected using standard PPS (probability proportionate to size) procedures. An interviewer makes j screening calls at points within a cluster that are relatively close geographically. (For specificity, we can assume that these might be housing units on blocks within the same census tract.) If a screening call yields an eligible household, then additional calls are made sequentially until k' additional eligible households are located. If a screening call does not yield an eligible household, no additional screening calls are made. Thus, if h of the j screening calls yield eligible households, then additional calls will be made sequentially until hk' additional eligible households are located. This is an unbiased sampling procedure that is a direct extension of the method of the previous section.

Note that this procedure, unlike the one discussed for telephone and mail screening, produces variability in the total number of completed cases in a cluster. The number of completed cases will range from $k' + 1$ to $j(k' + 1)$. This variability increases the sampling variance, as does the clustering. Even so, it may be shown that this procedure is optimum in some cases.

Assume that j screening calls can be made on a single trip, so that no additional travel costs are required. These j calls will yield $0 - j$ eligible units. For each eligible unit found, continue screening until k' additional eligible units are found. It is assumed that one additional trip will be required for interviewing in a segment once an eligible unit has been found. More complex cost functions describing travel may be used, but the general result will still follow.

It can be demonstrated that for most applications this is more efficient than either conducting only a single screening call per segment or conducting a very large number of screening calls in every segment.

To decide which procedure is optimum for a given cost, one would compare the variances or the equivalent n values, which are simply the sizes of simple random samples required to yield the same variances as for the proposed cluster designs. For a single cluster, $\sigma^2_c = \sigma^2_{\text{SRS}} (1 + \rho k)$, so that $n_{\text{equivalent}} = n/(1 + \rho k)$.

If one takes the cluster sizes as fixed and now considers the clusters as units, the variance for a design with j clusters can be approximated as a function of the variance of the single cluster design (Hansen, et al 1953): $\sigma^2 j$ clusters $= \sigma^2$single cluster $[1 + \rho'(j - 1)]$, so that $\sigma^2 j$ clusters $= \sigma^2_{\text{SRS}} (1 + \rho k')[1 + \rho'(j - 1)]$ and $n_{\text{equiv}} = n/\{(1 + \rho k')[1 + \rho'(j - 1)]\}$.

The expected cost of screening in j clusters is:

$$C_F = mj\,(k' + 1)\left[C_I + C_S\left(\frac{1 - t}{\pi}\right)\right] + m\left[\frac{jt}{\pi}C_S + C_T\left(\frac{\pi + 1}{\pi}\right)\right], \qquad 10.$$

and:

$$(k' + 1)_{\text{opt}} = \left[\frac{tC_S + \dfrac{C_T}{j}(\pi + 1)}{C_I\pi + (1 - t)C_S}\left(\frac{1 - \rho}{\rho}\right)\right]^{1/2} \qquad 11.$$

It must be recognized that these formulas are approximate and ignore the increase in variance caused by the variability in the total number of cases in a cluster. However, it turns out that solutions generally lead to only modest variability in the total number of cases per cluster, so that the approximation appears to be reasonably satisfactory.

The Use of Incomplete Lists

Earlier we discussed the use of lists, either with or without supplementation. In this section, we discuss efficient methods of supplementing the list if there is geographic clustering. Even incomplete lists may be very useful in identifying areas where the special population is located. In the simplest case, assume that a random (or systematic) sample of starting points is chosen from the list and that screening continues at each starting point until k additional eligible respondents are located. It is evident that this procedure is almost identical to those just discussed.

A cluster will have an initial probability of selection proportional to the number of members of the special population in it who are on the list. Although the definition of the cluster is somewhat arbitrary, it must be made in advance before the sample is selected. The telephone exchange of the unit selected from the mailing list would be a natural cluster for samples using mailing lists and telephone interviewing. (If not available on the list, this information would usually be obtainable from the telephone company.) For face-to-face interviewing, either the block or the zip code would be a natural cluster. Then, sampling within the cluster is inversely proportional to this probability, so that the ultimate sample is self-weighting.

The sample is biased, however, if there are geographic clusters that have *no* eligible respondents on the list. These clusters have no chance of selection. It is possible to measure the sample bias from such a procedure if one has an estimate of the total size of the special population. One would also estimate from the list the number of nonzero clusters and from the screening the average number eligible per cluster. The product of these last two is an estimate of the number of persons in the special population who have a nonzero probability of selection. The difference between the total estimate and the estimate of those with nonzero probabilities would indicate potential bias.

The cost function for using lists is very similar to those already discussed. Let C_L be the cost for a unit on the list. Then the total cost is represented by:

$$C_M = mk \left[C_I + \frac{(1-t)}{\pi} C_S \right] + m \left[C_I + C_L \right], \qquad 12.$$

and

$$k_{opt} = \left[\frac{C_I + C_L}{C_I + \frac{(1-t)}{\pi} C_S} \left(\frac{1-\rho}{\rho} \right) \right]^{1/2} \qquad 13.$$

The cost per case using optimum clustering is

$$C_I + \frac{(1 - t)}{\pi} C_S + \frac{C_L}{(k + 1)_{\text{opt}}}, \qquad 14.$$

and the cost per an equivalent unclustered case is

$$C_{ME} = (1 + \rho k) \left[C_I + \frac{(1 - t)}{\pi} C_S + \frac{C_L}{(k + 1)_{\text{opt}}} \right]. \qquad 15.$$

Use of Combined Methods

The use of combined procedures is common in survey sampling. A mail questionnaire may be followed by telephone interviews to a sample of nonrespondents. Telephone interviews may be combined with face-to-face interviews of households without telephones. The standard optimization methods allocate sampling rates to the procedures inversely to the square root of the ratios of costs. Bayesian allocation procedures result in the elimination of very costly procedures when the reduction in variance would be small and resources are limited.

In the screening of special populations, one would be very unlikely to use combined methods if a list is 95% complete, since the marginal reduction in total survey error would be negligible. Suppose, however, a list includes clusters where 50–90% of a special population live. Then, combined methods become necessary. Note that if one uses lists, the costs of the other screening methods increase, since one is now attempting to locate only those clusters with a zero probability of selection from the list.

Variations in Density of Special Populations in Nonzero Clusters

We now consider the situation where the special population is unevenly distributed among the nonzero clusters. This would be likely to occur with ethnic groups where most members live in a few clusters with high proportions of the population, but others are thinly spread among the general population. It is possible to have identified these clusters from earlier screening or Census data or by asking the first contacted household(s) to estimate π_j.

TELEPHONE SCREENING   Assume first that the nonzero clusters have been identified and categorized into strata where π_j is the proportion of the special population to the total population in stratum j. With telephone screening, no clustering is required, and the cost per case in the jth stratum is:

$$C_{P_j} = C_I + C_S/\pi_j .$$

An optimum allocation procedure would be to sample from the strata with rates inversely proportional to the square roots of costs. Thus, the relative rates in strata A and B would be:

$$\frac{r_A}{r_B} = \left(\frac{C_I + C_S/\pi_B}{C_I + C_S/\pi_A}\right)^{1/2} . \tag{21.}$$

If there is a screening or list cost, the procedures in the second section apply. Then, from Formula 5,

$$\frac{r_A}{r_B} = \left\{\frac{[1 + \rho(k_B - 1)]}{[1 + \rho(k_A - 1)]} \frac{\left[C_I + (1 - t)\dfrac{C_T}{\pi_B} + tC_S/(k_B - 1)\right]}{\left[C_I + C_S\dfrac{(1 - t)}{\pi_A} + tC_S/(k_A - 1)\right]}\right\}^{1/2} . \tag{22.}$$

FACE-TO-FACE SCREENING   Face-to-face screening would require clustering. Again assuming that the nonzero clusters have been identified, the total cost in the jth stratum would be:

$$C_{Fj} = mk\left(C_I + \frac{C_S}{j}\right) + mC_T , \tag{23.}$$

and

$$k_{opt} = \left[\frac{C_T}{C_I + \dfrac{C_S}{\pi_j}} \left(\frac{1 - \rho}{\rho}\right)\right]^{1/2} . \tag{24.}$$

The cost per equivalent case in the jth stratum is:

$$C_{EJ} = \left[1 + \rho(k + 1)\right]\left[C_I + \frac{C_S}{\pi} + \frac{C_T}{k}\right], \tag{25.}$$

and

$$\frac{r_A}{r_B} = (C_{EB}/C_{EA})^{1/2} . \tag{26.}$$

Effects of Disproportionate Sampling

Sometimes the special population is known to be more heavily concentrated in certain sectors of the population. These sectors may well be geographical areas, but they could equally be identified in some other way. For instance, another type of sector with a heavy concentration is a list frame, with unlisted members of the special population selected by area sampling. In such cases, the sectors may be taken to be strata, with the strata containing greater concentrations of the special population that is sampled at higher rates.

The justification for this approach is that it permits more of the survey resources to be devoted to collecting data from sampled members of the special population and less to screening out nonmembers. The gains from the approach are, however, often not as great as one might at first expect. Consider the simple case of two strata, stratum 1 with a relatively high concentration of the special population (P_1) and stratum 2 with a relatively low concentration (P_2); let the members of the special population have similar characteristics in the two strata. If the costs of data collection for sampled members of the special population are the same as the cost of screening out nonmembers, the optimum allocation of the sample for estimating a population mean is to sample stratum 1 at a rate $\sqrt{P_1/P_2}$ higher than the rate for the stratum 2. As Waksberg (1978) shows, the gains from using this allocation over a proportionate allocation are fairly small unless the concentration in stratum 1 is much greater than in stratum 2. Moreover, as Kalton & Anderson (1986) point out, the costs of screening out nonmembers of the special population may be appreciably smaller than the costs of data collection from members. When this applies, the optimum allocation is less skewed towards stratum 1, and the gains from the optimum allocation are even less than when the screening costs and data collection costs are the same.

Kalton & Anderson (1986) give tables that show that substantial gains from disproportionate stratification accrue only when P_1 is much greater than P_2, and when a high proportion of the special population—i.e. 80% or more—is in the first stratum. As an illustration, suppose that the costs of data collection for sampled members of the special population are the same as the costs of screening out nonmembers, and that the special population comprises 5% of the total population. Then, if $P_1 = 50\%$ and the percentage of the overall population in stratum 1 (W_1) is 5%, it follows that $P_2 = 2.6\%$ and the percentage of the special population in stratum 1 (A_1) is 50%. In this case, even though $P_1/P_2 = 19$, the optimum disproportionate allocation decreases the variance of a sample mean for the special population (other things being equal) only by a factor of 0.72. On the other hand if $P_1 = 50\%$, but W_1 is increased to 8%, then $P_2 = 1.1\%$, $A_1 = 80\%$, and the disproportionate allocation decreases the variance by a factor of 0.47. In the limit, if $P_1 = 50\%$ and $W_1 = 10\%$, all the special population is in the first stratum, so that $P_2 = 0$ and $A_1 = 100$; in this case the variance is decreased by a factor of 0.1 since no sampling is needed in the second stratum.

SPECIAL LOCATION SAMPLES

Special population samples may sometimes be defined by their activities, such as shopping, boating, hunting, camping, or traveling, either at a given location or as a more general activity. For some of these special populations it is far more effective to locate and interview respondents at the locations rather than at home.

Aspects of Sampling on Location

There are three major aspects of sampling on location: determining where to sample, when to sample, and accounting for the fact that different persons visit the location with different frequencies. Sudman (1980) discussed these issues with reference to shopping center sampling. Here we generalize to any location.

WHERE TO SAMPLE   Selection of respondents may be done as they enter or leave the location or as they move around within it. Selecting respondents as they arrive or leave is the simplest procedure because it does not require information on how much time has been spent in the location. This information is needed if the sampling is done within the location; otherwise persons who spend more time in it would have a higher probability of selection.

For sampling entrants, an unbiased sample requires that all entrances have some probability of selection. Sampling can be done at entrances even if the interviewing facilities are within the location. If, for convenience or because it is required, the sample selection is conducted within the location, locations should be selected randomly with probabilities proportionate to traffic, as with entrances.

TIME SAMPLING   The characteristics of persons visiting locations vary by season of the year, day of the week, time of day, and other less predictable factors, such as whether or not it is raining and whether there are special events. We assume, however, that the time period for the study has been determined so that seasonal factors can be ignored.

Time segments are essentially no different from geographic clusters and may be sampled in the same way. The first thing to decide is the length of the time segments to be sampled. Their length would probably depend on the length of the interview and other administrative considerations.

Though the simplest design is to sample all eligible time periods with equal probability, this is not an efficient design. Time periods in which there are few persons will yield small samples, and this will be inefficient. Note that the problem is identical to that of the method of selecting locations.

The solution is identical—sampling time periods with probabilities proportionate to the number of persons expected in the time period. Measures of visits by time periods can be obtained from previous counts. It would probably be necessary to have these counts over more than just a single week to average out the effects of climate and special events.

Once the probability of selection of a time period is determined, the sampling of persons in that time period can be made inversely proportional to that probability, so that the final sample of visitors is self-weighting to that point.

Although they are discussed separately, time and location sampling would be conducted simultaneously.

PROBABILITY OF VISIT   With location sampling, individuals' or households' probabilities of selection are a function of when individuals or members of households visit, where they enter, and how often. We have discussed how to obtain an equal probability sample of customers by when and where they visit—day of week, time of day, location, etc. It is important to sample these variables carefully because there is no practical way to control for them by questioning the respondent. It asks too much of human memory to determine from respondents all the "where and when" details of earlier trips. The probability of an individual or household being selected for the sample varies with the number of visits made to the location in the time period for the survey. Information on the number of visits made is thus needed to make weighting adjustments in the analysis. Respondents can report reasonably accurate estimates of their numbers of previous trips provided that the time period is sufficiently short.

LENGTH OF TIME PERIOD   Visits to locations, like other types of activities, are subject to two kinds of forgetting—omissions and telescoping (see Sudman & Bradburn 1974). The time period should be selected so as to minimize the net memory error. Also the sampling variability in the estimate is a decreasing function of the time period. For both of these reasons, periods that are too short (a week or less) or too long (several months) should not be used. On the basis of experience with medical events and consumer expenditures, a period of from two weeks to a month seems optimum.

The question could be asked in the following way: "How many other times, not including today, have you visited in the past two weeks (month), that is since (date)?" The assumption in using this question is not that all respondents can answer it perfectly, but that the net errors across all respondents are small and that these errors are unrelated to the topic being studied.

If sampling is done within the location and not at entrances, an additional question must be asked to determine when the trip started. That question might be phrased: "Do you remember what time you arrived here today?" The assumption in using this question is that the probability of selection of a respondent at a random point within the shopping center is proportional to the length of time that the respondent has been in the location.

Weighting

For samples of entrants to or leavers from a location, a sample estimate of a parameter for the population of visitors during the survey time period can be obtained by weighting inversely by the number of visits in that period. Thus, respondents who have not visited the location in the past period except for the current visit would have a weight of 1; those who visited one other time would have a weight of 1/2; those who visited two other times would have weight of 1/3, etc.

Similarly, for samples of visitors within the location, respondents could be given weights inversely proportioned to the lengths of their visits. To simplify this process, time would be measured in quarter or half hours because respondent estimates would probably be rounded off in any event.

The estimates obtained by inverse weighting are not unbiased; individuals who did not visit a location during the period have a zero probability of inclusion. An unbiased estimate can be made if one knows the fraction of the population not visiting a shopping center during the period and if one imputes the characteristics of the visiters who visited a shopping center once to this group.

In some cases, one would be interested not in the population of visitors of a facility, but rather in the population of visits. In this case the sample of entrants can be used without additional weighting.

Some of the methods proposed here for location sampling are similar to those that have been proposed for counting of mobile animal or human populations at selected locations. See for example Cowan (1982, 1984), Cowan & Malec (1984), Bailey (1951), Chapman (1954), Darroch (1958, 1959), Fuller & Goebel (1978), Hammersley (1953), Jolly (1965), Leslie (1952, 1953), Robson & Wright (1977), and Seber (1962, 1973). The key difference between human and animal populations is that humans can report past behavior, although not always accurately. Capture-recapture procedures would be preferred to asking simply for visits to a location when there was concern that a visitor could not provide reasonably accurate information on number of previous visits in a specified time period. It must be recognized, however, that human capture-recapture also has problems. Thus, in a study of homeless persons, one must determine whether a person who is sampled during the recapture study was also sampled during the original capture study. Especially in cases of difficult mobile populations, this identification may also be difficult.

SUMMARY

We have described a wide range of alternative methods that can be used for careful sampling of special populations. The use of single or multiple lists, even when incomplete, is generally efficient, although if the list is too incomplete supplementary procedures may be necessary. Since screening is so expensive, the use of telephone procedures and sometimes mail techniques can reduce costs substantially.

If special populations are clustered, the following alternative methods should be considered for reducing screening costs:

1. Telephone or mail screening to determine and eliminate zero segments by initial contact with a single unit.
2. Use of two or three initial contacts per site if face-to-face screening is required.
3. Use of lists to identify nonzero segments, if the percentage of the special population living in areas not covered by the lists is small.
4. Use of combined methods, such as telephone and list screening or telephone screening and face-to-face interviews, if no single procedure is sufficient.
5. Reducing the sampling rate in nonzero areas that have relatively low densities of the special population.

If members of the special population are very heavily concentrated in certain areas with only a few members in other areas, it will be worthwhile to oversample the denser areas. In some cases it may be reasonable to omit the very lightly populated areas entirely.

For some populations, obtaining additional information from respondents about members of their networks can substantially reduce the amount of screening required if this information can be obtained with reasonable accuracy. Snowball samples are a special example of this and are efficient if the total population is small and can be completely identified.

Finally, some special populations are defined by their activities and can be sampled at special locations where they participate in these activities. For these special populations it is important that there be some measure of intensity of usage.

The use of this range of alternative sampling procedures for special populations should be carefully considered before resorting to ad hoc convenience samples, especially if one wishes to generalize to the total special population.

Literature Cited

Bailey, N. T. J. 1951. On estimating the size of mobile populations from capture-recapture data, *Biometrika* 38:293–96

Bergsten, J. W., Pierson, S. A. (1982). Telephone screening for rare characteristics using multiplicity counting rules. *Proc. Sect. Surv. Res. Meth., Am. Stat. Assoc.,* pp. 145–50. Washington, DC

Biernacki, P., Waldorf, D. (1981). Snowball sampling: Problems and techniques of chain referral sampling. *Sociol. Meth. Res.* 10:141–63

Blair, J., Czaja, R. (1982). Locating a special population using random digit dialing. *Public Opin. Q.* 46:585–90

Brown, C., Ritchie, J. (1981). *Focussed Enumeration. The Development of a Method for Sampling Ethnic Minority Groups.* Policy Stud. Inst. Soc. Community Plann. Res., London

Chapman, D. G. (1954). The estimation of biological populations. *Ann. Math. Stat.* 25:1–15

Cowan, C. D. (1982). Modifications to capture-recapture estimation in the presence of errors in the data. Proc. Am. Stat. Assoc., Biometrics Section. Washington, DC

Cowan, C. D. (1984). *The effects of misclassification on estimates from capture-recapture studies.* PhD thesis. George Washington Univ., Washington, DC

Cowan, C. D., Malec, D. J. (1984). Capture-recapture models when both sources have clustered observations. Proc. Sect. Surv. Res. Meth. Am. Stat. Assoc., pp. 461–66 Washington, DC

Czaja, R., Warnecke, R. B., Eastman, E., Royston, R., Sirken, M., Tutuer, D. (1984). Locating patients with rare diseases using network sampling: Frequency and quality of reporting. In *Health Survey Research Methods, 1982,* ed. C. F. Cannell, R. M. Goves, pp. 311–324. Publ. No. (PHS) 84-3346. US Dep. Health Hum. Serv., Washington, DC

Darroch, J. N. (1958, 1959). The multiple-recapture census I & II. *Biometrika,* 45:343–59, 46:336–51

Deming, W. E. (1977). An essay on screening, or a two-phase sampling, applied to surveys of a community. *Int. Stat. Rev.,* 45:29–37

Fuller, W. A., Goebel, J. J. (1978). On the estimation of season total number of different households utilizing a park, *Biometrics* 34:139–41

Greeley, A., Rossi, P. H. (1966). *The Education of Catholic Americans.* Chicago: Aldine

Groves, R. M., Kahn, R. L. (1979), *Surveys by Telephone: A National Comparison with Personal Interviews.* New York: Academic

Hammersley, J. M. (1953). Capture-recapture analysis. *Biometrika* 40:265–78

Hansen, M. H., Hurwitz, W. N., Madow, W. G. (1953). *Sample Survey Methods and Theory,* Vol. 1. Wiley: New York

Harris, D. R. et al, (1982). *Compensation and Support for Illness and Injury.* London. Macmillan

Hartley, H. O. (1962). Multiple frame surveys. *Proc. Soc. Stat. Sect., Am. Stat. Assoc.* pp. 203–6. Washington, DC

Hartley, H. O. (1974). Multiple frame methodology and selected applications. *Sankhya C* 36:99–118

Hunt, A. (1978). *The Elderly at Home.* London: Her Majesty's Stationery Off.

Jolly, G. M. (1965), Explicit estimates from capture-recapture data with both death and immigration—stochastic model. *Biometrika* 52:225–47

Kalton, G., Anderson, D. (1986). Sampling rare populations. *J. Royal Stat. Soc.* 149: Forthcoming

Kish, L. (1965). *Survey Sampling.* New York: Wiley

Leslie, P. H. (1952, 1953). The estimation of population parameters obtained by means of the capture-recapture method I & II. *Biometrika* 38:269–92, 39:363–88

Nathan, G. (1976). An empirical study of response and sampling errors for multiplicity estimates with different counting rules. *J. Am. Stat. Assoc.* 71:808–15

Robson, D. S., Wright, V. J. (1977). Estimation of season total number of different households utilizing a park. *Biometrics* 33:421–5

Rossi, P. H., Crain, R. (1968). The NORC permanent community sample. *Public Opin. Q.* 32:261–72

Rothbart, G. S., Fine, M., Sudman, S. (1982). On finding and interviewing the needles in a haystack: The use of multiplicity sampling. *Public Opin. Q.* 46:408–21

Seber, G. A. F. (1962). The multi-sample single recapture census. *Biometrika* 49:339–49

Seber, G. A. F. (1973). *The Estimation of Animal Abundance and Related Parameters.* New York: Hafner

Sirken, M. G. (1970). Household surveys with multiplicity. *J. Am. Stat. Assoc.* 65:257–66

Sirken, M. G. (1972). Stratified sample surveys with multiplicity. *J. Am. Stat. Assoc.* 67:224–27

Sirken, M. G. Graubard, B. I., McDaniel, M. J. (1978). National network surveys of diabetes. *Proc. Section Surv. Res. Meth., Am. Stat. Assoc.* pp. 631–35. Washington, DC

Sirken, M. G., Royston, P., Warnecke, R., Eastman, E., Czaja, R., Monsees, D. 1980. Pilot of the national cost of cancer care survey. *Proc. Section Surv. Res. Meth., Am. Stat. Assoc.* pp. 579–84. Washington, DC

Snow, R. E., Hutcheson, J. D., Prather, J. E.

(1981). Using reputational sampling to identify residential clusters of minorities dispersed in a large urban region: Hispanics in Atlanta, Georgia. *Proc. Section Surv. Res. Meth. Am. Stat. Assoc.* pp. 101–6. Washington, DC

Sudman, S. 1967. *Reducing the Cost of Surveys.* Chicago: Aldine

Sudman, S. 1972. On sampling of very rare human populations. *J. Am. Stat. Assoc.* 67:335–39

Sudman, S. 1978. Optimum cluster designs within a primary unit using combined telephone screening and face-to-face interviewing. *J. Am. Stat. Assoc.* 73:300–4

Sudman, S. 1976. *Applied Sampling.* New York: Academic

Sudman, S. 1980. Improving the quality of shopping center sampling. *J. Marketing Res.* 17:423–31

Sudman, S. (1985a). "Efficient screening methods for the sampling of geographically clustered special populations. *J. Marketing Res.* 22:20–29

Sudman, S. (1985b). Experiments in the measurement of the size of social networks. *Soc. Networks* 7:127–51

Sudman, S., Bradburn, N. M. (1974). *Response Effects in Surveys: A Review and Synthesis.* Chicago: Aldine

Waksberg, J. (1978). Sampling methods for random digit dialing. *J. Am. Stat. Assoc.* 73:40–46

Waksberg, J. (1983). A note on locating a special population using random digit dialing. *Public Opin. Q.* 47:576–79

Welch, J. (1975). Sampling by referral in a dispersed population. *Public Opin. Q.* 39:237–45

Ann. Rev. Sociol. 1986. 12:431–49

TOWARD A STRUCTURAL CRIMINOLOGY: METHOD AND THEORY IN CRIMINOLOGICAL RESEARCH

John Hagan

Faculty of Law, University of Toronto, 78 Queen's Park Crescent, Toronto, Ontario, Canada

Alberto Palloni

Department of Sociology, University of Wisconsin, Madison, Wisconsin 53706

Abstract

This paper calls for a structural criminology that is distinguished by its attention to power relations and by the priority it assigns them in addressing criminological issues. Dominant criminological paradigms both imply and deny what structural criminology requires. That is, our theories often imply that crime is a product of power relations, but our methodologies commonly ignore this premise. We make this point first with a preliminary review of prominent sociological theories of crime and then by a more systematic review of three research literatures: on class and criminality, on criminal sentencing, and on the family and delinquency. The paper concludes with an argument that a new focus on the relationship between gender and crime can provide a new starting point in the development of a structural criminology that is a more sociological criminology as well.

INTRODUCTION

Methodology is a term with many meanings. The meaning we adopt in this essay is suggested by Hirschi & Selvin (1967:4) when they note that the core of

431

0360-0572/86/0815-0431$02.00

methodology "lies in the relation between data and theory, the ways in which sociologists use empirical observations to formulate, test, and refine statements about the social world." Sociologists who study crime frequently have failed in their methodology because they have ignored a sociological premise that underwrites much criminological thinking. This premise, sometimes implicit and sometimes explicit, is that the meaning and explanation of crime is to be found in its structural foundations. This premise distinguishes what we will call *structural criminology*. Before we argue the value of this premise, we first clarify what is meant by it.

Social structure is formed out of relations between actors. These actors may be individual or corporate in form, and their relations may be ones of affiliation as well as subordination. These structural relations are organized along both horizontal and vertical lines.

Structural relations organized along vertical, hierarchical lines of power are of greatest interest to criminologists. Perhaps this is because crime itself implies a power relationship. To perpetrate a crime is often to impose one's power on others, while to be punished for a crime is to be subjected to the power of others. Structural criminology is distinguished by its attention to power relations and by the priority it assigns them in addressing criminological issues.

Dominant criminological paradigms both imply and deny what structural criminology requires. That is, our theories often imply that crime is a product of power relations, but our methodologies conventionally ignore this premise. We make this point first by assertion and then by a more systematic review of three research literatures.

Consider the following. Labelling theory (e.g. Becker 1963, Lemert 1967) focuses on the roles of crime control agents in defining crime; the theory makes clear that there can be no crime without reactions to it by empowered others. Yet research guided by labelling theory seldom has *measured* the power relations of interacting actors and reactors. Similarly, conflict theory (e.g. Turk 1969, Quinney 1970, Chambliss & Seidman 1971, Taylor et al 1973) focuses on the roles of class and status group characteristics in guiding the reactions of crime control agents to the group-linked behaviors of others. However, research in the conflict tradition seldom has measured class or status group memberships in the kinds of relational terms that determine the location of individuals in positions of power. Finally, control theory (e.g. Hirschi 1969) focuses on links between individual actors and institutions like the family. However, research by control theorists is often more concerned with measuring the attitudinal consequences of these links than with studying the linkages per se and the group-linked power relationships they reflect.

Our argument does not diminish the above theoretical traditions. Each is important for its unique explanatory insights. Each has helped spawn new research literatures. And, most importantly for our purposes, each calls attention to a role of social structure in defining and explaining crime. The problem is the translation of these theoretical insights into the structural study of crime. Methodologically, the structural implications of these theoretical traditions have been ignored. Thus far, we have made this point by assertion. This point can be made empirically with evidence drawn from three research literatures: on class and criminality, on criminal sentencing, and on the family and delinquency. Each of these literatures is highly influenced by one or more of the theories we have considered. Each, we argue, can be better guided by a methodology that is more consistent with the structural premises of the theories.

CLASS AND CRIMINALITY

The literature on class and criminality is important, complicated, and controversial. It is important because so many of our theories are based on assumptions about the relationship between class and criminality (Hirschi 1972). However, this literature is also complicated by the many meanings and measures that attach to the concepts of class and criminality. Edwin Sutherland (1945, 1949) raised (without resolving) many of these issues, while inventing one of modern sociology's most popular concepts: "white collar crime."

Sutherland's approach to the study of white collar crime was explicitly structural in his acknowledgment of differential social organization, his insistence that white collar crime was organized crime, and his use of corporations as units in his most famous research (1949). Nonetheless, Sutherland's definition of white collar crime, "as crime committed by a person of respectability and high social status in the course of his occupation" (p. 9), has troubled researchers (see Geis & Meier 1977). This definition shifted attention away from corporations as the units of study, and it grounded the measurement of class position in reputational notions of "respect" and "status." Structural measures of class position, grounded in relations of ownership and authority, speak more directly to the kinds of theoretical issues (i.e. issues of power and its corporate corruption) that interested Sutherland. Structurally conceived variables speak directly to these issues by measuring location in positions of ownership and authority, rather than indirectly by making inferences from titles of occupations or scales of occupational prestige (see, for example, Wright 1977, Robinson & Kelly 1979). In this sense, structural measures of class not only locate individuals above or below one another, they locate individuals in terms of their relation to one another in the social organization of work. This argument has been made most prominantly in the study of class relations by Erik Wright (e.g. Wright 1977), but the point has a broader application.

For example, the substitution of relational measures of class for reputational and gradational measures clarifies one aspect of the relationship between class position and white collar criminality that has often remained moot. It does so by making explicit that owners of businesses and persons with occupational authority are located in positions of power that allow use of organizational (usually corporate) resources to commit larger crimes than can persons located in employee positions without authority. It is this element of power in the social organization of work and the kinds of crime this power allows, apart from the simple relationship between status and the size of these crimes, that is of theoretical interest and importance (Hagan & Parker 1985). As Wheeler & Rothman (1982:1406; see also Clinard & Yeager 1980) note, the corporation and access to its resources "is for white collar criminals what the gun or knife is for the common criminal—a tool to obtain money from victims." Status measures obscure this structural insight.

However, meaningful measures of class are only part of the issue of class and criminality. Sutherland anticipates our further difficulties in his assertion that some civil offenses are also crimes. Insofar as there exists a "legal description of acts as socially injurious and legal provision of a penalty for the act," Sutherland (1945:44) insists that these acts are crimes (cf Tappan 1947). Today this position is not so much disputed as ignored in the class and criminality debate; thus, the advantages of using relational measures of class are obviated.

For example, statistics on sometimes deadly white collar crimes have the potential to change the way we think about the class-crime connection. Consider one kind of white collar crime: Schrager & Short (1978:333) call it "organizational crime"—those crimes of corporate actors (individuals and collectivities) that cause physical harm to employees. Such "occupational deaths" far outnumber deaths resulting from murder (Geis 1975). It is estimated (e.g. Page & O'Brian 1973, US Department of Labor 1973, Glasbeek & Rowland 1979) that every year more than 14,000 Americans are killed in on-the-job accidents, while more than 2,000,000 are injured. Job-related illnesses may cause as many as 100,000 deaths a year. Schrager & Short (1978:334n) indicate that in the United States comparable common crime statistics for 1970 include 16,000 cases of murder and nonnegligent manslaughter, approximately 7,000 cases of manslaughter caused by negligence, and 335,000 cases of aggravated assault. In Canada (see Reasons et al 1981), "occupational deaths" rank third after heart disease and cancer as a source of mortality, accounting for more than ten times as many deaths as murder.

All or most such deaths may not result from employer intent, but neither do they result predominantly from employee carelessness. One recent estimate (see Reasons et al 1981:7) is that "approximately 39% of the job injuries in the U.S. are due to illegal working conditions, while another 24% are due to legal but unsafe conditions. At the most, a third of accidents are due to unsafe acts." Meanwhile, there are numerous examples of employers intentionally, knowingly or negligently, creating hazards; failing to follow administrative orders to alter dangerous situations; and covering up the creation and existence of such hazards. The case of asbestos poisoning involving administrative decisions within the Johns-Mansville corporation is one of the best known of these examples. Ermann & Lundman (1980) argue that such deaths occur in large numbers, and Swartz (1978) concludes that they should be recognized as a form of murder, or what sometimes is called "corporate homicide."

We need not here debate the fine points in defining corporate homicide or establish precisely how many such homicides occur. It is enough to note that such deaths occur in great numbers; that corporate homicides involve, in addition, many consumers and other members of the general public; and that corporate homicides seem likely to rival or exceed in number the deaths resulting from homicide conceived in traditional terms. Our immediate interest is in the meaning of corporate homicide for the class-crime controversy and the structural study of crime.

However, we first must make several points about more conventional forms of crime and delinquency. The birth cohort analyses of Wolfgang and his colleagues (1972) and the work of Greenwood (1979) reveal that while the prevalence of "street crime" may be low in the general population, the incidence among those few offenders involved in these acts can be quite high. Wilson (1975) uses these findings to argue for selective incapacitation. However, a broader methodological point is also made. That is, while a behavior may not be highly prevalent in the general population, its high incidence among selected members of that population may still be of great importance in developing an understanding of the behavior and its distribution across the population. Because of their reliance on central tendencies, correlational techniques may obscure this point. This is especially likely when correlational techniques are used to analyze self-report surveys of the general population. Such surveys are unlikely to locate many of these behaviors and are further compromised for these purposes by the difficulties of sampling small class segments (e.g. the employer or capitalist class makes up a minute part of the general population) and by the inadequate operationalization of categorizing concepts such as class.

So if crimes such as corporate homicide occur with high incidence but low prevalence, among highly selected subpopulations (for example, particular employers in particular kinds of industries), they are unlikely to be identified in meaningful ways with correlational analyses based on self-report data and the measurement of status rather than class. Relational measures of class, more revealing measures of crime, and modes of analysis that are unaffected by highly skewed distributions are required.

Finally, implicit in our discussion of street crimes of violence and corporate homicide is the likelihood that crime is not a unidimensional concept. Class measured in relational terms is connected to various kinds of criminal and delinquent behavior in different ways. For example, among adults, while class probably is related *negatively* to street crimes of violence involving direct physical attacks (Nettler 1978), it is also likely that class is related *positively* to harms caused less directly, through criminal acts involving corporate resources. Similarly, among juveniles it may be that some common acts of delinquency are related positively to class (Hagan et al 1985; see also Cullen et al 1985), while other more "serious" acts of delinquency are related negatively to class (Colvin & Pauley 1983; Braithwaite 1981; Elliot & Ageton 1980; Hindelang et al 1979, 1981; Kleck 1982; Thornberry & Farnsworth 1982). It frequently appears that reputational or gradational measures of status are not related to crime and delinquency at all (Tittle et al 1978). Nonetheless, there is increasing reason to believe that class measured relationally is connected to crime and delinquency in interesting, albeit more complicated, ways. We develop this point further in our discussion of the family and delinquency below. Meanwhile, a structural criminology urges us to incorporate relational measures of class, to reconsider what is meant by criminality, and to move beyond the assumption that the relationship between class and criminality is linear or additive in form.

CRIMINAL SENTENCING

If power relations influence criminal behavior, it seems likely that they also influence reactions to these behaviors, although perhaps again in more complicated ways than is commonly assumed in the methodology of this research. The research on criminal sentencing is probably the most highly developed literature on reactions to crime (see, for example, Hogarth 1971, Blumstein et al 1983). Perhaps this is because the issue of equality in sentencing is such a visible and symbolically important part of the criminal justice system (Arnold 1967). It may be a prerequisite that such a symbolic issue is addressed in simplified ways; that is, for an issue to become important symbolically, perhaps it must be framed in simple terms. In any case, this seems frequently to have been true in discussions of equality in sentencing, to the detriment of research in this area.

The measurement of class is again a prominent factor in this research literature. While the largest volume of research on equality in sentencing has focused on the issue of race (Kleck 1981), it may be that class is the more salient factor (Hagan & Bumiller 1983). Once more, however, this point has been obscured by the substitution of status for class measures (e.g. Chiricos & Waldo 1975). Structural—that is relational—measures of class make more explicit the ways class might influence sentencing. For example, relational measures highlight positions of persons who are unemployed (e.g. Hagan & Albonetti 1982). It is likely the fact of *unemployment,* more directly than low social status, that leads to punitive sentencing decisions. That is, it is probably the position of powerlessness that unemployment directly implies, rather than a relative deprivation of status, that better accounts for punitive sentencing decisions. Indeed, the law scarcely bothers to deny this.

Many sentencing guidelines and criminal codes designate unemployment as a legitimate criterion in determining pretrial release and the use of probation (Bernstein et al 1977, Nagel 1983). Perhaps this is why the research literature on sentencing has not devoted much attention to the direct and indirect influence of unemployment on sentencing decisions (although see, for example, Lizotte 1978). The search has been for extralegal influences that would discredit sentencing decisions in the very terms the system itself defines as illegitimate. Race is clearly illegitimate and therefore receives the greater attention. The structural significance of unemployment and of its embeddedness in the decision-making rules is overlooked.

Meanwhile, race also is often considered astructurally. Typically, the significance of race is assumed, apart from whom or what the offender has offended against, and without consideration of the period or place of sentencing. This may be because the influence of race is so clearly understood as illegitimate. However, the structural context in which race operates may be determinative of its influence. That is, the significance of race may derive from specific power relationships.

The best understood examples of this involve the role of race in sentencing when the race of the victim is also salient. For example, homicide and assault are characteristically *intra*racial offenses. When a black offender assaults or kills a black victim, the less powerful position of the black victim often combines with the paternalistic attitudes of white authorities to justify lenient treatment (Kleck 1981; see also Myrdal 1944, Garfinkel 1949). Rape, on the other hand, is more frequently *inter*racial. When a black violates a white victim, the high sexual property value attached to the white victims (which derives from the power positions of their significant others) and the racial fears of authorities serve to justify severe treatment (LaFree 1980; see also Wolfgang & Riedel 1973). Robbery is also increasingly interracial. The higher value attached to white property by its more powerful owners and the fears of white authorities may here also lead to more severe sentences for black offenders (Thomson & Zingraff 1981).

Note, however, that the above studies only consider crimes involving victims of interpersonal violence (homicide, assault, rape), or the threat of it (robbery). Such offenses constitute a small, albeit important, part of the American crime problem. However, this kind of structural analysis can be extended to include the so-called "victimless" crimes. For example, during a Nixon administration antidrug crusade (see Peterson & Hagan 1984), a set of relational distinctions was developed involving the identification of victims and villains within the drug trade. This crusade involved a compromise between conservative and liberal impulses; the "big dealers" were identified as villains, while middle-class youth and blacks (but the latter only insofar as they were rarely big dealers in a racially stratified drug trade) were reconceived as victims. The assignment of victim status was prompted by the relative power of middle-class parents and was generalized to ordinary black drug offenders (Peterson 1985). The most dramatic effects of this new conceptualization were the increasingly punitive treatment of big dealers in the place and period studied (1969–1973 in the Southern Federal District Court of New York City), combined with lenient treatment of ordinary black drug offenders and the very severe treatment of black big dealers. More generally, these findings suggest that while there may be a trend toward equality in American criminal sentencing, patterns of differential leniency and severity only become apparent through consideration of the structural contexts in which sentencing decisions are made (see also Zatz 1984). When focused on a single period and place, without consideration of how variation in contextual variables affect relational conceptions, studies miss a key element in the structural understanding of reactions to crime.

A structural understanding of criminal sentencing also includes consideration of the different kinds of actors, corporate as well as individual, that are involved in criminal cases. We have noted that the organizational form of the corporation is crucial to understanding the class-crime connection (see also Reiss 1981, Ermann & Lundman 1980, Wheeler 1976), and more generally it is apparent that "those interests that have been successfully collected to create corporate actors are the interests that dominate the society" (Coleman 1974:49). Corporate actors are powerful participants in the legal process. But the corporation is a "legal fiction," with, as H. L. Mencken aptly observed, "no pants to kick or soul to damn." So corporations are "juristic persons" that the law chooses to treat, for many practical purposes, like "natural persons." However, the limits noted by Mencken are apparent in the impossibility of imprisoning or executing corporations. A result is that little research has been done on the relative experiences of individual and corporately organized actors in the criminal courts. Nonetheless, important possibilities do exist.

One possibility in studying the sanctioning of white collar criminals is to make the use of corporate resources a central variable in examining the treatment of offenders. Wheeler & Rothman (1982) illustrate how such measures may be applied, and recent work (see Hagan & Parker 1985) demonstrates that such measures are important in determining how alternative kinds of statutes are used to prosecute white collar offenders. This work suggests that employers are becoming increasingly adept in using the power that derives from their structural location in the social organization of work to distance and disengage themselves from the crimes that they encourage subordinates to commit (see also Farberman 1975, Baumhart 1961, Brenner & Molander 1977). The effect is to leave the latter more open to the application of criminal sanctions (Hagan & Parker 1985, Schrager & Short 1978:410, Dershowitz 1961).

A second possibility involves studying the role of corporate actors in initiating and influencing prosecutions of individual actors. Grocery stores, department stores, drug stores, and many other kinds of commercial establishments are heavily involved in bringing charges against individuals. This makes possible the analysis of the relative influence of corporate and individual actors in using the criminal courts. Although little research has been done, there is some evidence (Hagan 1982, Albonetti 1985, Krutschnitt 1985) that corporate actors are more likely than individuals who bring such cases to obtain convictions, and the likelihood of conviction increases with organization size. Further, when corporate actors are in the role of complainants, there is some evidence that sentencing disparities by characteristics of individuals decrease. Corporate actors may encourage formal rationality, simultaneously increasing convictions and decreasing sentencing disparities. More research is needed, but it is clear that the power of corporate and individual actors to influence case outcomes can be compared in significant ways.

Differences also exist in the power of actors within the courts to influence outcomes, although this too remains largely unstudied. Actors in the judicial system do not simply exist alongside one another, but in relation to one another, with variation in the power to determine outcomes.

For example, while common sense may dictate that judges alone control sentencing, Eisenstein & Jacob (1977:37) note that "the judge does not rule or govern, at most, he manages, and often he is managed by others." Probation officers and prosecutors often are involved in sentencing by giving sentence recommendations. Probation officers prepare presentence reports that usually offer evaluations or recommendations for sentencing. Carter & Wilkins (1967; see also Myers 1979, Hagan 1975) cite the close relationship between recommendations of probation officers and final dispositions and suggest that probation officers are a source of disparities in sentencing. However, prosecutors also have a stake in sentencing, as a means of ratifying plea bargains, and judges are sensitive to this. As Simmel (1950) noted, triads are inherently unstable, making the power relationship among probation officers, prosecutors, and judges in sentencing of additional interest. Research (Hagan et al 1979) suggests that prosecutors are more powerful than probation officers in determining the final outcomes. Sentencing may indeed be a lonely task, as judges (e.g. Frankel 1972) lead us to believe. Nonetheless, sentencing does not occur within a social vacuum: Judges too are social actors, influenced by the power relationships that surround and organize their work.

How all of this is perceived by the general public returns us to the symbolic aspect of criminal justice decision-making. Criminal justice is a variable and symbolic phenomenon, open to systematic variation in perception. One reflection of this is that persons located in different power positions vary in the quality of the criminal justice they perceive. Again, the social structure of these perceptions involves the location of individuals in class positions. Members of the surplus population and blacks are more likely than others to perceive criminal injustice (Hagan & Albonetti 1982). Beyond this, however, it appears that black members of the professional managerial class are particularly likely to perceive criminal injustice. Speculation as to why this is the case brings us back to the decisions made. Albonetti et al (1985) demonstrate that black offenders (relative to whites) experience a poorer return on class resources (i.e. income and education) in bail decisions. It may be that black professionals experience various kinds of harassment from authorities, harassment that they had expected their class resources would finally end. Again, the meaning of race varies with the power relationships within which it operates and is experienced.

THE FAMILY, GENDER, AND DELINQUENCY

Power relations may also play a role in mediating links between the family and delinquency, and perhaps adult criminality as well. Indeed, the family may be a crucial link between gender relations and class relations in the causation of delinquency.

Wilkinson (1974) notes that family breakdown was first emphasized as a causal factor in delinquency research at the turn of the century; it was accepted as an important variable until about 1930. For the next 20 years, family breakdown was rejected as a causal factor. Although some signs of renewed interest emerged in the 1950s, to date, concern with the family remains limited. In explanation, Wilkinson suggests that in the early 1900s the family was seen as important because of its near exclusive control over the development of children, and because of a very negative attitude towards divorce. However, in the 1930s many of the family's protective, religious, recreational, and educational functions shifted to other institutions. Meanwhile, attitudes toward divorce were softening. Wilkinson concludes that, ". . . the decline in concern for the . . . home . . . came about not because scientific evidence provided conclusive grounds for rejecting it, but because cultural and ideological factors favoring its acceptance early in this century became less important . . ." (Wilkinson 1974:735).

Meanwhile, the form and significance of the family has indeed changed, with important implications for the understanding of delinquency. Current conceptions of the family derive from an ideal-type patriarchal structure that has characterized western industrial societies. At the core of this kind of family is a separation of roles at work and home, such that women are assigned primary responsibility for domestic social control (Hagan et al 1979). In such families, mothers become instruments and daughters become objects of domestic social control. The essential feature of this kind of family is that mothers (more than fathers) are expected to control their daughters more than their sons. This structural relationship is the key to what Rosabeth Kanter (1974) calls the "intimate oppression" of informal social control, and what radical feminist theory calls "social reproduction" (Vogel 1983). This structural relationship is postulated, in a formulation we call power-control theory (Hagan et al 1985), as the basis of gender differentials in crime and delinquency. Our thesis is that it is this kind of power relationship that keeps girls less delinquent than boys, and women less criminal than men. These same family relationships produce males who are relatively free to offend, often with women as their victims. The theoretical meaning of these family relationships may have been obscured by the tendency of past research to interpret measures of social control within the family as indicators of affection or attachment rather than power and authority, and by the tendency of prior work to overlook the gender stratification of these relationships.

What may make the study of family relations and delinquency important to the understanding of class relations and delinquency is the fundamental premise that work relations are a source of family relations: for example, that patriarchal relations in the household follow causally from male domination in the workplace. These are the class dynamics of the family. Power-control theory argues that to understand the effects of class position in the workplace on crime and delinquency it is necessary to trace the manner in which work relations structure family relations, particularly the instrument-object relationship between mothers and daughters described above.

The approach we are proposing suggests that the class analysis of delinquency, and ultimately of adult criminality as well, should become more fully relational (Hagan et al 1986). It encourages, for example, a focus on workplace relations between actors, and on how these relations position spouses relative to one another in the home. Of course, the ideal typical western industrial family, with the father employed in a position of authority outside the home and the mother not so employed, is only one possibility in a changing world of work relations. The structural theory we are proposing focuses on resulting variation in gender-specific authority relations between parents and children in the home. The theory predicts that these authority relations, and therefore gender differences in delinquency, will be particularly acute in patriarchal family structures and less acute in more egalitarian family structures. The interlocking relationship of work and family structures suggests a link between class and delinquency that has eluded past criminological research, and this holds open the possibility of developing an understanding of a combined role of gender and class in the causation of crime and delinquency. Ironically, a focus on crime and gender might have provided a better beginning to the study of crime in the first place. In fact, it may yet still hold the key to a new start in the development of a structural criminology. To develop this final point further, we must go back to the beginnings of sociological criminology and consider as well some contemporary disagreements about the role of sociology in criminology.

STARTING OVER

Sociology can be considered the scientific study of social relations. The development of a relational methodology in criminological research is therefore not only a call for a structural criminology, but a call for a more sociological criminology as well. The sociological tradition has long been ascendant in criminology (see Gibbons 1979), but today it is increasingly under attack. On the one hand the attack comes from those who see criminology as its own "fully autonomous discipline" (e.g. Thomas 1984), and on the other hand from those in other disciplines (eg. Wilson 1975) who believe their own or some grander combination of disciplines provides a better approach to the study of crime. The structural approach outlined in this paper opposes the separation of criminology from sociology, arguing that the structural foundations of sociology make its explanatory role necessary to the understanding of crime and delinquency.

In this regard, recall how sociology came to the study of crime in the first place. In its formative period, American sociology was unique in its willingness to consider social problems that other established social sciences deemed unimportant or uninteresting. The study of criminal and delinquent behavior is one example. However, the importance of sociology to the study of criminality was more clearly appreciated as it was recognized that most criminal and delinquent behavior occurred within the context of particular social groups that other social groups then attempted to control. These group-based relations were a natural focus for an emergent structural sociology, as represented, for example, in early efforts to develop American sociology at the University of Chicago (see Hinkle 1954).

As satisfying as these early explanatory efforts may have been to sociologists, however, they failed to satisfy those who more single-mindedly sought ways to prevent crime. There is evidence that the meliorative effects of treatment strategies developed out of early Chicago work have been underestimated (see Schlossman 1983). Nonetheless, modern critics, including most notably the political scientist James Q. Wilson (1977; but see also Scheingold 1984, Jacob 1984), have reasoned that the sociological focus on "ultimate" structural causes of criminal and delinquent behavior has impeded the formation of effective crime policies. Wilson (1975:3) writes that "ultimate causes cannot be the object of policy efforts precisely because, being ultimate, they cannot be changed." Regardless of whether one accepts this judgment about the malleability of the causal factors sociologists emphasize, it seems clear that Wilson and representatives of rival disciplines wish to develop criminology as a form of policy analysis.

It is interesting that one of the effects of the new policy analysis of crime is to shift attention away from criminal and delinquent behavior and onto the strategies used by control agencies in response to these behaviors. Sociologists, too, particularly labelling and conflict theorists, have been much interested in the actions of control agencies. However, a fundamental premise of a structural criminology is that a one-sided attention to only these reactions of control agencies misses much of what we initially set out to study, and beyond this makes impossible a full understanding of the phenomena (i.e. both criminal behavior and reactions to it) we wish to explain. The policy analysis of crime leaves off where the sociological study of crime and delinquency began. Sociologists may still be uniquely suited to pursue the causes of behaviors regarded by others as disreputable.

Why, then, have sociologists who study crime *themselves* become collectively less interested in exploring the causation of criminal and delinquent behavior? In part, the answer may lie in an unnecessary legacy of criminological positivism. Certainly much of the early dissatisfaction with the etiological study of crime was expressed in the form of attacks on criminological positivism (e.g. Matza 1964). These attacks were often deserved, given the fashion in which early European efforts to bring natural science methods to the study of crime causation were selectively given prominence in early American criminology. Structural criminology not only assigns renewed importance to the study of the causes of criminal and delinquent behavior, but also emphasizes the role of the methods of natural science in criminological research. A brief reconsideration of criminological positivism may therefore be in order. This reconsideration also forms the basis for a reassertion of the importance of gender relations in the development of a structural criminology.

Criminological positivism usually is traced to the Italian School, including the work of Cesar Lombroso (1910), Raffaele Garofalo (1914), and Enrico Ferri (1915). Our point is that criminological positivism might as reasonably and more usefully have been traced to the work of Adolphe Jacques Quetelet (1842) or William Bonger (1916). If it had been, American criminology might today be more structural and sociological in form.

With the advantage of hindsight, it is distressingly easy to see why the Italian school initially was so popular. Lombroso (1895) captured the biological imagination of America, which was highly developed during the early part of this century. As is noted in the opening lectures of most introductory criminology courses, Lombroso saw criminals as biological "throwbacks" to an earlier, primitive, or "atavistic" stage of evolution. One might therefore have expected Lombroso to argue that men were more criminal than women because they were more atavistic. Instead, he argued that woman was "atavistically nearer to her origin than the male" (Lombroso 1895:107). As a result, Lombroso needed to posit something further that restrained woman's atavistic inclinations. His assumption was that, "in ordinary cases these defects are neutralized by piety, maternity, want of passion, sexual coldness, weakness and an undeveloped intelligence" (p. 151). Lombroso went so far as to trace woman's passivity to the "immobility of the ovule compared to the zoosperm" (p. 109). It is plausible to speculate that Lombroso's theory of female criminality gained currency because it both asserted woman's biological inferiority and warned of the dangers of arousing her passions or developing her intelligence.

In another era, Bonger (1916) might have captured the American imagination, or at least its sociological imagination. Bonger was aware of biological explanations of sex differences in crime. However, he argued that "the smaller criminality of woman is not to be sought in innate qualities, but rather in the social environment" (p. 477). Bonger reasoned that as class position declines, so too do differences in the social circumstances of the sexes, and therefore their relative rates of crime. Assuming this was the case, Bonger believed there was a straightforward way of demonstrating the social basis of sex differences in crime:

> A very conclusive proof of the thesis that the social position of woman is what explains her lower criminality is as follows. The difference in the manner of life of the two sexes decreases as we descend the social scale. If the social position of woman is then an important determinant of her lower criminality, the figures ought to show that the criminality of men differs more from that of women in the well-to-do classes than in classes less privileged (p. 477).

It is the structural position of woman, therefore, that determines her relative criminality. More generally, "if the life of women were like that of men their criminality would hardly differ at all as to quantity, though perhaps somewhat as to quality" (Bonger 1916:478).

The theories of Lombroso and Bonger could hardly differ more in their identification of the causes of criminal behavior and, therefore, in their explanation of sex differences in crime. Where Bonger places an emphasis on structural causes and so anticipates a structural criminology, Lombroso places the emphasis on biological predisposition, a tradition that makes the conceptualization and measurement of social relations secondary at best. Nonetheless, what made both of these theorists criminological positivists (and might have allowed them to do more than simply talk past one another) was their common way of addressing the issues of explanation.

Both began with an observed correlation: Men are more criminal than women. Assuming the correlation was real, and not simply a product of gender bias in the response to crime, Lombroso and Bonger sought to test their causal theories. Although their results were entirely different, they proceeded in similar ways. Each specified other variables that could account for the observed correlation. Lombroso looked for what he believed to be the innate qualities that distinguished the sexes; Bonger looked for differences in their structural positions. Both anticipated a style of quantitative reasoning and a logic of causal analysis that persists as a foundation of modern criminology. While today Lombroso's biogenetic theory is not taken seriously, Bonger's theory has been tested with positive results (Hagan et al 1985).

From the Old Positivism to the New Structuralism

Given the attention Lombroso's work received, and the neglect of Bonger's work, it is perhaps not difficult to see why criminologists gradually lost interest in the study of the causes of criminal and delinquent behavior. The kinds of assumptions that surrounded Lombrosian positivism rendered suspect the efforts of others to revive Lombroso's or Bonger's causal interests, regardless of whether the new theories were structurally or otherwise inspired. It was as if criminology needed to be purged of Lombroso's misguided thoughts before etiological theory could begin anew. Labelling and conflict theories became a mechanism by which this occurred.

Ironically, however, it is feminists (among others) who bring us back to etiological questions. For if criminological theory has entered a period of relative silence on the causes of criminal behavior, feminists are anything but silent about the causes of gender differences in these among many other types of behaviors. Unencumbered by Lombrosian positivism, feminist scholars take for granted that gender differences in criminal behavior, as in other kinds of behavior, are the product of informal as well as formal (i.e. official) processes of social control (e.g. Simon 1975, Adler 1975). The gender stratification of social control and its consequences are insidious, pervading the workplace, the family, and official agencies of crime control. Both formal and informal processes of social control are socially structured in terms of gender and are available for study as such. Consider the feminist Catherine Mackinnon's (1982:193) response to a one-sided focus on the law and its agents:

> Initiatives are . . . directed toward making the police more sensitive, prosecutors more responsive, judges more receptive, and the law, in words, less sexist. This may be progressive in the liberal or the left senses, but how is it empowering in the feminist sense? Even if it were effective in jailing men who do little different from what nondeviant men do regularly, how would such an approach alter woman's rapability? Unconfronted are *why* women are raped and the role of the state in that. Similarly, applying laws against battery to husbands, although it can mean life itself, has largely failed to address, as part of the strategy for state intervention, the conditions that produce men who systematically express themselves violently toward women, women whose resistance is disabled, and the role of the state in this dynamic. Criminal enforcement in these areas, while suggesting that rape and battery

are deviant, punishes men for expressing the images of masculinity that mean their identity, for which they are trained, elevated, venerated, and paid. These men must be stopped. But how does that change them or reduce the chances that there will be more like them? Liberal strategies entrust women to the state. Left theory abandons us to the rapists and the batterers.

It bears reiteration, then, that a fundamental assumption of a structural criminology is that the understanding of criminality must be built on an analysis within and between groupings of individuals in their many social settings, for example, in the family and in peer groups, at school and at work, as well as in relation to the state. We have argued with examples: That to understand the class-crime connection it is necessary to take into account the relational position of individuals in the social organization of work as well as the ways in which their behaviors are defined by law; that to understand variations in sentencing decisions and by implication other kinds of criminal justice outcomes it is necessary to take into account relationships between offenders, complainants, and victims, as well as power relationships between persons involved in the decision-making process; and that to understand interconnections between gender, class, and delinquency, it is necessary to consider the relative positions of heads and spouses in households and the impact of these work-based relations on the gender stratification of domestic social control.

Note that in each of our examples there is a necessary focus on action and reaction in the production and reproduction of crime and its control. The power relations that underwrite a structural criminology cannot be developed, explored, or tested with one-sided methodologies. The subjects we study require a relational, that is sociological, method of analysis. Relationally measured concepts better capture the mechanisms of criminal behavior and its control.

But structural criminology obviously cannot answer all questions about crime and delinquency. Rather, its purpose is to formulate more clearly how meaningful questions about crime and delinquency can be asked as well as answered. However, important questions remain. For example, we began with an assumption that vertical, hierarchical relations of power and subordination are more important in the study of criminality than horizontal, nonhierarchical relations of affiliation and solidarity (for interesting developments along the latter lines, see Ekland-Olson 1982, 1984). Both may be important, and a key to explanatory success may involve conceptually linking the two kinds of relations among actors and groups. We also began with an implicit assumption that power relations deriving from both ownership and authority in the social organization of work are crucial to the meaningful study of crime and delinquency. When and how these separable sources of power and subordination exercise influence remains unsettled in the study of social stratification as well as in the study of criminality. The fates of sociology and criminology are closely entwined. The purpose of a structural criminology is to suggest a methodology by which this work can usefully proceed.

Literature Cited

Adler, F. 1975. *Sisters in Crime*. New York: McGraw-Hill

Albonetti, C. 1985. *Decisions to prosecute: The effects of uncertainty*. Unpublished manuscript. Urbana: Univ. Ill.

Albonetti, C., Hauser, R., Hagan, J., Nagel, I. 1986. Criminal justice decision-making as a stratification process: The role of race and stratification resources in pre-trial release decisions. Submitted

Arnold, T. 1967. The criminal trial. In *Law, Politics and the Federal Courts*, ed. H. Jacob. Boston: Little, Brown

Baumhart, R. C. 1961. How ethical are businessmen? *Harv. Bus. Rev.* 39:5–176

Becker, H. 1963. *Outsiders: Studies in the sociology of deviance*. New York: Free Press

Bernstein, I., Kick, E., Leung, J., Schulz, B. 1977. Charge reduction: An intermediary stage in the process of labelling criminal defendants. *Soc. Forc.* 56(2):362–84

Blumstein, A., Cohen, J., Martin, S., Tonry, M. 1983. *Research on Sentencing: The Search for Reform*. Washington, DC: Natl. Acad.

Bonger, W. 1916. *Criminality and Economic Conditions*. Boston: Little, Brown

Braithwaite, J. 1981. The myth of social class and criminality reconsidered. *Am. Sociol. Rev.* 46:36–57

Brenner, S. N., Molander, E. A. 1977. Is the ethics of business changing? *Harv. Bus. Rev.* 55:57–71

Carter, R., Wilkins, L. 1967. Some factors in sentencing policy. *J. Crim. Law, Criminol. Police Sci.* 58:503–14

Chambliss, W., Seidman, R. 1971. *Law, Order and Power*. Reading, Mass: Addison-Wesley

Chiricos, T. G., Waldo, G. P. 1975. Socioeconomic status and criminal sentencing: An empirical assessment of a conflict proposition. *Am. Sociol. Rev.* 40:753–72

Clinard, M., Yeager, P. 1980. *Corporate Crime*. New York: Free Press

Coleman, J. 1974. *Power and the Structure of Society*. New York: Norton

Colvin, M., Pauly, J. 1983. A critique of criminology: Toward an integrated structural-Marxist theory of delinquency production. *Am. J. Sociol.* 89(3):513–51

Cullen, F., Larson, M., Mathers, R. 1985. Having money and delinquency involvement: The neglect of power in delinquency theory. *Criminal Justice Behav.* 12(2):171–92

Dershowitz, A. 1961. Increasing community control over corporate crime: A problem in the law of sanctions. *Yale Law J.* 71:289–306

Eisenstein, J., Jacob, H. 1977. *Felony Justice*. Boston: Little, Brown

Ekland-Olson, S. 1982. Deviance, social control and social networks. In *Research in Law, Deviance and Social Control*, ed. S. Spitzer, R. Simon, pp. 271–99

Ekland-Olson, S., Lieb, J., Zurcher, L. 1984. The paradoxical impact of criminal sanctions: Some micro-structural findings. *Law Soc. R.* 18:159–78

Elliot, D. S., Ageton, S. S. 1980. Reconciling race and class differences in self-reported and official estimates of delinquency. *Am. Sociol. R.* 45:95–110

Ermann, M. D., Lundman, R. 1980. *Corporate Deviance*. New York: Holt, Rinehart, Winston

Farberman, H. 1975. A Criminogenic market structure: The automobile industry. *Sociol. Q.* 16:438–57

Ferri, E. 1915. *Criminal Sociology*. New York: Appleton

Frankel, M. 1972. *Criminal Sentences: Law Without Order*. New York: Hill, Wang

Garfinkel, H. 1949. Research Note on Inter- and Intra-Racial Homicides. *Soc. Forc.* 27:369–81

Garofalo, R. 1914. *Criminology*. Boston: Little, Brown

Geis, G. 1975. Victimization patterns in white collar crime. *Victimology: A New Focus*, Vol. V, *Exploiters and Exploited: The Dynamics of Victimization*. ed. I. Drapkin, E. Viano, pp. 89–105. Lexington, Mass: Lexington

Geis, G., Meier, R. 1977. *White-Collar Crime*. New York: Wiley

Gibbons, D. 1979. *The Criminological Enterprise: Theories and Perspectives*. Englewood Cliffs, NJ: Prentice-Hall

Glasbeek, H., Rowland, S. 1979. Are injuring and killing at work crimes? *Osgoode Hall Law J.* 17:506–94

Greenwood, P. 1979. *Selective Incapacitation*. Santa Monica, Calif: Rand

Hagan, J. 1975. The social and legal construction of criminal justice: A study of the pre-sentencing process. *Soc. Probl.* 22:620–37

Hagan, J. 1982. The corporate advantage: The involvement of individual and organizational victims in the criminal justice process. *Soc. Forc.* 60(4):993–1022

Hagan, J. 1985. Toward a structural theory of race, gender and crime: The canadian case. *Crime Delin.* 31:129–46

Hagan, J., Albonetti, C. 1982. Race, class and the perception of criminal injustice in America. *Am. J. Sociol.* 88:329–55

Hagan, J., Bumiller, K. 1983. Making sense of sentencing: A review and critique of sentencing research. In *Research on Sentencing: The Search for Reform*, ed. A. Blumstein, J. Cohen, S. Martin, M. Tonry. Washington, DC: Nat. Acad. Press

Hagan, J., Hewitt, J., Alwin, D. 1979. Ceremonial justice: Crime and punishment in a loosely coupled system. *Soc. Forc.* 58:506

Hagan, J., Parker, P. 1985. White collar crime and punishment: The class structure and legal sanctioning of securities violations. *Am. Sociol. Rev.* 50:302–16

Hagan, J., Simpson, J., Gillis, A. R. 1979. The sexual stratification of social control: A gender-based perspective on crime and delinquency. *Br. J. Sociol.* 30(1):25–38

Hagan, J., Simpson, J., Gillis, A. R. 1986. Class in the household: Deprivation, liberation and a power-control theory of gender and delinquency. Submitted

Hagan, J., Gillis, A. R., Simpson, J. 1985. The class structure of gender and delinquency: Toward a power-control theory of common delinquent behavior. *Am. J. Sociol.* 90: 1151–78

Hindelang, M., Hirschi, T., Weis, J. 1979. Correlates of delinquency: The illusion of discrepancy between self report and official measures. *Am. Sociol. Rev.* 44:995–1014

Hindelang, M., Hirschi, T., Weis, J. 1981. *Measuring Delinquency*. Beverly Hills, Calif: Sage

Hinkle, R., Hinkle, G. 1954. *The Development of Modern Sociology*. New York: Random

Hirschi, T. 1969. *Causes of Delinquency*. Berkeley: Univ. Calif. Press

Hirschi, T. 1972. Social class and crime. In *Issues in Social Inequality*, ed. D. Theilbar, S. Feldman, pp. Boston: Little, Brown

Hirschi, T. 1973. Procedural rules and the study of deviant behavior. *Soc. Probl.* 21:159–73

Hirschi, T., Selvin, H. 1967. *Delinquency Research: An Appraisal of Analytic Methods*. New York: Free Press

Hogarth, J. 1971. *Sentencing as a Human Process*. Toronto: Univ. Toronto Press

Jacob, H. 1984. *The Frustration of Policy: Responses to Crime by American Cities*. Boston: Little, Brown

Kanter, R. M. 1974. Intimate oppression. *Sociol. Q.* 15(2):302–14

Kleck, G. 1981. Racial discrimination in criminal sentencing: A critical evaluation of the evidence with additional evidence on the death penalty. *Am. Sociol. Rev.* 46:783–805

Kleck, G. 1982. On the use of self-report data to determine the class distribution of criminal and delinquent behavior. *Am. Sociol. Rev.* 43:427–33

Krutschnitt, T. 1985. Are businesses treated differently? A comparison of the individual victim and the corporate victim in the criminal courtroom. *Sociol. Inquiry* 55:225–38

LaFree, G. 1980. The effect of sexual stratification by race on official reactions to rape. *Am. Sociol. Rev.* 45:842–54

Lemert, E. 1967. *Human Deviance, Social Problems and Social Control*. Englewood Cliffs, NJ: Prentice-Hall

Lizotte, A. 1978. Extra-legal factors in Chicago's criminal courts: Testing the conflict model of criminal justice. *Soc. Probl.* 25:564–80

Lombroso, C. 1895. *The Female Offender*. New York: Fisher Unwin

Lombroso, C. 1918. *Crime, Its Causes and Remedies*. Boston: Little, Brown

Mackinnon, C. 1982. Feminism, Marxism, method and the state: Toward feminist jurisprudence. *Signs* 8:185–208

Matza, D. 1964. *Delinquency and Drift*. New York: Wiley

Myers, M. 1979. Offended parties and official reactions: Victims and the sentencing of criminal defendants. *Sociol. Q.* 20:529–40

Myrdal, G. 1944. *An American Dilemma*. New York: Harper

Nagel, I. 1983. The legal/extra-legal controversy: Judicial decisions in pre-trial release. *Law Soc. Rev.* 17:481–515

Nettler, G. 1978. *Explaining Crime*. New York: McGraw-Hill

Page, J., O'Brian, M. 1973. *Bitter Wages*. New York: Grossman

Peterson, R. 1985. Discriminatory decision-making at the legislative level: An analysis of the Comprehensive Drug Abuse, Prevention and Control Act of 1970. *Law Hum. Behav.* 9:243–70

Peterson, R., Hagan, J. 1984. Changing conceptions of race: Towards an account of anomalous findings on sentencing research. *Am. Sociol. Rev.* 49:56–70

Quetelet, A. 1842. *A Treatise on Man*. Gainesville, Fla: Scholars' Facsimilies & Reprints

Quinney, R. 1970. *The Social Reality of Crime*. New York: Little, Brown

Reasons, C., Ross, L., Paterson, C. 1981. *Assault on the Worker*. Toronto: Butterworths

Reiss, A. 1981. Foreward: Towards a revitalization of theory and research on victimization by crime. *J. Criminal Law Criminol.* 72:704–13

Robinson, R., Kelly, J. 1979. Class as conceived by Marx and Dahrendorf: Effects on income inequality, class consciousness and class conflict in the United States and Great Britain. *Am. Sociol. Rev.* 44(1):38–57

Scheingold, S. 1984. *The Politics of Law and Order: Street Crime and Public Policy*. New York: Longman

Schlossman, S. 1983. The Chicago Area Project Revisited. Santa Monica, Calif: Rand

Schrager, L., Short, J. 1978. Toward a sociology of organizational crime. *Soc. Probl.* 25(4):407–19

Simmel, G. 1950. Quantitative aspects of the group. In *The Sociology of Georg Simmel,* ed. K. H. Wolff, pp. 000 New York: Free Press

Simon, R. 1975. *Women and Crime.* Lexington, Mass: Lexington

Sutherland, E. 1945. Is 'White Collar crime' crime? *Am. Sociol. Rev.* 5:1–12

Sutherland, E. 1949. *White collar Crime.* New York: Dryden

Swartz, J. 1978. Silent killers at work. In *Corporate and Governmental Deviance.* ed. M. D. Erman, R. Lundman New York: Oxford Univ. Press pp.

Tappan, P. 1947. Who is the criminal? *Am. Sociol. Rev.* 12:96–102

Taylor, I., Walton, P., Young, J. 1973. *The New Criminology: For a Social Theory of Deviance.* London: Routledge & Kegan Paul

Thomas, C. 1984. From the Editor's Desk. *Criminology* 22(4):467–71

Thomson, R., Zingraff, M. 1981. Detecting sentence disparity: Some problems and evidence. *Am. J. Sociol.* 86:869–80

Thornberry, T., Farnsworth, M. 1982. Social correlates of criminal involvement: Further evidence on the relationship between social status and criminal behavior. *Am. Sociol. Rev.* 47:505–18

Tittle, C., Villemez, W. J., Smith, D. 1978. The myth of social class and criminality: An empirical assessment of the empirical evidence. *Am. Sociol. Rev.* 43:643–56

Turk, A. 1969. *Criminality and the Legal Order.* Chicago: Rand McNally

United States Department of Labor. 1972. *The President's Report on Occupational Safety and Health.* Washington, DC: USGPO

Vogel, L. 1983. *Marxism and the Oppression of Women: Toward a Unitary Theory.* New Brunswick, NJ: Rutgers Univ. Press

Wheeler, S. 1976. Trends and Problems in the Sociological Study of Crime. *Soc. Probl.* 23:525–34

Wheeler, S., Rothman, M. 1982. The organization as weapon in white-collar crime. *Mich. Law Rev.* 80(7):1403–26

Wilkinson, K. 1974. The broken family and juvenile delinquency: Scientific explanation or ideology. *Soc. Probl.* 21(5):726–39

Wilson, J. Q. 1975. *Thinking About Crime.* New York: Basic

Wolfgang, M. 1972. *Delinquency in a Birth Cohort.* Univ. Chicago Press

Wolfgang, M., Riedel, M. 1973. Race, judicial discretion and the death penalty. *Annals Am. Acad. Polit. Soc. Sci.* 407:119

Wright, E. O. 1977. Marxist class categories and income inequality. *Am. Sociol. Rev.* 42:32–55

Zatz, M. 1984. Race, ethnicity and determinate sentencing: A new dimension to an old controversy." *Criminology* 22(2):147–72

Ann. Rev. Sociol. 1986. 12:451–78
Copyright © 1986 by Annual Reviews Inc. All rights reserved

SOCIAL IMPACT ASSESSMENT

William R. Freudenburg*

Department of Rural Sociology, Washington State University, Pullman, Washington 99164

Abstract

This article reviews the large and growing literature on social or socio-economic impact assessment (SIA). Sociologists and other social scientists have been examining various "impacts" or consequences for decades, but the field of SIA emerged during the 1970s as a response to new environmental legislation. Both in its origins and its contributions, SIA is thus a hybrid, a field of social science and a component of the policy-making process. SIAs are generally anticipatory—efforts to project likely impacts before they occur—but empirical SIA work has looked at a broad range of social consequences. The largest subset of empirical SIA work has focused on relatively specific construction projects, particularly large-scale energy development projects in rural areas. Important advances have taken place in documenting economic/demographic and also social and cultural impacts. Further developments in findings, theory, and techniques will be necessary to meet the challenges of the future. The field is showing increasing consensus on a number of earlier controversies, e.g. on the need for SIAs to cross the usual disciplinary boundaries and to develop original data where "available" data are not sufficient. The main issue on which consensus has not yet emerged involves the question of how best to incorporate scientific input in what will remain largely political decisions. The field's efforts to deal with this fundamental and perhaps enduring question, however, may provide useful guidance for other efforts to include scientific input in political decision-making—efforts that may take on growing importance as society begins to deal with the increasingly complex risks posed by technological developments.

*Current address: Department of Rural Sociology, University of Wisconsin, Madison, Wisconsin 53706.

451

0360-0572/86/0815-0451$02.00

INTRODUCTION

> Technology is neither good nor bad.
> Nor is it neutral.

> Kranzberg's Law.

Social impact assessment (SIA) is a hybrid, an offspring both of science and of the political process. Its lineage is ancient, but its emergence is recent, a response to society's increased concern with environmental degradation and the social implications of technology. For the most part, the hybrid has only begun to bear fruit within the last decade.

Reflecting SIA's hybrid heritage, this review will discuss both the policy and the scientific aspects of SIA. Of necessity, the review will be limited to what might be called mainstream SIA literature, which tends to form a subarea of "environmental sociology" (Dunlap & Catton 1979). SIA also draws heavily from other traditions in sociology, such as human ecology, social change, social problems, social indicators, and evaluation research, but these and other bodies of work are outside the scope of the present review.

Under some of the broadest definitions, SIA can be seen as including all of the social sciences and a good deal more besides. In general, however, *social impact assessment* refers to *assessing* (as in measuring or summarizing) a broad range of *impacts* (or effects, or consequences) that are likely to be experienced by an equally broad range of *social groups* as a result of some course of action. Although SIA is among the policy sciences and has a certain similarity to evaluation research (Carley & Bustelo 1984, Wolf 1977), it is also distinctive in at least three main respects. First, SIA tends to focus on the consequences of technological developments—usually developments that lead to alterations in the biophysical environment—while evaluation research tends to focus on programs or policies, especially social policies. Second, while evaluation research commonly focuses on stated or intended goals of public policy initiatives, SIA generally focuses on unintended consequences of developments that are often initiated by private, profit-oriented firms (cf Merton 1936). Third, under most definitions, SIA is a planning tool, prospective rather than retrospective—an attempt to foresee and hence avoid or minimize unwanted impacts—while evaluation research tends to take place after a policy has been set into motion.

As is noted below, however, there are many variations around these central tendencies. Despite the future-oriented focus of SIA as a whole, for example, some of the most important contributions to the field have been empirical analyses of impacts actually experienced after development has proceeded. Most practitioners in the United States appear to see SIA's major role as one of providing information and analysis to be taken into account in political decision-making. Yet SIA practitioners also often work to involve the public in the decision-making process (Daneke et al 1983), and the practitioners range from academic scientists who strive for dispassionate analysis to political activists whose analyses are impassioned indeed.

These and other forms of diversity make it difficult to provide a simple review of the entire field, but the task is aided by a number of excellent summaries that have become available recently. Accordingly, this review provides an overview at a somewhat broader level of abstraction, referring to more specific works as appropriate. It is divided into three main sections. The first deals with the historical development of the field as we know it today. The second notes some of the main empirical findings about social impacts and controversies about social impact assessment that have become the focus for SIA scholarship over the past decade and a half. The third and final section turns to some of the implications that grow out of the accumulated literature, including implications for the broader role to be played by science in the policy-making process.

HISTORICAL DEVELOPMENT

The Policy Context

The phrase "social impacts" means something like "social consequences," and the scientific genealogy of SIA can be traced back to the earliest days of sociology—to the concerns of Toennies and Durkheim, for example, with the social consequences of the Industrial Revolution. But the field as we know it today can be traced to legislation that took effect in 1970.

The first presidential act of the 1970s was the signing of a law passed just a few days earlier: the National Environmental Policy Act of 1969, or NEPA. This short and apparently simple act, five pages long in its entirety, has had enormous repercussions. Under NEPA, before a federal agency is allowed to take actions "significantly affecting the quality of the human environment," it must first prepare a balanced, interdisciplinary, and publicly available assessment of the action's likely impacts or consequences—an assessment now known as an environmental impact statement, or EIS. It is in the EIS context that much if not most SIA work is done, at least in the United States.

Section 102 of NEPA requires Federal agencies to make "integrated use of the natural *and social* sciences" in "decisionmaking which may have an impact on man's environment" (emphasis added). Like many provisions of the Act, however, those dealing with the social sciences were not immediately grasped. "Integrated use" is sometimes difficult to find even today, but it was virtually impossible to find in some of the earliest EISs. In one notable example, the *total* assessment of the social impacts to be created by relocating a community consisted of the following sentence: "Acquisition of approximately 130 acres used by [the community of] North Bonneville will affect the human population that resides there and also some mouse, rat, and domestic animal habitat that is normally associated with intense human use areas" (US Army Corps of Engineers 1971 : 3.1). The agency's concern for the community was later increased, but only after almost a decade-long battle had been fought in agency corridors, the media, and even the halls of Congress.

One major reason for the early lack of integrated use may have been the low proportion of NEPA lawsuits that had social impacts as a major focus. Before NEPA had been in effect for its first full decade, over 12,000 EISs had been prepared, and over 1,200 EIS-related lawsuits had been filed, but virtually none of the early suits focused on the social impact portions of the EISs (Freudenburg & Keating 1982). The few early suits dealing with social impacts, moreover, could scarcely have been less propitious for establishing legal precedents. Most of the cases were efforts to require the preparation of EISs on "socioeconomic" grounds alone, in cases where Federal decisions had negligible impacts on biophysical environments. Two important early examples were the closing of a military base and the development of a job training center on a site where a campus had previously stood. In both cases there were actually to be fewer people on the sites—generating fewer impacts in the form of air pollution, dust, noise, etc—than would have been the case previously. Not surprisingly, the courts ruled that no EISs were required in these and similar cases.

The US Council on Environmental Quality, the agency charged with overseeing implementation of NEPA, issued regulations for implementing the procedural provisions of the Act in 1973 and then again in 1978. The official 1978 regulations have clarified the situation: "Social and economic effects by themselves do *not* require preparation of an EIS," but if an EIS must be prepared because of physical environmental impacts, and if the social and bioenvironmental impacts are "interrelated," then the EIS is required to discuss "*all*" of these impacts on the human environment" (US Council on Environmental Quality 1978 : 29; emphasis added).

Even after these clarifications were issued, the flow of SIA-related litigation could scarcely be said to have created a heavy burden for courts: It appears that the first case making clear use of social science expertise was not decided until 1983, and the first case presenting the type of issue envisioned in the Council on Environmental Quality's regulations was not decided until May of 1985. The 1983 decision involved an effort to require the Nuclear Regulatory Commission to prepare an EIS before permitting the undamaged nuclear reactor at Three Mile Island to resume operation (the reactor happened to be shut down for refueling when its twin unit malfunctioned). The case argued that restarting the undamaged unit would damage the psychological health of citizens living nearby, that psychological health is a form of "health" protected by NEPA, and thus that an environmental impact statement was required even though no other environmental impacts were alleged. A high court in the District of Columbia agreed with the citizens' contention, but the US Supreme Court—in *Metropolitan Edison Co. v. People Against Nuclear Energy*, 460 U.S. 766, 103 S. Ct. 1556 (1983)—did not. While noting that psychological health could be a form of health as defined under NEPA, the Justices ruled that they had not been shown "a sufficiently close causal connection" between the physical act of restarting the reactor and the hypothesized increase in mental health problems. A group of respected mental health researchers had reached essentially the same conclusion about one year earlier (Walker et al 1982; for fuller discussions of the case and its implications, see Jordan 1984, Meidinger & Freudenburg 1983).

It was not until May of 1985, more than 15 years after the Act was passed, that the first decision was rendered on the type of case envisioned in the Council or Environmental Quality regulations (and presumably in NEPA itself). The case—*Northern Cheyenne Tribe v. Hodel*, No. CV 82-116-BLG (D. Mont. May 28, 1985)—involved the largest federal coal lease sale that had ever been held. While the Department of the Interior had prepared an EIS on the affected area (the Northern Powder River Basin of Wyoming and Montana), the EIS included virtually no discussion of the sale's likely social, cultural, or economic impacts on the Northern Cheyenne Tribe, and thus the Northern Cheyennes sued to have the EIS overturned. They succeeded. In a strongly worded decision, Judge James F. Batten overturned the EIS, voided the sale of over 350 million tons of Federal coal (with a market value of well over $4 billion), and chided the Department of Interior for failing to turn its "ostensible concern" with socioeconomic impacts into "any meaningful analysis of the extent of such impacts on certain groups of residents within the affected area, particularly the Northern Cheyenne Tribe" (pp. 14–15; see also the discussion in Freudenburg & Keating 1985).

The Social Science Context

The early years under NEPA, from roughly 1970–1975, were a time of humble beginnings for the field, with most SIA work being a relatively straightforward continuation of research that had been underway before the Act was passed. Some of the earliest signs of the emergence of a self-conscious field of SIA came when the Council of the American Sociological Association (ASA) authorized the formation in 1973 of a committee "to develop guidelines for sociological contributions to environmental impact statements" (Dunlap & Catton 1979:246). Given the newness and relative lack of development of the field at the time, the Committee ultimately disbanded without making formal recommendations on EIS criteria (Wolf 1975), but its efforts prepared the groundwork for establishing the Environmental Sociology Section of the ASA.

In addition, the field of SIA could also be said to have emerged from the efforts of the Committee—especially its chair, C. P. Wolf, described by some as the founder of the field but by himself as its "finder" (Wolf 1977). Wolf was also the convener of the Ad Hoc Interagency Working Group on SIA that began to meet in Washington, DC in June of 1974. In early 1974, he organized a session on social impact assessment at the annual meeting of the Environmental Design Research Association and later turned the session into the field's first published volume (Wolf 1974). June 1975 saw publication of the first special journal issue on SIA (*Environment and Behavior*, Vol. 7, No. 3), again with Wolf as its editor. In January 1976, he turned over his earlier *Environmental Sociology* newsletter to the ASA and established a second newsletter, *Social Impact Assessment*. This he still edits for a subscription list that has grown to more than 1000; it remains the field's most important channel of communication. At about the same time, he was also working with Kurt Finsterbusch on *Methodology of Social Impact Assessment* (Finsterbusch & Wolf 1977), which led to a second edition and then a sequel (Finsterbusch et al 1983). The original was identified in a later survey of practitioners (Davidson 1983) as the most influential volume in SIA. (Both the original volume and its successors are useful sources on SIA methodologies, which receive little attention in this review.) When the ASA's Section on Environmental Sociology established its award for Distinguished Contributions to Environmental Sociology, the Section's Council unanimously chose Wolf as the first recipient.

If the first few years after NEPA were a period of humble beginnings, the following years (from roughly 1975–1980) might be identified as a second era—a time of not-so-humble claims and aspirations. Agencies were accustomed to measuring "adequacy" in terms of following official procedures, rather than in scientific terms, and they desired procedural guidance for dealing with SIAs. One of the results was a multiplying of how-to manuals and a dramatic growth in the enthusiasm of their claims. Unlike the Ad Hoc ASA committee, writers of these manuals indicated little difficulty in deciding what to include in SIAs. One claimed, for example, "All of the information necessary to conduct a social assessment, analyze data, present findings, and make recommendations is contained within this book" (Fitzsimmons et al 1977:3). While the manual making this claim received mixed reviews (Flynn 1976, Shields 1976), it was still one of the more widely respected of the early guides—along with the more sociological guide produced for the US Forest Service by Richard Gale (1975)—and it was the first to be commercially published. Even so, such a claim would have required more than a little bravery, particularly at such an early state of the development of the field. It also may have proved to be less than entirely convincing—a conclusion suggested by the proliferation of other publications on "How To Do Social Impact Assessment," numbering roughly two dozen at last count. (Other agencies, such as the Corps of Engineers, also considered producing their own manuals but decided instead to draw on empirical case studies—R. Love, personal communication.) More recent volumes often reflect more modest goals, such as producing "a reference manual that can be consulted either for general advice or for more specific direction on particular problems" (Branch et al 1984:3), although, the advertising for a manual being published as this article went to press claimed without qualification, "with this book you can conduct socio-economic impact assessments."

The enthusiasm of the claims was not simply a response to agency needs, however. Some of the field's most important early progress did in fact occur in adapting established social science methods (such as surveys, demographic projections, and field research techniques) to the new demands of SIA (see e.g. the collections in Finsterbusch & Wolf 1977, Wolf 1974). In addition, the field's growth during the late 1970s was exceptional. In Canada, for example, a 1975 study found only two dozen SIAs, and even that only "by stretching the definition of social impact research" (Boothroyd 1978:131). At the time of a nation-wide conference three years later, participants were able to identify over 3000 SIAs (D'Amore 1981). Also, SIA practitioners may have been influenced by the broader culture of the industrial developments they assessed, and during the late 1970s, this culture was dominated by "big thinking" and massive projects—to say nothing of consulting opportunities—particularly in the field of energy development.

Conversely, during the third post-NEPA era of SIA, extending roughly from 1981 to the present, the field began not only to think more seriously about the "bust" side of development but to experience those very problems itself. In the United States, a new President took office, one who placed relatively low priorities both on social science and on environmental protection and who tended to view impact assessment as a form of "paralysis by analysis." In addition, the combination of a recession and the increasing effectiveness of energy conservation led to the cancellation of one large-scale energy project after another. As the projects were cancelled, so were formerly lucrative consulting contracts for SIA firms, many of which were forced to scale back, close branch offices, refocus their efforts in other areas of work, or even go out of business entirely.

Yet an examination of SIA literature reveals that the early 1980s were a time not of disastrous decline, but of exceptional productivity—a time of retrenchment, to be sure, but also one of reflection and reconsideration, resulting in what may be a higher level of quality than was found in previous periods of SIA work. While there can be little doubt that many factors were at work, three seem to have been particularly important. First, researchers who had previously been in high demand for project-specific assessments, one contract after another, began to find time to do the more detailed analyses that many had wanted to do all along. Second, a pair of important conferences were held in summer and fall of 1982—the Alaska Symposium on the Social, Economic and Cultural Impacts of Natural Resource Development (many of the formal papers from which were published in Yarie 1983) and the International Conference on SIA, held in Vancouver, British Columbia, Canada, two months later. These conferences gave researchers the opportunity to consider the contrasts, complementarities, and contributions to be gained from those whose contexts and philosophies differed from their own. This cross-national cross-fertilization seems to have been particularly important for US practitioners, who had previously paid too little attention to developments in other countries. Third, a lag of several years is common before work in any field begins to climb the learning curve and to appear in scientific journals; SIA was not immune from this general tendency.

It is mainly in the past few years that the accumulating evidence has begun to permit more confident statements about the actual impacts of projects. The first "SIA textbook" to focus not on how to do SIAs but on what was known about social impacts was published in 1980 (Finsterbusch 1980), and the first books to summarize literature on the impacts of a given type of development (rapid community growth) appeared at roughly the same time (Murdock & Leistritz 1979, Weber & Howell 1982). A special issue of *The Social Science Journal* (Vol. 16, No. 2) was devoted to "the social impacts of energy development in the West" in 1979, and a July 1982 special issue of *Pacific Sociological Review* (Vol. 25, No. 3) was devoted to sociological research on boomtowns in particular. The Westview Press series on social impact assessment, which included only four titles before 1981, roughly quadrupled its number of titles by the end of 1985. And finally, as this list reflects, the proportion of SIA discussions appearing only in the "underground" literature or technical reports has declined since 1980, and publications have begun to appear increasingly in refereed journals and other mainstream publications.

MAJOR FINDINGS AND FEUDS

Empirical Findings

Empirical work in SIA has been extraordinarily varied, studying "social impacts" associated with sources as disparate as highways and high technology (Llewellyn et al 1982, Berardi & Geisler 1984). Some work has gone beyond technology to urge an emphasis on local regional-/ or national-level programs and policies (see e.g. Cramer et al 1980, Dietz 1984, Freeman et al 1982); some has even gone beyond strictly human actions to look at the social impacts of natural events such as disasters (Dillman et al 1983, Erikson 1976).

An important area of early research focused on forests and recreation; indeed, this work provided an impetus for the development of the entire field of environmental or natural resource sociology (Dunlap & Catton 1979). Particularly significant studies included those dealing with the impacts of increased population densities on the experiences of outdoor recreationists (Lucas 1964, Wagar 1964), the impact of the outdoor setting per se on the activities of recreationists (Burch 1965), and the impacts of forestry management practices on recreationists and other social groups (Hendee et al 1978). Related work, using a somewhat different definition of SIA, has looked at "social impacts" on quasi-natural systems such as National Parks of the human populations living nearby (e.g. Baxter et al 1984).

Entire reviews could be devoted to forest recreation or many of the other topics noted above. In addition, a number of authors have stressed SIA's potential to contribute to broader policy considerations (e.g. Finsterbusch 1984, 1985; Carley & Bustelo 1984; Wolf 1977). To date, however, the largest and most important area of empirical work in SIA has dealt with relatively specific construction projects.

In the earliest days after NEPA, the most important types of projects may have been water resource developments such as dams and urban undertakings such as highways. Work on water resources led to what appear to have been the first set of actual agency guidelines, namely those issued by the US Water Resources Council. In addition, some of the empirical studies from this era remain among the best yet done on the social impacts of reservoir construction and relocation. For example, Burdge & Johnson (1973) used a longitudinal design, included interviews with people who had actually been relocated by reservoir development, and focused on social and psychological impacts as well as easier-to-quantify economic impacts. They found, among other things, that younger, more affluent, and better-educated migrants fared better in the relocation process than those who were older, poorer, and less educated. The primary beneficiaries of development were found to live in different locations than the victims; in addition, those who refused to accept initial offers for their land were found to receive higher prices, and those who were relocated were found to express dissatisfaction with their interpersonal as well as economic dealings with the agency building the dam (Burdge & Johnson 1973; see also Andrews 1981, or the compilation by Field et al 1974; see also the later summary provided by Finsterbusch 1980).

Similarly, some of the most important work on urban highway construction dates from the first few years after the passage of NEPA, and some of the significant work on urban renewal dates from the period before NEPA was enacted (e.g. Fried 1963, Gans 1962). By the mid-1970s, studies showed that (at least after the Uniform Relocation Assistance and Real Property Acquisition Policies Act of 1970) relocatees generally received sufficient payments to allow them to move into comparable or superior housing. One notable study found that about 80% of the relocatees moved into equal or better housing and neighborhoods, that 50% of the previous renters became homeowners, and that a portion of the cost of the improved housing was borne by the government, although a portion was also borne by the relocatees themselves (Buffington et al 1974). Only 6% of the relocatees in this study thought that they had down-graded the quality of their housing. Another study found that "sixty percent of the respondents were more pleased with their new homes than the old, while the reverse was true for 27 percent" (Burkhardt et al 1976:34). The bad news is that relocation was found to lead to declines in neighboring and neighborly assis-tance, use of neighborhood facilities, and participation in neighborhood orga-nizations (Burkhardt et al 1976:46–50). In addition, as was the case with rural relocation for reservoir construction, the stresses of relocation appear to have been greater for long-term residents and the elderly (Buffington et al 1974; Fried 1963). Fried (1963) also noted problems related to spatial identity—i.e. for those persons having especially strong ties to their neighborhoods (see also Fellman & Brandt 1970). For more detailed reviews, the most extensive treatment available is the seven-volume compilation by Llewellyn et al (1982); see also Finsterbusch (1980).

But projects such as new highway construction and urban renewal became increasingly rare after the early 1970s, just as the larger field of SIA was beginning to crystallize. This fact may reflect both the increased national concern with protecting natural and human environments that led to NEPA and the effectiveness of NEPA itself in giving expression to such concerns. In addition, the "energy crisis" that followed the oil embargo of 1973–1974 led to a decline in gasoline consumption and hence in the revenues for new highway construction. That same energy crisis, however, led to a remarkable growth in opportunities for rural SIA work in studying the impacts of large-scale energy development, particularly in the Rocky Mountain region of the United States and Canada.

As did other areas of SIA, this one draws on work that was underway before NEPA (see especially the summary by Summers et al 1976), but this area saw explosive growth during the late 1970s. Until the middle years of that decade, studies of rural industrialization had tended to view even large-scale de-velopments in rural areas as generally beneficial, providing "an important tool for solving the twin problems of rural poverty and urban crisis" (Summers et al 1976:1). Even after NEPA, environmental impact statements tended to note in detail the likely economic benefits of growth and the need for expanding municipal services but to say virtually nothing about the broader range of potential sociocultural impacts. In the later 1970s, however, reports from so-called "energy boomtowns" frequently (but by no means always) began to note a pattern of problems similar to the "social pathologies" that Durkheim, for example, might have predicted—suicide attempts, increased crime, and drug abuse problems, and so forth—and the field became the focus for considerably increased controversy and contention.

To oversimplify only slightly the picture that has since emerged, the major conclusion appears to be that the impacts have neither been as positive as claimed by project proponents nor as negative as claimed by opponents. Most rural communities in the United States continue to favor industrial developments (Murdock & Leistritz 1979, Stout-Wiegand & Trent 1983), with the clear exception of nuclear facility development (Freudenburg & Baxter 1984), although the support appears to be more a reflection of general cultural favorability toward development than the expectation that a respondent will benefit personally from growth (Gartrell et al 1980; Gates 1982).

Where local benefits have been expected from large-scale projects, the focus has been primarily economic, specifically including jobs for local unemployed or young persons, whether in the large-scale developments themselves or in the so-called secondary, ancillary, service, or spin-off employment—i.e. in local restaurants, clothing stores, filling stations, and other services set up or expanded to serve the workers brought in by development. Virtually all service employment benefits appear to have been overestimated. First, as Murdock & Leistritz (1979) note, early impact projections commonly incorporated "multipliers" of approximately 1.6 and 2.5, respectively, during the construction and operational phases of major facilities; these imply the creation of 0.6 and 1.5 secondary jobs, respectively, for each job on the development project itself. Empirical evaluations have produced far lower numbers. Summers et al (1976:55) found "the most significant aspect" of findings on the operation of facilities to be the "very low multipliers—half of them are below 1.2." In other words, only 2 additional jobs were created for every 15 that had been anticipated. An analysis of 12 major power plant construction sites (Gilmore et al 1982) calculated actual construction-phase employment multipliers to be 1.2 to 1.3 for sparsely populated areas and only 1.3 to 1.4 even for areas with moderate population densities. In another retrospective analysis of 12 nuclear power plants, Pijawka & Chalmers (1983) estimated actual local employment multipliers to have averaged 1.16 during construction and 1.23 during operation of the facilities. The major monitoring effort on the Huntly Power Project in New Zealand (Fookes 1981) also developed an estimate of 1.125 for the local construction employment multiplier.

An analysis of the accuracy of 1980 population projections from 225 EISs found that "many statements simply ignore the socioeconomic dimensions entirely, others fail to provide necessary baseline or impact projections and still others do not provide data for jurisdictions that are useful for local and state-level decisionmaking." Even for EISs providing projections on identifiable jurisdictions, the analysis found their projections to be "of questionable value" (Murdock et al 1984:292). The mean error in cities' projected populations was over 50% and was apparently "not merely a result of the rapid growth or small population sizes of the projected areas" (Murdock et al 1984:291). Much of the inaccuracy, however, was due not to social scientists but to engineers who significantly underestimated the construction workforces needed (see also Braid 1981, Dietz 1984, Finsterbusch 1985, Gilmore et al 1982).

Most of the in-migrating workers tend to come from within the state or at least from within a thousand miles or so of a project (Mountain West Research 1975, Murdock & Leistritz 1979, Wieland et al 1979), and sizable minorities or even majorities of the workers tend to report having lived "in the area" at least briefly prior to taking employment at the facilities (Mountain West Research 1975, Chalmers 1977). The proportion of "local hires" tends to be higher where the host area populations are larger and/or the projects are smaller (Dunning 1981, DeVeney 1977, Malhotra & Manninen 1980). Even so, local employment often falls below initial expectations, for three reasons. First, local workers tend to be concentrated in the less-skilled job categories (Summers et al 1976, Mountain West Research 1975), although even these jobs often provide higher wages than are otherwise available in many rural areas (Murdock & Leistritz 1979). Second, the projects do not generally appear to lead to a decrease in the local unemployment rate, apparently in part because "new jobs often do not go to the local unemployed, underemployed, minorities and marginally employable persons likely to be near or below the poverty level" (Summers et al 1976:3). Third and finally, while such projects generally do halt or even reverse patterns of population decline, they apparently do not increase the propensity of local youth to stay in their home communities (Summers et al 1976, Seyfrit 1986).

Just as the anticipated benefits of development may not prove to be as substantial as sometimes hoped, however, there is also increasing evidence that *negative* impacts of growth may not be as severe as sometimes feared. Outside of the area of housing, the "soaring costs of living" often mentioned in the early SIA literature (and sometimes asserted even in more recent documents) have proved difficult to find in practice (Thompson et al 1979). Aggregate-level statistics do often reflect significant increases in per capita indicators of disruption, particularly in the areas of crime, substance abuse, and the need for human services more generally (Thompson et al 1979, Bacigalupi & Freudenburg 1983, Baring-Gould & Bennett 1976, Colorado Division of Criminal Justice 1981, Freudenburg 1982, Lantz & McKeown 1979, Lovejoy 1977, Milkman et al 1980, Montana Energy Advisory Council 1975, Suzman et al 1980). The interpretation of many of these statistics, however, remains highly controversial (see Weber & Howell 1982, Murdock et al 1985, or the July 1982 issue of *Pacific Sociological Review*, Vol. 25, No. 3; for aggregate-level statistics on crime rates in particular, compare Colorado Division of Criminal Justice 1981 to Wilkinson et al 1984). Despite these community-level statistics, surveys in affected communities have repeatedly failed to find evidence of psychological pathologies in the general population (England & Albrecht 1984,

Freudenburg 1981, Gartrell 1980, Krannich & Greider 1984, Suzman et al 1980). Similarly, empirical evidence has provided little support for the assumption that energy boomtowns are particularly stressful for the elderly (Gilmore et al 1982, Freudenburg 1982) or for women (Freudenburg 1981; but see Moen et al 1981, Stout-Wiegand & Trent 1983). On the other hand, more careful empirical analysis (Freudenburg 1984) has shown evidence of significant disruption in a group often identified in early SIA work as being likely to benefit from growth, namely the young people of rapidly growing communities (see also Seyfrit 1986; for further reviews, see Cortese & Jones 1977, Finsterbusch 1980, Freudenburg 1982, Murdock & Leistritz 1979; for a comprehensive set of reviews, see Weber & Howell 1982; and for a "critical review," see Wilkinson et al 1982).

Controversial Conceptions

As noted at the outset, SIA is not merely an area of empirical social science; it also draws from and contributes to the policy-making process. Particularly given the increasing availability of empirical summaries of SIA work (see the specific items cited above; see also Finsterbusch 1985), it would be inappropriate for this review to focus exclusively on the empirical work. Instead, something like equal space needs to be devoted to the large and increasingly important body of scholarship dealing with what might be called the metatheoretical issues of SIA—efforts to conceptualize and clarify the field. As in the case of the empirical literature, the metatheoretical literature can only be summarized here in greatly simplified form (for further discussions, see e.g. Boothroyd 1978, 1982; Bowles 1981b; Carley & Bustelo 1984; Cramer et al 1980; Dietz 1984; Finsterbusch 1984, 1985; Freudenburg & Keating 1985; Gale 1984; Jobes 1985; Murdock et al 1985; Tester & Mykes 1981; Wolf 1974, 1977).

The task is aided by the fact that many of the issues that would have been considered controversial and deserving of mention in the late 1970s appear today to be the focus of much higher levels of consensus—or more accurately, of pluralism. For example, many authors speak not of social but of "socioeconomic" impact assessment. The two terms have become essentially interchangeable in common usage, but in earlier years, the "*social* social impacts" were so often ignored that many "socioeconomic" assessments were strictly economic, rarely going beyond roads, sewer and water systems, and the other facilities and services making up what might be called "the edifice complex." Today, both "social" and "socioeconomic" impact assessment essentially refer not just to sociology, economics, or any other single discipline, but to interdisciplinary social science efforts. The general consensus appears to be that noneconomic or sociocultural variables need to be examined as well as economic or demographic ones (Albrecht 1982; Branch et al 1984; Carley &

Bustelo 1984; Finsterbusch 1980, 1985; Freudenburg & Keating 1982; Murdock et al 1979, 1985; National Academy of Sciences 1984).

Similarly, arguments might once have centered on several other issues that no longer appear to warrant extensive discussion—e.g. the role to be played by quantitative vs qualitative data, the importance of attitudes vs those impacts not mediated by attitudes, the need for original vs publicly "available" data, or the appropriateness of combining all impacts in terms of a single metric (whether dollars or some other system such as a listing of pluses and minuses). In general, just as the leading practitioners in the field appear to have moved away from analyses based narrowly on a specialist's own disciplinary background, most appear to be in agreement today on the inappropriateness of limiting the SIA to whatever data may happen to be available (see e.g. Finsterbusch 1980, Freudenburg 1982, Little 1977, Schnaiberg 1980). They recognize that SIAs should not be limited to variables that are easily quantified and/or politically salient (Carley & Bustelo 1984, Dietz 1984, Freudenburg & Keating 1982, Holden 1980, Murdock et al 1985, Wolf 1977). Agreement is also growing that, while decisionmakers should be provided with a concise summary of likely impacts, the attempt to "add" or otherwise combine incommensurables goes against the intent of NEPA, which is to provide relevant information for a decisionmaker's judgment, not to hide the analyst's own judgments behind a single, overall figure. Science provides no basis for combining impacts that may be as dissimilar as apples, oranges, and orangutans; efforts to add incommensurables may merely hide the value decisions that are inherent in the analyst's efforts. A decision as simple as dividing a category into two subcategories, for example, can effectively "double the weighting of the original category" (Boothroyd 1978:130; see also Flynn 1976, Holden 1980, Shields 1976).

Perhaps the main issue on which increasing consensus is *not* evident is the manner in which scientific and political considerations can best coexist. In some views, SIA is essentially synonymous with applied social science, while in others, SIA becomes almost synonymous with the political process (Carley & Bustelo 1984:10, discussing Torgerson 1981). Divergent opinions on this issue were brought out particularly clearly by the First International Conference on SIA. In his comments on the Conference, for example, Boothroyd (1982) noted the divergence between the "technical" and "political" approaches to SIA, while Carley & Bustelo (1984:7) later differentiated between "research" and "participatory" approaches. Numerous practitioners have since commented informally if a bit inaccurately about the "U.S." and "Canadian" approaches, respectively.

There have been important examples of empirical work in Canada (for a summary, see Bowles 1981b), as there have been in a number of other nations that have received little attention in this review, particularly including New

Zealand (Taylor et al 1982), Australia (Armstrong 1982), and a broad range of third-world countries that are the focus of social impact research in the context of international development (Finsterbusch 1985, Bailey 1985). The key difference is that in the United States, most "action" efforts have taken place inside the normal channels of agency decision-making; social scientists have served as important "internal proponents" for community interests and also have produced extensive bodies of work on efforts to "mitigate" or lessen the negative impacts (see e.g. Metz 1980, Davenport & Davenport 1979; Halstead et al 1984). "Action" orientations in other countries have often been more politicized—in the sense of working directly with affected communities, helping to organize opposition to projects, etc—and some of the most articulate spokespersons for this approach have been Canadians (see e.g. Carley & Bustelo 1984 or the collection in Tester & Mykes 1981).

The institutional settings for SIA differ greatly between the United States and Canada. While Canada has important environmental laws and regulations, along with agency traditions that some practitioners view as being more neutral toward development than those in the United States, Canadians do not have a statutory basis for SIA comparable to the National Environmental Policy Act. Instead, it is only a minor exaggeration to note that, if SIA in the United States can be traced to NEPA, SIA in Canada can be traced to the Berger Commission (Berger 1977). Justice Thomas R. Berger of the British Columbia Supreme Court was appointed by the Canadian Government to examine the social, economic, and environmental impacts of "the greatest project, in terms of capital expenditure, ever undertaken by private enterprise anywhere" (Berger 1983 : 22)—a proposed pipeline along the Mackenzie Valley that would have brought natural gas from the Arctic to midcontinent. The pipeline would have crossed a region as large as western Europe but inhabited by only 30,000 people, half of them natives. Berger held hearings skillfully and empathetically, complete with native translations, in a series of northern communities; his inquiry helped to educate his countrymen about their neighbors to the north as well as to investigate the implications of the pipeline itself. His final recommendation—to delay pipeline permits for 10 years to allow settlement of native claims—did not carry the force of law, but it had a greater impact on policy outcomes than have most social impact recommendations in the United States.

Particularly since the time of the International Conference, US practitioners have devoted increasing thought to the political dimensions of SIA. Before that time, the general if unspoken consensus appears to have been that, if SIA could be said to have possessed a "bias," whether in its practice or practitioners, that bias would have been a "conservative" one, in the sense of working against disruptions or other changes in preexisting communities. It is clear that developers have tended to see SIA practitioners in this light—if only because SIAs, like EISs in general, have rarely been used to build a stronger case for development but have sometimes identified reasons why developments should not proceed (but see Allee et al 1980, Finsterbusch 1985). Indeed, social scientists in agencies have sometimes served as internal advocates for community interests that were otherwise being ignored by development-oriented agencies. As a number of writers have recently pointed out, however, there actually may be a pro- as much as an anti-development bias in SIA, although the pro-development bias may operate at a deeper and more subtle level.

Two key factors that tend to make assessments more supportive of development are the selective availability of data (Schnaiberg 1980) and the analysts' tendency to focus on certain questions while ignoring others (Susskind 1983). In addition, analysts work within a system that contains its own biases—although those biases may not be consciously recognized—a possibility perhaps indicated by the common terminology. EISs will often weigh local "preferences" against a national "need" for energy, for example, rather than balancing a national "preference" for cheap energy against the "need" to preserve the vitality of local communities. Assessments on particularly controversial facilities (e.g. for nuclear waste) claim to assess both "real" and (locally) "perceived" impacts, rather than assessing both the impacts that are "acknowledged" by (project-hired) experts and those that are not. From another perspective, some of the "non-acknowledged" nuclear waste impacts result from the credibility problems of the nuclear industry and the Department of Energy, which are unable to "sell" their claims about the safety of planned facilities because communities contrast early industry claims about clean and cheap nuclear power against more recent news reports about cost overruns, management difficulties, leaks of radioactive waste, and efforts to cover up damaging evidence. Similarly, the mitigations proposed in most EISs have to do with changes that are suggested for local communities, rather than for the proposed developments. EISs and SIA practitioners will often conclude that the decent and humane thing to do is to "help communities cope" with developments that are "destined to go ahead" as planned, rather than helping *developers* learn how to do a better job of adapting to the ways in which local communities do business (Bowles 1981a). In short, while it would be inappropriate in the extreme to drop efforts to improve the empirical quality of SIA work, it also needs to be recognized that the work is affected in both subtle and significant ways by the context within which it takes place (for further discussion, see Jobes 1985, Freudenburg & Keating 1985).

IMPLICATIONS

The Policy Context

As the foregoing discussion should suggest, NEPA and SIA are worthy of increased sociological interest for more reasons than merely the new setting for applied sociology they helped create. In the empirical realm, SIA has led to important new opportunities for testing and extending the hypotheses drawn from the broader body of sociology. Perhaps in part because SIA requires a focus on change over time, it holds promise for its practitioners to rethink and to contribute to basic research in a variety of areas, such as human ecology and community change, that will help to make those fields more dynamic. In the policy context, NEPA has helped to institutionalize what is in many ways a new approach to the use of scientific information in political decision-making. This section will turn to the latter of these contributions first.

As Frank (1932) pointed out in a classic law article, societies have long shown distrust for the "human" element in decision-making. Under what might be called the first models for dealing with this problem, the early modes of trial—ordeals, judicial duels, "floating" tests for witches, etc.—were "considered to involve no human element. The judgment [was] the judgment of the supernatural, or 'the judgment of God' " (Frank 1932:582). The nineteenth-century equivalent of the earlier distrust for human judgment, according to Frank, was reliance on a body of impersonal legal rules. Under this second model of decision-making, "rationality" was thought to emerge through a dependence on rules that were derived from self-evident principles, thus reducing the human element in decision-making to a minimum (for a fuller discussion of this second approach, also known as "formal jurisprudence," see Monahan & Walker 1985:1–31). In the twentieth-century, largely in response to a school known as "sociological jurisprudence" (e.g. Pound 1912), the emphasis on such abstract "universal principles" declined, and a third model emerged, placing increased emphasis on empirical evidence. One could even argue that with society's increasing replacement of the sacred by the secular, this model attempted to replace the presumably fair or even sacred decisions of the supernatural with those of the scientist, where in the extreme case the scientist would replace the judge or the elected official as the actual decisionmaker. Perhaps the illustration with which social scientists would be most familiar is the cost-benefit analysis: Rather than having public works projects built primarily on the basis of pork-barrel politics, the argument goes, a dispassionate and scientific analysis should be used, and the project should only be built if the benefits outweigh the costs.

Yet it may not be that simple. One of the major points of Frank's article was that "the human element in the administration of justice by judges is irrepressible. . . . [T]he more you try to conceal the fact that judges are swayed by human prejudices, passions and weaknesses, the more likely you are to augment those prejudices, passions and weaknesses. . . . For judges behave substantially like the human beings who are not judges" (Frank 1932:580–81). Similarly, "scientific" decision-making has come under fire more recently, as in the case of the cost-benefit analysis, for being anything but value-free. It appears that scientists also tend to behave much like the other human beings who are neither scientists nor judges. Fallibilities include a susceptibility to political pressure and a sensitivity to the conclusions desired by clients; purportedly scientific assessments have sometimes succeeded not so much in eliminating human fallibilities and political pressures as in hiding them behind a statistical smokescreen (Schnaiberg 1980, Hoos 1979).

The approach taken by NEPA is a fourth and very different one; indeed, one way of viewing the extent of the difference is to see how often the law is misunderstood. Despite many references to a "balancing" of costs and benefits, both in legal decisions and in the technical literature, NEPA is a radical departure from the more familiar cost-benefit assessments of old. While the law does ask at least implicitly for an identification of the full range of significant costs and benefits that are likely to result from a given action, the key provision is the way in which the identified information is incorporated into decision-making. In a nutshell, the EIS must contain a full and fair discussion of likely impacts or effects (along with possible measures to lessen or "mitigate" negative impacts). The EIS is then distributed to interested parties, first in draft and then in final form, before it is used by policymakers (along with political considerations) as a basis for making an actual decision. Notably, NEPA does *not* require a policymaker to come up with a "right" or "best" decision, and it does not require projects to be stopped if they would be likely to create negative impacts. It merely requires that these impacts be publicly disclosed, and that the impacts and their potential mitigation be "considered" by policymakers, before certain federal actions may be taken (US Council on Environmental Quality 1978; see also Caldwell 1982, Freudenburg & Keating 1985).

This approach has aroused more than a little controversy. Perhaps the most common criticism is that the law has been wasteful of time and other human resources, encouraging greater emphasis on "paperwork" (the EISs) than on actual decisions and policy outcomes. Indeed, only a tiny handful of NEPA-related lawsuits have succeeded by attacking agency *decisions;* more successful by far have been the lawsuits focusing on the adequacy of EISs.

On a pragmatic basis, however, NEPA decisions are by no means the only area in which courts have been reluctant to intervene in the operations of government agencies. On the contrary, this is a well-established precedent in what lawyers call "administrative law" (for discussions, see Monahan & Walker 1985, Rodgers 1981), and it is also governed by other legal rules such as the Administrative Procedures Act. In addition, NEPA has by no means proved to be a "toothless" law. "What NEPA did was to change the rules of the game; the new rules have changed the pattern of access to decisionmaking, and they have shown definite signs of changing actual outcomes, as well" (Freudenburg & Keating 1982 : 77; for a fuller discussion, see Caldwell 1982). One indication of the change in access comes from a study that found "consumptive users" such as logging companies to account for nearly 80% of the personal business contacts of Forest Service personnel, but for only 17% of the public comments on Forest Service EISs studied. The EIS process caused agency decisions to be "altered to some degree in approximately half of the decisions" in which the authors of that study were involved (Friesema & Culhane 1976: 349–50, 354). In another study, an early evaluation of the Michigan Environmental Protection Act, Sax & DiMento found evidence of the effectiveness of actual litigation on a NEPA-type statute. Environmentalists won over 50% of the lawsuits they initiated; most of the cases were settled out of court for an average cost of less than $2,000 for the environmentalists, and even the cases that went to court had an average expense of only $10,000 (Sax & DiMento 1974: 7–8).

In a broader sense, moreover, it is the law's very focus on the adequacy of EISs that can strengthen the role of truly scientific analysis in decision-making. Unlike the case with the more traditional cost-benefit analysis, where it is to a proponent's advantage to have the analysis "slanted" in favor of a proposed development, the focus on adequacy and accuracy in EISs can place a premium on fair and full disclosure of impacts. In addition, as Dietz (1984) notes, the more effectively the EIS identifies the likely impacts and implications of the decision, the more clearly it can be seen that a given decision indicates that a policymaker sees one set of values or considerations as more important than another. Rather than using a thin veneer of scientific respectability to hide political considerations, in this view, the proper application of the NEPA model acknowledges that both facts and values are likely to play significant roles in political outcomes, and it helps to clarify the relationship between the two. In short, while the NEPA model is still an unusual and novel one, it may deserve greater attention in the future from those who are concerned with the role of science in societal decision-making.

The Research Context

In the case of empirical studies of social impacts, perhaps the most visible need is for a continued increase in the links between SIA and the broader body of social scientific research. The recent increase in empirical testing of what Wilkinson et al (1982) call the "boomtown disruption hypothesis" is a particularly noteworthy example of this tendency. The potential for advancement of empirical work will be further enhanced if several other recent trends are continued. The first is an increasing consensus that SIAs need to include a specific focus on *sociological variables,* instead of allowing the analysis to be guided by data availability, political pressures, or whatever "laundry lists" of potential impacts happen to be available (Little 1977, Cramer et al 1980, Murdock et al 1985, Finsterbusch 1985, Jobes 1985). This change is particularly heartening in contrast to an earlier tendency, still not entirely extinct, for EISs to deal in great detail with services and facilities but to become suddenly vague when dealing with human behavior. In early assessments, the matters of traditional sociological concern were sometimes dealt with, if at all, as being related to few if any considerations beyond the provision of municipal services. One scarcely needs to be a sociologist to know that people rarely attempt or commit suicide because of inadequate sewage treatment facilities, yet recognition of that fact by EISs has at times been painfully slow in coming.

A second development, related to the first, is increasing agreement on a key dependent variable, namely *quality of life* (Wolf 1974, Boothroyd 1978, Freudenburg & Keating 1982, Freeman et al 1982, Carley 1983, Dietz 1984, Branch et al 1984, Olsen et al 1985). The field of SIA is likely to remain a diverse one both empirically and theoretically, but a careful reading of the SIA literature suggests that it may now be possible to be more specific in deciding just which "social impacts" are deserving of study: Those that are identified by a relevant body of social science research as having specifiable implications for a social group's quality of life. Indeed, Burdge (1983:193) defines SIA in terms of this variable: "The purpose of social impact studies is to answer the following question: Will there be a measurable difference in the quality of life in the community as a result of what the proposed project is doing or might do in the future?" Quality of life is not as tangible as trailers and toilets, nor is it as easy to quantify as are dollars, but the concept has been the focus of a good deal of work, allowing SIA specialists to draw on established bodies of social science research. Most specialists agree that the concept can be measured reasonably effectively through a combination of so-called "subjective" and "objective" indicators (for discussions, see Carley 1983, Land 1983, Schuessler & Fisher 1985).

The third development is an increasing emphasis on *disaggregation* and *distributional impacts* (Elkind-Savatsky 1986, Flynn et al 1983, Gale 1984). In the literature on rapid community growth, one major reason behind the early overestimation of both anticipated benefits and drawbacks may have been the tendency for policymakers to search for an "overall" answer—"Well, so is the new mine going to be good or bad for the community?" Similarly, researchers often searched for "social pathologies" or "benefits of development" in relatively undifferentiated terms. One of the reasons for the improved progress of the field in recent years, on the other hand, may be researchers' increasing tendency to focus on specific population groups, notably women (Moen et al 1981, Freudenburg 1981), youths (Freudenburg 1984), "newcomers" (Massey & Lewis 1979), and native or other population groups that differ markedly from Anglo or "mainstream" cultures (Bowles 1981a, Geisler et al 1982, O'Sullivan 1981). In addition, researchers are beginning to focus more on the tendency of projects to redistribute resources, ranging from the broad level of national or even international changes (Lovejoy & Krannich 1982, Newton 1979) down to a microlevel focus on developments' implications for redistributing wealth and/or negative impacts in given localities. There is more than a little irony to the fact that the literature speaks so often of "socioeconomic" impacts and yet has tended until recently to avoid discussing the implications of projects for socioeconomic *status* and other distributional considerations (cf Schnaiberg 1980). As Freudenburg & Keating note (1985 : 15), "Even presumably 'public' projects will tend to have *distributive* impacts . . . [that] will rarely work to the disadvantage of the 'advantaged.' . . . Highways are generally built through poor neighborhoods, not rich ones."

The fourth and final development is an emphasis on *theories of the middle range*—of a level of abstraction high enough to allow conclusions from one setting to be usefully applied in another, but not of such high levels as to attempt to explain everything while in fact explaining very little. As Merton noted (1967 : 56), there is enduring truth in Plato's observation that "Particulars are infinite, and the higher generalities give no sufficient direction." An illustration of middle-range concepts can be drawn from the present author's own work on energy boomtowns. It may be that findings in this area are best understood not in terms of relatively global assertions about "damaged" or "improved" social functioning, but in terms of a narrower focus on a community's "density of acquaintanceship"—essentially the proportion of the community residents who are acquainted with one another. Rapid population growth and turnover in a boomtown can create a lowered density of acquaintanceship, but these changes do not lead to dramatic increases in the number of people who are truly isolated or "atomized." The decreased density of acquaintanceship may be responsible for disrupting informal mechanisms of watchfulness, socialization, and deviance control—and hence for frequent increases in boomtowns' crime rates—but the continued vitality of friendships and support networks may provide a kind of "social buffering" that greatly lessens any psychosocial disruptions that might otherwise be created (Freudenburg 1986).

The Challenges Ahead

A number of major issues are likely to prove important in the years ahead. Three that are currently discernible appear to be particularly deserving of mention.

"NON-PROJECT" IMPACTS   The first issue is one that is already being noted by a number of SIA practitioners (Finsterbusch 1984, 1985; Carley & Bustelo 1984; Dietz 1984; Wolf 1977). While the field is devoting increasing attention to the empirical impacts of specific, large-scale facilities in relatively isolated areas, there is a need to explore SIA's potential to contribute in "non-project" contexts—dealing with "impacts" that range from long-term but localized problems, such as the presence of toxic wastes or the erosion of a community's economic base, to short-term but broadly distributed impacts, such as those that result from changes in state or national policies or programs. These new contexts, moreover, may require the development of new approaches as well as creative adaptations of established SIA techniques, perhaps leading to a bridging of some of the gaps between SIA and evaluation research.

ASSESSING JUDGMENTAL BIASES   Second, SIA provides unique opportunities to contribute information on the decision-making process itself. In an increasing number of technological decisions, "expert" judgments have come to take on considerable significance. Particularly given the long-term social impacts that can result from what might appear at the time to be narrowly "technical" decisions, previous debates over expert "vs" citizen perceptions can take on new meaning. Unfortunately, "experts" are not infallible. Mumpower & Anderson (1983) and Hogarth & Makridakis (1981), among others, have provided excellent overviews of the types of judgmental errors that are as likely to be present in the predictions of purported "experts" as of the general public. By virtue of at least occasional membership in interdisciplinary teams preparing EISs and a familiarity with social science literature that many of their "more technical" colleagues lack, SIA practitioners may be in a unique position to see that such error-prone "expert judgments" are interpreted with caution rather than deference, both in the EISs and in decision-making more generally. Indeed, this contribution may prove to be particularly important for emerging field of risk assessment.

PLANNING FOR "SURPRISES"   Third, SIA practitioners may also need to devote more attention to the fallibility of their own projections. This point goes beyond Merton's (1936) conception of "unintended consequences." In addition to the potential for developments to create unintended impacts, external sources of "surprises" seem to be an inescapable fact of life in industrialized societies. SIA practitioners may need to explore approaches that differ in at least one significant way from the typical scientific tendency to make ceteris paribus or "surprise-free" projections. "All other things being equal," the analyst will say, "X is likely to lead to Y." In many ways, this approach is eminently reasonable, since the logic is explicitly stated, and the analyst does not expect variations in those "other things" (i.e. factors not included in the analysis). If other changes were expected, they could be explicitly taken into account. In other ways, however, recent experience seems to indicate that this approach is profoundly unreasonable. In practice, "other things" have shown very little inclination to remain "equal." The world-wide decline in petroleum prices in the 1980s was as unexpected as the sudden increases in petroleum prices during the 1970s, but in both decades, people who had based plans on apparently reasonable extrapolations from previous trends found their lives to be badly disrupted as a consequence. Particularly given today's changeability both in society and technology, perhaps what is needed from SIA is not only a set of "surprise-free" or ceteris paribus projections but also a more systematic examination of the implications of other things *not* being equal (cf Henshel 1983).

The most appropriate strategies for dealing with uncertainty per se can be quite different from those that are appropriate for dealing with whatever outcome is judged "most likely." An illustration can be provided by electric power planning. In earlier years, even when point estimates were bracketed by ranges of alternative projections, utilities tended to base their planning on whatever level of demand was projected to be "most likely" by forecasters. This approach worked quite reasonably as long as demand continued to rise at historically high rates—roughly doubling every ten years—but the approach put a premium on facilities with high generating capacities, especially nuclear power plants, and it turns out in retrospect to have had little flexibility. If the projections had been reasonably close to the mark, the utilities could have responded in a relatively straightforward way, slowing down planned construction or adding new or larger facilities to their schedules. Yet the very reliance on building nuclear power plants caused the planning situation to change. All nuclear reactors finished in recent years have cost far more than original estimates, and the increased electricity prices have contributed to a national trend toward energy conservation—leaving utilities with expensive problems of excess capacity despite the cancellation of almost half of all the commercial nuclear reactors ever ordered in the US (Rosa & Freudenburg 1984). In response to earlier problems, the Pacific Northwest (where the problem first became too obvious to ignore) recently adopted a policy of "planning for uncertainty." Rather than depending on the generating resources that appear most economical to meet a *given level of projected demand,* this approach emphasizes resources that can respond most quickly to *changes* in projected demand, thus placing greater emphasis on flexible, small-scale generators that can be put into operation quickly, and on manipulating the level of demand through conservation. It may be that future SIAs will need to explore similar approaches, emphasizing not relatively specific projections of impacts but the steps that appear best-suited for maintaining the flexibility to respond to a range of potential outcomes (for further discussion of the trade-offs between flexibility and apparent "efficiency," see Ayres 1980).

CONCLUSION

In short, much remains to be done. The mating of science and politics in SIA has often been uneasy, and further conflicts are likely in the future. While there are reasons for concern as well as for continued effort, however, fairness requires that the accomplishments as well as the problems of the field be noted. Like most teenagers, SIA has endured growing pains, identity crises, and overblown expectations. Further challenges lie ahead, as well, and the coming decade is likely to be a key time in the field's development. But in realistic terms, SIA has shown considerable growth and maturation in its decade and a half of existence. With the proper combination of support and guidance, this field has the potential to grow into the type of maturity that will contribute significantly to the legacy it has received both from its scientific and its political predecessors.

ACKNOWLEDGMENTS

Colleagues too numerous to mention have contributed the papers, ideas, and brainstorming time that helped make this paper possible. I thank all of them collectively here, and I hope they will all forgive me for not thanking them individually. The University of Denver Department of Sociology provided both a congenial setting and intellectual stimulation for developing this paper during the 1984–1985 academic year. Both the initial development and the final revisions of the paper were supported at Washington State University. During the process of writing the paper, reviews and particularly helpful suggestions were provided by Peter Boothroyd, Riley Dunlap, Kurt Finsterbusch, Cynthia Flynn-Brown, James Flynn, John Gartrell, Thomas Heberlein, Robert Jones, Ruth Love, Robert Mitchell, Steve Murdock, Thomas Rudel, Carole Seyfrit, and C. P. Wolf. Other helpful suggestions were provided by *Annual Review* referees. These valued colleagues are responsible, individually and collectively, for many of the strengths of this review, but they bear no responsibility for its shortcomings. This is Scientific Paper No. 7264, Research Project 0478, Agricultural Research Center, Washington State University.

Literature Cited

Albrecht, S. L. 1982. Commentary. *Pac. Sociol. Rev.* 25:297–306

Allee, D. J., Osgood, B. T., Antle, L. G., Simpkins, C. E., Motz, A. B., Van Der Slice, A. 1980. *Human costs of flooding and implementability of non-structural damage reduction in the Tug Fork Valley of West Virginia and Kentucky: IWR Research Report.* Fort Belvoir, Va: US Army Engineer Inst. for Water Resourc.

Andrews, W. H. 1981. *Evaluating Social Effects in Water Resources Planning: First Set.* Washington, DC: US Water Resourc. Counc.

Armstrong, A. F. 1982. *First Directory of Australian Social Impact Assessment.* Parkville, Victoria, Australia: Univ. Melbourne

Ayers, R. U. 1980. Growth, risk and technological choice. *Technol. Soc.* 2:413–31

Bacigalupi, L. M., Freudenburg, W. R. 1983. Increased mental health caseloads in an energy boomtown. *Admin. Ment. Health* 10:306–22

Bailey, C. 1985. The blue revolution: The impact of technological innovation on third-world fisheries. *The Rural Sociol.* 5:259–66

Baring-Gould, M., Bennett, M. 1976. *Social impact of the trans-Alaska pipeline construction in Valdez, Alaska, 1974–1975.* Testimony prepared for the Mackenzie Valley Pipeline Inquiry

Baxter, J., Cortese, C. F., Key, W. H. 1984. *The Social Impacts of Energy Development on National Parks: Final Report.* Washington, DC: Natl. Parks Serv., US Dept. Interior

Berardi, G. M., Geisler, C. C. 1984. *The Social Consequences and Challenges of New Agricultural Technologies.* Boulder, Colo.: Westview

Berger, T. R. 1977. *Northern Frontier, Northern Homeland: The Report of the Mackenzie Valley Pipeline Inquiry.* 2 Vols. Ottawa: Supplies & Services Canada

Berger, T. R. 1983. Energy resources development and human values. *Canadian J. Comm. Ment. Health* (Special suppl.) 1:21–31

Boothroyd, P. 1978. Issues in social impact assessment. *Plan Canada* 18:118–133

Boothroyd, P. 1982. *Overview of the issues raised at the international conference on social impact assessment.* Presented at Int. Conf. Soc. Impact Assessment, Vancouver, British Columbia, Canada

Bowles, R. T. 1981a. Preserving the contributions of traditional local economies. *Hum. Serv. Rural Environ.* 6:16–21

Bowles, R. T. 1981b. *Social Impact Assessment in Small Communities: An Integrative Review of Selected Literature.* Toronto: Butterworth

Bowles, R. T. 1982. *A quick and dirty profile of the social impact assessment community.* Presented at Int. Conf. Soc. Impact Assessment, Vancouver, British Columbia, Canada

Braid, R. Jr. 1981. Better work force projections needed for nuclear plant construction. *Power Engineer.* (April):91–95

Branch, K., Hooper, D. A., Thompson, J., Creighton, J. 1984. *Guide to Social Assessment: A Framework for Assessing Social Change.* Boulder, Colo: Westview

Buffington, J. L. Meuth, H. G., Schafer, D. L., Pledger, R., Bollion, C. 1974. *Attitudes, Opinions, and Experiences of Residents Displaced by Highways Under the 1970 Relocation Assistance Program.* College Park, Tex: Texas A&M Univ.

Burkhardt, J. E. Boyd, N. K., Martin, T. K. 1976. *Residential Dislocation: Consequences and Compensation, Final Report.* Washington, DC: NCHR Program

Burch, W. R. 1965. The play world of camping: Research into the social meaning of outdoor recreation. *Am. J. Sociol.* 70:604–12

Burdge, R. J. 1983. Community needs assessments and techniques. See Finsterbusch et al 1983, pp. 191–213

Burdge, R. J., Johnson, K. S. 1973. *Social Costs and Benefits of Water Resource Construction.* Lexington, Ky: Univ. Kentucky Water Resources Res. Inst. Rep. No. 64

Caldwell, L. K. 1982. *Science and the National Environmental Policy Act: Redirecting Policy through Procedural Reform.* University, Ala: Univ. Ala. Press

Carley, M. J. 1983. Social indicators research. See Finsterbusch et al 1983, pp. 151–67

Carley, M. J., Bustelo, E. S. 1984. *Social Impact Assessment and Monitoring: A Guide to the Literature.* Boulder, Colo: Westview

Chalmers, J. A. 1977. *Construction Worker Survey.* Denver, Colo: US Bur. Reclamation

Colorado Division of Criminal Justice. 1981. *Colorado's Energy Boom: Impact on Crime and Criminal Justice.* Denver, Colo: Colo. Div. Criminal Justice, Dep. Local Affairs

Cortese, C. F., Jones, B. 1977. The sociologi-

cal analysis of boom towns. *Western Sociol. Rev.* 8:76–90

Cramer, J. C., Dietz, T., Johnston, R. A. 1980. Social impact assessment of regional plans: A review of methods and issues and a recommended process. *Policy Sci.* 12:61–82

D'Amore, L. J. 1981. An overview of SIA. See Tester & Mykes 1981, pp. 366–73

Daneke, G. A., Garcia, M. W., Priscoli, J. D. 1983. *Public Involvement and Social Impact Assessment.* Boulder, Colo: Westview

Davenport, J. A., Davenport, J. Jr. 1979. *Boom Towns and Human Services.* Laramie, Wyo: Univ. Wyoming Press

Davidson, G. K. 1983. *Social Impact Assessment: A Survey of Its Practitoners.* Alexandria, Va: Santa Fe Corp.

DeVeney, G. R. 1977. *Construction Employee Monitoring.* Knoxville, Tenn: Tenn. Valley Authority

Dietz, T. 1984. Social impact assessment as a tool for rangelands management. In *Developing Strategies for Range Lands Management,* ed. Natl. Acad. Sci. Boulder, Colo: Westview

Dillman, D. A., Schwalbe, M. L., Short, J. F. Jr. 1983. Communication behavior and social impacts following the May 18, 1980, eruption of Mt. St. Helen's. In *Mt. St. Helens, One Year Later,* ed. S. A. C. Keller, pp. 191–98. Cheney, Wash: Eastern Wash. Univ. Press

Dunlap, R. E., Catton, W. R. Jr. 1979. Environmental Sociology. *Ann. Rev. Sociol.* 5:243–73

Dunning, C. M. 1981. *Report of Survey of Corps of Engineers Construction Workforce.* Fort Belvoir, Va: US Army Corps of Engineers Inst. Water Resources Res. Rep. 81–R0

Elkind-Savatsky, P. D. 1986. *Differential Social Impacts of Rural Resource Development.* Boulder, Colo: Westview

England, J. L., Albrecht, S. L. 1984. Boomtowns and social disruption. *Rural Sociol.* 49:230–46

Erikson, K. T. 1976. *Everything In Its Path: Destruction of Community in the Buffalo Creek Flood.* New York, NY: Simon & Schuster

Fellman, G., Brandt, B. 1970. A neighborhood a highway would destroy. *Environ. Behav.* 2:281–301

Field, D. R., Barron, J. C., Long, B. F., eds. 1974. *Water and Community Development: Social and Economic Perspectives.* Ann Arbor, Ann Arbor Sci.

Finsterbusch, K. 1980. *Understanding Social Impacts: Assessing the Effects of Public Projects.* Beverly Hills, Calif: Sage

Finsterbusch, K. 1984. Social impact assessment as a policy science methodology. *Impact Assess. Bull.* 3:37–43

Finsterbusch, K. 1985. State of the art in social

impact assessment. *Environ. Behav.* 17: 193–221

Finsterbusch, K., Llewellyn, L. G., Wolf, C. P. 1983. *Social Impact Assessment Methods.* Beverly Hills, Calif: Sage

Finsterbush, K., Wolf, C. P. 1977. *Methodology of Social Impact Assessment.* Stroudsburg, Penn: Dowden, Hutchinson & Ross. (1st ed.)

Fitzsimmons, S. J., Stuart, L. I., Wolff, P. C. 1977. *Social Assessment Manual: A Guide to the Preparation of the Social Well-Being Account for Planning Water Resource Projects.* Boulder, Colo: Westview

Flynn, C. B. 1976. Science and speculation in social impact assessment. *Soc. Impact Assess.* No. 11/12:5–14

Flynn, C. B., Flynn, J. H., Chalmers, J. A., Pijawaka, D., Branch, K. 1983. An integrated methodology for large-scale development projects. See Finsterbusch et al 1983, pp. 55–72

Fookes, T. W. 1981. *Monitoring Social and Economic Impact: Huntly Case Study, Final Report Series.* Hamilton, New Zealand: Univ. Waikato

Frank, J. 1932. Mr. Justice Holmes and non-euclidean legal thinking. *Cornell Law Q.* 17:568–603

Freeman, D. M., Frey, R. S., Quint, J. M. 1982. Assessing resource management policies: A social well-being framework with a national level application. *Environ. Impact Assess. Rev.* 3:59–73

Freudenburg, W. R. 1981. Women and men in an energy boomtown: Adjustment, alienation and adaptation. *Rural Sociol.* 46:220–44

Freudenburg, W. R. 1982. Coping with rapid growth in rural communities. See Weber & Howell 1982, pp. 137–69

Freudenburg, W. R. 1984. Boomtown's youth: The differential impacts of rapid community growth on adolescents and adults. *Am. Sociol. Rev.* 49:697–705

Freudenburg, W. R. 1986. The density of acquaintanceship: An overlooked variable in community research? *Am. J. Sociol.* 92. In press

Freudenburg, W. R., Baxter, R. K. 1984. Host community attitudes toward nuclear power plants: A reassessment. *Soc. Sci. Q.* 65:1129–36

Freudenburg, W. R., Keating, K. M. 1982. Increasing the impact of sociology on social impact assessments: Toward ending the inattention. *Am. Sociol.* 17:71–80

Freudenburg, W. R., Keating, K. M. 1985. Applying sociology to policy: Social science and the environmental impact statement. *Rural Sociol.* 50:578–605

Fried, M. 1963. Grieving for a lost home. In *The Urban Condition: People and Policy in the Metropolis,* ed. L. J. Duhl, pp. 151–70. New York: Basic

Friesema, H. P., Culhane, P. J. 1976. Social impacts, politics, and the environmental impact statement process. *Natl. Resource J.* 16:339–356

Gale, R. P. 1975. *The U.S. Forest Service and Social Impact Assessment.* Eugene, Oreg: US Forest Serv. Staff Paper

Gale, R. P. 1984. The evolution of social impact assessment: Post-functionalist view. *Impact Assess. Bull.* 3:27–35

Gans, H. J. 1962. *The Urban Villagers: Group and Class in the Life of Italian-Americans.* New York: Free Press

Gartrell, J. W., Krahn, H. N., Sunahara, D. F. 1980. *Cold Lake Baseline Study: Phase II.* Peace River, Alberta, Canada: Alberta Small Bus. Tourism, Northern Dev. Branch

Gates, D. P. 1982. *Social Profile: Rifle.* Craig, Colo: US Bur. Land Mgmt.

Geisler, C. C., Green, R., Usner, D., West, P. C. 1982. *Indian SIA: The Social Impact Assessment of Rapid Resource Development on Native Peoples.* Monograph No. 3. Ann Arbor, Mich: Univ. Mich. Natl. Resources Sociol. Res. Lab.

Gilmore, J. S., Hammond, D. M., Moore, K. D., Johnson, J., Coddington, D. C. 1982. *Socio-Economic Impacts of Power Plants.* Palo Alto, Calif: Electric Power Res. Inst.

Halstead, J. M., Chase, R. A., Murdock, S. H., Leistritz, F. L. 1984. *Socioeconomic Impact Management: Design and Implementation.* Boulder, Colo: Westview

Hammond, K. R., Mumpower, J., Dennis, R. L., Fitch, S., Crumpacker, D. W. 1983. Fundamental obstacles to the use of scientific information in public policy making. See Rossini & Porter 1983, pp. 168–83

Hendee, J. C., Stankey, G. H., Lucas, R. C. 1978. *Wilderness Management.* Washington, DC: US Forest Serv. Misc. Pub. No. 1365

Henshel, R. L. 1982. Sociology and social forecasting. *Ann. Rev. Sociol.* 8:57–79

Hogarth, R. M., Makridakis, S. 1981. Forecasting and planning: An evaluation. *Mgmt. Sci.* 27:115–89

Holden, A. G. 1980. *Estimation of social effects: Social science in the planning process.* Portland, Ore: US Forest Ser. Work. Pap.

Hoos, I. R. 1979. Societal aspects of technology assessment. *Technol. Forecasting Soc. Change* 13:191–202

Jobes, P. C. 1985. Social control of dirty work: Conflict avoidance in social-impact assessment. *The Rural Sociol.* 5:104–111

Jordan, W. S. III. 1984. Psychological harm after PANE: NEPA's requirements to consider psychological damage. *Harv. Environ. Law Rev.* 8:55–87

Krannich, R. S., Greider, T. 1984. Personal well-being in rapid growth and stable communities: Multiple indicators and contrasting results. *Rural Sociol.* 49:541–52

Land, K. C. 1983. Social indicators. *Ann. Rev. Sociol.* 9:1–26

Lantz, A. E., McKeown, R. L. 1979. Social/ psychological problems of women and their families associated with rapid growth. In *Energy Resource Development: Implications for Women and Minorities in the Intermountain West*, ed. US Commiss. Civil Rights. Washington, DC: USGPO

Little, R. L. 1977. Some social consequences of boom towns. *N. Dak. Law Rev.* 53:401–25

Llewellyn, L. G., Goodman, C., Hare, G. 1982. *Social Impact Assessment: A Source Book for Highway Planners.* FHWA/RD-81/023-029 Washington, DC: US Dep. Transport.

Lovejoy, S. L. 1977. *Local Perceptions of Energy Development: The Case of the Kaiparowitz Plateau.* Los Angeles: Lake Powell Res. Proj. Bull. 62

Lovejoy, S. B., Krannich, R. S. 1982. Rural industrial development and domestic dependency relations: Toward an integrated perspective. *Rural Sociol.* 47:475–95

Lucas, R. C. 1964. *Recreational Use of the Quetico-Superior Area.* St. Paul, Minn: US Forest Serv. Res. Pap. LS-8

Malhotra, S., Manninen, D. 1980. *Migration and Residential Location of Workers at Nuclear Power Plant Construction Sites,* 2 Vols. Seattle, Wash: Battelle Hum. Affairs Res. Centers

Massey, G., Lewis, D. 1979. Energy development and mobile home living: The myth of suburbia revisited. *Soc. Sci. J.* 16:81–91

Meidinger, E. E., Freudenburg, W. R. 1983. The legal status of social impact assessments: Recent developments. *Environ. Sociol.* No. 34:30–33

Merton, R. K. 1936. The Unanticipated Consequences of Purposive Social Action. *Am. Sociol. Rev.* 1:894–904

Merton, R. K. 1967. *On Theoretical Sociology: Five Essays, Old and New.* New York: Free Press

Metz, W. C. 1980. The mitigation of socioeconomic impacts by electric utilities. *Public Util. Fortnightly* 106 (Sept. 11):34–42

Milkman, R. H., Hunt, L. G., Pease, W., Perez, U. M., Crowley, L. J., Boyd, B. 1980. *Drug and Alcohol Abuse in Booming and Depressed Communities.* Washington, DC: Nat. Inst. Drug Abuse, US Dep. Health, Educ. Welfare

Moen, E., Boulding, E., Lillydahl, J., Palm, R. 1981. *Women and the Social Costs of Economic Development: Two Colorado Case Studies.* Boulder, Colo: Westview

Monahan, J., Walker, L. 1985. *Social Science in Law: Cases and Materials.* Mineola, NY: Found. Press

Montana Energy Advisory Council. 1975. *Coal Development Information Packet: Supplement I.* Helena, Mont: Off. Lt. Gov.

Mountain West Research, Inc. 1975. *Construction Worker Profile.* Washington, DC: Old West Reg. Comm.

Mumpower, J., Anderson, B. F. 1983. Causes and correctives for errors of judgment. See Finsterbusch et al 1983. pp. 241–62

Murdock, S. H., Leistritz, F. L. 1979. *Energy Development in the Western United States: Impact on Rural Areas.* New York: Praeger

Murdock, S. H., Leistritz, F. L., Hamm, R. R. 1985. The state of socio-economic impact analysis: Limitations and opportunities for alternative futures. Presented at Ann. Meet. So. Assoc. Agric. Sci., Biloxi, Miss.

Murdock, S. H., Leistritz, F. L., Hamm, R. R., Hwang, S. S. 1984. An assessment of the accuracy and utility of socio-economic impact assessments. In *Paradoxes of Western Energy Development*, ed. C. M. McKell, D. G. Brown, E. C. Cruze, W. R. Freudenburg, R. L. Perrine, F. Roach: pp. 265–96. Boulder, Colo: Westview

National Academy of Sciences, National Research Council. 1984. *Social and Economic Aspects of Radioactive Waste Disposal: Considerations for Institutional Management.* Washington, DC: Natl. Acad. Press

Newton, P. W. 1979. In the North, overseas priorities inhibit local identity, with ultimate economic and social costs. *Royal Australian Plan. Inst. J.* 17:189–92

Olsen, M. E., Canan, P., Hennessy, M. 1985. A value-based community assessment process: Integrating quality of life and social impact studies. *Sociol. Methods Res.* 13:325–61

O'Sullivan, M. J. 1981. *The psychological impact of the threat of relocation on the Fort McDowell Indian community.* Ph.D. thesis. St. Louis Univ., Mo.

Pijawka, D., Chalmers, J. A. 1983. Impacts of nuclear generating plants on local areas. *Econ. Geog.* 59:66–80

Pound, R. 1912. The scope and purpose of sociological jurisprudence. *Harv. Law Rev.* 25:489–516

Rodgers, W. H. Jr. 1981. Judicial review of risk assessments: The role of decision theory in unscrambling the Benzene decision. *Environ. Law.* 11:301–20

Rosa, E. A., Freudenburg, W. R. 1984. Nuclear power at the crossroads. In *Public Reactions to Nuclear Power: Are there Critical Masses?* ed. W. R. Freudenburg, E. A. Rosa. pp. 3–34. Boulder, Colo: Westview

Rossini, F. A., Porter, A. L. 1983. *Integrated*

Impact Assessment. Boulder, Colo: Westview

Sax, J. L., DiMento, J. F. 1974. Environmental citizen suits: Three years' experience under the Michigan Environmental Protection Act. *Ecol. Law Q.* 4:1–62

Schnaiberg, A. 1980. *The Environment: From Surplus to Scarcity*. New York: Oxford Univ. Press

Seyfrit, C. L. 1986. Migration intentions of rural youth: Testing an assumed benefit of rapid growth. *Rural Sociol.* 51:199–211

Shields, M. 1976. Review of *Social Assessment Manual. Soc. Impact Assess.* No. 6:16–19

Stout-Wiegand, N., Trent, R. B. 1983. Sex differences in attitudes toward new energy resource developments. *Rural Sociol.* 48:637–46

Summers, G. F., Evans, S. D., Clemente, F., Beck, E. M., Minkoff, J. 1976. *Industrial Invasion of Non-Metropolitan America: A Quarter Century of Experience*. New York: Praeger

Susskind, L. E. 1983. The uses of negotiation and mediation in environmental impact assessment. See Rossini & Porter 1983, pp. 154–167

Suzman, R. M., Voorhees-Rosen, D. J., Rosen, D. H. 1980. *The impact of the North Sea oil development on mental and physical health: a longitudinal study of the consequences of an economic boom and rapid social change*. Presented to Ann. Meet. Am. Sociol. Assoc., New York

Taylor, C. N., Bettesworth, C. M., Kerslake, J. G. 1982. *Social Implications of Rapid Industrialisation: A Bibliography of New Zealand Experiences*. Canterbury (New Zealand): Ctr. Resource Mgmt. Lincoln Coll.

Tester, F. J., Mykes, W. 1981. *Social Impact Assessment: Theory, Method and Practice*. Calgary, Alberta, Canada: Detselig

Thompson, J. G., Blevins, A. L. Jr., Watts, G. L. 1979. *Socio-Economic Longitunal Monitoring Project: Final Report: Vol. 1. Summary*. Washington, DC: Old West Reg. Comm.

Torgerson, D. 1981. SIA as a social phenomenon: The problems of contextuality. See

Tester & Mykes 1981, pp. 68–92

US Army Corps of Engineers. 1971. *Final Environmental Statement: Second Powerhouse, Bonneville Lock and Dam, Columbia River, Oregon and Washington*. Portland, Ore: US Army Engineer Dist.

US Council on Environmental Quality. 1978. *Regulations for Implementing the Procedural Provisions of the National Environmental Policy Act* (40 CFR 1500-1508). Washington, DC: US Council Environ. Qual.

Wagar, J. A. 1964. *The Carrying Capacity of Recreational Lands: A Review*. Washington, DC: Soc. Am. Foresters, Occas. Pap. No. 7

Walker, P., Fraize, W. E., Gordon, J. J., Johnson, R. C. 1982. *Workshop on Psychological Stress Associated with the Proposed Restart of Three Mile Island Unit One*. McLean, Va: Mitre Corp.

Weber, B. A., Howell, R. E. 1982. *Coping with Rapid Growth in Rural Communities*. Boulder, Colo: Westview

Wieland, J. S., Leistritz, F. L., Murdock, S. H. 1979. Characteristics and residential patterns of energy-related work forces in the Northern Great Plains. *Western J. Agric. Econ.* 4:57–68

Wilkinson, K. P., Reynolds, R. R. Jr., Thompson, J. G., Ostresh, L. M. 1984. Violent crime in the Western energy-development region. *Sociol. Perspec.* 27:241–56

Wilkinson, K. P., Thompson, J. G., Reynolds, R. R. Jr., Ostresh, L. M. 1982. Local disruption and western energy development: A critical review. *Pac. Sociol. Rev.* 25:275–96

Wolf, C. P. 1974. *Social Impact Assessment*. Stoudsburg, Penn: Dowden, Hutchinson & Ross

Wolf, C. P. 1975. Report of the committee on environmental sociology. *ASA Footnotes* 3 (Aug):15–16

Wolf, C. P. 1977. Social impact assessment: The state of the art updated. *Soc. Impact Assess.* No. 20(Aug):3–22

Yarie, S. 1983. *Alaska Symposium on the Social, Economic, and Cultural Impacts of Natural Resource Development*. Fairbanks: Univ. Alaska Press

SUBJECT INDEX

CUMULATIVE INDEXES

CONTRIBUTING AUTHORS, VOLUMES 1–12

CHAPTER TITLES, VOLUMES 1–12

492

Annual Reviews Inc.

NONPROFIT SCIENTIFIC PUBLISHER

4139 El Camino Way
P.O. Box 10139
Palo Alto, CA 94303-0897 • USA

ORDER FORM

Now you can order
TOLL FREE
1-800-523-8635
(except California)

Annual Reviews Inc. publications may be ordered directly from our office by mail or use our Toll Free telephone line (for orders paid by credit card or purchase order, and customer service calls only); through booksellers and subscription agents, worldwide; and through participating professional societies. Prices subject to change without notice. ARI Federal I.D. #94-1156476

Individuals: Prepayment required on new accounts by check or money order (in U.S. dollars, check drawn on U.S. bank) or charge to credit card — American Express, VISA, MasterCard.

Institutional buyers: Please include purchase order number.

Students: $10.00 discount from retail price, per volume. Prepayment required. Proof of student status must be provided (photocopy of student I.D. or signature of department secretary is acceptable). Students must send orders direct to Annual Reviews. Orders received through bookstores and institutions requesting student rates will be returned.

Professional Society Members: Members of professional societies that have a contractual arrangement with Annual Reviews may order books through their society at a reduced rate. Check with your society for information.

Toll Free Telephone orders: Call 1-800-523-8635 (except from California) for orders paid by credit card or purchase order and customer service calls only. California customers and all other business calls use 415-493-4400 (not toll free). Hours: 8:00 AM to 4:00 PM, Monday-Friday, Pacific Time.

Regular orders: Please list the volumes you wish to order by volume number.

Standing orders: New volume in the series will be sent to you automatically each year upon publication. Cancellation may be made at any time. Please indicate volume number to begin standing order.

Prepublication orders: Volumes not yet published will be shipped in month and year indicated.

California orders: Add applicable sales tax.

Postage paid (4th class bookrate/surface mail) **by Annual Reviews Inc.** Airmail postage or UPS, extra.

ANNUAL REVIEWS SERIES		Prices Postpaid per volume USA/elsewhere	Regular Order Please send:	Standing Order Begin with:
			Vol. number	Vol. number
Annual Review of ANTHROPOLOGY				
Vols. 1-14	(1972-1985)	$27.00/$30.00		
Vol. 15	(1986)	$31.00/$34.00		
Vol. 16	(avail. Oct. 1987)	$31.00/$34.00	Vol(s). _____	Vol. _____
Annual Review of ASTRONOMY AND ASTROPHYSICS				
Vols. 1-2, 4-20	(1963-1964; 1966-1982)	$27.00/$30.00		
Vols. 21-24	(1983-1986)	$44.00/$47.00		
Vol. 25	(avail. Sept. 1987)	$44.00/$47.00	Vol(s). _____	Vol. _____
Annual Review of BIOCHEMISTRY				
Vols. 30-34, 36-54	(1961-1965; 1967-1985)	$29.00/$32.00		
Vol. 55	(1986)	$33.00/$36.00		
Vol. 56	(avail. July 1987)	$33.00/$36.00	Vol(s). _____	Vol. _____
Annual Review of BIOPHYSICS AND BIOPHYSICAL CHEMISTRY				
Vols. 1-11	(1972-1982)	$27.00/$30.00		
Vols. 12-15	(1983-1986)	$47.00/$50.00		
Vol. 16	(avail. June 1987)	$47.00/$50.00	Vol(s). _____	Vol. _____
Annual Review of CELL BIOLOGY				
Vol. 1	(1985)	$27.00/$30.00		
Vol. 2	(1986)	$31.00/$34.00		
Vol. 3	(avail. Nov. 1987)	$31.00/$34.00	Vol(s). _____	Vol. _____

ANNUAL REVIEWS SERIES		Prices Postpaid per volume USA/elsewhere	Regular Order Please send:	Standing Order Begin with:
			Vol. number	Vol. number

Annual Review of COMPUTER SCIENCE

Vol. 1	(1986)	$39.00/$42.00		
Vol. 2	(avail. Nov. 1987)	$39.00/$42.00	Vol(s). _____	Vol. _____

Annual Review of EARTH AND PLANETARY SCIENCES

Vols. 1-10	(1973-1982)	$27.00/$30.00		
Vols. 11-14	(1983-1986)	$44.00/$47.00		
Vol. 15	(avail. May 1987)	$44.00/$47.00	Vol(s). _____	Vol. _____

Annual Review of ECOLOGY AND SYSTEMATICS

Vols. 1-16	(1970-1985)	$27.00/$30.00		
Vol. 17	(1986)	$31.00/$34.00		
Vol. 18	(avail. Nov. 1987)	$31.00/$34.00	Vol(s). _____	Vol. _____

Annual Review of ENERGY

Vols. 1-7	(1976-1982)	$27.00/$30.00		
Vols. 8-11	(1983-1986)	$56.00/$59.00		
Vol. 12	(avail. Oct. 1987)	$56.00/$59.00	Vol(s). _____	Vol. _____

Annual Review of ENTOMOLOGY

Vols. 10-16, 18-30	(1965-1971, 1973-1985)	$27.00/$30.00		
Vol. 31	(1986)	$31.00/$34.00		
Vol. 32	(avail. Jan. 1987)	$31.00/$34.00	Vol(s). _____	Vol. _____

Annual Review of FLUID MECHANICS

Vols. 1-4, 7-17	(1969-1972, 1975-1985)	$28.00/$31.00		
Vol. 18	(1986)	$32.00/$35.00		
Vol. 19	(avail. Jan. 1987)	$32.00/$35.00	Vol(s). _____	Vol. _____

Annual Review of GENETICS

Vols. 1-19	(1967-1985)	$27.00/$30.00		
Vol. 20	(1986)	$31.00/$34.00		
Vol. 21	(avail. Dec. 1987)	$31.00/$34.00	Vol(s). _____	Vol. _____

Annual Review of IMMUNOLOGY

Vols. 1-3	(1983-1985)	$27.00/$30.00		
Vol. 4	(1986)	$31.00/$34.00		
Vol. 5	(avail. April 1987)	$31.00/$34.00	Vol(s). _____	Vol. _____

Annual Review of MATERIALS SCIENCE

Vols. 1, 3-12	(1971, 1973-1982)	$27.00/$30.00		
Vols. 13-16	(1983-1986)	$64.00/$67.00		
Vol. 17	(avail. August 1987)	$64.00/$67.00	Vol(s). _____	Vol. _____

Annual Review of MEDICINE

Vols. 1-3, 6, 8-9 11-15, 17-36	(1950-1952, 1955, 1957-1958) (1960-1964, 1966-1985)	$27.00/$30.00		
Vol. 37	(1986)	$31.00/$34.00		
Vol. 38	(avail. April 1987)	$31.00/$34.00	Vol(s). _____	Vol. _____

Annual Review of MICROBIOLOGY

Vols. 18-39	(1964-1985)	$27.00/$30.00		
Vol. 40	(1986)	$31.00/$34.00		
Vol. 41	(avail. Oct. 1987)	$31.00/$34.00	Vol(s). _____	Vol. _____

FROM

NAME _____

ADDRESS _____

_____

_____ ZIP CODE _____

Annual Reviews Inc.

4139 El Camino Way
P.O. Box 10139
Palo Alto, CALIFORNIA 94303-0897

A NONPROFIT
SCIENTIFIC PUBLISHER

PLACE
STAMP
HERE